SUBJECTIVITY AND LIFEWORLD IN TRANSCENDENTAL PHENOMENOLOGY

SUBJECTIVITY AND LIFEWORLD IN TRANSCENDENTAL PHENOMENOLOGY

Sebastian Luft

Northwestern University Press
Evanston, Illinois

Northwestern University Press
www.nupress.northwestern.edu

Printed in the United States of America

10 9 8 7 6 5 4 3 2 1

ISBN 978-0-8101-4320-3

The Library of Congress has cataloged the original, hardcover edition as follows:

Luft, Sebastian.
    Subjectivity and lifeworld in transcendental phenomenology / Sebastian
Luft.
        p. cm.
    Includes bibliographical references and index.
    Collected essays, most previously published.
    ISBN 978-0-8101-2743-2 (cloth : alk. paper)
    1. Phenomenology. 2. Hermeneutics. 3. Husserl, Edmund, 1859–1938.
I. Title.
B829.5.L568 2011
142.7—dc22

                                                            2011012612

This book is dedicated, with love, to my family:
Stephanie, Julia, Hannah Elisabeth, and Robert Maria

Contents

Acknowledgments

The author would like to thank the following publishers for permission to republish the articles below as chapters in this book:

Chapter 1 was originally published in *Continental Philosophy Review* 31 (1998): 153–70.

Chapter 2, "Husserl's Theory of the Phenomenological Reduction: Between Lifeworld and Cartesianism," was originally published in *Research in Phenomenology* 34 (2004): 198–234.

Chapter 3 was originally published in German in *Subjektivität—Verantwortung—Wahrheit: Neue Aspekte der Phänomenologie Edmund Husserls*, ed. David Carr and Christian Lotz (Frankfurt am Main: Lang, 2002), 127–48. Translated by Jon Burmeister.

Chapter 4, "Facticity and Historicity as Constituents of the Lifeworld in Husserl's Late Philosophy," was originally published in German in *Phänomenologische Forschungen* 5 (2005): 13–40. Translated by Colin J. Hahn.

Chapter 5, "Husserl's Concept of the 'Transcendental Person': Another Look at the Husserl–Heidegger Relationship," was first published in *International Journal of Philosophical Studies* 13, no. 2 (2005): 141–77.

Chapter 6, "Dialectics of the Absolute: The Systematics of the Phenomenological System in Husserl's Last Period," was first published in *Philosophy Today* 25 (1999): 107–14. The present text presents, however, a significantly expanded version of the article in *Philosophy Today*.

Chapter 7, "From Being to Givenness and Back: Some Remarks on the Meaning of Transcendental Idealism in Kant and Husserl," was first published in *International Journal of Philosophical Studies* 15, no. 3 (2007): 367–94.

Chapter 8, "Reconstruction and Reduction: Natorp and Husserl on Method and the Question of Subjectivity," was originally published in *Neo-Kantianism in Contemporary Philosophy*, ed. Rudolf A. Makkreel and Sebastian Luft (Bloomington: Indiana University Press, 2010), 59–91.

Chapter 9, "A Hermeneutic Phenomenology of Subjective and Objective Spirit: Husserl, Natorp, and Cassirer," was first published in *The New Yearbook for Phenomenology and Phenomenological Philosophy* 4 (2004): 209–48.

Chapter 10, "Cassirer's Philosophy of Symbolic Forms: Between Reason and Relativism: A Critical Appraisal," was published in *Idealistic Studies* 34, no. 1 (2004): 25–47.

Chapter 11, "The Subjectivity of Effective History and the Suppressed Husserlian Elements in Gadamer's Hermeneutics," was published in *Idealistic Studies* 37, no. 3 (2008): 219–54.

Chapter 12, "Husserl's 'Hermeneutical Phenomenology' as a Philosophy of Culture," has been hitherto unpublished, though a shorter version of the present text was presented at the annual meeting of the Society for Phenomenology and Existential Philosophy in 2004 and at the Seminar for Phenomenology and Hermeneutics (Marquette University) in 2005.

Instead of recording my acknowledgments in a note at the end of each chapter, I would like to express my thanks right at the outset.

I would like to thank the following institutions for their support:

The Husserl-Archives at the Hoger Instituut voor Wijsbegeerte of the Katholieke Universiteit Leuven (Belgium) and their directors, formerly Prof. Rudolf Bernet and currently Prof. Ullrich Melle, for their permission to quote from unpublished manuscript material and for the free perusal of the archival material and the library.

The Alexander von Humboldt Foundation for granting a postdoctoral fellowship (Feodor-Lynen Fellowship) to pursue my work concerning the intersections between phenomenology and neo-Kantianism. Chapters 8 through 10 especially are a result of this work.

ACKNOWLEDGMENTS

The Department of Philosophy at Emory University for its institutional support in the years 2002 through 2004.

The Graduate School at Marquette University for several Summer Faculty Fellowships between 2004 and 2008 and the Way Klingler Sabbatical Fellowship in the years 2009 through 2011, as well as Marquette's Department of Philosophy for its support in the form of granting me graduate student research assistants between 2004 and 2011 who helped me assemble material and proofread my texts: Kyle McNeel, David McPherson, Nicholas Zettel, Celeste Harvey, John Westbrook, and Matthew Zdon.

Special thanks go to Andreas Friedrich of the Husserl-Archives in Freiburg im Breisgau and to Matthew Zdon for preparing the final manuscript as well as the index for Northwestern University Press. I also thank Jon Burmeister and Colin J. Hahn for translating chapters 3 and 4, respectively.

I thank Henry L. Carrigan Jr. of Northwestern University Press for accepting this manuscript and for encouraging me to push beyond initial hurdles. The present book would not have seen the light of day without his support. I would also like to thank my editor, Anne Gendler, and my copy editor, Paul Mendelson.

Since it is neither possible nor fair to measure the extent to which the following people have aided, influenced, inspired, and helped me in numerous ways to improve my work, I am listing them here in alphabetical order. My sincere gratitude goes to Lillian Alweiss, Markus Asper, Rudolf Bernet, Francesc Perenya Blasi, John B. Brough, David Carr, Paul Crowe, Steven G. Crowell, Andrew Cutrofello, Robert C. Dostal, John J. Drummond, Gottfried Gabriel, Hans-Helmuth Gander, Carl Friedrich Gethmann, Berndt Goossens, James Hart, Klaus Held, Burt Hopkins, Matthias Jung, Iso Kern, Nam-In Lee, Karl-Heinz Lembeck, Dieter Lohmar, Rudolf A. Makkreel, William McKenna, Ullrich Melle, Karl Mertens, J. N. Mohanty, Dermot Moran, Thane M. Naberhaus, Thomas Nenon, Søren Overgaard, Henning Peucker, Sonja Rinofner-Kreidl, Tetsuya Sakakibara, Michael K. Shim, Robert Sokolowski, Rochus Sowa, Andrea Staiti, Anthony J. Steinbock, Jürgen Stolzenberg, László Tengelyi, Pol Vandevelde, Thomas Vongehr, Roberto Walton, David Weberman, Donn Welton, Reiner Wiehl, Eric E. Wilson, Harald Wiltsche, and Dan Zahavi.

Special thanks go to Thane M. Naberhaus and Roberto Walton for their careful reading and insightful critique of my "Introduction."

Last but not least, I would like to thank all the students I have taught over the years at the universities of Leuven, Emory, Marquette, Graz, Puerto Rico, and Freiburg im Breisgau, who continued to pose penetrating questions and forced me to clarify my thoughts and ideas. Any clarity I may have achieved in shedding light on the philosophical matters under discussion here is in no little part thanks to them. All remaining shortcomings of this book are entirely my fault.

SUBJECTIVITY AND LIFEWORLD IN
TRANSCENDENTAL PHENOMENOLOGY

Introduction

We are now in the seventh decade after the death of Edmund Husserl (1859–1938), the founder of phenomenology, and 150 years after his birth. Now is the time to look back and venture a certain assessment, and there are reasons why this time gap was necessary for a proper view and evaluation of his work. If Gadamer is right that to be a classic requires a certain time gap between what is to count as classic and us today, then one can argue that we are only now beginning to be in a position to view Husserl as a classic author. But let us focus, for a moment, on the time gap itself and what has happened between Husserl's death and today. The story to be told here is by no means trivial but is part of the reception that made Husserl a classic philosopher of modernity.

There is something very curious about the unquestioned importance of Husserl on the one hand and, on the other, his reception, both of which are quite incongruent. When his first programmatic work, the *Logical Investigations,* appeared in 1900–01, Husserl was immediately heralded as founding a promising new philosophy with its novel method and programmatic outlook. After that, his philosophical contemporaries witnessed a series of further, primarily programmatic, works—*Ideas I, Formal and Transcendental Logic, Cartesian Meditations* (published "only" in French translation), and finally, the fragment of the *Crisis of European Sciences and Transcendental Phenomenology*—in which the founder of phenomenology portrayed himself as laying ever-new foundations, drafting ever-new introductions, repeating programmatic statements and grand announcements. But these promises were never fulfilled during Husserl's lifetime. The "detailed analyses" that supposedly make up the "body" of phenomenology were at best mere announcements, with the exception of the small publication of the lectures on time-consciousness, published in 1928 by Heidegger (at a time when Husserl's most famous pupil was already estranged philosophically from his teacher). Husserl did present some of his descriptions in his lecture courses as a university professor (all written out in full and read off without any rhetorical pomp), but as these are for the most part published now, one can immediately see that the students must have been utterly lost as to what Husserl was presenting from the lectern.

It was no surprise, then, that the "phenomenological movement," as Husserl was fond of calling his following, turned out to be a group of heretics, who built their own philosophical edifices by taking some building blocks from the "quarry" of Husserl's oeuvre, not infrequently mocking their founding father for his shortcomings and biased views in his allegedly "naive" descriptions. However, only Husserl's closest pupils and assistants were aware of the philosophical mountain range (to use a metaphor from James Hart) that Husserl was heaping up in his daily private meditations, carried out in his famous "research manuscripts." But the situation was even worse: neither Husserl nor his last assistants, Landgrebe and Fink, when they made an arrangement of the manuscripts for the purposes of setting up an "archive" in 1935, had the faintest idea of the amount, extent, and thematic range of manuscripts, which they guessed as being at "a few thousand pages." The more exact amount is, as we now know, at around 40,000 pages of research manuscripts written over the course of more than forty years. Most of these texts and the topics with which they dealt were unknown to the public. It was a hidden treasure that not even its creator wholly oversaw.

Hence there was a profound disconnect, as mentioned above, between Husserl as he was publicly known and the "real" Husserl as he presented himself (to himself only) in these private texts. The disconnect also extended to the style of philosophizing itself. Opposed to the public figure who proudly and boldly presents a new research program and style of method, there is in his private notes a philosopher who is forever searching, always tentative, brutally honest to and hard on himself, at times almost timid and halting and, above all, always inscrutably self-critical. And this disconnect accounts, just as profoundly, for the way Husserl was received by his contemporaries and successors. Hence, the reception of Husserl is not a trivial story concerning the simple transmission of the author's intention via his writings to the reader, who either grasped or misunderstood the author's meaning. Instead, it is the story of a false or at least highly ambiguous reception due to these contingent factors, most importantly, due to Husserl's hesitancy and apprehension to publish anything that he did not deem perfect and satisfactory to himself. The tragic history of Husserl's private work, as we now know, was that of conceiving ever-new projects and producing (in his eyes) ever-new failures, and what finally ended up with the printer—sometimes at the urging of his friends and colleagues—were at all times only preliminary works, to be followed by what he hoped would finally be a definitive presentation of his philosophy.

Thus, the picture presents itself as the following: the public Husserl was the author of few works, most of which had the character (and sometimes the title) of "Introductions" and which were of a programmatic and promissory—and hence incomplete and unsatisfactory—character. The private Husserl was a tireless worker who conceived his philosophy as an endless research program with vast regions of research, and who worked on a breathtaking array of problems concurrently, increasingly engrossed in his work and convinced of its truth, and hence ever more removed from his contemporaries. But the published writings, as programmatic as they may be, give not the faintest indication of the wealth of his private work. It is unimaginable what a loss for philosophy it would have meant had these manuscripts not been saved from their certain destruction at the hands of the National Socialists, who loomed menacingly over the philosopher of Jewish descent in his last years.

But as is known, things played themselves out differently and more happily. Husserl's literary estate, including his library and drafts produced by his assistants—all with marginalia by the master—were saved, and a critical edition of his collected works, known as the *Husserliana,* was begun after the war. The generations of researchers who worked on the many volumes of the *Husserliana* were able to make their way through the mountain range they encountered only slowly, first transcribing the material from Husserl's shorthand, then publishing it piece by piece. For certain editorial reasons, the first volumes contained out-of-print books and finished typescripts (such as *Ideas II* and *III*), and the actual research manuscripts were initially not published—at least not as the main texts of these editions—until some two decades into this enormous editorial project; all the while philosophers began studying these steadily emerging texts in one of the several "Husserl Archives" around the world. Gradually in the mid-1970s, and increasingly in the 1990s and the first decade of the twenty-first century, a great number of these texts began seeing the light of day, together with a ten-volume edition of Husserl's correspondence. To date (at the beginning of the second decade of the twenty-first century), more than sixty volumes have been published in the *Husserliana* series (including its subseries), and the edition—which will not publish every text Husserl wrote, but only what the editors deemed most important— is nearing completion within the second decade of this century.

The reason I have gone into detail in elucidating this historical-philological background is because it accounts—as I insist, in a *non-trivial manner*—to a large extent for the history of Husserl's reception. While the reception on the part of Husserl's contemporaries is known, it is also worthwhile to look at it after Husserl's death. Husserl, who was Jewish by birth, was a persona non grata during the Nazi reign, and after 1945 he became virtually unknown, as is evidenced by the fact that the Belgian Franciscan priest Hermann Leo Van Breda, the savior of Husserl's manuscripts, had to revert to a publisher outside of Germany to print the tomes of the *Husserliana*. Also, the general demolition (*Kahlschlag*) produced by World War II and the emigration, expulsion, or death of philosophers from Germany left Martin Heidegger virtually as the "last man standing" on the philosophical scene of the time. Heidegger, though barred from teaching after his denazification process, nevertheless published a series of works in the postwar period, making him the celebrated philosopher who eclipsed nearly every other thinker in Germany at the time. Since Husserl, as Heidegger's teacher, had been—so it seemed— "*aufgehoben*" (sublated) in his pupil, it was not considered necessary to have recourse to a figure who had busied himself with abstract and far-removed problems such as logical thinking, and who had built his philosophical edifice on problematic foundations, such as Cartesianism, that had long been "destructed."

But during the heyday of the Heidegger mania, and despite it, several younger philosophers began exploring Husserl's "real" work, the unpublished material, and set out writing "discrete" studies and monographs devoted to special problems of Husserl's work that had not been known about before. To these works belong studies that are to this day compulsory reading for anybody interested in knowing Husserl, by figures who have shaped not only Husserl scholarship but also phenomenology writ large, and who have been important figures in postwar and contemporary philosophy (and from whose works the present author draws heavily in this book). These thinkers—regardless of whether they were critical of Husserl and ultimately rejected his project—paved the way, along with the text material itself that has appeared in the meantime, for a greater understanding of Husserl. There are still aspects of his work that are little known or poorly understood and are currently being explored (such as the field of moral philosophy), but it is fair to say that the situation now is such that the entire oeuvre of Husserl is laid out for public view—both through Husserl's texts themselves and those of his interpreters. In short, we are currently in the "golden age" of Husserl research and finally at the level at which the "real" Husserl can be received. Perhaps this time of "ruminating" was necessary for the "real" Husserl to emerge in fullness. This is not to discount in any way the efforts on the part of previous interpreters; their work is forever part of the understanding of Husserl that we have today. But it means that we are now on the cusp of a new wave of Husserl scholarship that has before its eyes the entire mountain range of Husserl's vast oeuvre and that can rise above the skirmishes that have occupied—and distracted—research in phenomenology for so long, where philosophers have been fond of taking cheap shots at Husserl for the sake of motivating their own projects and where the scholarship siding with Husserl has responded in kind to counter these allegations.

Thus, to come back to the issue that started this introductory reflection, some seventy years after Husserl's death, we are only now in a position to really *begin* assessing Husserl's philosophy as a whole. Despite problems with which one might take issue in the details, one is now able to paint a general portrait of this philosophy, to describe its gestalt, as it were, by taking a step back. But to do so, moreover, is also to place this philosophy into the history of Western thought by comparing and contrasting it with the great achievements of Western philosophy. Such an endeavor of locating Husserl within the tradition is a curious one, since Husserl himself—who was trained in mathematics and had a comparably limited knowledge of the history of philosophy—was incapable of assessing his own position in the Western tradition, and as a result his own characterization of his own achievement was not always fair. Husserl himself believed that he had broken new ground, or rather, broken with the tradition—as his famous talk of "bracketing" or "putting in suspension" through the epoché suggests—and hence believed he could philosophize in an altogether new key. And indeed, many scholars have followed Husserl in this self-characterization and have ignored (and sometimes overlooked) the relations of his phenomenology to the tradition. The *originality* of Husserl's phenomenology, however, remains unquestioned and undiminished when one understands Husserl, despite all of his innovativeness and novelty, as deeply rooted in a certain tradition of Western philosophy. To assess Husserl's philosophy against the backdrop of the tradition and to properly place him into this tradition—*this* marks the real importance of his philosophy and is the only manner to offer a fair assessment, which cannot do without comparisons.

Hence, in the following I will attempt to draw a portrait of his philosophy as I have come to see it, namely, as a philosophy deeply committed to the Western ideal of the Enlightenment. After that, I will spell out what I take to be the main *innovation* and the *provocative main thesis* of his transcendental phenomenology. It is this main thesis that is supported many times over in this book in various forms and arguments, and it is a thesis that has become clear only piecemeal to this author over the course of time. Unfortunately, this provocation has escaped most readers of Husserl, and perhaps its provocative character lies in Husserl's *profound continuity* with the best attempts of modern philosophy. I will end this introduction by explaining the specific angle of interpretation and the tendency pursued in this book, as it unfolds over the twelve chapters presented here.

A Portrait of Husserl: A Thinker of the Enlightenment

Before defining Husserl's project by going into the actual and painstaking work of phenomenology, that is, its detailed work of description, it may be permitted to take a step back and look at the gestalt of Husserl's philosophy, viewing it like a piece of art. I deliberately say "philosophy" (and not phenomenology) because every philosophical effort—be it in the form of a system or a research program or even only in the form of fragments and snippets—reveals a certain shape when viewed from a distance, and as having such a shape, it can be compared with other shapes of philosophy. Since philosophy is an anthropological constant and appears, accordingly, in every human culture in one shape or another—linked usually in one way or another to religion or art or science or other cultural activities—such a comparison is legitimate. But this task is also extremely difficult, since the one comparing these different gestalten has to have an intimate knowledge of each of them, so as to make such a comparison meaningful. Though some scholars (including Husserl himself) have attempted to compare Husserl's philosophy with that of certain figures outside the Western canon, I shall limit myself to the latter, hence, Husserl's position in Western—or as he called it, European—philosophy. Since, according to Husserl, Europe is itself an anthropological type (alongside India, China, and others), such a restriction to the philosophy growing out of Europe—as its ideal philosophical shape—is legitimate as well.

Compared to the view from a distance, the view through the magnifying glass—the vista that Husserl preferred—does not yield the gestalt of Husserl's philosophy. This makes Husserl a rather frustrating object of the view from a distance, compared to other philosophers, who address questions as to the ultimate intentions of their philosophies head-on, preferably in their famous introductions to their *magna opera* (Kant, Fichte, Hegel, and Heidegger being perhaps the most impressive examples). None of the grand rhetoric accompanying these presentations is to be found in Husserl. But Husserl himself, surprisingly, was able to express this, his gestalt, when prompted. I say "his gestalt" with deliberate ambiguity, for there is a moment in Husserl's life when his *personal* sentiment expresses this very notion with respect to his philosophy. He intimates, namely, that doing philosophy and being a human being end up being, to him, one and the same thing, or that philosophy is done at the behest of demands voiced by the individual, and vice versa; something in the individual calls for him to become a philosopher. This inseparability of the man and his work is itself a performative act on the part of the philosopher Edmund Husserl. On his seventieth birthday, as is recorded by bystanders, Husserl said before a group of pupils who had assembled in honor of his celebration: "I *had to* become a philosopher; otherwise I could not have lived in *this* world" ("*Ich* musste *Philosoph werden, sonst konnte ich in* dieser *Welt nicht leben,*" quoted by Schuhmann in Hua-Dok I, 344). I take what sounds like an off-the-cuff statement in a mood of high spirits to be, in fact, the profoundest expression of Husserl's philosophical sentiment. More precisely, the gestalt of his philosophy expressed therein is, I believe, the gestalt known in the Western tradition as that of *Enlightenment.* To say why the following interpretation of the gestalt of Husserl's philosophy expressed in this highly personal statement would not be mere psychologizing requires an explanation of what "Enlightenment" means.

The definition of "Enlightenment" can, of course, only be given by an approximation to this philosophical gestalt, and it cannot avoid being somewhat "subjective." What I take "Enlightenment" to be is, simply speaking, the project of becoming enlightened, or to stay with the metaphor of light, to reach the state of absolute transparency. This transparency pertains to an illumination about *what and who one is.* And this problem cannot be separated from the question regarding *what one does.* What one does, finally, depends on *where, when, and with whom* one does what one does and is who one is. Now this "otherness" to myself—the location, the time and circumstance, other human beings—that I am nevertheless inextricably part of has been called *situation* by a school known as existentialism. This existential sentiment is expressed in Ortega's famous "*yo soy yo y mi circunstancia.*" To become illuminated with respect to who and what one is and does, therefore, is *inseparably linked* to my self's other, which I shall call, in one word, *world,* as the totality of all situations. Enlightenment, then, is the project of becoming illuminated about myself *in my inseparable relation and enmeshment with the world.* I cannot define and understand myself without the world and my relation to the world of which I am part, and vice versa; there is no comprehension of the world without a comprehension of the world in relation to me. "I" and "world" are just two infinitely distant poles of what I shall call *One Structure.* Just as I know that the world does not depend on me, that I do not create it, that I am just one object in the world among others, I *equally* know that the only way to experience the world is from my own perspective. It is through *my own eyes,* to use vision as *pars pro toto,* that I see the world, though this seeing "does nothing to" the world, does not "harm" it. The two viewpoints are not mutually exclusive, but compatible as statements following from two fundamentally different views on what I call the *One Structure.*

Indeed, this is where an Enlightenment account differs from an existentialist one, though they share the same starting point. Indeed, what sounds like a *dark riddle,* in Ortega's phrase (and one can find similar turns of phrase in Sartre, Heidegger, and others), is, to the one committed to the Enlightenment, a *task,* a *terminus ad quem,* a something that *can and needs* to be illuminated, that can be made sense of, that can be clarified thoroughly and "rationally." The traditional term for this process of making transparent by way of rational clarification is, since Kant, *critique.* Enlightenment is thus a process of critique whose goal—an ideal, a regulative idea—is transparency with respect to the *One Structure.* This One Structure is, to repeat, the *fundamental relation (or perhaps better: relatedness, interconnectedness), the co-relation of I and world.*

Now what this "making transparent" can actually mean may legitimately be defined differently. I said before that it is a *making understandable rationally.* But this definition, too, is located on a certain level of formality. Hence, what is reason? More appropriately asked, how is reason *utilized* and *applied*? Using reason as *logical reason,* utilizing logical propositions, formulating premises and drawing inferences and conclusions, is but one special application of reason, and a very specialized one at that. To *act* (to which belongs thinking) *rationally,* then, can take on many forms, such as judging, arguing, deliberating, reflecting, but also negotiating, convincing, asking, promising, and finally, acting and doing such as helping, defending, donating, giving, and so on. As one can see, this enumeration of verbs moves from individual to social acts, from theoretical to practical acts, implying no particular hierarchy or order (though it is possible that one might find one through more deliberation).

Is there any kind of common denominator in these acts, when construed as rational acts? I believe that here, too, the *One Structure* comes to the fore again: all acts that can count as rational have as their core the interrelatedness of I and world, which appears in the form of others, the environment, the situation, the time and place, and so on. The rational element in making understandable the *One Structure* consists in clarifying its manifold and in turn interrelated aspects in such a way that *understanding becomes a common phenomenon.* Understanding is never solipsistic, nor is the use of reason in any of the ways listed (an incomplete list, to be sure). To use a phrase from Husserl, understanding, rationality, and

Enlightenment are essentially and intrinsically *intersubjective* projects. In characterizing the task of philosophy as trying to make understandable something previously not understood—and perhaps something one had never thought one could ever understand—Husserl once uses the metaphor of the "torch of reason" that has be lit in order to bring light into this murky region. That is to say, to Husserl's definition of the Enlightenment belongs the *steadfast belief* that *everything can in principle be understood,* and that means nothing other than the *enactment* of the fundamental belief of the Enlightenment, namely, *that the world stands under laws.* And it is the task of science to discover, discern, and understand these laws. Science, then, is more than just natural science with a simple or singular model of reasoning (laws following strict causality, say); it is what is called *Wissenschaft* in Kant's philosophy: a rational scrutiny in the manner just indicated with respect to the *laws and their peculiar character* in each possible region of experience. This is a meaning that "science" retains from the German idealists and up to Husserl's notion of philosophy as *rigorous* science. To achieve this rational understanding by way of a making-understandable as a communal affair is the ideal task of the Enlightenment.

These reflections on the definition of the Enlightenment have brought us back to Husserl. I have interpreted Husserl's personal statement quoted above as an expression of (his understanding of) the Enlightenment (despite his personal misgivings about its historical manifestation). It is more than a personal and anecdotal little acceptance speech; or if it was, Husserl was, I think, speaking from the heart of his philosophical ethos, which had become fused with his personal one. Including what has just been said, one can "unpack" this statement in the following way. Husserl's statement that "otherwise I could not live in this world" is an expression of the *One Structure* of I and world. But this structure is that which made him turn to philosophy ("I had to become a philosopher"). In other words, there is a direct link between the problem of the *One Structure* and the task of solving it through philosophy. Or put differently, doing philosophy is never just a "mere scientific" affair, a "job" among others or a sophisticated mind game; instead, doing philosophy is motivated by the *existential problem* of "*yo y mi circunstancia.*" But the existential riddle that existentialists enjoy reveling in, is, for Husserl, merely the starting point for doing philosophy as enacting the Enlightenment, which is a *rational clarification and illumination of this One Structure.* In other words, and this is exactly where Husserl's existential concern ends and where his philosophizing begins, Husserl's philosophy is motivated by the quest to make the *One Structure* understandable scientifically. It is merely—as opposed to existentialism—the *terminus a quo.* Husserl's philosophy, thus, is the basic existential problem turned into a philosophical research program to make understandable, to illuminate, to reach, with the torch of reason, *into the One Structure,* to bring ultimate transparency into the *One Structure.*

What I call the *"One Structure"* here is, in Husserl's terminology, nothing other than *the correlational a priori,* the essential relation between constituting subject and constituted world. Philosophy as the enactment of Enlightenment, where the personal and the public can no longer be separated, thus can be defined as the endless project of illuminating the One Structure, the interrelatedness of I and World. It becomes illuminated through a rational analysis, that is, one that *makes understandable* this very interrelatedness *in manifold manners* as itemized above, with the ideal telos of an absolute transparency, which is equally a self-transparency as well as a transparency with respect to the World; they are but two sides of the same coin. This understanding has been framed as a *research program called phenomenology.* What this research program amounts to, what it means *in concreto,* will be discussed now, after the gestalt of Husserl's philosophy as a form of Enlightenment philosophy—or Enlightenment as such—has been defined. The *One Structure* becomes, in Husserl, concretized in his notion of the *correlational a priori.*

The Thesis of This Book: The Thoroughgoing Correlation, as Disclosed Through the Reduction

As a result of being a form of Enlightenment philosophy, Husserl's phenomenology is importantly a form of transcendental philosophy, or what amounts to the same, a philosophy committed to transcendental idealism. Once Husserl establishes phenomenology as transcendental idealism, he never wavers in this self-interpretation. What transcendental idealism establishes, in broadest terms, is the dependence of the world as experienced on the experience of the world. What is forever eliminated is the idea of a world independent of experience, or in Kant's terms, a thing-in-itself. The belief in a mind-independent world, which Kant calls empirical realism, is, in turn, only possible on the basis of transcendental idealism, simply because the statement "the world exists independently of experience" is a statement made on the part of an experiencing agent. There is no escaping transcendental idealism; boldly stated, it is impossible to leave the confines of our mind. But in Husserl's view, Kant had by no means exploited his main insight to the fullest. By briefly contrasting the two positions, the peculiarity of Husserl's transcendental idealism will become evident. (For a more thorough discussion of this contrast, see chapter 7.)

To be sure, one need not *restrict* the Copernican turn, as Kant did, to "assuming that the objects must conform to our *cognition,* which would agree better with the requested possibility of an *a priori* cognition of them" (Kant 1998, 110, B xvi, italics added). Instead, one can broaden this idea to assuming that the *world as such* conforms not only to our a priori cognition of it but, more elementarily, to our *experience* of it. Thus, the Kantian turn to transcendental idealism turns out to be a very specific application of a more general idea, namely, the Husserlian one that not only does our cognition of things in the world depend on our cognitive faculties, but our *experience of the world itself* depends on our *experiential faculties.* Time and space are not merely forms of intuition that receptively, that is, passively "take in" matter and that are "blind" without concepts, but they are constitutive structures that are active even in "just taking in" matter. Experience does not require concepts but actually generates them, "constitutes" them. Every experience of the world is a matter of constitution, all the way up to making synthetic judgments a priori.

Hence, the Kantian turn was motivated by the *factum* of synthetic judgments a priori, and the philosophical question generated by this fact was the famous "how possible?"—the question as to the conditions of the possibility of the fact. More precisely, the conditions of the possibility of synthetic judgments a priori pertain to, or amount to, the *justification* of this fact. How are we *justified* in claiming, rightfully, that synthetic judgments a priori are not only possible but in fact exist (in Newtonian science, at least so Kant believed on the basis of the scientific belief of his day)? It is from here that Kant's critical epistemology, replacing traditional metaphysics, unravels. The answer to the "how justified" is given in what Kant calls a "*deduction.*"

The Husserlian turn to transcendental idealism, by contrast, is motivated by the *factum of the world* and *its justification.* This is a question that the Kantian project must take for granted, or rather the Kantian question is located already on a much higher level than that of the justification of the reality of the world. The Kantian original question thus becomes rephrased as the conditions of the possibility of the experience of the world, and answering it clarifies the justification of the experience of the world, and hence of the world itself, since any notion of a "world in itself" (like a thing in itself) has been excluded with the turn to transcendental idealism. Hence, the Husserlian question asks about the conditions of the possibility of the experience of world, the "how possible" of our being justified about claiming that we do in fact experience the world. The answer to the "how justified" is given in what Husserl calls a *"reduction."*

"The reduction," therefore, is the term for Husserl's version of the transcendental turn, which leads to his specific project of a transcendental philosophy. The reduction, in other words, establishes phenomenology as transcendental philosophy. Every access to phenomenology must pass through this eye of the needle. It is no surprise, then, that the reduction has taken on such a decisive role in Husserl's thought and stands as *pars pro toto* for his entire philosophical enterprise. I shall not rehearse the methodological steps of the reduction or the different ways into the reduction here (but see chapters 1 to 3). But highlighting what I see as the most important aspect of it will bring us to the thesis of this book, the *thoroughgoing correlation* as Husserl's main contribution to the project of transcendental philosophy, phenomenologically reconceived.

The reduction (from Latin *re-ducere*) leads back from the natural attitude, in which I conceive of myself as a thing in the world and the world as existing independently of me (empirical realism), to the transcendental-phenomenological attitude committed to transcendental idealism. This is the stance in which the correlational a priori between constituting subjectivity and constituted world becomes disclosed. The reduction, thus, is not to be (mis)understood as a leading back to a Cartesian Ego as a "tag-end of the world" but as the disclosure of what Husserl in his earlier period calls the "immanence" of consciousness. The term "immanence" is misleading in many ways as well, for it could imply some sort of mental "interiority" in a self-enclosed mental realm, some sort of an "internal movie theater" detached from the world. But if one contrasts immanence with transcendence and understands the latter in the Kantian sense, as that which reaches beyond possible experience, then the term "immanence" as a designation of "that which does not go beyond" is appropriate and comprehensible. "Immanence," then, refers to the region of experience of the world on the part of an experiencing agent (who is always but an individual in a community, in an inter-subjectivity). Immanence, therefore, is made up of the two parts, experience-of and that which is given-in experience. The *terminus technicus* for this complex structure in Husserl is the *correlational a priori*. It is a rephrasing, after the transcendental turn, of what has been called earlier the *One Structure*. The reduction as leading-back, then, must not be understood as leading back from the world to the I, but rather from the *natural attitude,* in which I and world are conceived empirically, to the *transcendental attitude,* in which the correlational a priori discloses itself. The leading-back, therefore, discloses what Husserl also simply calls *"the transcendental"* as the title for the correlational a priori with its noetic-noematic structure.

The relation of both sides of the coin is that of a constant balance, an equilibrium, a harmony.

And this is where Husserl's transcendental idealism differs from that of Kant and other idealists, who place the emphasis on the subjective side of things as one case of overemphasis, instead of the objective side, which exists as well (to be discussed later). In Kant, the tendency towards the subjective is clear from the very manner in which the thought experiment guiding the first *Critique* is set up: instead of privileging the objects over the subject, which must conform to them, the experiment turns things around. This tendency toward a subjective idealism becomes exacerbated, as is known, in Fichte, only to be balanced again by Schelling's "real-idealism" and then, though differently, in Hegel's absolute idealism. Hegel's may appropriately be called a *methodological* idealism because Hegel's idealism is no longer committed to any stance but is an endless reflectiveness that has sublated all possible positions (theses) and ends up in an absolute mediacy, which amounts to an absolute immediacy (following the nature of dialectical thought). Whether or not Husserl's idealism may be compared to Hegel's will be discussed in chapter 6 and need not occupy us here; but what is important is to draw from this briefest of reflections on the history of idealisms after Kant the conclusion for a characterization of Husserl's form of transcendental idealism.

The reduction as leading back to the disclosure of the correlational a priori culminates in Husserl's peculiar notion of transcendental idealism. Opposed to any idealisms that place the emphasis on either the "subjective" or "objective" side of things, Husserl's *entire focus* is on the *thoroughgoing correlation of subjective and objective*. The correlational a priori is the *One Structure* transcendentally clarified, where neither of the two poles may be privileged over the other. Both stand in a thoroughgoing correlation, where in each case the *absolute balance* between both needs to be maintained. There is no subjective constitution without an objective *constitutum*. Nor is there an objective constitution (constitution of something objective) without a subjective counterpart, a subjective *constituens*. To say it in less technical terms: the world and the world-experiencing Ego are dancing—at all times, on all levels, in all forms and shapes—a tango. The correlation, as the balance, the collaboration and cooperation on all levels, is never upset; never is the relation severed, and it cannot and must not be severed. This co-relation is thoroughgoing, in other words, because it obtains on all levels of constitution, from lowest passivity to highest activity. Passivity and activity, which designate the two extreme poles of constitution, are thus not to be identified as, on the one hand, an absolute non-involvement of the Ego up to its opposite, and, on the other, an absolute involvement. All constitution involves Ego and world, and this is not just some lofty speculative statement but one that is demonstrated in detail in Husserl's rigorous scientific philosophy with all its descriptive wealth.

For instance, where a naturalistic or pre-transcendental, empirical theory would describe perception as a simple receiving of sense-data, the correlational a priori on this level of "passivity" (pre-predicative experience) consists in a givenness of the perceptual object in adumbrations, with a concomitant interaction with this givenness of the Ego on the level of a pre-predicative, lived-bodily experience of it. Likewise, any active engagement in the world, a self-conscious judging or deliberate acting, is based on a history of sedimented acts as acts in the world, and the world, therefore, is not just the stage upon which an Ego can act, but the world constitutes the situation I am in *as much as* I am able to shape, within my realm of possibilities, the circumstances of the situation. The freedom of the "I can" is at all times restricted by these circumstances limiting me. But the latter are, at the same time, the conditions of the possibility of acting freely. (Recall Kant's image of the "light dove," Kant 1998, A v/B viii.) Nor does the world simply dominate me; I do not simply shape and create the world. The term "constitution" refers to this complex mutual dependency. Unraveling it is the task of phenomenology.

These are just hints of examples of the thoroughgoing correlation, which, as being "backed up" by numerous detailed descriptions, any reader of Husserl will recall, and they demonstrate *in concreto* what Husserl means by transcendental idealism, his version of it, which is cashed out in terms of the theory of constitution. This is equally a transcendental theory of world-constitution (world being constituted by subjectivity) as it is one of world-constituting (subjectivity constituting the world). They are two sides of the same coin. I and world are merely the poles of a correlation, of the tango, where any notion of a pure I or a pure world (or world in itself) are abstractions. In truth, all worldliness is Egoic, and all egoity is worldly, but in such a way that they stand in a (co-)relation of mutual constitution. All of this is spoken, however, after the transcendental turn, and the talk is of I and world as *transcendental* notions, as conditions of possibility of the world appearing to an Ego, and of a world being giveable to an Ego. Thus, whenever Husserl speaks of Ego, it is shorthand for "the Ego constituting the world," and vice versa; "world" is shorthand for "the world as constituted by an Ego." This explains Husserl's only seemingly contradictory statements—statements that are used to criticize him for an overemphasis on either side—to the effect that either the Ego or the World are "apodictic." They are both *moments of the One Structure,* transcendentally interpreted and phenomenologically described. World and Ego each bear the respective mark of the other.

The advantage of this theory is that it always maintains this balance, never severs this correlation, while many forms of idealism can be interpreted as tipping the balance to one side or the other. But this tradition of tipping balances goes even further and continues in philosophies (or phenomenologies) that might not appear to be a form of idealism. In the latter case, the upsetting of the balance has resulted in a move away from the subject, as we shall see in a moment. But to understand this claim—namely, that what has appeared as a critique of Husserl still takes place within the confines of idealism—one might mention, as a supporting interpretation of the reduction, the one that was put forth already in Ernst Tugendhat's famous *Der Wahrheitsbegriff bei Husserl und Heidegger* (*The Concept of Truth in Husserl and Heidegger*) in 1967 and which, if true, has consequences for the entire phenomenological movement. If one can agree that the reduction establishes transcendental idealism as the basic fact of the correlational a priori, then phenomenology *as such* reconstructs the manner in which the world as it is experienced in the natural attitude comes about for an experiencing agent. In this very general characterization, then, all manners of doing phenomenology as describing consciousness or experience (of things, entities, other human beings, God, moods) under the paradigm of intentionality can only take place after having performed the reduction. This means, if such a reading is right, that phenomenology in any form presupposes the reduction and stands within the space of immanence; they all take place, explicitly or implicitly, within the "space" disclosed through the turn to transcendental idealism. To reject the reduction, then, would amount to rejecting the correlation of consciousness and world as the minimal common denominator of any definition of phenomenology.

If this interpretation of the reduction is essentially correct—and I emphatically believe it is—then the further history of phenomenology can be characterized as being a series of attempts to upset the Husserlian balance of the correlational a priori by privileging either of the two poles. This has happened, essentially, in attempts to dislodge the supposed subjectivism of Husserl by insisting that constitution moves not from I to world (and be it in the form of the Other) but the other way around. Phenomenologies that emphasize this otherness in the constitution of the Ego, rather than the reverse, are forms of "objective idealism." The mistake here is that Husserl is placed on the side of a "subjective idealism" in the form of Fichte, a position, as has become clear, that he never held.

A seemingly more subtle critique is the attempt to do away with this dualism altogether. This is, however, a different expression of essentially the same critical tendency. It is present when Husserl is charged with being caught up in a subject-object dichotomy (one of the worst ways to misrepresent the correlational a priori, because the world is never an object), a dichotomy which can be undercut (from whence?), for instance, when emphasizing that the "power" of the world, in the form of the tradition or history, is "stronger" than Husserl's notion of a constituting subject, which is not truly (self-)conscious but merely a "flickering light" in the closed circuits of historical events. All of these approaches, as ingenious and original as they may be, can be interpreted as attempts to tip the secure balance of Husserl's correlational a priori into a certain direction, all the while *arguing, mistakenly, that Husserl has occupied the opposite side,* or that his stance is a lopsided one. They all misunderstand Husserl's transcendental idealism as a thoroughgoing correlation of the One Structure with its poles, I and world. To repeat, the strength of Husserl's phenomenology as transcendental philosophy committed to transcendental idealism is the thoroughgoing correlational a priori as a *balance* between both poles in which they are "always already" intertwined, interrelated, dancing a tango. And it always takes two to tango.

There is yet another way to cash out the achievement of Husserl's stance by shifting to a slightly different language. The truth of transcendental idealism of whichever form—even the lopsided ones—is its insistence that there is *no direct access* to the world in itself. The world is always world-for-us, for an experiencing agent (in one way or another), and there is never merely "raw" experience that "then" becomes "interpreted" (conceptualized, constructed, etc.). Even in Kant, what is experienced is always already conceptualized ("schematized") in order to be an object for us. This insight perhaps reaches its peak in Hegel's idealism, whose whole point may be phrased as explaining the mediacy of the only seemingly immediate (the "this" of natural consciousness) as being on one grand path towards mediacy that has become transparent to itself *as* mediacy, and that hence achieves immediacy, but only on the level of absolute mediacy. To say it differently, the truth of transcendental idealism is that there is no such thing as immediacy, a direct access to the world "out there." This is the realist presupposition that has been shown up as naive. But if there is no direct immediacy, no direct access, the same must hold, following the correlational a priori, for the Ego itself. The Ego must be mediate *to itself* just as much as it is to the world.

This is the context of Gadamer's critique of what he critically refers to as the "philosophy of reflection" (*Reflexionsphilosophie*), as a philosophy committed to the (according to Gadamer) *mistaken* ideal that while my access to the world might be mediate, I still have a direct access to *myself* via reflection. Consciousness of the world might be mediate, indirect, but at least I have immediate access to myself in reflection, when I turn away from the world and turn upon myself. The most transparent view I can ever get is that of myself in the looking glass of isolated reflection. It is this notion of the "armchair philosopher" that Gadamer applies to (among others) Husserl; in other words, Husserl is interpreted as someone whose methodological ideal lies in this tradition. To be clear about the critique: it challenges the idea that while any access to the world, including to myself in the world as a "me" (as Sartre would call it), as an object in the world, is mediate, I can still gain this much-desired immediacy via self-reflection. But in this desire for immediacy, I encapsulate myself in a reflective stance, I enclose myself within (what amounts to) my own prison of the self, which is a fiction. Husserl, with his ideal of the "uninterested observer" established after the epoché, is, to Gadamer, a prime example of someone who chases the fantasy of having immediacy at the cost of disengaging oneself from the world, distancing oneself from it in order to reach a supposedly "safe" realm of absolute interiority (and to indulge in the myth of absolute certainty), in which I can finally be my "real self," truly "at home" with myself only.

To count Husserl among the "philosophers of reflection" turns out to be one of the most insidious, and also stubbornly repeated, criticisms of his phenomenology. The aim of countering it here is not to engage in a lengthy *Auseinandersetzung* with Gadamer (on this, see chapter 11). But in refuting it briefly, one can counter once more Husserl's alleged naïveté or insensitivity with respect to such critiques stemming from speculative thought. To begin with, Husserl's transcendental idealism, too, (of course) rejects any direct access, any immediacy, if one means by this notion the idea that there is something that stands "behind" the phenomena given. We are, as Husserl insists, immediately in touch with the world, but the world as it gives itself; Husserl the idealist is also, as he insists, one of the most hard-nosed realists. But Husserl would be hopelessly naive were he to imply that this did hold for the Ego once the phenomenological gaze came to rest upon *it* instead of on any other given phenomenon. Reflection upon oneself is just *one intentional act* alongside others. And as an intentional act, it, too, constitutes. The stance of the phenomenologist when he does phenomenology is that of epoché, of letting things be, keeping them suspended in brackets, not participating in any of the thetic modalities that characterize normal intentional life, such as taking something to be, to be certain, to be doubtful, not to be, and so on. In this sense, the acts of the phenomenologist, like all acts of thinking, constitute a reflective stance, even those that describe the concrete subject's practical engagement and those that critique the ideal of a disengaged observer. But phenomenological reflection, as has become clear, is reflection upon the correlational a priori. That is to say, once the particular act of the phenomenologist is turned to the Ego itself, this sort of act-direction cannot mean that the Ego would be isolated from its relation to the world. The reflective act, which constitutes the Ego *as* reflecting, cannot, then, describe merely a worldless Ego, but discloses the Ego-as-worldly-as-disclosed-by-a-reflective-act. Reflection, properly understood, is not an act, then, that tears us away from the world, but one in which this very fact of being intertwined with the world (the correlational a priori) becomes thematic.

In other words, the idea that reflection on the Ego might move us from a mediacy (the ego directed at non-Egoic things) to an immediacy (the ego directed at itself) is a completely wrongheaded understanding of reflection, for Husserl. Any access to myself, therefore, whether through reflection or, mutatis mutandis, some other form, will also *only be mediate.* I will never be able to reflect myself out of the correlational a priori! And this means that there is *no contradiction* between the mediacy established through the transcendental turn and the access to the self through self-reflection. Even the most "intense" self-reflection cannot escape the correlational a priori and will only give me access to myself *mediately.* Even the act of reflection, as *per definitionem* an act directed upon myself, is an intentional act, and for that reason it is defined by the mediacy that mediates between the poles of the correlational a priori. Self-reflection, therefore, has methodologically speaking no "higher dignity" vis-à-vis other forms of intentional life; on the contrary, *every* form of thematizing—what philosophy does when it focuses on things otherwise hidden in natural life—is a form of reflection. Just as all intentional life is a form of constitution and is beholden to the correlational a priori, all thematizing functions through the structure of latency and patency, to use Husserl's terminology: thematizing something (not necessarily in "thinking") makes something apparent (patent), while the thematizing stream of consciousness is in turn not apparent (latent), but can again be made patent by a higher latency, and so on. There is, thus, nothing mysterious or privileged about reflection. As a thematic focus on the self in its constitutive functioning, it discloses its contribution to the constitution of the world, to which belongs the constitution of itself; both constitute one another.

Thus, the result of this "meditation" (pun intended) is that it would be a grave mistake to count Husserl as a representative of *Reflexionsphilosophie* (disregarding the larger question of who exactly might count as one of its representatives). His is a philosophy of reflection in the minimal sense that any *thinking* requires a distancing (by making patent from the standpoint of a latency) from one's normal state of affairs. But this distancing is a distancing from the *situation of the One Structure,* which becomes thematic precisely after the transcendental turn, which itself is an act of reflection. It is not a distancing from the world in favor of the I—or its opposite, say, in a form of self-dissolution in the waves of the world. To correctly understand the correlational a priori is already to see that all focus on the world (*as well as* on the Ego) implies a form of decentering, in contradistinction from a view which believes that a unilateral path runs from Ego to the world (while not denying that any access to the world is from the standpoint of first-person experience). Hence, Husserl's is not a philosophy of reflection which asserts that access to the "true self" occurs in a self-isolating reflection and with the ideal that this reflection might possibly achieve a stance outside of history and its affairs. A reflection upon oneself as part of the correlational a priori is not a "somersault" out of history, out of the world, or out of the correlational a priori. Even an "epoché from all traditions," which Husserl ponders in his late manuscripts (see chapter 12), is not meant as such a somersault but as a reflective view that makes this very embeddedness in tradition transparent—while not giving the Ego over to a tradition entirely. Here, too, Husserl retains a balance between autonomy and heteronomy (where autonomy implies heteronomy and vice versa). A phenomenological reflection is, for Husserl, an act that, if carried out correctly, precisely discloses the correlational a priori as a structure that is to be described with phenomenological tools and methods. Without a reflective act that distances the reflector from his life in the natural attitude, it would be impossible to attain a stance that gains an overview of the correlational a priori, which is a noetic-noematic structure of experience and not some static opposition between subject and object. Were this so, Heidegger would be completely correct in calling it a *Scheinproblem.*

But we may yet ask—and this brings us to the last systematic point of this introduction—what exactly is it that is disclosed in self-reflection? It cannot be a self outside of the correlational a priori, outside of history and outside of relations to others. But what is it *positively* speaking? Are the issues of self-reflection and self-consciousness simply anathema to phenomenology? Certainly not. But what can they mean, if they cannot deliver on a promise to provide an absolute or immediate access to ourselves? Answering these questions, finally, brings us to the manner in which the formal theme of "thoroughgoing correlation" gets filled with concrete content in Husserl's method and in what it describes, namely, the lifeworld. The lifeworld is the world in which we live. Thematizing the lifeworld, therefore, means also thematizing the self. The two cannot be separated. This much is clear. But what can this mean, especially with respect to the self that allegedly becomes thematic in self-reflection? What does self-reflection yield, from the standpoint of the correlational a priori? What does the correlational a priori predicate about the subject and the world?

Husserl's Philosophy as a Hermeneutic Phenomenology of the Lifeworld as a World of Culture

Reflection, as this reflection upon reflection has shown, is a form of thematization, one in which the Ego becomes transparent—patent—to itself. But this is not the same as a privileged access to oneself in which that reflection discloses a private vestige, a "secret back room" of the self no one else has access to, where the only key to unlock it is through my own reflection and which would reveal the "true self" that is otherwise "dispersed" in the world. Such a vision of the armchair philosopher has been forever dismissed and certainly cannot be taken to be Husserl's view. But rejecting this vision is not inconsistent with the insistence, which is equally a defining trait of Husserlian phenomenology, that any access to myself is irreducibly mine, from the first-person perspective. A perfectly valid, albeit (to Husserl) incomplete, definition of phenomenology is, after all, that it is a descriptive enterprise from the first-person perspective; a standpoint that is radically mine and to which nobody else has access. Nobody can see "into my mind" the way I do; nobody can be hooked up to me to become "online" with me in the way two computers can be linked up, with one having access to the files of the other. From the methodological standpoint, this is an insight that is hardly disputable. But it is also prone to a grave misunderstanding, namely, that my private reflection upon myself (and it cannot but be private) would supposedly disclose an equally private self. This was the mistake that followed from the erroneous notion of phenomenology as a form of *Reflexionsphilosophie*. What is it, then, that *does* become disclosed in reflection?

As has become clear, reflection, for Husserl, is no mysterious access to "hidden vestiges of the soul," but merely a manner of thematization in which something becomes apparent that was not apparent before, simply because no intentional gaze was directed toward it. (It was operative but not thematic, like an ordinary act of perception that is constantly ongoing.) But reflection is *just one intentional act alongside others*. This means that it, too, is a form of constitution, and that it discloses, as a "global" overview over this sphere, the self as a transcendental subject, that is, as the "subjective" pole of the correlational a priori. Thus, any thematizing of the subject is a thematizing of it *as the subject correlated to the things "out there"*; there is no self without world. This relationship is not *created* by the reflecting Ego, but simply disclosed as that which is the defining characteristic of Ego: the fact that it forms a correlational a priori with the world. Hence, the idea that reflection discloses a "real self" *when torn from the world* is forever rejected; to the contrary, such a view of the self is one of the *gravest distortions* one can have of oneself. The phenomenological analysis of reflection reveals that the notion of a worldless Ego, even as an ideal, is an impossible notion; such an Ego is a *lucus a non lucendo,* not a sphere of light against the darkness of the world "out there," but in truth the darkness of the self. One can adopt here Sartre's talk of the "opaqueness" of the Ego, if we take it to mean the Ego as a worldless and isolated entity. What, then, is the "true self," if it cannot be construed as some form of privacy, a view which would *in truth* amount to a form of solipsism?

The idea of the "true self" as removed from the world and worldly affairs (no matter how it might become revealed) is nothing but a form of Romanticism with respect to the self, one that celebrates its ultimate climax in Heidegger's idea of authentic existence. This is a form of life which has departed from the sphere of the public as that of *das Man,* which stifles any attempt at an authentic existence. This is the place where an impression that might have crept in over the course of the above presentation of Husserl's correlational a priori needs to be dispelled. For the Ego, though its access to the world is always by way of the first person, is always a subject as part of an *intersubjective community,* for Husserl. The above presentation, as focused on the Ego, was thus deliberately (or necessarily) an abbreviation, an ellipsis. The individual subject and its personal perspective is always but an infinitesimally small "moment" of the full realm of subjectivity, which is an intersubjectivity (in its historical dimension, as disclosed in genetic phenomenology). And this is again where the existential sentiment becomes revealed as a mere *terminus a quo* for Husserl: where the existential dichotomy *"yo y mi circunstancia"* seems to imply an isolated I in the face of the world (which threatens to devour me, to leave me bereft of any individuality), it is revealed, after the transcendental turn, to be the two-sided structure of *I as a member of a community* and *the world as a world with, by, and for others.* The correlational a priori, therefore, as revealed through the reflective act upon my individual self, gets fleshed out, on the subjective side, as a constitutive intersubjectivity, and on the objective side, as a world as a historical lifeworld. Neither I nor world are single categories; they are essentially *plural.* Let me spell out the consequences briefly.

Let us focus on the objective side for a moment, that of the lifeworld. What does it mean that the lifeworld is the correlate of a subjectivity as *intersubjectivity*? As forming a thoroughgoing correlation, the constitutive structures on the side of the lifeworld must correspond to those on the "other" side. That is, the world, too, must have a historical dimension, a genetic development, and a "habitual style" in accordance with that of a certain community of human beings. A habitual style, however, is never just a unanimous sameness, but is differentiated into diverse styles, just like the style of a person is made up of many different substyles (one's manner of walking, of speaking, of listening, etc.—all of these are part and parcel of someone's character as a complex) and is always only presumptive. And furthermore, these styles have not just been created in an instant, but have a "tail" of sedimentations—in short, a history. To shift to the world: it is, as the situation of all situations in which my life (as part of a community) plays itself out, immediately there with a "causal style" and as such there for me as providing options, lifestyles in the broadest sense of the term, that is, manners in which I can *partake and participate* in the constitution of the world. The world, therefore, is a vast field of *projects*—a term for collective activities in the broadest sense— in which subjects have participated, which they have created, shaped, refined, and institutionalized, and will continue to do so. One may only think of the habitual playing with a ball, which has formed itself into a game with accepted rules, and has institutionalized itself in leagues up to the World Cup. Entering a football team is but one example in which an individual becomes part of, partakes in, and creatively shapes (constitutes) the world. The world as lifeworld is, to use a term preferred by Husserl's neo-Kantian colleagues, a world of *culture.* Culture is not meant here as some lofty term for what one ordinarily means by "high culture" in order to distinguish it from subcultures or what is not cultured, i.e., primitive. Culture is, just like the lifeworld, a transcendental concept in the framework of transcendental idealism, and it implies that there is no "raw" world to which one may have *immediate* access, a region of "wild being" that *then* becomes "culturally formed." But just as constitution takes place on every level, so does that which constitution creates: this is culture. There is, therefore, no immediate access to the world, and no worldly immediacy, as explained above, and conversely, all access to the world is *cultural* in character in the sense of *creating, shaping, and partaking in* culture. The lifeworld must, therefore, be understood as a world of culture from beginning to end; culture has no "higher" meaning in opposition to "primitive" life.

To see the world as *culture,* then, is the consequence of transcendental idealism. Just as the dream of access to an immediate and "absolute" self has been dismissed, the idea of a pure and pristine world prior to culture (with its undeniable excesses in science and technology) has been revealed as nothing but a naive Romanticism. Both are Romanticisms that contradict critical philosophy as realized in transcendental idealism. This means, with respect to the Romantic dream of a pure self and a pure world prior to any cultural contaminations on both sides: one's "true" self and the "real" world can only be disclosed as, on the one hand, an Ego as part of an intersubjective community, as part of an ongoing activity, as a project that it does with others and in which it is involved *nolens volens* in shaping culture. On the other hand, the Ego is now understood as inextricably bound to the world as a world of culture, that is, a world replete with projects and institutions and objects, all of which reveal "spirit" as objectified. And both are related in the form of the correlational a priori; their relation is always bilateral.

"Authentic existence," then, as the dream conjured up by Romanticisms of various forms, can occur only through partaking in one of the projects that define the human being as part of a culture, and which define culture as the product of human creation and activity. One's "true home" can, therefore, never be outside of culture as a communal project. One's "true self" and the "real world" are, hence, revealed only through the correlational a priori, and they can reveal "authentic existence" as possible only through the thoroughgoing correlation of subjectivity as intersubjectivity and the lifeworld as a world of culture. What defines us is our place in culture, and what defines the lifeworld as cultural is the manner in which it accommodates these practices, which in turn make a cultural and humane life possible. To become *authentic,* then, is only possible by embracing culture as a communal world of common affairs, rather than shunning it by retreating into a niche, or what is nowadays also called a subculture, as deliberately shunning the "dominant master discourse" that "silences." Such a view rejects what is its very condition of possibility.

Is this not replacing one Romanticism with another, that of culture and the place of humans in culture? No, it is not; for this view of subjectivity and lifeworld is not a description of the world-as-it-is, but of the world-as-it-ought-to-be. In other words, just as the kingdom of ends is, for Kant, a regulative idea, never realized but ever to be realized, so is this vision of the lifeworld as a world of culture an eternal regulative idea for Husserl. (He calls it "teleology.") Romanticism dreams of a world as it should be and will never be and is hence of a melancholy mood. The critical view does not dream but is animated by a self-prescribed optimism; it constructs an idea of how the world ought to be, knowing that it will never be that way completely but believing that it is an ideal worth pursuing and towards which one can make actual progress. As such, it is an ideal that will never be fully realized and that is constantly threatened by crises. But crises, more than ever, are moments for pause and reflection, for *Besinnung,* on what we can achieve with our best efforts. As such, this view of subjectivity and lifeworld is more than a description (with rose-colored eyeglasses), but a sober and rational *prescription* for the future. And as describing the status quo, it is also a form of *reconstruction* of the past, an ideal narrative with respect to the past. The past, therefore, becomes integrated into a teleology of culture as the ultimate *terminus ad quem* of any human progress. Phenomenology, therefore, disclosing these connections, is in Husserl's mature vision more than just a matter of descriptive analysis. This is then the final—methodological—element that defines Husserl's phenomenology of the lifeworld as a world of culture.

Husserl's phenomenological method would be grotesquely misrepresented were one to characterize it as beginning and ending in a description of intentional acts and what is given in them. This characterization is true only for what Husserl calls *static* analysis, which becomes deepened in his genetic phenomenology. Genetic phenomenology opens up the view for the sedimented past which is operative in the current constitution of the world. Any activity rests on former layers of passivity, which are still "active" as habitualized, sedimented aspects of the *One Structure.* Genetic phenomenology, therefore, is applied to the Ego as well as to the lifeworld. But reaching into the past, which *is* no longer, is not possible by way of a direct description. As will be shown in detail in chapter 8, disclosing the past (and, in general, the temporal) dimension of the correlational a priori has significant consequences for the phenomenological method employed in Husserl's project. Concretely, if description can only pertain to what is given in the now, and if the now (in the sense of the correlational a priori—as experienced in the now and the now as the now of the lifeworld) is constituted by a past, then this past cannot be described directly but must be *reconstructed* from the now. Reconstructing, questioning back from the now, takes on the character of interpretation, *Auslegung.* Phenomenology, as expanded into the genetic dimension, then, takes on a *hermeneutical* component, one that is no longer *just* descriptive but that is at the same time interpretive, hermeneutical. This is the last piece of evidence that Husserl's paradigm is no longer that of "apodictic evidence"—a Cartesian ideal—but reaches insight into the *One Structure* which is "evidencing" (to use a peculiar term) in any way possible; making visible, laying bare, laying out what can be described and reconstructed and interpreted with respect to the correlation of subjectivity and lifeworld. This "evidencing" is the actual *scientific* task of phenomenological analysis as Husserl in effect carries it out, mostly without further ado, in his numerous writings, most of which—to bring us back to the beginning of this introduction—took the form of his private meditations. These were certainly meditations *in* the armchair, but not *of* the armchair, as should be clear by now.

Hence, the final shape of Husserl's phenomenology in terms of its methodology is a descriptive-hermeneutic-interpretive analysis of the correlational a priori between subjectivity and lifeworld, where both are construed *genetically* and *intersubjectively*. Together, subjectivity and lifeworld constitute culture and the human being in the lifeworld as a cultured being. This construal of the human being as enmeshed in the world—*its* world—is another manner of rephrasing Husserl's vision of the Enlightenment. One does not have to be a philosopher to become a cultured being, but philosophy, in the form of concrete analyzing phenomenological labor, is the critique of this culture that Kant envisioned, that is, culture as rational through and through. Culture becomes, through philosophy, a justified communal enterprise—a regulative idea lying in infinity.

Thus, phenomenology, originally begun by Husserl as a rather dry inquiry into the nature of intentional consciousness (and oftentimes seen as merely thus), becomes a *hermeneutical phenomenology of the correlational a priori of the world as historical world, as a world of culture, and of subjectivity as intersubjectivity, connected in a history and a tradition.* This is the final and ultimate shape of Husserl's philosophy. It has remained, however, a torso, concerning the actual completion of the project. As a philosophical project "certain of the future" (as Husserl was convinced, however [and as the chapters in this book will demonstrate]), it is merely at the beginning and reveals Husserl in the way in which he defined himself in old age: as a beginner, but a true beginner who has laid foundations that are unshakeable grounds for future research. In his Herculean effort, he has elevated Western philosophy to a stage in which it could begin to be scientific philosophy in the manner he envisioned. It is up to us who follow him to seize on this philosophical vision—and it is we who are now finally in a position to see the mountain range of Husserlian thought with the nearly completed publication of his writings. It is up to us to climb it and further chart its territory—or admire it from afar. It remains, however, the mountain range that needs to be crossed in order to see what lies beyond. For contemporary philosophy, there is no escaping this arduous path, even if one concludes by rejecting some or even all of the results of Husserl's work. But such is the work of phenomenology. It is forever a working philosophy with open horizons and whose completion lies in infinity. What the critic rejects, then, is not so much the Husserlian system and its foundation as rather individual findings and perhaps faulty observations or conclusions. In this sense, one cannot escape phenomenological idealism, just as one cannot escape Hegelian dialectics (albeit for different reasons). We have seen history repeat itself, as postmodernism flashed its mocking grimace at the sober face of modernism, just as, earlier, Kierkegaard's irony mocked Hegel's absolute idealism. Who will "win out" at the end of the day is, then, more than a philosophical question; it is one that is motivated by one's stance toward our world as either one of dispersed and disjointed individual efforts and fractured meaning—or the view entertained by the Enlightenment, of our world as a communal space of reasons and meaning and culture. It is the latter vision for which Husserl has drafted, arguably, the most appealing image. Whoever is committed to the Enlightenment in this or a similar form will find Husserl's the most thoroughgoing and convincing philosophy in support of this ideal.

Chapter Overview

The chapters of this book are arranged in three main parts. They reflect and gradually unfold the trajectory that is followed in this presentation of Husserl: a hermeneutic phenomenology of the lifeworld as a world of culture and the place of the subject in culture.

Part 1, entitled "Husserl: The Outlines of the Transcendental-Phenomenological System," is only seemingly a "mere introduction" to Husserl. With the exception of chapters 1 and 2 perhaps (where the "introduction" into the sphere of phenomenology turns out to be a systematic problem of its own), this part's chapters are arranged to explicate the outlines of Husserl's mature thought. Following the distinction in chapter 1 between a methodological and substantial (or thematic) account, the presentation offered here gives a glimpse of phenomenology's peculiar method of the reduction, which at the same time cannot be divorced from the substantial findings of Husserl's phenomenological descriptions.

Chapter 1 lays out the "basics" for a comprehension of Husserl's mature thought. While some interpretations of Husserl's project focus on the manner of moving away from one's ordinary lifestyle and into the sphere of phenomenology via the reduction, it will be made clear here that the project of transcendental phenomenology must start out with an outline of that from which this entire enterprise begins, the "natural attitude," which in a sense is comparable—both descriptively as well as systematically—to Hegel's natural consciousness. As will become clear later, its correlate is nothing other than the lifeworld. Hence, the natural attitude and the lifeworld form a correlation, one that can only reveal itself after the reduction.

Chapters 2 and 3 focus on the method of the reduction itself. Chapter 2 lays out the method and its methodological steps and ways into the reduction, citing more recently published texts of the *Husserliana*. Next, chapter 3 follows the train of thought by presenting some of the main problems and issues Husserl's method of the reduction faces. The first three chapters form a unity insofar as they lay out the method of the mature Husserl, while also indicating where Husserl was struggling with the articulation of the full meaning of this method. But understanding the reduction is a necessary element of understanding Husserl's philosophical project as a whole, which is always linked up with the method of *properly accessing* the sphere of phenomenology.

Chapters 4 and 5 deal with more "substantive" themes in Husserl's mature phenomenology, themes which are presented as key issues of his late thought, and also topics that caused the most confusion and aroused the most criticism, namely the concepts of the lifeworld and transcendental subjectivity. In chapter 4, the lifeworld will be presented in its main "axes," facticity and historicity, and hence this chapter lays out the matrix into which the actual phenomenology of the lifeworld becomes inscribed. Chapter 5 will deal, especially, with the Heideggerian critique of the transcendental subject. Utilizing some hitherto unknown texts from Husserl's manuscripts, this chapter offers a rebuttal to the Heideggerian critique, but one that at the same time shows Husserl responding to this type of critique by enlarging the scope of transcendental subjectivity to encompass the "transcendental person."

Chapter 6 forms the conclusion to part 1, in that it pulls the systematic strings of these first chapters together and lays out, in a "speculative" manner, the systematics of the phenomenological system. It is a rather peculiar treatment of Husserl, insofar as the speculative elements, known from the German idealists, but now put to use in a novel manner, are not avoided but are explicitly utilized. Husserl himself was neither very comfortable nor familiar with this speculative manner of thinking, but it will be shown that had he known about these tools, he could have reached speculative heights that would have brought him into the vicinity of the German idealists. Thus, spelling out these speculative elements explicitly "helps" Husserl's philosophy, so to speak, to find a systematic form that satisfies the speculative demand, and thereby his own systematic ambition. The reflections in this chapter are, therefore, also to be seen as an anticipation of a broadening and expansion of the phenomenological method of *description* into a "constructive" and ultimately hermeneutical register.

Part 2, entitled "Husserl, Kant, and Neo-Kantianism: From Subjectivity to Lifeworld as a World of Culture," follows this trajectory of opening Husserl up to a tradition to which he truly belongs: the transcendental tradition following Kant. This tradition as it is interpreted here includes, besides Kant himself, the Marburg neo-Kantians, namely Hermann Cohen, Paul Natorp, and, most importantly, Ernst Cassirer. The reason this claim can be made is because this school of thought explicitly broadened the Kantian purview from a critique of reason into a critique of *culture*. Not only is this project, as will be shown, not in contradiction to Husserl's, but they are mutually inclusive. To show that this is the case will pave the way for a fuller account of Husserl's phenomenology as also a philosophy of culture.

One of the most important systematic claims that becomes enacted with Husserl's move, via the reduction, to phenomenology as a form of transcendental philosophy, is that of transcendental idealism. But Husserl's is a peculiar form of transcendental idealism, and these peculiarities are not to be ignored, nor should we forget its basis and systematic background in Kant's position. Chapter 7, therefore, compares and contrasts the two philosophers' forms of transcendental idealism. To both, "transcendental idealism" is not just some philosophical position for which one can argue (for or against); rather, it is the label for a life commitment on the basis of a philosophical theory, which is thereby not a mere theory but a *practical* and also *moral* demand.

Chapters 8, 9, and 10 form a certain unity, for they all highlight, in different ways, Husserl's relation to the Marburg school of neo-Kantianism. Chapter 8 explores Husserl's first encounter with this school via his contemporary Paul Natorp. Natorp worked somewhat in the shadow of the great leader of the school, Hermann Cohen, and developed a transcendental psychology as a counterbalance to the "objectivist" tendency of the "official" method of the Marburgers, the transcendental method of construction of reality in logical thought. By handing the staff back and forth, as it were, Husserl and Natorp profit from one another, but in the end, it is Husserl who exploits the best from Natorp's sketch of a psychology. But Husserl thereby also opens up his phenomenological investigation to what Natorp calls "reconstruction." Phenomenology is not merely concerned with description of given phenomena, it also traces their genesis. This move to genetic phenomenology, therefore, is importantly influenced by Natorp. But it is also the first step to what will later be called "hermeneutic phenomenology" in that Husserl explicitly acknowledges that the phenomenological method extends beyond the (seeming) limit of mere description and hence beyond the "principle of all principles." What can be properly called "hermeneutical," in Husserl, is intrinsically of a *constructive* character.

This line of interpretation will be expanded in chapter 9, which adds Cassirer to the picture. Cassirer broadens the "classical" Marburg account of construction by framing philosophy as a critique of culture, and the latter (culture) as a universe of symbolic formation. Influenced by Natorp as well as by Husserl's phenomenology, Cassirer develops a full-fledged transcendental theory of culture, one that has also been termed a phenomenology of *objective spirit,* since he focuses mostly on the forms in which "spirit" terminates. However, this account is incomplete without a phenomenology of subjective spirit, which is provided by Husserl. This is a somewhat speculative manner of comparing the two "systems." The conclusion to this chapter is that both accounts are not only mutually complementary, but that such a dual account is also already to be found in Husserl, though only rudimentarily so. Since the two accounts are not in contradiction with one another, this chapter has a key function in the whole of this book, insofar as it hints at what phenomenology as a philosophy of culture can mean and how it can proceed.

Chapter 10, then, focuses on Cassirer exclusively and gives an account of his objectivist account of symbolic formation. In this direction of analysis, more detail will be given as to what would have to be part of such a philosophy of culture. The chapter also defends Cassirer against some criticisms of his systematics. But the most important lesson of part 2 for the present purpose is that Husserl's phenomenology in no way stands in contradiction with the transcendental account given by these philosophers in the Kantian tradition. They mutually demand and require one another.

Part 3, finally, brings the argument of this book full circle by demonstrating in what way Husserl's transcendental-phenomenological project can and must be construed as a hermeneutic philosophy of culture. Chapter 11 lays the ground, as it were, by way of a detour through a critique of Gadamer's hermeneutics. While some of the positive aspects of Gadamer's philosophical hermeneutics will be spelled out—including some that make certain improvements over some impasses and problems in Husserl—the chapter ends with a critique of Gadamer's project. Though different from Cassirer, Gadamer, too, is critical of the subjective account, wanting to eliminate altogether "subjectivism" or a "philosophy of reflection" centered on subjectivity. This is the manner in which he reads this tradition from Kant via Hegel to Husserl. In refuting Gadamer's critique and making a case for a Husserlian vis-à-vis a Gadamerian "hermeneutics," the ground is prepared for an account of a Husserl-inspired "hermeneutical phenomenology." To present the latter is the purpose of the last chapter, chapter 12. By first laying out basic criteria that a philosophical hermeneutics must satisfy, I will argue that Husserl's phenomenology, in the way it has been portrayed in the previous chapters, satisfies the minimal requirements of a philosophical hermeneutics. I will then go on to sketch the way in which Husserl's mature thought can be construed as a "hermeneutical phenomenology" that is superior to the other, better known, forms of hermeneutics (Heidegger, Gadamer). Finally, I spell out the way in which such a hermeneutical phenomenology can be a philosophy of culture by going back to the understanding of Husserl's phenomenology as a form of Enlightenment philosophy and by comparing Husserl's philosophy with the main tenets of the Marburg school, whose members openly confessed to pursuing a philosophy as a critique of culture. In moving Husserl into close proximity with this form of Kantianism, I am emphasizing what I call Husserl's *lasting humanistic promise.*

With the exception of chapter 12, all the texts appearing here have been published as articles in journals or anthologies (edited volumes). They have been written and have appeared in the last decade and a half. In putting these texts, which I consider the better pieces I have written, together in one volume, it is my wish that they reflect a line of interpretation that I have been pursuing in this work since I began publishing on Husserl (and Husserl's position in twentieth-century philosophy). I would be pleased if the systematic approach I have taken to Husserl becomes manifest in them and in the order in which they are arranged. It will become clear to the careful reader that this order is in no way arbitrary but is the result of a circumspect deliberation and arrangement. It is my hope that this work might be received as a systematic work on (what I take to be) Husserl's mature philosophy in the way sketched in this introduction and not "just" another collection of essays centering around a vaguely defined topic.

Regarding the shape in which the chapters are now, it was tempting, of course, to apply the red pen and begin correcting and reworking these texts, adding additional notes and insertions. However, I have resisted this temptation and have kept my modifications to a minimum. The changes made were those deemed necessary, namely to (a) eliminate repetitions (we all have our favorite passages from "our" classics!) and (b) cross-reference between the chapters in this book. Thus, while the reader is encouraged to read the book from beginning to end, he or she may also begin reading at any chapter and will find many references there to other themes in other chapters and their relation to the theme at hand, so that the ideal reader will also get an understanding of the systematic order and concatenation of the themes treated in this work. The only items that were added were short transitions between chapters, which show how the chapters hang together. These transitions have the purpose of summarizing what has been said and linking it up with what is to come. All remaining infelicities the reader might perceive concerning my "take" on Husserl remain my own.

Odenthal (Germany), Spring 2011

Part 1

Husserl: The Outlines of the Transcendental-Phenomenological System

Husserl's Phenomenological Discovery of the Natural Attitude

Wir können nicht leben wie andere Menschen, naiv dahin und mit anderen streiten, wir haben den schlimmsten Feind in uns selbst.
   —from Husserl's letter to Fink, March 6, 1933, Hua-Dok III/4, 91

Introduction

Among the great themes of Husserl's phenomenology—such as intentionality, the reduction, transcendental subjectivity, intersubjectivity, the lifeworld—one generally does not consider Husserl's notion of the *natural attitude.*[1] After all, was it not Husserl's whole intention as a philosopher to overcome the naïveté and fallacy of the natural attitude and to move, employing the classical Greek dichotomy, from a naive *dóxa* to an *epistéme,* to a philosophy as "rigorous science" (Hua XXV, 3ff.)? However, if it is his claim, as it is, that all philosophy before him has failed to perform the phenomenological reduction, in other words, that all pre-phenomenological philosophy has unconsciously remained on the ground of the natural attitude, one can begin to see how central his concept of the natural attitude must be. The natural attitude is pervasive and dominant as long as the phenomenological reduction, inaugurating phenomenology itself, has not been performed. Hence I want to raise the question: *What exactly is* this natural attitude? How is it characterized, and what does it mean to overcome it? If this natural attitude is so fundamental that all philosophy before Husserl has overlooked it (or at least not fully grasped it, though some philosophers, such as Heracleitus or Descartes have glimpsed rudimentary fragments of it), how does it become explicit in the first place? This chapter will argue that the phenomenological discovery of the natural attitude, hence the natural attitude *itself,* ought to be considered one of the great themes of Husserlian phenomenology. The natural attitude already implicitly belongs to those previously mentioned themes and, even though it is Husserl's project to overcome it, its dominance can be seen by the fact that it ultimately acquires a late recognition and restoration in the *Crisis* (Hua VI, 176–77, "The Task of an 'Ontology of the Lifeworld'").[2]

Husserl never systematically worked out a full and consistent theory of the natural attitude. This notion is rather, to use Fink's (1976, 190ff.) often-quoted term,[3] an "operative concept" in Husserl's thinking that serves as an unthematical basis for further thought. The task of this chapter is thus to reconstruct a theory of the essential content of this natural attitude, as well as the way it becomes thematic in the first place. This task has two levels, a thematic and a methodological level: in speaking thematically about the natural attitude, describing it in its content (on the thematic level), we are obviously speaking from another standpoint. If the natural attitude is, as the name suggests, a title for our everyday life, then speaking about it means we have, in one way or the other, already superseded its boundaries on a methodological level. To put it as Hegel would: seeing the limit *as* limit means it has already been surpassed. A description of the natural attitude will therefore *nolens volens* stand outside of it, occupy or speak in a different attitude. So much is intrinsic to the thematization of this phenomenon.

The Two Levels of Description: Thematic—Methodological

What I have already stated gives us two clues as to how we should proceed. First, we have to differentiate, on the one hand, between a thematical *description* of the natural attitude in its content, and on the other, *our* position in *describing* it. Whereas the description gives us an account of the natural attitude itself (as the theme), the methodological reflection upon this description will give an account of what it means to be *in* the natural attitude. A phenomenological analysis of the natural attitude will have to make the difference, in other words, between an *object* level and a *meta* level. The object level will give a description of the natural attitude *itself,* whereas the meta level will clarify that which makes this attitude "natural." This will become clearer as I proceed. For now we can keep in mind that what makes this phenomenological account of the phenomenon of the natural attitude so interesting and yet curious is the interdependence and inseparability of theme and method.

Let us now see how these two levels of analysis are intertwined. If the natural attitude is in one way or another a title for our everyday life, and if thematizing this attitude already means being in *another* attitude, then it can be said that the natural attitude is constituted precisely by the fact that it is not thematical *in or by* the natural attitude. In other words, being in the natural attitude, I am unaware *of* being in this attitude. Hence, this is exactly the reason why this attitude is called *natural*. The natural attitude is hidden to itself; thematizing this attitude—discovering it, as the title of this chapter says—means already being in another attitude, namely, the philosophical attitude, of which we now know nothing. Therefore Fink is perfectly right to call the natural attitude a "transcendental notion" (Hua-Dok II, 104),[4] because it only ever *becomes* a philosophical notion, that is, it only becomes thematic, if one stands in the philosophical (read: transcendental) attitude. It only becomes thematizable to the philosopher who is defined precisely by the fact that he stands outside of the natural attitude. This, the first of the *three* main constitutive factors on the methodic meta level making up the full concept of the natural attitude, I shall call *naturalness,* alluding to the name Husserl gives to the phenomenon. I want to pin down the term "natural" to its etymological root from the Latin *nasci,* "to be born," "to grow": the natural attitude, speaking generally and very formally, undergirds the everyday life we live, as it were, naturally, that is, dealing in a "straightforward" way with other human beings, animals, plants, things, making plans, performing actions, pursuing interests, and so on. Myself, my surroundings, and the people I deal with are all just common and natural. To call this "situation" natural would be absurd for someone living in the natural attitude, yet making this mode of daily life explicit and thematic requires that we are no longer in it. The term "natural" thus gives a thematic description of our life as it is carried out "naturally," but the fact that this is so can only become explicit in *another* attitude.

Mentioning these modes of everyday existence—dealing with other beings, acting, planning, and so on—we already have a first *thematic* account of how life in the natural attitude is performed. In our life we are dealing with certain things, entities. This dealing-with them implies that they are in some way given to us. The structure of givenness and having of the object, as the reader will have noted, is based upon the general structure of intentionality. This, Brentano's great philosophical discovery, was more thoroughly developed in Husserl's *Logical Investigations*[5] and henceforth remained an essential category in Husserl's thought (Hua XIX/1). The way of givenness as our mode of lived-experiencing (*erleben*) any kind of entity is correlative to the manner in which these entities are given to us in and through our intentional acts. Intentionality is the general structure of human subjectivity that serves as the basic level of any kind of human life.[6] If this is so, it must be possible at least in part to develop a theory of the natural attitude from this doctrine.

The Extended Structure of Intentionality: Act—Situation—Attitude and Its Correlate: The Horizon

Intentionality is the structure of acts in which entities are given to me in general, but I can also send out active intentional acts (rays of acts) towards something. I can, as we say, "intentionally," that is to say, deliberately tune my attention to what is not seen presently by turning my head. Alternatively, I can view something in my surroundings more closely that was merely at the margin of my attention, for example, I can tune my attention explicitly to the teacup that before was next to my computer unnoticed. In doing so, I do not just see a three-dimensional x, but this "thing" is given to me as something from which I can drink. The way of givenness of something to me implies that it is always given to me *as* something. This structure of something-as-something (*tì katà tinós*) alludes to Heidegger's notion of the "hermeneutical as" (Heidegger 1993, sec. 32, 148; esp. 149).[7] It can, however, already be developed from Husserl's theory of intentionality: something is always given to our intentional acts in a way of givenness; however, this way of givenness reveals itself already *as something* in my daily life. For example, this three-dimensional x is given as a cup for drinking, this y as food to eat, this z as a person, more specifically as a friend or stranger, and so on. My surroundings are not just a formal system of intentional givenness, but a nexus of meaning.

When realizing this, I also notice that this way of givenness as something is not fixed once and for all, in the sense that I merely passively, receptively receive given entities as fixed.[8] On the contrary, my life is structured by a multiplicity of active *interests* governing my manner of dealing with things, and so on. I am never solely passive, but rather am devoted to certain things, I pursue certain goals, and so on. To use another example: if I were a realtor I would not primarily see a house as a place for living (or, for that matter, just a three-dimensional x), but as an object of sale and business. If I were an architect, I would view it under the perspective of its construction, of the order of the rooms, the way the windows allow for the light to come in, and so on. Hence, daily life, according to Husserl, is a life of interests (Hua VIII, 92ff.).[9] I am never indifferent to the things around me, but rather my view depends on certain interests: for example, I am hungry, or I am working in my job as a realtor, or I am devoted to my hobbies. Even when I am tired and losing interest in things generally and am thus only "interested," if we can call it that, in letting go and giving in to my tiredness, even then I am not indifferent. Interest, in the manner Husserl understands it, can also be illustrated by the Latin origin of the word: *inter-esse* means to be among things, to be within a certain context.

Let us now look more closely at this notion of interest. Different ways of being interested can coincide in one and the same person. I can look at this object *x* as an aesthetic object, as practical in a general sense, as *specifically* practical in this or that sense. Correspondingly, nobody is *just* a businessman, *just* a . . . Shifting from one interest to the other lies within my free will. The fact that I always perceive a thing in a certain interest I shall term *situation*.[10] I am always in a certain situation, in the sense that I always have a certain, specific interest in something. I do not live jumping from one situation to the next as if there were "gaps" in between. Rather, I always live in a certain context within a flow of temporal succession. Also, my interest within a situation is not limited to this certain entity, but can be shifted to any other entity in the same form of interest. It is here that the term *attitude* comes into play.

My specific interest in a certain entity, my situation in other words, is always embraced or surrounded by an attitude. The attitude is like a halo (or an aura) around a certain act of interest. Being in the attitude of the realtor, let me call it the "realtor attitude"; my intentional rays of interest will be carried out according to this attitude. Likewise, I can shift my attitude, as an act of my free will, to the architectural attitude, or I can shift to an aesthetic attitude and view the selfsame thing, the house in my example, as a work of art. Strictly speaking, my active life is always already carried out in a certain attitude of which there are many, some of which may still be unknown to me. More precisely, my daily life consists of many attitudes I live in or live through ("*durchleben,*" as Husserl would say), alternating with each other, which need not contradict each other but can rather referentially imply each other (*aufeinander verweisen*). This is why I usually do not notice the shifting from one to the other. Still, yet other attitudes might be in contradiction with others. This calls for a phenomenological description of the phenomenon of attitudes, which we will have to skip here.[11]

One constitutive element (an invariant), however, we can isolate from what it means to be in an attitude. Living through an attitude towards a certain thing in a given situation, this attitude is not limited to a certain entity. I can look at *whichever entity I want to* in the aesthetic attitude. In principle, there is no limit to that which I can view in the aesthetic attitude. Hence, an attitude is directed towards an open horizon of possible entities. Analogously to the way an act has its correlative intended object, we can also say that an attitude has a correlative. But if in a certain attitude there is no limit in principle to that which can become an object of this attitude, what could be the correlative of an attitude? This correlative Husserl calls an *open horizon* or also *a world* (Hua VI, app. 17, 459).[12] Thus, we have a correlative to this world-horizon, namely an openness on the side of the experiencing person. In a way this openness can also be called a horizon, albeit on the side of the subject.

However, if there are several attitudes, there must also be a multitude of horizons; for the correlative of an attitude—of which there are many in my living reality—is a specific world, as when we speak of the world of business, the world of sport, of art, and so on. My life as carried out in a succession of situations with their acts is hence always already engulfed by, or integrated into, a special attitude which has a horizon or has as its correlation a special world (*Sonderwelt*). For example, correlated to the aesthetic attitude is the world of aesthetics (or art) in the sense that there is no limit to that which I can view aesthetically. This horizon or world is not in itself an entity but that which harbors or bears within it all possible entities of a certain attitude in their way of givenness to me. When I speak of world, henceforth, it shall be understood phenomenologically as horizon;[13] for now, however, I am still speaking of a special world, for example, the world of business, sports, and so on. In the same way, one can speak of special attitudes: the business attitude, the sports attitude, and so on. Both correlative parts have their respective horizonal structure.

Now let us point to one characteristic of this world-horizon. Living in a certain attitude and thus viewing certain things within this horizon that correlates to this attitude, I will experience the *things,* but not the *horizon* in which they appear. This horizon or special world remains *unthematic, because* the object that I have thematically is that to which I tune my attention. I shall thus call this correlation of attitude and horizon a *schema:*[14] all things that are given to me, or that I am attuned to, I have in a certain attitude, which is an attitude not to a single thing, but towards a whole horizon of possible things. That which I view in this attitude is thematic, but the attitude itself will remain for the most part unthematic; I usually do not notice that I am in one attitude and shifting to the next. In the same sense, correlatively, the horizon is also unthematic, as my attention is attuned to a single thing that is given to me through a schema.[15]

The Correlation of Homeworld—Home—Attitude, and the Alienworld: The Notion of Naïveté

Returning to the notion of the naturalness of my daily life, we can now describe more closely how this life is carried out. I am always in one way or another dealing with things, people, in a word: entities. Furthermore, I am dealing with them in a situation with a certain attitude that surrounds this situation like a halo. But in my natural life I live through a multiplicity of attitudes, for example, my job attitude, my leisure attitude that may again be subdivided into the sports attitude, the traffic attitude, and so on. The special horizons that correlate these attitudes are not separated worlds, limited within themselves, but they referentially imply each other, "touch" each other or maybe overlap; they are not separate "worlds," but make up my life as a whole and the locus in which it is carried out. The universal notion (*Inbegriff*) or field of this structure of attitudinal multiplicity and the correlative horizons in my natural life as a whole Husserl calls *homeworld* (*Heimwelt*) (Hua XV, app. 11, 214).[16] By this he means the sphere in which we feel "just natural," at home and at ease. Hence this homeworld is not one world of a single individual, but an intersubjective world, a world of tradition, culture, religion (myths), collective values. It is the world we are, literally, *accustomed* to. Therefore, this homeworld is the world of a certain family, society, people, nation with their historical tradition, that is, a phenomenon of generativity.[17] This homeworld is correlated to a "home attitude," as I shall call it, with its multiple subattitudes.

The term "naturalness" is a pure description of my daily life and bears no negative connotation. However, the structure of naturalness can take on a pejorative connotation. This is just the flip side of naturalness and stems, etymologically speaking, from the same root. This side Husserl calls *naïveté* (Hua VIII, 20).[18] Why is this naturalness of the home attitude carried out in the homeworld *naive*? What does "naive" mean here, and in what respect is it a negative characteristic of the natural attitude? Naturalness was defined on the methodological level as the fact that being in the natural attitude I know nothing of being in it. This we can now elucidate thematically with respect to the above. Being in the home attitude, I live through concrete special attitudes, which correlate to special concrete horizons, and these horizons are essentially open horizons. This means that the horizon of the homeworld is principally not limited; it can be expanded *in infinitum*. Because this homeworld-horizon is the only horizon to the home-attitude, it is "absolute." The horizon might be limitlessly expandable, but it will still be understood in terms of the homeworld of or for the home attitude. Hence, the naïveté of the natural attitude not only consists in the fact that being in the natural attitude I do not know of being in it, but also in the fact that, since I do not know of it as an attitude, I live in the belief that it is the only possible "way of life."

In fact, my home attitude is only one of many other attitudes constituted in the same manner. Every individual sociality (family, people, nation) has its home attitude, but there are many different socialities, with their own sets of subattitudes, with their own customs, traditions, myths, and rules, and so on. This applies to all factual and possible socialities. The home attitude is in principle naive, because it sees itself as absolute. This does not mean that one home attitude perceives itself as the only existing attitude, but as the only *home* attitude for itself. All other forms of life it will view either as naive, or as primitive, or as simply *alien,* that is, incomprehensible. To set the home attitude as absolute means that no other attitude will become understandable as a *home* attitude, but only as an alien attitude correlating to an alienworld.

The Naïveté as Pre-Philosophical *Dóxa*

However, we need not talk of other cultures and their cultural presuppositions in relation to our homeworld to see that the natural home attitude is *in itself* naive. Daily life consists of a certain "casualness" concerning its way of carrying itself out; daily life deals with things as artifacts, with human beings as friends, foes, or strangers; it is practical and not theoretical (even if the "daily life" of, for example, a chemist consists of performing laboratory experiments). Daily life in this sense is, as Husserl says alluding to the Greek term, dogmatic.[19] It is made up of certain relative opinions or beliefs, for instance, that my senses tell me the truth, that tomorrow will be Wednesday, and so on. These beliefs make no claim to be "absolutely" true. From a theoretical (scientific) perspective, from the attitude of *epistéme,* these beliefs might well be wrong: before Copernicus no one questioned the "fact" that the world is a plane and not a sphere—which in fact turned out to be a "pure belief."

Thus, daily life consists of a set of opinions, including certain forms of knowledge, that do not even make the claim to be exact and *absolutely* true: to drive a car (to "know" how to drive it) I need not know the chemical reactions going on inside the motor, and so on. These beliefs are mere "*dóxai,*" they are not, and *need* not be, subject to an epistemic investigation. The naïveté of this daily life, its naïveté within its home attitude, thus consists in a limitedness or finitude with respect to its doxic beliefs. Even though the horizon of the home attitude is endless in principle, it at the same time reveals in this structure its own finitude: in extending the horizon this attitude will always understand new, "incoming" entities in its usual style. The style of understanding entities will be biased or, literally, presumptuous. This style will continue in a (homeworldly) concordance (*Einstimmigkeit*) with what is familiar. Thus, the naïveté consists in daily life's setting of its doxic style of understanding entities as absolute. The *dóxa* sets as absolute that which is in fact only relative. It does not realize that its beliefs are *mere* beliefs that could be wrong or perspectival, inadequate or biased.

Hence we now have introduced the second constitutive element of the natural attitude: its naïveté, which is but the flip side of naturalness. Again, the same meta-structure as in naturalness can be employed to clarify this: seeing the natural attitude as naive already means having left it, but in a way that is *not* naive. The term "*dóxa*" only makes sense in opposition to "*epistéme*." Is this not-naive attitude already the philosophical attitude? I want to suggest that it is not. I will do so by bringing two notions into relation to each other as I strive to understand the full structure of how Husserl views the natural attitude; these two notions are the *epistéme* and the home attitude.

The Motivation for the Scientific Attitude

In the home attitude I live with a certain set of beliefs and opinions. These, however, can be disappointed. The belief that a stick is straight is shaken when being held into water it becomes at first sight "crooked." This is a simple example of how my visual perception can be surprised and shows that certain beliefs of my daily life are naive, that is, dogmatic. Here we can see the origin of *epistéme*, of science, in the very basic sense of the desire to find out how things "really" are. I want to know their "real" being and not only one aspect of this being according to my opinion, which has been disappointed or has discovered uncertainties or contradictions within it. In other words, I want to understand *absolutely* as opposed to my relative opinion or belief. I start observing, experimenting, measuring, counting, and so on, that is, I *abstract* from the opinions and beliefs of my naive attitudes, I look away from them, set them aside; in other words, I "bracket" them.

This "bracketing" inaugurates the scientific attitude; I position myself explicitly in an attitude that leaves the beliefs of my home attitude behind. I do this because I want to move from mere "subjective" truths to "objective" truths, from relativity to absoluteness, from *dóxa* to *epistéme*.

This scientific attitude is essentially different from the subattitudes within the home attitude, as the latter only have relative truths: I can see the house as architectural phenomenon *or* as a work of art. Both attitudes are "true" within the boundaries of their own "logic," but not in contrast to the other. In fact, there is no reason to set them in contrast to each other. However, in the scientific attitude, say the attitude of the physicist, I deliberately bracket these subjective opinions. These have their relative rights. Within an attitude an opinion will never be "false," only inadequate or wrong. In this scientific bracketing, however, the physicist will instead view the house as a three-dimensional x with certain attributes, which have nothing to do with relativity. I as a physicist will not see it as an artifact, but as an example of a certain species. This means looking away from certain qualities (house, artwork) and focusing on others that quantify it as a physical entity. This quantification is carried out in the natural sciences at the highest level as a process of mathematization. In doing so, these mathematical formulas are never relatively, but absolutely true, because mathematics, the paradigm of absolute truth, is not limited to any homeworld. On the contrary, any human being, hypothetically speaking, from any homeworld can be taught to understand mathematics. Despite their homeworldly customs, myths, and specific ways of thinking, every normal human being of any culture can principally understand mathematics,[20] even though mathematics or formal logic and with this the process of mathematization happened to have occurred in the history of Western thought.[21]

Hence, the scientific attitude stems, or arises, from the home attitude. It is thus an attitude of a higher order that seeks to rectify or replace the relative beliefs of the home attitude with absolute truths by finding objective absolute knowledge as opposed to subjective relative opinions. This means that this scientific attitude with its sphere of absolute truths, however objective, *still rests on the ground* of the home attitude. It is an attitude on a higher level, but has its roots and its foundation in the home attitude, because initially it is the individual in his home attitude who realizes the limits and finitude of his relative home attitude and pushes himself away from this very sphere, now discovered to be relative, and strives to reach an absolute viewpoint. Although the process has only occurred in this one way—the mathematization of nature—in the tradition of Western thought (which says nothing about other intellectual traditions that discovered the ideal laws of mathematics), I want to insist on the fact that this scientific attitude has arisen from a *specific* home attitude and still rests on this homeworld. This is the case even though it is an absolute sphere that no longer has a necessary link to the home attitude it has sprung from. It is exactly this oblivion of its roots Husserl criticizes as "naturalism" or "objectivism" (Hua VI, 271).

The General Thesis of the Natural *and* the Scientific Attitude

In contrast to the home attitude and the scientific attitude arising from it, we are now prepared to fully grasp the entire notion of the natural attitude. The procedure that determines this, namely the eidetic variation, is quite easy to understand and is basic to Husserlian phenomenology. This method involves the sorting out of what a number of phenomena have in common by variating, that is, considering several possibilities or transformations. Once we perform this we will quickly see its simplicity and we will probably ask why we have not employed this procedure before. However, this is only possible after having introduced the multiplicity of attitudes as a field of possible variation. This will give us the full notion of what Husserl means by the natural attitude.

Let us recall. First, I introduced the multiplicity of attitudes in the homeworld. These attitudes fall under the title of the home attitude. Arising from this attitude there is the scientific attitude which is not relative as are the homeworld attitudes, but rather is absolute. What now, we can ask, do all these attitudes have in common? In my devotion to a certain action in a certain attitude, in my working, viewing, contemplating, experimenting, and so on, I still always believe that the reality of the world I am in, in which I am "doing" these things, *exists*. Also, if I am doubting a certain thing, if my perception is disappointed, even completely annulled—if I, say, believe over there in the distance there is something and it turns out to be a mere shadow cast by something else— I still believe that the surrounding world "around" this annulment exists. Even disappointments in certain things will not cross out the belief that the world itself will continue to exist. This general belief that the world exists Husserl calls the *General Thesis of the natural attitude:*

> "The" world is always there as reality, it is at the most here or there "different" than I thought, this or that is to be crossed out of it under the titles "mere appearance," "hallucination" and the like, [crossed out] out of [the world] which—in the sense of the General Thesis—is always existing world. (Hua III/1, 61)

The "content" of this General Thesis is that *"the world is,"* if it were spelled out (Hua VIII, 36). All attitudes implicitly and tacitly bear the belief that the world they are in, or dealing with in some way or the other, exists. They might believe in it in different ways, as this or that, but they always believe *that* it exists.

If this thesis is inherent in all attitudes, it is, of course, never explicit; we are naive towards it. To paraphrase this, we can vary Kant's famous statement by saying: *the belief that the world exists must accompany all my attitudes.* In this broad sense the natural attitude is a primordial and anonymous passivity (*anonyme Urpassivität*) or passive belief in a "fact" that nobody has ever set down as a thesis, as the somewhat incorrect title "General *Thesis*" might imply. It is the general belief that all our actions, all our life rests on. The world is absolute facticity. Now we can see why the natural attitude would be too narrowly understood if one said it was simply the title of our everyday life, and why I have instead called the form of our everyday life the home attitude. For the scientific attitude, even as distanced from the home attitude—that is, standing outside of *this* naïveté—*also* rests on this ground. In the scientific attitude, I still believe in the general or absolute fact that the world exists. The scientific attitude might not be naive about the dogmatic claims and beliefs of the home attitude, but it is naive towards its own belief that the world exists. It thus harbors a naïveté on a higher level: it does not know that it, too, is naive towards the General Thesis of the existence of the world.[22]

As we have said, the scientific, objective attitude can in principle be understood by all home attitudes. This is because the scientific attitude is merely an extrapolation, or abstraction, from a single home attitude, in this case, the attitude of Western thought, even as all possible home attitudes rest on the ground of the natural attitude as well. The scientific attitude thus stands in the midst of the several home attitudes like an island. The full notion of the natural attitude is hence the *universality of an in-principle endless number of home attitudes,* which in turn break down into sub-attitudes, all sharing the belief that the world they are resting on as the original *arché* (*Ur-Arche*) exists. This is the reason the home attitude must not be identified with the natural attitude, for it is the latter which under-girds a multiplicity of home attitudes; stated otherwise, from the other side, the natural attitude is built up or constituted by the multiplicity of home attitudes with their multiple subattitudes. However, the natural attitude is not the *sum* of all these special attitudes, but the totality or universal structure of what it means to be an attitude. Metaphorically speaking, the natural attitude is not the "roof" under which these attitudes dwell, but rather the *ground* on which they unconsciously stand. The correlate of this universal natural attitude is nothing but the lifeworld itself.

Normality, Abnormality, and the Possibility of Leaving the Natural Attitude

The multiplicity of home attitudes within the natural attitude leads to the third and ultimate methodological aspect that constitutes the full notion of the natural attitude, which can only be sketched out briefly. Each home attitude has its open horizon of the way entities can appear to and be understood by it. This open horizon is a horizon of understanding. In my home attitude I will understand things as this or that, according to any one of the many subattitudes within this home attitude. That is, in the home attitude I will always understand something in a certain in-principle *known* sense, if not one, then another. The world as my homeworld is to me a harmonious horizon; the style of my living in the world and understanding it is one of concordance (*Einstimmigkeit*). Husserl calls this universal style of concordance within my home attitude, without which the world as my homeworld would be simply absurd to me, *normality* (Hua XV, 133; esp. no. 11, 148–71). There might be things unknown to me, but they do not call into question normality as a mode of existence. I will understand what is obscure or strange in the style that has become normal to me in the normality and naturalness of my homeworld. However, do we not have here the risk of a fundamental misunderstanding?

Having left the naïveté of the home attitude, as we have, we have given a description of the natural attitude as bearing a multiplicity of home attitudes. Each of these attitudes has its own style of normality which is gradually, more fundamentally, or even absolutely different from one another. One can move from relative differences of a certain tribe as opposed to its neighboring tribe, go to a certain society, a nation, a whole culture. Thus, the attempt to understand one entity in a home attitude that belongs to *another* homeworld with *its* home attitude will never understand this specific, typical thing in its own essence. It will never become understandable to me in the *other* home attitude.[23] For example, though I as a Westerner might understand in my home attitude this thing as a reeking lump of rotten substance, someone from East Asia might understand it as a delicacy, or vice versa. Thus, the normalities of the particular home attitudes *collide*. To the horizon of the home attitude hence belongs a dark outer horizon. Since this home attitude is constituted by normality, this outer horizon will be the *abnormal,* that which is principally not integrateable in the normal style of understanding. But we can see that the entity which is abnormal to us in *our* normality might be normal to the *other* homeworld. Therefore, it is *not* an *absolute* abnormality, but rather an *other* normality that is abnormal *to us.* Husserl calls the outer horizon of this abnormality, correlative to the homeworld, the alienworld (*Fremdwelt*). In other words: that which is abnormal to our normality is necessarily conceived as alien. However, this alienity has its own, alien normality with its own concordance.

But if the home attitude has as its style of normality a limitlessly open horizon, how can I ever have a knowledge of this alienity? If the home attitude is constituted by concordance, if it is led by a normal style of understanding, how then can we ever experience the alien as alien? Coming out of my home attitude I will only be able to view the alien as abnormal,[24] not as a normality in *itself* that I do not (yet) understand. Husserl struggled with this paradox throughout his lifetime: How is it possible to leave the home attitude and ultimately the natural attitude? Is this not a paradoxical enterprise much like the legendary figure Münchhausen pulling himself out of the swamp by his own hair?

In conclusion, I want to suggest a possible solution. I believe the answer must lie in the concept of normality, which only makes sense as normality in contrast to the abnormal that lies outside the horizon of our homeworld. This is the alienworld. How *we* get there remains a riddle. The riddle is precisely that it does not lie within our power to achieve this. However, is it not rather that the alien and the abnormal offer and open *themselves* up to *us,* but *as* abnormal and thus alien? It is this that awakens and enlightens our interest in the alien as alien.

If this is so, it is not *we* who question, but rather the alien itself that intrudes *our* horizon and calls *us* into question. So the question coming from that which lies beyond our normal, natural home leads right back to ourselves, thus changing us. What is changed into abnormal and alien is that which is for us the *most* normal, well known, and homelike, that which we never know of in the first place: *the natural attitude itself.* The alien makes us perceive *ourselves* in our very everyday existence as alien. The alien outside our homeworld awakens the "stranger in us all." In experiencing this, we can never go back into our old self-evident knowledge of ourselves and our world. This is what the loss of naïveté is all about. It may well be said that in discovering the natural attitude Husserl has taken up the old Greek problem of the *dóxa,* but at the same time has reformulated it in the context of his phenomenology. This, and his late recognition of the natural attitude in the realization that all actions stem from it, is Husserl's contribution to Western philosophy. In this chapter, however, I only wish to show the first step to this huge project which starts out—and can only do so—as a discovery of the natural attitude in its two mutually constitutive methodological and thematical notions.

From the Natural Attitude to the Reduction

This first chapter gave a general outline and characteristic of the natural attitude. As has become clear, the natural attitude is the correlate to the lifeworld. A full comprehension of what the lifeworld is in Husserl thus entails an exposition of the manner in which one lives in it in the mode of the natural attitude. When we return, in the chapters to come, to the lifeworld problematic, it must be borne in mind that part of its complex structure is the natural attitude. This chapter, then, can also be seen as part of a *systematic phenomenology of the lifeworld*. To use the distinction between thematical and methodological employed in this chapter, the natural attitude is a necessary element of a thematic account of what can be seen as *the* theme of Husserlian phenomenology: an interpretation of the life in the lifeworld.

However, the thematical is only complete in conjunction with the methodological consideration; to separate them is to lose sight of the character of phenomenological inquiry. The methodological issue arising here can be phrased as follows, then: the natural attitude is the mode of life prior to entering the sphere of phenomenology. Yet, as became evident, a description *of* the natural attitude is already *from* the phenomenological standpoint. The condition of the possibility of a thematic description of the lifeworld is that it has already been left behind. This overcoming of the natural attitude and taking up of a novel standpoint is the central problem of Husserl's method: the reduction. The next chapter will give a systematic exposition of this central methodological tenet of Husserlian phenomenology.

Husserl's Theory of the Phenomenological Reduction: Between Lifeworld and Cartesianism

Introduction

Anybody attempting to give an account of Husserl's method of the phenomenological reduction finds oneself in an ungratifying position. After all, this theme has been one of the main topics in more than sixty years of Husserl research.[1] Furthermore, this topic has been so dominant in Husserl's self-interpretation that talking about it equals discussing Husserl's phenomenology as a whole. A general account of what Husserl "really intended" with his phenomenology risks being superficial, because it can only conclude with generalities that every traditional philosopher would claim as her or his telos: to express the truth about the world. Yet, were it true that "all great philosophers think the selfsame," we would either end up in trivialities regarding philosophical endeavors as such or we would miss Husserl's point as regards the *uniqueness* of his philosophical method. This notwithstanding that it was one of his late realizations that he could not simply do away with the tradition of which he himself was a part.

While Husserl's self-characterizations, especially in his last work, *The Crisis of European Sciences,* seem to put off readers due to their ceremonious formulations, an approach "from the bottom up" will be more fruitful than a presentation from the perspective of his late position. At that time, he already was convinced of the deep veracity of his phenomenology and "certain of the future" (Hua-Dok III/9, 75).[2] Nevertheless, Husserl insisted that the reduction as the method to enter the sphere of phenomenology is not a device that, once performed, is valid for all times. It does not entail that the one who has been "converted"[3] would remain so for the rest of one's life. Rather, the reduction must be practiced repeatedly, the greatest threat for the philosopher being to "fall out" of the mindset of the philosophical attitude. This "danger" is integral to the performance of the reduction. If the reduction is the only way into transcendental phenomenology, then it must be part of this theory to furnish an entrance in a "didactic" fashion. As Husserl once puts it, nobody becomes a phenomenologist by accident.[4] Thus, making an entrance into phenomenology is a problem involving an enormous amount of philosophical effort comparable to that of Hegel's *"Anstrengung des Begriffs"* in the process of becoming a philosopher starting from "natural consciousness."

Yet, every philosophical theory is an answer to a problem, in response to which the theory receives its meaning, and this also goes for the phenomenological reduction. The first piece of theory leading to the reduction is the concept of epoché. This methodological device was intended, following the Skeptic tradition, to gain a view unbiased by the misguided theories of the past. Yet, the figure of bracketing is more than just terminologically derived from the Skeptics; rather, it comes out of a well-established philosophical background. To this, Husserl *nolens volens* contributes, even if he purports to completely do away with all previous philosophical problems by way of epoché to reach a "metaphysical neutrality."[5] Thus, although his framing of the reduction only becomes understandable on the basis of his mature transcendental philosophy, the problem emerges from a philosophical context he did not create.

Thus, first I would like to expound the philosophical context, if only to show that Husserl distances himself from it. Husserl attempts to suspend traditional misconceptions in an effort to solve the fundamental philosophical problem of establishing "true and lasting knowledge." Nevertheless, he acknowledges the problem underlying his philosophical commencement, precisely that of the commencement *itself*. This problem is the "starting point" for his project and is equal to that of finding the true "entrance gate" to philosophy. This point of departure is *already* a problem of how to begin with philosophy. This presupposes that the act of philosophy is something "peculiar" compared to the "normal" execution of life. This issue, underpinning his philosophical enterprise, can be termed the *epistemological* problem. From here, Husserl progresses from a descriptive phenomenological psychology to a systematic universal "science" in a transcendental register. Where Husserl differs from Hegel, however, is that the problem of entering this emergent science is not a ladder to be thrown away once climbed. Rather, "the problem of entry" is, and remains, part of phenomenology itself.

In order to avoid lapsing back into an immanent reconstruction of Husserl's theory of the reduction, one must give a preliminary sketch of the epistemological problem that led Husserl to perform the transcendental reduction. The epistemological framing of the problem of introducing phenomenology will lead to an explication of the fundamental form of life, the "natural attitude." This explication, however, has a different systematic purpose than in the previous chapter; the problem of the reduction, with respect to the natural attitude, is not only a problem of *leaving* this life form in order to make one's way into phenomenology. It is in itself a problem of thematizing this "primal" attitude, and in doing so, one is already performing the first step of the reduction. From there, I shall discuss the different ways into phenomenology. While the epoché deals with overcoming the natural attitude, the methodological problems of making a concrete way into the transcendental "realm" only begin here. One can discern three chief ways into phenomenology and show a certain systematics in their unfolding. This will be the issue of the second section of this chapter. In the third section, I will discuss the meaning the reduction had for Husserl. It has essentially two consequences that stand paradigmatically as the significance he attributes to transcendental phenomenology at large. However, I want to assert critically that in these two directions Husserl *failed* to show their systematic connection. Ultimately, we are left with two "loose ends" that Husserl was not able to tie together, perhaps because this is ultimately impossible, at least in an orthodox reading. Chapter 12, however, will show a possible solution to this dilemma, resulting in what I call a Husserlian hermeneutic phenomenology.

Although the topic of the phenomenological reduction has oftentimes been an item of phenomenological research in the past—including the "defining" article by Kern (1962)[6]—one is now, nearly fifty years later, in a much better position to assess the meaning the reduction had for Husserl, especially in the light of manuscript material that has since appeared in the *Husserliana*. What I would like to attempt here is a renewed exposition of Husserl's theory of the reduction focusing on the concept of the natural attitude, the ways into the reduction, and finally, the upshot of the "meaning of the reduction" that leads to two, not necessarily related, focal points. While this discussion cannot be exhaustive, it should make apparent that the issue of Husserl's theory of the phenomenological reduction deserves a renewed look.

The Epistemological Problem: The Relativity of Truths and the Overcoming of the Natural Attitude

The epistemological problem concerns, simply stated, true knowledge and the means of attaining it. This issue comes about where it is noticed *as* a problem. Hence, is knowledge *eo ipso* true knowledge? This depends not only on the meaning of knowledge, but also on the context in which one employs it. The sciences represent one such field. The achievement and pursuit of true knowledge is vital to scientific practice and to the meaning of science. Whether one speaks of absolute truths (e.g., in mathematics or logic) or adequation to truth (e.g., in meteorology) the value of a science depends upon its reaching "true" knowledge.

The sciences, however, are not the only field in which knowledge is an issue. In opposition to them, there is pre-scientific life and the ordinary performance of life as carried out in the *lifeworld*. Whereas the problem of "absolutely true" knowledge seldom becomes a theme here, the question of truth is more crucial than one at first imagines. Consider, for example, the occurrence of a car accident. Imagine then the different "true stories" heard from different people involved: the drivers, a passerby on the sidewalk, and so on. Especially when some interest is at stake (who assumes the culpability), one will hear very (if not altogether) different "versions," all claiming "truth." These are "situational truths," and it is the task of a judge to "judge the truth," which might lie, as often implied, "in the middle." Obviously neither the notion of truth nor that of knowledge are taken emphatically (absolutely). The task of the judge entails the "distillation" of "the" truth from different stories. The result is only an approximation to what "really happened." Truth in this sense is an "idea." In the example, "truth" is an issue of rhetoric serving certain interests. There is no "absolute truth" about the car accident, not even as a regulative idea, although contradicting persons claim "true knowledge." The good judge, then, is someone who arrives at a measured and fair judgment. But this is not "the" truth, but rather a matter of a justification.

While in this example the justification of truths is debatable, there are other areas where we do talk of truth and true knowledge, but in an unemphatic manner. For example, in the marketplace one speaks of the "true" price of produce. The vendors fix the price anew each day depending on different circumstances (e.g., the season). Hence, the daily price of a fruit is its situational "truth," and it is debatable: one bargains over the individual price every day. This notion of "truth" is relative to the situation. Nevertheless, it will have its "authority" and "rigidity" that is far from mathematical rigor.[7] Knowledge of this truth is fashioned in a similar way. One calls the person experienced in employing these situational truths a good salesperson or a good bargainer, employing not "pure reason" but *common sense*. In a different context, Husserl mentions the example of the house to illustrate that a single object can yield differing "views" without invalidating others. What one perceives depends on who one is: a real estate agent views the house as an object for sale, an artist views it as a piece of art, and so on.[8] Within each perspective, these "interpretations" claim situational truths, although from an outside perspective, they are "mere" interpretations. None of these persons sees their views *as* an interpretation.[9]

Thus, in order for a situational truth to *be* a truth, it must block out other contradicting truths. The truth of the artist is different from that of the real estate agent, but has its own "right," because both do not stand in *competition* with one another. But why not? The answer lies in the notion of interest. What "constitutes" a certain situation, what marks it as relative to other situations, is that the pursuit of a certain interest circumscribes a *situation* and "constitutes" a self-enclosed domain. The interest determines the truth of the situation. The interest of the real estate agent in selling the house determines his situational truth. The artist, likewise, pursues her own interest. Life in general is a "life of interest"[10] containing a multiplicity of interests, each "creating" specific situations. However, one should not understand the situational "field" of an interest as exactly delineated. Rather, it has the character of a *horizon* that can expand and narrow, yet never comes to an end. There is no principal *limit* to that which can fall in the field of a certain interest. At the same time, these "fields" are self-enclosed due to the current interest in operation.

Situations are not islands in a sea. Rather, they are horizons extending over a partial stretch or field of being. As such, they are essentially limited (cf. Greek *horízein* = to delimit) and exclude each other. The metaphor of tinted eyeglasses best illustrates this. Seeing through red glasses makes green objects invisible, whereas they will become visible when seen with glasses of another color. Similarly, a situational attitude blocks out other situations. Moreover, the image remains the same despite different colorings of the glasses. The object is in each case the same; it is "raw being" or "hyletic stock." But this is an artificial notion produced by the philosopher. In the natural attitude, we can never see this object in its purity, for this would involve stripping the world of its interest. Yet, due to its intentional character, life always implements a certain interest. There is no unintentional life, and intentionality always strives toward fulfillment.[11]

The world has thus a "face of interest" that it always shows us in one way or another. Since it is essentially a world of interests, one can give another notion to characterize the world: if the execution of life occurs in a multitude of situations, then life becomes the situation of all situations, or the horizon of all horizons.[12] How is one to understand a "horizon of all horizons"? Husserl conceives of the lifeworld as the totality of life in its multitudinous facets. The lifeworld is the field in which life in general carries itself out in its everydayness. Whether Husserl calls this phenomenon lifeworld or "natural world-life," he alternately emphasizes either the noematic (the world) or the noetic (the subjective, living) aspect. The noetic-noematic structure designates the correlational a priori in its universal form.[13] It signifies the essential relatedness of world and conscious life. The correlate to the lifeworld is that mode of living in which this lifeworld is the horizon for any kind of action: the "natural attitude."[14]

In order to enter the sphere of philosophy and to assume a philosophical point of view, one evidently has to relinquish the natural attitude. However, it is not entirely clear why this would be necessary, since as of now there is nothing "negative" involved in its characterization. Are there compelling reasons for "overcoming" natural life? What do "natural" and "philosophical" designate here? As it becomes clear in Husserl's further fleshing out of the natural attitude, he intends an adaptation of the traditional distinction between *dóxa* and *epistéme*,[15] assigning a specifically "modern" interpretation to it that is localized on a higher level than that of "mere" prephilosophical naïveté and opposed to "mere" critical reasoning.[16] Thus, when Husserl conceives of the "natural" in opposition to the "philosophical attitude," this echoes the distinction between *pretranscendental* and *transcendental* standpoints as a modern "version" of the said distinction. The transcendental turn anticipated by Descartes, and taken by Kant, applies the realization of the subject-relativity of the world. The turn to the subject, the "reduction" to the *Ego* (*cogito*), becomes the foundation of science. The world is not an "absolute being," but is relative to the experiencing subject. All experience is worldly, but world is always an experienced world. Thus, Husserl interprets Descartes' turn to the subject and Kant's transcendental philosophy as rudimentary forms of his transcendental turn.[17] The realization of the essential subject-relatedness of *all* worldliness necessitates this transcendental turn.

To Husserl, this transcendental turn is identical with leaving the natural attitude, for the natural attitude knows *per definition* nothing of this correlational a priori. The distinction between "world" (as horizon of horizons) and nature ("stripped" of all apperceptions) illustrates the natural attitude's "naïveté." Because the latter knows nothing of this subject-relatedness, it lives in the belief that it can perceive the *world* as *nature*—independent of any experiencing agent. However, this is impossible within the natural attitude because it would foster the illusion of seeing the world stripped of any interest. However, this is not to say that it is impossible to gain an "uninterested" view. To the contrary, the recognition that all situations in the natural attitude are guided by interests means stepping beyond the natural attitude. Yet, the elements that motivate this turn must already be present in the natural attitude. Thus, the epistemological problem that started this discussion consists, in other words, in being *blind to the correlativity of world and experience*. The distinction of *dóxa* and *epistéme* "translated" into this conception means: philosophy that believes it can operate on a "realistic" level is bound to the natural attitude, and it cannot be critical in the sense of transcendental philosophy. This is not only Husserl's critique of pre-transcendental philosophy but especially of his pupils who neglected to pursue the transcendental path that he had taken up with *Ideas I* (1913).

This framing of the epistemological problem motivates the way into phenomenology, which is identical with becoming aware of the limits of the natural attitude. Phenomenology, for Husserl, is necessarily transcendental philosophy that entails adhering to the subject-relatedness of all experience.

The Performance of the Reduction: The Main Paths into the Reduction

Husserl conceived several ways into the reduction, the number of which has been subject to debate.[18] Of greater importance, however, is Husserl's belief in the systematic order of the reductions, regardless of the historic manner in which he discovered them. Within this systematics, none of these ways devaluates, but rather explicates and complements, the others. Hence, this reconstruction attempts to adhere to the systematic order Husserl envisioned and disregards their temporal order of development. Legitimization of this disregard owes to Husserl's assertion that the path first presented (and mostly criticized), the Cartesian way, retains its "right" and "validity"[19] despite the problems Husserl sees with it. We will see, however, how these different ways lead to two "opposed" tendencies indicated in the title: to the "Cartesian" and the "lifeworld Husserl."

The Cartesian Way

If the reduction is not an impossible endeavor, then there must be certain "proto-forms" of putting the normal pursuit of life out of action *within* the natural attitude. Husserl considers a simple example of such a proto-form: the suspension of judgment two people will practice when in discordance with one another. If both are unsure of the truth of their judgments, they will suspend it, until they have found out the truth.[20] Only when one asserts the truth of the judgment hitherto uncertain, will it again be put into action. In the time between doubt and confirmation the judgment ("it is so") is "bracketed."

When Husserl labels this bracketing as epoché, he takes it over from the Skeptic tradition.[21] In a similar sense, Descartes' method in his *Meditations* is to be understood, according to Husserl, as an epoché insofar as the decision to "once in his life" overthrow all knowledge is equally a radical "step back" from everyday life.[22] The question why the Cartesian epoché is the first way by which Husserl introduces the reduction is of great importance. When he later uses the term "reduction" for this method as a whole, he seems to identify both steps of epoché and reduction. This blurs certain nuances that one might want to retain for the sake of clarifying the details of this method. In addition, it is only from his later understanding of transcendental subjectivity that the concept of the reduction can become more dominant in the carrying out of this method. How does the epoché come about?

The natural attitude consists in viewing the world as "nature," as existing independent of an experiencing agent. This belief Husserl calls the *general thesis* of the natural attitude,[23] and it is a constant anonymous "stating as existing," for it is so fundamental that it is never actually uttered. It is comparable to a constant sound the ear blocks out. In Husserl's words: "It is, after all, something that lasts continuously throughout the whole duration of the [natural] attitude, i.e., throughout natural waking life" (Hua III/1, 53, §30). Thus, the epoché, as putting the general thesis out of action, can be seen as making explicit this constant baseline "below" the "natural" hearing level. The epoché does in no way devaluate or negate it, but rather puts it out of action momentarily in order to pay attention to that which remains unbracketed. In *Ideas I*, Husserl insists that this bracketing is a matter of our perfect freedom, that is, the freedom to inhibit what we want to and to the extent we want to (Hua III/1, 54).[24] He later considered both elements ("how" and "to what extent") of this "freedom" as problematic.

First, where does this freedom come from and how is it enabled? If the natural attitude is this self-enclosed field of everyday life, then why should, and how *could*, it be left by bracketing it? Second, even discussing the possible *extent* of the validity of the general thesis gives rise to an understanding of it as a field with a greater or smaller scope—ultimately like a continent within an ocean. Discussing a smaller or greater scope misconstrues the radicality of the epoché, which puts the general thesis out of action "with one stroke."

The general thesis of the natural attitude pervades every form of life, since all life is guided by a certain interest and hence (tacitly or explicitly) affirms being.[25] Putting this life-pulse of continuous asserting out of action can only occur as a totalizing act, and not piecemeal. There is either being *in* or *out of* action ("on" or "off"). However, whereas this radicality in fact calls for an equally radical motivation, this rigid "either/or" blurs the character of the "yes" of the general thesis and the possibility of "breaking its spell." It is a "yes" with respect to the character of the world as "existing," but this world is to be understood as existing in a manifold of ways, referring to the multitude of special worlds encountered in the natural attitude. How could it ever be possible to bracket all these modes of living with one single stroke?

Apart from Husserl's insistence that it is a matter of our perfect freedom, a motivation for this step lies precisely in the relativities of the situational truths. If all of these are merely truths for themselves *and* if the philosopher's aim is to reach "absolute" truth, then it will seem plausible to refrain from asserting any of the former. This realization can already be seen as bracketing, since understanding these relativities *as* relativities overcomes being immersed in them. Situational truths can only consider themselves *as* truths if they take themselves to be absolutely true, where *in fact* they are only relative. The relativity is determined by *not being aware of* their situational characters; because they do not know this, they take themselves as "absolute." Not being bound to situations means already having left their realm. Indeed, leaving these situations behind and putting the validity of situational truths out of action are the same. Yet, understanding the relativities of situations *as* relativities—and having thus left the natural attitude—does not entail that one has *consciously* grasped the meaning of the epoché. To Husserl, it can only be fully achieved when one has reflected upon its meaning.

Hence, upon closer inspection, the metaphor of bracketing is yet more complex, involving two sides: that within the bracket and that without. Following the example of a doubtful judgment one does not consent to: the judgment will only be put back into action when one has "evidence" about its truth. Yet, the brackets can only be removed by an Ego that has evidence and asserts (or modifies) the old judgment. The method of bracketing necessarily reverts to the Ego, which is the executor of any act directed at the world. Thus, the *"methodic expedient"* (Hua III/1, 54) Husserl takes over from Descartes—who carried out his method "for an entirely different purpose" (ibid.)—does not have the function of nullifying or negating the general thesis, but rather of motivating the turn to the subject that is the origin of the acts directed at the world. All situations are those of an Ego.

Thus, Husserl's main interest in the process of bracketing is to posit these brackets in order to determine what can be left "without." The universal doubt leaves over the doubting agent, a "pure" Ego stripped of any worldly meaning, and it is only this Ego that can claim for itself absolute evidence. What remains in spite of radical doubt is the *transcendental* Ego, which is not part of the world, but is that which "has" the world "opposed" to it as its universal correlate. This consciousness is the totality of the field of intentionality, as the correlate to the worldly totality given in intentional acts. As such, this subject cannot be a psychic entity in the world, but is consciousness "as such." Bracketing the totality of the world necessarily entails bracketing my Ego as *part* of the world. What "remains" is not, as Husserl asserts in 1931, as a critique of Descartes' (and in part his own misleading Cartesian wording in *Ideas I*), a *"tag-end of the world"* (Hua I, 63). Rather, the epoché reveals the pure Ego, consciousness as such, opposed to the world; it reveals subjectivity as such which I as human being can access.[26] Thus, the Cartesian way is the most direct path to the transcendental Ego, but its problem lies in its possible misunderstanding as "reducing away" all worldly things until one reaches the "last man standing" (the Ego), rather than seeing the Cartesian Ego as *already* transcendental subjectivity, though Descartes could not know this.

Yet, of the motivations to practice the reduction, the strongest one arises in this Cartesian impetus of finding a basis from which to found apodictic evidence in the self-evidence of the Ego.[27] This search for an ultimate and final apodictic foundation, which, following the Cartesian paradigm, can only lie in the Ego (*cogito, ergo sum*), is never given up by Husserl, no matter how much his actual emphasis might be directed at other "phenomena."[28] However, it is not yet clear how one is to found a new scientific discipline from this basis "outside the world." In fact, is not this claim of a non-worldly subjectivity a metaphysical construction; does not this very step of reverting to an absolute Ego lapse back into a Platonism?[29] Although Husserl never gave up the claim of having laid the foundation of phenomenology on the basis of a Cartesian Ego, it is difficult to see how a philosophical science could be "derived" from this absolute Ego, if one sticks, apart from a Cartesian *method*, also to his *concept* of subjectivity (as non-worldly). The answer to this difficulty lies in Husserl's notion of the grounding character of transcendental subjectivity. It is not a Cartesian grounding in an axiomatic ultimate principle, but a "grounding" of everything worldly in constituting transcendental subjectivity as intersubjectivity.

At any rate, Husserl's later self-interpretation intends to show that this way is merely one point of access among others and, furthermore, that a Cartesian notion of subjectivity as a "tag-end of the world" is unable to grasp subjectivity as a "field" of phenomenological intuition. Looking back upon Husserl's philosophical development after *Ideas I*, one can say that the Cartesian way remained dominant before he felt forced to broaden this approach, so as to stay "up to par" with the phenomenological conception of subjectivity he later attained. As we shall see, precisely his insights into the character of transcendental consciousness made it necessary to modify his way into the reduction. However, this modification was in no way an abandoning, but rather the extension, of this first way.

The Psychological Way

The Cartesian way was introduced with the intention of securing a field of apodictic evidence and, as such, to create a foundation on which apodictic knowledge could be built. Up until *Cartesian Meditations* (1931), Husserl employs Descartes' image of the tree of knowledge, whose branches are the positive sciences and whose trunk is the unifying *scientia universalis*.[30] Phenomenology purports to be this unifying science; in this sense "Cartesianism" means that only evidence of "Egoic" experience can give the Ego *apodictic* evidence, whereas experience of worldly entities is potentially doubtful, deceiving, and so on. This is so, essentially, because mundane experience can undergo modalizations. In *Ideas I*, Husserl considered the epoché as a turn away from the world and its existence as taken for granted to the realm of pure consciousness by virtue of bracketing the "reality claims" of the natural attitude, thus as a move from transcendence to pure immanence.[31]

The argument for this turn to "inwardness" as a basis for apodictic knowledge runs as follows. Nobody doubts the evidence of something given directly, in intuition. An external thing, a sensuous object, gives itself as itself, and is to be taken as such. The principle of all principles—to "take everything that gives itself in intuition originarily . . . as what it gives itself, but only within the boundaries in which it gives itself" (Hua III/1, 51)—is stated precisely to support this claim. However, upon closer inspection, what is seen of a perceptual object is merely its front side facing me. The back side will always be hidden; as I turn the object around to see its back side, its front side will again be hidden, and so on. An external object is always given in "adumbrations," and therefore the evidence of this object will never be absolute. Indeed, the manifest side gives itself with a certain evidence; in direct perception there can be no doubt about it. However, other unseen sides can always turn out to be different than anticipated. I will never see the totality of an external thing; the evidence regarding it will always be *presumptive*. Evidence about transcendent objects will never be apodictic. Since Husserl is searching for an *absolute,* apodictic foundation, the external experience of transcendent objects does not qualify. Immanent experience, on the other hand, does not adumbrate itself. It is given apodictically *and* adequately—or there is no difference between both forms of evidence, since there is no object to which this experience can refer once transcendent objects have been bracketed. Only inner experience can be the basis for apodictic knowledge, since there is no uncertainty regarding its evidence. "*A mental process is not adumbrated.* . . . Rather is it evident . . . from the essence of cogitationes, from the essence of mental processes of any kind, that they exclude anything like that [adumbrations]" (Husserl 1983, 77, Kersten trans.).[32]

To be sure, there is no back side to the anger I feel or reflection I carry out. If inner experiences do not adumbrate themselves, this means that they cannot have a "spatial" extension; the category of "spatiality" does not apply. It might be a form of intuition, but that which is intuited in inner experience is not spatial. While I can only imagine the external object as seeing it from its front side with its back side unseen, the imagination itself is given directly and absolutely. In other words, the *lack of spatiality* regarding inner experiences seems to be the criterion for not adumbrating. Whereas adumbrations are linked to spatiality, it will sound trivial to say that experience takes place in time. Following Husserl's analyses of time consciousness one can say that the time "of" these experiences is not external, natural time, but the time "of" the experiences themselves. Experiences are "given" in a temporal now in a "primal impression" within a constant flow of time consciousness. Experiences "flow away" from my current, living Now and are retained within a certain halo from my present Now, until they recede out of the periphery of my "mental eyesight" into the "stock" of my memory. "Periphery" connotes a certain spatiality, namely, a distance from my present Now. This distance becomes apparent when an experience slips out of my immediate retention into memory, when I forget what I had just heard or thought. The very "act" of forgetting questions the apodictic evidence of inner experience. Nevertheless, one need not revert to such an obvious example. Already the "fading out" of experience in retention challenges the claim of apodicticity in inner experience in its totality. Inner experience can even deceive me; memory might be false or incomplete, and so on. Having full and total access to all fields of my consciousness would mean that the Ego disposes over a divine consciousness.

Indeed, time can be seen as a certain analogue of space in the sense that, just as the spatiality of an object prevents us from gaining a fully transparent view of it, so does the temporality of lived-experiences keep us from "having" the totality of consciousness in one act. Since all actual experience is "had" in the lived present, the temporally extended nature of our mental life *evades* a complete overview.[33] Because I can only view my mental life in a reflective gaze, I cannot "step outside" of it, since I am bound to the now in which my experiences are "actual." I will always have experiences, also of reflection, *in a living present,* and this present will move to an ever-new present from which previous experiences will recede into recollection. Thus, Husserl's own concept of time-consciousness and its descriptions "behind his back" counter his own claim to apodictic evidence of inner experience. Accounting for this in actual analyses subtly moves Husserl away from the Cartesian motif of apodictic evidence on the basis of *Ego cogito;* for, were one to limit oneself to "Egoic" experience in apodictic evidence, one would have to content oneself with in fact a very small portion of subjective life.

Thus, the Husserl who wants to ground knowledge in phenomenology as a "first philosophy" and the Husserl who actually does the detailed work of describing phenomena split apart. It is in this descriptive work where Husserl, in a most creative manner, "loses" his way and "forgets" his agenda. The latter is actually the radical philosopher, who oftentimes is overlooked precisely because readers take him by his published word, where the "official" Husserl speaks "ex cathedra" and makes declarative statements about his "grand vision." Without acknowledging the descriptive work underpinning these statements, and its potentially explosive potential, one almost by necessity receives a one-sided and skewed impression.

Now if one, however, leaves aside the claim to apodictic foundation, a whole world of subjective life opens up, readily available to be explored. "This seemingly impoverished *Ego cogito* has opened up to us an endless realm of instrinsically intertwined phenomena, so to speak a phenomenological jungle. . . . Only as a transcendental Ego could he [the beginning philosopher] posit himself, and only his absolute life with *cogito* and *cogitatum* remains. However, it seems, an eternal manifold lies herein" (Hua XXXV, 93–94). Put otherwise, Husserl's insight into the extension of this cogito forces him to expand the sphere of the Ego itself. At the same time, one cannot do without the Ego, for there must be a synthesizing agent which binds the cogitationes together within one stream of consciousness. As Husserl says in the *Cartesian Meditations,* the form of *Ego-cogito-cogitatum* is the general form of all conscious life.[34] Including the *cogitatum* as the actual field of experience for the phenomenologist, wholly divored from "foundationalist" intentions, gives rise to a whole new sphere of experience, which will be dealt with by an equally novel discipline: phenomenological psychology. The questions, then, will be (a) how to characterize this "field" of *cogitata* and, more importantly, (b) how to account for it methodologically. Given the desideratum of such a new "transcendental science," Husserl has to give answers to two interrelated questions: what kind of analysis can there be of this phenomenal "realm" or "field," *and* how is this possible as a philosophical science, if this field structure in its breadth escapes the claim for apodictic evidence? What is the theme of phenomenological research, given that the Ego is more than a pure Ego? In a different terminology, how can one account for consciousness if consciousness itself has a "horizonal" structure?

From its inception in the *Logical Investigations,* phenomenology endeavors to analyze consciousness. The "positive" discipline for this is, naturally, psychology. However, phenomenology as rigorous science aims at moving from facts regarding the human consciousness to essences; it is an eidetic science of consciousness, as essentially characterized by the structure of intentionality. Yet, this intentionality is itself not a homogenous and "uniform" framework, but is a complex sphere, structured by the structure of *cogito–cogitatum.* Accounting for this "rich" structure calls for a whole "psychology" on the basis of the phenomenological principles (intentionality). Phenomenological psychology is this designated discipline performed on the basis of an eidetic description of conscious phenomena. Structuring this discipline has its own problems and difficulties, which shall not be discussed here.[35] Yet it is clear how it would be necessary to systematically carry this out as a "universal" analysis. Husserl reflected intensely on how to perform this task in a systematic fashion.[36] In short, he proceeds from a positive science within the whole of the human sciences. In this framework, psychology, as science of consciousness conceived as a single Ego, would be followed by the science of communal spirit[37] in the framework of a phenomenology of intersubjectivity. However, these considerations, according to Husserl, thematize subjectivity as part of the world and hence remain bound to the natural attitude.

Hence, psychology is at first the thematization of a systematic science of (worldly) consciousness, but not transcendental subjectivity, because psychology as a positive science, due to its methodological naïveté, remains blind to the transcendental dimension.[38] Thus, in numerous attempts, Husserl strives to show how phenomenological psychology can motivate the reduction from worldly to transcendental consciousness by pointing out its methodological shortcomings and by explaining why a phenomenological psychology must necessarily lead to the transcendental dimension. It might well be that the picture Husserl draws of such a pre-transcendental psychology is a mere caricature in order to expound his own "transcendental discipline" in contrast to it; yet Husserl was also a child of his time and influenced by contemporary theories of psychology, which he hoped to embed in a transcendental framework. How, then, is the shift from phenomenological psychology to transcendental phenomenology motivated, and more importantly, how is it possible? Both questions belong together, for Husserl's strategy for demonstrating the necessity of moving to the transcendental dimension is to uncover the problems and paradoxes that arise if one *remains* bound to a purely "psychological" concept of subjectivity. Thus, how can I gain an overview over subjective life if I remain bound to my experience in the "lived present"?

The answer lies in the doctrine of the splitting of the Ego, which addresses the problem arising from expanding the Ego to a field structure. If consciousness is more than an Ego (a *cogito*) but a whole sphere of conscious life, then the question of the *agent*, the "unparticipating observer"[39] carrying out this discipline, becomes pressing. An overview of this sphere—which is a sphere of intersubjectivity—harbors the danger of dissolving this very agent that strives to gain an uninhibited view over transcendental life. The life the Ego experiences by reflection is nothing but the life of this agent itself—but it is not entirely *her* life only, but of a community of agents. Yet, the Ego can only access this conscious life that it calls its own from its own first-person standpoint. Thus, reflecting on one's conscious life yields access to this consciousness, but it also creates the following problem: how can I have access to this conscious life as such if I can never step outside of my individual self's position? And even if I could gain access, how can I experience these regions, which are not mine alone, without losing my individuality? I *can* inhibit the general thesis of the natural attitude and turn to my consciousness. But how am I to characterize the relationship between myself, the observing agent, and that which I observe, if the latter is the *whole sphere* of consciousness, which is not mine alone? Would this not end up in a vicious circle?

In phenomenological psychology, as in any science, there is a region to be observed and an observer. Only here we face the curious situation that the observer and observed are of one and the same essence. Hence, only an artificial rupture, which splits the Ego into an observer and a thematic field, can establish this difference of the same: the Ego and her own conscious life. "In my living present I have in coexistence the doubled Ego and the doubled Ego act; thus the Ego, which now continuously observes [e.g.] the house, and the Ego, which carries out this act: 'I am aware that I am continuously observing the house'" (Hua VIII, 89). In principle this doubling has no limit. I can always again reflect upon that which I have just observed and reflect upon this reflection *in infinitum*. I can always make the part of the Ego that I reflect upon "patent," whereas the reflective Ego will remain "latent." However, the reflection by a latent Ego (which can occur repeatedly in "iteration") will render the latent

Ego patent, and so on.[40] This infinite regress, to Husserl, is "undangerous" because we are not dealing here with a logical foundation; rather, it reveals, over and over, the reflective "I can." Although the reflection upon yet another Ego yields no new insight, the possible "iteration" of reflection proves the feasibility of the reflective faculty of consciousness and asserts the Ego's "insolubility" and centered "stability" in ever-new reflective acts.

Whereas this iteration adds no new insight into the nature of consciousness, the splitting into the observer of conscious life and consciousness itself as a result of this activity can only occur as a radical split, a rupture within the originally unitary conscious life. "Naive" life has its breaks and ruptures, but is overall "one" due to the shared belief in the general thesis of the natural attitude. Hence, the break with the natural attitude in the epoché is to be conceived as a split between the philosophizing Ego and that which it observes, consciousness itself, in acting out its life intentionally in the form of the natural attitude. The epoché is hence a *radical splitting of the Ego.* The reflective Ego is no longer under the "spell" of the general thesis; it reflectively turns its attention to consciousness, which, in turn, is intentionally directed at the world. As all intentional life "shoots at" the world and is as such "enamored" with it—here Husserl plays on the pun *"verschossen"* (Hua VI, 179)[41]—this reflective turn requires a radical change of attitude, although the intentional character of the reflective Ego itself is not altered. An alternative formulation of "being intentionally directed at the world" is "being interested in its affairs." Hence, the term *"uninterested* observer" becomes understandable as not being interested in the general thesis of naively positing the world as existing in different ways. Husserl later prefers the term "unparticipating" to describe the "status" of this agent, as the term "uninterested" implies an indifference. To be sure, the observer is eminently interested in knowledge about consciousness—she is interested in a way the natural Ego cannot and never will be "interested" as long as it lives in the natural attitude. Alternatively, and more adequately, "unparticipating" suggests that the philosophizing Ego does not participate in asserting the general thesis of the natural attitude.

This splitting enables a view on the totality of conscious life. This is not a "view from nowhere" because that which I gain access to is nothing but my own life as experienced from the first-person perspective. The view upon my life after the split, however, is still from the first-person perspective, only from a higher stance. What can this tell us about the discipline of phenomenological psychology, as yielding a point of access to phenomenology? Is it necessary for it to be a transcendental discipline? Ultimately, it has to be, because this totality only comes into view *after* a break with the natural attitude. The splitting of the Ego *and* the break with the natural attitude are inextricably bound together. However, it *is* possible to practice an eidetic science of consciousness from the natural attitude. Here, too, there is the difference between a scientific agent and the region this science thematizes. But this does not suffice to gain a *total* overview over consciousness as such, because its topic is only one stratum in the entirety of the constituted world: the psychic (excluding the somatic, etc.). Thus, the consequence of the endeavor to thematize the totality of psychology's subject matter necessitates the transcendental turn, something that psychology by definition cannot accomplish. Thus, as long as this discipline does not inhibit the general thesis, it remains on the ground of the natural attitude as a positive science. Hence, paradoxically, mundane consciousness thematizes itself as part of the world. In the hierarchy of the foundational strata of nature and spirit this discipline deals with conscious life on the foundation of nature. The "personalistic" attitude, which psychology occupies and which is necessary to access subjectivity, is thus an abstraction from the natural attitude, which experiences the whole of constituted life, albeit without any knowledge of its own accomplishments of *constituting* the world for itself.

By contrast, transcendental subjectivity is not part of the world; it is the world's correlate as that which constitutes the world. Transcendental subjectivity is not *in* the world; it *constitutes* it. Only the splitting of the Ego makes it possible for the observer to have a "transcendental experience" while remaining a mundane Ego. The Ego is at the same time an object in the world and a subject for the world (Hua VI, 182–83).[42] Yet, a phenomenological psychology, based in the natural attitude, *is* indeed possible. The transcendental viewpoint, already accessed in the Cartesian way, clarifies that this discipline, as a positive science, remains incomplete and methodologically ambiguous. A true phenomenological psychology is necessarily *forced* to perform the reduction and move from a mundane to a transcendental account. Thus, despite psychology's philosophical inadequacy, phenomenological psychology and transcendental phenomenology are "parallel" disciplines. This parallelism, however, vanishes with the realization that mundane consciousness is nothing but transcendental consciousness once one has inhibited the general thesis. Or, viewed from the transcendental "side," mundane consciousness is an incomplete "part" or "layer" of consciousness that is not part of the world, but correlated to it. Hence, a methodological consideration of phenomenological psychology reveals "that the consistent and pure execution of this task of a radical reform of psychology had to lead, of itself and of necessity, to a science of transcendental subjectivity and thus to its transformation into a universal transcendental philosophy" (Hua VI, 203).[43]

Apart from psychology's yielding an entrance gate to transcendental phenomenology or conceiving of psychology as a preliminary discipline before a treatment of "consciousness as such," another result comes to the fore in expanding phenomenology into a full-blown transcendental discipline, namely, the unparticipating observer. Contrasted with the Cartesian approach, the establishing of this agent "saves" the philosophizing Ego from becoming "lost" or "drowning" within the vast transcendental field. Moreover, only this way of access to the transcendental as a sphere of experience opens the view towards transcendental intersubjectivity— as a community of subjects constituting a communal world. Yet, establishing this observer in a conscious methodological move *retains* the radicality of the Cartesian approach because it insists on a philosophizing agent practicing this introspection; it can be seen as a Cartesian remnant in a wholly different agenda. Only with the clear carving out of such an agent can the philosopher claim to take over responsibility for his or her own actions as a scientist and human being. Not by accident is *Socrates* the archetype of a radical inquirer, who has discovered the foundation of all knowledge in himself.[44] For Husserl, practicing radical self-introspection in the way outlined equates living the ethical ideal of self-responsibility. This explicit establishing of the philosophical observer thus opens the path to "ethical" considerations of the role of the philosopher, which are a crucial part of Husserl's late reflections.[45]

Thus, moving from the Cartesian approach to the way into phenomenology via psychology enables Husserl to harmonize the *two* requirements that satisfy his demand for rigorous science. The first task is that of founding a scientific discipline, which phenomenology claims to be; hence it provides more than "just" a philosophical foundation in an Ego (as an axiomatic principle), but rather a discipline of the *cogitata* of this *cogito* in the broadest conceivable sense. The second requirement is that of living up to the "epistemologico-ethical" ideal of fully legitimizing the actions of the philosopher. This is only possible because the epoché opens up an overview over the *totality* of consciousness that hitherto, and by necessity, was hidden *in* this totality. As such, this science presents an ideal for all other sciences, not in terms of substance but concerning the moral ideal guiding the scientist's actions. The idea of science as well as that of the scientist are products of a variation from the philosopher as the "model scientist," and hence apply to all factual appearances of them.[46]

Thus, the way via psychology becomes the "grand path" into phenomenology, since such a psychology leads necessarily into transcendental phenomenology, if taken to its methodological conclusions. Psychology is the "field of decision" for an adequate framing of transcendental phenomenology. Put differently, the modern separation of psychology and transcendental philosophy has led to the fateful development in modern philosophy, psychologism. Husserl's transcendental phenomenology can be seen as an effort to combine both strands gone astray into one transcendental discipline. If psychology is truly to be part of critical philosophy, it cannot be carried out from "an empirical point of view" (as Husserl's heritage from the Brentano school made him believe), but rather "according to critical method," as, for example, Natorp the Kantian conceived of psychology.[47]

The Way via the Lifeworld

In his last attempt to present an introduction into phenomenology in the *Crisis,* Husserl proposes yet another way, that via the lifeworld (the "ontological way").[48] Although he had already pursued this path in his earlier work from the 1920s, it is not until the *Crisis* that it achieves its most mature presentation as Husserl's "last word" regarding this topic. Without devaluating his previous attempts, Husserl considered this path the principal one, although he merely draws the consequence from his earlier reflections. What motivated Husserl to broach yet another path, and what are its main lines of thought?

Insight into the nature of transcendental consciousness reveals "the transcendental" to have essentially intersubjective and genetic dimensions. On the deepest level (passivity), it cannot even be called "subjective" any longer. Husserl uses different terms to describe it, from simply "the transcendental" to "transcendental world," and so on. The initial conception of transcendental subjectivity is expanded into two major dimensions: as a field of consciousness it is not "only" a subjectivity but always already an intersubjectivity. Furthermore, the description of this field is incomplete if only analyzed in a static register. The static description turns out merely to grasp the uppermost stratum within a universe of genetic development.[49] Phenomenology in this full sense as a theory of world constitution accounts for how transcendental consciousness "forms" the world as product of its experience. Thus, only a full understanding of this consciousness can give the philosopher an equally full concept of the world as *lifeworld.* Since transcendental consciousness as world-constituting and the lifeworld as the product of constitution are correlates, thematizing *either of them* yields a way into phenomenology. Hence, the way via psychology and that via the lifeworld *complement* each other. Whether I take my point of departure from mundane consciousness and reduce to its transcendental "counterpart," or if I inquire back from the pre-given lifeworld to its constituting achievements, I arrive at transcendental (inter)subjectivity as the "absolute being" that constitutes the world.[50]

This means, if inquiring back into transcendental consciousness reveals the world as what it truly is—a product of the transcendental constitution—then only transcendental phenomenology can render a real understanding of the world *as a lifeworld*. In other words, as long as the world is not framed within this correlation, it has not been fully understood.[51] This is also a critique of the positive sciences. It is not the case that they have relinquished their ideal of scientificity, that is, to account for the essence of the world, as much as they have pursued a wrong path and have become blind to the true being of the world insofar as they have abstracted from it and have forgotten its basic character, as a world of everyday life. This is one of the main themes in the *Crisis*, where Husserl tries to give a diagnosis of his time and to show how transcendental phenomenology can help solve this crisis. This "missionary" motif in Husserl's philosophy goes back to the *Kaizo* articles from 1922, in which he calls for a "renewal" of the European spirit.[52] When some fifteen years later he diagnoses a "crisis" in modern European culture, he reverts to the same topic. In both cases, Husserl proposes: the world must be saved through rigorous science, this science ultimately being phenomenology.[53]

What does the crisis of modern European science consist in? Science has departed from the lifeworld in modernity by its method of mathematization. This process is an abstraction that has converted the world into a mathematical universe; it has supplanted the "real" world with the world of numbers, as dealt with in science.[54] Two results, again correlative, follow: first, science abstracts from the "real" world and lives in its own world of formulae. It has "forgotten" the lifeworld.[55] As a consequence, it loses sight of the original lifeworld from which it has emerged and continues to emerge. In this process, science not only loses sight of the lifeworld but *replaces* it with the scientific world. The lifeworld has become covered up by a scientific view of this world that does not see the world as what it is in its original sense: a world of pre-scientific, pre-philosophical life. However, is not the scientific form of life also a form of life, and a very special one? In what sense can the lifeworld, accordingly, be pre-scientific? Whence this critique of science?

There can be no doubt about Husserl's undiminished high regard for science. One must never understand his call back to the lifeworld as breaking with the ideal of a "scientific" mastery of the world. This would be a crass misreading of Husserl's famous quote of the dream of rigorous science "ending."[56] Indeed, the phenomenological approach does thematize the world as a lifeworld and is conceived as a counterbalance to the positive sciences, but its goal is also, thereby, to bring the sciences back on track. Thus, phenomenology does in no way devalue the achievements of the positive sciences, but wants to embed them in an all-embracing scientific endeavor that should remain "in touch" with the lifeworld from which it has sprung. What, then, does Husserl mean by lifeworld?[57] The world of science is opposed to the *pre-scientific* world. The lifeworld is hence the world of the pre-scientific attitude; indeed, it is nothing but the world the natural attitude has as its correlate. It is the subjective-relative world of *dóxa* as opposed to the world of *epistéme*. Not only does modern science "leap over" this world, it has never precisely been *in* its pre-scientific character the theme of a scientific endeavor, because relativity (to the subject, in this case) was its decided *terminus a quo;* the *terminus ad quem* was objective truth (and not the "subjective" truth "of the marketplace"). However, the pre-scientific lifeworld is the basis of *all* human actions, natural *or* scientific. Hence, it is the task of phenomenological reflection, first of all, to thematize this lifeworld, that is, to re-cover it by uncovering the abstractive strata that have become laid over it. Husserl calls for a "reduction to the lifeworld" in the specific sense of an initial "opening up," because the lifeworld has been "forgotten" by modern man in striving for a scientific world domination. Strictly speaking, one cannot call this forgetfulness, since it never was thematized in the first place. Not thematizing this as a foundation *even for the sciences* means leaving the latter dangling in open space.

How is this "lifeworld reduction" executed? Paradoxically, one must carry it out as a scientific endeavor aiming at a universal "ontology of the lifeworld" (see *Crisis,* Hua VI, §51). As such, it seems it should be carried out in the natural attitude. This could be seen as contradicting Husserl's own intentions in that he seems to rescind the reduction. From the higher, transcendental standpoint, however, the natural attitude has been understood as a "lower" (naive) form of the former and can only "artificially" be restituted. Indeed, one has to insist that it is a *reduction* that allows us to see the lifeworld as such ("stripped" of idealizations). This "lifeworld reduction" reduces to the world *before* any idealizations and reveals the sphere of basic life as the fundamental "presupposition"[58] of any activity.[59]

An ontology of the lifeworld has been perhaps one of the most intriguing ideas in the late Husserl. What this ontology consists of and how it is to be carried out shall not be discussed in this chapter. However, the very conception of this discipline is important in the present context, because it also yields a way into the transcendental sphere once we realize that the lifeworld is a "product" of constitution. Indeed, this concrete world of the natural attitude cannot come into view without practicing a universal epoché. One *needs* the reduction to uncover the sphere of transcendental subjectivity that constitutes this world as the world of the natural attitude, from which any activity takes its stand. Only by understanding the transcendental as constituting can we have access to the world in its base-function, that is, as pre-philosophical lifeworld. The reduction must even go beyond the philosophical standpoint, and the phenomenologist has to make her way *back into* the natural attitude, without, however, forgetting its transcendental "origin." Husserl called this reverse movement "enworlding."[60]

Only through a universal epoché from the lifeworld can we attain a full appreciation of the correlation between world and transcendental subjectivity. As Kern puts it: "only the ontological way hence grasps subjectivity really as transcendental" (1962, 344). Accordingly, only a thematization of the lifeworld attains a view of the world in its universal dimensions. After all, the world of the scientist is also a "world," despite resting on its unthematic basis, the lifeworld. The world is thus a universal foundation. Since transcendental subjectivity and lifeworld are correlates in the framework of constitution, gaining a full grasp of either one *includes* the possibility of understanding the other; one *cannot* go without the other. Only from the standpoint of an ontology of the lifeworld can one practice the transcendental reduction. Likewise, only through a full analysis of transcendental subjectivity in its broadest dimensions can we understand the world as the product of constitution and thus as what it ultimately is: a *historic* world of *life* with its genesis, history, and a ground on which historic "subjectivities" have developed and can ever develop. Only from this mutually embracing perspective can phenomenology ultimately thematize the *transcendental* problem of history. Indeed, Husserl insists that the reduction is in no way an impoverishment or a "reducing" of the world to some singular transcendental Ego. In fact, the reduction opens up a view on the world by transcending the naïveté of the natural attitude towards a universal standpoint. What has sometimes been understood as a "dis-engagement" with the world turns out to be precisely the way to fully comprehend it.[61]

Furthermore, the discovery of the genetic dimension of world constitution reveals the lifeworld to be not only historical but also, in its historicity, to have "laws of genesis." Tracing back the history of the lifeworld in its decisive developmental steps—its primal institutings—reveals these as developments on the way to transcendental phenomenology *itself*. The sketch of phenomenological "archeology" Husserl performs in the first part of the *Crisis* in going back to the first rudimentary forms of mathematization in ancient Greece is a reconstruction of how science and philosophy have come about in a certain historical situation. It is a reconstruction of how science arose from the pre-philosophical lifeworld through a radically new idea, the mathematization of nature. But there is also a "progressive" side to this historical consideration. Husserl's reconstruction of the history of philosophy is also an effort to trace these "primal institutings" as coming ever closer to the discovery of transcendental subjectivity until it—in this very "Hegelian" manner—reaches its decisive breakthrough in phenomenology. However, neither history nor philosophy come to an end; rather, they should proceed from here—this was Husserl's hope—in a new and transcendentally enlightened style. Thus, by interpreting history teleologically as a critical history of ideas,[62] it can be understood as eclipsing in the reduction and from here as the way into a transcendental reconstruction of the historic lifeworld.

To sum up, I have attempted to systematically present the three principal ways into phenomenology. There is ultimately but one way, which may have its different procedures or emphases: the way through the lifeworld. In a self-critical note, in one of his last manuscripts from 1937, Husserl writes:

> I have drafted different introductions into transcendental-phenomenological philosophy . . . We shall see that this lifeworld is nothing but the historical world. From here, it becomes conceivable that a complete systematic introduction into phenomenology begins and is to be carried through as a universal historical problem. If one introduces the epoché without the historic framing, then the problem of the lifeworld, i.e., of universal history, remains unsolved and still beckons. The introduction in *Ideas* [the Cartesian way] does in fact retain its right, but I now consider the historical way to be more principal and systematic. (Hua XXIX, 425–26)

Conclusion and Critique: The Reduction Between Transcendental Ego and Lifeworld

In various ways Husserl tried to come to terms with what exactly he intended by the reduction. His sometimes emphatic or ceremonious formulations show that he has more in mind than just solving a specific epistemological problem. Rather, the epistemological problem in its full dimensions is of such importance that solving it is comparable to a full "conversion of humankind." However literally these characterizations are to be understood, Husserl emphasizes that he considers the reduction his greatest discovery; he is convinced that it is also the most diffi-cult part of his philosophy. "The reduction" is much more than a purely methodological device.[63] At times it becomes a synonym for his entire philosophy. Let us look at the consequences to which this leads.

The discussion of the ways into the reduction has shown that there are *two* focal points the reduction leads to: the lifeworld as a constitutive product of the full scope of the transcendental, on the one hand; and, on the other, the transcendental Ego that, discovered by the unparticipat-ing observer, is the basis for any apodictic evidence upon which to build the edifice of science. What are Husserl's intentions in focusing on these two phenomena?

Let us start with the Ego of the phenomenologist. Establishing this observer vis-à-vis transcendental life in the process of constituting the world puts the philosopher in the position of accounting for this tran-scendental life, which he "partakes" in. This life is, in the last instance, nothing other than "my own." Accounting for it is more than an episte-mological task. Since the phenomenological scientist has to legitimate her actions, she has to give account of them responsibly and ultimately for herself. Accounting for one's own deepest "self" is more than just per-forming another scientific "job"; it is a task of the highest responsibility possible. The "dignity" of the philosopher's activity stems from his duty to act responsibly as a researcher. "Acting rightfully" in doing philosophy is so much an ethical issue that one cannot conceive of philosophy as being only a "job." It is rather a "vocation." In this Husserl alludes to the German *Beruf* (job) as derived from *Berufung* (vocation).[64] Being a "good philosopher" becomes an ethical ideal, in analogy to being a good human being. Contrary to the view that the epoché enacts a "disengage-ment" with the world, the position of the phenomenological observer is precisely a radical giving an account of this life, the famous *lógon didónai*. This is possible because the "unparticipating" view first makes a universal "overview" possible. This is not to say that *everyone* ought to become a phi-losopher. However, becoming one means not only achieving the highest dignity humanly possible but also living humanness, which consists in rationality, to the fullest.[65] Becoming a philosopher as the one who has performed the reduction and discovered absolute life "within" oneself means fulfilling a "self-forming of the Ego through absolute reflection to the absolutely genuine human."[66] It is an ideal task of justifying all of one's actions and taking responsibility for them. This lies within the tele-ology of human (rational) faculties. If practical rationality is a question of *freedom,* then the philosopher's actions in her "phenomenologizing" activity are a genuine pursuit of freedom. Moreover, the philosopher is even grander in this pursuit of freedom since she has become aware of this freedom as a full instantiation of rationality discovered in leaving the boundaries of the natural attitude. It is a freedom understood, rather than "blindly" acted out.[67]

Yet, the transcendental life I discover within myself is more than *my own* life. The reduction yields the insight that transcendental achievements never belong only to me; the world is never a product of my activity alone but of a transcendental intersubjectivity. Individual subjectivity becomes formed only in terms of others, the ones before me and after me, the ones I have never encountered and never will encounter, and so on. All of these have "contributed" to the world as it is. Thus, the reduction gives access to transcendental life as such, and hence breaks the spell of solipsism. In and through transcendental intersubjectivity we are bound together in one "spiritual" totality. Thus, Husserl calls the philosophers the "functionaries of mankind." They can assume this function insofar as taking over responsibility for myself directly leads to all the others as united in the totality of "monads." The philosopher, then, has a *double* task. On the one hand, he interprets the life of humankind in an "absolute" view. On the other, the philosopher in his activity of discovering this truth has to give account for the actions of mankind in their relative ways of life and in the multitude of (special) worlds. Giving a description of this life in this world is the first step in judging human actions. Thus, Husserl states programmatically, "phenomenological explication does nothing but explicate the sense this world has for us all, prior to any philosophizing, and obviously gets solely from our experience—a sense which philosophy can uncover but never alter" (Hua I, 177).

Thus, the philosopher's role is that of calling mankind back to its preconceived, teleological path. This is also the role that the philosopher and citizen Husserl assumed in the *Crisis* at a time when not only science had deviated from its designated path but a whole nation had gone astray, blinded by a frenzy of nationalism and racism. Husserl's calling for a reform of science in the light of the political upheaval in Nazi Germany might seem utterly naive to us. However, one must bear in mind what science meant in the whole of human culture to Husserl: scientific and ultimately philosophical activity are the highest realizations of human life as such. In this "emphatic" sense the philosopher's role might well be described, with Nietzsche, as a "doctor of culture." Indeed, a "crisis" can also be understood in medical terms as the crest of a sickness. Thus, the philosopher cannot directly intervene in the course of history—the sense of the world is one that can "never" be altered. Rather, one can only react to a disease that has already taken its course; that is, the philosopher has the duty to point out where and why, from which motives, this deviation from the "good" path has occurred and show possible ways out of the crisis by way of reconstructing it.

However, despite the emphasis on the philosopher's role as standing in lieu of humanity, Husserl insists on the "uniqueness" and "personal indeclinability" of the philosophizing Ego (Hua VI, 188). Despite Husserl's emphasis upon intersubjectivity, he holds that the agent can never be "reduced" to an irrelevant, contingent mode within an inter-monadic totality:

> The "I" that I attain in the epoché . . . is actually called "I" only by equivocation—though it is an essential equivocation since, when I name it in reflection, I can say nothing other than: it is I who practice the epoché, I who interrogate, as phenomenon, the world which is now valid for me according to its being and being-such, with all its human beings, of whom I am so fully conscious; it is I who stand above all natural existence that has meaning for me, who am the Ego-pole of this transcendental life, in which, at first, the world has meaning for me purely as world; it is I who, taken in full concreteness, encompass all that. (Husserl 1986, 188)

Thus, Husserl's philosophy *remains* a critical transcendental philosophy that can never do without an absolute Ego as the foundation and starting point of all reflection. It is precisely this "Cartesianistic" motif that Husserl never gives up, because it is connected to the idea that there is ultimately an apodictic foundation, an "Archimedean point" that provides a final foundation in the evidence of the Ego. The consequence of the reduction pursued thus far leads to a partial validation of the "Cartesian" Husserl. It is from this approach only that he can interpret the role of the philosopher in the framework of the cultural activity of mankind. In order to secure this cultural implication and to enable the philosopher to be more than a citizen of an ivory tower, Husserl "needs" Cartesianism.

However, on the other side of the balance, there is the issue of the lifeworld, which becomes increasingly important to the later Husserl. Some scholars, most forcefully Husserl's own former assistant Landgrebe, have interpreted Husserl's turn of attention to the pre-scientific world as a "departure from Cartesianism,"[68] as Landgrebe famously phrases it. His argument is that Husserl realized that he could not lay an apodictic foundation in the Ego. Therefore, he (more or less consciously) abandoned this project and instead turned to the lifeworld as the actual working field of phenomenology. Performing an "ontology of the lifeworld" is the true task for phenomenology. In order to do this, one does not need a Cartesian reduction to a transcendental consciousness. Hence, the departure has already occurred behind Husserl's back, the moment he turned to the lifeworld as his primary field of interest. This reading of Husserl's late philosophy was very dominant in the first decades after Husserl's death and was clearly influenced by Heidegger, more precisely by the notion that Husserl himself was (subconsciously) influenced by Heidegger's hermeneutics of facticity.[69] This is evidenced, supposedly, by Husserl's unfinished sketch of a lifeworld ontology. The fact that this ontology was never worked out in detail and only hinted at in the *Crisis* was taken as an implicit proof that the problem of the lifeworld was merely an "afterthought," a glimpse of something radically new that Husserl was not able to give account of ultimately.[70] It was an idea hinted at rather than clearly seen in view of its consequences, namely, that it would lead to an abandoning of his transcendental project.

However, in the past decades a good deal of manuscript material from Husserl's *Nachlass* (literary estate) has been published showing that a "theory of world apperception"[71] is in fact not only worked out in great detail; indeed, Husserl had been working on a lifeworld interpretation already since the early 1920s. Since this material has become known, the "departure" thesis has become highly problematic, and there is consensus among scholars that Husserl ultimately was not able to "achieve" this last step.[72] More importantly, it could never have been his intention to leave Cartesianism behind. But how can both tendencies be reconciled? Although Landgrebe's assessment of Husserl's late thought is clearly incorrect, and if one, furthermore, "subtracts" the Heidegger-inspired overtones of this interpretation, did Landgrebe perhaps see something that is not altogether wrong?

As has been shown, transcendental and lifeworldly, "ontological" analysis complement each other to Husserl. Therefore, the reduction is needed in order to access this lifeworld, since in all "normal" pursuit of life it is unthematic and *remains* all the more un-thematized in modern science. That is, by science's abstracting from the lifeworld, it is nevertheless bound to it unknowingly. Thematizing the lifeworld, as that which always remains un-thematized in the natural attitude, means already having left the natural attitude. Nevertheless, this does not mean *doing away* with it. To the contrary, it *remains* the basic form of life (the philosopher *remains* a citizen, a father, a mother, etc.). From the transcendental standpoint one understands the natural attitude as a "lower" stance, or which says the same, the natural attitude is already transcendental, yet without knowing it. The natural attitude is "implicated" in the transcendental perspective.[73]

For an ontology of the lifeworld, this entails that Husserl's "restitut-ing"[74] of the natural attitude in order to attain a standpoint to analyze it cannot mean that we, the analyzing philosophers, are to "forget" the perspective gained in the reduction. Going back into the old attitude, resuscitating the old naïveté, is impossible, as Husserl points out. Rather, this step back must be understood as a quasi-imaginary move: I pretend to go back into the "old" attitude, and from there description of the lifeworld can proceed in analyzing what life in the natural attitude was like before I became aware of it. We can understand "restitution" in this context as "reconstruction" of something that has been "un-built" in transcendental analysis.[75] This is why performing the reduction, rightly understood, does not stand in contradiction to the task of a lifeworld ontology. Tersely put: without the reduction, we would never gain an uninhibited view of the lifeworld.

Yet, although this ontology is "enabled" through the transcendental turn, it is also true that this discipline soon takes on its own character. Describing the world from its most primitive elements, through first formations of communal life to higher-order personalities and ending up finally in cultures, home-worlds, alien-worlds, and so on is a gigantic field of research. The rich methodological instruments Husserl has forged in his development of a genetic phenomenology provide the tools needed to pursue this task. In fact, one can say that this method takes on the character of a hermeneutics of the lifeworld, as it is the world given to experiencing subjects. It is a description of how the world we live in has come to be and how it functions. The term "hermeneutics"—which Husserl uses in a similar context—is designated to mean precisely this. It is rather a *descriptive* than a normative discipline. Where Husserl attempts such descriptions—for example, in analyses of Greek culture and philosophy—the "genetic" is oftentimes indistinguishable from factual-historical analyses.[76] It is thus not surprising that quasi-philosophical disciplines such as sociology, political theory, history, and pedagogy have taken up Husserl's ideas on the lifeworld. Furthermore, it cannot be accidental that the term "lifeworld" has become almost a household name that nowadays has little to do with its origin. *The very "mundaneity" of the problem of the world of life suggests its remoteness from transcendental questions.*

Thus, the interpretation presented here attempts to overcome the common assertion that there is a "contradiction" between Husserl's Cartesian position and his account of the lifeworld. I have tried to show that a philosophical thematization of the lifeworld is not possible without a transcendental question as to its origin in (inter)subjectivity. In Husserl's eyes, both agendas are correlates. At the same time, I would like to insist that Husserl's Cartesian account of the subject and his lifeworld ontology present *two distinct* and, in this sense, *separate programs*. They are projects Husserl pursues with different aims: whereas the "Cartesian Husserl" pursues a path of scientific grounding and foundationalism, the "lifeworld Husserl" is interested in what can be called a hermeneutics of the world of everyday life. Both projects are set squarely against each other, *not* in the sense that they contradict or cancel each other out, but in that they pursue two different *agendas*. They are located on two different "maps." One *can* pursue one while completely neglecting the other. It is possible to pursue a "theory" of the lifeworld without being at all interested in transcendental ("constitutional") problems. Likewise, one can immerse oneself in transcendental matters in the tradition of Kant and German idealism, and fruitfully utilize Husserl's contributions to transcendental theories.[77] In the wake of fundamental criticisms of reason and rationality especially in the second half of the twentieth century, it is understandable why this path has been of less interest than the former. This, however, cannot be a reason to discard this aspect of Husserl. In fact, neglecting the Cartesian Husserl leads to fundamental misunderstandings. These disregard the fact that Husserl never came close to considering transcendental phenomenology and the idea(l) of rigorous science a dream, let alone a dream that could come to an end.

This leads, however, to the concluding critical observation. Namely, Husserl *failed to combine* these two major aspects of his philosophical endeavor. There is *neither* just the "Cartesian" *nor* the "lifeworld Husserl." There is of systematic necessity both. However, there cannot be a *systematic principle* uniting both, since formulating such a principle would make the problematic step of considering one of the two projects as absolute and the other derivative. Favoring one would result in devaluing the other. It is inconceivable how foundationalist questions following the Cartesian paradigm would fit into a lifeworld ontology, precisely because this ontology is based on "the transcendental" as necessarily an *inter-subjectivity*. Likewise, it is not clear why such a lifeworld ontology would "need" foundationalist clarifications other than clarifying the role of the philosophizing agent, who is but a minimal focal point of experience *of* the lifeworld. Metaphorically speaking, on the "map" of the lifeworld, the Cartesian Ego is an infinitesimally small point. On the Cartesian "map," the problem of the lifeworld comes very late, so that it lies almost on another "continent." This is the consequence of the Janus head of the phenomenological reduction. A sign of Husserl's keen philosophical view is that he had looked in both directions, "backwards" into the depths of transcendental life and "forward" into the world. But, as profound as Husserl's instinct was, this view is either one-eyed or squinting.

The reduction thus has the *double* meaning of calling humanity to its utmost possibilities, to the "true" and "genuine" rational human being within one's self, on the one hand. On the other, its task is to convey an all-embracing understanding of the world we live in, including ourselves as dwellers in this world of interests and distinct activities. The conflict of *absolute* humanity and *relative* life pursuit remains, however: we are left with the *paradox of human subjectivity,* the resolving of which nobody else can decide but history itself in which reason unfolds teleologically— or where it can always disperse and even become lost. Performing the phenomenological reduction, to Husserl, is nothing but the constant attempt to "come to reason," although there might be factual hindrances on the way to this ideal—a way which necessarily leads through the lifeworld. Hence, the history of phenomenology itself will demonstrate the success of the program conceived by its founder—or its opposite. But this is not up to us to decide.

With the reduction, Husserl has touched upon the fundamental issue of freedom, the freedom to be oneself, or, which is to say the same, the freedom to open oneself to reason as the true meaning of humanity. The possibility of performing the phenomenological reduction would thus be identical with the extent to which freedom is possible.[78] The critical assertions mentioned notwithstanding, the reduction is Husserl's contribution to philosophy in the tradition of the Enlightenment that does not uncritically accept rationality as a given, but wants to conceive of it within a transcendental and intersubjective account of subjectivity. There might be no way to unify the issues of lifeworld and Cartesianism, but there might also be no other way to go than into these two, opposite directions.

From the Reduction to the Problems Arising from It

As has been shown in this chapter, the reduction, rather than solving all problems of method once and for all, as Husserl had hoped, is more than anything else something that raises even more issues. It comes as no surprise, then, that further concerns become pressing. Husserl worked on these until he laid down his pen; but they are not left entirely open and unsolved. Yet, they continue to pose challenges for any reader of Husserl, whether or not this reader wishes simply to understand his transcendental phenomenology, or to critique, go beyond, or refute it. There is no way, for anybody interested in phenomenology, around the purgatory of Husserl's version thereof.

While the previous chapters were largely reconstructive and expository—while certain problems were of course already hinted at—the following chapter will highlight some problems that emerge from these methodological reflections in conjunction with the reduction. The chapter will make clear why and to what extent "the reduction," more than anything else, remained the title for a whole set of problems where the basic question of interpretation must be, above anything else, whether or not this set of problems displays, in itself, a systematic order. The following chapter operates under the assumption that these problems, rather than being an unorganized heap, do have a systematic structure, which is reflected by four basic problems that are discerned in conjunction with the reduction. These problems are only comprehensible, however, after having digested the general conceptions of the reduction and the lifeworld discussed thus far; chapters 1 and 2 thus function as a foil for the following, chapter 3.

3

Some Methodological Problems Arising in Husserl's Late Reflections on the Phenomenological Reduction

Introduction

For some years now the phenomenological reduction has enjoyed a significant popularity both in phenomenological circles and within other philosophical orientations inspired by phenomenology. This is largely attributable, at least initially, to interest coming out of France, but which in the meantime has affected philosophers in other countries, an impulse affecting philosophers who explicitly subscribe to the "phenomenological movement" or those who have only a vague relationship to phenomenology of the *classical* variety.[1] It is due to this reconsideration that the founding father of phenomenology is also again being given more attention. Some hundred or more years ago he was, after all, the initiator not only of phenomenology but above all of the method of *phenomenological reduction* as a particular mode of access to philosophy in a decidedly transcendental form. Husserl's philosophy is often virtually identified with his method of reduction, and it is thus rightly believed that by a reconstruction of this procedure one can grasp phenomenology as a whole. Indeed, the reduction can be said to have been phenomenology's "primary institution" (*Urstiftung*) as a transcendental enterprise.

Husserl is of interest for contemporary philosophizing in general for reasons other than just the reduction. Yet the problems which arise particularly in his late work only become comprehensible when one has gained an understanding of the method of reduction, a method which for him is invariably connected with the paradigm of a philosophy of reflection and subjectivity.[2] In the difficulties which confronted Husserl, the fundamental problems—and also the limits—of a philosophy oriented in this manner can be seen. Not so long ago one might have received the impression that postmodernity and all forms of "post-isms" had outstripped Husserlian phenomenology; yet, more than seventy years after his death (and after the subsiding of Heidegger mania), it is widely recognized that Husserl can in no way be filed into the archives.[3] It is precisely the increasing publication of his *Nachlass* that has allowed a total picture of Husserl to emerge, one infinitely richer than the one known solely through his published writings.[4]

The assessment of the phenomenological reduction and its philosophical meaning has also shifted, both in taking up Husserl and in going beyond him; for contemporary phenomenological efforts have not always expressly based themselves on Husserl—to the contrary. Often the (new) approaches to and reconsiderations on the theme of "reduction" were formulated precisely as a *critique* of Husserl. While one might emphatically welcome Husserl's efforts toward a "reduction" as a grounding of a new philosophical method and a new philosophical-scientific ethos on the basis of subjectivity, one might in the same breath also criticize him by saying that he did not carry out this ideal *radically enough*.[5] Further, one might claim that because of his prejudices which, despite all the efforts of the epoché were nevertheless present, he remained trapped within unexamined paradigms. So went the tendency, to some extent, to carry out always newer and more radical reductions, in order to push forward into spheres which, because of Husserl's fixation on evidence and intuitability (*Anschaulichkeit*), necessarily had to remain hidden from him.

Yet, in the focus on always more radical regions made accessible through the reduction, it was seldom asked *what* "reduction" even means, and if "reduction" can even be methodologically appropriate for such operations of thought (*if*, that is, one is still within the realm of thought). The meaning of "reduction" is *either* taken as self-evident *or* is generalized in a way which has very little to do with Husserl's original idea—but which also, thereby, does not contradict it. Moreover, the obvious question as to whether it is even possible to *detach* the method of reduction from Husserl's basic orientation focused and dependent on his theory of subjectivity is not addressed. The methodology of reduction is neglected in favor of a thematization of that *to which* one reduces (and *can* reduce). Husserl's *philosophy* of the phenomenological reduction is taken to be a *method*—and *only* this—while in his last years it gained for him a far more universal meaning and is directly connected with his "metaphysical" standpoint. He viewed it as the most important component of his phenomenology as a whole, and the *latter's* success depended for him first and foremost on a correct execution and exposition of the reduction. It is above all for this reason that he devoted his final works to ever-new "introductions" to phenomenology—ultimately, new expositions of the reduction.

It cannot be our task here to defend Husserl's method of phenomenological reduction from an orthodox perspective, and it is in no way possible in this short space to give a systematic and complete exposition of it. Neither should the problems with the reduction be denied, nor *can* the method be presented in its systematicity; for, in the end, not even Husserl was capable of this. Instead, I would like to attempt to present the main themes around which Husserl's late thoughts on the phenomenological method revolve, and to "reduce" them to the essential philosophical points. At the same time it should be noted that Husserl's late manuscripts seldom allow themselves to be subsumed under *one* main theme. In his manuscripts he begins with one problem, jumps immediately to another, and comes back to an earlier theme in order to finally end with a "completely different" problem. Along with this comes the tendency in the late Husserl—be it flightiness or a flagging resilience of spirit—to only refer to themes instead of fully carrying them out, and to compress thoughts to such a degree that the linguistic exposition suffers for it. In short: Husserl's late texts demand an enormous interpretive effort from the reader. The difficulties are heightened by the balancing act between "getting inside" of Husserl's mind as he wrote these private notes and remaining on the outside enough so as to not get sucked into complete "immanence."

What will thus be presented here is a kind of tableau in which I have summarized Husserl's thoughts regarding the reduction writ large into *four main themes.* There is no outline from Husserl which serves as a basis of this compilation of themes; it simply represents an attempt to bring order to Husserl's serpentine lines of thought. The presentation thus cannot avoid a certain arbitrariness, and the author alone is responsible for any inadequacies. It was also not possible to lay out the whole context of the problem, since Husserl's late philosophy must be presupposed as known (but see chapter 2). Additionally, I am eager to quote as much as possible from the manuscript material—some of which is published in the meantime—so that Husserl can speak for himself, instead of simply making a report about him. The four main themes are (1) the motivation for the reduction, (2) the parallelism between phenomenology and psychology, (3) the relation of the worldly and the transcendental Ego, and (4) enworlding (*Verweltlichung*).

The Motivation for the Reduction

As one knows from his drafts and sketches as Husserl's assistant and also from the *Sixth Cartesian Meditation,* it was above all Husserl's last assistant, *Fink,* who urged Husserl toward the problem in which one is to see the motivation for the reduction. First of all it should be stated that this presentation of the problem is "homemade," for it first originated out of Husserl's mature understanding of the *natural attitude*. The natural attitude as a correlate of the natural pre-scientific world is, in this horizonal-intentional relatedness to the world as lifeworld, also in principle not separable *from* it; both form an a priori correlation. All human behavior is to be treated phenomenologically under the title "intentional acts," which have their objective correlate that in turn appears in the framework of a horizon. *All* acts take place in the world and in the belief in their existence, and this is simply to say: on the ground of the natural attitude. Due to its intentional relatedness to the world, the natural attitude thus appears to be unabolishable, because ultimately *all* acts have a worldly correlate. In other words, all behavior proceeds naturally attuned, taking place on the ground of the natural attitude. Seen more precisely, the question of the motivation for the reduction is two- or, indeed, threefold: (1) *Is* it even possible to leave the natural attitude? If the response to this question is affirmative, we can further ask: (2) *How* is it possible to leave the natural attitude—in other words, (3) *In what* is the motivation for this departure to be seen?

While according to *Ideas I* the question of the possibility of such a departure presents no problem at all—it is a matter of our "perfect freedom"—it imposes itself now precisely *as* a problem. In considering the departure a matter of leaving the natural attitude as "merely" an act of perfect freedom, the question as to its motivation had already, in effect, been skipped. The problem is, to use a metaphor previously employed, that it seems as if the natural attitude were conceived as a bubble which one can morph and expand in certain ways[6] but can never actually burst (since otherwise one would hang suspended in midair as a worldless subject). Admittedly, Husserl *must* answer the question of the possibility of a departure in the affirmative, for otherwise his whole project of a transcendental philosophy would be nonsensical from the outset. He must, hence, determine and motivate this very departure from the natural attitude. Additionally, Husserl would never have been content with Merleau-Ponty's assessment that the reduction is never completely achievable.[7] The reduction is achievable, and completely so—or it is not at all.

It seems that Husserl himself occasionally in his late manuscripts feels the paradox into which he has brought himself. How is one to depart from the natural attitude, when all acts in their intentional relation are relative to the world? How can this "spell" be broken? Even acts such as those of reflection which explicate this very relation are, as acts, once again related to something worldly (in this case, earlier psychical acts).

Indeed, Husserl never doubts the possibility of bracketing the natural attitude, but he continually poses the question of what this could mean and searches after ways to achieve this concretely, in a certain sense in order to convince himself of this possibility. It puzzles him to have to reconstruct something which he had already performed unwittingly. This search pertains to the *second* question, in which the motivation for such a departure is to be seen. If one can provide such a motivation, then one has already implicitly answered the question of its fundamental possibility. However, the fact that Husserl sees himself as always compelled once again to seek such grounds of motivation is an indication of his unacknowledged uncertainty regarding this question. Finally, the problem of the departure from the natural attitude can only be completely grasped when one accepts the theory of enworlding, which allows the manner of this "departure" to appear in a new light (see "The Enworlding of the Transcendental Ego" in this chapter, below). But Husserl did not reflect on this issue until very late.

Indeed, one could surmise that the problem of the "departure" has become, through the *fact* of phenomenology, obsolete: the fact that the reduction was accomplished and is thus "in the world" proves that the principal doubt about its possibility is meaningless (or one must concede that the transcendental phenomenology founded through the reduction is in the end only psychology or a form thereof). With the reference to the mere existence of phenomenology one would have rid oneself of the problem in far too simple a manner. That Husserl did not, however, take things this lightly is shown by his reflections on this theme, which sometimes sound like answers to the questions discussed by him and Fink. Although Fink is not our theme at the moment, it should be mentioned that *here* most of all one can determine the influence on the part of his last assistant. Husserl's deliberations read as defenses of his position against a productive provocation. While Husserl's reflections in the context of the Sixth *Cartesian Meditation* are published and therefore known, in his "private" investigations he follows another strategy.

What Husserl discusses in the latter context can be characterized as certain "proto-forms" of the epoché, specific and "primitive" lifeworldly modes of comportment, which can be seen as the first seeds for a total-epoché, insofar as in them the naturally consistent flowing of the normal stream of life is in some way modified. Even if Husserl would agree with his previous assessment in *Ideas I* that a total epoché from the natural attitude is a matter of "complete freedom," this act of radical freedom must still be carefully prepared, indeed explicitly "motivated"; in phenomenological terms, this means: it must be *founded*.

Viewed more closely, the natural attitude turns out to be utterly rife with and indeed virtually dominated by such proto-forms, even though the person living in the natural lifeworld never becomes reflexively conscious of them. They are nothing other than modifications of the "normal" straightforward progression of the life of consciousness. The basic idea is that the life of consciousness is itself an *abiding* modification, that is, it does not exhibit breaks occasionally and sporadically, but rather exists precisely *out of* them. A first reflection on the manner of carrying out our natural life shows us that this life *never* proceeds unbroken and unmodified. Indeed, under closer consideration it becomes clear that the unmodified life in a normal, undisturbed process of awareness is an *idea* lying in infinity. Intentional life is a continual self-modification and being-modified. The "normal" progression of this life is a constant process of the experience of breaks, which insert themselves into the progression of the intentional life, thereby creating a new harmony: "Consciousness *proves to be* in each phase essentially a modification. More precisely: the wakeful Ego is essentially a pole of the Ego, is intentionality continually overflowing into one another [*ineinander überströmender Intentionalität*], and this overflowing-into-one-another is, as reflection shows, a flowing-intentional being-modified [*ein strömend-intentionales Modifiziertsein*]" (B III 8/6a, from fall 1930).[8]

To what extent can this modification be seen as a proto-form of the "general overturn" in the epoché? The designation "proto-form" should no longer imply that they are first approaches, still having a long way before them before something like the reduction as radical modification of *total* life becomes possible. In the sense of the order of constitution, however, such modifications are indeed the lowest levels of founding for the higher-level (explicit and consciously enacted) modifications. Put precisely, the idea that what is modified does away with what is unmodified needs to be corrected, since a completely unmodified entity is merely an idea. Such everyday-lifeworld modifications *found* these conscious modifying acts, which are genetically of a higher level. If the normal progression of life is already understood as abiding modification, modifications add nothing fundamentally new to life. Reflection as modification does not genetically overcome something *unmodified;* if that were so, one could not explain the transition from what is unmodified to its modification. Rather, *all life of consciousness* is an abiding modification. Everything depends on *bringing* this modification *reflectively to consciousness*—whereby reflection *itself* is a modification *kath' exochen*. Such a reflection is indeed that which, fully developed, first pushes out beyond the natural attitude. As a universal modification it is admittedly more radical, but not *fundamentally* different from other modifications. Said otherwise: the natural attitude as something apparently unmodified over against the modification of reflection simply does not exist. The important insight here is: the natural attitude is not at all so "naive" but rather much "more critical" than it first appears. This also has a bearing on the traditional relation between naïveté and critique, which needs to be revised; it is not a dialectical relation, but one of mutual embrace, mutual interpenetration, and mutual foundedness.

Husserl's strategy in the question of a motivation for the reduction is clear: before something like a radical modification, which completely changes normal life, can be postulated, this must as a possibility be grounded or, more specifically, founded (on founding acts). This grounding lies in the fact that the life of consciousness *as such* is an abiding alteration and transformation. Reflection as a radical modification of consciousness is nothing but an extrapolation and radicalizing of the normal progression of consciousness, one which proceeds always and unavoidably as modifying: "Such a ["normal"] modification, which is essentially possible if not necessary, is first of all what reflection is; it is essentially a 'potentiality' ['*vermöglich*'] for the Ego" (B III 8/5a).

In reflection, however, the fundamental fact of modification becomes conscious; for it is "intentionally implied" in the natural and normal life of consciousness, whereby it constitutes a "new life of consciousness" through its own activity. "Every such new and—in particular here—reflective turn of the life of consciousness is something new; it is clearly not a mere variation which places something alongside something other, but rather is an 'intentional modification,' a new life of consciousness in which the modified as such, as intentional alteration, carries in itself the altered consciousness" (B III 8/5a).

With that said, the mode in which radical reflection functions is admittedly still not clarified, but for the former context this is not (yet) significant; for initially, in the sense of a genetic reconstruction, it has to do with the general characteristics of the life of consciousness, of which reflection is *one* form—namely, the form of making modification conscious to oneself explicitly. Reflection as becoming-conscious precisely of the fact of modification is already a perspective which *per definitionem* cannot be acquired from the natural attitude, and as such it is a *break* with the same. This provides the crucial evidence for how Husserl wishes to understand the departure from the natural attitude: it is not a radical break in the sense that a new life would originate ex nihilo, but instead is a change of perspective and attitude which, motivated out of the modifications of consciousness, is itself such a modification—but which in its specificity must still be clarified.

To summarize: Husserl's conception of the natural attitude leads to the problem of how it is possible to overcome it, or more precisely, to "escape" it. Husserl must be able to locate within the natural attitude itself certain "proto-forms" which found something like a radical reflection as the latter's conditions of possibility. Putting matters this way, it becomes apparent that the natural attitude can never be seen as an unmodified primitive condition onto which an "unmotivated" reflection "imposes" a modification. Rather, reflection is "only" a modification which, while being more radical than every "natural" modification (even "natural reflection"), is founded genetically in the lifeworldly modifications of various interests. When one has provided evidence that natural life is always an abiding flow of modifications, then reflection in its deepest levels of founding is genetically explained. Reflection is a change of perspective from this natural life, but one which is not in principle different from the "normal" act-life. As a break with the natural attitude, reflection is a "splitting of the Ego," that is, a radical change in perspective. However, the order of founding makes clear: the first splitting of the Ego is not reflection, but rather is *life as such,* as is already described in *First Philosophy,* "continually-in-an-active-comportment-of-self-splitting [*Sich-immerfort-in-tätigem-Verhalten-Spalten*]" (Hua VIII, 91). This complex structure has now become concrete: this abiding self-splitting in which a new harmony is continuously produced is nothing other than "modification." Simultaneously, an original notion of the natural attitude is refuted that it would be a primitive condition unbroken by any modification, a condition which would be comparable to life in an intellectual wasteland. Such a state of mind has never existed nor will it ever exist.

The Parallel Between Phenomenology and Psychology

The problem of the relationship of phenomenology to psychology is "old hat" for Husserl studies. Both its configuration and also the fundamental problems of this differentiation—which ultimately comes down to an indissoluble parallel between the two disciplines—have been extensively discussed and are sufficiently known.[9] Less well known, and thus not to be overlooked, is the fact that this problem was such a large one for Husserl that he produced an enormous mass of manuscripts on this theme. One cannot avoid receiving the impression that here Husserl twists and turns and nevertheless always just comes to the same familiar conclusion: that phenomenology and intentional psychology are completely parallel disciplines and that they differentiate themselves from each other simply—although the whole problem is concentrated in this "simply"—

in the (not-)completed change of sign [*Vorzeichenänderung*]. For Husserl, the inadequacy of psychology here becomes manifest precisely through the fact that it does *not*—as it must, if it is to understand itself—comprehend itself as *incomplete* in view of its actual form as transcendental phenomenology. Psychology is insufficient and naive, and simply does not know it. Husserl's tactic here is to bring psychology's inadequacy before its own eyes, and this occurs through the continually re-demonstrated evidence of its essential "paradox."[10] While the general nature of this critique of psychology is known (see chapter 2), Husserl intends to demonstrate in his manuscripts in greater detail the nature of this "paradox."

In what way is psychology, according to its own conception, a "paradox"? It is initially "naive" insofar as it is not clear about the actual purpose of its work, a telos predetermined for it by *its own task*. As the science of the soul, it must *eo ipso* thematize the life of the soul in its totality, and from there the totality of the world given to experience; as such it is the positive science of psychical intentionality. But "soul" is merely a part of the human Ego as a psychophysical whole. In order to maintain the soul as the exclusive subject matter, psychology must bracket out the *physical* dimension of the human and limit itself purely to the immanent-psychical. This methodological step is what Husserl terms the "psychological reduction." It is very much *comparable* to the phenomenological reduction, although different from it on a decisive point: while the psychological reduction reduces (leads back) to the psychical, it continues to keep in validity the being of the world. Psychology as the science of the soul, which brackets out all that is extra-psychical, still stands in the midst of the world, and in so doing it thematizes only one layer within this world. Simultaneously, it believes that it is able to thematize the totality of all beings *from out this psychical layer,* insofar as all that can be experienced must present itself in the psychical as the content of experience (immanent experience). Because the thematization of the totality of the world occurs from this level, this totality is apparently accessible *only from and out of it.* Psychology "finds itself" in merely one layer of the world (the psychical), but simultaneously claims to be able to illuminate the totality of the world from this one level. It stands in an essential paradox, that of psychologism.

In what precisely does the paradox consist? It lies in the fact that psychology is not *able* to achieve what it *claims* to achieve according to its own job description, namely, a thematization of the totality of the world out of the psychical perspective; or, *vice versa,* it does not anticipate the dimensions which it *must* claim to reach according to its own task. The psychologist finds himself in a paradox because he does not see that, in order to be a complete psychologist, he must recognize the psychical itself as part of the world (an insight already apparent from his constitution as having a body as an organ of his functioning), which must then lead him to a bracketing of this psychical dimension as well. The psychologist, as Husserl portrays him, is always a *failed* phenomenologist and no researcher in his own right, like every other positive scientist, who can find his area of investigation in the pre-given realm of the world.[11]

All the same, even in psychological research one must not unconditionally seek to comprehend the totality of the psychical dimension:

> As long as we have not thought this idea of universality through to its end, and what it presupposes as purely psychical, and indeed regarding its method of experience and knowledge of experience, as long as we do so, we do not in principal encounter any difficulties. (B I 14/57b, from July 1931)

If one attempts to do justice to this self-legislated claim of universality—or, stated more plainly, if one is simply consistent—then this consideration leads already into the transcendental, and we stand "already in the transcendental attitude" (B I 12/57a).

The attitude of the psychologist is *from the start* a paradoxical stance, and the reason for this is that he feels comfortable in this naive stance and, in this naïveté, can make no claim to the status of itself as science. The psychologist is trapped in the natural attitude which, as a result of his job description as overcoming any naïveté, leads him into an absurd stance. While the natural attitude in its own naïveté has its "own right," the psychologist is in an absurd position *precisely because* he remains caught up in the natural attitude. Psychology is the highest discipline on the way to transcendental phenomenology and thus should not be content with this wavering position between science in the natural realm and transcendental science; it is thus also the "field of decisions" (Hua VI, 207) with regard to the fate of transcendental philosophy. Its paradox consists in the fact that it, in its universal scope, is not *able* to be a *positive* science of the universal life of the soul.

Ultimately, it is within psychology that the paradox of human subjectivity concretizes itself, which is reduced to the central argument repeated time and again and in different formulations: "What is individuated in the world and in space-time as actuality and possibility can never be the world and space-time themselves" (B I 14/55a). Therein consists the "paradox of subjectivity."

In the same sense, that which appears in the world as something constituted can never accomplish the constitution of the world. Ultimately, the paradoxical situation of psychology is simply a characteristic of all such paradoxical (pseudo-)scientific undertakings, which Husserl designates as "anthropologisms"; these undertakings all commit the error of declaring a layer of the world to be the fundamental layer and ground without seeing that this is simply *one* layer in the framework of the layers of constitution, be it the psychical or the average everyday factical existence.[12]

Nevertheless, Husserl insists, the parallel between phenomenology and psychology remains. The parallel disciplines correspond to "parallel lines, which intersect only in the infinite realm out of which they came,"[13] but the metaphor does not solve the problem of how both disciplines are to exist alongside one another *and* as one leading into another. The question thus arises concerning the sense in which psychology in general can still exist if reflection about the scope of the universal psychical sphere indeed oversteps this sphere *eo ipso* into the transcendental and annuls it in its parallelism to the transcendental. Admittedly, such a discipline has never existed, and it appears as though Husserl *needs* the dimension of the worldly psychical sphere as a foil of argumentation, in order to elucidate in it the contrast with the transcendental sphere.[14] Ultimately, and regardless of how one can solve the problem of psychology's status, the issue comes down to the fact that psychology and phenomenology are two disciplines of *one* phenomenon, the life of consciousness. The parallel of both disciplines, thus, is a reflection of their subject matter: consciousness. In general and independently of the scientific question concerning the relation of the disciplines, then, the more fundamental question is, how is the difference of what is psychical and what is transcendental itself to be understood, and *is* it actually a difference? Apparently it is a matter of the consideration of one and the same phenomenon from two perspectives, which are nevertheless always possessed by one Ego. What then is the relation of the mundane and the transcendental Ego? *This* is the basic issue that is at stake in the question concerning the relation between psychology and phenomenology, and it is to be discussed now.

The Relation of the Worldly and the Transcendental Ego

Just as with the parallelism of psychology and phenomenology, Husserl's attempt to determine the relation of the worldly and the transcendental Ego occupies *thematically* a prominent place and *quantitatively* an expansive space in his manuscripts. Primarily this has to do with the question of what the reduction "changes" in the Ego and what the reduction to a transcendental, non- (or pre-)worldly Ego can amount to. In this change one can, so to speak, "read off" the accomplishment of the reduction; for there must be a difference "in" the Ego *before* and *after* the reduction; otherwise, this methodological procedure would have absolutely no "return" and consequently make no discernible sense.[15] Of course, the reduction cannot change the "being" of the Ego—one remains a human being in the world, with all of the abilities, duties, and so on related to this. What is changed through the reduction is the view and the understanding the Ego has of its own self and of the world in which it is situated *as* worldly. Determining the relation of the mundane and the transcendental Ego is, in other words, a matter of a correct understanding of the transition from the natural to the phenomenological attitude as that attitude which reflectively sees through the relativity of the mode of comportment of the natural attitude as such.

Negatively expressed: the reduction does *not* change the fact that the Ego is a person in a practical, social (etc.) world; no new life-task is allocated to it.[16] The reduction remains for Husserl a reflexive operation; it can—to take up Husserl's description of phenomenology as "the hermeneutic of the life of consciousness"[17]—be designated as a "hermeneutical turn" within the life of the Ego, one which makes possible a new and expansive transparence of the Ego regarding its own self. For Husserl, this has a revolutionary significance.[18] The Ego *recognizes* itself as through and through "rationally" determined; for a universal transparence of the Ego regarding its own self makes clear to it the fundamental synonymy of subjectivity and reason, provided that "reason" is understood to be not simply pure reason, but all of the capacities of consciousness subject to describable rules.[19] This recognition of its own self *after* the reduction— this is the decisive factor—is not an "abstract-theoretical" recognition in contrast to the *concrete* of the natural life of interest. Rather, the reduction *reverses* the founding relation of the natural and mundane Ego. That is to say, the Ego after the reduction experiences itself as expanded beyond its natural horizon, insofar as it has now learned to see the sphere of transcendental being—*its* transcendental being—as world-constituting. It realizes through this procedure that before the reduction it had lived in a constricted horizon that is now *recognized as* constricted. As separated from its transcendental origin of life, the Ego lives abstractly prior to the reduction, as a plant without roots would be "abstract," that is, cut off from its rootedness in its supporting soil.

While in an *objective* respect the reduction is an act in the history of a concrete consciousness and *temporally* comes, as an episode, very late in the natural, straightforwardly lived life, the reduction reveals that natural life is "essentially" *always already* transcendental, without knowing or being *able* to know of this while *in* the natural attitude. The Ego lives in the natural attitude, unreflectively, intentionally "infatuated" with the things of its interest, and without knowing about the transcendental life which constitutively accomplishes these things. The blindness or one-sided sight about its transcendental origin is "inborn" to the mundane Ego; from childhood on it has habitually learned to see nothing else, but this does not mean that this sight cannot be acquired. The *capability* for this belongs essentially to the human Ego; it is only a matter of awakening it. Husserl expresses this relation of the Ego *before* and *after* the reduction with numerous metaphors, which not coincidentally are also to be found in descriptions of religious experiences of awakening: blindness—seeing, sleeping—awakening, unconscious—conscious, latency—patency, muteness—speaking.

Natural life turns out to be simply the "final layer" in the all-encompassing process of world-constitution. Because it is blind with respect to this constitutive process, it lives in an *abstraction* from this knowledge, insofar as it knows nothing of the concretion of the world resulting from the process of constitution, and simply lives in the layer of "final constitutedness." The reduction inverts the sequence of founding: the absolute, world-constituting transcendental life is the *próteron te physei* which has laid itself, qua constitution, back into the world and lives an abstract, incomplete life:

> I in the phenomenological reorientation, the transcendental, in transitioning, gain as a thematic horizon of experience my *concrete* transcendental subjectivity, my transcendental Ego-subject (the pole) as the center, as the substrate of the *concrete totality* of my potentialities [*Vermögen*], as the center of my current and potential [*vermöglichen*] life of consciousness, or my current and capable subject matter, *under which* fall my worldly subject matter and my natural world as the world of my natural-habitual life. The natural existence in the synthetic achievement of the previously hidden achievements (which constitute the Ego of naturalness as the unity of the manifolds) is then, in the concretion of transcendental subjectivity, an *abstract layer*. The natural form of life is then recognized as a *limited* form in which the Ego actualizes its capability in prefigured habitualities and so actively accomplishes an Egoic existence, a mode of self-preservation or rather of a striving for self-preservation which does not account for a higher, richer manifold of possibilities. (B III 8/10a, from fall 1931, italics added)

The richer possibilities of the transcendental life consist not in a *factical* broadening of the possibilities of human life—not to mention the fact that it is provided with a realm of infinite research—but rather in the fact that the Ego recognizes that all of its mundane ways of life carry a transcendental "*index*"; in an image Husserl appreciates, the *two-dimensional* surface of the world is given a *third* dimension, and thereby becomes "richer" in the transcendental dimension.[20]

> Through the transcendental *epoché* I experience and recognize my *absolute* being, moreover, that everything of the universe for me is purely *relative*. I recognize that my being as a human and my being as being-in-the-world, in the world experiencing, thinking, valuing, acting living-into it [*Hineinleben*], is a *particular* mode of my absolute being and life, a mode of consistently bringing worldly being to validity in my apperception [*weltliche Seiendes in meinen Apperzeptionen zur Geltung <zur> bringen*], from which this being for me affects me and is destined to multiple abilities and in the process apperceives me and my performing life itself in a certain psychical mode, and thus has and preserves it as something psychical in the validity of being [*Seinsgeltung*]. . . . This being and life of the Ego, in which and through which its particular performance and structure of performance the world constitutes itself as something existing for me and with its whole content of meaning [*Sinnesgehalt*], is not itself something worldly existent, it is *in itself prior to* the world in general and every particular worldly being. On the other hand this world is, as out of its [= the absolute Ego's] performance receiving the sense of being, nothing separated from it, something separated from the absolute Ego, not something next to it as something having a relation to it. The relation the world has to the absolute Ego is like the relation in it of something constituted to something constituting, and this relation lies completely *within* absolute subjectivity, transcendental subjectivity. (B II 4/82a/b, from 1929/30, italics added)

The natural attitude is thus simply one single, and indeed a limited, mode of life of the Ego in its concretion; by this it becomes understandable what Husserl meant with his claim in *Cartesian Meditations*—cryptic without this background—that the natural mode of life is a "mute concretion" which must be "brought to the expression of its own sense." This full concretion of transcendental life is mute as long as this life, which is *awakened to itself* through the reduction, lends it no voice.

In this context, more than ever, idealist-speculative tendencies are unmistakable when it comes to characterizing the relation between the "absolute" and the worldly, and it once again raises the question of the influence of Fink. His "Hegelian" interpretations of Husserlian phenomenology are well known from the *Sixth Cartesian Meditation*, so it is necessary here to confront the widespread opinion that these speculative formulations are actually Finkian, and no indication of Husserl's thinking. To the contrary, Husserl's *Nachlass* is full of such hints, and not just beginning with the manuscripts from 1929—that is, after the time of Fink's assistantship—but already from 1922 on and with great frequency starting in 1926,[21] and the first impulse for this came most likely from the neo-Kantians.[22] An assessment of this idealizing tendency cannot be accomplished here, and a comprehensive evaluation of these manuscripts in addition to a comparison with the systems of German idealism remains to be done.[23] But to conclude this exposition, *one* theme must be still be addressed, one in which Husserl's characterization of the reduction is *consummated,* and in which he wished to form this into an organic (or perhaps better: dynamic) whole.

The Enworlding of the Transcendental Ego

If the reduction has clarified how to depart from the natural attitude and how to gain access to a "dimension of the depths" of the transcendental sphere, the "correlative" question is raised *after* the reduction of how the transcendental Ego comports itself toward its *constituted* appearance or "manifestation" in the world. This self-objectification of the transcendental in the world appears under the title *enworlding.* If enworlding thematizes the *countermovement* of the reduction, one can rightly say that enworlding takes the "eccentric path" (Hölderlin) of the reduction, that is, of departing from oneself in order to return, and that the reduction would therefore, without the process of enworlding, remain incomplete. Enworlding is an integral component of the reduction and, not coincidentally, follows upon it necessarily; in it, the movement of the reduction first becomes transparent to itself, provided that the transcendental Ego becomes reflectively conscious of itself as its mundane being. Enworlding is thus a self-critique of the phenomenologizing capacity, which is also proven in that it is the central theme of Fink's transcendental doctrine of method which follows the "doctrine of elements" in the Sixth *Cartesian Meditation,* commissioned by Husserl.[24]

Enworlding is not a function which the phenomenologizing Ego *deliberately* exercises. To the contrary, it is always already in process when the phenomenologizing agent practices his experiencing activity (his theorizing). Because every experience "ontifies" what is experienced, that is, makes it into a being for a consciousness, the transcendental *in the act of phenomenologizing* is equally ontified. Since experiencing and what is experienced are structures of the Ego—albeit after the transcendental turn—the process of *ontification* presents itself as pyschologizing. Every phenomenological act psychologizes its intentional content simply through the fact *that* it experiences it. This enworlding through the phenomenologizing agent is thus not something which would be willful or deliberate and over against the "first" enworlding *secondary* in the constitution. The phenomenologist has no choice but to enworld through his acts of experience, which are a constitutive performance like every other. However, in his *first* straightforwardly executed research he is still naive, insofar as he has still not engaged in any reflection upon his own doing, and thus has not made its necessary ontification conscious to himself. It is necessary in the higher-level critique to see the enworlding of this research *through* this research and a fortiori to correctly interpret it: the enworlding psychologizes the transcendental components of meaning. It is not otherwise possible for it to enworld through the act of its becoming experienced, that is, to become a constituted part of the world. It is thus imperative to understand this enworlding correctly. "The phenomenological activity becomes[25] human activity, a psychological activity of the ordinary human Ego, belongs to the world and is thereby a historical event in the history of philosophy" (B I 5/156a, from December 1931).

Through this enworlding, which is an "enshrouding" of the transcendental as psychological, there arises the situation of transcendental semblance [*Schein*], insofar as the "result" of phenomenologizing, like other psychological or philosophical statements, stands "in the world" and thus can be taken as such. To *overlook* this self-veiling of the transcendental as something worldly—that it thus always appears *as* something worldly—is the danger of which the self-critical phenomenologist must be conscious:

> Can this act [of the phenomenologist] still have a place in the world? And thus all acts of the phenomenologist and he, the phenomenologist himself? He is not a human who simply phenomenologizes among another activity. He is the absolute transcendental Ego which discovers in the natural attitude the human being and its world with all of the worldly determinations, who performs human activities, perhaps scientific ones, but, on the other hand, in reflectively and consequently reducing finds the absolute transcendental being and the world as transcendental formations [*Gebilde*]. *To be a phenomenologist, this is something that only the phenomenologist can experience and discern.* He, who is a naive human, knows only of the worldly and can only discern what is psychical in the human. (B I 5/157a, italics added)

Nevertheless, this does not mean that the parallelism of transcendental and natural truth is lost for the phenomenologist, even if transcendental truth has its necessary natural appearance:

> As soon as I return to the natural attitude, . . . I posit *eo ipso* the whole world in its validity and myself as a human in its validity. . . . But now I have gained *two kinds of knowledge* and have them in habitual validity [*Gültigkeit*], the worldly, in the worldly subject matter, and the transcendental in that of its subject matter. Indeed, I have forgotten neither of them. Although I engage myself again in worldliness and work scientifically, I must now know that all of this worldly behavior and its scientific results simply as worldly have their transcendental constitution and thus are transcendental formations [*Gebilde*], that I myself am a transcendental formation of transcendental subjectivity, of its self-objectification. (B I 5/160b, italics added)

What does this insight change in my life and for my scientific research as a human being and as a scientist? Strictly speaking—nothing. I "simply" gain a new insight into that which is (and how it is). The transcendental knowledge that is now enworlded teaches me to see that all natural truths—invisible to the natural attitude, (having become) visible to the phenomenologist—point toward their transcendental meaning; this fact does not, however, amount to a theory of two truths (perhaps in the sense of two language games), but rather makes possible a correct understanding of the world *as constituted*. Consequently, the relation of the constituting and the constituted—the transcendental and the natural world—can be comprehended in a correct manner only through a *transcendental* understanding, which embraces the natural comprehension:

> Now that I recognize the world . . . in its transcendental meaning of being [*Seinssinn*], the world as a questioned phenomenon and as transcendentally accessed is indeed the theme decided upon in transcendental knowledge, but not simply as a naive theme encapsulated in naïveté. But of course, it is a *completely different* theme. I no longer live as a natural human, I live, so to speak, in an unnaturalness [*Unnatürlichkeit*]. But when I now keep my transcendental interest bracketed—*I can no longer actually abandon it,* at least not its former gains—now, then, I live as a human being and perhaps I do research as a human being, only I do so knowing that all of this has an absolute, a transcendental meaning. (B I 5/162a/b, italics added)

To use an unorthodox metaphor: through the reduction, a contrast agent is, as it were, injected into the world, making visible the transcendental components of meaning—namely, to the phenomenologist. At the same time, they remain in the world as worldly formations, but they can now be understood in their transcendental meaning. Ultimately, everything worldly is a product of transcendental constitution, but with those statements, which indicate transcendental-philosophical truths, the insight is particularly "virulent"; for, as statements expressed by the phenomenologist, they, too, are enworlded *as* explicated ("logified") and *through* their becoming uttered. They express *transcendental* truths—truths of phenomenology—which have their enworlded form only in a manner which is veiled and yet *not otherwise possible*. Everything that is, is worldly, even the phenomenological utterances, but it is only correctly recognized *as worldly* when it is recognized in its *transcendental* origin. On the other hand, not all statements which "appear" *as psychological* are veiled transcendental truths, even if they are constituted, worldly, and as such, psychological. All that is transcendental appears in the world, be it genuinely transcendental and thus only apparently worldly *or* genuinely worldly with a transcendental index. In other words: there is not a *secondary* enworlding in the act of phenomenologizing in addition to the *primary* enworlding, that of "simple" constituting. All experiencing constitutes, and that is: enworlds, be it that of someone in the natural or in the phenomenological attitude; the difference is that the "phenomenologizing" Ego brings the transcendental-enworlding acts to consciousness once again in a higher reflection, and in so doing is critical with regard to its own manner of cognition.

That the transcendental enworlds itself thus signifies a self-objectification and self-explication of the veiled "knowledge of the depths" of subjectivity. Husserl expresses this process with another metaphor by saying that the transcendental "streams into" the world: the transcendental becomes worldly, and this means knowable; what is worldly becomes transcendental, and this means unveiled in its hidden layers of meaning, "fitted" with a transcendental index. But all of this comes to consciousness only in the self-consciousness of the radically self-questioning and self-criticizing phenomenologist in his first-person perspective. With this, the circle is closed: the reduction makes possible the radical break with the natural attitude, insofar as it establishes an attitude which allows the natural world-life and the world itself to appear in a new light. But ultimately, when this new attitude in turn becomes transparent to itself in a higher-level self-critique and again in this higher-level condition sees itself as worldly, the phenomenologist arrives at a—if you will, dialectical—determination of the relation of both fundamental attitudes, between which phenomenology remains indissolubly fixed.

Conclusion

In summary, it can be said that Husserl's philosophy of the phenomenological reduction is not a matter of an esoteric, mystical procedure (or whatever other similar misinterpretations might exist) but rather is a matter of, in the words of Landgrebe, a genuine, phenomenological "access to metaphysics (admittedly in another sense)," by means of systematic reflection which always subjects every level of reflection again and again to a novel reflection. In addition, it has to do with a strict and responsible grounding and justification of all rational knowledge, that is, of *science,* through a self-grounding and self-justification. The comprehension of the true sense of the world as a product of transcendental constitution is the crucial insight here and that which can only be precipitated through radical reflection, and this is ultimately also the highest level of reflection that phenomenology can establish—and is also that by which the limits of phenomenology are set. Phenomenology is and remains a radical philosophy of *reflection,* and if one considers this—that the ultimate level to be reached is still a matter of reflection, that is, of subjectivity and first-person access—to be a shortcoming, then phenomenology is indeed altogether deficient.

In Husserl's late reflections on these matters, one can catch sight of more concrete deliberations which he was only able to hint at in his published texts, deliberations which reveal his struggle for concretion, understanding, and—ultimately—absolute self-transparency. The procedure for such a reflection, which is to be actualized always anew, is, and remains, the reduction. To carry out the reduction means not so much to make the case for a specific view of philosophy and metaphysics—on this question Husserl, to the end, never committed himself; rather, the reduction bears witness to the will to become a radical philosopher and not to take this task lightly—but rather to concentrate all of one's effort of thought upon it, in order to carry it through up to the (reflexively revealed) ultimate limit in a self-responsible manner.

Translated by Jon Burmeister

The Main Theme of Transcendental Phenomenology After the Reduction: The Lifeworld

With this chapter, the reflections on the methodology of entering the sphere of phenomenology—world-constituting transcendental consciousness—come to a preliminary close, at least in that they are the main focus of attention. In the next two chapters, "constitutive" issues will be taken up, which come to the fore once the reduction has been carried out. Chapter 4 will focus on what is arguably the main theme of Husserl's mature transcendental phenomenology: the lifeworld; while chapter 5 will deal with the problem of the person (or personhood) from the vantage point of transcendental phenomenology. The problem will be assessed by way of a discussion of *the* notorious topic within the phenomenological movement: the Husserl–Heidegger relation. But the interpretation offered in this book is that both themes—lifeworld and subjectivity—cannot be separated; how they penetrate one another will already become clear in the following two chapters.

In the next chapter the main theme of Husserl's mature oeuvre, the lifeworld, will be treated. However, to this day, there exist a plethora of misinterpretations or simple misunderstandings of what the lifeworld is to Husserl. Only recently have his manuscripts on this topic been published (in Hua XXXIX), which, albeit in selection, amount to almost 1,000 pages of text. The actual minute details of this peculiar science cannot be expounded here; rather, the two main "axes" of its coordinate system shall be laid out. By characterizing the lifeworld via the main "axes," facticity and historicity, the lifeworld as a *transcendental theme* will take on a greater richness and plasticity than it is usually assumed as having. This presentation also counters the common assumption that Husserlian phenomenology has little to say about facticity and history, topics which are supposedly not discussed within the phenomenological tradition until Heidegger and the existentialists following him. The main insight, then, is that these themes, which seem to be *the* topics of existential philosophy or hermeneutics, remain deficient and incomplete without their being framed within the transcendental correlational a priori in the way Husserl did.

Facticity and Historicity as Constituents of the Lifeworld in Husserl's Late Philosophy

Introduction

There is no doubt that "world" is the fundamental theme of Husserl's late phenomenology. Starting from his earlier analyses of thing-perception from around 1905 and his characterization of the "world of the natural attitude" in *Ideas I* of 1913, the concept of world is progressively expanded and finally thematized as the universal horizon of meaning, which leads to the final shape of Husserl's thought. In this ultimate stage, initially documented publicly in the *Crisis*, this universal horizon of meaning appears in the form of the notorious term "lifeworld" (*Lebenswelt*). This term is not, as was initially conjectured, an entirely new concept, which would stand askance to Husserl's phenomenology as an eidetic analysis of consciousness,[1] but rather synthesizes in a felicitous manner Husserl's efforts concerning an encompassing noetic-noematically directed transcendental phenomenology. Lifeworld and transcendental subjectivity form the two poles of a universal correlation.

All of this is well known; however, a closer look reveals problems and difficulties. For "lifeworld" is not simply a concept for "the world in which we live" in the sense of a colloquial or even partially scientific language, but is a complex *terminus technicus* in the framework of Husserl's late philosophy under the title of *genetic phenomenology*. Genetic phenomenology analyzes not only the structural constitution of intentional acts, but also their development in an "intentional history." In this sense Husserl's mature philosophy, as *transcendental* phenomenology, likewise claims to thematize historicity, that is, not history as *factum*, but its interpretation with respect to its transcendental dimension. Only in this way can the facticity of the lifeworld be correctly clarified, that is, insofar as it is understood as the locus of sedimentation of intentional acts. The facticity of the lifeworld is thus not to be fully appreciated without the transcendental question as to its "conditions of possibility." All of this is still further complicated in that Husserl endeavored, in his late phase, to form his phenomenology into a system. Husserl's phenomenology undertakes a systematic reconstruction of the transcendental constitution of the lifeworld. That, at any rate, is a (very) rough sketch of Husserl's idea of a phenomenological systematic as a static-genetic clarification of the constitution of the world.

The final form of Husserl's philosophy presents itself at first sight, however, rather as a confused knot of problems than as a stringently worked-out system. But this is not to say, on the other hand, that one cannot make out a systematic concatenation of these themes. As Donn Welton emphasizes, Husserl's "systematic" late philosophy does not so much present a system but rather a *systematic method,* which evolves in the last two decades of Husserl's life.[2] The present contribution undertakes in this sense, starting from this thesis of Welton's, to pursue the more humble task of reconstructing the systematic connection between lifeworld, facticity, and historicity in Husserl's late work. These are not, however, arbitrarily chosen terms from the late work but central concepts, which give an insight into Husserl's phenomenology of the lifeworld; a theory or rather method that is not laid out in a fully fleshed-out manner, but rather stands, as it were, as an unfinished building shell. Given the plethora of manuscripts on this theme that have just recently been published[3] and the fact that the concept of "lifeworld" seems to be but a catch-all phrase—a phrase that suggests that everything on this topic has already been said—it is worth considering Husserl's phenomenology of the lifeworld anew under the stated aspects. Here one can find, as will be seen, many still-unsolved problems and interesting aspects. Indeed, given the newly published volumes of the *Husserliana,* the reception of this theme in scholarship has just begun.

Welton's and the preceding reflections stand in a certain tradition which goes back to the work of Ludwig Landgrebe, among others, that concentrates in particular on Husserl's reflections on history. According to a well-known phrase of Landgrebe's, the phenomenology of Husserl in its mature form—apart from or in addition to a phenomenology of the lifeworld—is a "transcendental theory of history."[4] History is—this is itself a phrase of Husserl that is frequently cited by Landgrebe—the "grand fact of absolute being."[5] Facticity, which is thematic here, is—one can speculate—none other than that of the lifeworld, insofar as the historical life of humankind plays itself out in a world formed by human beings and their achievements, hence in a lifeworld in the pregnant sense of the term. But that, in turn, presupposes a very broadly developed, special concept of *facticity* which needs to be explicated in its specificity. If by "facticity" is meant not simply what Heidegger discussed, for example, in his "hermeneutics of facticity," then this concept must be elucidated in its conjunction with the transcendental register in which Husserl framed the question. This is the peculiar challenge for the interpreter of Husserl's late work.

On the other hand, without wanting to declare overly large generalities, one can say that that history of which Husserl's phenomenology is to deal as a "transcendental theory" is likewise that of the lifeworld, since all worldly life proceeds, in essence, historically and as such terminates in the world. In what precise sense "history" is spoken of is equally in need of clarification. That there *is* a relation among lifeworld, facticity, and history is, hence, not all that controversial. However, in previous research the question as to their systematic connection has been mostly unfurled from the side of history or from the question of to what extent phenomenology can function as a philosophy of history.[6] Instead of the question as to how the lifeworld is an element of historicity or of transcendental history, however, I would like to invert this problematic and ask to what extent a phenomenological theory of the lifeworld, conversely, needs historicity for a clarification of its constitution.

What holds for the concept of history in the framework of phenomenology, one can also assert for the second term of this chapter's title. In this case, too, scholarship has also, rather, been interested in what "facticity" is to mean in the late Husserl in isolation from other terms and considered in itself and what its relation to, say, other forms of facticity is, whose "hermeneutics" can be seen as the antithetical program to Husserl's transcendental-subjective methodology[7]—instead of connecting this problem up with a reflection concerning the program of an ontology of the lifeworld. "Facticity" or "*factum*" is mostly understood in opposition to "essence" or "transcendental," whereby, in my opinion, the question of this alleged "opposition" is the really crucial one. The question as to how "facticity" is defined in the late Husserl is inseparably connected with the status of his phenomenology as *transcendental.* Without wanting to dismiss these questions—say, the relation to Heidegger—again as senseless or wrongheaded, what interests me here is the converse question: to what extent facticity, precisely in its relation to the sphere of transcendental consciousness, must be a component of a mature theory of the lifeworld. It thus is not sufficient to understand facticity as mere "actuality" in a trivial sense and the lifeworld, accordingly, simply as the "factical world of life"; rather, it must be explained to what extent facticity in its peculiar meaning is a necessary component of the lifeworld and outlines, or at least pre-delineates, in this highly original sense *together with* the phenomenon of historicity the coordinate system of an "ontology of the lifeworld." Finally, the internal connection of these phenomena must be made explicit, if both elements are not to be merely treated as subordinate elements of a more comprehensive theory of the lifeworld, but must rather have a systematic function in and for it.

Initially, we shall reconstruct Husserl's mature program of an "ontology of the lifeworld." It will be shown that a full-fledged reflection concerning the interpretation of the lifeworld leads, *eo ipso,* to the phenomenon of history. In the second part we shall explain how the characterization of history in the framework of the transcendental question amounts to a peculiar characterization of facticity. Finally, we will show how Husserl's definition of the relation between transcendental and factical is decisive for his understanding of the *historical* lifeworld and its "meaning."

The Program of an "Ontology of the Lifeworld" and the Problem of History

Above all, two fundamental and intrinsically interconnected developments in Husserl's late philosophy—one methodological, one substantial—lead as of the 1920s to the late conception of the lifeworld and its "ontology."

From Static to Genetic Phenomenology

Husserl's "turn to history" in the *Crisis* was in truth prepared more than a decade earlier[8] through the expansion of "static" phenomenology into the genetic dimension.[9] The fundamental insight here is that the life of consciousness—as the analysis of time-consciousness already shows—has a procedural, dynamic character which escapes the static (constitutive) description of noetic-noematic act relations, which merely researches on the surface. Noesis and noema are thematized, in the first presentation, as merely "rigid," "finished" constitutive phenomena. Such a focus is only possible if one intentionally puts out of focus the temporal character of consciousness, as Husserl did in *Ideas I,* from 1913 (and subsequently criticizes this in his own presentation in the *Nachwort* of 1930).[10] If one imagines, metaphorically, that static analysis is two-dimensional, then the genetic analysis thematizes the third dimension, the depth dimension. All intentional processes (those of the "surface") refer to a "depth dimension" in which a present act was "prepared," that is, it had its genesis, be it in earlier acts that have sunk into "passivity," or "purely passive" processes, which precede in advance the acts in the actual ("active") sense of the term. All current behavior is founded on earlier acts, as well as on passive "act-processes" such as, for instance, motivations and associations. In connection with the description of these dynamic relations and their lawfulnesses, Husserl speaks firstly—and not entirely by accident with an eye to German idealism—of a "history" of the life of consciousness, leading to self-consciousness.[11] This history of consciousness itself has lawful forms of carrying itself out, and these can be unearthed and described as such in their essential lawfulness. Genetic phenomenology, thus, is and remains eidetic. A historicity described thus, as genetic essential lawfulness, initially governs and forms something like the factical development of the concrete life of consciousness of a human being, for example, the development of characteristic properties or a concrete habit.[12] Thus, every habituality, every habit of the concrete human being is preceded essentially by a history of habitualizations, which in turn refer back "eidetically," lawfully, to a primal instituting (an *Urstiftung*) and from there passes through a developmental series according to an "inner" lawfulness. Hence, every factical development has an essential structure of progression. The task of genetic phenomenology is to exhibit "laws of genesis" as rules governing a factical development (Hua XI, 336). This is the context in which Husserl first thematizes the phenomenon of history—as the history or genesis of the life of consciousness according to essential forms.[13] The meaning of history at stake here is, however, not yet precisely worked out, insofar as it refers to *both* the factical historical development (genesis) within a concrete consciousness, a "monad," but *also* to the essential laws of genesis, according to which the concrete monad develops lawfully (historicity).

From Object to Horizon

Husserl's investigations into the structure of intentional consciousness lead him to an expansion of the original intentional relationship between act-performance and the object given therein, which becomes the phenomenon in the transcendental-phenomenological reduction. The method of the epoché and reduction, in so doing, brackets the naive belief in the being-in-itself of the world and reduces it to being-experienced, correlated to giving-itself in particular modes of experience (meaning, judging, valuing, etc.). That which appears in experiencing consciousness becomes thematic in its givenness for this consciousness and is analyzed in the essential manners of its givenness; in the paradigmatic case of perceptual analysis, something is analyzed in its givenness through adumbrations. So far, the framework of investigation opened through the phenomenological reduction is pre-delineated. What is new in Husserl's analysis in the time after *Ideas I* lies, however, in the following decisive insight, which hangs together with the phenomenological method of epoché and reduction. Specifically, the epoché universally brackets the same belief in the world that is taken for granted in the "natural attitude." This means: what gives itself in this attitude is always already given in a *field* or *context* of something co-conscious, co-given, but not presently conscious or given. An individual intentional act manifests itself as actually a realized act from an endless number of "potential" (*vermöglich*) others. To these potentialities of act-performances, however, corresponds something on the noematic side. Initially, potential acts, seen noetically, refer to an endlessness of *entities* towards which one can turn. On the "subjective" (noetic) side, this fact is expressed in the concept of attitude: an attitude is a general stance "from" which potential acts (endlessly many) can emerge potentially with a particular "meaning" (*Meinung*).[14] A specific attitude is characterized through the stance of interest, that is, in the attitude of the artist, of the scientist, and so on. An attitude is thus determined such that an interest can pertain to all potential objects (and thus is not directed to a fixed number of entities) or only perceives that which serves the interest.

Something analogous plays itself out on the "objective" (noematic) side: at first the perceptual object can appear in endless adumbrations and can present itself endlessly differentiated in these adumbrations. The object is thus not a mere "X" with certain determinations, but a field of possible facets of appearances; Husserl calls this the "inner horizon." Yet the "outer horizon" of an object is also endlessly undetermined, insofar as a structure of references runs from given presences to ungiven, but giveable, presences: the seen house shows itself from the front side, whereby the back side is "implicit," but it refers at the same time to the associated, but presently unthematic, co-meant garden, and so on. This endlessness correlates not to a (more or less unlimited) quantity of entities, but to an openness, wherein entities come to givenness. This field is nothing other than what Husserl calls "horizon." Everything that appears gives itself in a horizon, which is currently unconsciousness but is co-conscious, and into which one (in the case of external perception) can penetrate in actualization of kinesthetic possibilities (I can move around the house, view the back side and enter the garden lying behind it, touch the plants, etc.). This horizon as the sphere of current and potential givenness Husserl now also terms *world*. The surrounding world of the known garden, in which the children play, and so on, is embedded in the larger horizon of the city; the latter is in turn embedded in the county, and so on. The recurring use of "and so on" here is thus no accident. The world as a structure of reference has the fundamental character of "and so on." The lifeworld as the title for the "horizon of all horizons" is thus to be understood before the background of this expansion of the theory of intentionality. In the same sense, the natural attitude as the fundamental character of all human behavior is understood as the "attitude of all attitudes," which is characterized through the "general thesis" ("the world exists").[15] On both "sides" of the noetic-noematic structure of intentionality, thus, the decisive new development comes to the fore: the discovery of the phenomenon of horizon.

Considering this structure more closely, there is above all a pair of concepts—givenness/pre-givenness—that Husserl analyzes extensively and which hangs together with the horizonality of experience; in this context, the phenomenon of the temporality of experience newly comes into play.

If the given is "embedded" in a horizon, from which it appears and from which it can only be given, then it follows that the horizon itself has a priority "before" the individual appearances.[16] Givenness presupposes a pre-givenness. "Givenness" and "pre-givenness" are the pair of concepts that run parallel to the structure of appearing thing and horizon. The "pre" in pre-givenness obviously has also, and predominantly, a temporal meaning.[17] Every givenness of something experienced presupposes itself a pre-givenness, which logically as well as temporally precedes the givenness and sets up or "makes possible" its appearing. In the temporal understanding of the concept, "pre-givenness" implies *earlier* givenness. Every presently given, lived-through presence of something experienced, as well as the presence of experience itself, *is* always only "from" the past, which was an earlier present. The "living present" is living because it has a dynamic temporal structure, in which it proceeds onward from present to new present, but has also already proceeded with certain events—and will further proceed in a presumptive future that is still uncertain, but with more or less distinct anticipations. The presence of experience is the famous standing-streaming "living present." This entails, however, that the present has a certain structure, which is pre-delineated for it from the pre-givenness of earlier experienced presents. Givenness is always "from" pre-givenness, and the latter pre-delineates—through verification and correction—the structure and type of givenness for the currently experienced living present. Givenness has its typicality and its "ontic style" from pre-givenness. Pre-givenness thus refers back to genesis, that is, it is a product of such a development. Since the experience of consciousness proceeds temporally, the present experience can proceed in no other manner than in a type, which is pre-delineated from earlier experiences. This type is, however, not something static, but something that was, for its part, temporally formed and is in a constant flux. For this reason, Husserl was fond of the Heraclitean metaphor of the standing-streaming flux.

The following two features are, in sum, the essential expansions in Husserl's late philosophy, which enter into the phenomenological determination of the lifeworld:

1. Acts of consciousness in their noetic-noematic constitution are not merely phenomena to be described in static analysis, but have a temporal-dynamic structure. Experience, which is always experience of the world, is itself structurally subject to a genesis. Thus the history of the experience of the world is to be clarified phenomenologically, insofar as this is a reflection in the transcendental attitude, which thus focuses on, not the world itself, but experience of the world. That is *in nuce* the meaning of Husserl's transcendental idealism.[18] The demonstration of the lawfulness of the genesis is thereby of a special significance. This genetic consideration is thus (a) eidetic, insofar as it concerns "laws of genesis," and (b) transcendental, insofar as it concerns not the world or concrete worldly experience, but the conditions of the possibility of the experience of the world. Just as the body is a condition of the possibility of external perception, *pre-givenness* is a condition of the possibility of present *givenness*.

2. Acts of consciousness are not merely directed to an experienced object in the manner of its appearing, but always also inexplicitly ("attitudinally") to the horizon in which the object is given. The horizon is the correlate to an attitude. This horizon, in and from which givenness currently occurs, is "always already" pre-given, just as acts are always already led by interests, that is, attitudinal. Entities give themselves "from" the pre-givenness of the world, that is, logically presuppose the latter. Pre-givenness is, however, also to be understood temporally, insofar as givenness rests upon past and sedimented givennesses, which have made the respective present into that which it is. The horizon is therefore nothing other than the broadest possibly unfolded notion of intentionality in noematic respect.

Now, both elements complement themselves in the following respect: experience of the world is historical insofar as it has a history of experience "behind it," "in its back," as it were, which has shaped the typicality and the style of its life through confirmation and pre-delineates it in its further development with a certain typicality (which is, of course, constantly in flux); and experience is horizonal, insofar as it is embedded in a horizon, which pre-gives a structure of givenness. This horizon is itself subject to a genesis in its givenness, and thus subject to a historical process, which for its part has its "laws of genesis." In both cases it concerns the structures of experience, and in both cases one is referred to a temporal, that is, historical, dimension: the historicity of experience of the givenness of the world and the historicity of givenness or of the development of the worldly horizon itself; both are two sides of the same coin. Insofar as this principally concerns the structures of experience as conditions of possibility, wherein the world builds itself up for an experiencing consciousness according to ideal laws—in Husserl's words, "constitutes itself"—such reflections are transcendental-phenomenological ones. The structures thus explicated are therefore the conditions of the possibility of a concrete (factical) experience, for example, of a human being on planet Earth.

For a phenomenological theory of the lifeworld (as a title for the universal horizon of experience), this means: this theory must describe the world *reconstructively,* in that matter in which it gives itself for an experiencing consciousness, that is, in its worldly pre-givenness and in the genetic structure, in which the experience of the world has built itself up and has developed for an experiencing consciousness—and in further respect *anticipates* how it can or will unfold (presumptively). In both cases one is referred to a "historical" dimension, or one literally bumps up against it; in the one case, one is confronted with the history of experience itself; in the other case, with the history of the world, as it formed and developed itself in pre-givenness up to the one that is currently given in the living present, and that means, to the one currently given and lived-through. World, however, constantly functions as a meaningful horizon for an experiencing consciousness and is inconceivable, therefore, independently from consciousness, that is, for the type of investigation phenomenology does, it is anathema. As can be clearly seen, these are not two isolated manners of consideration, but the noetic and noematic relata of one co-relation. From here it becomes understandable how theory or "ontology" of the world of experience conceived in this manner is, or must contain, an element of transcendental phenomenology, that is, how transcendental phenomenology is or must contain an ontology of the lifeworld in the described sense. There is thus in fact only one ontology, whose "method" is phenomenology. Or, as Husserl formulates it in a manuscript from 1934: "Ontology in the full and complete sense is the ontology of all apodictic (or 'a priori') truths of the world as a world conceivable in any way [*einer überhaupt erdenklichen Welt*]" (Hua XXXIV, 469; from spring 1934).[19] Ontology, methodologically understood as phenomenology of the world as the lifeworld, is thus no discipline separate from transcendental phenomenology—as a transcendental science of consciousness. Any separation of "ontology" (science of the lifeworld) and "epistemology" (science of consciousness) would be artificial. Transcendental phenomenology is, rather, a theory of the world as the lifeworld, that is, as the world of experience, and ontology only makes sense as a "transcendental" discipline, that is, as a science of the pre-given world, whose correlate is transcendental subjectivity.[20] How this correlation is now to be understood more precisely is the topic of the next section.

History versus Historicity: The Transcendental Ego and Transcendental Humanity: The Transcendental Horizon of the Lifeworld

So far everything may be more or less known, even if the systematic connection of these structures in Husserl may not always be entirely clear. There is now, however, another "axis" in Husserl's late philosophy, which in some way stands squarely to what has been explained up to this point. Following the latter, one arrives at the problem of facticity, and one can approach it through the following question: if consciousness has its own history, which can be disclosed through genetic questioning-back (*Rückfrage*), what is then the relation of this history to what one normally means by "history," that is, what in fact justifies simply superimposing the ordinary sense of history on consciousness?[21] Obviously history here is spoken of in an equivocal sense; more precisely, in a twofold equivocation. The *first* difficulty consists in an ambiguity regarding *whose* history is meant. In the manner in which Husserl introduces the phenomenon of history in the framework of the genetic method, it becomes clear that it concerns in the first instance the history of a conscious subject, a monad. At first the history of an individual subject is thematic, and not that of a group of human beings, a people, or an epoch. The "history" of consciousness means thus initially the history of intentionality of an individual subject as the history of the development of its habits and not history writ large, as the history of a group of humans, a people, or even an epoch. Both may not be simply taken together without further ado, but form levels of subjectivity, starting from individual subjectivity, ascending to a plurality of subjects, even if the individual subject always enjoys a methodological priority for Husserl. In both cases, however, one is dealing with history as the factical progression, with the *res gestae*.

Second, Husserl initially does not distinguish between history as *res gestae* and as historicity. Let us set aside for now the distinction between individual and communal history. History can, as is already seen, denote either the factical progression of events—the factual happenings and what can be chronicled and dated—or what Husserl also refers to as "inner history" in the sense of genesis. What is the relation of both to each other, and can the difference between both be methodologically justi-

fied? What is hinted at here is nothing other than the classical phenomenological distinction between external and internal intuition (*Außen-*
and *Innenbetrachtung*).[22] This distinction is not identical with that between
history (as account of the *res gestae*) and what one might ordinarily mean
by historicity; historicity, say, as an essential feature of a human life, which
has passed through its events that are to be reconstructed causally. In the
framework of a genetic clarification of the course of consciousness, the
specifically phenomenological internal consideration deals with a clarification of meaning (*Sinnesaufklärung*), which is precisely *not* to be causally
reconstructed. Rather, causality here is meant in a different sense, since
it does not concern natural events, but rather those of the spiritual world
with its own laws. According to Husserl, one may thus not fall prey to a
naturalistic reductionism. Not the events themselves in their causal succession—which they must naturally display in "external consideration"—
are of interest to the phenomenologist, but rather the clarification of
the motivational structures of meaning, which have "made possible," that
is, motivated, factical events. Opposed to "external" history (*res gestae*)
there is hence an "inner" or "internal" history. From this, again, one has
to distinguish an "inner history *of a second level*," which subjects this inner
history again to the transcendental reduction; thus, methodologically
seen, this is a reconstruction of the spiritual motives, which may not be
understood naturalistically, that is, in a reductionistic manner. We are
thus not talking about "internal history," for example, of the American
people, which formed the specific "national character" of Americans—a
problematic method anyway—but rather about the historicity of bodily
subjects-in-themselves. This manner of consideration is only possible if
consciousness is not considered naturalistically as a part of the objective
world, but as something which "forms" the world in its constitutive acts and
therefore is essentially not worldly. That is to say, this manner of consideration is only possible after carrying out the transcendental reduction.

Opposed to "history," Husserl also therefore alternates between "*Geschichtlichkeit*" and "*Historizität*" (both to be rendered as "historicity" in
English) as what the genetic reconstruction discloses after the transcendental turn. Insofar as the motivational structures of the inner history
of transcendental consciousness first form external history—they are, as
it were, its conditions of possibility—Husserl describes the history that
becomes accessible in internal consideration opened by the transcendental reduction as *transcendental history*. After "historicity of the first level"
(reconstruction of the "essence" of a concrete person or concrete group
of people), "transcendental historicity" now concerns a "historicity of
the second level." Husserl's phenomenology is interested, therefore, neither in the individual history of a person (as, say, in psychoanalysis or

historiography—"How did Hitler become a dictator?") nor of a group of people (as, say, in a sociological-historical consideration—"How could the German people turn to National Socialism?"), but rather is interested in the laws of genesis of consciousness, insofar as it, whether as individual- or group-consciousness, lives into a world and forms ("constitutes") this world through its passive and active intentionalities. This distinction between history and historicity runs squarely to the distinction between fact and essence insofar as every progression, whether factical or transcendental, has its own essential genesis to be described respectively. History relates to historicity like description (of past events) to interpretation (of their meaning). Interpretation means, however, in *transcendental* phenomenology not a *causal* reconstruction of the meaning of history, but rather—to raise the level of abstraction still further—a clarification of the genesis of meaning itself.

Undoubtedly, this distinction is difficult to make sense of. Therefore, all comes down to the question of the relation between the internal and external consideration, or, to employ Husserl's terminology, of the relation between "transcendental" and "factical." What Husserl means by transcendental history can only emerge in contrast to factical history. On this topic, Husserl makes clear statements that relate back to the earlier, but deferred, question of *whose* history is actually meant. The starting point of all transcendental reflections—and such reflections are constantly at play in the framework of Husserl's theory—is always the I, which initially, as one's own I respectively, is thematic as an individual Ego of a reflecting person, on one's primordial level. The individual I, as a factical reflecting person (as "phenomenologizing") finds, in the transcendental-phenomenological reduction, the transcendental Ego, initially its own. Husserl never relinquishes this "solipsistic entryway," the first-person access, through one's individual reflection. Accordingly, one must first determine the relation between the transcendental and the factical Ego; what is said with respect to *their* relation must, a fortiori, be transferred over to the relation between the transcendental and the factical as such. How are, thus, the factical (concrete) and the transcendental I related to each other?

Against an obvious, and therefore oft-repeated misunderstanding, it must be emphasized that with the transcendental and factical Ego, Husserl does not mean two I's or a dualistic conception of the subject. For Husserl, rather, they concern two moments of one structure which are to be distinguished *methodologically*, which are merely differentiated through their particular perspective (attitude), that is, they only become distinguishable through the respective perspective on them. It is in either case the I, as it is lived through (unthematically) in the natural attitude *and* as the transcendental-constituting I, as it becomes thematic in the reflecting ("phenomenologizing") attitude. The factical Ego is thus itself not at all thematic to itself; this is precisely its "distinction" in the "natural" attitude. The natural attitude is thereby characterized in that it is never thematic *as an attitude*. As Husserl says in an interesting marginal note to a manuscript, "The world as the universe is generally speaking no theme in the 'natural attitude,' accordingly, it may actually not be called an *attitude*. The world is pre-given, it is the field of all natural attitudes in the actually thematic sense" (Hua XXXIV, 14, note). The difference between the transcendental and the factical Ego is thus that between the Ego that first becomes *thematic* and the Ego that lives in the world but lives "lost in the world" (*weltverloren*), intentionally "infatuated" in the world, unaware of its world-constituting achievements. In the phenomenological consideration, accordingly, the Ego does not become thematic in a random manner, but rather as an intentional field, which intentionally achieves for itself the world through its own experience as the *world of experience* for itself.

But generally speaking, the I is equally transcendental, as it always already apperceives itself psychophysically in the world, that is, as it finds itself factically. The transcendental Ego has always already, in Husserl's words, "enworlded"[23] itself. As a worldly Ego, it can, after the transcendental reduction (after the transcendental "questioning back"), disclose its transcendental "being," but this unveiling through the phenomenological reduction always temporally succeeds the enworlded apperception of itself as a human person and its being as transcendental. The transcendental Ego is indeed the *próteron te physei*, but not *pròs hemâs, pròs moû*, to be precise. The worldly I has no transcendental Ego behind it, as it were, in its back, to which it "owed" its worldly being; instead, the transcendental I "encompasses" the natural-factical I. The natural I is a "mode" of the transcendental I.[24] This means that all factical givens of the Ego must be transcendentally interpreted—that is, with respect to their constitutive functions—but they are thereby "sublated" (*aufgehoben*) in their facticity. The phenomenological viewpoint discloses simply a structure of meaning, which cannot come into view without a *break* with the natural attitude; what hereby comes into view is the correlative structure of the intentionally constituted life of consciousness, yet not simply only in its facticity, for the latter is only interesting insofar as this offers an opportunity for the eidetic analysis:

> Human being or world indicate a certain transcendental structure of
> transcendental subjectivity. If I segue from the factical world (which
> for me has the factical meaning of "my and our world"), considering

essential possibilities, to a possible world in general, then I have varied my factical human being and that of the human beings existing with me and for me; I have thus modified *implicitly,* however, also my *factical transcendental* monad, my *factical transcendental* humanity [*Menschentum*], and that of my co-monads. Thereby is it the case, however, that we all, we human-monads, thus are concurrently world-constituting, and in a world which must include us monads objectively as human beings existing alongside each other. (Hua XXXIV, 155, from August 1930, italics added)

This transcendental consideration thus discloses that the self-enworlding of the world-constituting, transcendental Ego as factical, that is, as *unconscious* of itself as constituting, is itself an essential law of the Ego. Or what is the same: to "shroud" itself in its transcendental accomplishments is thus itself an essential law of the Ego!

Although Husserl in this quote already goes above and beyond the primordial level, let us remain at it a bit longer. Here it is an essential fact, and not only for human facticity, which can never be sublated and modified through reflection, that the Ego is constituted as with a *lived body,* which can therefore not go beyond this fact in eidetic variation. To have a lived body is a condition of the possibility to be a factical Ego (whether it is human or another living creature), and is at the same time an essential component of a factical Ego, regardless of its "intellect." As Husserl says at one point, "The lived body presupposes itself" (A VII 12/64a, from February 1932), that is, it is, as an unsublatable moment of the human being, what radically individualizes the particular factical Ego, here: the particular human, on the one hand. But on the other hand it is also what, as it were, creeps up on the Ego even without a special reflection and which is, as such, without a "presupposition"; a bodiless consciousness (just like a worldless one) would be nonsense for Husserl. What does this mean now for the enworlding of the transcendental Ego in a *genetic* perspective?

Due to the constantly occurring process of enworlding as natural-human self-apperception in the course of the constantly occurring world-experience on the part of the human being, the factical history of the psychophysical human being is itself *per definitionem* the enworlded form of its transcendental history. What can this mean? To understand this is of the utmost difficulty, and the interpretation may not level the distinction between factical and transcendental.[25] The factically lived-through history of the human being "realizes" the transcendental history of transcendental subjectivity, since its life (or life as such) cannot proceed other than factically. "To proceed factically" means now that it proceeds without a *consciousness* of its own achievements. It has, as Husserl also says, a "transcendental index," but natural consciousness lacks, as it were, the *"toolbox"* of how to make this index thematic. "Factical" means therefore not only "concrete" (in opposition to abstract or eidetic), but at the same time "naive" in the sense of the naïveté of the natural attitude. Through transcendental questioning back, which the phenomenological internal viewing makes possible, the human transcendental constitution of meaning is indeed disclosed, its "inner history," its "inner logic" as it were, according to which factical history occurs and plays itself out (i.e., must play out lawfully). It is, however, the history initially of an Ego, which cannot abandon in this bodily *functioning* this form of facticity. The functioning of the lived body is itself something that is not only not thematized in natural consciousness but that was altogether unnoticed in philosophy itself up to now. Husserl is correct, therefore, to emphasize that the distinction between body (*Körper*) and lived body (*Leib;* as functioning subjectivity) is one of the most original discoveries of constitutive phenomenology.[26] Corporeality (*Leiblichkeit*) lives itself out, however, necessarily in a factical (i.e., constituted) world, which is formed in the first instance by the lived body (through acting and working). Thus the I as factical (qua lived body) and world belong inseparably together, insofar as the world is the stage upon which lived-bodily functions play themselves out. All relatings to the world are intrinsically bodily and not something bodily "mediated," since there is no mean point between the transcendental Ego and the world. Ego and world are, as Merleau-Ponty would say, "from one flesh."

Landgrebe already hinted at this connection early on, when he interpreted the identification of the facticity and transcendentality of the Ego in the late Husserl in the sense of the *bodily functioning* of the factical subject.[27] This brief suggestion can be expanded, after what has been said above, such that the natural Ego as bodily constituted is nothing separate from its transcendentality, but that the natural-factical Ego is a "mode"—namely unrevealed, unaware of its transcendental origin—of the wholly clarified Ego as transcendental. The "natural attitude"—and not the natural Ego itself—is a "mode of transcendental subjectivity."[28] It is, however, an essential law of a factical Ego to be "caught up" in an attitude, just as it essentially always lives bodily in a world. The theme "living body" will not be pursued further in the following—there is nothing like an "intersubjective living body"—but serves in the preceding context only for a further characterization of what "facticity" means with respect to the Ego. The bodily functioning of the Ego is rather a supplementary "guarantor" for the claim that the Ego is "worldly" through and through, belongs to the world, since it is essentially of the same "matter" as the latter. The living body is the captive "anchor" which couples the I with the world. Further, it belongs essentially to being in an attitude to initially not know *anything* about this being-in-an-attitude. The naïveté of the natural attitude is thus no accidental condition, which could be simply overcome, but an essential fact of a factical Ego. Hence, only a radical *break* with the natural attitude can free the Ego from this essential "self-enshrouding."

However, one may not now remain, like earlier, in a "solipsistic" manner of consideration. Accordingly, the world is essentially a communal world, in which the I exists with others.[29] The transcendental Ego as a "transcendental Robinson Crusoe," as it may initially appear after the reduction, is an abstraction. World is always already a common world. If the Ego in its factical enactment lives its own transcendental historicity in community with others, then this holds analogously for the world as intersubjective, so long as the world is an always historically grown communal world, in which the acts of a multiplicity of subjects have sedimented themselves,[30] and this, too, is an essential discovery: "The world bears an essential historicity in itself: prior to the question of factical history" (A VII 11/8b, from September/October 1932). This "bearing-in-itself" must be interpreted as an inclusion of the worldly in the transcendental and shows once more that there is, for Husserl, no division or split between both "spheres," but that they present the moments of *one* structure. As subjects live worldly, the world is for its part not only historical in the sense of *res gestae,* but *historical* in the sense of the transcendental register. The historicity which is spoken of here is nothing other than that of transcendental intersubjectivity, which so far has been considered only from its primordial level. The relation of transcendental and factical transfers from Ego and "its" world to the Ego-community and world itself, insofar as it is a world of collectively functioning subjects (including those who have functioned and will function). But nevertheless, this can only be unveiled from the primordial I: "My apodictic factum as transcendental bears within itself the apodictic transcendental monadic subjectivity, existing in transcendental temporality, and its being in a relative historicity, ordered [*gegliedert*] in transcendental 'humanities' [*Menschheiten*]" (ibid.).

From here follows, as Husserl continues in this manuscript:

> The world is a historical formation of my immanent temporal historicity of my "humanity" ["*Menschheit*"] transcendentally implied within me, in which I, transcendental-temporally, am myself implied transcendentally "objectified" as a monad and have, as such, a socially interconnected coexistence. But in a peculiar manner: I as a transcendental timeless

monadic I and my transcendental "humanity" are[31] in historical development. (A VII 11/8b)[32]

Several things are especially noteworthy in this—extremely dense—passage: the transcendental Ego is initially termed a monad, which "as such" is socially constituted. Husserl's monads thus, as we know, have windows. Moreover, the transcendental Ego as a "timeless" I has a historical development; this points to the above-elucidated essential circumstance that it belongs to the *eidos* Ego to be historical. Finally, the sequence of functioning proceeds conversely to that of the discovery on the part of the phenomenologist: history as factically proceeding is something in which I occur as a factical Ego with my "living history." World history itself is in turn the enworlded form of transcendental intersubjectivity, that is, of the transcendental universe of monads. Just as the factical Ego in its history "bears" in itself its transcendental history (implies it as an "index") as its own history of meaning, in the same manner does the factical history of the world have its constitutive history of meaning prior (pregiven) to it, which precedes it not temporally as an act is preceded by a decision, but which functions as its depth dimension, which is concealed to the natural attitude; the depth dimension is thus always present, but unthematic. Rather, transcendental history "precedes" factical history logically, not only in the sense of an essential structure, according to which factical history plays out concretely. Transcendental history is also the history of "transcendental humanity,"[33] which finds itself enworlded and "comes to itself" in a group of people which reflect upon themselves, clarify themselves and their own existence; this is the endless succession of generations of philosophers. The latter is necessary if this knowledge is to assume a worldly form, or what is to say the same, that knowledge becomes conscious in reflection in factical human beings, who abandon their limited horizon of the natural attitude, and thus become transcendentally reflecting philosophers. That is to say, the questioning-back discloses essential structures of genesis, not the sequence of genesis itself like a secret "script" to which one could gain access in a mysterious way. It is thus a rational activity, through and through, on the part of reflecting human beings, who thereby take up a particular rank within society (the philosophers as "functionaries of mankind").

This scenario points to science and philosophy as forms of human existence in which this initially concealed knowledge realizes or manifests itself. These monads are then "awakened" instead of "sleeping" in their normal day-to-day living in the "natural attitude." Just as it belongs eidetically to an Ego to shroud itself with respect to its transcendental dimension, it belongs essentially to a community of people to initially be naive, but to prefigure certain individuals who can break out of this self-forgetfulness and are destined "to open the eyes of humanity" and "to discover the true meaning of the world."[34] The latter indicates the *teleological* dimension in Husserl's philosophy of history. A humanity—at bottom a group of subjects—only comes to itself because there are individuals who break through the ordinary habit of life that they take for granted. *And* the individual Ego comes to itself only when it elevates itself above the natural attitude and views itself as part of a humanity striving ever upwards, to which it belongs actively and in original creation: "Further progressing, I [as the meditating philosopher] understand that through every transcendental existence, not merely individually but in the intersubjective communalization and as an intersubjective totality, goes a striving of unity to '*perfection.*' It is *no accident that the human being*, constantly occupied with particularities of experience, of valuing, of desiring and achieving goals (purposes), *never comes to contentment*" (Hua XV, 404, from 1931).

That the transcendental enworlds itself in factical history, then, means that the "meaning" of history is not to be sought outside of itself—neither in a divine transcendence nor in a solipsistic "immanence"—but lies in itself, once the acts which have achieved it are disclosed in their transcendental function, and once the world is disclosed as the constitutive product and order of meaning. The progression of history as formed by subjects is itself its meaning, whose meaningful development can be impaired or interrupted only through crises. Only the transcendental manner of consideration can disclose this meaning, insofar as the meaning of history concerns not the *res gestae* of particular humanities, which one could simply re-narrate. Rather, Husserl's manner of consideration makes it possible to reconstruct the internal motivations of meaning, which only make possible, initially, something as a factical development in its causal succession.

What, now, concerning the task of an "ontology of the lifeworld" as an interpretation of our communal quotidian world? The lifeworld is, as a product of constitution, the result of transcendental formation of meaning, which is to be construed as a genesis of constitutive achievements. This transcendental formation of meaning in genetic lawfulness is nothing other than the transcendental history of the lifeworld. The lifeworld thereby becomes conceivable as an essentially historical world and refers back to its transcendental history as "internal" history, which, however, is not an anonymous occurrence but the deed of acting subjects. This "referring back" is to be understood such that the lifeworld as a factical historical world "bears in itself" this transcendental horizon. An "unorthodox" way to formulate this would be to say that history as the factical progression of a humanity is thoroughly permeated by subjectivity, by the achievements of functioning agents; not a historical progression which—as a "destiny of being" or "history of effects"—simply comes over us as an anonymous force. This perspective radically calls humanity back to responsibility with respect to itself, its lifeworld, and its history. This is the Husserlian understanding of what "Enlightenment" can mean in the framework of transcendental phenomenology.

Once these essential connections have been understood, the order of foundation is turned upside down: the transcendental horizon bears "in itself," as embracing it, the factical horizon. Just as the human being only occurs in the world as bodily constituted and individualized, there is also only one world that, however, as factical-historical realizes its transcendental history, that is, enworlds it and as such first makes it "real." Only the transcendental dimension opened through the phenomenological reduction discloses the lifeworld as what it is in the deepest sense, but which cannot be known without transcendental questioning-back.[35] To describe the lifeworld without the transcendental horizon in which it is genetically constituted would be like trying to describe humans as merely factical and to naturalize the sphere of the spirit, without a knowledge of its transcendental dimension: one would fall back into a pre-philosophical naïveté and would simply do anthropology (or sociology or historiography) as positive sciences, in the same manner as a factical science of consciousness is "only" psychology (for example, as "descriptive," even as eidetic) and can never be philosophy as the clarification of the grounds and conditions of possibilities. Likewise, a genetic phenomenology without a transcendental index would only be a historiography of random subjects without an apprehension of the meaning that occurs in history; a meaning, however, which is itself constituted and is a "coming to being" (*"Werden zum Sein"*). One would attain, just as one can give an "external consideration" of the human being as psychophysical—and thereby would have precisely overlooked its distinctive characteristic as a person—an external consideration of history as a causal reconstruction of the *res gestae*, instead of a phenomenological internal consideration, which is, for Husserl, the only appropriate consideration as a *transcendental-philosophical* one. Such an "external consideration" would be, say, a reconstruction of a "history of effects," which accepts the effects of a certain cultural formation purely as given (as "classical"), instead of taking the internal perspective and inquiring into the grounds, motives, and conditions that make it possible that something can *become* classical in a certain epoch and community of people.

Summary and Conclusion

As one can glean from these last remarks, with this discussion we stand only at the beginning of the actual investigations on the constitution of the historical lifeworld; yet they provide the framework into which these analyses fall. The "coordinate system," as was earlier said metaphorically, is hereby only roughly sketched; but this also means that the concrete and detailed descriptions which Husserl carried out in the context of the "theory of world apperception"[36] can only thereby become understood in their systematic content. To sum up: how do facticity and historicity thus systematically hang together in the framework of the ontology of the lifeworld?

All science—and the ontology of the lifeworld just presented also has an eminently scientific character—is in the most general sense science of the world. Insofar as one starts out, in the framework of transcendental phenomenology, from this world as the world of experience on the part of human, factical life within it—one could also, if such an experience were accessible to us, start out from creatures on Mars and their world— it is to be questioned as to its transcendental constitution of meaning. The achievement of transcendental constitution terminates, however, in this factical world, that is, its facticity is an enworlded mode of transcendentality, unaware of itself. In this context, facticity thus means—besides being bodily constituted—also to be "unaware of the transcendental-constitutive dimension." There is thus only one world, which essentially "bears in itself" its concealed transcendental depth dimension, but which also constantly "enworlds" the latter, whereby the transcendental achievement of meaning at the same time constantly "blurs its tracks." In this sense, one could say that the world is itself "the absolute," insofar as transcendental life and the lifeworld are the moments of *one* structure. This "Finkian trick" is thus already present in Husserl, even though Husserl reserves the term "absolute" for constituting consciousness.[37] However, this is purely a terminological dispute. The constituting of the meaning of the lifeworld is now the result of a genesis or history in the transcendental sense of the term, as the internal history of the transcendental universe of monads, which bears in itself a transcendental historicity and continually enworlds this historicity and, along with it, itself in the constitutive process (and thus is always also initially concealed to itself). Thus, the genetic dimension is irrevocably inscribed in the theory of the lifeworld. The ontological status of transcendental humanity, however, is— at least in this respect—to be understood such that it always finds itself as factically enworlded in a world which has a historical character "thanks" to the transcendental history of acting subjects in it. Its facticity is only to be understood as a continually enworlded transcendental occurrence of meaning. Historicity and facticity in the sense thus explicated necessarily belong together like two axes, into which the ontology of the lifeworld "inscribes" itself.

At the end of the deliberations from the manuscript from which I quoted here (A VII 11),[38] Husserl notes:

> This is the phenomenology which discovers, questioning back from the pre-given world, worldly historicity as formation of transcendental historicity and now forms, instead of the naively constituted human world, the absolute monadic world as existing in its historical omnitemporality, as continually developing, forming itself and forming within itself continually itself as objectivating world, with worldly human beings and animals, forming worldly human beings as humane, as forming in themselves willingly humane self-formation. (A VII 11/11a)

The reflections in this manuscript conclude: "With this, however, phenomenology is not at an end" (ibid.). On the contrary, in terms of the analytic-descriptive work to be carried out it only just stands at the beginning. It demands, however, as was suggested, over and above this, in a certain sense a developed humanity which can disclose these nexuses of meaning, which thereby first elevate this humanity to a "true humanity" by overcoming its naive stage and striving towards an *ideally* anticipated goal which it has gotten to know through these reflections. The beginning towards this new departure comes thus only at a relative end point of a long development, which makes possible a new beginning. This suggests that one would have to consider for future analysis in this connection another theme, hereby inseparably related to it, which was of great concern to Husserl especially in his late phase, namely the problem of *teleology*, which however cannot be further discussed here. Yet, as Husserl suggests, a teleology of scientific rational humanity cannot be carried out without a preceding "transcendental archeology." How such an "archeology," for its part, is to be understood has been reconstructed here.

What Husserl means by "transcendental history" and the lifeworld has hereby become comprehensible in outline; but this discussion also makes clear, in all sharpness, the highly complex, ultimately perhaps even problematical character of Husserl's talk of "transcendental life" and its relation to facticity in the last phase of his work. What Husserl had in mind when he claimed that the transcendental and the factical are apparently "moments" of *one* structure must thus continue to be the theme of philosophical efforts. The preceding remarks aimed to clarify Husserl's late philosophy of the lifeworld in its complexity, but also in its full degree of abstraction. As has become apparent, Husserl was occupied up to the last in working out his systematic phenomenology as a *systematic method*. The final form of Husserl's thought is therefore certainly not easier to grasp, but at least it has become visible in its richness that is still scarcely exhausted. The "open horizons" of which Husserl spoke with respect to phenomenology as a "working philosophy" is therefore no empty phrase, but the task for future intellectual efforts that take seriously the concrete facticity and the historicity of human life. Whether the human species will ever be able to attain the telos of a fully enlightened rational humanity, as Husserl anticipated, remains, nevertheless, more in question today than ever. But here, too, the factical is no case in point against Husserl's analyses carried out in a transcendental-eidetic register.

Translated by Colin J. Hahn

The Relation of Transcendental and Factical: From Lifeworld to the Subject as Person

The relation of "the" transcendental and "the" factical, which has been the focus in this chapter, continues to be a neuralgic point in Husserl's late philosophy. Indeed, it becomes even more pressing as this relation becomes "applied" to the subject itself, or as the subject becomes framed in this tension. This problematic has already been hinted at in chapter 3 in conjunction with the problem of "enworlding," and in this chapter in conjunction with the question as to the exact status of the subject as both a transcendental agent and as situated in the factical lifeworld as a *person* due to its lived body. Focusing on the subject itself, with respect to its "double life" (as Rudolf Bernet has called it), and concerning the question of its status as *both transcendental and factical,* leads us to one of the deepest, but also most difficult and problematic aspects of Husserl's thought.

This difficulty is compounded by the fact that it was no less than Husserl's most ingenious pupil, Heidegger, who both criticized Husserl's concept of subjectivity and formed his own notion of the human subject as *Dasein* in his *Auseinandersetzung* with his teacher. One can say that both "profited" from this mutual encounter, although both certainly did not see it that way. To Husserl, his "master student" had—like so many of his other pupils—simply not grasped the phenomena such as "lifeworld" or "transcendental subject" that emerged after the reduction. To Heidegger, his "old man" had simply not understood the novelty of his own critique and had lumped him together with a newly emerging trend called "existentialism," which Heidegger found unjust and incorrect. Hence, the following chapter shall present both trajectories: Husserl's, insofar as his thoughts defending himself against Heidegger culminate in his notion of the "transcendental person"; Heidegger's, as he departs from his teacher's project of an eidetic science of the transcendental. Yet I do not want to simply side with Husserl and repeat the old mantra that Heidegger had not understood Husserl—or, for that matter, the opposite concerning Heidegger, whose proponents make the same claim. Instead, I hope to come to a measured conclusion that correctly and fairly assesses both paths of thought, while concluding that both simply parted ways. The conflict cannot be mediated, but the best that an interpreter can do is to demonstrate how both indeed entered different paths, which simply cannot be brought to harmony or "synthesis." That this interpreter has more sympathy with Husserl's path is a different story (and explained in greater detail in the "Introduction").

Husserl's Concept of the "Transcendental Person": Another Look at the Husserl–Heidegger Relationship

Introduction

It is fair to call the Husserl–Heidegger relationship *the* classic topic of phenomenology. It was at the heart of the phenomenological debate even before the publication of Heidegger's groundbreaking *Being and Time* (1927) and has received attention again in recent phenomenological scholarship.[1] Many philosophers, and not only those affiliated with the phenomenological movement, have developed their own philosophical standpoint by associating themselves with the Husserlian or the Heideggerian versions of phenomenology (and derivations of them), or by thinking through the dispute between the two thinkers in order to become clear about their own philosophical standpoint.[2] With regard to the *nature* of their relationship, some have claimed, on the one hand, that Husserl and Heidegger have very little or almost nothing in common. Others, on the other hand, have argued that they are in fact working on the same philosophical project without being aware of it. Because of its complexity, this has been a long-standing issue, and not only within phenomenology, which has contributed to the way phenomenology as a whole has been received by the philosophical world at large. Lastly, given their difficult personal relationship, one should regard Husserl's and Heidegger's respective views of one another with great suspicion. Indeed, a great deal of misunderstanding, deliberate or otherwise, led to their dispute and to the feud that ultimately ended their friendship.

In this chapter I am focusing on a specific topic that will offer one pathway into this difficult field, namely, the question of *personhood* or of a phenomenological *anthropology*. What is at stake, moreover, is the question of phenomenology as *transcendental philosophy* that, for Husserl, could only be based on consciousness framed in a transcendental register. To Heidegger, phenomenology—leaving aside the question as to its status as transcendental—must begin with considering concrete *Dasein*, which, however, is just a point of access to the question of *Being* as the actual telos of his project. Historically, the last philosophical debate between the two took place during their collaboration on an entry for the *Encyclopaedia Britannica* (on "Phenomenology") which Husserl was asked to write in 1927. Perhaps because Husserl already sensed the differences in Heidegger's understanding of phenomenology (he did not read *Being and Time* until 1931), Husserl called on his former assistant to help him draft this text. The differences arising here are paralleled by passages in Heidegger's *Marburg Lectures* as well as in *Being and Time,* where Heidegger (in §7) famously defines "phenomenology" purely in terms of a formal method of "letting things be seen in the way they show themselves" (1993, 34)—and in so doing, severs an immediate link to consciousness. Indeed, he divorces phenomenology abruptly from that which for Husserl could ever be the topic for phenomenology, namely, consciousness or subjectivity conceived as transcendental, that is, as distinct from worldly subjectivity. Yet, disconnecting the phenomenological method from a method for analyzing consciousness does not mean that Heidegger did not thematize subjectivity in his own way—as factical being-in-the-world, which he termed *Dasein.* Heidegger clearly wanted to move away from the tradition of what Gadamer has called *Reflexionsphilosophie,* that is, a philosophical inquiry that gains access to the question of subjectivity by reflection, or more generally, theory. Regardless of his often scathing critiques, the question of man is, certainly up to *Being and Time,* at least one very important aspect of Heidegger's overall project. At the end of 1927, Heidegger writes the following remarkable sentence to his Marburg colleague, the theologian Rudolf Bultmann: "The foundation of [my work] is developed by starting from the 'subject,' properly understood as the human *Dasein,* so that with the radicalization of this approach the true motives of German idealism may likewise come into their own."[3]

It will be my claim that Husserl and Heidegger (the Heidegger of the "phenomenological decade" 1919–29)[4] had this very paradigm "subjectivity" in common. This claim will not be met with resistance if it can in principle be agreed that Heidegger's hermeneutics of facticity in division 1 of *Being and Time* is at least a minimal account of what it means to be a human subject.[5] By "paradigm" I mean, furthermore, that subjectivity was both Husserl's and Heidegger's *methodological* foundation in developing their respective philosophical "systems," regardless of where this foundation led them—Husserl, to a full-fledged eidetic science of consciousness, Heidegger, to a new ontology that thematizes the Being of the entities. Also, both had important *thematic* things to say about human subjectivity itself. However, the difference in the way they *understood* subjectivity can be seen as the central topic around which their dispute evolved. Although Husserl considered Heidegger's redrafting of phenomenology as a hermeneutics of facticity fundamentally flawed—derogatorily rendering it "anthropologism"—the criticisms that Heidegger leveled against Husserl's concept of the transcendental subject, for example, in his comments on Husserl's draft of the encyclopedia entry, remained in the back of Husserl's mind and resurfaced in peculiar contexts in his later manuscripts. It is my contention that the curious term "transcendental person" that Husserl employs in some of these manuscripts, while being consistent with his earlier discussions of personhood (especially in *Ideas II*), is a direct reply to his pupil's objections. It is this concept on which I would like to focus centrally in this chapter, as it both forms a memorable catchy term for Husserl's standpoint and yields an optimal target for Heidegger's critique.

In the first section of this chapter (after the introduction), I shall sketch both Husserl's and Heidegger's project of a philosophy of human subjectivity. It will become clear that Heidegger's critique of Husserl's "unparticipating observer," if plausible, has fatal consequences for Husserl's project as a whole. Husserl acknowledges this critique to a certain extent and responds with a recasting of the transcendental subject in terms of the subject's "concreteness," for which the "transcendental person" functions as a key term. In the second section, I shall set Husserl's concept of the transcendental person in the context of his mature concept of constitution. This will prepare for a presentation of Heidegger's critique of Husserl's concept of the transcendental subject in the third section. In the fourth section, I shall try to elucidate Husserl's counter-critique of Heidegger's objections and shall attempt to reconstruct Husserl's position, drawing from the scattered remarks that Husserl makes throughout his research manuscripts.

It is my intention to recount Husserl's arguments against Heidegger as convincingly as possible, not to judge the ultimate veracity of Husserl's position. In fact, a last assessment will, I believe, have to come to the conclusion that Husserl, probably more than Heidegger, wore blinders that simply did not allow him to see beyond the polemic context and terminology in which Heidegger dressed his novel thought. Scholarship in this field made it clear that it was up to interpreters who did not belong to either Husserl's or Heidegger's camp to see the issues at stake more clearly. Their insights will be incorporated as much as possible in the course of this chapter. The purpose of the chapter is to *present* Husserl's alleged arguments against Heidegger as he penned them in his private study in his last years. This includes Husserl's way of understanding *Heidegger's* attack—regardless of the fact that today we can perhaps no longer agree with Husserl's judgment. Whether Husserl understood Heidegger correctly—ultimately, I believe, he did not—must be left open to further interpretation, as it goes beyond the scope of this chapter. The chapter does not argue in favor of or against "Husserlian" or "Heideggerian" phenomenology, but is meant as a further look at their relationship. I shall draw on Husserl's hitherto unknown manuscripts in the context of his reflections on the phenomenological method that culminate in the concept of the "transcendental person."[6]

Philosophy as "Anthropology" and Heidegger's Critique of Husserl's Concept of the "Unparticipating Observer"

One can say, rather superficially, that Husserl's philosophy had subjectivity as its topic, Heidegger's the question of Being. Nevertheless, one can make the case that Heidegger's emphasis, at least up to *Being and Time,* was on subjectivity as well. This is warranted by pointing out that the subject, qua *Dasein,* is the focus of the fundamental ontology in division 1 of *Being and Time,* an analysis that is supposed to lead, ultimately, to the question of Being. The difference between them is that Heidegger conceives of this subjectivity radically differently from the way Husserl did; to the point that Heidegger considered "subjectivity" or "consciousness" inadequate terms altogether. Heidegger's critique of Husserl in *Being and Time* is first and foremost a critique of Husserl's conception of *subjectivity,* or more precisely, his framing of subjectivity along the lines of Cartesianism[7] and in terms of transcendental philosophy.[8] Yet, in this reading, Husserl merely stands at the end point of a development gone awry since Descartes.[9] Heidegger's counter-concept of *Dasein,* a "being in the here and now" as the term for that being which we ourselves are (as essentially finite, caring beings), stands in stark contrast to Husserl's teleological concept of subjectivity as an endless field of research accessed by (potentially) endless reflection. In this sense, and not completely without legitimacy, Heidegger's approach has been portrayed as that of a "hands-on," pragmatically oriented philosophy of practical subjectivity and Husserl as an over-theoretical "armchair philosopher" who seems to have no interest other than describing in endless detail the inkwell he sees standing before him on his desk.[10] Both readings are certainly exaggerated and to a certain extent unfair; yet they were the ways in which, falsely or not, the contrast between the two was often perceived—and in fact, by Husserl himself. A closer look at both will reveal their inadequacy.

Indeed, to overlook the fact that Heidegger's characterization of what it means to be a human *Dasein* is a piece of "theoretical" philosophy is fundamentally to misread Heidegger. Thus, the characterization of Husserl as the "theoretician" and Heidegger as the "practitioner" is an oversimplification and ultimately grossly misleading. They have in common a phenomenology of the subject, in Heidegger's emphasis on *Dasein's practical* behavior and relation to itself, the others, and the world, and Husserl's focus on science and eidetic intuition in order to bring out general characteristics of transcendental subjectivity. However, this distinction still does not get to the core of the matter with regard to the question of subjectivity. Getting to the "things themselves" for Heidegger meant getting back to the original and concrete sense of what it means to be a factical concrete human subject. In a sense, this is no different from what Husserl wanted in his lifeworld ontology, except that Husserl never seemed to get beyond the foundations and in the end never arrived where Heidegger already was. Indeed, as we shall see, one of Husserl's criticisms is that Heidegger took his point of departure "too high up" ("*zu hoch angesetzt*" is a recurring complaint of Husserl's) vis-à-vis Husserl's approach "from the bottom up." Husserl also could not overlook the compelling and genial simplicity of Heidegger's designation of the human being as *Dasein* as being-in-the world. Heidegger was "with one stroke" where Husserl always wanted to be, as he was always busy with laying adequate foundations. Thus, it was Heidegger's strong emphasis on the "concreteness" of subjectivity which, I believe, in turn prompted Husserl to recast or reformulate his own conception of transcendental subjectivity in terms of the "*transcendental person.*" The term "transcendental person" appears only a few times in Husserl's entire work (and only in his private notes), as though Husserl was insecure about employing it. Although it features only in some later manuscripts, I am inclined to call it a key concept regarding what Husserl himself considered his main discovery, that is, transcendental subjectivity in its universal dimensions (ultimately as intersubjectivity).[11] Thus, to Husserl, only when one thematizes the person from the standpoint of *transcendental* phenomenology will one be in a position to arrive at the subject's fullest and concrete being. Accordingly, Husserl believed that Heidegger's fundamental ontology had no bearing on transcendental philosophy. Along with the irritation one must feel regarding the peculiarity of the term "transcendental person" itself, what is perplexing is the motive which led Husserl to introduce this term, namely, the defense of his standpoint against Heidegger's attack—and with Heidegger, the entire budding "existentialist movement."

Apart from immanent developments in Husserl's thought with respect to the concept of personhood from *Ideas II* onwards,[12] I believe that the strongest motive for employing this term comes as a reaction to *Heidegger's* critique of Husserl's conception of phenomenology as transcendental idealism. Although the opposition between idealism and realism might be a tired philosophical distinction (especially since Husserl's peculiar idealism at the same time has a strong realistic tendency),[13] it seemed to many phenomenologists in Husserl's circles that traditional "idealisms" imply claims that seem almost impossible to reconcile with the character of phenomenology. Indeed, phenomenology is dedicated to the analysis of concrete phenomena, "things themselves," instead of seemingly artificial distinctions that idealism makes, such as that between a mundane and a transcendental subject. Heidegger was, in *this* sense, decidedly an anti-idealist, although it is another question whether or not he subscribed to the transcendental turn. To Husserl, rejecting idealism included rejecting the transcendental turn. Heidegger's critique of Husserl in this respect is most explicit in his famous comments on Husserl's *Encyclopaedia Britannica* article as well as in certain passages in *Being and Time. Being and Time* can certainly be read in its entirety as a philosophical program set up against or in competition with Husserl's. One can speculate that these issues—Husserl's transcendental project and Heidegger's developing systematics—were the topic of the discussions that Husserl and Heidegger had at least up to 1929. And in 1931, the year in which Husserl gave his talk "Phenomenology and Anthropology" throughout the German Kant societies—with "anthropology" designating the adversarial philosophies of Scheler and, especially, Heidegger—Husserl concluded that Heidegger's philosophy presented nothing but a pre-transcendental, that is, naive, anthropology—"anthropologism"—and not a transcendental phenomenology as a first philosophy in the sense that he, Husserl, inaugurated it.[14]

This is not to say, however, that Husserl's phenomenology cannot also be understood in a certain "application" as an anthropology, if one understands by this term a philosophical science devoted to the question of the human subject. Indeed, this would be an anthropology with a special meaning of *anthropos* and in a transcendentally clarified framework. Hence the term "anthropology" is used here not as a term for a positive science but as the title for a philosophy that considers the question of the human being as a basis for further inquiry. In *this* sense, all transcendental philosophy since Kant can be called "anthropology." Regarding Husserl's reading of Heidegger, it is thus highly indicative that Husserl picks up mainly on Heidegger's concept of *Dasein* and treats this as the center of *Being and Time,*[15] a reading, in other words, that made it possible for Husserl to term Heidegger's philosophical project *altogether* an "anthropology." We know that Heidegger repeatedly complained that many of his contemporaries understood his philosophy as just another version of existentialism—that is, a philosophy that has human existence as its basis—rather than fundamental ontology. This was, in Heidegger's eyes, a standard misunderstanding of his philosophical position, which was, instead, purportedly devoted to the *gigantomachia peri tes ousias* (the "giant battle concerning being") inaugurated by Plato and Aristotle—and forgotten since. We must leave aside the question of what Heidegger's philosophy, at least in the period of *Being and Time,* was "really about"; the only point made here is that it is not unreasonable to read *Being and Time* as a highly original sketch of an anthropology (of *Dasein*), and that, furthermore, this was the way *Husserl* read it, as did so many of his contemporaries. If, however, one concedes that Husserl's transcendental phenomenology is a question regarding the human subject as well, and if one goes along with Heidegger's own assertion in *Being and Time* that the question of Being can only be dealt with from the perspective of a fundamental ontology of *Dasein,* then one can say that the question of a philosophical anthropology—as a philosophy of the subject—lies at the heart of the discussion between the two. This assertion can be further supported if one means by anthropology a philosophy that poses the question of the human being in "fullness," as a *person*.[16] For an anthropology of this sort, the main question would be what exactly *constitutes* this full-fledged personhood. It is in this respect that Heidegger's critique of Husserl's concept of the transcendental Ego exerts its fullest force.

Essentially, Heidegger holds that Husserl's consideration of the Ego as a transcendental "entity" is far too abstract to account for the human being in her everyday life. "Abstract" means here that the theoretical locus that Husserl seems to assume is not where *Dasein* actually takes place "first of all and most of the time": in its factical, average everydayness (*durchschnittliche Alltäglichkeit*). It is this quotidian existence in its finitude that Husserl overlooks, in Heidegger's opinion. This is due to the neglect on Husserl's part—and with him the entire Western philosophical tradition—to pose the question of the being of that entity which *exists* and as such *understands* itself and the world, rather than simply being *present-to-hand* (*vorhanden*). It is only a hermeneutics of *Dasein*'s quotidian facticity or average everydayness that can account for the person's "true" being, even if the primary mode of this being might be inauthentic. Thus the phenomenological account must first of all pay attention to this basic mode of *Dasein*'s existence and, since it is non-thematic, one must actually learn to see it, thereby not dismissing this basic mode of life. Indeed, Husserl's concept of the subject as transcendental Ego, according to Heidegger, tacitly "leaps over" the question of the mode of being (*Seinsart*) of this entity (as well as the world it lives in), and, furthermore, leaves the question unanswered as to whether this transcendental Ego is the same as or different from its "factical" mundane counterpart. In framing the subject as transcendental Ego, that is, as different from any other worldly entity, Husserl sees that there is a difference in being between the subject and other entities. Yet he does not exploit this insight. Heidegger's question of the being of the subject, as distinct from other *vorhanden* and *zuhanden* entities, is only possible on the basis of Husserl's discovery. In this sense, one can say, Heidegger is presenting not so much a critique of Husserl as an immanent modification of his insight.

Heidegger's critique aims not only at the concept of the transcendental Ego (its exact ontological status), but also at Husserl's methodological "device" or agent inextricably involved in analyzing it, namely, that of the "unparticipating observer." Of course, Heidegger was not so naive as to overlook the fact that in his own account the analyzing agent must somehow distance itself from its own entanglement in the world—since it is one and the same *Dasein* that now lives "naturally" and later philosophizes. However, he wants to undercut the theory–practice distinction altogether.[17] In this sense, it is Heidegger's contention that Husserl's concept of the "unparticipating observer" also *reflects* Husserl's theoretical or all too abstract methodological approach to the question of the subject. This might account for the fact that an explicit analysis of the philosophizing agent is missing in *Being and Time*. Thus, because of the "detached" stance of the "unparticipating observer," Husserl does not "see" the worldhood of the world and the human being's engagement in it in their *concrete* modes. Or, as Merleau-Ponty famously phrased it: the reduction cannot be completed, for if it were, we would be disembodied spirits. Even to pose this deliberate detachment as an ideal is Husserl's *proton pseudos*. This is not to say that Heidegger completely *rejects* the transcendental reduction—perhaps there is a reduction in Heidegger of a completely different kind.[18] Rather, what he questions is the problematic methodological intention implied in proposing an "unparticipating observer" in the course of the transcendental reduction.

The purpose of Husserl's unparticipating observer is to assume a standpoint, an "attitude," that enables a description of the world and man after an epoché from (a bracketing of) the "natural attitude." The natural attitude is Husserl's term for our unreflecting ("naive") everyday living in the world. To do philosophy, to Husserl, implies a break with this unreflecting lifestyle. Moreover, this change of attitude from the natural to the philosophical standpoint also by necessity entails a transcendental turn from the naively living human Ego, who takes the existence of the world for granted, *to* the Ego that *experiences* the world. As such, the transcendental Ego is the agent that "constitutes" the world in intentional acts. Thus, although the transcendental turn is that which *enables* Husserl first of all to open the view upon the "natural attitude," from reading the "Fundamental Reflection" in *Ideas I* one could argue that at the same time, and precisely with this methodological step, he closes the door to a genuine *recognition* of this sphere of the "natural attitude." Indeed, living in the lifeworld is discussed and then dismissed in a few pages. In short, if one needs to take a step away from the "natural attitude" in order to view it in the first place, one has taken the wrong approach from the very start. In this sense, Heidegger's insistence on the facticity of *Dasein* must also be conceived as a general attack on one of the fundamental principles of Husserl's phenomenology which, according to Heidegger, takes too abstract a stance to give a truly phenomenological account of the human being as existing in her lifeworld. As Landgrebe, Husserl's former assistant, rightly remarks, "in Heidegger's rejection of the 'unparticipating observer' lies an attack on one of Husserl's core thoughts,"[19] namely, his notion of philosophical theory. Such a stance accounts for an abstract view of subjectivity and cannot represent its true concretion. In other words, because of his "theorizing" presupposition, Husserl failed to really get "to the subject itself." The upshot of this critique is ultimately that the distinction between a "mundane" and transcendental subject is impossible, and it is ultimately a rejection of Husserl's conception of transcendental phenomenology as a theory that can only begin its work after breaking with the "natural attitude." Certainly, Heidegger considers his fundamental ontology in *Being and Time* a piece of transcendental phenomenology as well, insofar as, according to Gethmann, Heidegger's phrase "meaning of being" is shorthand for "the apriori *condition of the possibility* of entities *and* the possibility of relating to them. 'Meaning of Being' is, as it were, the term that succeeds Kant's aprioric synthesis" (1993, 11).[20] However, Heidegger criticizes Husserl's concept of transcendental philosophy as relying on the break with the natural attitude. In other words, the "natural attitude" is a phenomenologically impermissible construction.

While this critique is widely known, there are some hitherto unknown points that Husserl has made to oppose these objections and which further clarify both his method's status and its focus on subjectivity. I think that Husserl was aware of the critique (at least *this* critique) made by Heidegger, and some of the passages from the *Nachlass* will help to support this assessment. Yet, Husserl's arguments are at the same time nothing but a logical continuation of his mature concept of intentionality and constitution, and they highlight a certain aspect of his peculiar concept of "the transcendental." The "transcendental person" evoked here can be interpreted as a particular emphasis on the Ego's *concreteness,* which is not opposed to but further clarifies Husserl's concept of "transcendental." Hence, in the next section of this chapter I shall reconstruct this concept. In the third section I shall briefly summarize Heidegger's arguments against Husserl's position. Perhaps Husserl has gotten Heidegger entirely wrong in this critique, and perhaps the project of "fundamental ontology" has more to say about these issues than Husserl's somewhat reductionist and simplifying understanding of his pupil's intentions. In any case, the scholar interested in giving a just account—this author, that is—has to acknowledge that Husserl *did* understand Heidegger in this way, and that this understanding might have been a *mis*understanding or a different one from that which Heidegger would have preferred or deemed adequate. Yet, a reconstruction of Husserl's arguments cannot disregard the presuppositions that guided him, even though they may be ultimately skewed. Subjecting Husserl's understanding of Heidegger to a critique is a project for a different study.

The "Transcendental Person" as Concrete Unity of That Which Constitutes World

Husserl's analyses dealing with the problem of the human person start out from the methodological assumption that a certain *position* is required with regard to that which is to be described. Whereas one can analyze objects in the world "objectively" in the way the positive sciences, such as biology, physics, and even to a certain extent psychology, do, Husserl points out that this type of description speaks from a certain perspective or *attitude.* What makes this attitude "objectivistic" is that it talks about objects as existing in themselves, that is, without the "import" of the viewer's perspective. This objectivistic attitude, however, cannot grasp the essence of subjectivity because, to use Nagel's famous terminology, it will only give a "third-person perspective" account of what is and can be experienced only from a "first-person view." Indeed, subjectivity in its germane essence can only be grasped when performing a shift to the first-person perspective. Unlike the "objectivistic" or "naturalistic" attitude (Husserl's terms) that reconstructs causal relations between objects, the "personalistic attitude" views human activity and interaction with the world in its genuine mode of existing (analyzed under the heading of "motivation").[21] Opposed to the scientific "view from without" (the third-person perspective) is the "view from within," the first-person perspective, and a discipline doing justice to the *experience* of the human subject must be conceived of in this sense as a "science of the first-person perspective" that avoids the fundamental category mistake of framing this science with the basic categories of the natural sciences. This will suffice for a summary of Husserl's view of the fundamentality of "attitudes" and his insistence on taking a special standpoint—the personalistic attitude—in order to analyze subjectivity.[22]

Distinguishing the first- and third-person perspectives and explicitly shifting to the first-person perspective are not yet sufficient to establish phenomenology as a rigorous science. What makes phenomenology different from a psychological account? Phenomenology gives us access to the "view from within" and thereby thematizes the multitude of ways in which we experience the world subjectively. This "view from within," this experience *of* world, breaks down into many types of experience and attitudes. Phenomenology is certainly a "rigorous science of the subjective" in analyzing the different attitudes the subject takes toward the world. Phenomenology's main insight is that the world is in a certain way *given,* and phenomenology's task is to analyze and categorize these modes of givenness.[23] Yet, merely shifting to the first-person perspective from the previously occupied third-person perspective is not enough to establish a science. The question, then, is how to frame the first-person perspective adequately to make such a *scientific* account possible. Depending on this framing, a certain type of science will result. Since the personalistic attitude differs substantially from the naturalistic attitude, one can also expect that the epistemological character of a science of the personalistic attitude will be different from that of a science of the naturalistic attitude. Indeed, when Husserl insists that phenomenology—the science of the personalistic attitude—is a "*rigorous* science," he is intent on *carrying over* this rigor from the natural sciences, but with a fundamentally different sense of rigor. What makes the natural sciences rigorous is that they are exact and produce repeatable results under reproducible conditions and what they ascertain is *laws of nature.* However, their results pertain to *factual* entities in nature (plants, animals), and the laws they formulate are laws with respect to factually existing entities. The laws can only be formulated on the basis of things existing in nature. Phenomenology's rigor, on the other hand, consists of the fact that its results are not just lawful but *eidetic,* that is, true of *any* subject or consciousness and at *all times,* whether such a subject exists or not. Phenomenological laws are laws as well; they are not laws of ephemeral nature, but laws of "spirit." Phenomenology as eidetic science deals not with specifically human consciousness but with *consciousness as such,* regardless of whether it is human, animal, or divine.[24] Transcendental phenomenology is an *eidetic science of transcendental subjectivity.*

In order to clarify the special status of phenomenology as an eidetic science of consciousness as such, Husserl contrasts it with psychology as an *empirical* science of the first-person perspective. Given that Husserl claims to have founded a radically new science, he must clarify what distinguishes it from *traditional* psychology. The personalistic attitude is customarily occupied by the psychological observer, that is, the psychological scientist who has *not* made the shift from specifically *human* consciousness to analyzing *consciousness as such.* In Leibniz's terminology, psychology only establishes *verités de fait,* not *verités de raison.* For Husserl, therefore, the psychologist's methodological stance is inconsistent for several reasons. First, because it considers only the human psyche in its accidental disposition and not psychological states of affairs "as such," it leads into psychologism. A psychologistic account amounts to a relativism that, because it is merely describing factual consciousness, is relative to the specific character of the accidental human subject, and not normative or eidetic. Should the psychological states of affairs or, for example, the hard wiring of the human brain change, so could the structure of consciousness, which contradicts the essence of consciousness. Husserl's famous sentence "The tree burns but the essence of the tree does not burn" applies to the essence of consciousness as well. This critique can be traced right back to the *Prolegomena* of the *Logical Investigations* of 1900.

Following from this psychologistic mistake, psychology considers its position *fundamental* in order to describe the way the world is given to a subject, and in so doing disregards the fact that it is merely one way of describing among others—it wears epistemological "blinders." It takes its point of view as absolute, whereas it is merely relative to its specific perspective. In Husserl's terminology from the *Crisis,* psychology is indifferent to the "paradox of subjectivity," that the subject is an object *in* the world, and as such an object for disciplines of the third-person perspective such as psychology or biology, *and at the same time* a subject *for* the world, a subject which "has" in the first-person perspective the world as its correlate. Therefore, psychology, precisely by taking the seeming fundamentality of its position for granted, declares its stance to be absolute and continues to maintain on the epistemological level a problematic duality between two different accounts that is not plausible phenomenologically. Indeed, psychology does not even see, let alone attempt to solve, the paradox of the two accounts and their basis in the two fundamental perspectives.

The phenomenological reduction and the transcendental attitude attained therein purportedly solve these problems. First, the attitude of the phenomenologist is *neither* naturalistic *nor* even personalistic in a simple and straightforward way, in the sense of naturalism. It is "personalistic" in the purely formal sense of adhering to the first-person perspective; however, it goes beyond the perspective of the psychologist as it aims at an *eidetic science* of subjectivity as such. The phenomenological attitude is an attitude that commits to neither epistemological position naively and is hence neutral with regard to any absolute ("metaphysical") truth claim. Rather, it is an "absolute" stance in the sense of attempting a "bird's-eye view" that is aware of the partialities of other attitudes which *take themselves* as absolute without being *entitled to* (because they are merely relative).[25] It is not a stance *beyond* the distinction between first- and third-person perspective; it is firmly a first-person perspective in a non-naive ("critical") way, that is, by being *aware* of its particularity. It is this "metaphysical impartiality" that Husserl intends with the "unparticipating observer."

Thus, the *transcendental* (*phenomenological*) attitude shares with the personalistic attitude in principle the "view from within." What makes it transcendental, however, is the fact that it considers the "conditions of the possibility" of consciousness *as such* and not of a specifically human or any other (kind of) consciousness. For example, a condition of the possibility of having perception is to have a body not as a mere physical body (*Körper*) but as an organ of conscious activities (a *Leib*). Even a God could not have disembodied perception, because it belongs to the essence of "external perception" that things are given in adumbrations that are only revealed in bodily interaction with them. Furthermore, consciousness is framed in terms of *intentionality*.[26] This means that it does not consider only a certain *stratum* of consciousness, such as the soul (as opposed to, or "above," or somehow appended to the body), but conscious life *as such* which is intentional in every respect when experiencing a world. Indeed, stipulating a priori formal distinctions such as mind and body without looking at the "things themselves" is unphenomenological. The uninhibited and impartial look at our experience of world teaches us that the world is given in a manifold of ways and is given to different stands we take with regard to it. Yet, in spite of this multiplicity, we experience this world as a unity or totality. Thus, despite its multilayered experience, conscious life in general "constitutes" the world for itself through intentional acts.

Husserl's paradigm of intentionality in the framework of his mature theory of transcendental constitution indicates that the world as the totality of what consciousness experiences is "built up" from intentional acts. These acts can be conscious acts in the discrete sense of acts of thought (such as reflection or imagination), but also such "physical" actions as walking around a three-dimensional object, touching it, dealing with it in certain contexts. The latter are not merely physical movements (i.e., without conscious "Ego-involvement"), but are ways in which consciousness, necessarily as embodied subjectivity, experiences world, even "unconsciously." Thus, the famous analysis of perception is an example of an eidetic account of how subjectivity on a very elementary level ("passivity") constitutes three-dimensional objects. If we look at "experience of world," we do not at first find any kind of duality; we just have "givennesses" for consciousness. "Consciousness," however, is *equally* not some kind of abstract entity "tacked on" to the body, but is my subjective awareness of myself and the world on any given level, no matter whether I am dreaming, feeling pain or "physical" distress, or performing an intellectual activity such as doing phenomenology. Thus, viewed from the perspective of the phenomenologist, how we interact with other human beings emotionally and affectively, how we deal with them not only as physical bodies (*Körper*) but as "besouled" *lived*-bodies (*Leiber*), is a form of constitution. Even purely "intellectual" acts such as willing or desiring, when they are factually carried out, involve a "physical" component when my willing results in an action or when a certain emotion changes my countenance. *All* ways in which conscious life in an embodied manner experiences the world fall in principle under the rubric of constitutive analysis as an eidetic account of consciousness. In other words, intellectual acts are just one type of acts. *All* experiences, each in their own way and specific manner, contribute to constituting the world for a subject, not a specifically human subject but a *subject as such* that is necessarily constituted as having a lived-body, living in a world as the totality of givenness for consciousness.

From this perspective, it becomes clear that the term "transcendental person" is the most consistent translation of these matters into one concept, assuming that "person" is a term that formally designates a conscious being as such in its fullest dimensions, not just as psyche or as a psychological researcher reflecting solipsistically, but a conscious and responsible agent living in a social setting with others and with rules, living in a state of affects, emotions, and so on, and as essentially embodied. "Person" is the conscious being in the fullest account of constitution, that is, the highest level that "contains" all other, partial strata. Taking the transcendental Ego in its "fullest" dimensions means expanding "Ego" into "person." The term "person," moreover, implies a unity or identity, namely, that acts are carried out from a single identical pole. Whereas this conception of "person" is fairly standard (and deliberately so), employing the term "transcendental" in this context is original. By "transcendental," Husserl does not mean any categorical determinants or principles a priori; "transcendental" does have the meaning of "conditions of possibility," since the transcendental framing of the person comprises that which is essentially needed for a consciousness to experience a world, for example, a body as the organ of its acts. "Transcendental" indicates, furthermore, that the methodological tools used to analyze subjectivity in its genuine sense cannot be those of other "worldly" entities. Transcendental phenomenology is a genuine separate discipline that thematizes a region encapsulated within itself (*ein in sich abgeschlossenes Gebiet*), that of pure consciousness. This broad understanding of "the transcendental" opens up a wide array of phenomenological research into personhood, following Husserl's definition of phenomenology as "transcendental empiricism,"[27] that is, as a "positive," descriptive science of transcendental life. Hence, although this concept of transcendental is quite distinct from its traditional, Kantian heritage, what Husserl means by the term is quite straightforward when combined with "person." The transcendental person is the human being in its broadest, that is, intersubjective and genetic, dimensions as *viewed from the standpoint of the transcendental theory of constitution.* Of these dimensions, factical *human* life is but one instantiation of various potentialities; in other words, eidetic laws of transcendental life are valid, no matter if any life factually exists. The transcendental person is man in "fullness" or "concreteness" with *all* actualities and potentialities. It is not an entity different from that of the "mundane person"; rather, it is the same human being viewed from the standpoint of the rigorous scientific first-person perspective of transcendental phenomenology. One quotation will suffice to outline this concept:

> I, the human being in the world, living naturally only as this human being and finding myself in the personal attitude as this human person, am thus not *another* Ego which I find in the transcendental attitude. . . . The transcendental Ego as pole and substrate of its potential totality is, as it were, the transcendental person which is primally instituted [*urgestiftet*] through the phenomenological reduction. This Ego will be framed henceforth in terms of the universality of the concrete transcendental and takes on for itself the all-embracing life that brings into play all potentialities and that can then actualize all possible modes of self-actualization. It will become apparent that natural personal existence and life is only a particular form of life, a life that remains identical in view of all potential changes, i.e., [it is] the actual and possible unity of life, centered through the identical Ego-pole, which remains the same in all these potential changes. (Hua XXXIV, 200–201)

The transcendental person is thus not an abstract or "theoretical" moment of the human person, but the person viewed in its fullest "concretion." As such, it is just a different term from the more familiar concept of the monad that Husserl employs sporadically in 1910[28] and prominently in the 1920s (in Husserl's quite "un-terminological" manner of thinking). The "monad" as a term for the transcendental Ego entails (having recourse to Leibniz) that the Ego, as a sphere of experience of world, implies the world within it. It also, moreover, reminds us of the Leibnizian distinction between factual and eidetic truths, the latter of which phenomenology strives to ascertain as truths of the subject as person *in its concretion.* "Person" and "monad" highlight different aspects of one and the same structure, and it is especially its appeal to "concretion" that presumably leads Husserl to shift terminology to the "transcendental person."

To summarize: phenomenology is an eidetic science of transcendental subjectivity, that is, it formulates eidetic laws of consciousness as such. In this sense, it is not bound to a specific type of consciousness, for example, that of *Homo sapiens,* and thus avoids the problem of psychologism and skepticism. The full-fledged consideration of consciousness on all levels of constitution, however, renders the transcendental Ego actually more adequately a transcendental *"person."* Husserl intends a universal discipline of *experience-of,* and to counter the misunderstanding that this experience-of is merely a "mentalism" (a study of merely intellective acts), he employs the term "transcendental *person.*" The concept "person" grasps the entirety of what it means to be a conscious being on all of its levels, that is, in its fullest *concretion.* One possible explanation of why Husserl reverts to the term "person" in this context, apparently out of the blue, is that the concept of the monad does not sufficiently account for the "concretion" he feels he needs to emphasize in order to counter Heidegger's critique, to which we shall turn now.[29]

Heidegger's Critique: The Questionable Mode of Being (*Seinsweise*) of the Transcendental Ego

While Heidegger presumably did not know of Husserl's reflections with regard to the status of the transcendental Ego as transcendental person (these sparse comments are from the manuscripts of the 1930s), the thrust of Heidegger's critique is clear: it comes from the presumption of the fundamental role—or, for that matter, Husserl's disregard of the fundamental role—of human *existence* (*Dasein*) in determining the nature of the human being. It cannot be grasped in its unique and genuine character by considering it from an "abstract" stance such as

Husserl's alleged "unparticipating observer." This attitude fails to bring *Dasein* into view, not because it could not possibly *focus* on *Dasein* (for, as mentioned above, an analysis of *Dasein* also implies a "distanced" stance), but because it treats *Dasein* in an all too theoretical fashion. A theoretical consideration will only thematize consciousness, not *Dasein*. To restate Husserl's position, the establishment of the "unparticipating observer" goes hand in hand with his shift from the natural to the transcendental perspective, that is, from practice to theory. Although the "natural attitude" might be the first *for us* (*pròs hemâs*), it is not the first *by nature* (*te physei* or *kath' auto*), because it is a *product* of constitution and therefore cannot be a basis for philosophy as genetic, constitutive analysis. Hence the natural attitude as the *product* of constitution must be relinquished by the philosopher, who, instead, explains its coming-about. Husserl's point here is, with respect to Heidegger, that *Dasein* is a term for the subject *living in the natural attitude*.

For Heidegger the fundamental mode of *Dasein* is its factical existence, and this is also the methodological foundation from which to approach any analysis of its "essence," an essence which lies precisely in its existence as *caring* for its own being. And only through *existing* can *Dasein*'s being become known in a fundamental way. This does not mean, to Heidegger, that existence is opposed to doing theory. Rather, theory for Heidegger is a *derivative mode* of factical existence. Human *Dasein* as an essentially *understanding* entity is *always already* in the mode of understanding and interpreting itself. *Dasein* exists always already in the mode of self-interpretation (*Selbst-Auslegung*), and doing theory is just one, explicit, mode of life. We would misunderstand Heidegger's critique of Husserl's ideal of the "unparticipating observer" if we thought that such a stance is impossible for Heidegger. Rather, Heidegger's critical point is that to Husserl it is, in fact, an *ideal,* a model stance of phenomenological description. In a polemic phrase, presumably aimed at Husserl, Heidegger holds that one cannot gain any genuine knowledge of the things in our surroundings merely by "gaping" or "staring" at them as Husserl's distanced observer would supposedly do, but by being actively involved with their usage. Instead, the character of *Dasein* and its primary mode of knowledge is that it is "already-being-with" the world and its artifacts, and we do not need to *construct* an "intentional connection" between subject and object first. Heidegger writes:

> Initially, this already-being-in-the-world is not solely a rigid staring [*Begaffen*] at something merely objectively present [*vorhanden*]. Being-in-the-world, as taking care of things, is *taken in* by the world which it takes care of. (1996, 61)

This practical involvement is nothing other than *Dasein*'s specific way of being as being involved in dealing with these artifacts. The analyzing and the acting Ego cannot truly be separated; philosophical analysis is just a self-unfolding and making-explicit of everyday activity. To analyze subjectivity "theoretically," that is, by being at a distance from oneself by a "splitting of the Ego," as Husserl would have it, means to *lose* it in its primary mode of life. Thus, it should not be a transcendental observer that theoretically analyzes the subject's constitution of the world. Rather, it is a factically existing *Dasein* that not only understands the world "always already," but also has to analyze it in this factical mode in making this mode explicit to itself. But it is a making-explicit that it always already carries out in *doing* things. Husserl's doctrine of "constitution of world" by a transcendental subject leaps over the *factum* that this constitution is actually *carried out* by a factical *Dasein*. In his comments on the *Encyclopaedia Britannica* article, Heidegger writes, quite provocatively: "Transcendental constitution is a central *possibility* of the existence of the factical self" (Hua-Dok III/4, 146; italics added). What kind of possibility is this? It is significant that Heidegger does not even mention the term "transcendental subject" because it is, to him, not really a subject in the strict sense of the term. So in order to determine the meaning of "transcendental subject," one needs to address the *ontological status* of that being which constitutes the world:

> That which constitutes is not nothing, thus it is something and existing, yet not in the sense of the positive. The question of the mode of being of that which constitutes cannot be avoided. . . . What is the mode of being of this absolute Ego—in which sense is it the *same* as the factical Ego, in which sense is it *not* the same? (146)

One must be clear that these seemingly rhetorical questions contain a fundamental criticism, for one can easily spell out their consequence: if the absolute Ego *is* the same as the factical Ego, then the whole project of *transcendental* phenomenology with its ensuing theory of constitution essentially collapses, that is, it becomes obsolete as a discipline *divorced* from "factical" considerations; and if it is *not* the same, then this analysis can tell us nothing about the existence of factical *Dasein*. Husserl's *transcendental* phenomenology, in other words, cannot inform us about anything substantial concerning the status of that which is essentially a caring *Dasein* in the world, the human subject.[30] Performing the transcendental turn is simply the wrong way to attempt to get at *Dasein*. While Husserl wants to get to the subject, he in fact is turning away from it.

If, therefore, Heidegger suggests, the question regarding the being of the absolute, constituting Ego must be posed in order to determine its status—and that means its status vis-à-vis that of the "mundane" Ego— and if accordingly, as Heidegger further claims, transcendental constitution is merely a *possibility* of the factical Ego, then this amounts to saying that the transcendental Ego in fact cannot have the "ability" to constitute the world through its own "power." This is the case not only because its mode of being has not been clarified, for to clarify it would mean, to Heidegger, becoming aware of its problematic status. Moreover, if its status is merely that of a *"possibility"* of concrete *Dasein,* it cannot be treated as an "entity" of its own. It is merely a stance that *Dasein* takes at certain times. *Dasein* lives as understanding *already,* and making this understanding explicit (i.e., in theory) is only something that occurs occasionally. Finally, the attempt to clarify the status of the transcendental Ego is completely pointless. One cannot speak of it as an Ego proper precisely because this transcendental Ego as world-constituting *cannot in itself* be *part* of this world and hence cannot *be* in the sense of *existence.*[31] In Heidegger's reading, Husserl "stumbles" over his own claim that that which constitutes the world is in itself not a worldly "entity." Husserl's problem is that he does not address the question of the *being* of the transcendental, a question that poses itself naturally if one considers the world-constituting agency not itself an entity of this world. Had Husserl done so, he would have seen that "transcendental subjectivity" is merely an abstract stratum (defined in terms of "possibility") of concrete subjectivity rather than an entity of its own type that can be described by a reflective turn to immanence.[32] Husserl conceivably shied away from this question because he believed that by virtue of the epoché he could be neutral with regard to any metaphysical or ontological claims. Yet, given the plausibility of Heidegger's critical points, his unarticulated conclusion (in a letter to his teacher, after all, from which these quotations are taken) is that the very idea of a transcendental Ego is absurd—*if,* that is, one does not make the attempt to salvage this concept of the transcendental by somehow "linking" it to the factical Ego as *Dasein.* But already the dualism involved here is problematic. "Transcendental Ego" is a concept without any meaning *of its own,* but only "in conjunction" with the concrete factical existing Ego that *exists,* over against other entities with their own modes of being (as *zuhanden* artifacts and *vorhanden* things). In other words, "transcendental Ego" is, for Heidegger, merely an *abstract moment* of the full concept of *Dasein* as factically existing in a factical world. It is dependent on the factical subject rather than the other way around—whereas for Husserl, the concrete subject is "merely" a "mundanized" transcendental Ego.

This means, to Heidegger, that the question of the human being can only be tackled by addressing its concrete existence in the unity of her lived-experiences immersed in a world—*Dasein* is to be understood as essentially "being-in-the-world." In this sense, *Dasein* is a transcendental concept as well, but Heidegger does not endorse Husserl's equation of the transcendental attitude with *theory* as a distanced act of reflection. Husserl's transcendental approach does not really get us to the "things themselves," that is, to *Dasein*'s existence in the world and interaction with artifacts and tools, and to understanding oneself and one's own being *in* such interactions. An analysis of *Dasein* thus does not preclude it from being carried out in a transcendental register. This means, however, that Heidegger's hermeneutics of facticity does deal with the human being's existence in this very world of practical engagement and with (self-)understanding in and through this engagement. Although Heidegger would reject labeling his attempt as "anthropology," the main category of personhood and the traditional topics of anthropology are nevertheless present in his analysis of *Dasein*, categories ("existentials") such as understanding, language, affects, moods. "Anthropology," it will be recalled, was the name Husserl gave to Heidegger's project in *Being and Time*. Even though Heidegger criticizes traditional anthropology for passing over the question of human being's existence—and it is known how Heidegger shuns the traditional canon as a whole—Husserl is not entirely mistaken in reading *Being and Time* as a phenomenological anthropology, insofar as Heidegger does not reject the basic themes of traditional anthropology—in focusing on the concept of *life* as in Dilthey's hermeneutics or even in nodding to Husserl's insistence on the concept of intentionality.[33] Rather, what Heidegger rejects is their methodologically inadequate treatment (in not posing the question of *Dasein*'s being) as well as an implicit acceptance of a traditional philosophical canon that would place anthropology alongside other positive sciences dealing with the same "entity," such as sociology and biology. Rather, hermeneutics of facticity is *fundamental ontology of Dasein,* that is, this "discipline" (again, an inadequate term for Heidegger's intentions) is foundational for all other philosophical and scientific "disciplines." This means that the being of *Dasein* is fundamentally different from the being of other entities. Hence a fundamental ontology of *Dasein* that gives us the basics of an ontology of the human being. Moreover, a fundamental ontology of *Dasein* is destined to let us gain access to the more fundamental question of Being, which is the true goal of Heidegger's endeavor. However, this access will only be granted by reframing the question of the human being or the person by conceiving of it as *Da-Sein,* that is, as having an intrinsic connection to Being (*Sein*).

This is why division 1 of *Being and Time* (§§9–44) presents merely a "preparatory fundamental analysis of *Dasein*." For without an analysis of *Dasein,* preliminary as it may be, we cannot gain an appreciation of the question of Being. It is this ultimate aim that motivates Heidegger to reject framing the question of the human being in the traditional discipline of anthropology (and, as we know, to reject other traditional disciplines, such as ethics). Nevertheless, as Heidegger states in §10 of *Being and Time* ("The Delimitation of an Analytics of *Dasein* Against Anthropology, Psychology, and Biology"), he deems it a valid and necessary task to "determine positively ontologically the mode of being of the person" (Heidegger 1993, 48). It is in this context also that Husserl is mentioned alongside Scheler and Dilthey as failing to solve the problem of *Dasein*'s true being—although framing consciousness in terms of intentionality makes some headway in overcoming problematic traditional paradigms, for example, the metaphysics of "substance."[34] Thus, Husserl is correct in reading Heidegger's analytics of *Dasein* as also ultimately a consideration of the personhood of the person, however different from Husserl's transcendental framework, carried out from the standpoint of *Dasein*'s concrete, average quotidian existence and its own manner of doing "transcendental philosophy." Despite his more general interest in the question of *Being,* Heidegger's project of fundamental ontology presented in *Being and Time* can be termed a "pragmatic" (as opposed to "theoretical") phenomenology of concrete human existence. It is different from Husserl's transcendental phenomenology insofar as "transcendental" in Husserl implies performing a splitting of the Ego into transcendental and mundane parts and henceforth divorcing theory from practice, a move that Heidegger fundamentally criticizes. Thus, because Husserl completely ignores Heidegger's *Seinsfrage,* or disregards its importance, he can see in Heidegger's *Being and Time* merely a naive, pre-transcendental anthropology of *Dasein.* Yet, this impression is not completely unwarranted from reading division 1 of *Being and Time.*

Husserl's Critique of Heidegger's "Anthropologism" and Transcendental Phenomenology as "Philosophically Genuine Anthropology"

While the reader of Husserl's manuscripts dealing with Heidegger (to which we shall turn now) can see that Husserl acknowledges Heidegger's critique to a certain extent—at least the one mentioned in the previous section—Husserl in turn touches on a weak (or at least dark) spot in Heidegger. Husserl might have been blind to many aspects of Heidegger's approach, but he saw very clearly that Heidegger's critique of the transcendental Ego and the concomitant theory of transcendental constitution amount to a critique of Husserl's ideal of philosophy as "rigorous science," that is, as eidetic science of transcendental subjectivity. To Heidegger, the actual phenomenological analysis cannot be carried out by an unparticipating observer who stipulates eidetic truths, but must and can only be performed by factical *Dasein* itself in its individual concrete existing and its always already occurring self-interpretation. In other words, an "eidetics" of the human subject understood primarily as *transcendental* subject is absurd, not because such an eidetics is impossible, but because such an eidetics of *transcendental* subjectivity cannot let us gain insight into the fundamental mode of subjectivity, factical existence. Such a project is, to Heidegger, fundamentally flawed in wanting to do justice phenomenologically to human *Dasein*. Rigorous, that is, eidetic science is pointless with regard to an entity whose *essence* (*eidos*) is to *exist*. This is one reason why Heidegger insists in §7 of *Being and Time* that the phenomenological method has to take its cue from the specific topic in question, rather than approaching an entity with a methodological presupposition that does not do justice to this entity.[35] It does not do justice to *Dasein* because *Dasein*'s mode of being is fundamentally different from that of other entities. An eidetics can hence only be "existential," not categorical, which is to say, it can retain its rigor, but not in the sense of "naive eidetics." Husserl thought, in turn, that a project of phenomenology as an eidetic discipline, that is, a rigorous science, means that it is either rigorous science or else mere *Weltanschauung*, that is, an articulation of human being's view of the world, a mere description without normative claims. Husserl understood Heidegger's critique of the questionable mode of being of the transcendental Ego and the method of doing this as going against Husserl's even more fundamental claim that philosophy is a rigorous science. To Husserl, rejecting this fundamental tenet ultimately accounts for the *crisis* of European sciences in general. This makes it understandable why, to Husserl, giving up the connection between science and philosophy has such fatal consequences. Hence, it will come as no surprise that this is the first point where Husserl attacks Heidegger.

Thus, Husserl asks, what is the theoretical status of Heidegger's analyses of factical *Dasein*? More generally, what is Heidegger's stance concerning theory or science? Heidegger, too, claims a certain philosophical validity to his analyses and not just a personal truth pertaining to one's own private *Dasein*. In other words, the emphasis on *Dasein*'s facticity cannot mean to Heidegger that his results are arbitrary or "merely subjective." It is here that Husserl launches his counter-critique. In spite of Heidegger's explicit rejection of philosophy's "scientificity" and in spite of *Being and Time*'s strong emphasis on a certain methodological solipsism based on the specific mineness (*Jemeinigkeit*) of *Dasein,* Heidegger does claim a certain generality, or in Husserl's words, attempts to establish "rational" and "general human truths" regarding *Dasein*'s existence. No matter how one defines "rationality" or "truth," any theory that calls itself philosophical (and does not merely claim biographical or "subjective" truth) aims at "*the* truth" or at least has it in its purview as a regulative idea. In this sense, Heidegger's analyses must inevitably *presuppose* a "theoretical" stance as well. An analytics of *Dasein,* even in its focus on *Dasein*'s facticity, cannot preclude a "scientific," that is, rational, intersubjectively consensual account that *in some way or another* requires a theoretical stance. It is not that Heidegger *does not* take such a stance; of course he does, as we have seen, and he knows this. Husserl's point is that this theoretical stance *necessarily entails* the claim to rationality and scientificity. The opposition is not between the theoretical Husserl and the atheoretical Heidegger: Husserl maintains that doing theory *implies* the very idea of rationality and scientificity. Husserl writes of Heidegger:

> The philosopher doing anthropology believes that he can be a philosopher and in any case aims at truths, i.e., eidetic truths, at the least general human truths, whose nexus is a theoretical nexus that has its origin in a theoretical interest. This interest could be a mere passing one, it could be motivated practically, ethically, religiously, in the hope of bettering human beings by these insights, to spare them from intellectualistic or rationalistic aberrations, etc. Yet, if one can identify *science* and *rationalism,* then every anthropology, no matter how it is characterized and no matter how it may thematize human "existence," is equally rationalism. (Hua XXXIV, 258)

As Husserl clearly saw—and as has been pointed out time and again by scholars[36]—*Being and Time* notoriously excludes the question of that *Dasein* which describes factical *Dasein:* the description cannot be other than from a "theoretical" standpoint and the results of its analyses cannot but be "rational," that is, generally true findings (whether or not they are eidetic, i.e., *verités de raison*). According to Husserl, the seeming omission of the Ego of the philosopher or her "theoretical attitude" accounts for Heidegger's rejection of the necessarily scientific character of philosophy. To Husserl, statements such as "*Dasein*'s being is distinguished by the fact that, in its very Being, that Being is an *issue* for it" are in principle not different from "every object in three-dimensional space gives itself in adumbrations," even though the subject matters to which these statements pertain might be fundamentally different. Nevertheless, making such statements is *nolens volens* a scientific endeavor. To Husserl, the argument against philosophy as science (not just rigorous science!) amounts to a skeptical argument which criticizes general truth and in so doing itself claims general truth. Moreover, Heidegger's emphasis on "doing" rather than "theorizing" cannot be a critique of the methodological paradigm of theory because such a critique must itself assume a "theoretical," "reflective" perspective. Although this has long been noticed by critics of *Being and Time,* it is important to point out that Husserl too reconstructs Heidegger's rejection of philosophy as science from this perspective. In the end, as has been shown above, Husserl was flogging a dead horse by insisting on the unacknowledged "theoretical status" of Heidegger's project. However, it is not easy to see from one's first readings of *Being and Time* what Heidegger's view of the status of theory is. Indeed, it requires a great deal of interpretation to see what he has in mind when he deliberately *brackets* the question of the philosophizing *Dasein.*

Next, Husserl raises the issue of the alleged fundamentality of *Dasein* in its factical existence. What exactly legitimizes Heidegger's claim that *Dasein*'s life in its factical being-in-the-world is in fact the most fundamental level? In other words, what does it mean to be a fundamental level? Does it mean that it cannot be transcended or "penetrated" in a *transcendental* questioning regarding its origin, that is, the conditions of its possibility? And even if this factical level is the most fundamental, it is still not self-evident that it should be *privileged* over other dimensions of meaning. To Husserl, acknowledging that concrete existence is a fundamental stratum does not *prohibit* questioning its origin.[37] In other words, factical existence might be *fundamental* in the sense of a basis of our everyday life, but this is not to say that it is an *absolute* ground upon which everything is relative. What Husserl has in mind is, of course, the depth dimension of the natural attitude that can only be accessed by a *genetic* analysis. Fundamentality and absoluteness are not automatically coextensive, as Heidegger seems to assume. Declaring the level of *Dasein* as fundamental means, to Husserl, rejecting the transcendental question concerning the *constitution* of *Dasein* that can only be clarified in a *genetic* inquiry. With respect to Heidegger's claim to the fundamentality of the fundamental sphere of *Dasein*'s life, Husserl remarks:

> The radical question is now whether this natural ground of judgment (the ground that is presupposed by concrete life in all its activities and thus also theoretical life in which the sciences of this primal ground, the positive sciences, originate) is indeed a primal basis with regard to which one can no more inquire into the grounds of its validity, or

whether it has, as we shall see, an origin which is, to be sure, deeply concealed but which can be revealed, a most complicated foundation systematically to be analyzed, a constantly living but always concealed foundation, as absolute life and absolutely concrete being of that subjectivity which we ourselves are. (Hua XXXI, 258–59)

"Anthropologism" is Husserl's term for that kind of inquiry which considers this "factical ground" as absolute. It is a "false philosophy by absolutizing a positivistic world" (259),[38] "positivistic world" being shorthand for "the world of the natural attitude." The acknowledged fundamentality of concrete existence, which Husserl would not reject, does not preclude the claim that this life has a deeper level, which is hidden from this life *because* this life is merely living in the "natural attitude." The natural attitude is characterized by being "intentionally infatuated" (*verschossen*) with things in the world. Life in the natural attitude is blind to intentional achievements that make experience of world possible, in other words, to the transcendental dimension. All being is relative upon being experienced; hence the only absolute upon which everything is relative is "transcendental consciousness." For Husserl, Heidegger's fundamental ontology of *Dasein* amounts to a *philosophy of or in the natural attitude,* that is, a "naive" philosophy, just like every philosophy that does not perform the phenomenological reduction. This critique of Heidegger has to do only in part with the fact that factical existence is first and foremost active and not contemplative. Certainly there can be, Husserl maintains, contemplation in the natural attitude; nevertheless, the activities of the "natural attitude" and the sciences arising on its basis are by definition "positive," that is, they take place on the basis of the natural attitude that takes the existence of the world for granted. To Husserl, however, this basis is itself something that is *constituted,* and it can only become explicit through a radical *break* with the natural attitude. One could even say, with Husserl, that the fact that this factical life does not *know* of its deeper, constituting level is precisely the "proof" that there *is* such a deeper level. It is only accessible through a *break* with the traditional way of seeing things; this was the whole point about the natural attitude's "naïveté," as discussed in chapter 1. Nothing is "wrong" with the natural attitude; a problem arises, however, when the *philosopher*—not the human person *living* in the natural attitude—absolutizes it. This is why for Husserl, doing philosophy requires a *break* with the natural attitude, and the only place the philosopher[39] can "go" after leaving the natural attitude is the transcendental sphere. For Husserl, doing *philosophical theory* can only mean doing transcendental philosophy. And doing transcendental philosophy means *turning away* from the natural attitude, a break which Heidegger did not accept. From Heidegger's point of view, Husserl completely overlooked the fact that Heidegger already tacitly stands in the realm of the philosophical dimension opened up by Husserl, since Heidegger clearly took over, if in a modified fashion, fundamental phenomenological paradigms such as intentionality (as *already being-with* entities). Heidegger's claim, however, is that doing philosophical theory is but a radicalization of a "reflective" tendency inherent in *Dasein*'s everyday life, rather than an inherently "unnatural" or "artificial" performance.

While Husserl, oriented to the "things themselves," in principle applauds the approach from concreteness and fact-oriented analysis, this does not mean to him that this sphere, which we find ourselves in and live in first and foremost, is an absolute sphere upon which everything would be relative. After all, Heidegger's own analysis presupposes a theoretical attitude from which to describe even this concrete everydayness. How to conceive of this concreteness, which both sought, is certainly an open question. It may well be that Heidegger and Husserl mean different things by this category. More precisely, Husserl feels deeply misunderstood in assuming that the stance of the "unparticipating observer," who gives a description of how an embodied consciousness constitutes world, only describes this constitution in terms of *theoretical* or *intellective* acts. The unparticipating observer does not merely, or even primarily, describe an unparticipating *agent.* Here we can recall Husserl's concept of the transcendental person: only the person viewed in this way as experiencing world in a manifold of acts and activities and from the unity of its Ego-pole can account for the subject's life in a world. The totality of experience and its corresponding phenomena are grasped by the term "transcendental constitution." This constitution is not a mere *possibility* of the factical Ego, but that which the Ego "always already" does in *all* of its factical, practical, willing, thinking, and so on activities, including the philosophical. This constituting activity is not a rigid structure, but a continuing process in the transcendental history of self-enworlding subjectivity. Apart from Husserl insisting on the importance of the "unparticipating observer," and thus his methodology, Husserl's abbreviated remarks can also be construed as indicating the importance of a genetic analysis in the constitution of something like the natural attitude or everyday life, a dimension that is indeed missing in *Being and Time.* The genetic sphere, however, only reveals itself when we break with the natural attitude and assume the transcendental stance that for the first time opens up the sphere of constitution. Furthermore, transcendental constitution is not merely a potential, abstract moment of the Ego that would depend on its "actualization" by factical existence; on the contrary, factical existence is the concrete "actualization" of the transcendental as the totality of Egoic potentialities. Speaking of Heidegger, Husserl writes:

> Is it not precisely the method of "classical" phenomenology, by opening up pure conscious life primarily in its most general forms and then progressing to the constitutive problems, that it also opened the way towards a reflection of the world which views any scientific world constitutively in its concrete relation to constituting subjectivity? Is not *practical* subjectivity also constituting, was it ever the intention of my phenomenology merely to reveal the nature of natural science constitutively? When one starts out, as I do, by explicating a natural concept of the world in a transcendental-aesthetical manner, then this signifies, as I still believe despite Heidegger, a necessary and a priori first system of tasks, that I have chosen the method of abstractive theoretical consideration only differently, but in a certain sense I have chosen it more primitively than Heidegger. (Hua XXXIV, 260)

Thus, the concept of the transcendental person as that which constitutes the world in *all* forms of experience is intended to counter the critique that the transcendental Ego is too abstract a concept to grasp the true personhood of the person. Husserl feels that Heidegger wrongly understands transcendental consciousness as a mere transcendental *Ego* and not what it truly is, the transcendental person. Yet, framing the transcendental person as that which constitutes in *all* manners of intentionality also has consequences for Husserl's own conception of the unparticipating observer. This observer might be "only" theoretically interested as well, but this theoretical work is equally constituting and as such carries out a "continuing constitution"[40] of the world itself in terms of covering new ground in phenomenological analysis. In terms of constitution, there is no difference between theory and practice—since all acts constitute—and any such distinction, like that of mind and body, is dogmatic. Husserl's late realization that this observer constitutes as well must be conceived as a clear concession to Heidegger's critique. However, Husserl is not willing to give up the idea of a break with the natural attitude in order to cross the threshold into phenomenology.

These points by Husserl are meant as a counter-critique to Heidegger's assertion that factical existence is the absolute sphere whose transcendental origin cannot be questioned. The "philosophically true anthropology" that Husserl proposes in the form of his transcendental phenomenology—presumably the type of phenomenological theory he anticipated Heidegger was to carry out—is an account of the transcendental which is, rightly understood, the absolute of philosophy. As absolute, it still has the general character of "consciousness" as something that needs theoretical reflection in order to describe it. For only this view yields the perspective upon the universe of subjectivity's concrete potentialities that can only be "thought up" in reflection, through eidetic variation. This overarching "absolute" essentially comprises the transcendental person as that which constitutes the world in all of its actualities and potentialities *and* the world as the necessary correlate of this constant process of constitution.[41] Only in this universal consideration can one claim to have reached true concreteness, in contrast to which the purely "mundane," factical existence of *Dasein* is but an abstract, that is, *limited* stratum. It is abstract because it absolutizes factical existence—in Husserl's terms, the natural attitude—without seeing that a different attitude or perspective on the world is also possible, no matter how one wants to characterize this account, as "theory," contemplation, unparticipating observation, or otherwise. In a "hermeneutical" twist, one could rephrase Husserl's point as insisting that one can only reach true concreteness when naive concretion has been *understood* from a different standpoint. Being naive equals remaining in an abstract position; hence:

> Natural *Dasein* in the synthetic achievement of the formerly concealed . . . life turns out to be an abstract stratum in the concretion of transcendental subjectivity. Natural life becomes understood [i.e., after the transcendental turn] as a limited form in which the Ego actualizes its potentialities in pre-formed habitualities and in this way carries through an Egoic *Dasein* . . . which holds a higher, richer manifold of possibilities out of consideration . . . (Hua XXXIV, 198)[42]

In other words, where no real case can be made for why the factical foundation should be fundamental in an absolute sense, why (in other words) it could not be subjected to a *constitutive* analysis, the project of "fundamental ontology" is necessarily flawed. Husserl argues that phenomenology can only be carried out as "transcendental." This means, to him, making a radical turn to subjective experience (more precisely, subjective experience as such) that, in turn, can only be achieved by a break with the natural attitude. Husserl believed that Heidegger's sketch of a hermeneutics of facticity was just an account of factical *Dasein* in the natural attitude (the first criticism discussed). Furthermore, Husserl questions the "fundamental" ground of the natural attitude as an "absolute" basis. What he merely hints at here is his draft of genetic phenomenology that reconstructs the natural attitude we currently live in as a product of genetic layers of constitution (the second criticism discussed).[43] It should be clear from the previous section that the first criticism is unfair to Heidegger's fundamental ontology of *Dasein*. Just because Heidegger omits an explicit analysis of the philosophizing agent does not mean that he has no position on the matter. As the last quotation from Husserl shows, however, doing theory as self-explication of already-present self-understanding is simply not enough. For Husserl, one needs to become a "complete theoretician" in order to perform an eidetic variation of all "Egoic possibilities," which cannot become available without reflection. But Heidegger's point seems to be that this performance is itself the realization of such a possibility, a possibility of the "factical self." To Husserl, this last point may well be true, but trivially so, since factical and transcendental Ego are ultimately identical. And this second criticism—the absence of the genetic dimension—does point to a dimension that at least seems to be absent in *Being and Time*. Whether such a genetic account could be supplied in the framework of *Being and Time*'s fundamental ontology is another, open question.

Conclusion

In conclusion, Husserl's insistence on the concreteness of the transcendental Ego as transcendental person *as well as* his insistence on the concreteness of the phenomenological analysis of transcendental constitution in these late texts is indeed peculiar, especially since some of these statements are made in contexts where Husserl explicitly addresses Heidegger. The reading presented here is intended to highlight a certain aspect of Husserl's theory, and the claim is that Husserl's insistence on this aspect is motivated by Heidegger's critique. Husserl's critique of Heidegger results partly from Husserl's clear misunderstanding of Heidegger's intentions. Still, Husserl's critique articulates his serious concern regarding the lack of a genetic dimension in Heidegger's sketch. An analysis of *Dasein,* because it seems to be missing a "depth dimension," cannot give us a notion of human subjectivity's concretion, although this is what Heidegger seems to want in his insistence on "facticity" and approach from "quotidianity" (*Alltäglichkeit*). At the same time, the concept of the transcendental person is but a continuation of Husserl's concept of constitution which is already present in Husserl's earlier analyses of personhood, although Husserl did not employ this terminology at this early stage. Although Husserl's analyses of the person do describe, for example, the person's bodily involvement in her activities, and thereby reach a very high level of "concretion," Husserl was still under the impression that his (mostly unpublished) analyses were not convincing enough given the popularity of Heidegger's existential philosophy. Heidegger's critique merely presses Husserl to reframe his already operative concepts. The persistence with which Husserl presents this claim for concreteness shows that he is intent on salvaging his approach from the attack on his phenomenology launched so forcefully by his former favorite, and undoubtedly most talented, pupil. It is clear that this is an attack to be taken seriously, although Husserl seems to dismiss it rather lightly, which conceals the deeper and more problematic issues, the difficulty of which I have tried to indicate.

To Husserl, Heidegger merely stands at the peak of what he calls the "fashionable philosophy of existence" (Hua XXXIV, 257) which has abandoned the ideal of rigorous philosophical inquiry as well as the transcendental turn and indulges in factical, finite existence. But this criticism—although it sounds rather like the typical complaint of the older generation against the thoughtlessness of the newer—stands for fundamental issues that Husserl has with Heidegger's project of fundamental ontology. The problem is precisely the question of the *foundation* that Heidegger seems to take too lightly in Husserl's view. This is perhaps Husserl's strongest case in point against Heidegger: because of its unjustified claim to an absolute status, fundamental ontology cannot be transcendental philosophy, and if it cannot be transcendental, then it cannot have the status of rigorous science. This is why Heidegger's philosophy cannot be a valid anthropology (as it could have been had it been manageably contained), but is instead merely a problematic "anthropologism." It could have been a veritable phenomenological anthropology, Husserl believed, if it had remained within the framework of constitutive phenomenology. A phenomenology of the human person could have had a valid place as part of Husserl's sketch of an ontology of the lifeworld, and not as a project so radically *divorced* from Husserl's. However, by absolutizing the sphere of *Dasein,* Husserl thought that Heidegger—who did not mince his words in his critique of the "old man"—made a radical break with his teacher and turned against the latter's project—more radical than it should have been, to judge from Heidegger's own intentions. Articulating Husserl's standpoint, Alweiss correctly asserts that *Being and Time* "could have succeeded in its departure from Husserl only by returning to Husserl and by acknowledging its indebtedness" (Alweiss 2003, 166). So the conflict between the generations worked both ways.

In order to pose and answer the question of man, Husserl suggests, one needs an anthropology which has to proceed in a transcendental register and as an eidetic science, concretely as a constitutive, genetic analysis of the correlation of consciousness and world. Any claim to the fundamentality of *Dasein* blocks the way to subjectivity's concreteness which lies not in a given "facticity" but in a "transcendental concreteness," which in turn understands a given facticity, even that of doing philosophy, as a realized possibility of the universe of Egoic, transcendental potentialities.[44] For Heidegger, in turn, Husserl took the right path in framing subjectivity in terms of intentionality, but stopped short at a premature stage—consciousness—and did not break through to the question of the *being* of consciousness. But Heidegger's step beyond meant breaking with the very paradigm of consciousness and its firm link to "unparticipating theory," a move which Heidegger was very well aware of. Yet, Heidegger wanted not to disregard the question of the human being, but to free it from its confined concentration on the notion of *consciousness*. To be fair to Husserl, one has to insist that he *did* articulate the human being's "practical, valuing, willing," and so on activity, but he continued to articulate his philosophy in what sounded like a language of mentalism. Heidegger wanted not to dismiss Husserl, but to bring him into his own. It is this move that Husserl could not comprehend.

Regarding the question of the person: in Husserl's eyes, Heidegger took his point of departure on much too high a level in trying to frame subjectivity's concreteness in terms of its factical fundamentality. The whole constitutive problematic after Husserl's genetic turn *precedes* an analysis of factical subjective life, which Husserl took to be a "static" analysis. In his hermeneutics of facticity, Heidegger has tried to construct a house without first laying the foundations, and the foundations, to Husserl, could only lie in absolute, world-constituting consciousness. Although Husserl in turn might have been all too quick in criticizing Heidegger as simply going with the flow of the zeitgeist, he did have a keen sense of Heidegger's thought as breaking with fundamental principles of his thought, which, in turn, Heidegger merely wanted to bring to full fruition rather than abandon altogether—although at times his rhetoric might have sounded otherwise. To Husserl, the question of personhood has to be further refined, and that means expanding constitutive analysis into a genetic, intersubjective account of how the lifeworld is built up through constitutive strata. The analysis of the "natural attitude" is only the last word in a long story. To Heidegger, such an analysis of *Dasein* was not the last word either; indeed, one can more adequately call it "the first word," since the "fundamental ontology" of *Dasein* was only a preliminary stage in a continuing project that was dedicated to thematizing the Being of the entities. Ultimately, therefore, the topic of personhood had only a passing relevance for Heidegger's project as a whole. The question whether Husserl rightly understood Heidegger's greater intentions must be left undecided here. There can be no doubt, however, that

Husserl had a clear sense of the thrust of Heidegger's critique as well as of its potentially devastating consequences for his transcendental phenomenology. It was this critique that Husserl tried to counter with the tools and methods available to him and which culminated in the concept of the "transcendental person." It was these "tools and methods" that Heidegger was no longer willing to use, though he was indebted to his teacher's phenomenology in almost every respect. Yet, one can see clearly how both Husserl and Heidegger took their departures, distinct as they may be, from the person living in the natural attitude or *Dasein*'s average everydayness.

Venturing a Glimpse into the Outlines of the System

After discussing the natural attitude, the reduction, the lifeworld, and the concept of subjectivity, one can conclude that the most dominant elements of Husserl's mature transcendental phenomenology have been sufficiently discussed, problematized, and defended, even against a critique as powerful as Heidegger's. The previous discussion will not have "solved" the lingering problems, but will at least—hopefully—give the reader an idea of the impressive scope of Husserl's wide-ranging thought. Not trying artificially to solve these issues and problems and then to move on, it should become clear that Husserl's idea of phenomenology as a "working philosophy" (*Arbeitsphilosophie*) is to be taken seriously, in that the issues discussed here are more or less titles for actual "construction sites" where Husserl continued to revise, reassess, refine, and expand his theories. Husserl himself did not think he sufficiently clarified matters so as to have solved them once and for all, but that is no fundamental critique of the theories themselves and the ideas expressed therein. To the contrary, they were left as "open construction sites" whose absolute solution was an ideal lying in infinity, just as phenomenology as a finished system was an infinitely improveable task. Yet Husserl believed that he had laid the ground stock and foundation, whence at least the hope of being on the trajectory of making headway was not in vain.

Yet, despite these open problems, Husserl did venture glimpses into the system of phenomenology once completed. Such glimpses must be taken with a grain of salt, however; they cannot be taken as part of "classical" phenomenology, which analyzes intentional acts and their contents (in a static, genetic, intersubjective register). Instead, they are explicitly considered "speculation" or "construction" by Husserl, that is, reflections that need not be able to be "cashed in" by the "small change" of concrete analyses, as one of Husserl's favorite metaphors would have it. At times, Husserl allowed himself to deal in "large bills" to glimpse beyond "daily business." How the outlines of such a system would look is the topic of the next chapter. That chapter concludes this first part, which dealt entirely with Husserl and his transcendental phenomenology.

Dialectics of the Absolute: The Systematics of the Phenomenological System in Husserl's Last Period

Introduction: Broaching the Issue of Systematicity

This chapter's title indicates three central concepts: dialectics, the absolute, and system. It is especially the notion of system that indicates the goal of this chapter: namely, to bring together these three notions in a systematic coherence in order to elucidate the character of Husserl's late philosophy. Such a task seems to call for a "speculative" and not a phenomenological treatment—at least in the common usage of the term "phenomenological," which seems to preclude freestyle speculation. For this reason, it might seem rather futile to attempt to apply these notions to Husserl's phenomenology. Husserl's initial reservations towards systematic philosophy are well known and have often been discussed (and shall not be repeated here). They have led people to believe that Husserl has nothing to say on these matters. As I shall show in this chapter, this general image of Husserl is quite skewed. Husserl not only had systematic ambitions, but also carried out quite extensive and intricate reflections on the systematicity of his mature transcendental phenomenology. These will be the topic of this chapter, which concludes part 1 of this book.

Indeed, there are numerous motives for Husserl's later move towards a decisive and explicit "will to a system." This will is manifested in his many attempts at a systematic outline or sketch of his system—both published and unpublished—and in many letters to friends and colleagues. That Husserl never published a "system of phenomenology" is not to say that such systematic ideas are not present in his late texts. Given his earlier reservations, why did he even desire to forge a "system of phenomenology"? One dominant motive is certainly his perceived competition with the system builders of his time, especially the neo-Kantians, which led him to attempt to formulate and work out his phenomenological system in his mature years. Thus, one obvious external reason was clearly his wish to establish phenomenology as a system alongside other competing options.

Yet there must also be immanent reasons for this effort—and also for his great distress in failing to achieve what he had set out to do. In his last years, when he realized he would not be able to complete his task (or even if completed, would not be able to publish it in Nazi Germany), he at least wanted to reflect this systematic scope in his manuscripts in order to leave to his phenomenological successors a useful source of material in the form of unpublished texts.[1] Hence, the most obvious *internal* reason was the wish to leave the bulk of his work, which lay in the infamous 40,000 unpublished manuscript pages, behind in a systematic manner, not just as a heap of disorderly scribblings. As we now know through the nearing completion of the *Husserliana,* this wish was more than just a "last will," but Husserl's *Nachlass* represents a *systematic approach and a systematic research agenda* called phenomenology, although this systematicity might not be obvious at first sight.[2]

But the internal systematics of his phenomenology was to have a most significant bearing on the movement he started. Indeed, as an infinite task, the phenomenological movement *itself* was supposed to carry out and in this process constitute the system of phenomenology as the decisive figure in the history of Western philosophy. Phenomenology itself, this was Husserl's hope, was, as a unified school, the completion of the system in its generational nexus, which had been primally instituted by Husserl himself, just as other schools of thought had been primally instituted by philosophical individuals in the history of Western philosophy (Plato, Descartes, Kant). Husserl had laid the unquestioned ground, fixated once and for all, and already in his lifetime Husserl began "farming out" different areas of his constitutive phenomenology to his pupils to till the soil of regions he simply could not till (to speak in a metaphor Husserl appreciated) due to his own finite existence. This way, Husserl speculated, the system of phenomenology would be carried out in future generations on the basis of the foundations laid by him.

If a speculation on this sort of speculation on Husserl's part may be permitted, it is quite likely that the history of the phenomenological movement would have evolved very differently had Husserl managed to produce a minimally satisfactory systematic sketch of "the system of phenomenology" in broad strokes; a systematic sketch that could have been read and handed down as a "manifesto" to which one could "sign on." We know now that the opposite happened, that phenomenology split apart as a movement already well before Husserl's death. But since the tides of postmodernism have washed over us, and the Heidegger-mania, which dominated "continental" philosophy in the last decades, has also died down, it is perhaps possible to restart the strain of a tradition that was simply interrupted—not least by the upheavals and catastrophes of the twentieth century—and carry on a legacy that lay latent in Husserl's unpublished texts; a legacy which is beginning to flourish in novel reception.

A conversation about the relevance of phenomenology in our times would probably have to start out with Husserl's notion of phenomenology as "first philosophy," as the grounding discipline for all other sciences. This would demonstrate how phenomenology is "always already" engaged with other sciences. Here, however, the cue shall be taken "from the other end," as it were, namely from the systematic scope of phenomenology *itself*, irrespective of the issue of phenomenology being a founding discipline for other disciplines. A full consideration and appreciation of Husserlian phenomenology would have to, certainly, pursue this two-pronged approach, that is, of spelling out the systematics of transcendental phenomenology, on the one hand, and taking phenomenology as the self-encapsulated discipline Husserl always held it to be—which will be the sole focus of this chapter. On the other hand, however, phenomenology as the founding discipline for all other sciences is the other aspect of phenomenology that was perhaps almost equally important to Husserl. Finally, a full assessment of Husserlian phenomenology would have to reflect on the *tension* between these two prongs of the Husserlian project. Hence, the systematic locus of these reflections on the system of phenomenology itself in the present chapter exists alongside that of placing phenomenology in relation to the "mundane" sciences. The question as to the system of phenomenology is thus (and ironically) not the whole story.[3] The whole story is phenomenology's role within the concert of the other sciences—and ultimately in the midst of culture writ large. The question of phenomenology as a possible philosophy of culture, or complementing the latter, will be broached in chapters 9 and 12. For the "real" domain of phenomenology lay in the sphere of the transcendental constituting the world, not the world itself as constituted—or rather, both may not be separated.

But let us return to the "immanent" question as to the systematicity of the phenomenological system. As mentioned, Husserl unsuccessfully attempted several times to work out this system, roughly between 1920 and the time of his death, though he indicates in his correspondence that he wanted to form his phenomenology in a "systematic fashion" already much earlier. Moreover, the development of the phenomenological movement—a term coined by Husserl himself with this very intention of establishing a "systematic" (read: "scientific") philosophy—after his death can be interpreted as a refusal to carry out his master plan, insofar as it meant that each phenomenological scientist would have to participate in this endless task. Yet even given these factual obstacles which left the system unfinished, we cannot simply pass over this "will to a system," as seems to be the tendency in a great deal of Husserl scholarship today.[4] To neglect this "systematic Husserl" is to do an injustice to Husserl's innermost intentions. If the will to a system is so apparent—as is the case in the late Husserl—the duty of an honest interpreter is to at least attempt to understand what Husserl had in mind, even if such an attempt leads to the consequence of having to question this systematic conception, precisely for the same reasons that guided Husserl's initial formulation of this system. But much in such a rejection of Husserl's systematic ambition depends on what "system" is to mean in conjunction with his transcendental phenomenology.

It is one fundamental insight of the late Husserl that phenomenology cannot do without a systematic conception serving as a guiding clue for its research as well as embedding the intricate detailed analyses into a systematic totality, which is to be more—to play on Kant's distinction—than an aggregate, "put together by mere estimates," a mere collection of items without a guiding clue. Kant goes on: "hence [the idea of a complete, systematic science] is possible only by means of an *idea of the whole* . . . , thus through their *connection* [of the concepts belonging to this science] *in a system*" (Kant 1998, 201, B 89). Husserl would be deemed overly naive had he not had this general idea of a system in mind, as being more than just an aggregate, that is, the sum total of all analyses belonging to phenomenology, but as a systematic whole guided by an idea. It is in his late thought that such an idea begins to take on shape. It is this idea on which I will attempt to zero in here.

Indeed, to develop such an "idea of the whole" may be exactly what marks his departure from his earlier project of a "critique of reason" in the years after the *Logical Investigations*. This project can be seen as the first systematic ambition in Husserl, but it is very different from his later reflections on the matter. In this early project of an eidetic description of all classes and types of acts (logical, volitional, valuing, etc.), the *implicit* idea seemed to be that just finishing this task by a mere enumeration would constitute "the system." The system was the finished set of descriptive analyses. This comparable naïveté on Husserl's part was certainly also owed to his philosophical background in the school of Brentano, who deemed such efforts as a wasted labor of love. But anybody who has made an effort to comprehend the great systematic ambitions of a Kant or Hegel, say, can only judge this knee-jerk reaction on the part of the Brentanians as immature and silly. By the time Husserl had come to his mature philosophical position of phenomenology as transcendental philosophy, he had made large strides from his earlier stance, which he himself deemed naive. He had left the early realists far behind him and was now ready to face the challenge of the great systematizers.

Husserl's later reflections on the systematicity of transcendental phenomenology were, as we shall see, highly complex and sophisticated and can, in this sense, well be compared to the systematic aspirations of the German idealists and also his contemporaries, especially the neo-Kantians mentioned above. It was no less than Husserl's colleague in Marburg—philosophical enemy, personal friend—Natorp, who finished his life's work with a "Phenomenological Systematics,"[5] attempting to pull together the strings of his work and leave it to posterity. The grand sytem, with which one could step down, could be considered as a guiding clue, a sort of "manual" for the entirety of the work carried out. It is for this reason that the final systematic sketch need not amount to a large tome, but could be read like a short but dense manual of instructions to the actual content of one's work. In this sense, and apart from internal reasons to complete the task of one's efforts into a system, it was also considered a necessary last and public step to finish one's life work with a systematic sketch, especially since Husserl's idea was to have merely laid the foundation for future generations of phenomenologists. The systematic form was, thus, the formal conclusion and closure to a lifelong philosophical project, which might not have stood clearly before the eyes of its creator at all times. From this highest vantage point, everything on the path of thinking could or should be interpreted as necessary, even what seemed like deviations at the time.

One reason, of course, why systematizing has received so little attention with respect to Husserl is that system-building has been out of fashion since the countercurrent in modern philosophy beginning with Kierkegaard and Nietzsche. Though Husserl had little, if any, overlap with the likes of Nietzsche, his early philosophical stance, hidden in the guise of "descriptive psychology" intentionally divorced from all "grand" philosophical questions of the metaphysical sort, might actually be quite similar to someone like the great nihilist, to whom system-building was a great intellectual "dishonesty." But such pure sentiments, when diagnosed under the sober gaze of the philosopher, quickly vaporize into thin air. As Nietzsche himself might have been able to notice, there is no utterance that is not "theory-laden." The intellectual dishonesty then lies in turning one's back on this very theory. The later Husserl certainly saw through this naïveté.

Despite these critics of philosophy, which they equated with system-building, one must not overlook that this "synthesizing ambition"—

which begins with Kant (who also spoke of "all future metaphysics" that should be derived from his system of critique), continues with the German idealists, the neo-Kantians (Rickert, Cohen, Natorp), and is alive to this day, to mention only Luhmann, Habermas, Schmitz, Brandom, McDowell—is the dialectical antithesis to the former destructive attitude. The sentiment expressed here—explicitly or implied—is that to construct a system from the pieces one has assembled is the true and the only manner in which a philosophy may be expressed. And, concomitantly, it is the only manner to justify *oneself,* not only as a philosopher or public intellectual, but also as a private individual. The motif of responsibility— for oneself, for one's community of fellow-humans—runs through Husserl's late thought, and with it, he never claims to say anything new; it is the sentiment expressed in the philosophies of Kant, Fichte, Cohen, Natorp, Rickert, to which he consciously nods. To counter a Kierkegaardian trope, there is no conflict or antithesis between the system and the individual. The system contains the individual; the individual expresses the system.

With very few exceptions—even Heidegger had a systematic ambition during a phase of his life—every significant Western philosopher since Kant has attempted such a system, but it is equally noteworthy that many of them either failed miserably (at least in the judgment of their peers) or left their system incomplete. The incompleteness might be due to either the character of the system itself—which was to be seen deliberately as an "open system," as in Cohen, Rickert, Cassirer—or to an actual failure in that its author simply fell short of the task set by himself. To which category Husserl belongs shall not be judged here, though enough of his systematic efforts will be laid out in the following to enable the reader to make his own informed decision. What is important to note, however, is that Husserl, who had begun modestly with his attempts to solve problems in the philosophy of mathematics, ended with a systematic outline of a "philosophy of the future" which is no different from these philosphers just mentioned, who might be more famously known for such efforts.

With respect to Husserl more specifically, taking into consideration the nature of this systematic totality has always already tacitly given an answer to the question of systematics. That is to say, even though Husserl might not have reflected upon this systematics explicitly, no answer *is* an answer; the answer lay in his substantial analyses themselves, even without a methodological or "speculative" reflection on them. But the fact that no explicit "theory of method" is to be found in Husserl's writings does not imply that passages without an explicit declaration of "speculation" do not bear such a quality that must be spelled out. But, for all that, we need not go as far as Fink did and critically assert that phenomenological analysis without speculation "is not worth a dime."[6] Instead, we need only acknowledge that an implicit understanding of a systematic totality is always presupposed. Yet does not harboring unchecked presuppositions contradict the very principle of phenomenological analysis? Is it not phenomenology's task to achieve a universal and completely self-transparent understanding, which can only be reached when we thematize this understanding and which in turn calls for an understanding of this understanding? Thus, to spell out these presuppositions is actually to do Husserl a favor. Husserl himself knew that he was not well suited to this task and he was happy to rely on Fink to do it; hence with the help of Fink—though also critical of the latter's speculative engagements—this shall be attempted here in outline.

In the spirit of Husserl, neglecting to subject the results of phenomenological analysis to an interpretation regarding their meaning and their sense—in other words, their position within a system—disregards the fundamental intention of phenomenological inquiry, namely, to practice radical self-introspection and self-critique and to give an account (the famous *lógon didónai*) for these results. If all data experienced in the lived-experience of transcendental life calls for a critique, this critique in turn calls for a critique. It is thus a—*systematic*—consequence of the nature of phenomenological analysis to perform a "critique of a critique" or what says the same thing, a "phenomenology of phenomenology" or, to put it in yet different words: to reflect on the systematics of the phenomenological "system" is equal to performing a self-critique of the acts of the phenomenologist himself. All of these figures of thought are used in the late Husserl; hence, it is the interpreter's task to weave these pieces together in a systematic manner. But since Husserl himself was not able to pull them all together, this interpretive task is, to be sure, one of the most difficult ones that a phenomenology in the Husserlian style faces.

Although Husserl was guided by a strong "will to a system" by the 1920s, that is, when he worked out a universal transcendental conception of world constitution, it is noteworthy that at that time he hardly reflected on the nature of this phenomenological system in a more sustained manner. His calls for a "critique of the critique" quickly die away, and where he mentions the need for such a self-critique, his demands remain promissory.[7] It is not until his last assistant, Fink, who was, as a young man, enthusiastic about the great systems of German idealism and who was also able to take in the influence of Heidegger, that Husserl is pushed towards these systematizing ideas and demands arising from the idealist systems. Fink joined Husserl at the time of his retirement and stayed with him in the last decade of his teacher's life. Though Husserl will ultimately not follow his assistant, his reflections not only on the phenomenological system itself but, more importantly, on the *nature of a system of phenomenology* become much more refined and subtle. It is with the help of Fink that Husserl is pushed towards speculation, though it is also Fink who is the "Trojan horse" in wanting to allow inimical ideas to enter the system of Husserlian phenomenology. Husserl felt this danger in his closest pupil darkly; but he also appreciated the challenge that Fink brought to bear on his thought.[8] As such, Fink was also a catalyst who helped certain ideas and thoughts see the light of day. In all of these responses to Fink, we encounter Husserl as one knows him; yet Fink helped Husserl make certain things explicit that otherwise would have remained in the dark.

In the following, I will present Husserl's subsequent reflections on such a systematic conception, which are guided by the insight that phenomenology cannot do without a somewhat "speculative" approach. Husserl certainly would not have accepted the term "speculation" for his efforts. To put it in his own words, phenomenology has to move from being a merely "regressive" phenomenology (that of constitutive analysis) to a "constructive" exercise in reaching for, and spelling out, the contours and limits of the system of transcendental phenomenology. As being located at the fringes of the system, that is, of that which may be considered phenomenological and what not, Husserl also practices, in a good sense, the method of critique invented by Kant. This form of critique is, *nolens volens,* a self-critique, as the investigation of what can be cognized is always necessarily an investigation of the agent who cognizes. If one replaces cognition with consciousness, one can easily apply the Kantian method of critique to the Husserlian enterprise. But the historian of philosophy also knows that it was Hegel who believed that such a method is naive, as it does not see that the stance presupposed by this act of critique is already one above the alternatives of "within" and "without" the bounds of reason (or consciousness). Only the dialectical approach to the problem of a self-critique could lend hope to tackle this issue in a philosophically responsible manner. Though Husserl never read Hegel in greater detail, he was certainly sensitive to these matters, and most likely through the mediation of Fink.

Hence, I am purposely placing Husserl's attempt to come to grips with a phenomenological system under the very un-Husserlian, speculative title "Dialectics of the Absolute." It is obvious that the term "dialectics" is not a typical Husserlian notion.[9] My aim, however, is not to employ these terms in their traditional sense (neither Platonic, nor Kantian, nor Hegelian), though the Husserlian sense is certainly not completely novel. Rather, it is my goal to present a phenomenological conception of these terms in a Husserlian vein, so as to give Husserl's attempt at a phenomenological system a freer treatment than his own terminology allowed for. Or conversely, I will "translate" Husserl's systematic thought into the terminology of speculative idealism. After that, and from within the framework of this systematic conception, I will formulate a critique of this system which arises consequentially from its very conception; namely that phenomenology wants to "sublate" the natural attitude. I shall conclude, however, by dismissing this critique, which has been voiced many times over, as a misunderstanding and misreading of Husserl's philosophical vision. Indeed, it is nothing but a "cheap shot" against a systematic sketch that is—however unwittingly—as sophisticated as that of Hegel's. Although an *Auseinandersetzung* with Hegel's Logic cannot even be attempted here, this much should become clear: that it is a task for future philosophy to spell out Husserl's systematics, and (in order) to compare it with the best in classical German philosophy, and—perhaps, as a distant idea—to come up with a unified account of transcendental idealism. With the addition of the efforts of the neo-Kantians (in part 2 of this book), the outlines of such a unified vision of *transcendental philosophy* (no longer only phenomenological) will become visible.

Husserl's Late Conception of Phenomenological Systematics

In realizing that the work of the phenomenologist can never come to an end for reasons having to do with the very project, Husserl attempts to at least glimpse the tail end of the grand lines of phenomenological inquiry under the title of a "phenomenological metaphysics" or teleology.[10] Such an attempt, however, calls for a special justification, for a methodological problem arises here: in looking beyond what is given in apodictic evidence of the living present, one cannot maintain this ideal of evidence—one cannot have any evidence, that is, any experience of, for example, one's own birth or death or of a dreamless sleep. They mark the limits of what can be experienced. As a result of such reflections to which one is pushed simply through phenomenology's research program, there must be a reconsideration of the method to be employed here. Husserl's name for this methodological expansion of the original scope of phenomenological investigation is "constructive phenomenology." Whereas static phenomenology can be called (purely) descriptive, and genetic phenomenology reconstructive (i.e., reconstructing "past" layers of constitution), these givennesses on the margins need to be explicitly *constructed* to *be* phenomena. This constructive method serves not only as a way of accessing primarily "ungiven" phenomena, but more especially and concurrently, it is a reflection upon that which is actually going on in phenomenological analysis, as the very modes of access and description *on the part of the phenomenologist* come into view. In other words, while constructive phenomenology searches at the fringes of the given (or ungiven, for that matter), there occurs at the same time a self-distancing from the living present in which the analysis itself is carried out. In this split between descriptor and descriptive phenomenon, the "locus" of phenomenological analysis itself comes into view. The reflection on this locus is nothing other than the called-for self-critique, which is at the same time a reflection on phenomenology's systematicity. This connection may be made by recalling that to Hegel, the system is defined by the position in which the system is carried out. "The absolute," in Hegel, is the absolute standpoint of "science" once consciousness has been led through the thorny path of doubt and the despair of skepticism. By practicing phenomenology as a science, Husserl unwittingly already occupies this absolute standpoint. The reflections on the activities of the phenomenologist hence occupy the same systematic locus as in Hegel's *Phenomenology of Spirit.*

Generally speaking, phenomenological analysis is located in that sphere accessed by the reduction, transcendental consciousness, and it is a critique thereof, first and foremost in the direct sense of inquiry, investigation, and justification. As accessed by a turn away from one's normal manner of life as straightforwardly directed at worldly entities, it is *eo ipso* a manner of reflection. Insofar as it retreats from the world as constituted, this reflexive critique of transcendental consciousness is carried out in a regressive method—as an unbuilding (*Abbau*) of its constituted strata. But this reflection upon myself as a constituting agent upon my always ongoing constitutive activities is also, as Husserl says, a splitting of the Ego into the latent Ego, which constitutes, and the patent Ego, which becomes explicit in the gaze of reflection, which is again carried out on the part of an Ego which is, in turn, latent, and so on. The Ego, which is doing the actual analyzing, thus is equally hidden, as are other "fringe phenomena," and analyzing it itself calls for a constructive consideration about what goes on in the process of this analyzing. It has to be constructed in order to *make* it into a phenomenon. In other words, insofar as "straight" phenomenology is by definition a critique of transcendental subjectivity, reflective phenomenology, which attempts to analyze the agent who does phenomenology, calls for a critique of this critique. The order of this higher-order critique can be seen structurally in the terms Husserl employs: phenomenological metaphysics, which thematizes limit phenomena such as birth, death, or "grand facts" such as history, in general *facta* of life, is *second* philosophy.[11] *First* philosophy to him is and can only be philosophy of the Ego as constituting agent, including its self-constitution. Thus, methodologically the higher-order critique must begin with an analysis of the Ego regarding its own "doing." Its status as "higher order" is, in fact, to be seen as the first in the order of things, in the sense of "first for us" (*pròs hemâs*). From this perspective, phenomenology in its entirety may be characterized thus as a thorough "philosophy of what is first for us."

Given this trajectory to an ever more radical reflection on the Ego, it becomes understandable that Husserl in his later years increasingly turns his eye towards *that* Ego, which carries out phenomenological analysis. Thus, within the framework of a first philosophy, phenomenology as an eidetic science of the constituting Ego, the higher-order critique is that of the *philosophizing* Ego. This agent Husserl determines as the famous "unparticipating onlooker"; it necessarily has distanced itself, via a splitting of the Ego, from that which goes on in transcendental life, which, of course, it itself is. Hence, the phenomenology of the phenomenologizing Ego must be seen as the *first necessary step in determining the nature of the phenomenological system.* One can see how Husserl's understanding of system has changed in the direction of an idealistic understanding: a system can only be developed from an underlying idea guiding all "aggregates"; this idea is the basic assumption a reflective phenomenology must make, that is, that it must "make its departure from the Ego." As Schelling puts it, the "Ego is the principle of all philosophy," but as a principle in phenomenological terms, it is not an axiom, but is a principle that follows from the thoroughly held paradigm of adhering to the radically reflective standpoint, the first-person perspective, and to consider everything else—in one word: the world—as "emanating" from the Ego. This is an idealistic restatement of Husserl's theory of constitution.

That the self-critique of phenomenology, in the manner explicated, leads to a critique of the phenomenologizing agent is a direct consequence of the critique of Husserl's first systematic conception: the "first" critique as inquiry into transcendental constitution of the world cannot come to an end because world constitution will always continue, just as it has never begun. As constituting the world, in which things begin and end, these categories cannot be applied to transcendental consciousness. When Husserl says, in some late texts, that "the transcendental subject does not die," he is not positing some kind of divine consciousness; rather, such statements must be understood in the sense of Augustine's analysis of time, where questions as to what God did "before" he created time are simply absurd questions. Thus, as a constantly streaming process of constitution, there is no way to escape it *if* one remains at this level of constitution, and a systematic conception of phenomenology that reaches some sort of "closure" will be impossible. Rather, one has to move to the level of a critique of this critique. One has to move, in other words, from a doctrine of elements to a doctrine of method which determines, in the words of Kant, "the formal conditions of a complete system of pure reason" (Kant 1998, 627, A 707/B 735–36). This higher-order critique that Husserl frequently calls for is not performed for the sake of finding yet another higher level of critique to be analyzed; if this were so, it would lead to an endless regress of iterative reflections. Though the method of the splitting of the Ego appears as if it were a constantly "iterable" (repeatable) process with no discernible result (comparable to looking at oneself in the mirror with a mirror in one's back), this would be a misunderstanding. The "iterability" of reflection means that it is possible, at every juncture in the process of description, to move to the meta-level of self-critique, which is the same as a critique of the critique. Indeed, this self-critique of the phenomenologist serves instead as the first step of reflection upon the nature of the phenomenological *system*. The system can only come into view *in and through* this self-critique.

If the reflections upon the systematics of the phenomenological system start out with the analysis of the unparticipating onlooker in the manner indicated, then the very activity of carrying out this reflection is equivalent to a *self-explication of the system itself;* for the one expressing the system and the system itself cannot be separated, just as the splitting of the Ego points to one selfsame Ego. Put trivially, without a phenomenologist, there can be no phenomenology. Phenomenology, in other words, needs not only an agent doing phenomenology; the agent's activities, in the manner in which they are carried out, are a *constitution of the system itself,* just as simple acts on the lower level constitute the world. However, thematizing this agent in the higher-order critique requires a self-distancing in the form of a split between the thematized and thematizing Ego. This, too, is a higher-order split, that is, not just between constituting and constituted, but between the Ego as constituting and the Ego as analyzing this constituting, which is, in turn, a higher-order constituting. Only *this* thematizing, thus, is a self-critique, performed by the philosophizing Ego in regard to itself through the split. This splitting not only calls for an explication of what it is that we acquire in this splitting, but it also problematizes the primal unity of the Ego. The Ego is but one, though it comes to be known as one through a split. In terms of Hegel's *Logic,* it is both identical and different, and in this difference identical and different in its identity.

It is at this point that I want to introduce the notion of dialectics,[12] taking the cue from Husserl's *other* assistant, Landgrebe, who suggests that "this splitting [of the Ego] is precisely the problem that [Hegelian] dialectics is attempting to solve, apparently in a way such that dialectics is inseparable from every form of 'transcendental reflection'" (Landgrebe 1980, 25).[13] The splitting of the Ego obviously cannot mean that the result of this split is two (or more?) completely unrelated pieces; or as Husserl also says, commenting on the metaphor of the split, that one ought not to imagine it like a split-apart tree trunk (Hua VIII, 90). They are *relata* of one original unity, and as such there has to be a tension between them. Insofar as these are (a) the Ego that constitutes straight-forwardly, though unknowingly of its constitutive achievements, the Ego of the natural attitude, and (b) the Ego that analyzes these constitutive achievements themselves, one may conclude that this splitting occurring through the phenomenological reduction is that between the Ego of the natural attitude and that of the phenomenologist, or between empirical and transcendental Ego, that is, the Ego as constituted, living in the mode of the natural attitude, and the Ego as transcendentally constituting, living in the mode of the phenomenological attitude. Husserl, as is well known, tried to elucidate the relationship between these Egos and took pains to do so, one of the reasons for his trouble being that he was not in a position to employ the speculative terminology needed for this task. Indeed, the speculative figure of identity-in-difference, whose relation is that of a dialectics, that is, as opposite of one another and yet identical in this opposition, might have helped him express this relation. It is a "speculative" or "logical" figure of thought, as it cannot be filled with intuitive content. But it is operative in Husserl's thought in this very aspect. This leads to the conclusion that there was indeed a certain type of "dialectic" at work here into which Husserl was "forced."[14] But this being "forced" is not to be seen as a bad thing; to the contrary, this dialectics helped Husserl's systematics come into its own. As always, the influence that other philosophers exerted on Husserl was indirect and not easily visible. But we will quickly see how this dialectic comes to life in Husserl's late thought.

Husserl's reflections on this curious relationship peak in the "paradox of subjectivity." Let us see now how a dialectics is at work in this paradox. The paradox consists in the constellation that the Ego is at the same time an object *in* the world *and* that *which* constitutes the world of which it is part. The phenomenologist knows this; the one living in the natural attitude does not, and yet they are one and the same, but living in different attitudes. Hence the question as to the relation between the two within the paradoxical nature of the Ego becomes the question as to the relation between these two *attitudes*. On this relationship, Husserl says that the natural attitude is a "mode of the transcendental attitude."[15] Both attitudes are in the relation of mutual embrace, but this very statement can only be made from the transcendental attitude. Although the phenomenologist leaves the natural attitude, he will remain a human being in the world. All of his activities, although performed in a different attitude, *remain* worldly activities with an "index" referring to their meaning as transcendental; one lives the same life in a different attitude, respectively. In Husserl's terms, the phenomenologist is *always already* "enworlded"—there is no "secondary enworlding," as Fink calls it, which would take place "after" the "first" enworlding in "normal" constitution, because the phenomenologist does not first perform an analysis and then secondly "bring it" into the world like sending a letter to his "mundane address." Rather, phenomenological analysis is always already worldly, and as such it becomes necessarily (mis)understood as a positive science of consciousness: as psychology.

> Thus, the phenomenological activity becomes a human, psychological activity of the normal human Ego, [it] belongs to the world and is a historic event within the history of philosophy. (B I 5/155a, from November 1931)

The Ego is transcendental, yet it is enworlded by virtue of its mundane disposition as a psychophysical entity, concretely, by his or her lived-body.[16] However, what is so paradoxical about this relationship? Why not say, as Kant, that this Ego is a "citizen of two kingdoms" and that it is split in two due to its psychophysical constitution, where the physical part accounts for its being part of the causal world of nature and the mental or rational as part of the world of freedom? To Kant, this dual consideration of the subject is such a paradox, an intrinsic dualism that may, perhaps, point to a deeper unity that, however, lies beyond the limits of reason, as does the dualism of intuitions and concepts. Already the idealistic critics of Kant, especially Hegel, rejected such a dualism as the last word; seeing the dual nature *as* dual means occupying a higher stance. The paradox is only one if one does not occupy a higher standpoint from which one sees the two as antithetical. Kant was in effect already at this higher position but refused to acknowledge it. His "humility" was hypocrisy, if anything.

This Hegelian reaction to the Kantian dualism is, now, an exact parallel to Husserl's solving of the paradox. Indeed, to Husserl, this kind of scenario, whereby the dualism must remain and cannot be sublated (*aufgehoben*) in a synthetic higher stance, was not satisfactory either. But why can one not, to Husserl, accept a scenario whereby the split must be acknowledged as revealing the paradoxical nature of the subject once the break with the natural attitude has occurred and a higher stance has been occupied? Why can't the Ego be made up of an intrinsic antithesis, and why can't one say that the antithesis only becomes apparent to the phenomenologist who has to bear this split between being a philosopher and a citizen, father or mother, and so on—and that the natural attitude remains a splendid primal state of affairs unruptured by philosophical thought? This would mean that the paradox becomes a constant tension between two attitudes within one person, just as someone might be split between someone being a neutral judge who has to preside over the case of a friend. This would mean that the paradoxical nature, once the split has occurred, can never be overcome. However, paradox to Husserl is never a state to be satisfied with but rather a situation to be overcome, where "overcoming" means a mediation in the form of the dialectical three-step. Once the higher stance has been occupied after the reduction and acknowledged through the higher-order critique, the paradox vanishes or is *aufgehoben.*

Moreover, introducing another speculative figure of thought, clinging to the paradox would presuppose characterizing the split solely in a static register. However, the paradox itself is the product of a genesis in the same way the dichotomy of natural and transcendental attitude is not a fixed fact but occurs through a shift or a radical break within the natural attitude. Although "in every human being 'lies' hidden a transcendental Ego" (B I 5/157a), breaking through the boundaries of the natural attitude, and hence becoming a philosopher, is a process, and a difficult one, to say the least. Once one has established oneself as a phenomenologist, one can see, through the universal correlational a priori, that the entirety of being is the product of transcendental constitution. In other words, the constituted world is *relative to* constituting transcendental consciousness or, in other terms, transcendental consciousness is *absolute.* It is not a metaphysical absolute, as it is not some kind of substance, divine or other; one may call it the *phenomenological absolute,* as the sphere, where the being of the world manifests itself, to which it is relative. But this is the product of a reflexive stance, where the insight has been reached that everything worldly is a product of constitution and hence *intrinsically subjective.* The absolute stance, thus, is not in this respect comparable to a Hegelian mediation of all doubts and differences in an absolute standpoint; rather, it is here that the Husserlian sentiment turns back to the Kantian sense of transcendental philosophy: Kant's critical project is first and foremost one of *justification* of claims to cognition. If one starts at the lowest possible level, however, that of simple experience of the world in perception—Husserl's starting point—then the thesis of the relativity of everything worldly to an absolute, which is consciousness, amounts to the project of a *justification of all forms of experience as constituted in transcendental consciousness.*[17]

The genetic relation between natural and transcendental consciousness can hence be called that relation between the absolute and the relative. The question now is to what extent we are justified in calling this relationship a dialectical one. Phenomenological analysis, in Husserl's eyes, is not a strictly methodological device that once practiced is valid for all times. Rather, it is a development that unfolds step by step, and by this unfolding, phenomenology itself unfolds. The strata of transcendental life are not simply "there" with the reduction, but are hidden and have to be dismantled by deepening transcendental analysis. If transcendental life is the absolute, this step-by-step unfolding reveals the absolute itself in always deeper inquiry (into its genetic and intersubjective dimensions; see chapter 4). However, the concrete research is carried out by myself, a concrete human being, and as such it is always already enworlded. Employing the dichotomy of absolute and relative, we can say that every knowledge in which we discover more of this absolute life immediately sets it in relation to our relative worldly existence; it becomes "localized" in the world. Concretely speaking: it is I, myself, who discover previously hidden strata of my own life as transcendental consciousness (even if I discover it is not mine alone). If this transcendental life is nothing but the complete "system of reason," insofar as all types of constitution stand under laws, then it becomes understandable how, on Husserl's account, performing the reduction—and thereby gaining knowledge of the absolute—is equal to instantiating humanness as rationality in its full possibilities. The actual carrying out of the system of phenomenology is thus equal to fulfilling the promise of the Enlightenment.

Phenomenology thus is more than an epistemological undertaking, but pursues an epistemologico-ethical (*erkenntnisethisch*) goal. The dialectics going on in transcendental reflection consist in the constantly oscillating movement between the transcendental and the natural attitude, which always learns more about its hidden transcendental absolute life and which in the process of this learning acquires more of this life and hence becomes itself "more absolute," while at the same time never leaving the relativity of the situated bodily existence in the lifeworld. Partaking in the absolute means partaking in the infinity of this transcendental life and overcoming the finite confines of factual existence. Husserl's is a philosophy of the infinite, as precisely the deed of phenomenology frees the finite individual from the confines of his "homeworld." The following passage may thus be understood as a manifesto against all forms of existential philosophies, philosophies, that is, that revel in finitude:

> Through the phenomenological reduction as "transcendental reflec-
> tion" the Ego frees itself from the confinements of the naturalness of
> its existence [*Dasein*], those [confinements] of "naive" humanness, [it]
> frees itself, as it were, of the blinders that render invisible [*abblenden*]
> to it its absolute, its completely concrete existence, or which is to say
> the same, that render invisible to it an infinite richness of possibilities
> of life, in which those [possibilities] of natural existence are included,
> however in which they are, so to speak, abstract-incomplete. (B II 7/28a,
> from October 1930)

However, with this "primordial" analysis, that is, as focused on the
individual investigator, we still remain within the confines of phenomenology as a "solipsistic" enterprise, which is, to be sure, an abstraction.
Although Husserl's phenomenology is decidedly a "philosophy of reflection," the phenomenologist must of course be open to other researchers, first in phenomenology, but by extension also in other disciplines.
The scientific community is—to use a modern term—a matter of collective intentionality. The single phenomenologist is part of a philosophical movement with other scientists, and therefore phenomenology
is itself only one element—albeit the decisive one—within the history of
Western philosophy. Phenomenology can only develop from being embedded in the scientific community and is no *creatio ex nihilo*. Hence, the
same dynamics that go on within the philosophizing individual are applicable to the grand scheme of history. The process of science in general,
according to Husserl, is itself the unfolding of hidden reason and as such
science is en route to the realization of reason. Although the sphere of
the transcendental had not been discovered until Descartes and Hume,
and only truly seen by Husserl himself, the decisive figures of philosophy
have glimpsed at this transcendental life in true introspection, and even
religious founders such as Buddha have had intuitions thereof, but without the interest of subjecting it to philosophical rigor.[18] To those objecting to this highly selective historiography, one must reply that this
is an ideal reconstruction, not meant as historically faithful. Given this
proviso, one can say with Husserl, science is en route to reason or, put
another way, science aims at transcendental consciousness.

However, this unfolding of the absolute in history stands in constant
tension with the natural attitude, or what is the same, pre-scientific life.
Yet, the same structure as in the single Ego applies here too: theoretical
results of science do not remain in the heads of scientists or locked up
in libraries. They become part of the pre-scientific world: "enworlding"
occurs the moment that truths previously unknown to pre-scientific life
settle into this life in the form of scientific technology, education, and

even common sense, as scientific results of the highest complexity become trivialized (to mention only evolutionary theory or the theory of relativity). Though this "trivialization" can take on a negative function—as when trivialized theories are utilized to further political or ideological agendas—the enrichment of pre-scientific life with "more reason" is, generally speaking, indeed a success story. The history of the unfolding of reason is at the same time a constant enrichment of pre-scientific life with scientific truth. This means that the relativity of pre-scientific life itself strives towards the absolute, since the absolute in that very instance of being discovered becomes enworlded in the form of the scientific community. In this sense, every discovery is equal to the process of enworlding. In Husserl's (surprisingly speculative) words:

> Once science has developed in the world as a cultural formation [*Gestalt*], the world has taken on the form of a world which knows itself. Universal science is the developing self-knowledge of the world, carrying itself out as a spiritual structure of deeds [*geistiges Werkgebilde*] of the researching subjects, who themselves belong the world. . . . In the awakening to reason and to universal philosophy, the totality of monads grows to its self-realization which ascends in steps, and thus one can also say of the constituted world, it is a world that has awakened to self-consciousness. (K 11 5/11, undated, probably from the thirties)

Against any inclination to take this as a completely naive vision of history, one has to insist that Husserl explicitly calls this reconstruction of this development a "fiction," even a "story." He never claims to be true to the factual historical development of European history and the history of science, and it is not important, either. It is an ideal-typical reconstruction of the history of reason (with its primal and final institutings, *Ur-* and *Endstiftung*) within the "anthropological type Europe" (also an ideal type), which has followed its consequent development to that form of science that has at last opened up a perspective to rigorously work out a science of absolute, transcendental consciousness. What is more, only such an *ideal* reconstruction of this historical development, which requires constructing an ideal line towards an ideal truth, can construct an ideal for a *factual* telos, which would be the complete instantiation of reason in the world *as we know it*, or the full enworlding of the absolute in this world, or, correlatively, the sublation of the relativity of the factual world into the all-embracing absolute, which is properly understood as absolute facticity, since it is always in the streaming and dynamic process of enworlding. If the highest realization of reason is in fact enabled by phenomenology or if phenomenology *itself* is the highest realization of reason, then one could surmise that Husserl's highest ideal is that the natural Egos become phenomenologists. *"The world has to be phenomenologized"*; this could be a paraphrase for Husserl's master plan.

Now, how can we characterize the systematic conception underlying this ideal? If this higher-order reflection, this critique of what phenomenology is doing, is itself a part of discovering the absolute, then the difference between a doctrine of elements and a doctrine of method itself becomes ultimately sublated.[19] If all transcendental insights immediately become enworlded by the very fact of being discovered by the phenomenologist, then the systematic considerations about the system cannot be separated from the system itself: *the facticity of the historic development of philosophy itself tells us the story of what the system is. History itself is the system.* "History is the grand fact of absolute being" (Hua VIII, 506); this oft-quoted slogan can only become fully understood now. The only way to constitute a systematic conception of this system, then, is to tell a story (*eine Geschichte*) of this history. Thus, the act of phenomenologizing is itself a narrative, but in this sense but the peak of a narrative of universal scope.

This story is not normative; it does not construct one grand "history of being" or "spirit." Rather, it is a reconstruction, and as such it is intrinsically humble and open to corrections and is only ever presumptive. This is where it differs—once more—significantly from Hegel. It is a story of reason unfolding, but one that always has to regain its concordance through breaks and inconsistencies; and this applies both to its reconstruction of the past and especially to its draft of the future. The story does not come to an end with absolute consciousness, but is a narrative that continues as long as the facticity of human beings in a world exists. And only the facticity of history can prove the story that we are part of right or wrong. This reconstruction has to act as a corrective instance where a misdevelopment has become so commonly accepted that it is not even perceived as such any more. This is exactly the situation of the crisis Husserl found himself in during his last years. It is a symptom of this crisis that the enworlding of reason in history is not perceived as an absolute facticity, but mocked at as a mere dream, a dream moreover, which is "over" (*ausgeträumt*).[20] Only a crass misreading of Husserl's intentions could interpret this famous quote as expressing a fatalism. It is this fatalism to which Husserl's entire philosophical efforts provide one powerful response.

A Critique of Husserl's Systematic Sketch

Very briefly I want to formulate a critique of this ideal. It shall not primarily concern the criticism of Husserl's claim of humanity essentially becoming phenomenologized or, more concretely, that every person should become a phenomenologist. This vision has been amply criticized as "elitist" or overly naive and need not be repeated here. One could counter this critique by asserting it rests on a misreading or that at the very least Husserl has remained ambiguous on this point. One possible reading of the "phenomenologization of humankind" thesis could be that not everybody has to become a phenomenologist in a phenomenologized society, that neither presents an ideal, but that everybody plays his or her part in this society under the spiritual leadership of the true functionaries of mankind, the phenomenologists (see the *Kaizo* articles).[21] But the functionaries of mankind are no philosopher kings. They are scientists who in *this* respect do not differ from other scientists in that they have a defined method and a clear goal. They might have a task of a higher "cognitive dignity," but are not higher humans. However, I do not want to pursue this train of argumentation here, as it presents more than anything a "cheap shot" against Husserl.

Another line of critique could run as follows. If it is Husserl's idea to phenomenologize the lifeworld, no matter how this is to be attained and no matter how much this projects the future as getting closer to this limit idea, the general direction is clear: our lifeworld is to become a philosophically understood and enriched world. However, this ideal amounts to essentially the same crucial step for which Husserl criticizes modem science: it has as its consequence an idealization of the lifeworld. Even if science does so in an objectivistic sense—in the sense of objective science that obliterates the subjective-relative lifeworld—the general direction in which phenomenological science treats the lifeworld is the same. It pursues the ideal of transforming the world into a philosophical world. In doing so, the phenomenologist would be destroying the ground on which he stands. Husserl's grand plan to merge science of the lifeworld with that of transcendental consciousness would then have to be deemed impossible because it would entail *reducing one to the other.* In both cases this is not feasible, or what says the same thing, the result would be dissatisfactory: we would, on the one hand, end up with an idealized lifeworld—even if it were *phenomenologically* idealized—and, on the other, we would be left with a transcendental consciousness that is identical or indifferent to a psychological entity; that is, we would abandon the project of transcendental philosophy. In both cases, we would do injustice to the phenomenon at stake. Thus, in order to preserve either, we need both in their mutual absolute antithesis. However, it then seems that, without conceding the possibility of a synthesis, Husserl's project of absolute dialectics collapses. Not only is the paradox of subjectivity insolvable—already the attempt to do so is a paradox.

Conclusion: Phenomenology as the Enlightenment Restated

Countering this critique can, in conclusion, yield the opportunity to re-iterate the systematic ramifications of Husserl's system of phenomenology and to connect it to the meta-topic of Husserl's contribution to the Enlightenment. To repeat this last critique, the threat involved in an ever-increasing enrichment of the lifeworld with transcendental consciousness is, as it were, a mutual assimilation of the transcendental and the mundane, making both indistinguishable and thereby doing an injustice to both, and ultimately leveling the distinction altogether. What we are left with is enlightening neither for the philosopher nor the one living in the natural attitude.

But such a reading of the process Husserl calls "enworlding" is a misunderstanding. It is true that the lifeworld is subject to an ever-increasing enrichment of scientific knowledge. And in this enrichment, the constitutive accomplishments that made these scientific "things"—by which I mean not only theories, but also objects derived from them, such as cars, microwave ovens, and so on—is no longer visible. To remind the reader of an example from chapter 1, nobody driving a car can in the least imagine the "brain power" that went into its making. Indeed, each new development of technology stands on the shoulders of previous inventions and would be impossible without them. Thus, in the case of science, enworlding means both a trivialization or popularization of its theories and can also lead to a forgetfulness of the theory altogether, as in the example of the car, whose technology is based on a complex of highly intricate theories. As a result, the threat is that the lifeworld becomes theorized altogether and thereby "denatured." This is the scenario that Husserl lamented as the crisis of modern science: it has turned the world into a technicized universe and the world, which once was the enchanted region of nature, becomes thematic only insofar as it can yield a practical use for humans, be it as the forest which provides lumber, or the oceans that yield oil, which, if accidentally spilled, destroys the sandy beaches, thus harming tourism. Of this scenario Husserl was certainly neither the first nor the only critic; it has been voiced as early as the Romantics, who witnessed the ascent of the Industrial Revolution, and it has been repeated in different variants by this "romantic" strain in modern philosophy, such as Heidegger's critique of technology and the Frankfurt school with their diagnosis of the "dialectics of the Enlightenment." But is this critique really applicable to Husserl's transcendental phenomenology?

No, it is not. First, the "space" opened up by phenomenological inquiry is not another area of science of the world, which could in some way or other become technicized, that is, utilized for a practical (social, political, technical, economic) purpose. The space of phenomenology is the *space of meaning* (to use a phrase from Steven Crowell). Phenomenology clarifies the conditions of the possibility of meaning, that is, where and how and the manner in which it is constituted. Hence, as with all other philosophies or philosophical theorems, one would do it a grave injustice to ask for its "practical applicability." Whoever asks for such a practical usage has not understood the nature of philosophical theory and speaks from the standpoint of the natural attitude. But that philosophy has no "practical usage"—at least in its naive understanding—applies *especially* to Husserlian phenomenology. Husserl's phenomenology is—despite all its rhetoric—a special form of philosophy of reflection, to borrow a characterization from Gadamer. That is to say, it is and will always remain a reflective undertaking that can only have as its ultimate goal an enlightenment of oneself and ultimately of humanity. To what extent such an enlightenment as attaining clarity about one's innermost being will ever have an "applicability," as "the rubber meeting the road" (or whichever images one may favor), will forever remain unmeasurable and fickle.

What "gain," then, does phenomenology yield? It is nothing more and nothing less than a novel insight into meaning as constituted through consciousness. This is Husserl's ultimate insight, which is his contribution to the project of the Enlightenment. The world and world-constituting transcendental consciousness are the two relata of one correlation, which together is the absolute, but which can only become known, come to consciousness as meaningful, in the self-questioning, self-reflection, and introspection on the part of the individual who has left behind the confines of the natural attitude and has become a philosopher in Husserl's sense. Becoming a philosopher is an ongoing and never-ending process which requires a dialectical movement between both poles of existence, the natural and the philosophical standpoint. And this is where Husserl differs from Hegel, despite all similarities with him, as spelled out above.

The absolute standpoint, to Husserl, is an ongoing process of reflection *in relation to and in discussion with* the natural standpoint. It is, in other words, not a standpoint where the philosopher could ever claim "satisfaction" or come to rest. It is, strictly speaking, no standpoint, but a descriptive *stance* that investigates consciousness in its many forms. It is, thus, a research program, not merely a standpoint that has productively overcome skepticism. Though skepticism was a problem for Husserl as well—as his narrative of the history of philosophy as caught between system-building and skeptic destruction shows[22]—its specter is not the main threat in Husserl's descriptive analyses; they are not threatened by skepticism, but are only threatened by one's own faulty or incomplete description. Indeed, it was the refutation of skepticism in the form of psychologism—the confusion between acts as mental episodes and their (ideal) content—that opened the door to his phenomenology as eidetic science.

Second, Hegel wanted to complete the Enlightenment by reaching absolute idealism, which would overcome all incomplete or one-sided attempts at the same, once and for all. The absolute standpoint was the ultimate transparency one could reach by relegating all one-sided standpoints to the story of the history of self-consciousness, properly told. Husserl, too, is a philosopher of the Enlightenment, but to Husserl, the latter cannot consist of an absolute standpoint in the sense just characterized. The absolute standpoint is by definition detached from other forms of knowledge. All positive claims to knowledge, as practiced in the sciences, are necessarily one-sided, thus the philosopher in Hegel's scenario cannot partake in such efforts. But to Husserl, the standpoint of the philosopher practicing phenomenology is decidedly not detached and removed from other forms of knowledge and a fortiori cultural activities. It is in this sense, as mentioned, that Husserl's idea of Enlightenment remains closer to that of Kant: phenomenology is the enterprise of *justification of claims to knowledge and cultural activities*. It justifies them by showing (describing, reconstructing) how they arise and become possible—their conditions of possibility—out of achievements in consciousness.

The system is thus an unending, never-completed process of descriptive analysis in the phenomenological style (intentional analysis, in its broadest definition), only the ground of which has been laid by Husserl. The *systematicity* of the system consists in its relation to natural consciousness, the common sense of the natural attitude, which it enlightens by showing how its achievement arises out of consciousness. The dialectical relation between both, then, is a constant back and forth ("zigzag"), which can more properly be defined as a hermeneutical circle spiraling upwards. Husserl's ideal is not an ultimate *Aufhebung* (sublation) of the natural standpoint, but an increasing transparency on the part of the philosopher who allows the natural standpoint to remain just that, though he can be an exemplar of a formation of a group of people—in this case, the scientific community—who unite under one idea, which they have explicitly formulated and which henceforth guides their lives, in a mutually responsible manner and in constant scrutiny and mutual justification. It is here where Husserl's social philosophy, as inspired by Fichte and culminating in the personalities of higher order and ultimately a global community of love (*Liebesgemeinschaft*), is systematically located.[23]

The dialectics of the absolute, in the manner specified in this chapter, is the realization of the promise of the Enlightenment. It achieves, as a general reflective insight and concurrently as a never-ending research program, transparency about the character of ourselves and the world, as receiving their meaning in meaning-bestowing transcendental subjectivity as intersubjectivity in a genetic and generative nexus. Phenomenology's programmatic character, hence, is informed by Hegelian dialectics, but ultimately sides with Kant and his philosophical vision—and that of his followers. How Husserl's philosophy relates to Kant and his followers—the Marburg neo-Kantians in their project of transforming the critique of reason to the critique of culture—will thus be the topic of the next part of this book.

Part 2

Husserl, Kant, and Neo-Kantianism: From Subjectivity to Lifeworld as a World of Culture

From Being to Givenness and Back: Some Remarks on the Meaning of Transcendental Idealism in Kant and Husserl

> Kant's oeuvre contains gold in rich abundance. But one must break it and melt it in the fire of radical critique in order to bring out this content.
>
> —Husserl, from a manuscript from ca. 1917, Hua XXV, 206

> Essentially, already the phenomenological reduction, correctly conceived, implies the marching route to transcendental idealism, just as phenomenology in its entirety is nothing other than the first rigorous scientific form of this idealism.
>
> —Husserl, from the lecture *Erste Philosophie*, 1923/24, Hua VIII, 181

Introduction

In a letter to Cassirer written in 1925, Husserl reflects on his philosophical journey. Influenced in his early development by his teacher Brentano and his school, he was initially "adverse to Kant" and "unreceptive to the genuine sense of Kant's philosophy." After forging his method of the phenomenological reduction, however, "I had to realize that this science further developing in me encompassed, in an entirely distinct method, the entire Kantian problematic . . . and that it confirmed Kant's main results in rigorous scientific founding and in their limitation" (Hua-Dok III/V, 4).[1]

Like many philosophers who succeeded Kant, the mature Husserl both recognized Kant's towering genius and saw himself in the tradition of Kantian philosophizing, though he never wanted to become a member of a school. Instead he intended, in his way, to wrest the true kernel from Kant's philosophy, even if this meant reading him against the grain and "understanding the author better than he understood himself" (Kant 1998, 326, B 370). As the date of the letter quoted above shows, it was very late in his career that Husserl realized that he was furthering the true intentions of Kant's thought. Indeed, in *Ideas,* book 1, dating from 1913, he explicitly conceived of his phenomenology as a form of *transcendental* philosophy with a reference to Kant's critical philosophy.[2] He espoused, even embraced, the Kantian concept of transcendental idealism and utilized this term frequently to describe his philosophy, though he pointed out that his *phenomenological* idealism was different from all traditional idealisms.[3] Husserl's transcendental idealism, like Kant's, allegedly solves all one-sided -isms through a new method, with the difference that Husserl believed that he was finally *doing* it instead of merely announcing it.[4]

In what sense is Husserl's phenomenology a transcendental idealism? Indeed, such a notion seems curious when we look back at the founder of this doctrine, for Husserl rejected what was precisely the main tenet of Kant's transcendental idealism, that is, the distinction between thing-in-itself and appearance, as "mythology."[5] Instead, the manner in which Husserl conceived of his phenomenology as transcendental was by grounding all knowledge and, more broadly, all experience of being in constituting, meaning-bestowing subjectivity. *This* was the sense—the correlational a priori—in which Husserl believed that his phenomenology could be interpreted as transcendental idealism: that all being receives its meaning in meaning-bestowing acts of transcendental subjectivity. So from the standpoint of phenomenology, a distinction between a *thing-in-itself,* to which we have no access and about which we can know nothing, and its *appearance,* of which we have experience and knowledge through our cognitive apparatus, makes no sense. With his distinction, Kant might have opened the door to a "science of appearances," phenomenology,[6] but the very distinction is a mythical construction. The "gold" in Kant's genius was the Copernican turn back to subjectivity. In this endeavor, Husserl saw Kant acknowledging Descartes' turn to the *Ego cogito* and expanding upon this ingenious first beginning.[7] Moreover, Kant's philosophy presented to Husserl the ideal of *scientific* philosophy, that is, philosophy as a metaphysics that would henceforth emerge as science, as "rigorous science" grounded in human lived-experience of the world. This is the sense in which elements of Kant's philosophy can be adopted and others shunned. Only in this way is the promise of Kant's Copernican revolution fulfilled.

So much for Husserl's interpretation of Kant and his own self-interpretation vis-à-vis the Sage of Königsberg. But it is of more than just exegetical interest to ask whether Husserl was really correct in this assessment of the Kantian project and the concept of transcendental idealism. I would like to argue that Husserl's rejection of Kant's notion of transcendental idealism rests on a misinterpretation of the true meaning of this doctrine. Presenting Kant's achievement in a new light will do more than rectify an erroneous—and, if true, absurd—interpretation of his transcendental idealism. My main aim is to show that a more plausible reconstruction of Kant's type of idealism will also give us deeper insight into a genuine *phenomenological* sense of transcendental idealism that is not so far from Kant's own, though with some significant advances over Kant. *Kant*'s transcendental idealism can, in turn, help clarify *Husserl*'s version thereof. A reconstruction of Husserl's phenomenology as transcendental idealism stemming from the Kantian approach is helpful for understanding the Husserlian project, and is the *only* way to understand the mature Husserl's transcendental standpoint.

First I will show how Kant's concept of transcendental idealism is a much more interesting and promising project than it first appears to be. With this reading of Kant stemming from a certain tradition in Kant scholarship, I will then turn to Husserl and reassess the latter's project as it appears in this light. Only from this perspective will the transcendental-phenomenological reduction and its real intention become understandable. Finally, I will present the "new" shape of transcendental idealism and transcendental philosophy as it appears in the mature Husserl. One way in which Husserl moves beyond Kant's metaphysical outlook is in framing phenomenology as a rigorous science of appearances, in other words, an eidetic science of being as it is *given* (to an, and in fact *any*, experiencing agent). Yet, the real force of Husserl's phenomenology is a novel concept of being as *validity*. Husserl's version of transcendental idealism shows us a path to the true *being* of the world, rather than leaving us stuck with an irritating duality between thing-in-itself and appearance.

I will conclude with some remarks on Kant's and Husserl's views on the relation between theoretical and practical reason, suggesting that Husserl ultimately aligns himself with the systematic scope of Kant's transcendental philosophy as it makes a transition from knowledge to action. Kant's entire system is geared towards reason's practical application and has an elaborate moral philosophy in the transcendental vein, as a result of revealing reason's limits. Husserl, too, attempts to show a transition from cognition to action, stemming from his interpretation of being as validity, thereby underpinning Kant's practical postulates on a deeper level. It is Kant's emphasis on practical reason which Husserl acknowledges, while interpreting the practical import of reason slightly differently. Husserl, though merely making meagre gestures towards ethics (at least following this idealistic approach),[8] thereby remains ever more forcefully in the framework of Kantian philosophy.[9]

From Being to Givenness: Kant's Copernican Revolution

In order to understand Kant's groundbreaking Copernican revolution, it helps to distinguish two moments of the overall argument which correspond to the two steps in which Kant introduces it in the "Transcendental Aesthetic" and the "Analytic," respectively. The two steps in the argument together make one sustained argument for transcendental idealism.[10] Let us recall the overall point of Kant's revolution, which he introduces as an experiment:

> Hence let us try whether we do not get farther with the problems of metaphysics by assuming that the objects must conform to our cognition, which would agree better with the requested possibility of an *a priori* cognition of them, which is to establish something about objects before they are given to us. This would be just like the first thoughts of Copernicus. (Kant 1998, 110, B xvi)

The point of the experiment is to inquire into what happens to the question of metaphysics—true cognition of being—when we turn the tables and assume not that it is *our* cognitive apparatus that conforms to *objects,* but rather that it is the *objects* that must conform to *us* if we want to have any knowledge (*Kenntnis*) and even cognition (*Wissen*) of them. But in order to talk about real cognition (a priori), we must *first* assume that objects are *given* to us. Being is only knowable as given. Objects can only be known to us if we can have *experience* of them, if they are *Gegen-stände,* if they appear to us, stand over against us. Hence, the way we can have experience of objects is as *appearances,* but not as they "really" are. We know nothing of objects as things-in-themselves. This basic distinction marks Kant's notion of transcendental idealism: we can have no experience and knowledge of things-in-themselves, but only of things as they appear to us; it is our subjective makeup that enables things to be given as appearances. But Kant goes one step further: our way of experiencing objects is *to us* the only way the things are. Hence it is *we* who "put" something "into" the objects, and beyond that, things-in-themselves are in no way constituted in this way outside our experience.[11] Things-in-themselves *have in themselves* no epistemic conditions; epistemic conditions exist only *for* epistemic agents.[12]

What is this shift about? The move to subjectivity is surely in the Cartesian tradition, but there is more at stake here. Allison has portrayed this move as one from the "theocentric" to the "anthropocentric" model of cognition (1983, 14). What is the theocentric model? Its claim is that we *can* (ideally, once we have attained a Godlike perspective) have direct access to things, that is, to things as they really are. The human standpoint, from which we experience things, is irrelevant with respect to the cognition of things. We have direct access to things, and the way we experience them is how they really are. In other words, the *perspective* on things does not count. We see the world as any agent—God, humans, creatures from Mars—from its standpoint would cognize the world. The Kantian shift is thus to take *this perspective* seriously, more precisely, to see it as *constitutive* for the experience of things. Moreover, let us assume that the standpoint actually does something *to* the object. This is not a manipulation of its "true" being. But a standpoint on something has a certain perspective. What is seen shows a certain *aspect;* from a perspective objects show themselves as *appearances*. This is what the move to an anthropocentric model of cognition is about: it is a consideration of the specific human standpoint on things, as opposed to a view that the standpoint on things does not matter.[13]

This, then, is how Kant's Copernican revolution must be understood, as a two-standpoint theory. In Allison's words: "The distinction between appearances and things in themselves refers primarily to two distinct ways in which things (empirical objects) can be 'considered': either in relation to the subjective conditions of human sensibility (space and time), and thus as they 'appear,' or independently of those conditions, and thus as they are 'in themselves'" (1983, 8). Yet one has to be more precise: things-in-themselves "considered" (thought) as they are in themselves means considered as they are *not experienced* by any subject. Any subject that has experience has a standpoint *in order to* have experience. Hence things-in-themselves are objects that are *not experienced*. The realist claim is that we are able to have access to objects without experience. To Kant, this is absurd. So the true distinction between objects and things-in-themselves is about considering the object as given from a perspective, and the object *"given" without a perspective ("only cognized")*. The two-standpoint theory is really about the distinction *"with or without* a standpoint." Kant also calls the thing-in-itself a *noumenon*[14]—it is a mere *Verstandeswesen;* we can *think* it, but we cannot know what *experience* of it would be like. As subjects, we must have experience to have knowledge of objects. Things can be *given* to us only in experience.[15] God does not need a perspective from which to experience things, but we cannot know what Godlike knowledge is like.

In this move to an *anthropocentric* model of cognition, Kant proposes to investigate the world *as it is given from a perspective,* and this perspective is, for us, the *human standpoint,* the only one we know of (though we can conceive that other creatures have theirs). Hence, Kant introduces a radically *finite* perspective to human cognition, as Heidegger has rightly pointed out,[16] insofar as a standpoint puts limitations on experience: I cannot simultaneously see an object from the front and from the back. God's bird's-eye view can "do" this, but this is not *experience* in the way we know it. Heidegger is completely wrong, however, if this means that therefore our *cognition* is finite. For the point of Kant's entire critical project is precisely to justify the belief that *despite* our subjective perspective on things, we *can* have objective, a priori cognition. As a priori, it is a-perspectival. Cognition exists, as *human* cognition, but it *is* a priori cognition. This leads us to the next step in which Kant unfolds this notion of transcendental idealism.

The first step was the Copernican turn itself, from the object of experience to the experience of objects. More precisely, objects appear in space and time, but as appearances for us: space and time are our manner of experiencing objects. This is the *factum* that is established in the "Transcendental Aesthetics" and addresses the *quid facti* question. The *factum* from which Kant begins his enterprise is that objects *are* experienced as existing in space and time as our forms of intuition. Yet, this is still not enough to establish a "thick" sense of experience, for experience to Kant is more than just intuition.[17] For although intuition is all we have in order to establish *givenness,* we do also have *a priori cognition* of objects when we do science (modeled on the ideal of Newtonian physics). The crucial question of the *Critique* is: *How is this possible?* For cognition exists! The question is not just about the possibility of synthetic judgments a priori, but "How are we *justified* in making these judgments?" This is the *quid iuris* question addressed in the "Transcendental Deduction." The positive impact of the first *Critique* is justifying how for us, as human beings with standpoints, it is possible to have a priori cognition. We are justified in making this claim because, although we have a finite perspective *qua experiencing observers,* we do have access to pure concepts *qua rational creatures.* The problem that then remains to be solved is how to connect our rational and our empirical nature. Kant answers this question in the notoriously obscure "Schematism" chapter, the success of which we will need to leave undecided here.

When these two aspects are put together, the achievements of Kant's Copernican revolution and the doctrine of transcendental idealism are

(a) to move from a theocentric to an anthropocentric model, that is, to introduce the aspect of *perspective* into our specifically human cognition; and

(b) to establish the legitimacy of a priori cognition *in spite of our necessary perspectivity*. Kant wants to acknowledge the limitations of the human standpoint[18] while finding a way to justify what to him was a fact, namely, that we have access to universal truth.[19]

For the purposes of the next section of this chapter, (a) is of greater interest, though we will address (b) in the section after that. Concerning Kant's influence on Husserl, we can assert that Kant was really the first to frame the concept of being as being-given, as appearing. Appearing is the "noematic" side of Kant's Copernican turn to the experiencing agent; appearing-of and givenness-to are two sides of the same coin. Correlatively, being, as we can experience it, must be being-given from a certain perspective and is, for us, nothing other than being given; it is *phaenomenon*. In this sense, Kant can be said to be the first phenomenologist. His doctrine of the thing-in-itself is less "mythical" than Husserl *himself* thought, if we frame transcendental idealism as a doctrine that introduces the idea of perspective to experience, as opposed to a self-contradictory "view from nowhere," that is, a perspective without a perspective.

From Givenness to Givenness-as-Such: Husserl's Transcendental-Phenomenological Reduction

This brief reconstruction of Kant's transcendental idealism had the purpose of connecting Husserl with the Kantian project. I will now present Husserl's transcendental idealism with a focus on the following two aspects: Kant's anthropocentric model of cognition and the *quid iuris* issue. I will deal with anthropocentrism in this section, and the *quid iuris* in the next.

Husserl himself acknowledged that the transcendental-phenomenological reduction is his way of rephrasing the Copernican revolution.[20] So I will first reconstruct the reduction in the light of what was said about Kant, which will give us an interesting perspective on Husserl's original advance over Kant.

The first move into transcendental phenomenology occurs when Husserl introduces the epoché, the bracketing of the natural attitude. This putting-in-suspension gives rise to a turn towards the subjective acts in which the world is experienced *in* the natural attitude. The natural attitude is oblivious to these subjective acts. In the natural attitude we experience the world as existing independently of us. The natural attitude's implicit epistemology can be characterized as empirical realism: in the natural attitude, we think that the world exists *independently of anybody experiencing it.* It takes the being of the world for granted. Hence the "general thesis" of the natural attitude, "the world exists," with "existing" meaning simply that it exists as in-itself.[21] What Kant presented as two epistemic positions—transcendental idealism and empirical realism—becomes, in Husserl, *mapped onto* the relation between the natural and the philosophical standpoint. In this shift of attitude, Husserl's "Fundamental Reflection" exposes the theory-ladenness of the natural attitude. So we see Husserl already operating within the Kantian framework when he introduces the reduction. Natural and philosophical *attitude,* as he calls them, are two standpoints on the same thing: the world. But the natural attitude is really no attitude at all; for if "it" were to be asked to clarify its opinion of the world, it would respond: the world is; the fact that it might be given and only in this way experienced is irrelevant. This implicit epistemology is naive.[22] The naïveté is comparable to Kant's empirical realism, which considers the world "independently of those conditions" in which the world is experienced. The natural attitude does not deny these conditions; it is simply oblivious to them.

How does the philosophical attitude, then, view the world? It sees it in the Copernican "style" after the epistemic claims of the natural attitude have been suspended: the world is only world *for us,* insofar as it is experienced. The reduction "reduces" being to being-given and the world to a phenomenon, a universal sphere of givenness. Being-given is correlated to the agent that experiences this givenness, the world-experiencing subject that, as *experiencing* the world, cannot at the same time be *part* of it. This is the famous paradox of subjectivity: the subject is at the same time a subject that experiences the world and an object in the world, depending on the viewpoint. The paradox can only be reflectively clarified when one understands that it arises from two different views on the same "thing," the subject.[23] It is as paradoxical as a trompe l'oeil in that one cannot "see" both items that the picture displays—Freud's head, the women—at once, though one knows that they are both "there." Once one takes the philosophical standpoint, this experiencing agent comes into view. As the paradigm of intentionality underlying this concept of subjectivity implies, the subject is always intentionally related to something experienced; its experience is always experience-of. In the sense that Husserl already stands in the Copernican mindset, so, too, does Kant already have an implicit notion of intentionality when shifting from thing-in-itself to appearance as appearance-for the human subject.[24]

With respect to the subject's experiences, all being is only experienced when given, and this is the only way in which it can be spoken of by the subject that is, qua experiencing, intentionally related. Thus, "intentionality" implies the relatedness between being and experiencing agent. Being is *relative to* the experiencing subject. This experiencing subject is, hence, the "*absolute*" as that to which all being is relative. This is merely another way of phrasing the basic idea of transcendental idealism: being can only be experienced from a perspective, and hence is relative to the perspective from where it is experienced or from where it shows itself as appearing. That to which being appears is absolute being, which is not an "absolute" standpoint (as should be clear from the previous chapter). What is absolute is the existence of *a* reference point from which being is experienced. Every being that appears, appears *to* this experiencing being and is, for us, the only being we can experience. It is an affirmation of transcendental idealism when Husserl writes (in 1908!): "There is only a being-in-itself outside absolute being; it is that which comes to be given through real and possible consciousness of being-in-itself (of things, of nature etc.). . . . It belongs to the essence of being to be-able-to-be-given" (Hua XXXVI, 32).[25]

Yet Husserl does not stop here. For while he does distinguish being for us vis-à-vis being-in-itself, he insists that it belongs to being's *essence* to be experienced. He uses the term *being-as-such,* which cannot but be being-given. As he writes, "To the essence of *all being* belongs a relation to consciousness" (Hua XXXVI, 36; italics added). How can Husserl say that, if this is not meant to be another form of anthropomorphism? To recall the Kantian shift from the theocentric to the anthropocentric model of cognition, why does Husserl not simply stop where Kant stopped, limiting himself to our specific human standpoint? The motive for rejecting the anthropocentric model goes back to the original impetus of Husserl's philosophizing: to stop at the human standpoint would be a form of *psychologism:* the thesis of the relativity of all being would again be relative to the *human* subject! The statement "To the essence of all being belongs a relation to consciousness" is an ideal statement, not pertaining to any particular consciousness.

One might object that, for all we know, creatures on Mars *could* have direct access to objects, without any relation through givenness. But this is absurd! *If* Martians have experience, and if this experience is mediated through sensibility, then they also can only have experience of appearances. As Husserl famously says, even God, if he had experience—that is, if God had some form of sensibility—could only see the object as given in profiles.[26] Thus, Kant was right to frame being as givenness, but he reduced this statement to givenness for us humans, thereby relativizing it. Hence the anthropocentric model leads to a relativism or subjectivism.

This, then, is the advance that Husserl's transcendental reduction introduces over the Copernican turn: Husserl is not talking about a concrete (human) subject in *this* world, but about consciousness-as-such, which has intentional experiences and something given *in* these experiences. In Husserl's terminology, Kant performs a *phenomenological* reduction and a turn to the subject, and maybe one could even speak of a *transcendental* reduction in Kant's focus on the *subjective forms* of intuition, but there is no *eidetic* "reduction" which moves from the *human* subject to *subjectivity-as-such*. Only this move can attain a truly scientific philosophy, which has to be about *vérités de raison,* not *de fait.* This is what Kant, too, wanted; but *vérités de raison* cannot be bound to, and relative to, any specific factual creature, such as the human being. Husserl's phenomenology in its transcendental-*eidetic* shape is a doctrine of experience-as-such, consciousness-as-such, and, correlatively, appearance-as-such. Phenomenology is not about the specific *human* manner of experiencing; rather, the human experience is only one possible manner in which a concrete subjectivity experiences world.

Husserl's phenomenology provides, hence, an eidetics of experience-as-such, of being-as-such being given *to* a subject-as-such.[27] Husserl *radicalizes* Kant's anthropocentric model by lifting it to the eidetic level— "rigorous" science—in considering *consciousness-as-such.* I shall term this a move from an anthropocentric to a *noocentric* concept of cognition (Greek *nous*), as moving from human consciousness to *consciousness-as-such,* whereby "consciousness" is shorthand for perspectivalness with its two foci: being as givenness and experiencing agent as having a standpoint. These are encompassed in Husserl's term "transcendental subjectivity."[28] Kant was right to emphasize the perspectivalness of the experiencing agent, and correlatively the status of being as givenness, but stopped short of *universalizing* this insight into an eidetics of experience.

But is such an abstraction to consciousness-as-such possible? One might object that it is *we* who say this. Indeed; but what we experience is all we have to go on, and it is from here—and only here—that we can begin eidetic variation, that is, abstraction from our personal standpoint. However, Husserl's point of abstraction is *not* to move *away* from a standpoint. The generalization that Husserl enacts is not one from standpoint to *no* standpoint, but from *our* standpoint to *standpoint-as-such.* And that this is possible is proven by mathematical abstraction: to speak of being as givenness, to say that being is experienced and hence is perspectival, is just as ideal a judgment as when in geometry we abstract from a triangle in the sand to the ideal triangle. The drawn triangle can give rise to geometrical insights—eidetic claims—without their being bound to our forms of intuiting it. In other words, our human standpoint does not bar us from making eidetic claims. And the eidetic claim here is that being, when experienced, can only be given to an agent with a standpoint, a "consciousness." Given Kant's insistence on the a priori status of pure geometry, Kant did not have to limit himself to our specific human experience in the "Transcendental Aesthetic." He would only have had to insist upon the specifically human standpoint as the necessary starting point for a philosophical inquiry. While Husserl would agree that a standpoint imposes a limitation, it was too much of a limitation on Kant's part *not* to include the idea of limitation on the *ideal* level. The noocentric account, too, includes this general notion of limitation, without sacrificing the status of *ideality.*

Hence, the transcendental-eidetic reduction universalizes Kant's "Transcendental Aesthetic": if being exists, it can be known only through experience—or through being's necessary relatedness—and experience presupposes a standpoint; hence being can only be known as given. It is nonsensical to speak of a being *outside* being given, because it, too, would presuppose experience without that which is *constitutive* of experience: a standpoint. This holds universally; it is the *essence* of external perception and gives a new meaning to the idealist doctrine of *esse est percipi.*[29] This move from an anthropocentric model of cognition to a noocentric model entails, thus, a reformulation of the *quid facti.* The *factum* is not that human cognition exists, but that *experience-as-such exists. This* is the *factum* whose conditions of possibility transcendental philosophy must clarify.

The question arising, then, is what bearing this noocentric model of cognition has on the question of a priori truths that we, according to Kant, are justified in having, in synthetic judgments a priori. Is not Husserl's transcendental idealism a *new* form of subjectivism, based entirely on experience? Where does a priori cognition, which is crucial to Kant, come into the picture? Let us see how Husserl avoids this subjectivistic consequence, which would go against the grain of his philosophy, and how he reconciles his insistence on the necessity of a standpoint with his conception of knowledge.

From Givenness Back to Being: Being as Valid Meaning and the Question of the *An-Sich*

To Husserl, Kant still remains within the strictures of rationalism by positing a distinction between two stems of cognition—sensibility and understanding—that have no relation (known to us)[30] to one another. Given this distinction, it is, in Kant, only the understanding that can, through the use of categories, produce cognition. We can see now how Husserl's "universal noocentrism" undercuts this very distinction by framing the notion "object of experience" in the broad sense of anything that can be *given*—be it to "external" or "inner" experience—phenomenologically, an artificial distinction. The phenomenological concept of *experience* denotes anything that shows itself in (its own forms of) evidence, but also only in the manners and boundaries in which it can show itself—this is the "principle of all principles" (Hua III/1, 51). Phenomenology's gaze, hence, encompasses *anything* that gives itself, with its two-sided structure (givenness-to and appearance-of). We *always* "gaze," internally or externally. Any distinction within the notion of "givenness," might refer to different types of givenness (perception, memory, phantasizing, etc.), but it is in principle *all givenness (to an agent)*.

Transcendental phenomenology is in this sense "subjectivism," if this means that Husserl is proposing a science of experience. But what kind of cognition can such a subjectivism produce? How do we get from subjective experience to objective knowledge? To address this issue, we must ask what concept of being as givenness Husserl's phenomenology proposes. What precisely is *givenness*? Answering these questions will let us see how Husserl's philosophy relates to the *quid iuris* question and the question of a priori cognition. Certainly, a universal noocentrism cannot be a sellout of rigorous scientific philosophy, though it entails a modification of Kant's original view on a priori cognition.

The phrase "being as givenness" is still an entirely formal concept. *What* is the given *given as*? The answer is that the object, the *x*, is given *as something*. There is no mediation or interpretation necessary in order to experience something *as something*. What I see is a car, and I hear a noise (the rattling of the muffler). The object is given immediately with a *meaning*;[31] what is experienced is in one way or another given with a specific *validity* (*Geltung*). *Es gilt* can be translated as "it holds," and can also have the sense "it holds meaning." This meaning is not a fixed entity. Rather, it depends on the standpoint that I occupy, and it can vary and change altogether.[32] The object is seen as an "independent" thing in the natural attitude, but as relational from the philosophical standpoint, that is, as it *gives* itself, and this "giving" is always accompanied by meaning. Hence, I can see a tree as a source of shade, a provider of produce, an object of sublime beauty—or "just" a "natural object." The object is experienced, given as *meaningful.* It has, in Husserl's terminology, a *noematic sense* that is valid for me. Things in the world *make sense.*[33] This sense, however, is given to an object by subjects who have bestowed this meaning upon it—not necessarily I myself, but other subjects before me, *a* (group of) subject(s). To see this object here as a wine glass is *already* a perception of a very complex, meaningful object, that is, of something as a container for potable liquid, with an aesthetic quality. But in any event I can say that the object, *as a meaningful thing in my surroundings,* has received this sense through (somebody's) meaning-bestowing acts. That is what we do when we experience: we experience something *as* something with a certain meaning. It is not a "raw" thing-in-itself that *then* receives meaning; what is heard *is the sound of a car, the meowing of a cat,* and so on.

The meaning-bestowing on things in their givenness Husserl calls *constitution.* We, and subjects as such, are *constituting* when experiencing, which is not a construction or production. Things in their givenness constitute *themselves* in our experience, and as meaningful they have a certain validity for us.[34] Indeed, this validity of something like a cultural object, a wine glass, is already very complex and presupposes an enormous number of simpler constitutive acts. Since acts are all we have to go on in our knowledge of this object, we can glean the type of work that the phenomenologist is to carry out: her task is to give an account of the full constitution of objects *in their noematic sense* in every possible layer, sphere, and dimension.[35] This can be carried out empirically—as by a cultural historian—but Husserl's goal is a transcendental-philosophical account, asking "How is it possible?" This marks the genetic dimension of Husserl's transcendental phenomenology: starting from the simplest acts in which an object becomes constituted—experienced *as something with a meaning*—the task is to give a description of experience of objects on all levels. Concerning external objects, one would begin by describing the kinesthetic interactions with it: the eye movements, touching it, seeing the front, anticipating the appearance of the back. This is what Husserl carries out in great detail in his genetic logic, which might also be called a universal noocentric account of experience by an embodied agent[36] as meaning-bestowing on a multitude of levels, beginning from the simplest and proceeding to the most complex ones, such as social, intersubjective acts, in which intersubjective agreement is achieved.[37] This is not cultural anthropology, but a transcendental account of how consciousness-as-such bestows meaning in different ways and in different complexities.

Thus, according to the noocentric account, consciousness-as-such is generally meaning-bestowing in its experiencing. What is experienced is always something that has meaning. But the specific noematic sense of the experienced *x* is not fixed. The meaning depends on the perspective and changes accordingly. But there is no normativity or dominance of one meaning over others. Depending on the perspective it can be seen as this or that (container of liquid, aesthetic object). It would be absurd to say that one would be "better" than the other. They are simply different noematic meanings depending on the standpoint one wishes to take. Even the standpoint of the scientist, while striving at objectivity, *remains* a standpoint.[38] Objectivity is in itself something constituted. This will have consequences for the very idea of objectivity.

The meaning within a specific perspective is always unfolding and expanding, and will never be fully revealed. The object will always disclose more aspects that enhance the meaning of the thing in its validity for me. But more experience of the thing does not necessarily continue to enhance the *specific* noematic sense. It does not have to "keep going." The sense can "explode," can turn out to be non-sense; the validity can be annulled. I may think I am certain that the object I see every day is a house, until one day I discover that it is a stage prop with no back. This discovery happens through some new experience that bestows new permutations of meaning. But in this case, the noematic sense *itself* is annulled; it is simply not what I expected it to be. But this can always happen. The meaning is only meaning *as long as . . .* , "until further notice." Yet, through the striking-through of a certain noematic sense, *automatically and immediately* a new one will arise: it is not a house, it is a stage prop— it is *x*, then non-*x*, which is immediately *y*. While the meaning-bestowing will always continue, it can be interrupted and annulled, but it immediately gives rise to a new meaning. It is always a meaning *of something*, the experience of which can change, but will always be experience in its constituting dynamic process.

In Husserl's words, experience is always only *presumptive*, is always only *for the time being*, and always has to affirm itself; the thing experienced has meaning only insofar as it has not been contradicted by new experience, something which is *always possible*. Thus, while the meaning can always change (the specific *vérité de fait*), this in itself is an eidetic law *of* experience (a *vérité de raison*), which is immutable. Hence, the general law is: all experience is contingent in constituting validity. Even the meaning of the world itself as a meaningful universe is only presumptively true and can always turn out to be a chaos, from which a new meaning arises. There can be no guarantee that the meaning that things have for us cannot change and be annulled. But a new validity will always arise. Experience is in this sense always *holistic and meaning-generating*, while the meaning is constantly subject to affirmation (*Bewährung*).

After these analyses we can return to Kant's *quid iuris* question and assess Husserl's reformulation of it. Kant's *quid iuris* presupposes the distinction between the two stems of cognition and clarifies why we are justified in making a priori judgments when applying categories to experience. The a priori judgments that Kant has in mind are scientific judgments, that is, a priori judgments about the world as it is experienced scientifically. The *quid iuris* question presupposes that we indeed *have*, as *factum*, truths of "necessary and universal" dignity. *Husserl's* point is: when it comes to experience and judgments based on this experience, there *can be* no a priori judgments (universal and necessary). It *is* universally and necessarily the case that all judgments about something experienced are *presumptive*, which does not question their truth, but all truth about experienced being is only truth *at this point in time* and can always be annulled. Truth with respect to objects of experience—not eidetic laws of experience itself—can be objective, but only *for the time being*, with the possibility that it will be modified or annulled, yielding new truth. Thus, the *quid iuris* question, to Husserl, cannot be taken to be asking about the a priori that Kant had in mind—the synthetic a priori. Husserl's notion of a priori is *dynamic*. The only thing we can say with unchanging certainty with respect to objects of experience is that all experience about worldly things is presumptive; the cognition of them is ever changing. Scientific judgments about them make a claim to objectivity, which is perfectly legitimate if one understands objectivity as in principle fallible.[39]

Husserl hence transforms the question of *quid iuris* into that of *quid valoris*. The claim to the legitimacy of making objective judgments about objects of experience is not in itself rejected. Instead, this question turns out to be already situated on a higher level of experience and becomes *underpinned* by the question concerning the *validity* of objects as they give themselves in experience, *prior* to cognitive claims being made about them. The legitimacy of making such claims must be grounded in experience itself. The transcendental question, then, must be phrased as follows: how are we justified in experiencing objects as having a certain *validity*, which is *validity for us*? The general answer is: through meaning-bestowing acts from transcendental subjectivity. *This* is the *factum*, being as givenness to an experiencing subject *as validity*; the "how possible" question is hence not about the legitimate category application to experienced objects, but about the how of givenness and meaning-bestowing on *each* specific level of experience, all the way up to experience where truth claims are constituted. Kant's *quid iuris* question *presupposes* not only that we have objects *given* but that we experience them *with a certain validity*, which need not be *scientific* validity. Regarding types of validity, scientific validity is no "better" than aesthetic, commonsensical, or religious, and so on, validity.

Kant was right about the *constitution* of synthetic judgments a priori, that is, as a matter of synthesis enacted by a part of the subject, the understanding, which is to Husserl a mental capacity not in principle different from other subjective "accomplishments." Moreover, Kant had a mathematical concept of a priori, which means that his analysis is located on a very high level of experience, the discourse of science. Accordingly, what Kant meant by "objects of experience" are those of the scientist, not the objects in the lifeworld, which are constituted as well, albeit on lower levels of constitution.[40] Husserl writes, with reference to Kant's *quid iuris* question: "The transcendental question as to the essence, the meaning of every right [*Recht*, Latin *ius*] . . . metamorphoses into the question whether and to what extent [this right] is *valid, can* be valid. This pertains comprehensively to all positive *world*-cognition and thereby in fact to *all* positive sciences" (Hua VII, 271). Here Husserl is placing Kant's question in the genetic perspective. Kant is not "wrong," but starts "too high up," presupposing the meaning of "right" and *its* constitution. The legitimacy of category application in a priori synthetic judgments presupposes this same ability on much simpler levels of discourse and, in terms of our complex life in the world, is a far too limited account of experiencing things as meaningful. The *lifeworld* is experienced as meaningful, and scientific ("objective") meaning is just one of many types of meaning. This in no way mitigates the legitimacy and importance of science, but emphasizes the need to see it in a layered account of the constitution of the lifeworld from simplest to most complex experiences. In terms of the *Crisis,* Kant is guilty of the forgetfulness of the lifeworld.

Finally, what does this interpretation of being as validity say about the status of the *An-sich* of objects? Husserl obviously rejects the notion that there is a thing-in-itself *behind* the appearance. Yet appearances are, of course, appearances *of the thing;* the noematic sense is the sense of the object as it is intended to be (as house, as prop). All of these senses are "true" in their own right, as we said, and there can always be new noematic senses, new perspectives. And the specific noematic sense itself is never exhausted; I can always find more aspects of the thing. But these are aspects *of the thing,* not a mere appearance with a true object behind it. It is the real thing that we experience, *despite* its givenness in profiles. There is thus a positive way of retaining a sense of thing-in-itself, as an *idea* of all aspects, all noematic senses with all their profiles and perspectives, *experienced at once.*[41] It is a Kantian (regulative) idea. As it lies in infinity, the thing's experiences are never exhausted, but we *experience the thing.* We are immediately in touch with it in the way that it appears to us in a specific attitude as noematic sense with a certain validity. This is a sense that can always be struck through, and a new sense can be given. We *are* immediately in touch with the *An-sich* of the thing, though *through* the specific noematic sense, which is not a "filter," but a way of experiencing through a perspective, and we can occupy only one perspective at one point in time. Thing-in-itself and thing-as-experienced (noematic sense) differ not as two different viewpoints on the same thing, or as two different considerations. They are, rather, distinguished *within* the philosophical consideration. The difference concerns the object as experienced *now,* at point, and the (idea of the) object experienced at *all* points in time, all of which would only show *appearances,* but appearances of the *real thing "in the flesh."*

In sum, Husserl has given us a new sense of transcendental philosophy. Kant's original idea was to introduce a perspective on our experiencing; this is the first and most basic sense of transcendental idealism. Thereby, however, Kant's view remained anthropocentric. To Husserl, Kant's philosophy cannot really be a *science* of subjectivity, only a transcendental metaphysics of the human mind, construed in pure formality. Husserl expands the range of subjectivity towards subjectivity-as-such, bringing philosophy to the level of "rigorous science." One result of this universal noocentric discipline is the expansion of the scope of experience as the mode in which givenness is received (constituted), undercutting Kant's two-stems doctrine. The science of experience as such starts on a much more primitive level. Kant's understanding of experience was the cognizing experience of the scientist; Husserl's concept of experience is the everyday experience in the lifeworld, from which higher-order types of experience, such as scientific experience, arise. The lifeworld is the world experienced from the standpoint of the natural attitude, from which the transcendental questioning-back must begin as an inquiry into the conditions of possibility of this validity. Where for Kant the transcendental question was about legitimate category application to sensible objects, it is, in Husserl, first about meaning application to being, thereby creating ("constituting") meaning with validity. In every experience, we experience meaning that can always turn out to be false, but there always *will* be valid meaning. Husserl's transcendental question concerns the *quid valoris.*

Finally, whereas Kant saw an unbridgeable gap between objects as given and the thing-in-itself, which we cannot know, Husserl has brought us back to the thing-in-itself. It is the thing-in-itself as a limit idea lying in infinity, to which we, however, have direct access through our experience, which is always from a certain perspective and always only presumptive. His conception is thus closely connected to modern philosophy of science, which sees all truth with respect to experienced objects as provisional and in principle falsifiable.[42] In all of this, Husserl has furthered certain insights already present in Kant and made significant headway himself. Kant had an ingenious insight in the form of the Copernican turn that intrigued many thinkers who succeeded him, including Husserl. Regarding the basic insight of transcendental idealism, being as givenness, Husserl is in complete agreement with Kant. He only forcefully brings home the point that this move, instead of taking us away from the world as thing-in-itself to some speculative realm, is the grand path, the *only* path, to the *world itself* and is the only way to account for it philosophically. Such an account must *begin* with experience on the most basic level up to scientific judgment, in which objective truth claims become articulated. Husserl thus reconstructs philosophically what was the very starting point for Kant's entire endeavor: the synthetic a priori itself.

Conclusion: From Being to Action: Kant's and Husserl's Practical Postulates

I have tried to reconstruct a trajectory from Kant's project to Husserl's by showing that the Kantian move from the theocentric to the anthropocentric model of cognition becomes radicalized in Husserl's noocentric model of experience. The question of cognition in Husserl becomes more deeply founded in that of experience, that is, the question of a priori truths about experienced objects becomes reframed as that of their validity for the experiencing agent, ultimately for a community of interacting agents. This community is that from which scientific judgments, among other achievements—works of art, buildings, poetry, television shows—are generated. The validity of objects in their noematic sense is a Kantian idea. This introduces a new notion of transcendental idealism that salvages Kant's original impulse, while breaking with Kant's rationalist paradigm of the synthetic a priori.

But let us take a look back at Kant's systematic scope. While it is the *positive* function of his philosophy to carve out a new sense of metaphysics, a realm in which we can rightfully lay claim to a priori truths, this is only one aspect of his project. The other, negative, function is to *delimit* the boundaries of knowledge, thereby "making room for faith."[43] This faith is that in mankind's progress to gain access to the Kingdom of Ends, the realm of freedom. Thus, the entire project of delimiting theoretical reason was to make space for *practical* reason, to show how the limits of *thinking* lead to the possibility of *action*. The entire purpose of Kant's critique was to demonstrate the noumenal character of freedom and the practical necessity of attempting to realize it precisely through the intrinsic limitations of theoretical reason. Given this apparent imbalance between theoretical and practical reason in Kant, one is compelled to ask if one can find anything similar in Husserl's "system."

Husserl saw this connection between cognitive Is and moral Ought. His statement concerning his relation to Kant in the letter to Cassirer ends rather cryptically. Listing a number of problems remaining unsolved in Kant's philosophy, he concludes: "To these belong the problems of facticity as such, those of 'irrationality,' which . . . can only be addressed in an expanded method of the Kantian postulates. The latter are perhaps the greatest of all Kantian discoveries" (Hua-Dok III/5, 6).

As Kern has pointed out, the postulates that Husserl is talking about here are Kant's postulates of practical reason.[44] This suggestion can be supported by a manuscript from the same period, entitled "Kant's Doctrine of Postulates" (Hua VIII, 354–55),[45] in which Husserl illuminates the above passage. Human life, he muses, when viewed "in transcendental introspection," can always end in chaos and absurdity, and certainly will end in death. "The whole world will end, my people, with its entire value system of European culture and ultimately every world culture" (Hua VIII, 354). Further, with respect to the fact that a culture has been established with its abiding structure and continual meaning-bestowal, the question of *its* validity and its necessity arise as well. What happens when we consider the final goal of the world as we know it? Is this necessary? Indeed it isn't—it is just as presumptive as anything else, a merely contingent fact. This gives rise to the next question: "What if the course of passive and active constitution and thus a subjective life in the form of a human lived-body in relation to its constituted surroundings were an 'accident'—and if the conditions of the possibility of a continuing valuable life . . . were only contingent and only partially and temporarily fulfilled?" (Hua VIII, 354–55). The answer is, "It may well be the case"; there is no reason to believe that the course of our history, or any history, has any internal connection to a transcendent and necessary truth to which it approximates itself. As Husserl says, alluding to Kant, nothing in this world, which I know through experience, can make me believe with necessity that it all makes *any* sense. It could all be illusion and idle and futile attempts.

In view of this possibility, there are only two alternatives. One result could be utter negation and a life in "constant despair," which excludes action, in a sort of Schopenhauerian resignation.[46] The other alternative is "affirmation" of a world that *is* meaningful and replete, not with an illusory meaning, but with fulfilled, real sense. Whence does "affirmation" derive its force? This sense, since we cannot *know* that it in fact exists, can only be hoped for and demanded in the form of a *moral Ought*. This unconditioned Ought, Husserl asserts, is found in the Kantian categorical imperative as an absolute demand to action. Given this Ought, Husserl concludes: "Such a demand can only have meaning if I live; and if I live for it fully and absolutely, then I also believe, even if perhaps I am not clarifying this for myself, precisely because this belief is necessarily co-given [with this demand]. But when I reflect [upon these matters] I see: one [the belief] is impossible without the other [the demand]. If, however, I believe and become conscious of this belief, and enact it from this practical source *freely,* then it gives meaning to the world and to my life, gives the joyful confidence that nothing is in vain and all is for the good" (Hua VIII, 355).

What Husserl seems to say in this enigmatic passage is that viewing (cognitively!) the world as a meaningful whole is *in itself* a moral Ought. While the insight into the presumptive nature of our world *could* lead to despair, it can also lead to an absolute affirmation in the form of the demand stemming from the moral Ought, in which meaning is created through my belief in the moral law. It is, hence, the belief in a thoroughly and truly meaningful world that can save me from the existential despair into which I could fall given Husserl's transcendental idealism, according to which all cognition, and my entire culture, is only presumptive and potentially falsifiable. So it seems that Husserl needs the hope for a meaningful world more desperately than anybody else! Given the potentially bleak outlook on the meaninglessness of the world, one needs to feel the *moral* demand to fill this potential void.

The interesting Husserlian point, vis-à-vis Kant, would be: Kant believes in the certainty of *some* a priori cognition, but thereby acknowledges the *limits* of cognition, relegating these limitations to the hope that we can help in creating a better world through *action*. We *ought* to act, as we can understand from the moral law in us. But the success of practical action is always uncertain, prone to error and mistake. Kant's move is from *limited* certainty to *boundless* hope, for we cannot know what this Kingdom of Ends would be like. It is a noumenon. Thus, Kant's transcendental idealism extends into the ethical realm as well, and necessarily so, as the limiting part of the critique of reason is the gateway to action. For *Husserl,* from the essential uncertainty of theoretical cognition follows precisely the morally *prescribed* certainty that the world has meaning *because* I know that I can attempt to realize this meaning through practical action. The certainty we are talking about, then, is not *cognitive* certainty, but "joyful confidence that all is for the good." It is a certainty restored based on the rejection of Kant's notion of a priori cognition. This follows from Husserl's transcendental idealism: the world is meaningful if we choose to *perceive* it as meaningful, if we wish to *give* it a sense and decide to act accordingly. We are the authors of this optimism concerning human capabilities. And only this optimism, for which there is no other reason than the moral demand, gives us *any* incentive to act at all. Hence we can only *act* morally in a world *after* the theoretical insight that the world *ought to* make sense. Husserl's notion of Ought is thereby theoretical, not practical; it is first and foremost a theoretical insight that must then be acted on practically. But when we act, we realize theoretically that we cannot *avoid* acting in a way that is meaning-bestowing *while* the meaning we bestow can always turn out to be wrong. Morality's demand, hence, *begins* already on the level of meaning-constitution. We cannot *help* but try to come up with a *valid* meaning and implement it actively. The success of both—meaning-bestowal and realization—must forever remain doubtful, but creating such a final vision is a regulative idea that can fill us with hope, while we are active in this creation. Joy occurs in the creative process itself, though disappointment always looms.[47]

In the end, Husserl's phenomenology is a solid affirmation of the Kantian postulates, which can be summarized essentially as: what cannot be thought, must be done. This is the only way in which we can hope to get any closure in a world that is never perfect, but contains meaning; a meaning it receives through us, and only through us—though we can always fail, but also must never despair. Not to despair *in itself* is a moral demand. In this light, Husserl has remained a "true Kantian" in the best sense as both a firm and an "idealistic" (in the everyday sense of the word) believer in the human capacity to create a better world, with the realistic sense that we can always fail. The positive as well as the negative aspects of Kant's *Critique* are thereby satisfied in equal measure.

From Kant to the Neo-Kantians: Subjectivity and Its Method of Analysis

This chapter first merged Husserl explicitly with the intellectual realm of transcendental idealism in the specifically Kantian form. It makes clear to what extent, but also in which limits, Husserl is a necessary and intrinsic part of the tradition of classical German philosophy. Thus, historically the first thinker in this line of tradition is Kant; but it was Husserl's contemporaries, the neo-Kantians, especially of the Marburg school, who first made him familiar with this tradition. Especially Husserl's contemporary Paul Natorp in Marburg was Husserl's most intimate connection with Kantianism, more so than the Southwest German representatives. To focus on this productive *Auseinandersetzung,* thus, must be the next chapter in the story of Husserl's relation to transcendental philosophy. But the irony of the story is that Natorp's influence on Husserl did not *primarily* pertain to the question of transcendental philosophy, but rather to that part of *phenomenology* which was traditionally believed to be the one *farthest removed* from Kant and the neo-Kantian tradition, namely the question of subjectivity as a field of research, not just a formal principle (be it as "I think" or "I posit"). Thus, Natorp was able to "help" Husserl in the domain that was considered the true achievement and lasting "possession" of the phenomenologists. To shed light on the relation between Natorp and Husserl is another argument for the claim, implicit here, that both traditions were not as far apart as is usually thought. Thus, regarding Husserl's conception of subjectivity and the question of analyzing it, the Kantian tradition related to Husserl by way of Natorp was *at least as important* for Husserl's development as that thinker and his school from which he stemmed and which was so inimical to Kant and the Kantians: Brentano and the Brentanists. The next chapter continues the as of now largely untold story of the relation between Husserl and the transcendental tradition.

Reconstruction and Reduction: Natorp and Husserl on Method and the Question of Subjectivity

Introduction

Paul Natorp's influence on the development of Edmund Husserl's phenomenology, especially on the transcendental reduction and genetic method in Husserl, has been vastly underestimated. Husserl's contemporary, Natorp (1854–1924) was an exact observer and critic of Husserl's philosophical development from before the publication of his *Logical Investigations* (1900/1901) and up to Natorp's death. Moreover, Natorp was the single contemporary philosopher with whom Husserl had the most intimate contact, as is witnessed by their extensive correspondence.[1] Natorp provided the "interface" through which Husserl came into contact with the neo-Kantianism that was then prevalent in Germany philosophy, as well as with Kant himself.[2] As Husserl acknowledged after his transcendental turn, it was his discussions with representatives of the transcendental tradition, that is, the neo-Kantians, that aided him in developing a full-fledged *transcendental* phenomenology. His closest ally among these erstwhile opponents was undoubtedly Natorp.[3]

The relation between phenomenology and neo-Kantianism remains to a large extent an untold story, though the intersections between both schools are extensive. But to tell this story will prove decisive for the development of twentieth-century philosophy and beyond, and disentangling the many strands of these interactions has more than just historical merit. The present chapter can only be the beginning of this story, which will be continued in the next two chapters, and it will focus on the relation between Natorp and Husserl and the most important issue that fueled their discussion. This issue is that of the status of transcendental philosophy, especially as it purports to be the method proper for the analysis of *concrete subjectivity*. The original impulse to undertake such an endeavor came, interestingly, from Natorp, whose philosophical psychology—in contradistinction to other brands of psychology, such as Brentano's "descriptive psychology"—intended to carry out such an analysis within the framework of the "Marburg" transcendental method inaugurated by his teacher Hermann Cohen. In so doing, however, Natorp was already in a sense going beyond Cohen's methodological confines. He found in Husserl a kindred spirit in such an attempt, as shall be shown.

While Husserl was striving to develop his own philosophical method and school—this tendency called the "phenomenological movement" is akin to what was frequently called the "movement back to Kant"—he nevertheless with one eye, and competitively, peered at the neo-Kantians. Husserl's philosophical method of phenomenological reduction and his turn to transcendental phenomenology were developed in close discussion with Natorp. This was so much the case that many of Husserl's followers believed, upon reading *Ideas I* (1913), that he had become a Kantian himself and had thereby fallen back into the naive or speculative idealism that phenomenology had supposedly overcome once and for all.[4] However, it is more appropriate to say that the influence that representatives of the neo-Kantian tradition exerted on Husserl helped him come into his own. Natorp's influence on Husserl also extends to the very way phenomenological description should be carried out. As has been argued by Iso Kern in his *Husserl und Kant* (1964)—the first study to address this topic—and again more recently by Donn Welton in *The Other Husserl* (2000; 443n38), the development of Husserl's later genetic phenomenological method is inspired by Natorp's concept of a "reconstructive" analysis of consciousness. Put more strongly, Husserl would have been unable to attain this late stage without Natorp's influence.

Hence, this chapter will claim that Natorp was the decisive factor that led Husserl to develop both the phenomenological reduction and his later genetic phenomenology. Although their philosophical presuppositions and education, as well as their understanding of the nature of philosophy, were quite different from the outset,[5] Natorp and Husserl were working on parallel problems and in close proximity, which enabled them to benefit from each other. For his part, Natorp was attempting to draft a philosophical psychology that intended to counter the "objectifying" tendency of the transcendental method developed by his teacher Hermann Cohen. This was called for, according to Natorp, in order to recapture the concrete life of the subject. And indeed, the same philosophical motivation lay behind Husserl's phenomenology and its call to the "things themselves." Yet it was, ironically, Husserl who exploited and executed the project for which Natorp strove but himself later abandoned (and the many attempts on the part of neo-Kantians to "overcome" their original positions would be another, perhaps final, chapter of the story that is only begun here). Thus, the relation between Natorp and Husserl does not point to a simple one-sided "learning" of one from the other; instead, it bespeaks a genuine *symphilosophein* on issues which were commonly held to be vital for doing transcendental philosophy. Especially in the light of Husserl's later self-interpretation, phenomenology is conceived (in line with Natorp) as critical philosophy and is committed to transcendental idealism, as the ultimate scope of his philosophical project demonstrates when it finally does justice to the concrete subject and its lifeworld as a world of culture.[6]

Husserl knew what he owed to the neo-Kantians: "After having learned to see Kant from my own perspective, I am now able, and especially in the last years, to receive rich instructions from Kant and the true Kantians," Husserl writes to Ernst Cassirer in 1925 (Hua-Dok III/5, 4).[7] By the time Husserl composes the *Crisis* in 1936, however, he again obfuscates most traces of contemporary influence and mentions only the most outstanding philosophers in the modern Western tradition (Descartes, Kant, the British empiricists) as having had any significant impact on him.[8] One reason for this omission may have been the historical fact that after Natorp's death and the emigration of many German philosophers of Jewish descent after 1933—Cassirer among them—the neo-Kantian movement had all but died off in Germany. Nevertheless, as of 1913 Husserl had shared with the neo-Kantians an agreement on the fundamental issues of philosophy—points of convergence, which Husserl's first presentation of phenomenology in the *Logical Investigations* of 1900–1901 had explicitly shunned. There are certainly immanent reasons for Husserl to widen his philosophy from a descriptive psychology to a full-fledged transcendental phenomenology, first in a static, and then in a genetic register. But there is a somewhat unhealthy tendency in Husserl scholarship to ignore, or at least downplay, the influences Husserl was exposed to early in his career, especially if they issued from thinkers outside of the Brentano school. Exposing the intersections between Natorp and Husserl will help to rectify a skewed view of Husserl and the influences he incorporated into his mature system. But this chapter is not just about Husserl; instead, we shall focus on the philosophical issues *common* to Husserl and Natorp. Rather than playing one off against the other, this discussion will demonstrate how the accommodation of certain theoretical elements in both thinkers led to a richer account and philosophically more satisfying theory of subjectivity in its "concreteness" within the framework of transcendental philosophy.

Hence, in this chapter Natorp's and Husserl's theories of subjectivity and their respective methods for analyzing it shall be compared. Their philosophical disciplines are termed, respectively, psychology (Natorp) and phenomenology (Husserl). I would like to point out differences and also draw out commonalities, but most importantly to show how both are working on the same project: namely, an attempt to analyze subjectivity in its most *original concreteness*. Both Natorp's method of reconstruction and Husserl's method of reduction add decisive elements to such a theory. Although Natorp rejects any experience of the life of the subject through reflection (or "introspection"), Husserl takes over, in a modified way, the former's idea of a reconstructive method, which he employs for a *genetic* account of subjectivity. Hence, this debate is also about the methodological principle of *phenomenology*, which, as it turns out, cannot restrict itself to pure intuition alone. For a phenomenological account of subjectivity, this is an insight of the highest importance.

While Natorp is critical toward his own method and in the last step of his philosophical development moves toward a "general unifying logic"— a doctrine of categories that unifies both "objectifying" and "subjectifying" tendencies—it is, ironically, *Husserl* who actually carries out Natorp's "grand vision" of a truly philosophical psychology. Natorp's method and conception of psychology proved a dead end for Natorp himself, but had a lasting importance for Husserl's late conception of subjectivity, which needed to be framed in a genetic register in order to capture subjectivity's "full concretion." Husserl's mature phenomenology, thus, can rightfully be considered phenomenological *as well as* neo-Kantian. Husserl thus recasts the method for analyzing subjectivity in a way that cannot remain strictly phenomenological in the traditional sense of pure description. His mature method goes beyond the common scope of phenomenology with the help of the methodological tools that he took over from Natorp. Husserl was able to adopt Natorpian elements because both shared in principle the same goal—to analyze the concreteness of subjectivity *without* succumbing to a pre-transcendental, naive philosophy of "existence."

The following sections will develop these issues by following the historical order in which Husserl and Natorp interacted with each other between the 1890s and 1924—the year of Natorp's death—though Natorp's influence can be discerned up until Husserl's death in 1938.

Natorp's Theory of Reconstruction and Husserl's Method of Reduction

Natorp's Position: Subjectivation versus Objectivation

Since Natorp's position was already well established by the time Husserl developed his phenomenology, it deserves to be discussed first. Natorp drew the conclusion of the Marburg reading of Kant, especially for the discipline of psychology. He presented his theory in an article of 1887, "Ueber subjective und objective Begründung der Erkenntniss" ("On the Subjective and Objective Grounding of Cognition"), as well as in his short book *Introduction to Psychology According to Critical Method* (*Einleitung in die Psychologie nach kritischer Methode*) of 1888. This concept of psychology was further developed in the completely reworked *General Psychology According to Critical Method* (*Allgemeine Psychologie nach kritischer Methode*) of 1912 (1912a).[9] As mentioned, the problems with this conception later led Natorp to abandon his psychology altogether and to develop, in his late work, what he called a "general logic." In this late conception of logic—which was sketched in his posthumously published lecture courses, *Lectures on Practical Philosophy* (*Vorlesungen über praktische Philosophie*, 1924) and *Philosophical Systematic* (*Philosophische Systematik*, 1954)—Natorp comes close to Cassirer's conception in the *Philosophy of Symbolic Forms*. As we shall see in the following chapters, one could even make the claim that Cassirer's philosophy was but the execution—with some important modifications—of Natorp's sketch of a philosophical systematics; and that, in this respect, both Natorp and Cassirer moved beyond the neo-Kantian project of a science which lays ultimate foundations, the *Grundlegungswissenschaft* inaugurated by Hermann Cohen.

The Marburg neo-Kantian position can be best characterized by the so-called *transcendental method*.[10] This method, first explicated by Cohen in his interpretations of Kant's *Critique of Pure Reason*, was further developed by Natorp and exploited for the discipline of philosophical psychology. Natorp's early work defined this task as filling a gap in the framework of Cohen's transcendental method. This is to say, what Natorp means by "psychology" is not an empirical discipline but a subdiscipline under the rubric of transcendental philosophy. Husserl understands it, quite correctly, as "aprioric psychology."[11] How does this fit in with the transcendental method, and what is the transcendental method about?

The starting point of philosophy, for Cohen, is the given reality as a *factum*. However, the *factum* that Cohen claims is primarily the *factum* of the positive sciences (*das Faktum der Wissenschaften*). *The factum* is not a *factum brutum*, but itself cognition. After all, neo-Kantianism arose in the midst of the scientism of the second half of the nineteenth century, when there was seemingly nothing left for philosophy to do apart from providing a foundation or explanatory basis for the activities of the positive sciences. However, Natorp insists—and this is where his own thinking sets in—that the *factum* is in effect a *fieri*, that is, something that is *made* through cognizing acts in the sciences: what is ascertained in the sciences is the product of theoretical activities. Through these activities the scientist explains the world as governed by a priori laws. The world is in this sense *constructed* through cognizing activities. We shall see, however, that the scope of Natorp's epistemology already goes beyond this limitation to scientific cognition. The term Natorp uses is *Erkenntnis,* which has the known ambivalence of meaning both explicit, specifically scientific or philosophical "cognizing" as well as simply "knowledge" as that *which is known—and* it is *both* meanings that Natorp wants to grasp.[12]

Hence, the transcendental method is about giving a logical justification regarding the conditions that govern the construction of reality through subjective, cognizing acts. The construction of reality is the deed of the scientist, but the philosopher thematizes the a priori conditions that factor into this construction of reality. Insofar as these cognizing acts ascertain something *lawful* through their activity, these laws can be called "objective." In short, the transcendental method of constructing reality can also be called "objectifying." It is about constructing objective reality through subjective acts, insofar as they cognize something objective, something with the character of a *law.* The law is a subjective production but, as objective and "fixed," is *no longer* subjective. Subjectivity thus becomes *objectified;* it is *in* objectifications that we find subjectivity. The method of objectivation—that is, the transcendental method—is about the objective founding and constructing of knowledge. Knowledge, insofar as it can be called scientific knowledge, has the character of lawfulness. Laws, in turn, are not fleeting or dynamic, but static and abstract vis-à-vis their appearances in the subject. This is precisely what makes them "objective."

Natorp goes on to argue, however, that not just cognizing ascertainments with the character of laws are objectifying: subjective life as such is objectifying, although it may not always be lawful. This becomes most visible in utterances. All judgments are objectifying insofar as they claim *something.* This is the character of "objectifying cognizing [*Erkenntnis*], scientific *as well as* pre-scientific: . . . to make objects out of appearances [*Erscheinungen*]" (Natorp 1912a, 193; italics added).[13] In other words, the transcendental method can and in fact must be expanded to cover not only objectifying acts in the sciences, but all activities of a subject which are objectifying *in one way or another,* and of which lawful cognizing in the *emphatic* sense of *Erkenntnis* is the highest (and thus the norm for all other judgments). In this respect, Natorp claims that his constructive method proceeds teleologically, beginning *genetically* with the lowest form of objectifications in everyday utterances (which have no explicit truth-claims), and up to the highest *forms* of objectifications in scientific discourse.[14] Thus, to sum up: the transcendental method of constructing reality in *Natorp's* interpretation is about ascertaining objectifications and their conditions by means of subjective acts, precisely by *objectifying* them. With this turn to the subjective, however, Natorp is already departing from Cohen's transcendental method, for which the objective laws alone are of interest.

What then, asks Natorp, about the subjective "side" of things? Where do subjectivity and its study, psychology, stand in regard to this project? The method or process of objectivation raises a significant question: If all subjective acts *objectify* in a given way, then what about the specifically *subjective* character of these acts? What happens with subjectivity? If subjectivity is objectified in the construction of reality, and if all subjective activities are objectifying, what about those pertaining to subjectivity itself? Obviously they, too, will be objectifying.[15] The result of this objectification is that subjectivity will be treated in the same, constructive way; the result is psychology as a scientific discipline, which in this sense is not different from biology, which objectifies biological affairs. However, in so doing, that element which precisely makes for the subjectivity of the subject—its dynamic, fleeting, concrete life—is lost. There can be, according to Natorp, *no direct description* of the subject in its genuine state of living, since every thematization is objectifying. As Natorp adds dramatically, that which makes the subject a subject is "killed."[16] In thematizing the subject one thus deals, metaphorically speaking, with a corpse instead of a living being. *All* traditional psychology supposedly proceeds in this way: it ascertains *facts* about subjectivity, and in this process loses the subject. The "spirit" of the subject vanishes in thematizing it, for thematization is objectivation. Thus it seems that psychology, at least in the sense of a description of states of affairs, is rendered impossible from the outset. This is indeed Natorp's answer, *unless* one construes psychology as a philosophical discipline which pays heed to the special character of subjectivity: this is the task that Natorp set for "transcendental psychology."

What is needed, then, for a philosophical psychology is a method which allows for a thematization of subjectivity that is *not* objectifying or constructive. This method is now the opposite of construction; rather, it is reconstructive. The method, which is opposed to objectivation—namely subjectivation—is that of a *reconstruction* of subjectivity by going back, regressively, from its objectifications. Whereas the objective method focuses on the relation between an opaque subject, which constructs objectivity, and this objectivity itself, the subjective method turns 180 degrees and looks at the relation of the (constructed) object to the (constructing) subject. As such, it is the *inverse method* of objectivation, and Natorp also speaks of it as a "turning inside out" (*Umstülpung*) of objectification. Whereas construction proceeds teleologically toward objective laws, which are abstract and unifying, the reconstructive method is genetic: it goes back to that which has constructed reality—the dynamic structures of consciousness, subjectivity's concrete life. Whereas objective laws are always mediated through constructions, the method of reconstruction goes back to the *immediateness* of subjective appearances, to conscious phenomena. It is about a "reconstruction of the immediate in consciousness" (Natorp 1912a, 199). Natorp also calls these conscious givennesses "phenomena." Thus, quite phenomenologically, the reconstructive method is about a recovery of the phenomena of consciousness, which are otherwise only objectified. In the *Introduction to Psychology* of 1888, Natorp even uses the term "reduction" for this move: "Thus for all spheres" of consciousness, he writes—for instance, "scientific representations as well as unscientific representations such as fantasy, but also the regions of feeling, desiring, willing"—"the same task is posed, [namely,] that of a *reduction of the always already and in some way or other objectified representation to the immediate of consciousness*" (Natorp 1888, 89; italics added). It is no exaggeration that Husserl can be interpreted as taking over *the term as well as the project* of this reconstructive procedure.

Before asserting critical questions, one should point out the valid philosophical motivation for this move: in his insistence on the difference between objectifying (constructive) and subjectifying (reconstructive) methods, Natorp clearly intends to preserve the radically different character of subjectivity vis-à-vis the sphere of objectivity. The distinction between subjectivity and objectivity is so strong that it can almost be considered an "ontological difference." It is about doing justice methodologically to "subjective *qualia*" which, if one were to treat them in an objectifying manner, would vanish precisely *in* their qualitative character as the dynamic, concrete life of the subject.[17] It is not so much that Natorp denies *any* access to subjectivity; rather, he merely warns that in *describing* consciousness one is already objectifying it. But this does not mean that consciousness, in its genuine character, cannot be *thematized* altogether; this thematization simply cannot be a *direct* description, but rather must be a reconstruction. It is not descriptive as such, but explanatory: it retroactively explains subjectivity in going back from its objectivations and explaining the specifically subjective moments which were involved in a given objectivation. Whereas objectification is teleological, subjectification is a "reverse teleology": it is a *causal* reconstruction of objectifications.

Hence, "objectivating" and "subjectivating" methods are nothing but opposite movements on an identical line.[18] One can proceed positively and reach the objectivations in construction, or move in the opposite, negative direction in order to "undo" the objectifications into subjective structures. The method of subjectivation is about regaining the dynamic, flowing subjective life *from which* fixed, crystallized objectiva-tions have been constructed. Thus, on the side of objectivation there are *laws,* which are unified and abstract. On the side of subjectivation there are *phenomena,* which are plural and manifold and concrete because they have not been objectified—and these must be preserved as such by the subjective method. Subjective life cannot be directly described but only reconstructively explained. The only "positive" and irreducible structure of consciousness (*Bewußtsein*) that one can discern is the *fact that it has (something) conscious* (*Bewußtheit:* "conscious-ity," "the fact of having some-thing conscious"). This having (something) conscious, Natorp calls sub-jectivity's fundamental character of "relation" (*Verbindung* or *Relation*). Thus, the fundamental trait of subjectivity is *having (something) conscious,* yet this "something" has always already been objectified. The pure rela-tion of *being conscious-of,* however, is the original structure of subjectivity into which one cannot further inquire.[19]

Husserl's Critique: Natorp's Reconstructive Method Is Blind to Intentionality

Husserl first discusses Natorp's position in the first edition of the *Logical Investigations.* Here he is critical of several points in Natorp's account, most famously that of the "pure Ego"—of which, however, Husserl later says that he "has learned to find it" (Hua XIX/2, 374, note). Hence Hus-serl's rejection of Natorp's notion of the pure Ego is a moot point for the Husserl of the *Ideas* of 1913. As he adds in the second edition of the *Logical Investigations* (also 1913), Husserl left this passage (§8 of the Fifth Investigation) nearly unchanged for the sake of documenting a historical and (according to him, at least) dated debate, because Husserl, being originally "metaphysics shy" with regard to the question of a pure Ego, had allegedly moved on in the intervening years. Thus, what Husserl calls "pure" Ego in his early critique of Natorp is nothing but the latter's concept of *Bewußtheit.* The fact of having (something) conscious, Husserl holds (in full agreement with Natorp), has a necessary relation *to whom* something is conscious. Hence, the concept of *Bewußtheit* implies a pure Ego as a "unifying referential point" (Hua XIX/2, 372).[20] This is the only positive discernible moment of subjectivity, but as such, it is empty or in-describable for the reasons mentioned above. Hence it is "pure" of any kind of descriptive content—it is a mere *center* of any conscious relation. In Husserl's reading, this center is nothing that can be "seen" (intuited), but it must be assumed as an idea. If it cannot be intuited, however, its status is highly problematic. Yet, Husserl suggests, if we leave these "meta-physical" questions aside we *can* describe subjective acts—"lived experiences" (*Erlebnisse*)—regardless of how we may *characterize* them. No matter how we determine them within a putative philosophical "system," the fact is we *have* subjective lived experiences and experienced phenomena. Thus, Husserl already at this stage presupposes a certain methodological epoché, which leaves aside questions regarding a pure Ego (as well as the question of the object of experience) and focuses on that which we experience and describe, the "in-between"—that is, intentional acts in their *relation* to their fulfillments. The "relation" of *Bewußtheit* that Natorp exposes is, to Husserl, none other than that of *intentionality—intentional* acts and their *fulfillments* (*contents*).

Hence, Natorp holds that consciousness is fundamentally a relation, while Husserl fleshes out this relation. The fact that relation is the basic character of consciousness does not mean that this relational character cannot be described. To say that consciousness is a relation is far too general; thus Husserl writes in the margin of his copy of Natorp's *General Psychology:*

> Consciousness is not, as in Natorp, relation as such. The fact that all relating occurs *consciously* is not to say that a relation is *within* consciousness. And further, the Ego's relating itself to the object is not to say that consciousness itself is a relation, as if the Ego would posit itself in relation to the object, as if it would posit "right" in relation to "left." (BQ 342, 27)

Thus, Husserl's point is that relation is not merely a structure *within* (rather than of) consciousness as always intending *something*. The character of intentional consciousness is that it relates itself to something, no matter how one wishes to characterize that something (as a meant object, a meaning, a content, etc.); and this relation is not something immediately and evidently seen but can only be known by reflection *on* this relation: "What the *relation* between Ego and intentional object (as objective [*gegenständliche*] relation) presupposes, as fundamentally relative, is reflection on the lived experience and reflection with identification of Ego and object" (BQ 26). Thus, precisely *in* the process of objectification there are experienced phenomena or appearances and corresponding lived experiences which can be reflectively described *in* the process of experiencing them.

Accordingly, Husserl notes beside a passage in Natorp's *Introduction to Psychology:* "The appearances *before* objectivation are [supposedly] the problem? No, the appearances *of* the objectivations, I would say, are the problem, maybe even the appearances *before,* but first and foremost, especially the appearances *in* the objectivation" (K II 4/104a, excerpts from

1904 or, more likely, 1909). In other words, no matter how one characterizes objectivation and its difference vis-à-vis subjectivation, the fact is that even in objectivations there are lived experiences that "have" phenomena, and these can be described *not* just reconstructively but reflectively precisely *in* the process of constructing objectivity. Thus, Husserl disregards these supposedly "metaphysical" questions of the fundamental character of subjectivity as "relation" and as pure Ego, and simply focuses on the phenomena that are seen in reflection. However, in "simply" focusing on the realm of intentionality, Husserl implicitly criticizes the relation to the pure Ego as a pointless addition. Instead of reflecting on the relation between *Bewußtheit* and Ego—which Natorp himself says cannot be described, and which is therefore an empty notion—Husserl focuses on the relation *of Bewußtheit* itself, that is, on that which is conscious. The Ego is hence to be found "in the object" it intends and, on the level of description, there is nothing wrong with this.

As Konrad Cramer claims in what has become a classic article, Husserl was very well aware of the theoretical problems with Natorp's construction, and *not* going along with Natorp in this respect was therefore a deliberate decision: "If there should be difficulties with Natorp's theory that cannot be alleviated by means of his own approach; if, furthermore, the reasons for the emergence of these difficulties are representative of a whole tradition of theories of consciousness, then this will protect Husserl's objective conception of Ego at least from *that* suspicion that he was theoretically naive" (Cramer 1974, 548). Husserl purports to be "naive" in a "positive" sense of focusing on the "things themselves" given in *Bewußtheit,* regardless of any "interpretations" of their ontological or "metaphysical" status.

By thus leaving aside the question of the pure Ego—the subjective, essentially opaque "side" of the constructive process—Husserl at the same time avoids the problem of having to describe this subjective side or in general of having to take a position on it. To express it in his later terminology, in the *Logical Investigations* Husserl focuses only on the *progressive* side of the constitutive process (in Natorp's terminology, "construction") of world constitution. And "within" the noetic side there is no place for a pure Ego other than perhaps as an idea—a "unitary Ego" corresponding to the "unity of the object." But more importantly, this is also about the methodological tools to be employed for describing consciousness—a concept which, at this point in Husserl's development (and as a legacy of Brentano), can be called "consciousness without a subject." The method Husserl employs is that of phenomenological description based on direct evidence: again, in his later terminology, it is a static description of lived experiences in their intentional "functioning."

This method, Husserl claims, is in no way speculative or indirect (i.e., reconstructive), but is directly based on evidence in phenomenological introspection or reflection. This is to say, Husserl goes along with Natorp's method of construction in his analyses of intentionality, only that Natorp was blind to this very intentionality *in* this process, due to the restriction Natorp placed on describing subjectivity *as* objectifying. Husserl rather focuses on the intentional elements precisely *in* the process of objectification. This description is in no way especially difficult or mysterious: one merely has to avert one's eyes from objects as transcendent and focus on the acts in which objects are given in psychic immanence. This description tacitly employs an epoché from the object as transcendent, as well as from a pure Ego from which these acts supposedly come forth. In fact, it is in this context that Husserl first introduces the phenomenological reduction, in 1907: the reduction means primarily going back to pure immanence, into a sphere that can be described purely and in evident intuition.[21]

Metaphysical Implications of Natorp's Transcendental Method for Husserl's Transcendental Turn

The "pure Ego" that Husserl was able to "find" by 1913 due to his transcendental turn was, of course, the "transcendental subject."[22] This is not the place to reconstruct Husserl's development between 1901 and 1913.[23] But here one can point out some metaphysical implications in Natorp's method to which Husserl was receptive, once he opened up toward "transcendental questions." Natorp's method of construction was, after all, a *transcendental* method in the sense of tracing the conditions of possibility of the construction of cognition in subjective "deeds." Natorp tried to emphasize this transcendental aspect by directly opposing the methods of objectivation and subjectivation. This move suggested a critique of Cohen's method, as well as implying that not only were the two methods (supposedly) radically opposed, but so were the *domains* or *spheres* to which they pertained; namely, objectivity and subjectivity. We have called this Natorp's "ontological difference." This could be seen by the fact that Natorp denies any direct access and description of subjectivity, because any such description would *nolens volens* revert to the method(s) of objectification. Another way of phrasing this is that the "objectifying" language pertaining to reality and its cognition cannot be applied to a sphere that is utterly different from reality. If subjectivity, in a manner which is indescribable for us, *constructs* reality, then it cannot be of the same *ontological kind* as reality itself. The subject that constructs objectivity is not itself objective *but—transcendental.* Because it is transcendental, it cannot be *described* by means and methods of objectivity. Although Natorp's actual *execution* of a subjectifying method may have serious problems, as Husserl will point out, one can retain the metaphysical implication of his theory. It was this implication that Husserl was shying away from in his first draft of phenomenology as "descriptive psychology."

It is clear that Husserl would be critical of the term "construction." Already in the *Logical Investigations,* however, he does use the term "constitution" to refer to the activities in the sphere of intentional life. One can understand this use of "constitution" entirely free of metaphysically loaded implications: objectivities constitute themselves in intentional acts; objects are intended in certain (types of) acts and have their ways of giving themselves or appearing in certain ways of experience. However, a "metaphysical" overtone is inevitable if one *generalizes* this structure—as Husserl indeed does later—to say: reality *in general* or *as such* (and not just its cognition) is constituted in intentional acts, in the immanence of subjective life. In other words, subjectivity *constitutes* objectivity—and this relation is, furthermore, a *correlation* that is valid for all types of subjective experience: the correlation is a priori. This at the same time marks a "fundamental essential difference" between *"being as lived experience* and *being as object,"*[24] and can be termed (as we have also termed it for Natorp) an "ontological" difference (Hua III/1, 87). Thus, if one posits a "correlational a priori" between constituting subjectivity and constituted objectivity (as the world in which I am also an object), then the question as to the "ontological" status of this "primal" subjectivity arises: that which constitutes the world cannot in itself be a worldly entity. Husserl's transcendental turn can also be interpreted as *admitting* this "metaphysical" consequence of the theory of constitution. To be sure, (Husserlian) *constitution* is not (Natorpian) *construction,* but both share the idea that the two "regions"—that is, the constituting and the constituted, the subjective and the objective—are radically different in nature, whether or not one wants to label this difference "ontological." While there are certainly more motives that factor into Husserl's transcendental turn, it is safe to say that it is this "metaphysical" implication that Husserl embraced as he came to characterize his phenomenology as "transcendental idealism." Transcendental idealism means, in the phenomenological sense (which Husserl also calls "constitutive idealism"), that being is only being insofar as it is experienced by a real or ideal subject, and that this subject, insofar as it constitutes being, cannot in itself *be* in the sense of worldly being. This state of affairs is later, in the *Crisis,* treated as the famous "paradox of subjectivity."

Husserl's Method of the Transcendental Reduction as a Reconstruction of the Natural Attitude

Seen from this perspective, it is conceivable that Natorp's idea of methods that are specific to objectivity and subjectivity, respectively, becomes attractive again for the transcendental Husserl. One element of subjective (intentional) analysis that Husserl deems fundamental to this analysis—and which Natorp flatly denies—is *reflection* in order to access this intentional life. This presupposes, however, a primal way of subjective life prior to reflection—a life that is "straightforward" (*geradehin*)—that experiences the world and as such constitutes it. The latter is certainly in line with Natorp's idea of the method of objectivating being through construction: the scientist, like any normally living human being—Natorp also speaks of "natural consciousness" (Natorp 1912a, 194)[25]—"constructs" reality, yet without any explicit knowledge of the transcendental elements which make this constructing possible, as conditions of possibility *of* construction. In Natorp, all normal execution of life (and not just science, as Cohen would construe it) is objectifying, and thus knows nothing of subjectivity's constructing deeds, which would have to be reconstructed. For Husserl, however, simple reflection is already capable of accessing this constructing subjective life in intentional acts. This means, however, that normal life is directed at *objects* and not at the intentional life that *constitutes* them: it lives in a state of blindness with regard to intentional life. As of *Ideas I*, Husserl calls this way of life the *natural attitude* (as discussed in chapter 1). It is characterized as being unaware of the subjective life that intentionally constitutes reality as it is experienced. This sphere of intentional life can, consequently, only be accessed by a *radical break with the natural attitude.*[26] This break is one key element of the phenomenological reduction. What emerges, hence, is a new attitude—namely, the phenomenological attitude of the philosopher who has broken with the natural attitude. The natural and phenomenological attitudes are thus two absolutely distinct ways of viewing the world: the natural attitude lives in a state of naïveté with regard to constituting intentional life; the phenomenological attitude thematizes precisely this life, and studies how it constitutes the world in which the human being lives *in* the natural attitude.

In short, the transcendental reduction as a break with the natural attitude can be interpreted as a *reconstruction* of how the natural attitude has come to be constituted through intentional life. It reconstructs how it has "happened" that normal human beings encounter the world as "fixed" and "complete" *after* a process in which it has been constituted; a process which, significantly, is never actually brought to a halt but is merely "bracketed" for the sake of investigation. It is clear, however, that this philosophical method must be fundamentally different from the natural attitude. The latter is guided by a certain "metaphysical" belief, namely that the world exists independently of any experiencing subjectivity (and as such, it is a "naive metaphysics"). Husserl calls this the "general thesis" of the natural attitude. Life in the natural attitude is not itself a method, like the method of a given science. However, it is Husserl's claim that the positive sciences themselves rest on this tacit base of the general thesis; they are "sciences of the natural attitude." That is, they have developed certain "objectifying" methods, but they share with the natural attitude of everyday life a belief in the subject-independent existence of the world. This echoes Natorp's levels of objectification, which begins genetically with everyday quotidian utterance and culminates in the objectifications of scientific judgments. Furthermore, Husserl also sees the need of a wholly different "method" of inquiry into subjectivity after a break with the natural attitude. On the one hand, the thematization of intentional life that has constituted the world—now we can say, the world of the natural attitude—is about describing how precisely this world *in* the natural attitude has arisen *in* and *through* these intentional acts. On the other hand, the term Husserl uses to access this sphere of immanence—namely, "reduction"—already implies that there must also be a genuine method that is adequate to what he also calls the "depth sphere of transcendental life."

It is thus from here that Husserl, after *Ideas,* is in general attracted to Natorp's method of reconstruction. As we shall see, however, Husserl is also critical of a crucial aspect of it, due to the theory of transcendental constitution that he developed in the meantime.

The Reduction Overcomes the Problem of Natorp's Method of Reconstruction

Let us turn back to Natorp briefly. So far, his theory of reconstruction as the method for an a priori psychology has remained a sketch. His psychology reconstructs subjectivity by going back from "fixed" and static objectifications to the dynamic, flowing life that has constructed the former. The method of reconstruction thus goes the *opposite* way of construction; it is its simple inversion. But so far this is mere theory. How is it actually carried out, and what new element does this a priori psychology *add* to the transcendental method? If it is merely reconstructive and, as such, comes *after* the accomplished work of construction, is there anything significant that this subjectifying method can add to the transcendental method? The answer is negative. Natorp's *General Psychology* is, as he points out, at least in the presentation of 1912, merely a promissory sketch—a "foundation of the foundation" of psychology.[27] But this psychology is never actually carried out, and for a simple reason—there *remains* essentially nothing to be done. What can it mean to follow the same constructive path in a negative, reconstructive direction? And what can it mean to "undo" constructions, other than to point out that subjective life is radically different—namely, in its dynamic and flowing character—from its objectivations?[28] Indeed, Natorp conceived of his psychology as "philosophy's last word" (Natorp 1913, 202)[29]—but his attempts to enunciate this last word lead him to completely modify his method.[30]

As Husserl sees it, however, Natorp's reconstructive attempt is not fundamentally flawed; rather, Natorp's mistake is that he does not carry it through to the end. It is, as we have seen, Natorp himself who tries to make a case for the radical difference between the spheres of objectivity and subjectivity. However, the "pan-methodist," as Natorp has been called,[31] does not transfer this substantive difference to the methodological level. Natorp is rather a "methodological monist": the methods of construction and reconstruction are, for him, essentially the same and differ merely in their direction. Had Natorp acknowledged the *ontological* difference he emphasizes so strongly, and then accounted for it on the *methodological* level, then the thematic *object* of investigation would also by necessity have had to be different as well. In other words, an ontological dualism stands here against a methodological monism, and this methodological monism was then translated into an ontological monism, regardless of the fact that Natorp himself insisted on the radical difference between subject and object.

Husserl's theory of the phenomenological reduction can now be seen to solve Natorp's dilemma. Instead of presenting a method of subjectivation and then claiming any analysis of its very subject matter (namely, subjectivity) as a "no-go" area, Husserl precisely accounts for the difference between objectivity and subjectivity on the *methodological level*. This allows Husserl to avoid the *problem* altogether by shifting to a different level of reflection from the natural to the transcendental attitude. If one concedes that a different method of analysis is possible—one which does not take the existence of the world for granted but studies its constitution in subjective *acts*—*then* one can acknowledge that the "structure" (to avoid the term "object") to be studied also is by necessity radically different. However, in keeping with this radical difference, this structure is to be analyzed by a method which is, in equal measure, radically different. Thus Husserl writes in the margin of his copy of Natorp's *General Psychology:*

> The opposition of object-subject that is at play here finds its compre-
> hensive resolution only through the phenomenological reduction, viz.,
> in contrasting the natural attitude—which has givennesses, entities, ob-
> jects as pre-given—with the transcendental attitude, which goes back to
> the *Ego cogito,* i.e., which passes over to absolute reflection, which posits
> primal facts and primal cognition, i.e., absolute cognition of possible
> cognition that has nothing pre-given but that is purely self-having cogni-
> tion *(sich selbst habendes Erkennen).* (BQ 342, 22)[32]

Thus, the distinction between the natural attitude as objectifying intentional tendency *and* the reflective, transcendental attitude which studies the constitution precisely *of* the natural attitude, is Husserl's solution to the problem that Natorp had posed but was himself unable to solve. Acknowledging this difference, however, makes way for a genuine study of subjectivity *as* constituting intentional life. Husserl also calls the way reduction pursues a "regressive analysis" (or simply "regression," *Rückgang*)[33] since it goes back from the "finished" constituted world as it is experienced in the natural attitude to constituting, subjective life.

Let us look at an example of how this works in Husserl, in contrast to Natorp. In Natorp, the objectifying method proceeds teleologically in constructing reality; the reconstructive method, since it is a mere inversion of the former, proceeds causally (although Natorp points out that subjectivity itself is not causally determined [Natorp 1912a, 209]). Nevertheless, since both methods are essentially the same, there is no other way in which to reconstruct subjective data than such a causal manner. To Husserl, however, causality is but one way of explaining processes in the world: it is a naturalistic type of explanation in accordance with the methods of the positive sciences (in the "naturalistic attitude"). However, if one concedes that subjective life, seen in its own domain and with the adequate "attitude," is not objective, then one can also apply a different method of analyzing it, the "personalistic attitude." This is where the classical phenomenological distinction between causality and motivation comes into play. Motivation is that type of "causality" which applies specifically to subjective life.[34] A "reduction" to this subjective life by means of attaining a different level of reflection and a subsequent regression into this life allows for an investigation of subjectivity in its true way of functioning, for instance, by using motivational structures as guiding clues.

Consequently, subjectivity is conceived of as a sphere of experience that can only be accessed in its genuine nature by a *break* with the natural attitude, and this entails a break with the *methods* of the natural attitude. Indeed, this break opens up a whole new region of experience in which nothing of the natural attitude is lost, but merely comes to be seen from a radically new perspective: not the world, but that consciousness which *has* world as its intentional *relatum,* is absolute being. This makes possible what Husserl envisions, with phenomenology, as a universal "transcendental empiricism." Although this would be a *contradictio in adiecto* for a Kantian, it was, ironically, Natorp who first envisioned it, though from his standpoint he was unable to take advantage of its discovery. Whereas the very consequence of Natorp's psychology is to render such a study impossible, it is Husserl who exploits it in his transcendental phenomenology. Interestingly, in his reflections on the idea of a "universal empirical science of consciousness" in 1926—when he had already reached his mature, genetic standpoint—Husserl mentions Natorp's "grand premonition" of such a universal psychology as a laudable exception vis-à-vis all other (!) imperfect attempts at a "pure psychology."[35] Yet Natorp's sketch of a psychology proper—unlike the interesting epistemological reflections accompanying it—has not, for essential reasons, been able to contribute to any actual psychologically valid insights, while Husserl's has. As Helmut Holzhey sums up his comparison: "Natorp's groundwork of a philosophical psychology supplies us only with modest contributions to a theory of subjectivity, contributions that are oriented to traditional psychological dispositions. Husserl's phenomenological analyses present incomparably richer material and have accordingly, also in the positive sciences, been more intensely received" (1991, 18).

Natorp's Epistemology and Husserl's Phenomenology Form a Correlation

At the outset it was suggested that Husserl's and Natorp's ideas together can yield a richer insight into the nature of subjectivity. With regard to Natorp's psychology, however, we have seen that it is ultimately flawed. The only reason it was worth acknowledging *seemed to be* that it aided Husserl in developing first his concept of transcendental phenomenology as the science of transcendental subjectivity, and then (as we shall see later) his draft of a genetic phenomenology. One can nevertheless retain an aspect of Natorp's theory which in fact complements Husserl's; a feature which is, indeed, for the most part lacking in Husserl. It is this aspect that can potentially *enhance* Husserl's phenomenology, and it was, in fact, taken up by the late Husserl. (Cassirer, as we shall see in the following chapters, took a similar and very fruitful path in his draft of a "philosophy of symbolic forms" in which Natorp's theory was his explicit point of departure.)[36] This aspect is, curiously, Natorp's interpretation of the transcendental method—that is, the method of objectivation.

As has been shown in preceding sections, the methods of objectivation and subjectivation (or epistemology and psychology) form a correlation. As correlative methods, what they have in common is that they are both to be carried out in a transcendental register. They are both about the "grounding of cognition" in objective and subjective senses, respectively. Given that the psychological method has nothing substantial to contribute to an account of the subject and that, consequently, any "hint" of the subject is only to be found (according to Natorp) *in* its objectivations, then it might be appropriate to call Natorp's objectivating epistemology a "psychology in disguise." After all, it *does* thematize subjectivity, albeit only *ex negativo*, as objectivated in its constructing activities, and primarily with regard to the logical justification of the conditions of possibility of not only scientific but also everyday cognitions.[37] Transcendental epistemology identifies the logical and functional principles at work in cognizing activities and thought-contents[38] of the thinking subject. As mentioned, it is about *fixed* laws of cognition vis-à-vis the *dynamic* life of the subject, or more precisely, the lawfulnesses *in* subjective cognitions. This is why epistemology's task (namely, discerning these laws in the acts of cognition) is primarily linked to construction in the positive sciences and only secondarily to "natural consciousness." But indeed, it is also about the "structures"—which can be called "logical" or "lawful" only in a vague sense—that govern everyday judgments and thoughts. Still very much in the tradition of a formal conception of the a priori, Natorp's epistemology thematizes the forms of thinking rather than the actual (intentional) thought processes that phenomenology analyzes—what Scheler famously termed the "material a priori."

In this sense one can say that what Natorp provides is, however mediated, nevertheless an account of subjectivity; to be sure, one that lacks the concreteness of a direct description of subjectivity that the phenomenological account is capable of. Yet his epistemology thematizes— to use Natorp's term *Bewußtheit*—the basic relational character of consciousness *with regard to the object of cognition*. The relation as such and in its "inner functioning" are not analyzed—that would be an account of intentionality—rather, this objectively oriented epistemology discerns the a priori preconditions *of* the processes in intentional acts *in* their objectifying activities, that is, in their relation to the object. As such, this epistemology takes place within a transcendental framework and remains close to Kant's objective deduction in the B edition of the *Critique of Pure Reason*.[39] It is a transcendental account of consciousness with regard to the *object* of cognition (and of experience in general), and this object can only be grasped as a fixed entity—the constructed object or law that is constructed by subjective activity. Psychology goes backward, inverting this objectivating tendency, but stops short of delving into the depths of subjectivity; the subject is a pure a priori principle and as such an eternally distant, ideal point.[40]

Husserl, however, has shown that it *is* possible to trespass this threshold when one practices the reduction and attains a different perspective from which to analyze subjectivity in its proper nature. In *this* sense, both accounts form a correlation insofar as—in Husserl's terminology—Natorp thematizes the *transcendental-noematic*, Husserl the transcendental-noetic aspect of subjectivity. In other words, Natorp's epistemology is not only about a construction or constitution of objectivity in general; it is also a *formal genetic account* of how objectivity has become "constituted" from simple acts up to the highest forms of judgment. Furthermore, this objectivity differentiates itself into distinctive spheres of objectivity; following Kant, it is not only about the constitution of theoretical and scientific cognition, but of "all other regions of objectivation: ethical, aesthetical, and religious" (Natorp 1912a, 198).[41]

Although Natorp never carried through with his program, this "noematic" account of the "objectifying" tendency of subjectivity was the starting point for Cassirer's account of the different symbolic forms. It might have also been an inspiration for Husserl's later draft of an ontology of the lifeworld with its different sub-forms (the so-called "special worlds") as ways in which transcendental subjectivity "enworlds" itself—the "worlds" of science, of everyday life, of art, and so on. Thus, Husserl also looks at the noematic side of constitution. The transcendental-noetic account proper, on the other hand, is represented in phenomenological psychology, which Husserl also calls "Egology," emphasizing the specifically Egoic structures of the acts of the *Ego*. It is also concerned with the *cogitatum,* but this *cogitatum* is always already embedded in a sphere of objectivity or, more simply speaking, a sphere of "meaning"—a "world." Constitution is ultimately a constitution of worlds as horizons of meaning, and instead of focusing on the constituting process that forms the world, one can look at the world as a *product* of constitution, and that means, as something that *always already has been* and *is always and at every moment* in time being-constituted. Although Husserl's transcendental method is primarily interested in world-constitution and more specifically in different "spaces of meaning," it is an insight of his late theory of passive genesis that these meaningful contexts have not been constituted by an individual self; rather, they are worlds which a self has been endowed with, and can only be taken over as given horizons of objectivities. This is to say, "world" is something that is constituted by transcendental subjectivity, but this subjectivity is properly speaking an intersubjectivity embedded in a history of world-constitution.

The methods of Husserl and Natorp thus form a correlation insofar as, on the one hand, Husserl thematizes subjective, constituting activities as the accomplishments (*Leistungen*) of transcendental subjectivity. As constituting intentional acts, they constitute *something*. This something, however, is ultimately a world, which is not something a single subject does by itself but rather an intentional activity that has always already been carried out by a community of subjects, and to which the individual merely contributes. On the other hand, Natorp's method thematizes the objective forms *into which* these accomplishments flow as they construct reality. As objectified constructs, however, they have already formed and become differentiated into spaces of meaning—the spheres of science, ethics, aesthetics, and religion (here Cassirer would add myth and language). These in turn have formed specific formal conditions that need to be adhered to when carrying out specific acts—acts of (scientific) knowledge, ethical acts, and so on. These would be transcendental-noematic questions; in a manuscript where Husserl takes this neo-Kantian position, he calls them "*a posteriori* questions of a 'transcendental kind'—such as: 'What would a *world* have to be like in order for it to be accessible for human cognition?'" (Hua VII, 383).

The Husserlian account can thus be called phenomenal or even dynamic, whereas the Natorpian account is structural or "functional" (as Cassirer has called it); both present *two sides* of one coin. Whereas the Husserlian account takes place within Egology as a "first philosophy," Natorp's account can be considered (as Husserl would have it) as a "last philosophy" (Hua VII, 385). This indicates that such a "last philosophy" is not at all excluded from the horizon of Husserl's philosophy. Rather, Natorp's "last philosophy" points to a sphere of questions which Husserl sensed would have to be answered at some point—spheres which he clearly anticipated.[42] To pursue such a "correlative" transcendental inquiry, then, seems to be a fruitful path of further research, and it shows how Husserl's phenomenological and Natorp's critical accounts can be reconciled, yet also stimulate each other.

Husserl as the Executor of Natorp's Reconstructive Method in Genetic Phenomenology

Let us focus now on the Husserlian method, that is, on the transcendental-noetic analysis of subjectivity in its intentional process of world-constitution: what has been thematized thus far is an account of subjectivity *insofar as it constitutes world*. As directed at the world, Husserl also calls this type of intentional analysis "progressive." This method as investigating the world-constituting activities of subjective accomplishments is the first and foremost task of phenomenological (as intentional) analysis.

However, it was Natorp who criticized this method as remaining on the level of a "static Platonism" in his review of *Ideas I.*[43] Natorp believed that in this method the transcendental Ego was treated like a Platonic, that is, *a static and unchanging* idea, and that Husserl did not consider the human subject in its dynamic and ever-changing character. Instead, Natorp insists that world-constitution is a *genetic* process that proceeds in essential "levels of consciousness."[44] Put on the defensive, Husserl replies to Natorp in a letter of June 1918 to the effect that "already for more than a decade" (Hua-Dok III/5, 137), he has "overcome the level of static Platonism" and has posed "the idea of transcendental genesis" as the main theme of phenomenology.[45] Indeed, Husserl asserts that analysis of subjective intentional acts—purely in their "progressive" tendency of constituting—grasps merely the uppermost stratum of this intentional life. Subjectivity, however, when seen in its fullest dimensions, is a "thick" and dynamic structure, of which a purely static description catches merely an "abstract" layer and not its full "concretion." Although, methodologically, static analysis is the first,[46] one cannot remain there; it is first *for us* but not *for itself,* to employ the Aristotelian distinction. Rather, the phenomenological observer has to delve into dynamic, genetic depths of subjective life in a *regressive* analysis.

Since this regression is not to be understood in a causal or any other "mundane" manner, it proceeds backward according to the genuine structures of transcendental subjective life. And as such, Husserl's regressive analysis in the framework of genetic phenomenology actually goes the "subjectifying" way, and thereby fulfills Natorp's original idea—namely, to actually observe subjective *genesis* from a new standpoint (after the reduction). Husserl himself refers to the neo-Kantian transcendental method interchangeably as "regressive" and "reconstructive" and claims that the neo-Kantians (and he means mainly Natorp) never truly understood their own project correctly: "All regressive, 'transcendental' method in the specific sense of regressive—often used by Kant and most prominently preferred in neo-Kantianism—operates with presuppositions that were never systematically sought for, never scientifically established and, especially, that were not grounded on a pure, transcendental basis" (Hua VII, 370).[47]

This regressive move is a "regression to origins, namely a transcendental phenomenological inquiry into the constitution"; that is, into the *"origins of objectivity in transcendental subjectivity,* of relative being of objects out of the absolute . . . in the sense of consciousness" (ibid.). This regression, however, is a move back to dimensions of transcendental life that lie—genetically as well as *logically*—*prior* to the acts in the "here and now" viewed in static analysis. It is not simply a regression back to subjective life as such (something that Natorp would reject). Rather, it goes further back and beyond *current* subjective life as witnessed in the "lived present," and back into the passive ("hidden") dimensions of subjectivity; dimensions for which Husserl uses different notions such as latency, the unconscious, "sleeping" subjectivity, and so on.[48] This implies that a regressive analysis regresses into spheres that *cannot* be made intuitively evident in the lived present of the subject (for instance, certain past primal institutings). There can be, accordingly, no *direct description* of these spheres, but only a certain explanation or "interpretation." Structurally, one can discern certain eidetic "laws of genesis," but sedimented phenomena *in* this genetic process can only be retroactively explained and consequently interpreted. The phenomenological *Urmethode* of intuition finds its limits in the realm of "passivity." In a remarkable passage, Husserl concedes that actually *all* genetic analysis is based on interpretation; the passage concludes as follows: "This [type of genetic inquiry] is 'interpretation': but obviously it is not arbitrary, but an unfolding [*Auseinanderwicklung*] of an explicatable intentionality. Or rather, such unwrapping [*Aufwicklung*] is *from the very start* interpretation; and all intentional analysis, all self-clarification [*Selbstverständigung*] of consciousness that finds its expression in description is interpretation" (A VII 13/62b).[49]

What kind of original evidence can this interpretation be based on? If these "depth structures" of subjectivity cannot be accessed directly, but only regressively, and hence cannot be described but only explained or interpreted, then the method of making such structures evident can only be a *reconstruction*. Although Husserl prefers the terms "regression" or (as just cited) "interpretation," there can be no doubt that this type of consideration might equally be called a "reconstruction"; and Husserl at certain places does indeed use this term.[50] What is at stake, however, is more than merely a terminological issue (to whatever extent Husserl may have adopted a Natorpian term). It is about a *significant modification* or *transformation* of the very principle of phenomenology: it is a tacit acknowledgment that the conception of intuition is too narrow, so that Husserl broadens the scope of phenomenological descriptive analysis by allowing the use of reconstructive or regressive analysis as an interpretation rather than a direct description of intuitively evident phenomena. This is called for because these phenomena in genetic analysis *are* not and cannot be *made* evident in direct intuition. This insight would have been quite foreign to the Husserl of *Ideas I* with its "principle of all principles": "that every originary presentative intuition is a legitimizing source of cognition, that everything originarily (so to speak, in its 'personal' actuality) offered to us in 'intuition' is to be accepted simply as what it is presented as being, *but also only within the limits in which it is presented there*" (Husserl 1983, 43–44, italics added).

As Kern states, this "type of phenomenology"—namely, the type employed in genetic analysis—"Husserl also calls 'explanatory' in opposition to the descriptive character of static [analysis]. 'Explanatory' science to Husserl essentially goes beyond the realm of the intuitive. In this sense, he concedes explicitly a non-intuitive, constructive element for *genetic* phenomenology" (Kern 1964, 370). To allow "genetic" dimensions to become at all thematic for phenomenological analysis requires a modification of the phenomenological method from a purely descriptive account of static intentionality to a *genetic* dimension of subjectivity based on reconstruction or interpretation. Thus, it was again Husserl who saw the "hidden truth" in Natorp's method, and it was this that he exploited after his turn to genetic phenomenology. Indeed, the regressive or reconstructive method with which Husserl was familiar was *proposed* by Natorp already in texts of the 1880s. Though this proposal was *opposed* by Husserl at the time, it is fair to say that he came to know of this option through Natorp, and that it heightened his awareness of the possibility of a genetic dimension of transcendental analysis—a possibility that Natorp proposed in his draft of an a priori psychology from the very start.

Husserl did not admit to this methodological shift, and instead presented it as a flowing development. Yet, given his original resistance to Natorp's regressive psychology, this seamless development is not as continuous as Husserl himself presents it. It is no exaggeration to say that Husserl's mature form of philosophy as genetic phenomenology would not have been possible without Natorp's interventions. Husserl might have stayed true to the "letter" of phenomenology in his later work, but in the actual execution of his analyses he overstepped the boundaries which he had previously set himself.

Conclusion

This chapter has attempted to reconstruct parallels between Natorp's psychology and Husserl's phenomenology with the intent of showing how each influenced the other's attempts to produce a method that would yield a rich account of subjectivity. Husserl and Natorp were on parallel tracks and dealt with similar issues, despite coming from different traditions. Following their philosophical instincts, they were each attempting to reach the "primal concreteness" of the subject. At a certain stage in this continuing discussion, Natorp had a view that was superior in certain respects to Husserl's because he was willing to consider "metaphysical" questions regarding the Ego that Husserl refused to broach. However, as of Husserl's transcendental stage—which was influenced by Natorp—Husserl in turn went beyond Natorp in overcoming the restrictions imposed by Natorp. Indeed, it was the transcendental reduction that "cashed in" on Natorp's wish to have direct access to the life of the subject; a wish that Natorp deemed unrealizable. Moreover, elements of this continual *Auseinandersetzung* then factored into Husserl's late recasting of phenomenology as a genetic analysis of transcendental consciousness. Hence, this comparison should help to highlight some of the important features of each thinker's views and how they influenced one another in their concrete work. It also shows that many insights taken to be "possessions" of phenomenology proper have been inspired in decisive ways by neo-Kantianism.[51]

Finally, what is at stake in this discussion between Natorp and Husserl and which still is at the heart of the discussion concerning *phenomenology itself* is the question of what method is to be employed for an analysis of subjectivity. Largely unacknowledged by Husserl, the deepening of the intuitive by a "reconstructive" method breaks with the methodological paradigm of self-giving evidence, which is sometimes believed to be the "holy grail" of phenomenology. Indeed, one can hardly underestimate the importance that this discovery had for Husserl's method, as well as for a reassessment of his phenomenology as a whole. But its importance is also due to the fact that Husserl strove, in the 1920s, to develop a philosophical system inspired by the idealistic thinkers of the first half of the nineteenth century. Whether openly admitted or not, Husserl's genetic phenomenology is influenced by the idea of a "history of self-consciousness" as professed by the German idealists, a kinship which he dimly felt through his interaction with the neo-Kantians. And since Husserl came into contact with the *latter* tradition by way of Natorp, a tradition so different from the one in which he came of age philosophically, the present chapter intends to contribute no less than a reopening of a philosophical dialogue between phenomenology and Kantianism in general, and to recovering the dialogue between Husserl and Marburg neo-Kantianism in particular. If the sketch of the Natorp–Husserl relationship which is provided here is in any way convincing, it should be clear that there are intricately connected and provocative dialogues which philosophers, particularly since the Second World War, have wrongly considered to be concluded.

Appendix: Works of Natorp Studied by Husserl

"Ueber objective und subjective Begründung der Erkenntniss." *Philosophische Monatshefte* 23 (1887): 257–286.
Einleitung in die Psychologie nach kritischer Methode. Freiburg: Mohr, 1888. (In Husserl's library under the signature: BQ 326.)

Both texts, which appeared at nearly the same time, deal with the same issue of the possibility of a "subjective grounding" of cognition, vis-à-vis Hermann Cohen's critical (constructive) epistemology (the "transcendental method"). The 1887 essay is a programmatic text which emphasizes the possibility of a "subjective" direction of transcendental-philosophical research—a possibility that Cohen ruled out. Husserl studied both texts in the course of composing *Logical Investigations* (see especially Hua XIX/2, 372–76).

New excerpts in 1904 (?) and October 1909 on *Einleitung in die Psychologie,* on the occasion of Natorp's visit to Husserl in Göttingen on October 17, 1909. (Archive signature: K II 4/98–110.)
Allgemeine Psychologie nach kritischer Methode: Erstes Buch: Objekt und Methode der Psychologie. Tübingen: Mohr/Siebeck, 1912. (Archive signature: BQ 342.)
"Philosophie und Psychologie," *Logos* 4 (1913): 176–202. (Archive signature: SQ 111.)

Originally intended as a new edition of *Einleitung in die Psychologie* (1888), the *Allgemeine Psychologie* is rather a new work that is roughly three times the length of *Einleitung.* Some sections, however, are taken over *verbatim* from *Einleitung in die Psychologie;* Husserl marks these passages in the margins of his copy of *Allgemeine Psychologie.* Again, Natorp's book and article appeared at nearly the same time. His article lays out again the project of a philosophical psychology—a topic with which the *Allgemeine Psychologie* deals explicitly—in programmatic terms.

Both texts were studied by Husserl in August and September 1918, in Bernau.[52]

In the winter semester of 1922–23, Husserl holds a seminar on Natorp's *Allgemeine Psychologie* (see Archive signature N 126, class notes by the Dutch philosopher H. J. Pos). At this time, Husserl also rereads sections of the *Einleitung* from 1888, in order to compare Natorp's earlier and later positions on a transcendental psychology.

H. J. Pos writes an article in reaction to Husserl's seminar, on "the methodological difference between Natorp and Husserl concerning subjectivity": "Het methodisch verschil tusschen Natorp en Husserl inzake der subjektiviteit," *Tijdschrift voor Wijsbegeerte* 19 (1925): 313–30.

Expanding the Relation: Husserl and Natorp *and Cassirer*

We have traced how the Husserlian project could be reconstructed as arising (not least) from his *Auseinandersetzung* with Natorp. This is not to say that internal reasons were perhaps not as decisive for Husserl reaching the final and mature phase of his thought; after all, the idea of genetic analysis and of the noetic-noematic correlation, which is ultimately the correlation of transcendental subjectivity and lifeworld, lay indeed in the general horizon of Husserl's work. Nevertheless, the connections to Natorp's thought are more than obvious, as is the fact that Husserl came to embrace the notion of phenomenology as transcendental philosophy with its transcendental-idealistic implications through Natorp and—as mentioned—with him, the entire tradition of transcendental philosophy, starting with Kant and including the Marburg school of neo-Kantianism. Hence, it is in no way a diminishment of Husserl's achievements to consider Natorp a catalyst of the ideas that might have been present in Husserl already from the start, but which were drawn out and brought into their own by Natorp.

Another positive consequence and result of this chapter is the insight that phenomenology of the Husserlian type and the constructive approach of the Marburg school need not be considered as the stark contrast that it has been claimed (by Husserl himself, among others). Not only are there constructive elements in phenomenology, but there are descriptive elements in Natorp's psychology—and there is a lot of phenomenology, by extension, in Cassirer, as the next chapter will demonstrate. But more importantly, with the focus on transcendental-noetic (Husserl) and transcendental-noematic (Natorp) analysis, both methods—that of reconstructing subjectivity and of constructing objectivity, to put it schematically—can be seen as forming a *correlation*. It is this important insight that will be expanded upon in the following chapter. The hero of the latter direction of analysis will be Cassirer, who went above and beyond Natorp. But his philosophy of symbolic formation also cannot do without a "subjective" element. Hence, both taken together can form a full-fledged "phenomenology of subjective and objective spirit," to speak in Hegelian language. While the next chapter will introduce Cassirer into the story told here, chapter 10 will then turn to Cassirer exclusively in order to spell out his philosophy of the symbolic as an alternative (or supplementary) project to the Husserlian one. It is from there that we shall return, in the last (third) part of this book, to the Husserlian project, which has been expanded in the way indicated in part 2.

A Hermeneutic Phenomenology of Subjective and Objective Spirit: Husserl, Natorp, and Cassirer

Introduction

In the introduction to the third and last volume of his *Philosophy of Symbolic Forms* of 1929, entitled "Phenomenology of Knowledge," Ernst Cassirer remarks that the meaning in which he employs the term "phenomenology" is Hegelian rather than according to "the modern usage of the term" (1954/III, vi). What sense can it make, then, to invoke Edmund Husserl's phenomenology in this context? Yet if, roughly speaking, phenomenology can be characterized as the *logos* of *phenomena,* that is, of being insofar as it appears (*phainesthai*) to a conscious subject, then the sense of phenomenology need not be so different from what Cassirer terms "the modern usage."[1] Phenomenology in this more liberal sense would be an account of how consciousness experiences the world through different forms of experience and in different spaces of meaning. The addition "hermeneutic," moreover, points to a broader methodological scope than that which one usually associates with phenomenology, that is, the phenomenological paradigm of description based on intuition. "Hermeneutic" connotes an *interpretive* dimension that goes beyond mere description. It will become necessary to expand phenomenology in this direction, as has been shown already in chapter 6. This chapter will carry on with this interpretive trend, but will do so in comparing Husserl with neo-Kantianism in the form of Cassirer.

In this attempt at a comparison between Cassirer and Husserl, I shall employ this broad concept of phenomenology—with the addition "hermeneutic"—as a philosophical project that investigates how consciousness relates to the world. In this sense, it is neither solely Cassirer's nor Husserl's nor, for that matter, Hegel's, although the phrase "of subjective and objective spirit" undoubtedly has a Hegelian ring to it. Indeed, it points to a subjective and objective tendency that is present in Husserl and Cassirer, respectively. Moreover, "a hermeneutic phenomenology" indicates that both philosophical concepts and methods, phenomenology and neo-Kantianism, usually taken to be so different from the very outset, can be mediated and brought to a certain synthesis. This synthesis forms a correlation within an account that aims at *a transcendental theory* that elucidates *the interrelation of mind and world*. This comparison does not intend merely to compare terminology when employing the words "phenomenology," "hermeneutic," and "subjective and objective spirit" to characterize this enterprise. Instead, I propose to broaden the restrictive sense in which both philosophical schools have used these terms, in order to open them up towards a more encompassing account of transcendental philosophy in the spirit of phenomenology and Kantianism.

Indeed, Husserl's analysis of the constitution of the world through subjectivity's passive and active achievements and Cassirer's account of the symbolic forms as transcendental forms of intuition that constitute and structure the cultural "spaces of meaning" can and must be seen as forming a correlation. This correlation gives an account of the way the *world appears for an experiencing subject* in the framework of a philosophical doctrine that is committed to transcendental idealism. Idealism states that all being is being-for-consciousness, and this forms a correlation that cannot be severed. Both Husserl and Cassirer endorse this general doctrine, yet they pursue it in different but reciprocal "directions." Both the neo-Kantian and phenomenological methods in this sense are incomplete without one another. Certainly, for both Cassirer and Husserl this would have been asking a lot. Neither of them saw their philosophies as complementing each other in this way. However, both not only took over crucial elements of the other's theory and integrated them into their own; they were also working on complementary projects. Perhaps they were not able to really see eye to eye due to the belligerent character of the philosophical scene in Europe in the first decades of the twentieth century (though their direct personal contact was reverential and polite). Indeed, the vigor with which discussions were fought out in defending opposing philosophical doctrines at that time is hardly comprehensible some eighty-plus years afterwards. Philosophical convergences were both ignored and deliberately overlooked.

Yet to spell out these intersections and filiations after so much time has merit not only for the sake of historiography and for rectifying the tired image that neo-Kantianism was a floundering project that was rightfully superseded by phenomenology and existentialism. Reassessing the philosophical debate in this historical situation has significant systematic ramifications and points to a discussion that is ongoing in philosophy today; namely, the question of how to analyze adequately the subject matter germane to transcendental philosophy. A modern conception of philosophy—in this Husserl and Cassirer agree—could only be placed in a transcendental framework. This is a systematic claim of timeless character. Yet, in order to show how Husserl and Cassirer arrived at this conclusion, one cannot proceed purely systematically. This discussion requires a reconstruction of the historical developments in both thinkers. Indeed, their philosophies are not conceivable without the constant interaction with proponents of the other school that aided them in their own philosophical progress. Although proceeding historically, however, this should not cloud the fact that stating that there is such a correlation implies a strong systematic claim. After all, phenomenology has traditionally presented itself as forming a stark antithesis to Kantianism, especially to its alleged formalism vis-à-vis phenomenology's intuitive approach. To show that phenomenology and transcendental philosophy in a Kantian vein are complementary has crucial consequences for both philosophies. As contemporary discussions show, this is not a dated issue but one that is reemerging in scholarship today.[2]

This discussion hinges most prominently on the *method* used for giving an account of the field or region germane to philosophy. The debate over method lies at the heart of the dispute between phenomenology and transcendental philosophy in the Kantian tradition: in particular, it has consequences for phenomenology *itself*. The critique which has followed phenomenology like a shadow since its inauguration with Husserl's *Logical Investigations* (1900–1901, Hua XVIII; Hua XIX/1–2) is leveled at nothing other than what Husserl considered the most basic methodological premise, namely that of *pure intuition* which brings phenomena to clear and distinct *evidence*. In other words, the neo-Kantian critique aims at the method of direct, evident *description based on intuition*. Later (re)formulated in the phenomenological movement by Martin Heidegger and others following him,[3] it is nearly forgotten now that this criticism was already intensively discussed in the early years after the publication of the *Logical Investigations* among the prevailing thinkers at the time, including the proponents of hermeneutic (or life) philosophy and the neo-Kantians, most importantly Paul Natorp. This is more than merely a historical observation. Rather, Natorp's initial critique aided Husserl in transforming his phenomenology into a transcendental philosophy, as demonstrated in the previous chapter.

Husserl was well aware that his new method was a radical departure from those of these established schools. Proponents of these challenged, as a reaction, this intuitionistic paradigm, which seemed fundamental to the point of being trivial, by insisting that pure intuition rests on unclarified presuppositions. In other words—as Gadamer later formulated it—Husserl's ideal of presuppositionless description and presupposition-lessness was itself a presupposition. Accordingly, to stick entirely to description based on pure and evident intuition would result, for the most part, in trivial findings. Knowledge the way the Kantians understood it, as based on principles (not intuition), would never be reached. Through intuition one would not gain any true *understanding*, since understanding entails a certain interpretation whose basis is necessarily a specific type of construction, that is, it involves a cognitive activity. Description based on intuition might reach a high level of concretion, but it is neither the first task for transcendental philosophy, nor the last. Yet in spite of this critique, the merits of the phenomenological method were also acknowledged, within certain limits; description can certainly give a rich account of the lifeworld and consciousness that experiences it; but, truly philosophically, nothing much is gained by it. One needs more than just description in order to attain a *philosophically* satisfying method. Yet very few philosophers, least of all Natorp and Cassirer, were dismissive of the phenomenological method but saw it, instead, as a valuable tool to give an account of the *life* of consciousness. It was generally hailed as a method that was here to stay, while at the same time not being the last word on method either. Description needed to be complemented by *construction*.

Indeed, this critique did not have the power to overthrow phenomenology; rather, it could even potentially strengthen it precisely by *incorporating* elements which were originally considered alien to it; Husserl did precisely this but thereby moved in the direction of the neo-Kantians. Husserl himself was much more open to the neo-Kantian point of view than many others of the phenomenological movement who saw in his transcendental turn a mere aberration from his early principles. As such, this is certainly not merely a discussion from a Husserlian point of view intended to strengthen it at all costs. Rather, what is at stake is the method of doing philosophy within an enterprise committed to the transcendental turn. It was Husserl's being true to the principles of phenomenology that led him to make the transcendental turn. Likewise, it was the compelling nature of Husserl's phenomenological descriptions that led Cassirer to incorporate elements of Husserl's method into his own. In general, the methodological opposition between phenomenology and Kantianism can be seen as a paradigmatic debate over this question of adequately studying what one could call "the transcendental realm," and it is precisely a dispute over intuition versus construction as the basis for analysis with regard to the transcendental realm. The result of this chapter will be that in order to analyze this transcendental realm, one needs both methodological principles. The perceived contradiction concerning both methods need not be maintained. Instead it can be conceived as a complementary correlation. Moreover, in the *application* of this method, both the phenomenological and the Kantian approach adhere to their own subject domains, which *as well* turn out to be a correlation "within" the transcendental realm, that is, the "subjective" and "objective" side, respectively. Thus what is at stake here is a double correlation: *a methodological* and a *thematic* one regarding the subject domain of this method.

Besides Natorp and Husserl, there is yet another figure of crucial importance here: Cassirer's teacher and Husserl's personal friend Natorp. Natorp was one of the first to publicly criticize Husserl's method of phenomenological intuition and, later, Husserl's static method in *Ideas I* (Hua III/1); and it was with Natorp that Husserl had the most intense interaction of all contemporary philosophers.[4] As has been shown in the previous chapter, Natorp's sketch of a philosophical psychology in his *Introduction to Psychology* from 1888 and later in his *General Psychology According to Critical Method* from 1912 had a significant influence on Husserl. Moreover, it was the method expounded in Natorp's work that was to be the cornerstone of *Cassirer's* method of symbolic formation. Confronting Husserl with Cassirer is impossible without first walking the reader through the discussion between Husserl and Natorp. Although Cassirer himself rests entirely on the "Marburg method," the transcendental method proposed first by Hermann Cohen and expanded by Natorp by a critical psychology, Cassirer has significantly broadened and transformed its original scope. Thus, in order to properly assess this relation, one must take the historical route and discuss first the issues arising in the debates between Husserl and Natorp. Taking Natorp into this discussion also contributes to adding a largely unwritten chapter of the history of twentieth-century philosophy, as his influence both on Husserl and Cassirer is usually downplayed by scholars.

Hence this chapter is divided into two parts. The first part will reiterate the dispute between Husserl and Natorp and show how it helped bring about Husserl's full-fledged method that stands under the heading of *genetic* phenomenology. Yet Husserl's incorporating insights of Natorp's method into his own "softens" the opposition between both methods. Since Cassirer builds upon Natorp's method, the correlation between the phenomenological and neo-Kantian methods is already visible here. That is, Natorp's method, originally intended as a critique of the intuitive phenomenological method, can be viewed as a way to complement Husserl's phenomenology, because Natorp puts his finger on a weak spot in Husserl's method, namely his alleged "static Platonism." Husserl originally rejects Natorp's genetic method of reconstruction, yet he later realizes that he must make use of "reconstructive" elements as he moves toward his "genetic phenomenology." This much is known from the previous chapter, though these insights will be utilized in the present chapter for a slightly different conclusion, one that was already reached, however, via a different route in chapter 8. Namely, incorporating these reconstructive elements implies a self-critique of Husserl's intuitionism; indeed, certain "constructive" elements are *necessary* for his genetic phenomenology and hence for a full-fledged transcendental phenomenology.

The second part will illustrate how Natorp's method sets up *Cassirer's* own systematic approach precisely in overcoming Natorp's methodological shortcomings. Cassirer readily and openly acknowledges Natorp's influence. However, he views Natorp's method as too narrowly construed and thus *expands* it into a pluralistically conceived method. Husserl, for his part, makes a similar move that makes it possible to confront him with Cassirer. Having presented both the phenomenological and neo-Kantian methods, it will become clear how they can be synthesized into what I have termed "a hermeneutic phenomenology of subjective and objective spirit." This is not meant merely as a historical account of the relationship between Husserl, Natorp, and Cassirer. Instead, both methods together can help us gain a better understanding and yield a richer account of what transcendental philosophy is to accomplish. Both methods are neither unrelated nor unmediatable. They can—and in fact should—be unified. They complement each other in decisive ways that for the most part have not been acknowledged by representatives of either side of the "divide" to this day. In this sense, this discussion is, on the one hand, intended to reinvigorate a somewhat forgotten debate in the history of modern philosophy. On the other, it is a systematic contribution to overcoming the strict separation between the Kantian and phenomenological ways of framing transcendental philosophy.

Husserl and Natorp: Intuition *versus* Reconstruction, or Intuition *and* Reconstruction?

The dispute between Husserl and Natorp begins immediately after the publication of the first edition of the *Logical Investigations* in 1900–1901. To understand Natorp's objections, one should keep in mind that in most philosophical circles, especially in the early phenomenological groups in Munich and Göttingen, Husserl's call to the "things themselves" was perceived as a liberating turn *away* from questions regarding subjective foundational structures and categories and a *turn towards* the *object*. Although Husserl confusingly calls phenomenology "descriptive psychology" in the

preface to the second volume of the *Logical Investigations*[5]—after he had
just completed a refutation of psychologism in volume 1—the analyses
are object-oriented insofar as phenomenology talks about objects as phenomena, that is, as they appear in (or "fulfill" themselves in) intentional
acts, following the correlation of intention and fulfillment of the First
Logical Investigation. What was to be thematized in intentional analysis
was the intentional relation that governs "between" Ego and object. Consequently, in this early account Husserl took the stance of skepticism with
respect to a pure Ego synthesizing all these subjective acts; such would be
succumbing to an "Ego metaphysics"[6] that phenomenology had purportedly left behind.

Natorp was the first to press Husserl on the issue of the pure Ego,
and in the first book of *Ideas Pertaining to a Pure Phenomenology and Phenomenological Philosophy* from 1913, Husserl records that Natorp's arguments in his *Introduction to Psychology*—arguments that he reiterated in
his 1901 book review of the *Prolegomena* (Natorp 1973, esp. 10–12)—led
Husserl to reconsider the question of the pure Ego. As Husserl acknowledged, it was through Natorp that he had "learned to find" the pure
Ego (Hua XIX/2, 374).[7] It was in *Ideas I* as well that Husserl introduced
the phenomenological reduction, thus inaugurating the transcendental
turn for phenomenology, and, in so doing, estranging a good number of
followers of phenomenology. Phenomenology, Husserl realized, needed
to have recourse to an Ego as a foundation or center point synthesizing
all experience. While this was framed as a Cartesian motive, as method
of radical doubt, it is equally a concession to Natorp, who claimed from
the outset that intentional acts must have a "radiating center [*Ausstrahl-
ungzentrum*]." In Natorp's words, it is constitutive for "facts of consciousness [*Thatsachen des Bewußtseins*]" to have a "relation to the Ego" (Natorp
1888, 11). Performing the transcendental turn in the Cartesian way made
it unnecessary, if not impossible, for Husserl to deny the existence of
such a center within Egoic life. Also, closer insight into the nature of
intentionality made it necessary for Husserl to focus on the subjective
"side" of acts (the "noeses") and hence their character as constituting
or "transcendental." These acts are transcendental insofar as a critical
"epoché" was needed in order to thematize the structure of intentionality in its purity. Only such a "pure" thematization could be rigorously
scientific (eidetic). Husserl sees the epoché as "purifying" consciousness
of its worldly elements and "reducing" it to its essential structures, those
of intentionality. Intentionality, in turn, necessarily includes an Ego that
relates intentional acts around a center.[8] This is, however, already a presentation of the results of Husserl's reflections as a response to Natorp.
Let us backtrack to reconstruct how Husserl arrived at this conclusion.

Ironically, although Natorp is the one to insist on the existence of a pure Ego, he *himself* takes a skeptical stance with regard to a *description* of this pure Ego. Following Kant, the Ego is a mere transcendental, a priori, synthesizing principle that makes experience possible. Experience itself, however, is at all times a dynamic process. Paradoxically, the manner in which Natorp conceives of his "psychology," albeit framed "according to critical method,"[9] implies that a psychology later envisioned by Husserl— an eidetic, descriptive discipline of intentional structures—is impossible. Natorp's psychology has a different scope than an eidetic science, precisely due to the specific character of subjectivity. Psychology is supposed to tap into the concrete life of the subject, that is, precisely in its dynamic flowing that evades an eidetic characterization. What Natorp has in mind with psychology is not an experimental science but a *philosophical consideration of subjectivity* that heeds subjectivity's special and distinct character. As such, the question is whether it should be part of transcendental philosophy. So, first, what is the character of transcendental philosophy according to the "Marburg method," by which one means the method as construed by Cohen?

Transcendental philosophy according to the "Marburg method" has to do entirely with objectivity and how objectivity becomes *constructed* through subjectivity, through the conditions that make constructed objectivity possible. The realm of objectivity—reality—comes to be known through objectivating acts (perception, for example),[10] and continues to be objectively known, or simply *"objectivated,"* through positive sciences as higher-order objectifications. In simpler terms, experience *constructs* reality, and transcendental philosophy ascertains the conditions of possibility of this construction. This focus on the construction of reality, first through experience and then through science (and ultimately all other cultural activities), expresses the Marburg paradigm that transcendental philosophy has to take its departure from the *factum* that is primarily that of science (*das Faktum der Wissenschaft*).[11] According to this Marburg reading, Kant's critique of reason is first (if not exclusively) a doctrine of the "logic of scientific discovery," a theory of science. Hence, every scientific deed discovers and ascertains new "findings" and as such objectifies them. Transcendental philosophy consequently clarifies the lawful conditions of the possibility of these cognizing deeds. Now, in this "objectifying" consideration, where is the subject? Subjectivity is *"found"* in the objects it creates, and critical, transcendental philosophy clarifies solely what is involved in constructing these objects. Transcendental philosophy is directed at the object, and as such, is inherently constructive, that is, object-oriented.[12] Natorp's point now is that the *factum*, however, is a *fieri*, that is, something that is accomplished by human beings in their cultural activity. Psychology thematizes this *fieri* itself. Natorp thereby intends to fill in a dark spot that was left open in the original scope of Hermann Cohen's method, namely, by providing a discipline dedicated to the subjective "side" of this process, to the *fieri* itself. The originality of this method becomes clear when one sees that this aspect was considered an entirely unnecessary discipline by Cohen.[13] Natorp's key insight was that philosophy in some way or another needed to address this concretion of the life of the subject in its creative ("poietic," as he later called it) character, and it makes understandable why Natorp saw himself in alliance with Husserl's phenomenological approach from the outset. Yet, since he is steeped in the transcendental method, the character of his psychology is problematic.

Indeed, because experience is constructive and objectifying Natorp takes a skeptical stance with respect to a description of subjectivity itself: every utterance is objectifying. This holds also for that regarding subjective occurrences: the moment they are objectified, through whichever method, they are no longer subjective. But in this objectification—and one cannot avoid it—the subjective is lost; it is *made* objective. In objectifying subjectivity through experimental science, for example, that very element which accounts for the true meaning of subjectivity dissipates. The immediate subjective character has vanished, its dynamic nature is brought to a standstill and hence can no longer be recognized as what it intrinsically is, a dynamic process of concrete life. Objectifying subjective experience "inserts" subjectivity into another element in which it is treated like a doctor treating a corpse instead of a living being (Natorp 1912a, 191):[14]

> Because this is so, [consciousness] must be inaccessible to all further description; for all that through which one would want to describe it . . . could only be taken from the content of consciousness, that is, it would presuppose itself, the Ego. . . . Being an Ego means not being an object [*Gegenstand*] but, opposed to all objectivity, that *to whom* something is an object. (Natorp 1912a, 28–29; emphasis added)

It is psychology's task to "save" subjectivity from objectification. This does not mean that Natorp rejects an account of consciousness altogether; rather, there can be no *direct* description of consciousness in the way that there can be a direct intuition of a perceptual object or a direct cognition of a law of nature. Consciousness is not among, next to, or above other objects and objectivities; for it is *not an object*. Rather, it is *opposed* to all objectivity and as such the "foundation" of all objectivity as that from where construction takes its departure. Because Natorp insists on the special character of consciousness in the most radical way, it can never be conceived along the lines of or by any analogy to objective reality; there persists an "ontological difference" between subjectivity and objectivity. Natorp is keenly aware of the immediacy and absolute originality (Natorp 1912a, 29: "*absolute Ursprünglichkeit*") of the irreducible "first-person perspective" that renders his consequence this radical. Excluding this direct access to subjectivity is intended to preserve its very nature. Yet, although Natorp is correct in insisting on this radical difference, Husserl contends that he does not carry through with it completely on the *methodological* level. Let us thus briefly turn to Husserl before discussing Natorp's psychological method.

Although Natorp already makes these claims before Husserl begins his philosophical undertaking, it is clear that they contradict everything phenomenology stands for. Indeed, it is paradigmatic for any phenomenological approach—transcendental or "realistic"—to declare intuition based on subjective evidence as a foundation for any further philosophical inquiry. Phenomenology is, in its purest and most basic sense, description of consciousness based on intuition. This is formulated in Husserl's famous "principle of all principles," according to which everything philosophy builds upon must have a foundation in "self-giving evidence and intuition" (*Ideas I*, §24, Hua III/1, 51). However, this foundational principle does not entail just any intuition, such as basic sensuous perception. Phenomenological intuition comes into play when describing essences. This implies a claim concerning what is not yet truly phenomenological description. In this sense, where the phenomenological principle is carried out most impressively is precisely in thematizing consciousness eidetically. In this respect, *both* Natorp and Husserl are vigorously against "naturalizing" consciousness as not recognizing the radical difference between subjectivity and "objective" being, that is, nature. Whereas Natorp proposes an approach to consciousness that is different from the objectifying tendency, Husserl goes a different path, yet for the same reason, that is, to avoid naturalism. Yet precisely with this eidetic science he is also intent on getting back to the concrete life of consciousness.

Indeed, that consciousness Husserl wants to describe with the phenomenological-intuitive method is not the natural consciousness we find in our everyday experience. It is from this consciousness and having-of-world that we must practice an epoché and look at pure structures of consciousness-as-such. This "bracketing" of the natural attitude, which consists of believing in the existence of the world independent of subjective experience, reveals "absolute" subjectivity that is not part of the world but opposed to it as its transcendental correlate. The subjective structures that transcendental phenomenology describes are hence no longer those of worldly (human) subjectivity, but subjectivity-as-such. However, this subjectivity is only attained by a radical change of attitude, in which (Husserl insists) nothing is "lost" but is viewed from a radically different perspective. Phenomenology is conceived as the eidetic science of transcendental subjectivity, something Husserl also likes to term "transcendental empiricism,"[15] a provocation to any Kantian, neo- or otherwise. From here, Husserl comes to embrace transcendental idealism as the doctrine which is committed to the radical opposition between (constituting) subjectivity and (constituted) objectivity, both of which are related to each other in a "correlational a priori." It is clear, however, that Husserl operates with a novel concept of "transcendental." It is not a formal set of knowledge from principles a priori but a field of intuition into the subject after the epoché has occurred (and with it, a bracketing of the naive belief in the independent existence of the world); it is not merely a formal, but a material a priori that thematizes the *concrete life of subjectivity eidetically*.[16] Thus, consciousness can be described when one makes a shift from the naive, everyday perspective to the phenomenological standpoint.

In other words, as opposed to Natorp, Husserl insists that a description of subjectivity in itself is possible if one concedes that subjectivity is an experienceable region of conscious life to which one can gain access via reflection (or "introspection") when one breaks with the ordinary way of viewing things.[17] Yet Husserl agrees with Natorp that this description must not naturalize subjectivity and treat it as another worldly being; hence the shift via the phenomenological reduction to pure, transcendental consciousness. Yet, whereas Natorp employs his critique of intuition of consciousness as a criticism of phenomenology, for Husserl it becomes the very starting point for a transcendental recasting of the phenomenological method. From this perspective, the phenomenological reduction is a way out of the epistemological dilemma Natorp had described, that is, that describing involuntarily is objectifying. The problem is not solved but avoided by taking a detour via another level of reflection by breaking with the natural attitude. The transcendental standpoint attained in the transcendental reduction situates itself in another "dimension" vis-à-vis that of objectivity. This is possible because the phenomenologist practices a radical break with the natural attitude and thereby is in a position where she can intuit conscious structures, which are not her private structures but which belong to any subjective experience-as-such. Hence, the transcendental turn first truly *enables* phenomenological (eidetic) intuitionism; a pre-transcendental account would be by necessity naturalistic.

Although Natorp, in turn, agrees with Husserl's emphasis on intentionality and its discernible structures,[18] this structure is to him a mere formal framework which *in itself* does not yield the basis for any further "material" investigation. But this Kantian dilemma, according to which "transcendental" equals "formal," is solved when one realizes that what is attained with the transcendental reduction is a (both formal and material) sphere of experience. Accordingly, Husserl's method of the transcendental reduction is a critique of the Kantian paradigm that intuition into the true realm of subjective life—whether one wants to label it transcendental or not—is impossible without "killing" it.[19] However, while Husserl believes to have secured his sense of "transcendental empiricism," we will see that the opposition between "intuition" and "construction" is not so easy to maintain when actually doing phenomenological description.

This skepticism with regard to consciousness is not the last word Natorp has to say about the method of psychology; for if this were the case, obviously his whole project of a rational psychology would come to an end right here. So what is the method of Natorp's psychology? Rejecting the approach of direct intuition does not mean that nothing can be said about consciousness. To be sure, consciousness cannot be described immediately and directly, but why not indirectly and mediately? This is the way Natorp in effect proceeds. If subjectivity is radically opposed to objectivity and if the transcendental method is about constructing objectivity, it is conceivable that the method Natorp proposes for the subjective "side" merely goes the opposite way of the constructive method; namely, it is re-constructive. It takes its point of departure from the "finished," "crystallized" objectivities (the *facta*) and pursues the opposite direction in reconstructing the dynamic, flowing life from which objectivity has become constructed (the *fieri*). Natorp also speaks of a "turning inside out" (*Umstülpung*) of the constructive method in going the opposite path of reconstruction. This reconstructive method is indeed a form of reflection (Natorp 1912a, 20),[20] only with the clear knowledge that this reflection cannot directly access the immediacy of subjective life. It can only reconstruct it retrospectively, moving "backwards" from its objectified achievements. It is a "reverse" movement and in this sense is comparable to a "reduction" in making recourse from the immediately given unities (the seen object) in experience to the subjective multiplicities in concrete subjectivity, which "constitute" the former in "intentional" activities (the dynamic, ever-new acts).[21] Hence, the method of reconstruction is designed to bring back the concretion of subjective life, however mediately, for every direct description would be an abstraction. The reconstructive move goes backwards

> from the objectivations that are achieved by science and before all science, without any conscious intent, [in] every quotidian way of rep-

resenting things. It [namely, reconstruction] consists . . . in undoing the objectivations . . . in thought [= construction], by reinserting that which has been severed by abstraction into the original interconnections, by giving back dynamics to the fixed concepts, and in so doing by bringing them back to the flowing life of consciousness. . . . It is . . . a complete and pure turning-around [*Umkehrung*] of the method of objectifying knowledge, scientific as well as pre-scientific. (Natorp 1912a, 192–93)

It is for this reason that psychology comes at a point where the work of philosophy is finished; it is philosophy's "last word,"[22] as it presupposes the constructive work, that is, the objectification of *facta*. However, the question lingers, of what exactly it is that remains to be discussed for a general psychology if it is framed in Natorp's way, by merely giving a reconstructive interpretation of that which has already been thematized in constructive analysis. It should be remembered that Natorp's sketch of such a discipline in *General Psychology* has remained a fragment and never is carried out.[23] Despite the internal problems with this discipline, however, the main insight of his psychology is his emphasis on the dynamic character of consciousness as opposed to the fixed nature of *facta*. In this sense, Natorp at all times emphasizes that this reconstructive method proceeds "genetically" (Natorp 1912a, vii) in recapturing the dynamic life of the original, flowing character of consciousness, as opposed to the "static" constructive method which treats objectivities as "finished" unities. Natorp's reconstructive psychology does not become executed, but it makes the point that will become important for Husserl, that is, that an analysis that does justice to the life of consciousness *must* be cast in a manner that conforms to this dynamic life. What is furthermore problematic in Natorp is that, since construction and reconstruction merely differ in the direction they pursue (the "plus" and "minus" direction), their methodological *character* is also the same: whereas the constructive way is teleological, the reconstructive path is causal; it is a "reverse teleology," as was said in the previous chapter. Thus, contrary to Natorp's pronouncements, the way the reconstructive method treats subjectivity is still "naturalizing." This is also the reason why the reconstructive method does not really add anything new to the transcendental method, and certainly nothing to a genuine understanding of subjectivity.[24]

But let us now turn back to Husserl. Although Natorp's position seems weak with respect to Husserl's more elaborate method of the phenomenological reduction, it is this reconstructive method that forms the backdrop of Husserl's genetic turn, a method that essentially rectifies Natorp's legitimate intentions; and Husserl never questioned the agreement between Natorp and himself in these principal matters. In this respect, Husserl even reluctantly admitted Natorp's influence in taking over the "genetic" aspect of psychological description that Natorp declares the paradigm of reconstructive analysis (see Natorp 1912a, §9, 249–50). In fact, this is one of the only aspects where Husserl explicitly agrees with Natorp upon studying his works in 1918, although he presents it as though he came upon the genetic method on his own terms by predating it. During this phase (1917–18), Husserl explicitly begins drafting a genetic phenomenology.[25] In a letter to Natorp from the summer of 1918, Husserl not only underscores the importance of the genetic, dynamic account of consciousness, but also drops the rather offhanded comment that he has posited the theme of genetic analysis for phenomenology "for already more than a decade" (Hua-Dok III/5, 137).[26]

While one can say with certainty in the light of the development of Husserl's thought that this is incorrect, scholars have wondered what he meant with this comment, and the primary candidate is usually, and rightly, considered Husserl's analysis of internal time-consciousness. Husserl has dealt with this topic since 1905, and in his epilogue to *Ideas I* from 1930 he judges retrospectively that the omission of time-consciousness is one major shortcoming of *Ideas I*.[27] The phenomenology of internal time-consciousness is by no means already a genetic analysis of subjectivity. However, the discussion of time in the phenomenological context is the privileged path towards it. As Kern argues,[28] Husserl probably had this in mind in this letter to Natorp. So how does Husserl move from an analysis of time-consciousness to genetic analysis?

In short, Husserl's analysis of time-consciousness thematizes the temporality of the flow of subjective life itself. Conscious life is a dynamic flow of ever-new now-points in which the Ego lives in the "lived present." However, the "nows" are not discrete points (as, for example, in Aristotle's concept of time),[29] but each present consciousness is embedded in a temporal horizon, in that each now-impression is preceded by a previous one which is not "past" but which "lingers," and likewise, the present now anticipates a new now. Hearing a melody as melody (and not as a sequence of unrelated tones) is only possible if that which I just heard is retained while I hear a present note and the hearing of the note now anticipates another coming note. The analysis of the temporal structure of subjective life itself reveals that the primal impression of the now is embedded in a series of immediately past retentions and protentions immediately to come.[30] A phenomenological description of how the Ego experiences something in time must pay heed to this "internal time-consciousness" itself vis-à-vis objective, physical time. Or said differently, the way the Ego's intuition functions can only occur in this temporal fashion: to the intuition here and now belongs necessarily an original

presentation and a halo of de-presentation, past and future. To say it in
Natorp's words: the fundamental character of consciousness is that it is
dynamic, hence the method to analyze it must be *genetic (reconstructive).*

If this is the case, then one must concede that the focus on intuition
(in the "here and now") only grasps a very small aspect of conscious life.
It is a "static" description that is based on what is intuited in *this* here and
now only. If one wants to give a phenomenological description of other
dimensions of conscious life, such as memory or imagination, it is clear
that one cannot bring the past memory, as past, to direct evidence and
intuition. I can remember a past occurrence here and now, but only as
past and not now; this constitutes the very essence of memory.[31] If one
acknowledges that consciousness is dynamic, then one must accept that
there are aspects and elements of conscious life of which I can never
have direct intuition, although they certainly exist as having undoubtedly
contributed in shaping my current experience. Examples of such essentially unintuitable yet decisive occurrences are my own birth or death,
the subjective life of others (be they past or present), or the primal impression of a type of object I have known since shortly after my birth (or
which I have not constituted *at all* like a cultural object that was "given"
to me "ready made"). Yet these are the preferred topics in Husserl's genetic phenomenology. Hence, the method of intuition reveals its limits in cases such as these, where one thematizes, not static intentional
structures, but the dynamic flowing life that produces ("constitutes")
objects of experience. This was the brunt of Natorp's critique from the
very beginning, when he termed Husserl's analysis of act-intentionality a
"static Platonism" (Natorp 1912a, 288–89). Indeed, these dynamic phenomena are not topics externally related to Husserl's thought but his
own favorite examples and areas of research. However, the topic of transcendental phenomenology is—ideally—a description of the *totality* of
subjective life in all of its facets and dimensions. Hence, in thematizing
the temporality of subjectivity itself, Husserl realizes that a description
of "fixed" intentional structures of consciousness is merely a static description, which is blind to the dynamic, genetic dimensions ("layers") of
consciousness. Static description, in ignoring any notion of the subject's
temporality, catches merely the surface dimension of subjectivity, disregarding its "depth structure." Thus, seemingly in his own way, Husserl
discovers Natorp's "flowing" (dynamic, genetic) structures of subjectivity by expanding his view beyond mere givennesses in intentional acts
(which are merely thematized as given in the now) to their genesis. Yet
this insistence on the dynamic flow of subjective life is not only the bedrock of Natorp's psychology; it was also his strongest point of contention
with Husserl's static phenomenology.

In other words, as Natorp already proposed, the structural ("eidetic") account has to be supplemented by a dynamic ("explanatory") account. A genetic account can no longer be eidetic but moves into a "hermeneutic" dimension, as Husserl himself indeed likes to refer to his genetic analyses as interpretation (*Auslegung*).[32] Moreover, since this dynamic depth structure—which Husserl also calls a passive genesis[33]—cannot be brought to direct intuition, it can merely be made evident through a reconstructive method. Although Husserl prefers the terms "restitution," "unbuilding" (*Abbau*), or "regressive method," or even "interpretation," there are a few places in his manuscripts where he does indeed use Natorp's term "reconstruction."[34] While this is not the place to analyze the reconstructive elements of Husserl's genetic phenomenology—a description of the temporality and ultimately historicity of transcendental consciousness[35]—this alone should become clear, that Husserl's own intuitive method applied to consciousness as a whole cannot but revert to reconstructive elements in its attempt to grasp the full "body" of the transcendental realm. In other words, it is impossible for phenomenological analysis to remain at the purely intuitive, static level if it wants to do justice to consciousness as a whole. Static analysis per se bleeds into a genetic account in an organic expansion of its descriptive scope. Yet, when one enters genetic spheres the descriptions that one gives are not and cannot be based on intuition, at least not on intuition alone. The consequence is that *the difference between intuitive and reconstructive methods cannot be strictly maintained.*

Indeed, this difference is artificial, although Husserl takes pains to show that even interpretation rests on intuitive elements. Although he insists, rather stubbornly, on the paradigm of evidence, he is forced to concede the necessity of "explanatory" or "interpretive" analysis that is not based on evidence.[36] Thus, contrary to Husserl's own emphasis that such interpretation is interpretation of "evidencing intentionality," his latter claim, that "all self-understanding is interpretation," runs counter to his original claim. Intuitive evidence is in fact a very late phenomenon in the life of consciousness as well as for the phenomenological method, as it rests on the larger foundation of interpretation that can only proceed reconstructively. Although Husserl claims in the above-quoted letter genetic phenomenology as his own discovery, the genetic, dynamic dimension that is required to analyze subjectivity through reconstruction was the whole point of Natorp's psychology that he had already laid out in his *Introduction to Psychology* from 1888, which Husserl knew well before any talk of genesis in his own writings.[37] Thus, phenomenology as a description of consciousness needs to be complemented by a reconstructive account. In other words, phenomenology becomes *hermeneutical.*

Although Husserl's genetic phenomenology is in this sense crucially indebted to Natorp's reconstructive method, there is, however, one decisive difference. The subjectivity that phenomenology analyzes is not part of the world (of "objectivity"). The "reconstructive" method that phenomenology employs is not a causal reconstruction, since subjectivity in its original sense is not part of the world of objectivity; hence something like a "causal" account will not do justice to subjectivity in its "own" right. One *can* give a causal account of subjectivity, but that would treat it as a part of nature in what Husserl calls the "naturalistic" attitude. This was, as we recall, Husserl's earlier critique of Natorp's methodological naïveté. Indeed, treating subjectivity in its germane sense means occupying a position that reveals subjective structures in their own original character and lawfulness, a lawfulness that is radically different from that pertaining to the sphere of objectivity. The "causality" in the sphere of conscious life, which Husserl calls "motivation," functions according to its own, very distinct laws, such as association.[38] Again, this topic need not be discussed here; all that should become clear is the context of Husserl's specifically phenomenological approach to subjectivity through the genetic phenomenological method, which came into being only after having been exposed to a decidedly non-phenomenological conception of subjectivity, both thematically and methodologically.[39]

To summarize, one can say that both Husserl and Natorp employ a method which in each case can be termed reconstructive. However, the difference is that although Natorp proposes a reconstruction of the concrete life of the subject in the framework of his *General Psychology*, he stops short of actually "delving" into the "depths" of subjectivity. He proposes but does not *perform* an actual genetic analysis. The reconstructive method is solely meant to "undo" that which has already been achieved by objectivation. It can only revert back to reconstructing "subjectivity" from the objective achievements which stand before us as cultural objects. The label for all that the human being constructs is *culture* (the paradigm of the Marburg school). Ultimately, although Natorp had the crucial intuition, subjectivity in his method can only be known *ex negativo;* that is, Natorp does not cash in on his own legitimate intuition. Reconstructive work comes to an end with the pure Ego as merely an a priori principle, a sheer ideal zero-point beyond which one cannot trespass. Hence, a real philosophical "psychology" is not carried out, although he gives the main guiding clues to Husserl. Natorp's analysis has its "locus" in the transcendental realm; yet the "subjective side" of it is essentially a black box.

As has been argued, however, Husserl's whole endeavor is to demonstrate how such a description of conscious life is indeed possible *when* one takes seriously the ontological difference between both spheres (subjectivity and objectivity, attained in the transcendental and the natural standpoints, respectively) in the methodological sense. Indeed, Husserl's subtle descriptions of consciousness in his intricate analyses of time-consciousness, perception, memory, and fantasy belie any skepticism concerning the efficacy of such analyses. To be sure, Husserl's descriptions are also "object-oriented," as they thematize intentional acts (as intending-*something*). Yet they are intentional structures of experience, and as such they can be made thematic in a reflexive turning away from the world "out there" into its origin in meaning-bestowing intentional structures of consciousness. Yet the other point inspired by Natorp is that even these phenomenological descriptions cannot methodologically do without reconstructive and constructive elements, insofar as there are dimensions of conscious life which simply cannot be brought to direct intuition. They can be reconstructed, not causally as in Natorp, but in a new attitude that brings into view consciousness's specific character. This does not, however, mean a bankruptcy of the phenomenological method, but rather a deepening and an opening towards speculative, metaphysical dimensions, as already emphasized in chapter 6. Although Husserl throughout his lifetime steered clear from such designations of his phenomenology, in his later phase his analyses are full of such elements, especially in his speculative thesis of the inborn teleology of all consciousness. Although he never went beyond mere announcements concerning these speculative ideas in his published writings, Husserl openly acknowledges—and not only in his correspondence with Natorp—his connection with the innermost intentions of speculative idealism.[40]

Comparing Natorp's and Husserl's methodology, one can conclude that both of them represent "transcendental methods." Yet, while Husserl gained important insights through Natorp's method, Natorp's own psychology is methodologically flawed. What is not touched by this critique, however, is the original transcendental method of construction developed by Cohen and espoused by Natorp, a method that uses constructive elements to explain how it is possible for consciousness to experience the world as a world of culture. Thus we can return to the conclusion of the previous chapter, namely, while Natorp is oriented towards the object of the investigation, Husserl is oriented toward the subject, or (in other words) Natorp in the *objectifying*, Husserl in the *subjectifying* aspect of transcendental life. Seen from *this* perspective, the opposition turns out to be a *relative* one in that Natorp looks at the noematic, Husserl at the noetic side of the "transcendental realm" as that which makes experience of world possible. Both locate their philosophical projects *within* a transcendental register.[41] Although Husserl was himself not blind to this noematic dimension, he rarely thematizes this aspect as more than an afterthought, whereas Natorp, due to his dogmatic restrictions, shies away entirely from conceding a proper description of the noetic. Both positions, however, need not be mutually exclusive; they merely emphasize different sides of the same coin. Both thematize the conditions of possibility of experience of world in "subjective" and "objective" directions, respectively. Furthermore, Husserl's method, in going the reconstructive path, becomes thereby genetic. Thus Husserl, first, exploits Natorp's radical difference between subjectivity and objectivity to establish a methodological difference, enabling him, second, to access and analyze genetically the noetic side of "the transcendental." The important methodological conclusion of this section is that in this respect both methods form a correlation; one necessarily supplements the other. Whereas up to now this sounded like a purely formal correlation, it will be up to Cassirer, who was well versed in both Natorp's and Husserl's methods, to fill this "promise" with content.

Husserl and Cassirer: Noetics and Noematics Within the Pluralistically Conceived Transcendental Realm

To show how Cassirer fits into the picture, we first have to point out the shortcomings of Natorp's method as they appear to Cassirer. These shortcomings are not internal flaws in Natorp's psychology but rather appear as an unwarranted—and indeed unnecessary—restriction on Natorp's part, which Cassirer purports to overcome. However, Cassirer by no means does away with the Marburg method. Rather, he transforms both Cohen's transcendental and Natorp's reconstructive method. Specifically, Cassirer considers Natorp's method, although in principle correct, too narrow and in need of broadening. It is important to note that this is an insight the late Natorp himself had reached, which prompted, for example, Heidegger to rightly point out a methodological convergence in the late Natorp and the Cassirer of the *Philosophy of Symbolic Forms*.[42] In either case, one can say that both Natorp and Cassirer have, in their way, moved away from the original neo-Kantian focus on scientific experience without simultaneously giving up the general framework of transcendental philosophy in the spirit of Kant. The label that has been applied to neo-Kantianism by critics, that it merely provides a justification for the positive sciences, is both incorrect and, in the light of where Cassirer took the Marburg method, especially unfair.[43] Both Natorp and

Cassirer have proceeded to a novel and original concept of transcendental philosophy and of its subject domain, "the" transcendental, and it was especially Cassirer's conception that came close to that of the late Husserl. The decisive insight that both Cassirer and Husserl had independently of each other was that the transcendental realm is structured in a *plural fashion.*

To start out, Natorp was widely perceived as the most severe "methodological fanatic" of the neo-Kantian movement.[44] This characterization—which was not entirely positive—pertained to the fact that he seemingly wanted to reduce every factual philosophical problem to a methodological question within the transcendental method, and in a sense this judgment is correct. As he emphasized, every *factum* is a *fieri* and as such subject to the transcendental method. Method is the absolute of philosophy, or philosophy is *nothing but* method because the *method,* in the sense of *met-hódos,* retraces the steps of the *fieri.*[45] In this sense, Cassirer charges Natorp with a methodological monism[46] stemming from his alleged "metaphysical monism," that is, that there is just one objective reality which can only be broached by one method, that of objectivation. To Natorp the realm of objectivity is originally nothing but nature, indeed, the nature with which the positive sciences deal. Although there is no reason to believe that there is more than one reality, Cassirer asserts, this is not to say that there is only one type of or one way of experiencing reality, a point clearly influenced by Husserl's phenomenology in its analyses of "attitudes" (see chapter 1). Natorp's transcendental method, at least before changing his view in his late philosophy, does in fact pay heed to only one type of objectivity: it merely focuses upon that which the positive sciences cognize and claim as the product of their cognizing activity. His approach only considers what Kant had thematized in the framework of theoretical philosophy. This was indeed Cohen's point of departure, to focus on the *factum* as the *factum* of the sciences (*das Faktum der Wissenschaften*).[47] However, did not Kant himself insist, if not on different realities, then at least on different ways of thematizing reality, namely through the disciplines of ethics, aesthetics, and religion? Recalling the scope of Kant's critical philosophy, Cassirer states:

> The meaning of the moral ought, the meaning of the work of art, the meaning of the religious, all of this is only visible to us in a special attitude of spiritual regard [*geistiger Blick*]. . . . Can we set ourselves to rest with this manifold of "perspectives" [*Gesichtspunkte*]; shall we just accept it as a last facticity, as a factum of spiritual being and spiritual life that we can no further explain and break down? If this were the case, then the very *idea of philosophy* itself would threaten to get lost. (1925, 288)

In other words, was not reason more than *pure* reason alone? Surely, there is but one reason; however, as Kant already insisted, it has different applications and intentions.[48] Is therefore, as Cassirer asserts, reason not better understood as *spirit*? Seeing reason in a broader conception as spirit, there are, accordingly, different ways in which it can experience the world. Yet, although the move from reason to spirit seems like a mere repetition of Hegel, Cassirer moves in an entirely different direction.

Indeed, the world we live in and which is constructed through subjective activity—this transcendental paradigm Cassirer does not question—is not merely the world of science. Science is but one, and certainly not the most fundamental, manner in which the world is constructed. As one of reason's points of crystallization, science presents merely one type of the broader account of subjective activity, which is more properly conceived as spirit. Kant's canonical differentiation of the applications of reason into aesthetics, ethics, and religion is a start, but not enough for Cassirer. He goes even further so as to include all activities and achievements of subjectivity, insofar as they are principal ways in which subjects encounter the world in a meaningful ("spiritual") way. This is in keeping with Natorp, who does not differentiate between "rational" and "irrational" human activities; all human activities in their own peculiar manner contribute to the way the world is for human beings. The world is entirely a world of culture; even something like "pure nature" is a product of the sciences as cultural activities. To Cassirer, this is the consequence of the sense and tradition of what he calls "modern idealism," which is committed since the Renaissance to positing and further investigating the correlation between world and spirit.[49] He is merely drawing the most far-reaching consequence from the Marburg method that all experience constructs reality, namely, that different experience constructs *differently*. Following Natorp's train of thought but at the same time breaking with him critically, Cassirer asserts:

> Eye-to-eye philosophy stands again not only with the particular sciences but rather with the world of spirit, which comprises, besides science, law as well as morality, art as well as religion. All of these need to be investigated, they need to be understood *in their own immanent sense*, in the particularity of their structure. (1925, 290; italics added)

In taking over Natorp's constructive method, Cassirer thereby *multiplies* the process of objectivation. He, too, employs the "transcendental method"; this method, however, has many *forms* of application. Opposed to Natorp's methodological monism stands Cassirer's pluralism, again merely following an insight Natorp had but did not exploit methodologically.

Yet in this pluralization of Natorp's method Cassirer goes one crucial step further. The problem with Natorp's (Cohenian) method was that, again following Kant, he remained fixated on the *lawful* character of scientific objectification. As mentioned, in his late period Natorp did arrive at thematizing art and religion and other "spiritual" regions; Cassirer was aware of Natorp's last vision. Yet even then Natorp remained fixated on the laws that govern their constructions and characterize their internal structures; he did not overcome the paradigm of lawfulness.[50] Yet the criteria of "general truth" and "lawfulness" only pertain to science and not, say, to language or art as equally valid expressions of the human spirit. Where one talks no longer of a lawful type of experience as in science, the character of what it is to be a law changes as well. Science, for example, uses language, but in a different way and to a different end than that of everyday parlance. To be sure, everyday language has a certain regularity or general nature as well, but this is of a different kind and rigor than that of scientific discourse:

> The generality of linguistic "concepts" does not stand in the same line as that of scientific . . . "laws": one is not merely a continuation of the other, but each moves in different tracks and expresses different directions of spiritual formation. (Cassirer 1954/III, 66)[51]

The full range of reality as formed by spirit would be too narrowly understood if one only examined it through the categories of lawfulness and exactitude as guiding clues. We are not just embedded in and given over to nature but are constantly in the process of forming reality into a world of humankind, into a culture. Cassirer thus concludes his critical discussion of Natorp:

> If we want to gain a truly concrete view of the "full objectivity" of spirit on the one hand, its "full subjectivity" on the other, we must attempt to execute this methodological correlation, that Natorp posits as principle, *for all regions of spiritual creating*. It will become clear that the three main directions of "objectivation" that Natorp presupposes in close connection to the Kantian *Critiques* . . . do not suffice. (Cassirer 1954/III, 67)

Hence different spheres of experience require different guiding principles in ascertaining how they construct their specific reality. As shall be demonstrated in the following chapter, the main directions of spirit's objectivation are what Cassirer calls the "symbolic forms." His philosophy of symbolic forms only becomes understandable in light of the foundations laid by Natorp.[52] The symbolic forms are the ways in which reason, conceived as spirit, manifests itself and through which the world comes to be experienced in different forms of experience. These forms shape the "spaces of meaning" that conscious human beings occupy in the manifold of their activities. As opening and allowing for spaces for spiritual activities, these forms are functional contexts (of which constructing nature is but one type) in which spirit comes to reveal itself, in language, myth, art, religion, and, to be sure, science. They are "ways which spirit pursues in its objectivation, that is, in its self-revelation" (Cassirer 1954/I, 9). These forms are not empirically discernible modes of human behavior but dimensions in which *spirit* "lives" and comes to understand itself. They are, in their plurality, *transcendental forms* of intuition in the Kantian sense, but with different and distinct "internal" logics and manners of functioning, of which scientific "lawfulness" (or lawfulness in general) is but one. These forms are "symbolic" because, in the literal sense of symbol from Greek *sym-bállein* (to throw together), each individual object is tied into a functional context, it stands in and for a specific space of meaning. In totality, these forms shape reality in the universal sense of that which is formed by human spirit.

This totality Cassirer calls "culture." Hence, "the critique of reason becomes the critique of culture. It strives to understand and to show how all content of culture, insofar as it is more than a mere particular content, insofar as it is grounded in a general form-principle, presupposes an original deed of spirit. Only in this endeavor does the basic thesis of idealism find its true and complete realization" (Cassirer 1954/I, 11). The actual task of Cassirer's *Philosophy of Symbolic Forms* is to discern and to describe these symbolic forms in their own specific ways of functioning. For the factual implementation of these descriptions Cassirer does not hesitate to employ the term "phenomenology,"[53] insofar as this analysis attempts to be true to the internal functional structures of each of the symbolic forms and describes them in their essential and necessary traits. The phenomenological influence lies precisely in taking experience seriously in the way the spirit constructs different "spaces of meaning." His method is thus constructive as well as descriptive. In this respect, Cassirer also calls his project a "phenomenology of consciousness" (Cassirer 1954/III, 64),[54] with consciousness constantly being "objectified" in the symbolic forms as spiritual contents through which human beings understand the world. In this sense, it is phenomenological more in the Husserlian, descriptive sense than in that of Hegel. What is Hegelian is the move from reason to spirit. What distinguishes Cassirer most from the latter is, however, that there is no hierarchy involved in spiritual formation, but each symbolic form is an independent and equally valid expression of spirit. There is no teleology, but rather a centrifugal emanation of spirit in different directions. In this rejection of a teleology of spirit as reaching an absolute standpoint, Cassirer concurs with Husserl, yet both embrace the idea of progress; as Cassirer says (and to which Husserl could agree), culture is a process of the "continual progress of freedom."[55]

Yet Cassirer's *Philosophy of Symbolic Forms* comes with the same "objectifying" focus as Natorp's. Thus, Cassirer refers to his philosophical project as a phenomenology of "objective spirit" (Cassirer 1954/III, 65),[56] and in so doing explicitly makes recourse to Natorp's method of objectification. Only what is objectified is not reason but spirit. Cassirer's philosophy of culture represents a phenomenology of objective spirit, a spirit, however, that is pluralized into different symbolic formations with their own particular modes of functioning and "lawful" regularity. As such, he is both loyal to Natorp's transcendental method *and* the phenomenological paradigm of unprejudiced, phenomenon-oriented description. Whereas Natorp looks at the world purely formally from the standpoint of an absolute method, Cassirer actually immerses himself in the manifold traditions of human culture, as witnessed in his works on Renaissance philosophy, mythology, linguistics, and modern physics. Due to his impressive erudition, he is the first to truly bring the transcendental method to life.

Yet there can be no mistaking that in this original interpretation of Natorp's (and Kant's) method, Cassirer also buys into a claim of Natorp's that has been shown to be problematic. For the same reasons as Natorp, Cassirer denies any direct access to subjectivity or, for that matter, spirit. He insists that his analysis of spirit is equally a "reconstructive analysis" in the sense of a genetic account of spirit's formation (Cassirer 1954/III, 65). We can only ever speak about subjectivity by reconstructing it backwards from the end point of its objective achievements, the symbolic forms themselves. Yet as he insists even then, "spirit does not reveal itself in its essentiality" (Cassirer 1995, 52).[57] We are, as subjects, what our place in culture is.[58] We are spirit objectified. In other words, although Cassirer overcomes Natorp's methodological impasse by multiplying the types of objectivations to capture all realms of spiritual activity, he nevertheless remains bound to the neo-Kantian dogma of the inaccessibility of subjectivity. His talk of "spirit" instead of subjectivity clouds his position with regard to the latter, but his doctrine of the "symbolic forms" implies the paradigm of subjectivity's (or spirit's) inaccessibility; I am not spirit, I partake in it. The term "symbolic" implies this as well. There can never be a direct intuition of entities; all intuition is always mediated through a symbolic meaning. Each experienced entity, qua experience, is a functional element within a symbolic form. Entities can only be perceived as bearing a "symbolic pregnancy" that "connects them internally" to a symbolic form. We never experience being "eye to eye" but always through the "tincture" of symbolic vision, which is not an obstacle but a necessary precondition of our finite experience.[59] This symbolism does not distort being but is the way—the only way—in which we can have *any* experience.[60]

It is for this reason—experience can only be symbolic—that any analysis of subjectivity can only be indirect as well. There is thus a double reason for subjectivity's inaccessibility: not only do we not see subjectivity "in itself"; we only have access to it symbolically. All that can be said about it will be "reconstructive" and will only give a "negative" image by means of an explication of the symbolic forms and of what occurs within *them*. The reconstructive method will be genetic only with regard to the objectifying symbolic forms. Cassirer scholars might object that Cassirer does discuss subjectivity in the context of knowledge as a symbolic form of its own (in the third volume of *The Philosophy of Symbolic Forms*). Yet Cassirer's account only deals with the structures that are needed to clarify the functioning of cognition, not subjectivity itself, that is, the concrete dynamic life of the subject.[61] The dynamic vivacity of the subject remains (deliberately) untouched. Thus, although Cassirer expands the concept of objectivation in a most original and fruitful way, he still remains bound to the problematic Kantian paradigm of subjective analysis as a region that is "off limits."

However, as we have seen previously following Husserl, this alleged inaccessibility of subjectivity due to its non-intuitability need not be maintained. One can support this by conceding that a phenomenology of subjectivity (in the style Husserl has demonstrated it) need not and in fact *cannot* rest entirely on intuition. Rather, this "direct and evidencing intuition" is merely the uppermost stratum of a larger and multilayered structure, of which even subjectivity—as the rational, self-conscious personal agency—is but the abstract top stratum. It would be abstract, that is, if one were to isolate it from its larger, genetic "depth structure."[62] We have now come to the point where we can put the pieces together and see how Cassirer's "expanded" position of the neo-Kantian method and Husserl's mature standpoint form an encompassing theory that accommodates both the noetic and noematic direction of the transcendental realm. Let us first turn to Husserl.

Although no longer bound to strict intuition but also including construction or interpretation, Husserl's genetic phenomenology intends to show how the world is constituted for an embodied subject by the subject's very acts in his method "from the bottom up," that is, through an analysis of foundational strata beginning from the most primitive levels of perception and moving to the highest strata of judgmental and scientific consciousness. For instance, by showing how perceptual objects are constituted through our bodily interaction with them in primitive *kinesthesia,* Husserl gives a lucid account of subjective acts in which objectivity becomes "constituted," whether these descriptions be intuitive or not. Indeed, it is this reconstructive interpretation that enables Husserl to access this depth structure of subjectivity, a dimension he calls "passivity." This is precisely the meaning of "passivity" in genetic phenomenology: by describing how through primitive intentional acts more complex objectivities such as *cultural* objects and ultimately culture itself (as a universal horizon of meaning) are "built up," "passivity" means nothing other than "no current Ego-involvement."[63] In a perception of spatial objects in the here and now, I have things already of a higher order (as "cup" or "table"), that is, as cultural artifacts. It takes an analysis of *Abbau* or reconstruction to reach the primitive level of just perceiving an object in its "pure" and uncultured existence. Husserl's mature genetic phenomenology thus reconstructs acts that have been executed in the past—by myself, by others before me, alongside with me—but that nevertheless contribute, in sedimented and habitualized ways, to the manner in which I, here and now as a cultural person, perceive and understand the world as a world of culture.

To use an example, in reconstructing acts of a certain type of experience, say visual perception, we can "hit upon" a primal instituting (*Urstiftung*) in which a particular type of object ("tree") is given for the first time and from which "radiate forward" certain apperceptive guiding clues that prefigure future tree perceptions. To be sure, this reconstruction is not factual in that person X, reflecting back on her past experience, will "find" this first "actual" vision of a tree. The reconstructive analysis is reconstructive in that it goes back to what ideally must have been a first tree vision, and describes interpretively what this must have been like. These descriptions, though not themselves eidetic, generate such eidetic insights as the presumptivity of all perceptual world experience.[64] Thus, genetic phenomenology necessarily goes beyond intuition towards the reconstruction of that which cannot be made evident, but all of the structures it describes are those of intentional acts; acts, that is, of experience of world. This reconstruction cannot proceed causally when it talks about transcendental subjectivity. Causality can never be a law of passivity, for these "events" within the passive sphere are not guided by rational thought under "logical" principles. They are proto-rational acts, but as such subjective *activities,* unaware of what they may accomplish. For example, the movements of the eye are unconsciously part of the constitution of a physical object. In this sense, one can plausibly speak of Husserlian philosophy as a *phenomenology of subjective spirit* that strives to give a description of the subjective "conditions of possibility" that are involved in a concrete subject's having of world.

Now it is crucial to see that Husserl, similar to Cassirer, moves to a pluralistic conception of "subjective spirit" as well. Connecting this issue with what has been said about our life in attitudes and situations (in several chapters in part 1) should make this point clear. Although there might be one world, what is experienced in intentional acts in the normal pursuit of life is always something singular according to the "active" mode of experience. Different acts constitute different objects and spaces of meaning. Thus, in his later reflections on the nature of intentionality as world-constituting, Husserl ultimately moves toward a pluralistic concept of constitution that brings him in connection to Cassirer's plural conception of symbolic forms. Husserl's train of thought goes roughly as follows: he realizes that intentional acts, as ways of "having" objects, come forth from a "horizon" of intending. This horizon is a certain meaningful way of intending or having, not just singular *cogitata*, but a world. However, in each *cogitatum* is intentionally implicated a horizon of other possible objects of experience. Yet in the sense of the correlational a priori, the horizon has a correlate on the side of the acts as well. As is known, Husserl calls this "horizon" on the noetic side "attitude." An attitude is a perspective one takes with regard to that which one experiences. Depending on the perspective, one will experience wholly different phenomena. To remind us of Husserl's favorite example: something like a "house" will be something completely different to an architect, a real estate agent, or a potential buyer, with special interests guiding their perceptions in each case. Each attitude determines the specific "spiritual regard" that is different depending on the attitude taken. Husserl's house example has striking similarity with Cassirer's famous "line example"; the line in the form of a sine curve can be understood, depending on the "context," as a mathematical graph, an artistic ornament, and so on (see Cassirer 1954/I, 30). What consequence does the introduction of the concept of plural horizons have for the last stage of Husserl's philosophical development?

Moving from a "pinpoint" thematization of intentionality as intentional acts to "horizonal intentionality" opens up a whole new array of phenomenological research. What comes into view is a plurality of attitudes. Different attitudes "intend" different worlds (the aesthetic attitude intends the world of art, etc.), and henceforth one can speak of a plurality of worlds as meaningful "contexts" that are correlated to a plurality of attitudes.[65] Husserl focuses only on a few examples of attitudes and does not really develop this important insight. One may suggest that this would be a meaningful way to further develop Husserl's phenomenology of "subjective spirit"; indeed, Husserl merely began working on these issues in his late philosophy in the context of the lifeworld. Yet it is fair to say that Husserl, too, has thereby expanded the original scope of his transcendental method of constitution by multiplying the "forms" in which the world becomes constituted for us in a *plurality of meaningful ways.* However, all of these worlds as horizons of meaning have their ultimate foundation of constitution in transcendental subjectivity that is pluralized into different constitutive attitudes. He thus supplies the "subjective" dimension that is missing in Cassirer. Also, although Husserl acknowledges the plurality of types of subjective constitution through different attitudes—which equally may be called transcendental forms of intuition—he has not made the attempt to categorize them in the way Cassirer has done with his order of symbolic forms. Perhaps one reason why Husserl shied away from this task was that he intuitively feared a "constructive" element creeping into such an analysis. Yet one can take one's point of departure from meaningful contexts ("worlds") and move towards subjective structures that correlate to them and in this sense pursue Cassirer's systematic agenda that takes its departure from the "finished" spaces of meaning. In other words, there is no reason to believe that one should *preclude* a priori such a systematization in the context of Husserl's constitutive analyses.

By contrast, one could say that Cassirer's "system" of symbolic forms is perhaps too constructive or rigid to allow for other conceivable forms.[66] Yet despite this systemic outlook that is lacking in Husserl and arguably too strong in Cassirer, Cassirer's phenomenology of objective spirit cannot stand on its own and in this sense can be a "partner" with Husserl's. Said differently, once the lack in Cassirer has become apparent, there *can be no better partner* than Husserl. As shown, in his late philosophy Husserl presents a rudimentary form of a phenomenology of subjective spirit in the form of the plurality of attitudes that complements Cassirer's philosophy of objective spirit, in that Husserl strives to thematize the plurality of attitudes that constitute the different worlds of meaning that Cassirer calls symbolic forms. Yet the different symbolic forms depend on human beings and their activities. They are the "element" in which humanity dwells, and this dwelling cannot be separated from the activities that engender them. In Cassirer's terminology, the symbolic form of, for example, myth is constituted by a different way of subjective "comportment" than that of science. Yet the objectification of spirit must have a subjective, constitutive side to it that Cassirer ignores. And in this sense one can rightfully speak of Husserl's phenomenology of subjective spirit and Cassirer's phenomenology of objective spirit as correlative methods that are but two directions of the "transcendental consideration," directions that can be isolated only artificially. They are both committed to a transcendental account of the world, focusing, in Husserl's case, on the noetic, and in Cassirer's case, on the noematic side of "the" transcendental, both of which break down into a plurality of meaning-formation and meaning, respectively. Furthermore, both strive for a "phenomenological" analysis of their subject domain, and both use description (based on intuition) and interpretation (based on reconstruction) as the methodological tools to describe it. Yet, in so doing, just like Natorp and Husserl, they merely emphasize two different sides of the same coin, though Cassirer's system of symbolic formation is superior to Natorp's rudimentary sketch. Indeed, focusing on one side does not stand in contradiction to looking at the other, if one concedes that both of them will yield a different type of account. And in both cases, description as a static account (which Husserl would call "eidetic," Cassirer "substantial") necessarily leads to an interpretive or genetic dimension, which Husserl calls "explanatory," Cassirer "functional." Both phenomenologies can be subsumed under the title "hermeneutics" insofar as the descriptive account must be expanded into the explanatory, interpretive dimension.

This interdependence comes most clearly to the fore when one excludes one side of the correlation. In his mature philosophy, Husserl came to realize that constituting subjectivity and constituted world cannot be analyzed in isolation. The *Ego cogito* necessarily includes the *cogitatum* in its horizonal dimension as world. Only considerably late in his career did he come to focus on the noematic aspect of this correlation in thematizing the horizon into which intentional life is directed. This horizon as a nexus of meaning and referential implication is concentrated in the term "lifeworld." However, this lifeworld is anything but a homogenous *cogitatum*, but breaks down into different nexuses of meaning, which Husserl calls "special worlds" (*Sonderwelten*), the world of science, the world of the natural attitude, with its sub-forms of the world of business, art, religion, and so on.[67] These are meaningful nexuses of referential implication and as such not essentially different from the symbolic forms in Cassirer's sense, in that they are guided by a "spiritual regard"— a specific attitude—that shapes the specific space of meaning and the way entities are experienced in and through this specific attitude. However, Husserl achieved these insights too late to devote exhaustive treatment to them, something he realized with great dismay.[68] Moreover, his account lacks a systematic overview, a perspective maintained by Cassirer so rigorously from the start. Yet Husserl's realization was precisely that if one merely drafts a phenomenology of subjective spirit without giving a correlative objective account of the forms into which these subjective achievements actually "crystallize"—an account of the *constituens* without the *constituta*—one ends up with a random collection of narratives of subjective acts, of something he himself mocked as "picture-book phenomenology." Without a noematic account of that to which the achievements of subjective life are actually directed, subjectivity diffuses into thin air. In other words, how it exactly happens that transcendental life constitutes a world of *culture* with its plural forms is a task that, Husserl saw, would have to be completed if there was to be any lasting value for his phenomenology.

On the other hand, merely remaining on the "objective," noematic side of things, as Cassirer did, renders any type of subjective agency obsolete. Without a strong concept of subjectivity, the symbolic forms remain devoid of "life." The term "spirit," though sublime, ultimately fails to hide this dark spot in Cassirer's theory. One could even go so far as to suggest that this omission made it systematically impossible for Cassirer to draft an ethics.[69] Where there can be no access to subjectivity, any talk of moral agency, ought, volition, and personal responsibility is meaningless. Without a subjective (noetic) account supplementing the objective (noematic), Cassirer's objective spirit remains impersonal and ultimately dead. Spirit can have no agency of its own, though it may be spirit's necessary condition to be anonymous. Surely one cannot content oneself with what would be a renewed version of Hegel's vision of the sacrifice of individual subjects on the altar of absolute spirit. To keep spirit "alive," one needs to remember that it is actually a subjectivity, ultimately an intersubjectivity, that generates spirit, which forms culture in all of its activities. Taking over Natorp's paradigm of subjectivity's inaccessibility accounts for this weak point in Cassirer. In this sense, Husserl's counter-position vis-à-vis Natorp holds against Cassirer as well. Indeed, from a Husserlian standpoint, one would have to reject this anonymous notion of "spirit" because this seems to advocate an impersonal "agency" governing (in) the world. Cassirer's use of "spirit" bears too much idealistic weight to be satisfactory to Husserl. However, Husserl's expansion of the transcendental realm that incorporates intersubjectivity is equally in danger of losing sight of personal agency. In Husserl's late philosophy one can sometimes get the impression that the subject is but an insignificant "zero point" in the ocean of intentional acts that are not mine. With this caveat on both sides, one can still agree on a philosophically acceptable use of the term "spirit" as the totality of subjective activities in different "attitudes." Yet only a "noetic" consideration that Husserl gives fills spirit with life. And only a systematic "noematic" account of culture as constructed in various symbolic forms provides the necessary objective counterbalance to Husserl's act analyses.

Conclusion

In the forgoing I have sought to show that both Husserl and Cassirer can be seen as working on the same philosophical project, that is, a description of the subject and the world insofar as both form a correlation within a philosophy that can be termed transcendental idealism. It is a philosophical project that thematizes how the world comes to be experienced for subjectivity through a plurality of conscious processes that terminate in a plurality of meaningful contexts. Although both thinkers were darkly aware of this kinship, they did not, unfortunately, pursue this lead themselves. Indeed, Cassirer writes in an already-quoted letter to Husserl in 1925:

> Since the publication of the first volume of the *Logical Investigations* I
> have always held the conviction that between the tasks that phenom-
> enology sets for itself and the basic insights of critical philosophy there
> lies a deep commonality: to be sure, what is at stake for both of us is
> what you call . . . "the radically executed science of the transcendental,
> to be executed *ad infinitum*." (Hua-Dok III/5, 6)[70]

Yet both were too engrossed in their own mindset and their (partly erroneous) presuppositions about the other's standpoint to make it possible for either to truly synthesize their projects. This goes for Husserl and Cassirer and for Husserl and Natorp. Unfortunately, this is also true for most scholars focusing on either strand of the tradition. If one removes the blinders on both sides, one will find remarkable similarities in the way their mutual tasks are actually carried out.[71] Thus, this retelling of the history of Husserl's, Natorp's, and Cassirer's philosophical interaction—and this can only be a beginning—has the systematic result of revealing the commonalities in both methods, enabling them to contribute in the joint effort of critical transcendental philosophy.

In describing and reconstructing transcendental structures, broken down into an account of subjective acts on the one hand and of symbolic forms on the other, both Husserl's phenomenology and the neo-Kantian method are committed to a "phenomenology of spirit."[72] But it is in the realization of the limits of intuition and the necessity of incorporating constructive as well as reconstructive elements that the methodology of this phenomenology takes on a hermeneutic dimension. It strikes the reader as a compelling coincidence when Husserl characterizes his phenomenology—in a public lecture of 1931—as "hermeneutics of conscious life," and Cassirer for his part—in the drafts for the planned but unpublished fourth volume of the *Philosophy of Symbolic Forms*—writes: "Theory of knowledge is essentially nothing but a hermeneutics of cognition, a hermeneutics that in each case grasps a special 'direction' of cognition and uses it as a basis for interpretation" (1995, 165). Both only hint at what they mean by "hermeneutics," but if this term is employed here to characterize their mutual projects, it is used as the method of faithful description expanded into interpretation and directed into opposite but correlative directions. Drafting such an encompassing "phenomenology of spirit" is of course a truly Herculean task, one that can merely be hinted at from afar. Instead, I would like to end this discussion with the humbler but perhaps not less important suggestion that, with respect to the correlation between the noetic and noematic sides of the transcendental realm, the phenomenological method based on intuition need not stand in contradiction with the neo-Kantian transcendental method based on construction. Rather, both can and need to be mediated in the way attempted. They emphasize the two aspects of the same hermeneutic-phenomenological approach to transcendental philosophy as the proper way to analyze the transcendental realm in its "subjective" and "objective" dimensions.

Following the Objective Path: Cassirer's
Philosophy of the Symbolic

We have seen in two preceding chapters how a phenomenological and a neo-Kantian account of what transcendental philosophy is to accomplish can be mediated. Indeed, their approaches are more than just compatible, but mutually *demand* each other, such that their methods are truly correlates within a full account of transcendental idealism. Although this book is in its scope essentially about Husserl, it is nevertheless appropriate to devote one chapter to spelling out the consequences of an "objectifying" account in its fullest scope, and that is in Cassirer.

Indeed, Cassirer was the one who most prolifically and circumspectly pursued the leads of the Kantianism he encountered in the form of his Marburg teachers, Cohen and Natorp. In so doing, however, he merely carries these methodological paradigms through to their fullest consequence. Cassirer is thus not a philosopher who left behind his Kantian origins, but to the contrary, one who spelled them out most radically. At the same time, he provided us with a system that also incorporates a plural methodology correlated to the internal logics of the different symbolic forms. At the end, however, his philosophical vision is clearly compatible with Husserl, as Cassirer, too, battles the largest enemy of their day: relativism. Since we are at the point in this book where we have encountered Cassirer's neo-Kantian system from afar, it will be helpful for an understanding of the scope of transcendental philosophy to venture a glimpse into *this* system, before returning to Husserl in the last part of this book.

Cassirer's Philosophy of Symbolic Forms: Between Reason and Relativism: A Critical Appraisal

This chapter pursues the double task of (a) presenting Cassirer's *Philosophy of Symbolic Forms* as a systematic critique of culture and (b) assessing this systematic approach with regard to the question of reason versus relativism. First, it reconstructs the development of his theory to its mature presentation in his *Philosophy of Symbolic Forms*. Cassirer here presents a critique of culture as fulfilling Kant's critical work by insisting on the plurality of reason as spirit, manifesting itself in symbolic forms. In the second part of this chapter, the consequences of this approach will be drawn by considering the systematics Cassirer intended with this theory. As can be reconstructed from his meta-philosophical reflections, the strength of Cassirer's philosophy is that it accounts for the plurality of rational-spiritual activity while at the same time not succumbing to a relativism. The *Philosophy of Symbolic Forms* steers a middle course between a rational fundamentalism and a postmodern relativism.

Introduction: A Brief History of Ideas

I would like to commence this exposition with a brief history of ideas regarding Cassirer's own philosophy. This is no random narrative but employs Cassirer's own insight that systematic philosophical problems evolve from within and out of a historical setting and as such have their own history. Cassirer's peculiar method, ingeniously mixing historic with systematic analysis, may be applied to his own philosophy.

It is curious to note that a thinker as influential as Ernst Cassirer has almost entirely been forgotten in the country where he came in 1941 to teach first at Yale, then at Columbia University, where he died in 1945, and where he witnessed a considerable amount of success.[1] This success owes, on the one hand, to his many studies in the history of philosophy—most notably his four-volume *The Problem of Knowledge*—and to his systematic studies in the philosophy of logic and mathematics (*Substance and Function*) already prior to the development of his own philosophical approach. Finally his systematic masterpiece *The Philosophy of Symbolic Forms*, published from 1923 to 1929, established for him a solid international reputation. On the other hand, it owes also to the fact that Cassirer was able to maintain close contacts to the sciences and to current philosophical endeavors of his time. Finally, in his last work, *The Myth of the State*, published posthumously in 1946, he presented the public with a penetrating critique of fascism, equaling Adorno and Horkheimer's *Dialectics of Enlightenment*, yet with an original assessment stemming directly from his philosophical standpoint and with an ultimately positive, optimistic hope for the future of Western civilization.

Furthermore, in the United States, instead of translating his lengthy magnum opus, Cassirer wrote his two last works in English. It was especially *An Essay on Man*, where he attempted to introduce his systematic ideas in a popular fashion, which has remained widely read decades later. Yet his popularity was so great at the time of his death that already in the 1940s the majority of his larger works had been translated into English. However, beginning in the 1960s, Cassirer increasingly became a forgotten thinker whose style of philosophizing has often been considered "academic," due to the sheer learnedness of his writings, echoing the style of philosophizing of past epochs.[2] The waning of interest in his philosophy probably also owes to a general discrediting of reason in the wake of postmodern critique. It was not until the late 1970s and 1980s that his voluminous *Nachlass* (literary estate), collected at Yale, was rediscovered by American and German scholars.[3] It was especially these philosophers in the United States who reintroduced Cassirer into the German-speaking world by pointing out the riches of this collection of papers and who, having initiated an edition of his *Nachlass* and a new edition of his published work, have been mostly responsible for causing an impressive Cassirer renaissance in Europe. This reawakening began first in Germany but by now has spread to other parts of Europe, certainly to France and Italy,[4] and has recently begun to flourish in North America. Here, again curiously enough, the interest in Cassirer has been sparked by Michael Friedman, the famous Kant scholar and philosopher of science, who has made the intriguing attempt to reconstruct the "parting of the ways" between analytic and continental philosophy by going back to the celebrated 1929 Davos dispute between Cassirer and Heidegger, a philosophical conference which the young Carnap also attended. In Friedman's reading of this encounter and the ensuing developments, he presents, quite surprisingly, Cassirer as winning the day concerning the dispute over the role of logic in philosophical method (Friedman 2000; esp. chaps. 7 and 8, 111ff.).

However, upon closer inspection, one finds that Cassirer's thoughts have not entirely been forgotten. Certainly, stomaching a systematic work of more than a thousand pages interwoven with discussions of problems in the history of philosophy has gone out of fashion. Nevertheless, Cassirer's influence ranges from thinkers within the more proximate neo-Kantian movement to the—again, almost forgotten—American philosopher-aesthetician Susanne Langer, who utilized his ideas of symbolism for her aesthetic philosophy "in a new key" (1942).[5] Remaining in the field of aesthetics, it was especially one philosopher, again from the analytic tradition, who has taken up Cassirer's ideas of multiple symbolic forms, interpreted as worlds, namely Nelson Goodman in his *Ways of World-Making*—as we shall see, in a very fresh and creative, yet ultimately misled manner.[6] Furthermore it is no less a person than Jürgen Habermas who applauds the "liberating power of symbolic forms" in Cassirer's idea of the original plurality of reason.[7] Also, postmodernity in its insistence on the plurality and "différance" of truths and its dismissal of the paradigm of "logocentricity" echoes Cassirer's idea of the plural universe of "discourse."[8] Cassirer's exposition of a meaningful universe of symbols is taken up in modern semiotics, as Eco himself would most surely acknowledge.[9] Finally, although the allusions are few, Gadamer's philosophical hermeneutics as a universal method of understanding the world deserves a renewed close look in light of Cassirer's plurality of symbolic forms as principal ways in which we understand the world within a historical horizon.[10] And this is not to speak of his influence on anthropology, sociology, and psychology (especially Gestalt theory).[11]

Systematically speaking, Cassirer was able to exert such an influence because he was a thinker deeply immersed in the scientific and philosophical discussions and currents of his age. In his philosophy he took up divergent tendencies such as theories of mathematics and logic and the theory of relativity, and he remained a keen observer of newer developments in linguistics and mythological as well as anthropological research. Furthermore, he was in close contact with the most prominent figures of contemporary philosophy, such as, certainly, the neo-Kantians,[12] but also had an intimate knowledge of Bergson, Dilthey, and Simmel as well as the phenomenologists, especially Husserl, Scheler, and Heidegger. As is immediately visible—and was readily acknowledged by Cassirer—phenomenology has great import in his philosophy, which should make him interesting for contemporary "continental" philosophy. But to be sure, phenomenology is but one strain in his systematic position.[13]

As a Jew, Cassirer shared the fate of many other Jewish intellectuals who had to emigrate from their home country of Germany and start anew from "zero." The same went for their works, mostly written in German, which, after the war, were either mostly forgotten or simply out of print. Whereas the philosophical world could be so fortunate as to witness a critical edition of, for example, Husserl's unpublished materials see the light of day after the Second World War, thus making him accessible and recognized as one of the seminal figures in philosophy of the twentieth century, the public has had to wait another forty years to see Cassirer come to life again in a renewed joint editorial effort. Indeed, many indications point to a novel interest in one of the most impressive philosophical figures of the twentieth century. This can be best shown by shedding Cassirer's thought of its thick cloak of historical analysis and presenting his own systematic philosophical import.

Instead of problematizing a specific aspect of his thought, I would first like to give a short exposition of the basic systematic ideas of the philosophy of symbolic forms. I will then proceed to mention a number of problems with his approach, and try to resolve certain issues. In conclusion, I will point out where I think Cassirer's philosophical efforts can be of paradigmatic importance for contemporary thought by showing that Cassirer both broaches and offers answers to the problems of relativism and the plurality of reason. At the same time, he remains loyal to the ideal of rigorous philosophical method and philosophical systematics. This makes him especially interesting for current philosophical projects, which often seem to be gridlocked on either side of the divide between a rather "old-fashioned" belief in reason and a postmodern relativism. Thus, what has been remarked about Cassirer's character, that he was a "conciliatory" and mediating figure between extremes, may be applied to his philosophy. This is precisely what, to my mind, can place him in a meaningful way into the midst of contemporary debates.

Cassirer's Philosophy as Critique of Culture and the Plurality of Symbolic Forms

The idea of symbolic formation is prefigured in Cassirer's first systematic work of 1910, *Substance and Function,* and is, in hindsight, already operative here, although limited only to one specific sphere, that of logical formation of concepts in exact, e.g., mathematical, science. As is typical for Cassirer, he develops his systematic ideas in the discussion of problems in the history of philosophy (the latter of which he likes to refer to as epistemology).[14] As we shall see later, it is not merely by accident that Cassirer frames his systematic concepts in the seemingly larger framework of the history of ideas. He is perhaps one of the first to both understand

and implement the fact that philosophical, and more broadly, cultural problems not only stand within a historical setting but have a history of effects (*Wirkungsgeschichte*) without which it is impossible for us to understand any kind of problem within the world of spirit.

The distinction between substance and function is, simply put, that between different paradigms within the theory of scientific conceptualization.[15] The traditional, essentially Aristotelian account of scientific concepts is a substantial theory. It is based on the naive belief that there is a simple correlation between being and thought. Hence, concepts represent the thematic thing pure and simple. Concepts are thus *substantial*—they refer to substances that are somewhere independently "out there" in the world. Concepts are conceived as naively conceptualizing substances as existing objects ("things"). The objects in turn are substantial because they stand on their own ground and do not require another substance upon which they depend. Things to which substantial categories are applied are framed in the concepts of *substantia* and *accidens*. Substantial categories thus reflect the essentially substantial nature of things in the world and mirror a substantialist epistemology (or, since this is prior to the Copernican turn, ontology).

However, there is also another way of conceptualizing objects, namely in terms of their *function* within a certain "series" of relations. This goes especially for mathematical functions. The concept of number exemplifies this best. Whereas a number can be considered a substantial "entity" (the concept "4"), a natural number must also be conceived of within what Cassirer calls a series (*Reihe*), for example, the series of numbers 3, 4, 5, and in this series "4" has its function or "meaning." The number 4 can only be conceptualized and hence "understood" in the series of natural numbers and in relation to them. Thus, the "concept" of the number 4 seen as a representative of the series of natural numbers is not substantial but rather *functional* within a certain series of meaning: The concept "four" is not a concept unless or without being integrated into the series of natural numbers, where it stands as a representative of this series. Thus, it is not "substantial" as referring to an independent entity but only functional within this specific "context." Hence, the functionalist account can also be called "contextual."

While this can be understood as merely an alternative way of forming scientific concepts, this distinction also has significance within the development of modern science. Cassirer sees here a progress in the use of the concept of function over against that of substance. For example, in the view of modern physics, there can be no talk of "substances" when one speaks of electrons, but the concept of an electron is a functional term in the context of a certain physical conceptualization. It only becomes "visible" as a fact when seen in the framework of a certain functional series, in this case a certain theory. The scientific theory as a whole is this "functional series" within which the concept of "electron" takes on sense. As is known, in a different theory, the wave theory, the subject matter is thematized in terms of waves. When talking of certain concepts, it is the function *within which* they are used that determines the "reality" of what one talks about. There is no independent, "substantial" reality just as there is no independent, "substantial" thing such as an electron. Rather, an electron is a *"conceptual scheme"* within a certain theory as an encompassing "schematism" of conceptualization. Thus, there is no simple correlation between being and thought. Rather, it is always a certain way of thinking and hence conceptualizing that makes "being" apperceivable. Such concepts are, to speak in Husserl's terminology of the *Crisis*, idealizations or abstractions, which are not derived from a "substance" in the pre-scientific lifeworld, but are entirely mental formations, "figments" used in order to explain certain phenomena in a specific scientific theoretical context. In contrast to Husserl, however (at least according to a certain understanding of him), there is no lifeworld as a "raw being" "underneath" conceptualizations stemming from certain types of experience, but all experience is by necessity an abstraction (even the concept "raw being"!).[16]

Now, as mentioned, these two accounts, substantialist and functionalist, are not merely two alternative ways of scientific conceptualization, but also indicate to Cassirer the *progress* that scientific and logical theory have undergone especially since the Renaissance.[17] In fact, this is where Cassirer's own philosophical considerations set in. According to him, this development demonstrates—*avant la lettre*—no other than the ensuing *transcendental turn* that has taken place in modern philosophy.[18] As it turns out retrospectively, the critical historical study of *Substance and Function* is merely an exemplification of the change in framing philosophical problems in the wake of idealistic (transcendental) philosophy. The shift from a substantialist account, which conceives of objects as "substances," that is, *independent* of their conceptualization, to a functionalist account, which frames phenomena in a meaningful "series" of functions, is *equal* to the shift from considering objects as they exist independently to considering them *insofar as they are experienced*.[19] And in this experience, objects can only be experienced as functional, that is, in a certain meaningful context, having, or better, serving a function in a framework of scientific explanation. Even science, in a philosophical reflection on its method, has undergone a certain "Copernican turn" in that it cannot disregard the "import" of experience in its perception of its object of investigation, and insofar as it conceptualizes these experiences, the concepts are by necessity functional concepts within a "functional series," in other words, within a scientific theory or context. Everything factual, Cassirer liked to quote Goethe, "is already [laden with] theory," because it presupposes that it is "seen," that is, experienced within an "epistemic" and hence conceptual scheme (1994b, 322).[20] Seeing something means *understanding* the seen in a specific way. And depending on the theory employed, the constitutional principles of this "series" can change. This "series" is not necessarily a "causal" succession or theory, but has according to the specific theory its own laws of functioning. In sum, the Copernican turn that Kant took *consciously* had already taken place some two decades prior to Kant *unconsciously* and has evolved since. This reading stands in the tradition of the Marburg school, according to which Kant's achievement lay in lending the transcendental turn in modernity its voice. The transcendental turn consists in supplanting a substantialist with a functionalist epistemology, according to which—simply put—being is a *construction based on a certain interpretation.*

From here, it took Cassirer almost another decade to develop the full-fledged philosophy of symbolic forms. In the meantime, and not by accident, he worked mainly in a field popular in the early years of the twentieth century, namely the study of myth.[21] One phenomenon which fascinated many ethnologists and anthropologists was the discovery that the so-called primitive cultures were anything but "primitive." Rather, their religious belief did indeed have its own "logic" of functioning which might be different from our "modern" and Western "enlightened" society but which nevertheless had clearly definable laws and rules of function in their religious practice, in their beliefs, and consequently in their way of explaining ("conceptualizing") their world. The world of mythical societies is a world which has its *own* order and, as such, has its *own* sense and meaning. Yet this sense is no longer *our* sense, and it even contradicts it in certain areas. "Enlightened" societies no longer believe in cosmogonies and myths, unless they are understood in a demythologized way. To a mythological society, however, the meaning of myths was not something "behind" the stories, but was immediately and genuinely taken to be true, establishing a direct link to the transcendent realm. Cassirer drew the consequences from this assessment, and it is in this context that he first formulates his idea of a symbolic form.

Myth can be interpreted as *itself* a "functional series" in conceptualizing the world, insofar as myth can be called a "concept," that is, a narrative which establishes a certain "theory" in the "soft" sense of giving an account of understanding the (mythic) world. It is not an abstractly worked-out theory, but the schema or series of mythic thought in general—here Cassirer relies on anthropological research of his day—is guided by an underlying theory, which the theorist can spell out. Such a series has a certain function for the primitive human being; it is the *form* in which this specific way of understanding the world is conceptualized—be the concept a mythical tale, a rite, or another mythical "objectification." A certain tale is a representative of this mythological worldview: in Cassirer's words, a *symbol.* Myth is a form of meaning in which primitive man lives. It is a life of, or rather *in,* meaning or sense. The decisive step to the theory of the symbolic forms, and with the backdrop of the distinction between substance and function, is the realization that there is not merely *one* functional form, such as science, but that myth can also be thought of as such a functional series, and that there is in fact a *plurality* of symbolic forms which equally have a specific function, namely science but also others, namely language, myth, religion, and art.[22] What makes these forms *symbolic* is that they *point to* not merely one but *alternative* "functional series" to explain the world or in which world becomes apprehended and thus comprehended. In the world of meaning—and there is no other real world for us—there is not merely one perceived X as a substratum with different meanings, but what this X is understood as depends on the symbolic form *within* which it is viewed, that is, thematized. A tree is something completely different to primitive man than to the artist or the biologist. Cassirer calls these forms symbolic because the "X" in view is never a simple substance, but stands as a symbol for the form in which it has its function. It *points to* the meaningful whole or totality: to the world of myth, of art, of religion, of science. "Symbol," thus, is itself a concept freed from linguistic or semiotic concepts, but a general term within Cassirer's transcendental theory of symbolic formation.

What kind of "world" are we talking about here, and what is the relation between a symbolic form and such a "world of meaning"? In one of the few definitions Cassirer ever gives, he characterizes a symbolic form as follows: "Under a 'symbolic form' shall be understood every energy of spirit through which a spiritual meaning-content is connected to a concrete sensual sign and is intrinsically bound to that sign" (1983, 175). Thus, instead of interpreting a symbolic form as a meaningful world, a "special world," as, for example, Goodman has understood it, a symbolic form is rather that which *encompasses* the experiencing agent and that which that agent experiences. It is the "energy of spirit" *generating* a "space of meaning" in which we find ourselves together with that which we experience in and with a specific sense. A symbolic form is not itself a world but that which *forms* a world as a meaningful context or totality. Human life is a life "in" meaning in the sense that it is a "spiritual energy" that *overarches* every experiencing process and connects that which is experienced to a "spiritual meaning-content," that is, language, religion, myth, art, and so on. The single experienced object never stands alone but is always connected to a symbolic form, or the symbolic form bestows meaning upon a single X. In a striking metaphor, Cassirer compares the symbolic forms to the light which is necessary to see objects in this "openness"—only that there is not just *one* "light" (of "being") but it is the light *spirit* generates and which is broken into different refractions. What is seen can only be seen in the light, but this light is the light of spirit, which is not itself "one." In another characteristic phrase, Cassirer calls this state of affairs "symbolic pregnancy,"[23] in the sense that a single experienced object is "pregnant with meaning" as it stands in the context of a symbolic form in which it becomes understood as this or that (depending on the specific form "*in actu*"). Merleau-Ponty's talk of the world as being "pregnant with meaning"[24] is a direct allusion to Cassirer's concept of symbolic pregnancy. As already mentioned in the previous chapter, Cassirer himself here alludes to the original meaning of "symbol" stemming from the Greek "*sym-bállein*," i.e., literally a "throwing together" of two entities, in this case the concept of the object and its symbolic meaning in its specific form. This, in turn, reiterates Goethe's theory of the "primal phenomenon" (*Urphänomen*) of which Goethe says that one must not try to find anything behind it but that it itself "is what it teaches us" (*es ist selbst die Lehre*). What is experienced is not a "thing" but a phenomenon in the original sense of the word, that is, *something shows* itself to us as a representative of a certain form, "pregnant" with its meaning. Yet, in contrast to Goethe, not just single unique phenomena merit the title "primal phenomenon" as paradigm cases of this "showing"; to Cassirer, *every* object has a certain specific pregnancy—and can even have different ones, depending on the form within which it is apperceived (Cassirer's favorite example is the meandering line, which can be a sine curve or an artistic ornament).[25]

To phrase it in another, perhaps more familiar terminology, the symbolic form is the *schema* in which something is experienced and as such the form in which any experience is always already carried out. Coming from Cassirer's Kantian background, from what has been said it is clear to him: a symbolic form is the condition of the possibility of experiencing. It is a *transcendental form of intuition*. It has to be pointed out that in his theory of symbolic forms Cassirer remains a transcendental philosopher in the Kantian tradition. We are not talking about the object of experience but our *experience of* the object, with the necessary addition that this experience is in itself schematized in a plural manner. The symbolic forms are not "contexts" gathered from empirical data but a priori forms in which spiritual life carries itself out. However, whereas Kant focused primarily on the object of natural science—and in this narrow understanding he was mainly read by the Marburg school—Cassirer's realization is that *any* intuited object stands under laws or forms of intuition, only that these forms represent different "spiritual energies" which do not belong to the type of intuition that characterizes science and its ideal of exactness. To be sure, Cassirer does not revoke the forms of intuition, space and time. Rather, space and time mean something different in mythical than in scientific thought. In this sense, every form of intuition as energy of spirit represents a meaningful form that stands on its own ground and has its own "right." "The concept of truth and reality of science is different than that of religion or art" (Cassirer 1954/I, 24). Each symbolic form has its own way of functioning with its own cognitive meaning, telos, and veracity. The symbolic forms of language, myth, religion, and science neither form a hierarchy in which the higher one "sublates" the lower in a dialectical fashion, nor do they form strata that do not have any relation with each other. Rather, the symbolic forms are to be understood as parallel functional series with their *own* right and their *own* way of functioning serving their *own* cognitive function, however, not like impenetrable "vessels" but as forms which can realize their mutual independence. They are, to use a Heideggerian term, equiprimordial, they stand on their own ground and are irreducible to one another. As such, their relation to other forms is secondary, although they, too, might be described as "referentially implying" one another, as Husserl describes the different "special worlds" (*Sonderwelten*) as having a relation of "referential implication" (*Verweisung*).

Describing the plurality of these forms is thus the task of the *philosophy* of symbolic forms. Reiterating what was the main intent of the Marburg school, according to which philosophy is essentially a *philosophy of culture,* Cassirer terms this project a critique of *culture,* in this establishing a direct connection to Kant's critique of reason, which he purports to fulfill: "Hence, the critique of reason becomes the critique of culture. It seeks to understand and to show how all content of culture, insofar as it is more than merely a particular content, presupposes an original deed of the spirit. In so doing, the basic thesis of idealism finds its genuine and complete authentication [*Bewährung*]" (Cassirer 1954/I, 11). Yet, acknowledging different forms of spiritual energy ("deeds") does not mean that the different "truths" of these different forms are a random collection or that truth itself becomes relative. This has to be ruled out from the beginning, especially in the light of Cassirer's repeated invocation of Kant's critical philosophy, although Kant was, to Cassirer, too much fixated on reason. To say that the critique of reason becomes the critique of culture is the same as insisting on the observation that reason is not just *pure* reason alone. Reason can be better understood as spirit which has different ways of "manifesting" itself through symbolic forms generating specific objectivities (the objectivations of art, of language, of scientific theories, etc., and their corresponding meaningful "realms"). Reason remains reason; it is just no longer conceived as a monolithic structure. Where in Kant this transcendental project is mainly carried out for the sake of a system of knowledge,[26] we shall have to ask in the second part of this chapter whether Cassirer has the same goal.

To say, however, that reason is plural does not mean that it is split or ruptured into incoherent fragments. The plural forms of spirit all bear the mark of reason. Reason is plural and *therefore* universal—as spirit. The One of spirit is rather, as Cassirer likes to point out, quoting the Greek *"hen diapherómenon heautô,"* "one which is differentiated within itself." Or to say it in another famous quotation: *"to on légetai pollachôs,"* being is spoken of (!) in manifold ways—it might *be* "originally" one (which would be a purely metaphysical, speculative statement), but we are speaking in the transcendental register of our *experience of* being. As such, the energy of spirit is experienced as not only plural, but each symbolic form in which it asserts its spiritual energy has its own way of functioning and more importantly, has or serves its own and genuine cognitive purpose. As Cassirer reminds us, the "truth" or validity claim of myth is completely different from that of science. The pressing question, "which is the *real* truth?" can be rejected, paradoxically, as skeptical because the quest for exact and real truth is a specifically *scientific* question that has little or nothing to do with the "truth" of art or religion. In other words, demanding "exact truth" is a question that makes sense only in the symbolic form of science and cannot be applied to that of myth (just as "evolutionism" and "creationism" are not mutually contradictory, but only incompatible). To do so would mean committing a *metábasis eis allo génos.* One can *compare* these different truths but one cannot *"mix"* them by transposing the truth-*principles* from one form to the other. All "truth" is contextual, even that of exact science, because it is relative to the symbolic form in which it has its specific function. The true is the whole (*das Ganze ist das Wahre*), to quote Hegel once more, but each particular truth is relative upon its symbolic context. The whole is hence not any sphere-shaped absolute (to cite Parmenides' image), but the absolute is essentially the relative in its plural manifestations. It is impossible to rid oneself of symbolic forms and to see "absolutely" or "freely." We never see the "thing in itself" but only phenomena bearing a certain symbolic pregnancy. Likewise, we do not live in one world but in a plurality of meaningful contexts that have been generated by the energy of spirit, which is nothing but human reason conceived of in the totality of its achievements. Yet, as we shall see, this does not visibly overcome the threat of relativism, which Cassirer felt and sought to battle.

Problems with the System of Symbolic Forms and Possible Resolutions: Cassirer's Theory of Symbolic Forms as Ethical Critique of Culture

Problems arise (at the latest) when one makes the attempt to systematize these symbolic forms or to mold these observations into a philosophical system, which, one assumes (perhaps naively), was Cassirer's aim. The first question is, most obviously, how one is to imagine the relation of the different forms to one another. In other words, what is the systematic upshot of this theory? Is the claim to the plurality of symbolic forms a purely descriptive assessment allowing for further factual development, or does Cassirer have a certain fixed systematics in the back of his mind? Just how many forms are there—are there more than the ones Cassirer presents to us, and what about the ones he merely mentions (such as, in a few places, economy) (Cassirer 1954/II, ix) but does not analyze? And did he not mention more forms because there *are* no more or because he simply did not bother or was not interested in dealing with them? Is his philosophy of culture, like perhaps Husserl's, a "working philosophy" with open, even endless horizons for future researchers? And if the forms he mentions are indeed the only ones, by which criteria does he claim this and how does he know this? If all truth is contextual, what about the truth of the theory of symbolic forms itself? In this cluster of questions let us first turn to the question of a system of symbolic forms. I cannot claim that these issues can indeed be completely resolved, but want to point to possible ways of dealing with the problems arising from Cassirer's systematic approach. It is my belief that Cassirer does not in the end get caught up in a simple or trivial relativism but that his philosophy in fact presents an intriguing way out of relativism precisely in the *application* of his theory.

To begin with, with regard to the huge theoretical claim such as the one Cassirer makes with the theory of symbolic formation, the question as to a certain systematics of this sketch is not an external one. Rather, it is a question that the very disposition evokes. However, Cassirer would most likely feel misunderstood were one to think he intended to draft a full-blown philosophical system such as that of, say, Hegel. Although his draft of a "phenomenology of knowledge" especially in the third volume of the *Philosophy of Symbolic Forms* has many allusions to Hegel, as we saw in the previous chapter, Cassirer's own approach is far too critical ("Kantian") as to believe that the system of knowledge can be developed in a purely theoretical "logic"—let alone out of a single principle. Yet even a "low-key theory" such as Cassirer's needs to become clear about its own stance with regard to a systematics. Indeed, in this context, Cassirer insists—quite, again, in accord with Husserl, as demonstrated in chapter 6—on the difference between forging a philosophical system and *philosophizing systematically*.[27] It is especially in this respect that one can rightfully speak of Cassirer's departing from one of the main paradigms of neo-Kantianism, namely, the erection of a systematic edifice.[28] Yet as we shall see, there are, paradoxically speaking, systematic reasons for rejecting a philosophical system. Nevertheless, describing the symbolic forms is certainly a systematic task in Cassirer's in-depth demonstration of how certain symbolic forms function. The three volumes of the *Philosophy of the Symbolic Forms,* in total over 1,000 pages, demonstrate this impressively. What makes these descriptions "systematic" can well be compared to the systematic claim *Husserl* makes in describing certain regions of intentional life in the lifeworld. External perception, just as the symbolic form of language, has a certain "systematic" manner of functioning and unfolding. "Systematic," in Husserl's *as well as Cassirer's* parlance, is often synonymous with "essential" or "eidetic" insofar as the manner in which perception of an external object through *kinesthesis* functions is necessary for every being constituted as having a lived-body, *as do* certain grammatical structures hold for a certain branch of language, that is, Indo-European languages. In this sense, and Cassirer makes this very explicit, the method of his analyses is indeed phenomenological as it is about a proper and detailed description of the phenomena in question in a coherent, "systematic" manner.[29] "Systematic," then, does not contradict the term "phenomenological," if a description of a given symbolic form is to lay out logically, exhaustively, and consistently this form and its inner "logic."

However, the mere order in which Cassirer presents the symbolic forms—first language, then myth, then science, without claiming to be exhaustive—must bear a certain systematic significance; at least this question has puzzled interpreters. More simply put, there must be reasons why specifically *these* forms are discussed and in *this* particular order. Only on a few occasions does he actually reflect on these issues: myth, he claims, is the most fundamental symbolic form because in every culture it is the first state upon which higher cultural life develops. All other symbolic forms come forth from myth and develop their own structure in contrast to it: "the problem of the origins of art, of the origins of writing, the origins of law and of science lead back to a level in which they all still rest in the unmediated and undifferentiated unity of mythical consciousness" (Cassirer 1954/II, ix.). As far as systematic claims go, this is probably the only real apodictic one; but it is also perhaps not that very controversial. Yet why, then, does he not discuss this symbolic form first, instead of, as he in effect does, language? To make a case for Cassirer, perhaps one reason for this is that he does not want the plurality of symbolic forms to be understood in a hierarchy or as levels of spirit's self-unfolding as in Hegel's scenario.[30] In this sense, the seemingly random way of discussing the forms can be seen as an acknowledgment of the plurality and in this sense mutual independence of the symbolic forms and their irreducibility vis-à-vis one another. He is a "phenomenologist" in the sense of not wanting to have his view obstructed from the outset by systematic prejudgments.

Yet this assessment again becomes questionable in view of the claim that myth is the most fundamental form in which all others are rooted. Their supposed "equi-primordiality" can thus not be maintained. This becomes especially clear when one compares the different symbolic forms Cassirer lays out: whereas it is not too hard to imagine that art, religion, and science are alternative symbolic forms conceptualizing the world in their specific way, how can language be interpreted as a symbolic form of its own? Does language not *penetrate* all of these spheres, and this being the case, how can it then be a true symbolic form, that is, an irreducible form of its own? Would it not have to be appended to one, or even all of the symbolic forms? Perhaps it is *precisely because* language penetrates all spheres of human life—that is, spiritual life—that Cassirer considers language a symbolic form of its own, conveying—in a unique way—a meaning that only language can reveal. Instead of criticizing this approach one could even exploit it by saying that, again, Cassirer was so true a phenomenologist heeding to the things themselves that he was not concerned with systematic boundaries and limits prematurely cutting off internal or essential connections. Rather, he merely wanted to authentically describe these forms in which we understand the world in a manifold of meaningful ways. Nevertheless, declaring language to be a symbolic form remains problematic (for the reasons mentioned).

Yet there might also be a deeper, intrinsically systematic meaning for this apparent randomness, which we can explicate by turning to the issue of the *number* of the symbolic forms. As pointed out, Cassirer only discusses in depth the symbolic forms of language, myth, and science, and he mentions religion, art, and once even (in his later work) technology and economy, but does not offer a closer analysis of the latter.[31] Is this to be understood as (ultimately) an exhaustive account of the symbolic forms or are there even more which he simply does not mention? Are there perhaps even sub-forms within certain forms? Or rather, is this universe of symbolic formation comparable to an open, flexible system where, perhaps over the course of history, new forms can develop just as technology is a phenomenon of the more immediate past?[32] If this were the case, leaving open the question of "closure" would be a necessary consequence of the temporality of symbolic forms and their diversity, and Cassirer repeatedly makes it clear that he is merely making a beginning in his research of symbolic formation. Further differentiations and distinctions might make it necessary to discern yet another form, or history might be headed in a way that a new symbolic form arises due to special circumstances (for even an account of the way spirit has evolved up to now cannot rule out unexpected changes in the future)—or, finally, one can not a priori exclude as impossible that historical, archeological research might perhaps discover an as of yet unknown human culture which does not dispose of anything comparable to myth as a foundational level in the way it has been conceptualized previously. If correct, this would be another case in point for the above-mentioned hunch, namely, that Cassirer's philosophy of symbolic forms would be quite like Husserl wished to conceive of phenomenology, that is, a working philosophy with potentially endless horizons open for future generations of philosophers (and positive scientists). In other words, declaring a fixed number of symbolic forms would preclude the discovery of yet unknown forms. The fact that the symbolic forms are transcendental does not mean they are eidetic, that is, supra-temporal, outside of the realm of history.

Furthermore, even attempting to pronounce such a fixed number would be problematic for yet another reason, and approaching it reveals perhaps the most difficult point in Cassirer's theory. Principally, one of the main discoveries of the theory of symbolic forms is that every concept and statement is embedded in a functional conceptualization or, which says the same, every utterance is contextual or perspectival (or, if this was not in fact Cassirer's discovery, at least he attempted to draw systematic conclusions from it). Cassirer certainly was aware of the fact that this very claim must certainly hold for the utterances of the philosopher, as well. But what about these utterances? What about philosophy, what about the philosophy of symbolic forms itself? Would not philosophy itself fall under the contextuality of symbolic formation? In the three published volumes of his magnum opus Cassirer did not explicitly thematize the role of philosophy in the totality of the symbolic forms, and it soon became obvious that this could not be due merely to a forgetfulness on his part, but in fact represents, if unaddressed, a blind spot in his theory—

something he shied away from perhaps subconsciously on purpose? But as we shall see, more "lifeworldly" reasons account for him leaving this issue open in his published magnum opus.

Indeed, the question of the role of philosophy within the symbolic forms can be immediately linked to the question of their systematics. Again, the question must be: why does Cassirer not give an exhaustive overview of the symbolic forms, and is this not due to some shortcoming but for systematic reasons? The answer is implied: making a statement of this type would mean occupying in *itself* a certain perspective. It is an answer that the *philosophy* of symbolic forms itself is not permitted to spell out. This leads, *it seems,* to two consequences, both highly problematic: it could mean (a) that philosophy occupies a higher stance than the other symbolic forms: it would be a perspective overlooking these. Immediately one must ask how this is possible if one cannot escape the guise of symbolic experiencing. Such a perspective would be utterly impossible to attain. It would be a "view from nowhere"—where the point of the transcendental theory of symbolic formation is precisely that seeing "raw being" is illusory, be this "prior to" or "beyond" symbolic formation. In the framework of this philosophy as a *transcendental* account, there can be no "nowhere."[33]

On the other hand (b), if philosophy is not a view from nowhere and if one acknowledges the perspectivalness of every spiritual action, the consequence would be that philosophy would in fact constitute *in itself* a symbolic form. But this, too, has disastrous consequences: if the theory of the symbolic forms is but one form next to others, this would amount to a relativism as this "truth" would stand equally next to others. It would be merely one theory of conceptualizing a universe of meaning next to that of myth, art, religion, and so on. The theory would annul and cancel itself out. In other words, the implicit reason for Cassirer's shying away from a full-fledged system would be that he would have to give in to the consequence that asserting such a systematics would declare one symbolic form as absolute and render the others relative to it, where it is precisely the point that all the actual and possible symbolic forms are relative but legitimate. Thus, in this reading, Cassirer has shied away from *having to admit* that his philosophy is a relativism. His silence would be a mere cop-out.

As we shall immediately see, the philosophy of symbolic forms is neither of the two alternatives outlined. As it turns out, there is a third viable alternative, which Cassirer spells out in the unpublished part 4 of the *Philosophy of Symbolic Forms,* which was left unpublished for completely accidental reasons. In Cassirer's view, the philosopher does not stand above the energy of spirit; rather, she can "merely" describe it.

This "mere description," however, is in fact capable of quite a lot. Philosophy's primary task, according to Cassirer, is analyzing the different ways in which spirit manifests itself in the world and reducing this apparent manifold to irreducible forms (and within these forms to certain basic phenomena).[34] However, philosophical thought can and must never make a statement about their totality or anticipate their exact quantity, therein perhaps prematurely exhausting them. This is the only "systematic" caveat the philosopher must bear in mind. For the philosopher of symbolic forms does not and cannot stand detached from these forms but—like every other human being—is *immersed* in them, but different from the ordinary cultural dweller, wants to bring them to full fruition by trying to understand them both in themselves and in relation to each other. The philosopher is somebody who is no longer bound to one form, which hence exerts an "absolutizing" claim unto others. Rather, she as "disinterested" and uninvested observer has the ability, through philosophical reflection, to move from one form to another, without remaining "caught" in any of them. This reflection is "relativistic" in comparing different forms of spirit, but not a relativism which concludes that one is as "good" as the other (and which would be the slippery slope to an "I'm okay, you're okay" postmodernism).

Neither is it an "absolutism" because an absolute standpoint is merely an a priori presupposition *if* one were to claim the standpoint of absolute spirit, which Cassirer never does. For every claim to absoluteness jeopardizes the richness and mutual relativity of the symbolic forms and purports to speak from an absolute, ultimately preposterous standpoint. Thus, the fact that Cassirer, at least in his published writings, shies away from such "absolutizing" statements must be interpreted as intentional and stems from his intuitive distrust of any conception of "absolute spirit" into which every spiritual activity is eventually "sublated." There is a title for such an absolute standpoint: it is called ideology. Cassirer's thought is therefore also a fervent battle against totalizing theories, in philosophy in general and in the way certain theories factor into concrete historical situations in particular. Cassirer will ultimately turn this into an ethical reading and application of his thought.

The role of philosophy, that is, the philosophy of symbolic forms, is described best in Cassirer's unpublished drafts for a fourth volume of this work:

> This is the peculiarity of philosophical knowledge [*Erkenntnis*] as "self-knowledge of reason": it does not create a principally new symbolic form . . . but it *comprehends* the earlier modalities [of symbolic forma-

tion] as that which they are: particular symbolic forms. . . . Philosophy
is both critique and fulfillment of symbolic forms . . . Philosophy does
not purport to posit another, higher form in place of the old forms, it
does not want to replace one symbol by another; rather, its task consists in *seeing through the fundamental symbolic character of knowledge itself.*
We cannot cast off these forms, although the compulsion [*Zwang*] to
do so is innate in us, but we must grasp and *understand* it in its relative necessity . . . We cannot overcome [this compulsion] by throwing
off the cloak of symbolic forms and seeing the "absolute" face to face,
but only by grasping each symbol in its *position* and understanding it
as limited and conditioned by others. The "absolute" is always merely
the complete, the accomplished and systematically overseen relative—
and especially the absoluteness of spirit is not and cannot be anything
else. (1995, 264–65)

Philosophy thus has no "locus" of its own; rather, it is a spiritual
endeavor, mustering through, as it were, the different symbolic forms,
comprehending each of them in its peculiar place and *holding* each in
this place, seeing to it that they do not "cross over" and blend into one
another. Perhaps the role of the philosopher, to Cassirer, can best be
called that of a watch-guard ensuring that none of these forms turns into
an absolute stance and as such exerts a power which is not only unduly
but can also become potentially dangerous. From here one can approach
one field which Cassirer does not address explicitly and which one might
expect to be considered a symbolic form of its own, namely *ethics*. Although Cassirer never drafted an "ethics," his late work, written in the
wake of World War II, can be read as a certain rehashing or recapturing
of this seemingly neglected field in his earlier work.[35] However, it is not a
wholly new line of thought he is taking up here but merely a new twist to
his basic theory. As especially his last work, *The Myth of the State,* intends to
demonstrate, his whole philosophical intentions are in effect geared towards ethical application, and in doing so remain akin to the fundamentally enlightened character of his thought. As should have become clear
by now, the philosophy of symbolic forms is by no means a postmodern
relativism in simply acknowledging a plurality of meaningful contexts.
Rather, it shows us that this plurality is an intrinsic characteristic of reason itself. At the same time, Cassirer insists that each of these forms has a
certain cognitive function and truth in the overall framework of spirit. By
the same token, it is a philosophy dedicated to Enlightenment and thus
to taking over responsibility, namely to be watchful that this plurality is
maintained in a philosophical self-clarification. The plurality of spirit is

its universality, and maintaining it is no easy task. As such philosophy is devoted to the freedom of spirit (*Geist*) and battles any *Ungeist*. Hence, doing philosophy in Cassirer's spirit is itself an ethical deed.

This is the theoretical backdrop through which Cassirer comes to criticize fascism. One characteristic of the type of fascism the National Socialist dictatorship represented, according to Cassirer, consisted in, on the one hand, being acutely aware of the symbolic character of knowledge. Therefore, on the other hand, it was especially able to manipulate public or political discourse, specifically by finding ways of letting mythical thought reenter the public sphere. Contrary to this misuse, Cassirer strives to show that the political sphere is more than just a public arena of rhetoric, but the open discourse of civilized mankind, a sphere which has to be guarded against abuse and intolerance. Yet, seeing through the mechanisms of public discourse does not mean using them in an ethical way. Quite to the contrary: fascist rhetoric consisted precisely in mixing symbolic forms, deliberately overstepping boundaries, specifically with the attempt to enable the rational forces of a civil society to become weakened in such a way as to make it possible for other, especially mythical forces to invade this discourse of a society built on rational, democratic principles. This is in a nutshell his critique of Nazi ideology: that the symbolic form of myth consisting of irrational forces threatens to destroy modern civilization and its achievements in letting it enter unfiltered into this society, which was established on the basis of rational principles. For example, by reverting to categories such as "good" or "evil" and amplifying them by use of modern technology and media, they have the potential to overpower the rational and sober voice of reason. Myth in itself is not the problem to Cassirer—as is amply clear from thematizing it as a symbolic form—but utilizing mythological categories in rational discourse contorts rationality itself. What goes on here is a mingling of "truths" which is aimed at discrediting the truth of rational, democratic, intersubjectively consensual discourse. In spite of the problems pointed out with the systematic implications and intricacies of Cassirer's theory, his timeliness lies in his attempt to not only draft a universal portrait of reason in its different cultural forms within the world of spirit, but also in his intent to steer this seemingly high-spirited "academic" discourse towards an ethical employment in a state of a "crisis in man's knowledge of himself."[36] In this he has taken seriously Kant's admonition that reason cannot content itself with being pure reason alone but that its primacy lies in its practical application.

To summarize briefly, the following are the points in the case of Cassirer which make him especially attractive to contemporary thought.

Cassirer's thought has developed, and most likely only *could* develop, because it was linked so closely to two different spheres: (a) modern science and (b) the history of philosophy. It was only in close connection to both that Cassirer worked out his own theory and, conversely, was able to contribute theoretically to the sciences as well as the history of philosophy proper with a systematic intention, and not just as historiography. Philosophizing in an "ivory tower" was something neither to be desired nor even possible to Cassirer. Not to say anything more concrete about how Cassirer adhered to this method (this is not the place to discuss this), this is a "stylistic" ideal which contemporary philosophy would benefit by adopting or emulating.

Systematically speaking: although reason is one, this reason is better understood as "spirit" and as such it is always already in the state of plurality. Spirit is broken in refractions of independent, but not unrelated, symbolic forms. In this regard, Cassirer attempts to salvage the paradigm of reason without succumbing to a postmodern position where "anything goes" in different referential frameworks. Yet he pays heed to the diversity and plurality of spiritual life. Consequently, the symbolic forms are not arbitrary "language games" but genuine and clearly identifiable forms in which spirit generates meaning. Cassirer thus safely and in a most original way navigates between the Scylla of absolutism or rational fundamentalism and the Charybdis of relativism.

As such, following from this, there is a clear emphasis on spirit and its achievements. Cassirer's philosophy is rationalistic but not naively so. It should have become clearer what has been claimed in the previous chapter, namely, that it is justified to call his philosophy a "phenomenology of objective spirit" which frames the individual subject in terms of his cultural achievements, or, conversely, which highlights the objective, that is, intersubjective, accomplishments of human beings in a cultural world over against the emphasis on the single individual. Heidegger is therefore perfectly right to assert that there is no place in Cassirer's philosophy for what he, Heidegger, calls *Dasein*[37] because it is precisely this focus on "finitude" which the dimension of spirit is destined to overcome. In other words, Cassirer's philosophy attempts a *middle way* between adhering to a problematic and "old-fashioned" conception of reason, rationality, and Enlightenment, which has rightfully been subject to criticism after World War II, on the one hand; *and* a postmodern attitude of arbitrariness, on the other, precisely in linking the paradigm of plurality *to* rationality, conceived as spirit. His vision is neither pluralistic alone by binding the plurality of symbolic forms to spirit, that is, to a "rationalistic" way of treating each other in tolerance and mutual respect; nor is it rationalistic alone by declaring reason to be essentially all that human as *cultural* beings "do" in objective achievements, for example, in art, religion, politics, economy, and so on, which function with their own "logics" that are not always "rational." In opening up this scope of "spirit" the philosophy of symbolic forms is also a philosophical program that allows for further "filling in" of "blanks" that Cassirer has merely pointed to but did not himself broach. Thus, one can say that Cassirer has anticipated current debates, like those of relativism vs. absolutism or pluralism/diversity vs. unity, and has pointed to concrete ways of coming to grips with these seemingly unbridgeable concepts. Cassirer thereby remains a philosopher of modernity, not postmodernity, but as perhaps one of the "last" philosophers of modernity, he is also one who can become again a serious voice in a debate with Husserl and others who consider this very modernity "an unfinished project."

Appendix: A Note on Goodman

In his famous *Ways of World-Making*,[38] Goodman sets out to give an account of how it is that these different "worlds" we live in and by come into being (1978). He explicitly attributes this attempt to Cassirer's concept of symbolic forms, although he makes it clear at the very outset that there is more that separates them than what they share in common. It was instead some interpreters of Cassirer who have made the attempt to better understand Cassirer by comparing him to Goodman.[39] And indeed, there are many elements in Goodman's theory of "world-making" which seem to complement or at least shed light on Cassirer's original idea. I believe that this reading—as intriguing as it may seem—is deeply flawed but that *ex negativo* it can help us better understand what Cassirer's theory is about.

To begin with, Goodman is clearly committed to relativism, although it is a relativism "under rigorous constraints" (Goodman 1978, x): "The movement is from unique truth and world fixed and found to a diversity of right and even conflicting versions or worlds in the making" (ibid.). Not even his own theory, Goodman would most likely claim, needs to bear any unifying truth, and this is clearly not his agenda. What interests him is the multiplicity of "frames of reference" (1978, 2), which is another term for the "multiple actual worlds" we live in. In this sense, they are not entirely different from what Husserl calls the "special worlds" (*Sonderwelten*) as meaningful nexuses of referential implication (*Verweisungszusammenhänge*), but of course without that element that makes them "Husserlian," the theory of constitution: each "version of the world" is "right under a given system—for a given science, a given artist or a given perceiver and situation" (1978, 3). And it is in this sense that Goodman considers himself "like-minded" to Cassirer in that, according to Goodman according to Cassirer, the plurality of worlds is "irreducible to a single base" (1978, 4). So far so good: he concurs with Cassirer on the plurality of worlds—here leaving out whether symbolic forms are to be understood as "worlds"—and disagrees with him in that there is, or even is the need for, a unifying base or even unifying theory that embraces the special forms. However, as one continues in Goodman's analysis, what *really* marks the difference to Cassirer is something different.

Where Cassirer is mostly content to lay out a "phenomenology of objective spirit" in spirit's manifold manifestations, Goodman's agenda lies rather with *what one can do* with this theory, namely, as the title of his work indicates, "ways of world-*making*" (emphasis added). And it becomes clear that this is utterly divorced from anything Cassirer would ever allow for: Goodman is interested in *how* it is that *we* as active agents are in the position to *make* worlds—*new* worlds, that is, especially through art, but also through other not merely "artistic" activities. The brunt of Goodman's analyses is the actual laying out of *how* it is that we can make ("create") new worlds, as it were in giving a set of instructions for how to construct new frames of reference. These methods are (a) composition and decomposition, (b) weighting, (c) ordering, (d) deletion and supplementation, and (e) deformation.[40] These are nothing but concrete instructions of how to "build" worlds, and are not merely there to provide a "map" of the existing ones.[41] This "building" can be literally the forging of new frames of reference, as in creating a new style in art, among which counts even the philosophical task of explicating the different, implicit worlds we live in: "Comprehension and creation go on together" (1978, 22). In this sense, the philosopher not only observes what goes on in different human activities (as ways of world-making), but he is himself actively involved in world-making, and this activity is in no way superior to others.

The radical difference from Cassirer is clear: there is no transcendental framework in Goodman. Goodman is a "happy postmodernist." He is merely laying out empirical, even practical "rules" of how to go about creating new worlds as frames of reference, whereas Cassirer, in describing symbolic forms, is giving an analysis of transcendental forms of intuition which lie prior to any given experience. They are, in Cassirer, *laws* by which we experience the world and as such understand it. Furthermore, these forms of intuition are nothing that would ever be in our *power* to create but which are *there prior* to any experiencing and acting in the world. Transcendental forms of intuition can never be "made" but only described in their characteristics. They are the way spirit happens to be constituted, that is, differentiated into different symbolic forms, and these forms are prior to any actual "living." It is reason *itself* that has already differentiated *itself* into different symbolic forms. It is for this reason that Cassirer's approach can only be descriptive with regard to giving an account of the symbolic forms; it can only ever be a "phenomenology of spirit."

But this of course points to a problem. Who or what is this ominous "spirit" Cassirer is talking about? Saying that "spirit" is just another word for "reason" in its diversity only shifts the epistemological problem to another level without solving it. In other words: Cassirer only accounts for a phenomenology of *objective* spirit in highlighting the forms and the manifestations of spirit, but not accounting for, that is, in effect *characterizing* the actual *energy* which spirit is or constitutes. "Spirit" is a decidedly "operative term" in Cassirer's theory.[42] In conclusion, and thereby returning full circle to the Husserlian problematic, I would like to suggest that such a "phenomenology of *subjective* spirit" can be found in Husserl's mature analyses of transcendental subjectivity, especially in his draft of a "transcendental logic" in his late phase. Husserl's method of showing how the world for a subject is built up genetically through first "passive" and then "active" intentional acts can be understood and employed to actually flesh out how a "symbolic form" comes about. To be sure, Husserl only exemplified this in detail with regard to the perceptual lifeworld, but he anticipated the same kind of analysis for the world as an intersubjective and historical world of culture. In this, however, his philosophical system has equally remained incomplete. But this is not an argument against his system; it merely demonstrates, versus Goodman, how Cassirer's Kantian and Husserl's phenomenological accounts are complementary.[43]

From Culture and Philosophy of Culture Back to Phenomenology as a Hermeneutic Philosophy of the Lifeworld as World of Culture

After laying out the basics of Husserl's mature phenomenology in part 1, this second part has opened up the view towards a broader consideration of transcendental philosophy as a philosophy of culture. It was no doubt the neo-Kantian influence (in the form of the Marburg school) that pushed Husserl in this direction. Yet, as especially this last chapter on Cassirer showed, Husserl's philosophy is, in itself, by no means complete but demands to be expanded in the way presented. However, to repeat, neither project mutually excludes the other; complementing Cassirer in the way indicated brings him to Husserl, and vice versa. An image Husserl employed to characterize his relationship to Dilthey (albeit mainly concerning the question of history) may be applied here as well: that both were like mine dwellers who ground their way through the mountain, only to happily meet in the middle. The full account, hence, is that of the lifeworld as a world of culture, but one as constituted out of subjective achievements of human beings as cultural creatures. Phenomenology, then, is also, following the critique of Natorp's, more than just a descriptive discipline, it is also a *hermeneutic* one. This is its intrinsic consequence.

Before spelling out this ultimate consequence from the Husserlian perspective, it is appropriate to broach one last *Auseinandersetzung* between Husserl and a philosophy that has seemingly laid claim to the label "hermeneutics," namely Gadamer's philosophical hermeneutics. As I shall show in the following chapter, Gadamer, in taking some important cues from Husserl, goes too far in his claims to be acceptable within the framework of transcendental philosophy, which Husserl's phenomenology was demonstrated to be. To be sure, Gadamer does not follow the path of objective spirit, neither in Hegel's nor Cassirer's form; but in his rejection of the Husserlian theory of constitution through transcendental subjectivity, he falls, following Heidegger, into another extreme, which is to be rejected from the Husserlian perspective. The following chapter thus will criticize Gadamer by laying bare the extent to which he actually depended on Husserl and where he fatefully went beyond him. Making these extremes in Gadamer explicit will then allow me to ultimately spell out the elements of a Husserlian hermeneutics as a philosophy of culture in the concluding chapter.

Part 3

Toward a Husserlian Hermeneutics

The Subjectivity of Effective History and the Suppressed Husserlian Elements in Gadamer's Hermeneutics

It seems to me that there is a clear connection between [Husserl's] concept of passive synthesis and the doctrine of anonymous intentionalities and hermeneutic experience; a doctrine that at all times, when it has shed the methodological constraints of the transcendental way of thinking, corresponds to my phrase: "one understands differently, if one understands at all."
—Gadamer 1986a, 16[1]

Introduction

In this chapter, I am making essentially two claims: one is rather exegetical, the other systematic. The first, exegetical point is to show that there are genuine Husserlian elements in Gadamer's philosophical hermeneutics that are usually overlooked or not treated as such—that is, as genuine Husserlian. This is to say, they are *not* at the same time Heideggerian in the sense of a seemingly seamless development in phenomenology from Husserl to Heidegger. This is a claim that goes against what one might call the "standard interpretation." This standard reading consists in two related claims: (a) that there is a logical continuity from Husserl to Heidegger and Heidegger to Gadamer, and moreover (b), Heidegger and henceforth Gadamer supposedly exploited the "best" from Husserl, whereby one is well justified in treating Husserl as a "sublated" rung in a development of phenomenology. I will show that this standard interpretation, proposed among others by Gadamer himself, is both wrong and problematic.[2] It is wrong simply because one can show that one cannot map Heidegger on to Husserl in the way that some believe. And it is problematic due to the systematic claim that I make, as I shall show. The method for demonstrating this first claim will be a hands-on demonstration by delving directly into Husserl's late genetic phenomenology, the mature final stage of his thought. In so doing, I attempt to show how Gadamer's hermeneutics as an account of the effective history of the tradition decisively takes up some key insights of Husserl's that are *not* to be found in Heidegger; indeed, they go *against* Heidegger's intentions. If this demonstration is convincing, it will automatically disprove the standard interpretation. In other words, I intend to treat as separate two strains of thought that are usually taken as continuity and argue that they do not and, indeed, *should* not be treated as belonging together. The middle sections of this chapter, in which I deal first with Husserl, then with Gadamer, are hence more "phenomenological," that is, demonstrative, rather than argumentative.[3]

The second, systematic claim that I deal with in the last major section of this chapter states that the fact that Gadamer saw himself in alliance with the philosophical project of the later Heidegger, rather than Husserl, is problematic and ultimately counterproductive for a successful philosophical hermeneutics, for a genuine philosophical position rather than a mere "theory of interpretation." Positively speaking, it would have been more productive had Gadamer aligned himself more with Husserl and the tradition he represents. This tradition one can call the tradition of Enlightenment, whereas Heidegger represents a decidedly anti-Enlightenment tendency in twentieth-century philosophy.

This point in favor of Husserl is made not for the sake of appeasing disgruntled Husserlians who feel that "their man" did not get his fair share. Instead, Husserl is merely a representative of the Enlightenment tradition that Gadamer shunned under Heidegger's influence. Husserl, however, presents a particular strain within the Enlightenment tradition, a strain that can be associated with the project of "foundationalism" (*Letztbegründung*). The reason why Gadamer should have been more "Husserlian" turns on the question of foundationalism that Heidegger (among others)[4] perceived as a problematic offshoot of the Enlightenment. The main critique Heidegger has of the Enlightenment tradition in modern philosophy is of the idea of having to establish an ultimate foundation of knowledge in the subject. The problem is that, following Heidegger's anti-foundationalism in forming his concept of "effective history,"

Gadamer effectively gives up the main tenets of the Enlightenment and falls—similarly to Heidegger, albeit not quite in the radical gesture of his teacher—into an irrationalism, relativism, and fatalism, all of which are unacceptable for many reasons. Moreover, by shifting the weight from subjectivity to effective history as the "agent" in history, Gadamer falls back into a new sort of foundationalism that he wanted to overcome in the first place.[5] Effective history might not be an epistemological foundation in the way that Husserl and the neo-Kantians—these being Heidegger's and Gadamer's main enemies—saw the transcendental subject—as a constructing or constituting subject. Effective history remains, however, a foundation or ground in the sense in which Gadamer often likes to refer to Schelling's notion of the "unforethinkable" (*das Unvordenkliche*), that is, as a structure that functions as a background but which cannot itself be elucidated or made transparent but must be ultimately accepted and, what is worse, trusted as last authority.[6]

After spelling out this critique of Gadamer, I will conclude by emphasizing that it does not mean a wholesale dismissal of Gadamer's hermeneutics; an attempt that has, I believe, made some headway *against* Heidegger, whose ultimate radicalism Gadamer did not follow either. The problem in Gadamer's account of effective history can be remedied by insisting instead, in a Husserlian vein, on the *subjectivity*, that is, the thoroughly *subjective* character, of effective history.[7] While I think that there is some validity in Gadamer's critique of Husserl's idea of a *transcendental* genesis and philosophy as "rigorous," that is, eidetic, supra-temporal science, he chucked out the baby with the bath water when giving up the idea of human subjectivity as that which shapes and forms history. Acknowledging, rightly to my mind, our "passivity" in being born into a tradition does not justify seeing history as an anonymous force over which we have no control whatsoever. One need not dismiss the *subjective* element in the attempt to overcome a *transcendental* account of history. While Gadamer is, I believe, correct to put Husserl "on his feet" when insisting on the *factual* history and tradition of our inherited culture, he should have emphasized in the same instance that this history is one that is formed and shaped by subjects, by historically and (at least potentially) responsibly acting agents over the course of history. Effective history must be conceived as subjective through and through—even in its passive elements—in order to drive away the specters of fatalism, mysticism, escapism, and irrationalism. But this does not mean that one also needs to reject the Husserlian transcendental project. Gadamer's account has some merit as standing on the shoulders of Husserl's transcendental phenomenology; he follows a decidedly non-transcendental path in his hermeneutics. But the condition of the possibility of Gadamer's philosophical project lay in Husserl. Thus, while some of the critiques of Gadamer are justified, they do not *necessitate* the move beyond Husserl.

The first major section of this chapter (after this introduction) intends to provide the general contextual framework for the exegetical and systematic discussions to follow. Its purpose is to assess the issue of foundationalism and prepare the way for presenting Husserl's genetic phenomenology and Gadamer's philosophical hermeneutics as organically following from this first draft of what may be called a phenomenology of the historical lifeworld.

The Context of Gadamer's Hermeneutics

The Issue of Foundationalism and Gadamer as Anti-Foundationalist

Like so many philosophies in the twentieth century, one can, too, consider Gadamer's overall philosophical endeavor as an intent to dislodge and overcome the alleged major wrongdoing of modern philosophy: foundationalism.[8] In this attempt Gadamer could find himself in the company of his teacher Heidegger as well as other philosophers, such as the existentialists, logical positivists, pragmatists, and the early analytical philosophy, all of which, despite their differences, share an anti-fundamentalist bent. But to understand this critique, who is this common enemy? Foundationalism, as a term coined not until the twentieth century, begins with the Cartesian attempt to base all knowledge on the self-knowledge of the Ego as an absolute, apodictically certain foundation. In this sense, foundationalism is a spin-off of Cartesianism. As the standard story continues, this tendency was radicalized in Kant's transcendental philosophy and the Copernican turn and came to a climax in the attempts of the neo-Kantians in the late nineteenth century who proclaimed the transcendental subject as the ultimate foundation that grounds and justifies all knowledge about the world. This perceived need to anchor all knowledge in a constituting subject spilled over, the saga continues, into other philosophical schools, for example, the phenomenological movement, especially Husserl, thereby contaminating its original impulse of describing "the things themselves." In this sense, Heidegger could speak of Husserl temporarily "between 1900 and 1910" falling "into the clutches of neo-Kantianism" (1997, 193),[9] by which Heidegger presumably referred to Husserl's notorious *Logos* article "Philosophy as Rigorous Science" (1911)

THE SUBJECTIVITY OF EFFECTIVE HISTORY AND THE
SUPPRESSED HUSSERLIAN ELEMENTS IN GADAMER'S
HERMENEUTICS

and the transcendental turn presented in his programmatic treatise *Ideas to a Pure Phenomenology and Phenomenological Philosophy,* book I (1913).

Let us briefly review what Husserl claims here in order to see how Husserl formulates a version of foundationalism. In the article published in *Logos*—the main neo-Kantian publication outlet besides *Kant-Studien*—Husserl spells out the two fatal consequences when one does not follow a foundationalist agenda, thereby confirming his alliance with his erstwhile enemies, the neo-Kantians.[10] The common enemies are naturalism and historicism.[11] Naturalism, as the name indicates, naturalizes consciousness and thereby treats it as a mere phenomenon of the positive sciences. As a side effect, it also naturalizes ideas and construes them as mere occurrences in a contingent consciousness. Historicism holds that philosophical (like all other) theories do not have any atemporal validity but only historical relevance. Both tendencies, hence, deny the supra-temporal status of truth and end up in a relativism. In order to avoid this fatal result and attain these "absolute" truths, one has to make a shift to pure consciousness that equally has no empirical contaminations. The transcendental turn presented in *Ideas I* in the form of the transcendental reduction to a constituting transcendental subject was the mere cashing-in of the promise to battle naturalism and historicism and to establish philosophy as a "rigorous," that is, eidetic science that could attain results with a precision comparable to other rigorous sciences such as mathematics. To be sure, the Husserlian project of transcendental constitution of the world from the bottom up was different from the neo-Kantians, as discussed in the chapters of the previous part of this book. Husserl shared with them, however, the belief in a foundationalist agenda that lays its ground in a pure subject (or "pure thinking"). Thus, the main proponents of foundationalism around 1900 and 1925 were the neo-Kantians and Husserl—the big names in German philosophy at the time.

Gadamer, who had studied in Marburg under the aegis of the leading neo-Kantians, especially Paul Natorp, as well as under Husserl in Freiburg, knew all too well which enemy he was battling. In this battle he was, however, entirely following his teacher Heidegger who had early on fought against foundationalism. Heidegger's famous project of a "destruction of Western ontology" had as its main intention the overturning of the emphasis on the subject in modern philosophy, to him a fatal move that had begun already with Greek philosophy. Framing the human "subject" as *Dasein,* as Being-in-the-World, was a clear departure from this tradition; *Dasein* is not a founding subject of apodictic knowledge, but a site, an opening, where Being makes an appearance. It is this anti-foundationalism in Heidegger that Gadamer picked up on immediately. Indeed, in Gadamer's presentations of his teacher's philosophy, he always points out the continuity in Heidegger's early thought and the later philosophy after the so-called "turning" ("*Kehre*") that was merely interrupted by his "transcendental" phase in *Being and Time*. The early Heidegger's focus on the "worldhood" of the world and its character of "worlding" ("*es weltet*," "it worlds," being the operative term here) and his later reflections on the history of being in its process of uncontrollable revealing and concealing are attempts to overcome foundationalism. Heidegger's philosophy can be seen as the radical attempt to "destruct" the focus on the subject in a supposedly even more radical turn than Kant's Copernican turn. It is a turn from the subject to being itself that appears and gives itself to us, who are mere receivers.

Yet Heidegger's critique aims at more than just the idea of laying an absolute foundation in the subject; rather, Heidegger for his part tried to overthrow the entire subject-object distinction that has plagued Western philosophy ever since its inception in Greek philosophy and its cementation in Aristotle's substance ontology. The result in Heidegger's late philosophy was a mystically inspired new thinking that overcomes these oppositions and listens to the voice of Being and the coming of the new God in the age of nihilism.

Gadamer did not go quite so far and explicitly shied away from the later Heidegger's "mysticism," a term that he himself used to label Heidegger's last phase. He did, however, share with Heidegger the latter's assessment of modern philosophy's seeming obsession with foundationalism and the need to overcome it. What Gadamer proposed instead of Heidegger's reconstruction of the "history of being," and more modestly than his teacher, was a focus on tradition and what he called its "effective history" (*Wirkungsgeschichte*) in the way it informs our every worldview. The essential claim is that the way in which we understand ourselves is always mediated through a tradition in which we stand and that has a manner of "effecting" us historically, for example, through the prejudices that have been handed down to us or the things that we consider "classic" in our culture. In this effective history, however, the subject is—to quote Gadamer's famous phrase—but a "flickering light in the closed circuits of historical life." Though less radical than Heidegger, this is still intended as a clear departure from modern philosophy's foundationalism and the main paradigms of what is thought of as philosophy as we know it in the Western tradition. That is, philosophy, in the form of philosophical hermeneutics, is no longer concerned with laying ultimate foundations or "getting things right," nor even with the truth, if we mean by "the truth" the way things *really* are "in and of themselves."

Rather, philosophical hermeneutics is about mutual understanding and dialogue and emphasizes the truth of "classical" elements of our tradition and the truth of art. In Rorty's influential reading of modern philosophy in *Philosophy and the Mirror of Nature,* Gadamer is, interestingly, invoked as proposing a new style of philosophizing that is purely "edifying" and instrumental in continuing the conversation of educated and intelligent individuals and is unconcerned with absolute truths or foundations, "while sparks fly upwards" (Rorty 1979, 389) in thoughtful conversations. Indeed, this reading is, as we shall see, too extreme, precisely because Gadamer is not able to rid himself of foundationalist motives in the characterization of effective history. Foundationalism comes back with a vengeance. My point is not that Gadamer *should* have overcome foundationalism, but that he should have reframed it in the way Husserl attempted with his genetic phenomenology, although Husserl remained bound to transcendentalism. Gadamer might have had a valid point in criticizing Husserl's transcendental phenomenology, but went too far in overcoming his subjectivism.

The Standard Interpretation: Husserl as *"Aufgehoben"* (Sublated) in Heidegger

In view of Gadamer's alleged "departure from foundationalism,"[12] where does Husserl fit into the picture? If Husserl was such a clear foundationalist, as mentioned earlier, would it not seem that any connection to Husserl would be of little help? It is undeniable that Gadamer almost always mentions the founder of phenomenology in recounting his own philosophical development. Yet in the way Gadamer presents Husserl, he merely repeats the "standard interpretation" of Husserl's position in the history of twentieth-century philosophy. This interpretation stems essentially from Heidegger, and it has since been repeated like a mantra by most twentieth-century philosophers who see their own philosophizing as related to the phenomenological movement.[13] The standard interpretation holds that, essentially, Husserl founded phenomenology as a new style of philosophizing (with the vague and ultimately empty catchphrase "to the things themselves!") but was superseded by Heidegger's fundamental ontology. While Husserl's merit lay in opening up a new horizon of research under the new paradigm of intentionality and evidencing intuition, he was ultimately displaced and *"sublated"* in Heidegger's philosophy because Heidegger saw through, and overcame, the problematic paradigms that Husserl was not able to shed, most importantly his foundationalism or Cartesianism. In this story, Husserl's merit lay solely in "stylistic" matters, such as his devotion to detailed analysis, his shunning of systematizing speculation, and his unflinching adherence to the ideal of philosophy as "rigorous science."[14] What is understood as "rigorous science," however, has for the most part little to do with Husserl. Those within the standard interpretation who obey this principle see it not as implying a foundationalist agenda as Husserl had intended; rather, the label is often invoked by those who want to insist that their philosophizing is the opposite of "lofty," "vague," or "fuzzy."

The truth is, however, more complicated than that. Although this chapter is ultimately not concerned with Husserl exegesis, rectifying this oversimplifying interpretation has, in itself, no small merit. Indeed, upon closer inspection, Husserl was *equally* influential for Gadamer as Heidegger was. Gadamer's philosophical hermeneutics cannot be adequately assessed and appreciated without elucidating some Husserlian key insights. Indeed, these insights are originally Husserlian in the sense that Heidegger did *not* exploit them and thus they did not reach Gadamer via Heidegger—which is not to say that Heidegger did not himself also "borrow" heavily from Husserl, while always concerned with covering his tracks. That Gadamer adheres to the "standard interpretation" is displayed by the fact that Gadamer never was able to really recognize a decisive *difference* between Husserl and Heidegger but instead emphasized their continuity. Gadamer liked to refer to Husserl's phenomenology as a method that opened vast new horizons that Husserl himself was not able to penetrate to his own full satisfaction. Thus, the standard interpretation continues, Heidegger expanded, though with significant modifications, those horizons that were opened up by Husserl.[15] The tacit implication for Gadamer was that the same could be said for himself as well. Concerning Gadamer's own self-interpretation, one can adopt for Gadamer's relationship to Husserl what Tugendhat once said with regard to Heidegger's relationship to the founder of phenomenology: that Gadamer "from the very outset stands in the dimension that was opened up by Husserl and now merely unfolds it" in his own manner (1967, 263). This unfolding, however, takes its point of departure where Husserl left off prematurely. What is problematic in this "standard interpretation" is *not* that Husserl was not rightfully criticized in this manner by Heidegger and Gadamer. There are plenty of problems in Husserl's phenomenology in the shape that he left it when he died. What is problematic is that this "teleological" reading renders Husserl unnecessary and "obsolete" because all of his valid insights were already exploited by Heidegger. I propose, instead, that Husserl and Heidegger in their key intentions present two unrelated strains of thought that ultimately do not square with one another.

Gadamer's Foundationalism and Husserl's Genetic Phenomenology: A Preview

While there can be no doubt concerning Gadamer's kinship with Heidegger's thought,[16] there are certainly elements in Husserl's philosophy that Gadamer unequivocally rejects, mainly of course Husserl's Cartesian project of laying an ultimate foundation and his concomitant doctrine of the phenomenological reduction. However, Gadamer pays tribute to the Husserlian impulses that he incorporated into his philosophical hermeneutics.[17] When discussing Husserl, Gadamer always treats him with the greatest respect and commends him both for his original phenomenological discoveries as well as his eye for detail in his intricate analyses and his philosophical innocence that allowed him to see phenomena with new eyes.[18] In so doing, however, Gadamer, too, merely repeats the standard interpretation. That is, he sees himself as furthering Heidegger's agenda. In his hermeneutics, Gadamer merely replaces Heidegger's history of being with *effective* history as the way the tradition has an effect on us in our self-understanding and our prejudices that inform our judgments.

The problems begin here, however. What exactly is effective history? If this "instance" is supposed to be the remedy to the plagues of modern philosophy, it deserves a closer look. As I will show in more detail in the last section of this chapter, this "structure" is no longer to be conceived along the lines of subjectivity; rather, Gadamer sees it as an anonymous force that comes over us like the weather and over which we as acting subjects ("flickering lights") have no control.[19] It is the way the tradition reveals and gives itself to us and forms, as it were, the condition of the possibility of our understanding. As such, I would like to claim, it is equally an ultimate foundation, namely, a non-sublatable foundation of our understanding. It is the ground on which we stand and which we cannot leap out of due to our finitude. Effective history is the foundation forming our prejudices which, in turn, found our judgments and understandings in our daily lives in the world. In this sense, Gadamer, against all intents and purposes, has been unable to shed the notion of foundationalism; the main difference is that the role of the ultimate foundation has been shifted, from a constituting subject, over to effective history. But who or what is this effective history? Does the idea of such an anonymous force in history not amount to mysticism and fatalism with respect to the events in history, just as in Heidegger's history of being? Could it not equally be construed as exculpation from humanity's responsibility in this world as well as escapism from the "hard facts" of life? Finally, taking away the responsibility for the course of history from acting agents in history opens the door to an irresponsible and dangerous irrationalism. Gadamer's concept of effective history is, in truth, a *lucus a non lucendo,* a dimension that raises more problems than it solves and is, therefore, to be resisted at all costs.

But we must first see how Gadamer arrived at this doctrine. In the following, I want to show where Gadamer has drawn from Husserlian insights in the development of his philosophical hermeneutics. In this assessment, it is possible to entirely ignore Heidegger and focus on the genuine Husserlian elements of Gadamer's thought. Thus, I am not interested in enumerating where Gadamer "borrowed" from Husserl. Rather, I want to attempt to show where and how Gadamer fruitfully *expanded* Husserlian ideas. To Gadamer, there is a systematic necessity to advance Husserl's philosophy; yet, I believe, both work on the same issue. This issue is a philosophical account of the lifeworld construed as intrinsically *historical.* The lifeworld is Husserl's and Gadamer's *common problem.* As mentioned, in most presentations of Gadamer's thought scholars rarely explicitly focus on Husserl and immediately jump to Heidegger.[20] A closer look will reveal that Gadamer not only took up some decisive Husserlian elements; moreover, one can find traces of genuinely Husserlian thought in Gadamer that *Heidegger* himself shunned in his project of a "destruction of Western metaphysics." Indeed, two of Gadamer's key concepts, "tradition" and "authority," already indicate that he, *like Husserl,* was more interested in a creative appropriation of the tradition and the history of philosophy rather than overcoming it.

The obvious starting point for launching into the exegetical part is Husserl's theory of the lifeworld, stemming from the doctrine of *horizon.*[21] I shall first present in the following section, "Husserl's Late Phenomenology as Genetic Analysis of Transcendental History," the decisive elements of this theory of the mature Husserl, with an eye toward those points that Gadamer took up and integrated in his philosophical hermeneutics. Hence, this is not a mere repetition of the sections presenting Husserl's theory of the lifeworld in chapter 4; instead, it is a novel presentation with an eye toward those elements that Gadamer later focused upon. Then, in the next section, I will show how Gadamer expanded Husserl's original account into a theory of historical understanding in a world that is essentially "traditioned." What was only vaguely anticipated in Husserl finds its full-fledged presentation in Gadamer's philosophical hermeneutics, thereby, however, dropping Husserl's transcendental framework. Most of Gadamer's thoughts are truly phenomenological insights in working through some unresolved problems in Husserl. Most importantly, the concept of horizon, as well as Gadamer's notion of the *fusion* of horizons, expands on Husserlian elements that have no equivalent in Heidegger and ultimately do not agree with Gadamer's Heidegger-inspired notion of effective history.

Husserl's Late Phenomenology as Genetic Analysis of Transcendental History

The term "lifeworld" is a concept that Husserl does not employ until late in his career, although it is merely a terminological "lucky find" for the topics that Husserl had been working on ever since he declared intentionality as the main topic of his philosophical work.[22] It is fair to call intentionality Husserl's term for *experience*. When systematically unfolded, intentionality reveals the basic elements of what Husserl later expanded into a universal theory of the lifeworld as the world correlated to subjective experiencing. The basic character of intentionality is that all consciousness is always consciousness-*of* something, perceiving is perceiving-*something*, thinking is thinking *of* something, and so on. Intentionality is not merely an empty cognitive intending of something; instead, every intentional act bestows *meaning* upon that which is intended.[23] I intend this object here not as an empty X with a meaning "attached" to it in a separate act, but I see it and immediately *comprehend* it as, for example, a table. Intentional acts in their pursuit in different contexts always are meaningful in the sense of meaning-bestowing. Meaning reveals itself only *in* acts. This means that in intentional acts as conscious activities I *understand* (as Gadamer would say) things, artifacts, and persons in my environment as what they are. But how is this possible?

Certainly, a meaning-bestowing act does not come out of nowhere. The significant meaning in which I "approach" an object is not created in the instant that I carry out this act. Rather, the meaning must have already been established in my everyday life. This meaning is not one among a fixed set of propositions that I can revert to. It is a silent "pool" of implicit "knowledge" or "know-how" that I carry with me and that becomes "actualized" in a given act situation. Husserl metaphorically calls it a *"horizon"* in which I live at all times and from out of which single acts come forth. The horizon is a horizon of *meaning*. For example, in order to understand this thing here as a table, I must have dealt with tables or similar objects before, and I must know the context in which a table has a certain meaning, that is, in the context of a house, more specifically a kitchen, a dining room, and so on. This knowing is thus not propositional knowledge in the sense of cognition, but a horizon of meaning in which I am at all times immersed.[24] Thus, the concept of horizon is but an *expansion* of the intentional relation of act and intended object. Intentional acts are a concrete *instantiation* of our meaningful existence in the world as a horizon of meaning; intentions are, in other words, something that *always takes place within* a horizon of meaning. The discovery of horizon is arguably the most important innovation in Husserl's mature thought in expanding the original intentional relation of act and fulfillment. The horizon is the constant "background" or "halo" of individual acts and hence part of the intentional structure itself. Husserl will utilize this concept in two directions, as a horizon of *acts* (on the "noetic" side) and as the *context* at which acts are directed (the "noematic" aspect).

The horizon from which intentional acts come forth Husserl calls *attitude*. An attitude is the horizon of understanding that I always carry with me in living in a certain meaningful way. Yet, we do not just live in one way of understanding, but we have a manifold of such attitudes at our disposal, for example, the work attitude, the leisure attitude, the artistic attitude, and so on. Husserl illustrates this with the example of a house: there is no such thing as a "pure" seeing of the house, but this "X" will be understood as something depending on the attitude that one takes toward it (the—by now—[in]famous example of the house that can be viewed in different attitudes).[25] Attitudes are different intentional perspectives that one can have on an individual object and that will in each case render a wholly different "understanding" or "interpretation" of this object. In this sense, all experiencing is interpreting, because it takes place within a certain horizon of understanding. This point refutes any kind of realism: there is no "real thing" out there to which I can approximate myself with ever more descriptions. It is entirely what it is by the way it is intended and in the way it gives itself in different profiles ("adumbrations"). This is a phenomenological restatement of transcendental idealism. The thing in itself is nonsense for phenomenology; it is given as *phainomenon* in different ways of approaching it. The thing is in this sense an idea as the sum total of meanings that I can bestow upon it in different attitudes, but nothing beyond that.

Being in a specific attitude means, moreover, that no matter what I see, I can perceive it from the standpoint of this attitude; for example, the artist can potentially view *all* objects as works of art, the businessman can potentially perceive all objects in his surroundings in terms of their market value, and so on. Thus, an attitude is not limited to a certain fixed set of entities but can be expanded to all possible entities. An attitude is an intentional structure, not a literal standpoint. Now something similar can be observed on the "noematic" side: this potential "everything" intended in an attitude is, in turn, not a certain, limited set of objects but can be potentially anything upon which I set sight from a certain attitude. Everything that is present to me in an intentional act implies a co-presence of an innumerable amount of *possible* objects of intention. Thus, on the side of that which I intend, or can potentially intend, we also find a horizon. But what is important in the Husserlian account is that the horizon is not an anonymous "clearing" that opens itself up to me (or not); rather, it is the field of that which *can potentially* be intended. It, too, is an element, that is, the noematic correlate, of the intentional relation itself.

This horizon on the side of that which "gives itself" in specific attitudes is the phenomenological concept of *world*. A world is not a certain number of objects but a region or sphere of meaning that allows for objects to be understood in a certain way.[26] Yet the original meaning of "horizon" (compare the Greek *horízein*) is "to delimit." That is, one horizon of meaning that corresponds to a certain attitude (the artistic attitude correlates to the world of art) is merely one region of meaning besides others. "Region" here is an epistemological, not an ontological, term; it does not refer to regions of nature, but regions of *possible intending* and, correlatively, *potential meaning*. In point of fact, we always already live in different worlds of meaning, in different meaningful contexts, of which there are more than we can ever know. To align this observation with a Gadamerian interest: it depends on the processes of maturation, education, and learning—in a word: *Bildung*—to become acquainted with ever more worlds of meaning. To "know" many such worlds (in a non-epistemic sense) and to pass through them freely and easily is a matter of being *gebildet*.

Yet we all live in *one world*, Husserl maintains, but this world is already differentiated for us into special worlds of meaning that we always and readily inhabit in our everyday life, starting from when we wake up in the morning in our "home world" and switch to the "business world" on our job and pass through the "world of leisure" on our walk through the park. The totality of these worlds as horizons is the *horizon of* all these horizons. This is Husserl's formal concept of the lifeworld. The lifeworld is the horizon that makes possible all these horizons, as the openness that allows for all these different contexts of meaning. As such, it is also an idea, because we know that all of these different regional worlds ultimately coincide in one world, though we live in it differently. The one world, the lifeworld, is in this sense again not to be misunderstood "ontically" (e.g., as earth) but as the epistemological concept of region of all possible regions of potential and actual intending. The noetic correlate is the formal potentiality to be in an attitude. This formal structure Husserl calls the "natural attitude."

The lifeworld is, thus, a formal concept designating the totality of all possible regions of meaning that correlates to the totality of all potential meaning-bestowing intentional acts. That is, Husserl at all times construes intentionality as *correlational.* To the lifeworld corresponds on the side of the "subject" the total sphere or horizon of consciousness that enables all these horizons of meaning to be experienced. This is the "natural attitude," which is "natural" in that we take all of this for granted. Husserl's theory, hence, can be understood as a reaction to the following problem: How, despite the *plurality* of meaningful contexts, is it possible to have *one world*? How do we have *unity* in this *plurality*? Husserl's starting point—which will lead to a fundamental problem, to Gadamer—is plurality; the unity of the world is, as it were, a regulative idea in Husserl. However, one *can* posit it as such an idea because the world is essentially a world of meaning. There are no regions that we intend that would be meaningless; conversely, there are presumably regions of meaning that are not yet tapped into or discovered. Yet we always and for the most part live "in different worlds," even if we might live together in the same geographical location. The stockbroker and the artist might live geographically together in Manhattan, but have little in common. That we live in *one lifeworld* means, to Husserl, that the difference between horizons can in principle be bridged. Yet, the idea of the plurality of horizons that we inhabit while living in one world presents a problem in Husserl, which, as we shall see, Gadamer sought to overcome.

This account of horizons, which Husserl calls "static," raises the question of *where* these horizons come from. In order to answer the question of the *origin* of the horizons, we have to turn to genetic phenomenology. Husserl's transcendental theory[27] so far—the "static" description of conditions of possibility of experience—does not explain the *origin* of these horizons of meaning. This calls for a deepened account in expanding phenomenology from a static act-analysis to a "genetic phenomenology,"[28] a theory toward which, it is worth pointing out, Gadamer is very sympathetic.[29] The main insight that Husserl advances in his mature phenomenology is that the expanded theory of intentionality expounded so far is merely the top "stratum" of a "historical" process. Metaphorically speaking, the horizons have a third "depth dimension." Every intentional act that an agent performs comes forth from a horizon that this person did not *create on her own.* It is an Ego who intends and understands this thing here as a table, but the Ego created neither the table nor the horizon of meaning that enables her to identify this thing *as* a table. The horizon of meaning that one "has" is something that one has taken over, something that one is, literally, born into. It has been created before me obviously by other subjects before me, and those in turn have taken over their horizon from subjects before them, and so on. In this sense, we all stand on the shoulders of giants. A "static" description of horizons in reality *presupposes* a *genesis* of intentional activities. The "status quo" rests upon a layered structure of sedimented intentional activities that have been carried out before I came into being. My horizon is the product of a sedimentation of past intentionalities that have formed, and continue to form, the present horizon of understanding. Horizons are nothing that I or any *single* subject have constituted; rather, the horizons that have developed before my own "intentional contributions" *constitute me.* Since they are nothing that I constitute but that I can merely take over (in agreement or disagreement), Husserl terms this process with the peculiar cognate "passivity." My horizon is a product of a "passive genesis" for me insofar as I do not actively create it. Current acts with their meaningful attitudes and worlds in the here and now have a history, but this history is that of acts themselves. To remind the reader of the results reached in chapter 4, genesis is not simple history (*res gestae*), but a *history of intentionality.* Thus, clarifying this "passive genesis" is Husserl's answer to how it is that these horizons that we inhabit and that constitute us come about.

What does it mean for phenomenology to analyze passive genesis? As a reconstruction of the history of intentionality, such a genetic or developmental description is not a historical account (of *res gestae*). Rather, Husserl's aim is to account for the genesis of conscious interaction with the world, the history of intentionality *itself.* It is a *phenomenological* reconstruction, that is to say, it is about an *eidetic* account of how genesis *in general* is carried out and reconstructs "*laws of genesis*"[30] that govern this intentional history (Hua XI, 336–45). It remains within the framework of transcendental phenomenology, as genesis is the depth dimension of the conditions of possibility for experience. For instance, to clarify an understanding of the table in this act of seeing, we have to perform an "un-building" of this "static" description, as this understanding already takes place on a very high level of culture, that is, it takes a certain maturity of cultural knowledge to see this object here as a cultured artifact. Hence, un-building reverts to the most primitive level of simple perception and starts from there, a description of perception as intending something in profiles (the front side with the hidden back side). But this is not an isolated description; there is a continuity reaching up to the highest levels of understanding. The phenomenological description in the genetic register hence proceeds from the most basic level and reconstructs the developmental laws as well as intentional structures that build up the layered intentional structures that finally reach the "status quo" of experiencing this thing here as a sophisticated object, for example, a table designed to support components for a smart classroom. In this sense, Husserl's genetic account is inherently *teleological*.

Husserl's paradigm of this most simple stratum of intentionality is external perception. The analysis of perception reveals that this thing here is given first and foremost as a three-dimensional X that I see with my eyes, its movements along with the movements of my body. Due to my physical makeup I can only see this object from its front side with the back side hidden, in "adumbrations." From here, Husserl goes on to describe how this thing here becomes "constituted" through my bodily interaction with it. This simple process of perception, however, is a constant process of modification and rectification,[31] as my expectation of what I am about to see is always at least *somewhat* different than anticipated. Thus, the seeing of the back side can turn out differently than I thought, so that the new perception annuls my earlier anticipation. Yet, the old anticipation has not "vanished" but is sublated into a higher synthesis of a new unanimous perception of the thing (instead of "this round object" the newly established "this round object with a dent on the back side"). This is an excerpt of an analysis of a "genetic lawfulness" in the sphere of passivity. It is passive in the sense that this kind of "primitive" interaction is already presupposed on higher levels.[32] Hence, the horizons of meaning that we inhabit rest on a genesis of meaning that reaches far back but that always is a genesis of *subjective* interactions with the world as a lifeworld. Accordingly, passivity has different levels of meaning: a perception (of this thing as something) can be passive in that I do not have to go back to the primal instituting when I first learned about what it was; in this sense, it is passive with respect to *my own* intentional history. Going deeper, we find "absolute passivity" in that it is not a part of my history at all: it might have been established by people I never knew a long time ago. Yet, in all of these cases, "passivity" designates *some subject's activity at a given time in the past.* The "past" is here equally not to be understood as *historical time,* but it is a past in the transcendental account of internal time-consciousness. It is a past not in time but in temporality.

This example of a genetic account of perception gives a glimpse of how Husserl conceived of the genetic method. Obviously, this presents a gigantic field of research that Husserl envisioned. This is what Gadamer meant when he spoke of these "vast fields" that Husserl opened up but never succeeded in fully penetrating. For, concerning the actual execution of this project, Husserl never really achieved more than beginnings. The "perpetual beginner," as he referred to himself, always dwelled in these lower regions and, forever dissatisfied with his own work, never made his way up to the surface to draft a full-fledged phenomenology of the lifeworld. The literally thousands of manuscripts that Husserl devoted in the last decades of his life to this single task show that he simply got stuck. He made attempts to give an account of the lifeworld on "higher levels" and "personalities of higher order" such as communities, peoples, and societies. Yet he ultimately had to content himself with declaring phenomenology the task of an "infinite chain of generations" of researchers who would carry out this project.[33] Yet, Husserl at all times remains bound to the Cartesian, subjectivistic paradigm. Genesis is a genesis of meaning constituted by a genetic "buildup" of intentional acts of a *subject*. Factually carrying out a philosophical project—and the contingent factors involved in this—is one thing and itself cannot be an argument against a theory. There are, however, reasons why this theory is problematic from the standpoint of Gadamer, which shall be briefly spelled out in the following, before moving on to Gadamer himself.

Indeed, Husserl's theory is a *transcendental* theory in the framework of philosophy as rigorous, that is, eidetic science. Although Husserl ultimately wants to thematize the lifeworld in its full historical concretion, he never truly arrives at this concretion and factuality, and due to his concept of phenomenology as transcendental philosophy, he cannot. The reason for this is, however, *not* his subjectivist bent; rather, what prevents him from really getting to the concrete world is his ideal of philosophy as *rigorous science*. Husserl's original idea of phenomenology simply cannot account for the concrete world because that would mean giving up the ideal for the contingent. There simply is no connection between transcendental genesis and historical development. Husserl's phenomenology clarifies the transcendental conditions of possibility of concrete historical development and *therefore cannot* arrive at concrete history as a process of its own, divorced from the correlation with constituting transcendental subjectivity, ultimately conceived as intersubjectivity. The lifeworld remains an equally formal concept. Thus, one has to conclude with respect to Husserl's late thought: he never clarified the relation between genesis and history. In fact, there *is* no direct line from genesis to history. This is not merely an external critique, since Husserl himself wanted to thematize history in his late thought.[34] Hence, Husserl envisioned something that his own method did not allow him to reach. He simply was not able to drop the tenet of transcendental philosophy and his proclivity toward a philosophy as *rigorous science*, meaning an eidetic discipline establishing timeless truths for any conceivable subject. There is no way to square eidetics with history. In order to enter into the "fruitful bathos" of concrete life in its historical shape, one must leave the ivory tower of eidetic science. So much for a Gadamerian sentiment.

The claim to be made in the next section is that Gadamer's philosophical hermeneutics in principle has its locus within this direction of research and took up these threads, but essentially dropped Husserl's transcendentalism and ideal of philosophy as eidetic science. But this does not mean that one cannot retain Husserl's main phenomenological insight, the concept of horizon, in a "concrete" manner. To be sure, Gadamer sets a different emphasis and special priorities in his work—most notably in the role that *art* plays for understanding—but his philosophy can be understood as an ingenious *expansion* and, as such, a *transformation of Husserl's account of the lifeworld* by essentially *historicizing* Husserl's transcendental theory of genesis. In the following, I will show that Gadamer took up and modified the methodological elements that Husserl developed in his rudimentary account of the lifeworld. What Gadamer thematizes is also nothing but the lifeworld, although he takes his point of departure on a higher level and places the emphasis on seemingly different phenomena. Yet, he merely explicates elements that are implicit in Husserl and overcomes some problems in his theory. Gadamer builds upon the foundations that Husserl constructed.

The main lesson to be learned from this discussion of Husserl should be that *even those elements* that seem a-subjective, like history and horizon, are elements of *intentionality,* that is, *subjective* interaction with the world. This means that Husserl's concept of horizon is located on a *fundamentally different* playing field than Heidegger's account of truth as "clearing" or "unconcealment" of the world's showing itself. Husserl's remains at all times a "subjectivistic" theory, albeit with a very original sense of "subjective." Any attempts to harmonize Husserl's concept of horizon and Heidegger's notion of the worldhood of the world are, for this reason, wrongheaded.

Gadamer's Philosophical Hermeneutics as a Phenomenological Analysis of Factual Tradition

I will take my point of departure with Gadamer's concept of experience and understanding as presented in *Truth and Method.* Gadamer's account of experience neatly maps onto Husserl's structure of horizon. Perhaps the most familiar hermeneutic concept is that of understanding. The most crucial point about this notion is that it is not just a cognitive event in the present; instead, every experience is or rather already presupposes a certain understanding, because we already stand in a certain tradition that exerts its influence upon us, as its "heritage."[35] Thus, the "attitude" (in Husserl's terms) that we always already find ourselves in is in fact enabled by a *horizon of tradition*. This tradition obtains universally in that nobody is *without* a tradition when understanding. Tradition is our life's "element."[36] A horizon in the "genetic" consideration is a horizon of tradition as our current horizon's depth dimension. What Gadamer calls "tradition" is, hence, nothing but the depth dimension of our current understanding. It is not, however, that of transcendental intentional processes, but of our concrete, factual history, that is, a history of human cultural achievements. It is for this reason that Gadamer considers actual cultural artifacts such as poems when putting his hermeneutics to work.

How does understanding as standing in a tradition work on supposedly simple levels of experience? Consider the Husserlian example that I immediately understand this object as a table, i.e., that I first and foremost do not question its meaning. To see this object as a table without first questioning the validity of this experience as well as the meaning experienced in it is a certain *prejudice*.[37] Indeed, to have a horizon of meaning as a tradition means that I for the most part do not *question* the meanings that I inherit. As such, they are prejudices. My life is full of prejudices and biases that I harbor. The horizon that Husserl outlines is in fact a horizon of tradition, and a tradition is constituted by unquestioned prejudices that govern my daily life. For instance, it is a tradition to shake hands upon meeting; to adhere to this tradition is a prejudice in the sense that I do not give myself account for it rationally whenever I do it. It is inherited and has become part of my "second nature."[38] What Husserl simply conceived of as a horizon's "background" character in Gadamer becomes concrete as a field of prejudices, that is, notions, opinions, beliefs that normally never become explicit. They are constant prejudgments, not judgments, for then they would no longer have the character of prejudice and bias. The point about these prejudices is that, like in Husserl's concept of horizon, they are simply part of what it means to have experience and to make judgments and are not inherently a bad thing. Another way of saying this is that the horizon of our everyday understanding in Husserl only comes into view in his notion of the "natural attitude" with its unquestioned prejudices as something to be left behind by philosophical reflection. Whereas in Gadamer it becomes the explicit theme of philosophical hermeneutics as a doctrine that intends to *understand* how these prejudices have come about through a tradition.

Thus, the depth dimension of my horizon of understanding is a *tradition,* and this tradition exerts an *authority* over me in the sense that it is implicit in guiding my daily activities; I am usually not aware of any of my prejudices. Now contrary to the Enlightenment sentiment according to which prejudices are to be overcome, Gadamer contends that prejudices as horizonal background are not necessarily a bad thing. Gadamer's intention in the historical passages of *Truth and Method*[39] is to wrest the concepts of tradition and prejudice from the Enlightenment tradition whose intention it was to radically do away with all prejudices and base all knowledge on rational insight. This immanent critique of Enlightenment is entirely in keeping with Husserl's analysis of horizon and background as inherent parts of experiencing and judging. To believe that one can entirely do without all prejudices is *itself* a prejudice. This is impossible to accomplish, just as it would be to get rid of the attitude from which acts emerge. We can never *entirely do away* with the "fore-structure" of understanding, according to which all understanding rests upon a *pre-*understanding, a prejudice, that we did not create on our own but that we can reflect upon using certain methods (e.g., art or philosophy). It would be a wrongheaded attempt to achieve full clarity of all prejudices, it would be a misunderstood Enlightenment. This does not automatically make Gadamer a representative of an "anti-Enlightenment"; having prejudices is not simply a result of a lazy reason (although it could be). Indeed, Gadamer distinguishes between good and bad prejudices. Bad prejudices are those attitudes that we can *understand as* bad upon reflection and that out of rational insight should be abandoned, for example, in the many forms of discrimination, where other human beings do not receive the respect they deserve as being members of the same race as myself. This is the sense of prejudice that the Enlightenment battled in order to rid oneself of, in Kant's words, a "self-incurred tutelage," and Gadamer is adamant about being a part of the Enlightenment in this sense of the term. "What Kant calls Enlightenment in truth corresponds to what hermeneutics has in view. . . . The stubborn clinging to prejudices or even the blind appeal to authority is nothing but the laziness to think" (Hahn 1997, 287).[40] However, all other prejudices are "good" in the sense that they guide and underpin our daily interaction and our ordinary behavior in general. Prejudices *form* the horizon of our understanding. I am a functioning member in society when I act according to the prejudices of this society. Prejudices are the *contingent, empirical conditions of possibility* of any understanding.

Experience here and now is always already engrossed in tradition that we remember—unconsciously or implicitly. Concrete experience presupposes memory; memory *forms* our presence. Our current experience is merely the "static," uppermost stratum of a historical process that went on before my individual existence and that will continue after my death. History is the history of human beings and as such has a movement, the direction of which can only be vaguely anticipated. This means that we stand in a tradition that we did not create and choose to be born into;

this accounts for our essential finitude that Gadamer invokes, following Heidegger. But this does not necessarily mean that the self-reflection of the subject is nothing but a "flickering light in the closed circuits of historical life" (1989, 281).[41] One less radical way of reading this phrase—indeed proposed here—is that all experience, *especially* conscious reflection, is historical and is not possible without the horizon from which it stems. The horizon of understanding both allows us to transcend our present situation and accounts for our essential finitude in that it is not possible to elucidate *all* prejudices that guide my current understanding. In fact, normally I am not even interested in this kind of elucidation and it is not necessary to carry on with my life. Instead, I am steeped in tradition, and my subjective experience of something is merely an abstraction from my concrete experience as immersed in a tradition.

This "immersion" Gadamer captures in the concept of *situation* (not altogether different from Husserl's notion thereof). Being in a situation means that "one does not find oneself opposed to it and therefore cannot have objective knowledge of it" (1989, 307). In a situation (and not just an isolated act), I find myself together with what I experience as "both" being there in one totality. I *find myself* in a certain attitude correlated to a certain horizon of experience. For instance, when going into a museum, I "attune" myself to having an aesthetic experience. But this is not really what goes on in a situation; the situation *draws me in*, it *attunes me*. What I experience is given to me in its entirety, as it brings about a switch of attitude (coming in from the noisy street). Although I only experience an aspect of the possible horizon—a given painting—the horizon is given "holistically." The situation engulfs me. The process of a concrete experience, however, can readily be described with Husserlian tools: as I enter a certain room and see a painting and approach it, being drawn to it "magically," the experience of this painting will undergo a constant modification and will either confirm or alter itself; but it will certainly never stay the same. Even if a break of understanding occurs—the painting appears to depict a still life, but I understand the dead animals stand for life's finitude, thereby changing the overall perception—this break will immediately be integrated into a new totality. The process of experience will never come to an end. I will never know this work of art in its entirety; I can always be surprised. However, I will always understand *somehow*, as every new experience rests upon a historical background that prefigures my current understanding. Thus, to quote a well-known Gadamerian bon mot, "one understands *differently if one understands at all*" (1989, 302). There is no *one correct* understanding. The "difference" is due to the fact that the horizon of understanding displays a temporal structure, it is in constant change and flux and a "genesis" with no conceivable end. There is no one correct way in which human beings "must" view the *Mona Lisa,* yet my understanding in the year 2010 is inconceivable without a history of previous understandings that guide mine at this point in time. Thus, there is no way to eidetically prefigure the further experiences I, or mankind as a whole, will have of this work of art. All I can say is that, due to perhaps known, perhaps unknown prejudices of my understanding, this individual picture drew me in, whereas others in the same room did not. *Explicating* what it means to be in a situation transforms it into a *hermeneutical situation.*

The nature of a hermeneutical situation is such that the horizon in which I stand here and now has a "tail," as Gadamer alludes to Husserl's image of the tail of a comet as the way past experience is "retained" in our lived-present.[42] Experience is not only surrounded by a pre-thematic historical horizon as a background for concrete experience; the background also determines the way in which I conceive of myself in the present *and from there,* the past. In other words, my own horizon becomes explicit when confronted with another. For example, in the experience of something like a historical text such as a novel, I first of all explicitly *acquire* a horizon of understanding when I recognize the *difference* in the hermeneutical horizon of the novel and that of my own understanding. What Gadamer says about the understanding of historical documents, however, applies universally. In all experience, I cannot reflect my way out of the historical setting into which I have been born; and I cannot just "leap" into another historical setting, either. For this would presuppose that I was an essentially ahistorical subject that just happened to be in a situation by chance. As a finite being, I am "traditioned," and this means essentially *historical.* History has and at all times continues to exert its effect on me. History is a history of effects that at all times factors into my current understanding. Hence Gadamer's key hermeneutical concept of *effective history* (*Wirkungsgeschichte*).

Effective history is more than a mere descriptive category; it comes with philosophical claims: experience is about understanding, and understanding is a never-ending historical process effected by history itself, a constant modification with no possible *telos* or *perfection.* Nobody can ever "exhaust" one's understanding of the world, and humans never will as long as they exist. Understanding is a universal trait of human beings living in a historical world; this understanding is engrossed in a horizon of consciousness of the past that has an unceasing effect on us. The life-world is a historical world in that the horizons of our experience are horizons of understanding that govern our everyday life. The decisive difference that marks Gadamer's development from Husserl is that this is not an *eidetic* analysis that presupposes the transcendental reduction. Instead, it describes the structure of what happens to us always already in our daily lives and what governs our understanding as essentially historical beings, not as transcendental subjects. As historical beings, we are part of a collective consciousness that we call tradition. Consciousness that "happens" in history is a historically effective consciousness that we are part of as figures in a tradition, as "catchers of a ball" that has been "thrown toward us" from the world itself ("an eternal partner") within a game of which we are by necessity part—alluding to Rilke's poem that stands as a motto of *Truth and Method*.[43] History is the way the *world gives itself*, but this world is nothing but the correlate of subjects living *in* this world by projecting meaning onto it. Gadamer has brought Husserl's transcendental theory down to the level of the concrete, historical lifeworld.

Thus, Gadamer is not claiming to give us a radically new theory; instead, he merely explicates what always already governs our lifeworldly existence; namely, prejudices that form our horizon. We are to gain an appreciation for the fact that our life is essentially historically prejudiced and that this is nothing bad in itself but part of our "ontological destiny." In this sense, Gadamer's hermeneutics lacks Heidegger's radicality in wanting to overthrow the tradition and is in truth closer to Husserl's method of a sound description of the lifeworld as an essentially historical horizon. It is about making explicit what is commonly implicitly valid in our conscious activity. In this formal sense, Gadamer is following Husserl's intentions, with the difference that this account is not eidetic, and it does not involve a world-constituting transcendental subjectivity; instead it is about concrete, factual human beings and their achievements in all activities that we consider specifically human, that is, culture.

Now let us see how Gadamer makes headway with respect to this description of the lifeworld. Indeed, Gadamer overcomes a problem in Husserl's method that Husserl never answered satisfactorily. Husserl's transcendental turn is informed by the methodological consideration that in my normal life I am not aware of my subjective activities as constitutive of world. Hence I must make these implicit activities explicit, and the question is how this is possible. Gadamer raises the same question, but rephrases it in the following way: How it is possible in the first place to make implicit *prejudices* explicit? What motivates this? If it is the case that our ordinary life is governed by prejudices that we do not acknowledge, nor even understand *as* prejudices, how, then, can it be possible to make these explicit? In Husserl's terms: How is it possible to leave the natural attitude? Husserl's (by now, familiar) answer to this problem is that we must practice an epoché, a "bracketing" of this natural attitude in order to disengage ourselves from it to bring it into view. In a similar sense, Gadamer, too, suggests a *suspension* of the prejudices *as* prejudices in order to make their implicit character explicit.[44] But this is just mentioned as an aside in Gadamer's account of prejudices and plays no central role in his theory, yet it does for Husserl, where this bracketing is entirely a reflective activity. It is a matter of reflection, that is, an activity of a thinking subject that deliberately reflects back upon itself. The transcendental reduction is but a radicalization of this reflection and is carried out in order to establish a sphere of immanence, in which I reflect upon my intentional acts in their world-constituting activity. Yet this still does not answer the question as to how this is possible in the first place; What motivates this first move in which I realize that I have to bracket my ordinary way of life? And why should I do this at all? As we recall from chapter 3, this cluster of questions was the problem of the "motivation for the reduction."

To Gadamer, this is an artificial problem arising from Husserl's quest for an ultimate foundation. Instead of asking, "How is it possible to disengage myself from my normal way of life and access a radically different standpoint from where I can view the constitution of the world through transcendental acts?" Gadamer asks the analogous question, "How can I become aware of prejudices as prejudices?" Gadamer saw this analogy clearly and gives an elegant answer to this question in the context of his discussion of prejudices.[45]

Indeed, our own horizon becoming explicit is something that occurs at all times, and it comes about through the confrontation with *another* horizon, for instance through the study of humanistic achievements of past writings.[46] Especially in his interpretations of poetry, Gadamer gives numerous examples of how the confrontation with the hermeneutical situation of a certain poet not only shows us that poet's horizon of understanding, but in so doing *challenges* our *own* horizon.[47] The actual work of interpretation that we perform in trying to understand a certain historical text is *not* to interpret it according to the horizon of understanding of the *author* and *her* time. Interpretation does not mean a "leap into" her horizon as if both horizons were two separate, closed-off circles. This was the method of historicism that Gadamer criticizes, that is, the idea that one can re-create the author's hermeneutical situation as a necessary precondition for understanding the meaning of a certain work of art. Such a re-creation is possible, but does not get us to the heart of the poem's meaning. Rather, in interpreting a text and realizing its timely relevance in 2010, I make it understandable *for myself*. Only then can it speak to me meaningfully and is not just a remnant of the past that should be studied out of sheer reverence for a "grand tradition." The *explication* of the poem's meaning is at the same time an *application* to my own situation. Only in this way can I understand this text not as a dated, historical piece but as something that still *speaks* to me. If the poem has become "merely historical" it has lost the power to speak to me, that is, to effect me in my current understanding. If the text, however, does speak to me, it is, to Gadamer, *classical,* and this means it is also standard-setting for other texts and, by extension, lifestyles. To say that Shakespeare's plays are standard-setting, however, does not mean that we today should write or live like Shakespeare did. When we call him a classic we mean that he had the fascinating ability to be creative in a way that his writings have to this day not become historical in the sense of being dated. Thus, this application of the historical text to my current situation is in fact a *fusion of horizons.* In order for the text to truly "speak" to me requires that the gap between both horizons has been bridged. This does not happen automatically when understanding occurs—an event that can always fail. Yet it can only be successful if that with which I fuse my own horizon has been wrested from the historicizing tendency that is rampant in philological research. Interpretation of past material has to be in this sense "existential."

This is the "philological" background of Gadamer's hermeneutics, which was originally a doctrine of interpretation with respect to juridical and religious texts. "Fusion of horizons" is Gadamer's response to historicism in philology and philosophical historiography. The history of philosophy must not be written as a mere history of problems but as a history of effects that form our current horizon. Such a fusion, however, applies universally, and this is what Gadamer's attempt at *philosophical* hermeneutics is all about. Understanding, conceived universally, is not merely understanding a certain *item,* but also its horizon. Understanding is nothing but a fusion of horizons that is "always already" taking place. Understanding is in all cases a fusion of horizons. Application of the text to my own situation, if correctly carried out, is not a violent appropriation in the sense of exploiting the text for my own purposes. Rather, all effective explication of another horizon is already an application *to* my own—otherwise it would not make sense for me—and at the same time an explication *of* my horizon that was otherwise unthematic to myself. Without a fusion of horizons, the text would remain forever alien to me, on the one hand. On the other, I could not even get to know my *own* horizon *as* horizon. But this fusion is not the result of a reflective act, but something that happens *always already.*

To return to the Husserlian question: how is it possible to become aware of my situation *as* situated, that is, of my prejudices *as* prejudices? The answer is: my prejudices are *always already* being challenged by other prejudices, not only by texts, but also by others. Prejudices always already confront one another and not only when I visit, for example, a foreign culture and experience a fundamental unfamiliarity, which is an extreme (or at least extraordinary) limit-case. Confrontation happens all the time. This does not mean that both "sets" of prejudices cancel each other out. Rather, only in this way do they clearly come to the fore and, ideally, complement each other. This is what understanding is all about. The fusion of horizons is not a synthesis of different orders of prejudices into one "pool" of indifference or a higher synthesis. Understanding is comprehending the otherness of the other; an otherness that both challenges, questions, confirms, and expands *my own* horizon and, thereby, first *constitutes* it. This applies to the experience with other persons, societies, and cultures. In order for fusions to come about, it requires an interest and a close attention to the other as other, that is, to not "pull" her "into" my horizon but to accept her otherness and yet understand *why* she is different from myself. Thus, becoming aware of my prejudices does not automatically mean doing away with them—unless, of course, they turn out to be unfounded or unfair or in any other way "negative." I can realize that someone else will always remain alien to me and that means, conversely, that I might have prejudices that I *see as* prejudices but will never be able to fully give up, contrary to my better judgment.

The question hence, how it is possible to become aware of my prejudices, turns out to be an artificial problem. Gadamer's point is that it is more appropriate to turn the whole problem around by saying, to the contrary, that it requires a deliberate ignoring or narrow-mindedness *not* to recognize that my way of viewing the world is always surrounded by other competing worldviews. Anyone who shows but the slightest interest in the other is already willing to put one's own prejudices on the line and be prepared to be proven otherwise. Only unenlightened people consider their own opinions to be set in stone. Hermeneutics, as Gadamer emphasizes, is about listening to the other, and this listening presupposes the willingness to grant the other that she might be right, no matter how I may disagree initially. This principal readiness to reconsider my own position points to the moral dimension of Gadamer's thought especially emphasized in his last phase. The lifeworld as a moral playground is not a sphere of purely rational principles but of intersubjective relations guided by *phronesis*.[48] In this sense, Gadamer, while aligning himself with the Enlightenment and Kant's critique, has also pointed to the importance of the completion of Kant's critical business through the critique of judgment.[49]

Thus, the different horizons of understanding that we encounter are not self-enclosed spheres, as Husserl thought when he stressed that we need special methodological tools in order to switch from one attitude to another. The way he saw it, without such breaks through reflection the horizons are like endlessly expandable "bubbles." There is no limit to what I can view from the standpoint of a certain horizon. While this is descriptively true, it disregards the evident fact that we switch between horizons all the time, and this happens mostly without our own willing. Husserl never really considered possible this switch from one attitude to another other than through an unmotivated leap. In Husserl's scenario there can be no fusion; rather, there would occur a violent clash of horizons. Gadamer's idea of a fusion of horizons is a deliberate answer to this problem. When two horizons meet, a fusion occurs, but not in the sense of creating a new higher "synthesis," but—ideally—in resituating the agents' standpoints.[50] The fusion means, on the lowest level possible, recognizing the other standpoint *as* another standpoint that I *can* potentially understand, even if I may not be *willing* to do this. But *recognizing* the difference of the other horizon is already a fusion of sorts. Yet even a "full" fusion does not mean that I become "dissolved" in it.[51] I can conceivably do away with my own horizon willingly, but this is subordination under the dominance of another horizon, for example, in a wholesale takeover of another's standpoint (something that politicians will know well who run on a common platform of their party). A fusion of horizons does not mean abandoning one's own standpoint but finding one's place in the world vis-à-vis the multitude of possible horizons. The world in its plurality presents always already a fusion of these pluralities into a complex worldview—not as a grand synthesis but as a horizon that is essentially plural. The question is not, "How can I get from the plurality of horizons to the lifeworld as the horizon of all horizons?"; rather, the lifeworld is already "constituted" as a sphere of plurality of which a single, subjective standpoint is but an abstraction. Thus, Gadamer merely turns Husserl's paradigm on its head, without abandoning it altogether. This is a way of seeing the image of the subject as a "flickering light" in a new way, as the demand to assert ourselves in the wake of available standpoints in the world. Maybe it can even become an ideal to remain a flickering light that blows in different directions in considering different viewpoints, instead of lighting a torch that will not budge in any direction or, worse, igniting a bonfire that draws flies to the light.

Finally, it is a logical consequence that Gadamer's sketch of a philosophical hermeneutics in *Truth and Method* culminates with the turn to language and to the "logic of question and answer."[52] What is presented as a return to Platonic dialectics is equally a modification of Husserl's theory of intentionality with the structure of intention and fulfillment. From the standpoint of hermeneutics, however, there is no such thing as an isolated intention. As Gadamer would agree, every intention comes forth from an attitude or a horizon, which is a horizon of pre-understanding.

That which is intended finds its fulfillment from within this horizon of understanding. That is, every act is already an explicit articulation of a prejudice, for example, as a judgment that comes from a pre-thematic sphere of prejudgments. This means, however, that it can only become explicit when *questioned.* Thus, every intention must be understood as answering a question posed beforehand from someone else and in turn as posing a new question. Every fulfillment of my intention is an *answer* to a question that comes forth from the unthematic horizon of my pre-understanding. In this sense, every intention is *already* an answer to a question that has already been posed. Every intention is, in truth, merely a moment within a dialogical relation with others and is already an answer to their questions, and this answer in turn poses a question to the partner(s) of a dialogue. Intentionality, thus, is not a structure of a solipisistically conceived consciousness but articulates the logic that underlies communicative interaction that, in turn, is guided by language. *"Being that can be understood is language"* (1989, 450).

Thus, to summarize the exegetical sections of this chapter, Husserl's phenomenology offers a rich account of the lifeworld in the plurality of its meaningful horizons that correspond to a plurality of possible subjective interactions with, and comportments toward (through the concept of "attitudes"), this lifeworld. The turn to the "genetic" phenomenological method opens the view to the lifeworld as an essentially "historical" phenomenon. Yet Husserl only thematizes *transcendental genesis* as a history of intentionality, not factual history *itself* due to his transcendental commitment that is focused entirely on the "internal" genesis of intentionality as subjective "contributions" to the world, rather than on the history of the world itself as a world formed by human consciousness. Husserl's genetic phenomenology cannot (and, to be fair, does not want to) account for history itself. Gadamer applies the concept of genesis to the dimension of factual *history* and thereby *historicizes* Husserl's concept of genesis, that is, he applies genesis to history itself as a tradition that has formed our current horizon as a situation of prejudices. He thereby (as he sees it) "frees" Husserl's account of the lifeworld from his transcendental and eidetic bedrock. This is an important *transformation* of Husserl's original theory as it allows for an account of the lifeworld in its *historical concretion,* which is a different concretion from the one aimed for in Husserl's notion of concretion. It is a concretion that is equal to facticity, without the perceived need for a transcendental questioning-back. Yet this effort is not entirely naive, for in this recasting Gadamer *overcomes* problems in Husserl, such as the never clarified possibility of shifting back and forth between different horizons. At the same time, Gadamer *expands* Husserl's account of experience as taking place within a horizon of acts by adding prejudices as necessary elements for understanding. Lastly, Gadamer's concept of the *fusion of horizons* reveals Husserl's question as to how one can become aware of one's prejudices *as* prejudices as an artificial problem. It is a fiction to believe that we must take our starting point from one's singular horizon and see how one can gain access to another horizon. Instead, our own horizon only *forms* itself in the first place through a constant interaction and fusion with other horizons. The lifeworld is inherently a *communicative* structure.

The result so far is that Gadamer, though he departed from Husserl's transcendental-eidetic paradigm, fruitfully expands on Husserl's phenomenology of the lifeworld stemming from the theory of intentionality expanded toward a notion of horizon. He is thereby giving up on the transcendental-eidetic paradigm, but this is not to say that his positive suggestions could not be reintegrated into that very framework; there seems no reason why not. But with his critique Gadamer also believes that he is not following Husserl's foundationalism. He seemingly departs from Husserl's Cartesianism because, to Gadamer, there is no ultimate transcendental consciousness that constitutes history. This sketch presented here, however, also intended to question this image of Husserl's genetic phenomenology as being still "Cartesian." Insofar as Husserl conceives of transcendental subjectivity as *intersubjectivity,* and the lifeworld as a product of an *intersubjective* constitution, the label "Cartesianism" is not applicable, as has already become clear in part 1 of this book. It is thus not necessary to identify foundationalism with Cartesianism. The anti-foundationalist critique targets "the wrong guy." So far I was able to carry out this discussion entirely without reverting to the Heideggerian element that helped shape Gadamer's account of effective history. In the last section, I will first show how Gadamer's theory of effective history ultimately does take up anti-subjectivist elements and conclude by pointing out why I think this is a fatal mistake and that it is better to insist on the subjective character of effective history.

Why Effective History Needs to Be
Construed as Subjective

In order to criticize Gadamer's concept of effective history, we need to distinguish the non-foundationalist reading from the one just given. For this purpose, let us review some of the critiques that Gadamer has faced in the history of his hermeneutics' reception. In the wake of the critique of ideology in the 1960s (especially through Apel and Habermas), Gadamer was charged with an overemphasis and an "apotheosis" (Apel's phrase) of tradition. Accordingly, tradition in Gadamer can be read as an encompassing, overarching structure that one cannot escape and that leads to a fatalism over against the blind forces of history, very much in the sense of Heidegger's fate of being (*Seinsgeschick*) that humans can merely respond to but have no power to alter.[53] A refusal to rationally legitimate the meaning that "reveals" itself in history amounts to a "capitulation of reason" (Apel).[54] According to this reading, Gadamer went *too far* in his critique of Enlightenment and ends up, in effect, in an anti-Enlightenment (or pre- or post-Enlightenment) stance. Gadamer moreover supported this reading by insisting that the effective-historical consciousness is "more being than conscious-being" (more *Sein* than *Bewusstsein*) (1986a, 495–96)— a modification that Gadamer felt necessary to counter Heidegger's critique that *Truth and Method* remained bound to a traditional concept of consciousness that Heidegger himself had long left behind. It is fate to which one is given over rather than something over which we as rational subjects have any control. The difference to Heidegger is that this fate is, in Gadamer, history and the tradition itself, not being with a capital "b."

Thus, how does Gadamer characterize this effective history proper? So far Gadamer's account has mapped tightly onto that of Husserl with the necessary modifications discussed. Another element now enters as Gadamer actually describes the way in which the fusion of horizons occurs with respect to the past. While Gadamer would acknowledge that history and tradition are things that pertain to human beings, he does not think it is something that these subjects can control and actively shape or form. It is something that we as people of the present have no control over in the way this tradition has effected our current understanding. Rather, it is the "essence" of history itself that shapes the way we understand ourselves. This history effects us in its own manner and according to its own, impenetrable logic and is in this sense effective historical consciousness that is more being than conscious-being; it is *facticity* rather than reflection. What Gadamer battles with this concept is the ideal of reflective philosophy (*Reflexionsphilosophie*) as the philosophical belief that one could reflect one's way out of history to reach an ideal standpoint to reconstruct a teleological history of self-consciousness or from which one would be able to establish timeless, eidetic truths about humanity. This was his critique of Hegel and, in the same vein, also of Husserl. But this critique also entails a critique of the idea that the understanding of ourselves *in the here and now* is a matter of reflection rather than an unthematic understanding of ourselves as having been shaped by our prejudices. Understanding is, to say it paradoxically, something that *achieves us*, rather than something that *we consciously achieve*.

In this sense, Gadamer explicitly invokes Husserl's concept of horizon to account for this situation, with a special emphasis that the horizon specifically refers to man's *finitude* (1989, 307).[55] Finitude has a lineage going back to Heidegger and Nietzsche that departs from Husserl. To be finite means that we cannot reflect our way out of horizons (or to believe that we can is an utter naïveté). However, the character of horizon is its essential openness. Specifically, our current horizon of understanding is open toward the past. Our horizon is always already historical in the sense of having been formed by the past. Thus, our current horizon "embraces all that which historical consciousness includes" (309). This historical consciousness that forms our current understanding is, however, nothing that we constitute; rather, it constitutes *us* as it forms the structure of our prejudiced horizon. The past and its tradition "obtain" and remain valid through tradition's being given in the way it hands itself down to us. This is why Gadamer likes to employ the impersonal term *"Überlieferung"* ("being-handed-down") as something that hands *itself down* to us and *creates* our understanding as a fusion between past and present. Even if we attempt to accomplish such an understanding of the past—and hence our present—*actively*, consciously, it can at best be described as "wakefulness of historical-effective consciousness" itself (312). Tradition is something that obtains with its own force of authority "without reasoning" (285). In this sense, understanding is not something that we can accomplish; rather, it *happens in* us. Understanding is acknowledging the effective history in which we find ourselves when we realize that our current horizon of understanding is only what it is when it is open to the past. However, as we have seen, this past is itself an anonymous force that effects us without being able to say why—this is what our finitude is about. Thus, *"understanding is not to be conceived as so much like an activity of subjectivity but as moving into [Einrücken]*[56] *an event of Überlieferung in which present and past are constantly mediated"* (295). It is in this context that we find the already quoted sentence that the subject is but a "flickering light" in the closed circuits of historical life (281).

Gadamer does not say who it is that effects us, and deliberately so. For giving account of this "who" would again consider it as a subject that "does" something consciously—something he wants to overcome. History is a "closed circuit" and impenetrable by any kind of reflection on the part of a subject. Any such "penetration" is no reflection at all in the sense of rational thought. It is at the most a meditation upon the prejudices that we have been endowed with through our tradition. We cannot, Gadamer maintains, say why we have been given these rather than other prejudices. This is why "the classical" is Gadamer's prime example of how effective history functions. The classical is something that prevails through history as something that speaks to us, no matter how much time has passed. A fusion is always possible. Yet, what accounts for the fact that some items of our history speak more strongly than others, why Sophocles and not Kallimachos, why Shakespeare and not Marlowe, why Goethe and not Stifter? Gadamer's point is precisely: we do not and we cannot know. We cannot give *reasons why* this is the case: history in its anonymous functioning simply phases out one thing in favor of something else and can be quite relentless at that. We simply cannot give *reasons* as to why one item prevails while another perishes and is lost forever to our historical consciousness. To establish "classics" is history's way of "acting." The dominance and prevailing of the classical can be seen by the fact that we cannot fight it but only accept it. "We call classical what prevails in the face of historical critique because its historical dominance, the binding power of its handed-down and conserving validity, lies already before all historical reflection and prevails within it" (1989, 292). History, in establishing classical traditions, exerts a normative[57] effect on us, placing norms on us as to how we should think and act and how we must listen to history, for not listening to history would deliberately cut us off from that which has made, and continues to make, our current understanding possible. Thus, effective history is entirely a-subjective if we mean by subjective something rational, understandable, scrutinizable, and something that can be critiqued from (another) subjective standpoint. In this sense, Gadamer has attempted to move away from foundationalism. History cannot be described in any way as subjective. History can at best be conceived as a force that comes over us and in the light of which we can be grateful to keep the flame of our self-consciousness burning. This is the sense in which Gadamer considers his hermeneutics as anti-foundational and anti-subjectivistic.

I begin my critique with questioning Gadamer's assumption as to the normative force of the classical. Is it really true that we cannot know why something is classical whereas everything else literally goes down in history, rather than *going down as historical*? Is historical research, say literary criticism armed with the methods of history, psychoanalysis, sociology, and so on, really not in the position to say why we consider Goethe a classic rather than a more minor figure at the same time, such as an epigone? I would question this alleged impossibility and insist, rather, that one can—if not entirely, then at least to a very large extent and ideally in totality—reconstruct why Goethe became such a classic. The reasons would be, for example, that he was able to accomplish a combination of random factors such as the following. For instance, he tackled themes that were prevalent in his society not only in Germany but in larger Europe, that is, he had a special way of addressing what people were especially concerned with in his time. Furthermore, he wrote in a way that appealed to the masses due to his outstanding linguistic talent. Also, the society he lived in was especially susceptible to the type of art that he turned out, in this case, in a nation that had come to a high linguistic level and appreciation due to historical, cultural, and political circumstances. Moreover, due to these factors that made him famous already in his lifetime, he became a classic already before his death, raising him to a classic before the "time gap" that Gadamer deems necessary for a classic. And he remains a classic because, after all, the society in Germany and the societies in the Western world have not changed as significantly so as to make him obsolete.

However, the Western world has changed in a way that certain topics simply do not speak to us Westerners any longer, such as the much-talked about topic of mésalliance that only had an appeal before the possibility of divorce and at a time when the strata of society were still very rigid. However, this topic might speak to other cultures where this still presents an issue. Thus, in this sense it is entirely possible that what we consider classic—and that Western civilization has considered classic for over 2,000 years—ceases to be considered classic. There is no reason to believe that the classic will last forever or even as long as there is an established "tradition" (modern Europe, "the West," etc.). An element of historical consciousness is historical forgetfulness as its necessary downside. The reasons why something would cease to be classical can again be elucidated through historical, sociological, and so on research—for example, the advance of feminism and gender equality in Western nations that renders many of Goethe's presentations of gender relationships obsolete. Thus, it is true neither (a) that the classic has a normative effect for all times once established as classic; nor (b) that we cannot give reasons—historical, sociological, philosophical, psychological—for why something would *become* classic in the first place as opposed to something ephemeral.

These reasons just recounted for why one author or text became a classic are, however, nothing but an account of activities of *subjects* that did certain things in the past. These subjects did not merely answer to a tradition that came over them as a blind force, but history is a history of human subjects who do certain things, are engaged in certain projects, and effect each other, all for certain reasons. History and the way it shapes a tradition as the backdrop of our understanding is at all times a history of subjective acts. This does not mean that subjects have to be at all times aware of their deeds and thoughts and sentiments. The prejudices that I harbor might be unknown to me in my normal everyday life and deeply rooted, but I can make them explicit when I reflect upon them, or at the very least I can be made aware of them when stumped upon them by another person. Reflection need not be a solipsistic act. But, more importantly, prejudices (*Vor-Urteile*) were at one point someone else's active judgments (*Urteile*). As anonymous and implicit and hidden as they might be, they were at one point in time someone else's active and conscious judgments. These judgments need not be rational and reasonable or moral; they can be born out of hatred, disregard, disinterest, being misinformed, but they are judgments made by subjects like us out of certain motives that can always be reconstructed. This is essentially the notion of "passivity" in Husserl's genetic-reconstructive phenomenology: subjectivity is not the same as rationality, and rationality—in the sense of conscious thought and judgment—can be traced all the way down to pre-philosophical, pre-rational, pre-predicative *experience*.

Let us take the controversial issue of racism: the (to our enlightened minds) bad prejudices involved in discriminating against other human beings do not come out of nowhere and for no reason—admittedly no *good* reason, but reasons nevertheless. Racism as the perceived inferiority of a people due to certain racial traits stems from judgments that a given group of subjects made with respect to others based on their own prejudices, which were once someone else's judgments, and so on. They are judgments and subjective all the way down to experience, in this case, the experience of someone else's physical otherness. Indeed, only this recognition is the full enactment of Enlightenment, for only when this has been realized can one counter something like racism, *not* as some "weird belief" that certain people had at certain times that we can no longer understand, but as beliefs they held for certain reasons, even if, or especially because, these reasons are faulty, mistaken, misinformed, or malicious. It is a prime research topic for disciplines such as historiography or sociology to reconstruct how these terrible attitudes arose, from which "reasons" informed by ideology or similar motives. It is possible to *understand* the racist, without endorsing or sharing that view.

Hence, "empathy" for others is always possible, even if we from our standpoint deem these others as "incredible" and rightfully outrageous. Only this realization makes injustice and bad presuppositions understandable and not as beliefs that some people held whom we now consider monsters (e.g., slave owners). They might have been monsters, but *human* monsters that *therefore* can be understood. The remedy to avoid monstrous behavior in the future history of humankind can only be a reconstruction of how these presuppositions came about in the first place, and not as a happening that just occurred and in the face of which one can merely throw up one's arms in the attitude of *je ne sais quoi* or even angry or saddened disbelief or resignation. It would be cynical with respect to victims of past atrocities to simply say, "It just happened." One must at all times attempt to reconstruct the subjective viewpoints that informed people's actions. Only this is Enlightenment: to bring light to dark, murky regions of the human soul that make atrocities possible.

This is why effective history, if it is proposed as so fundamentally a-subjective, winds up as a fatalism and irrationalism with respect to the events in history, and it potentially exculpates mankind from its actions and responsibilities and the necessity to explore the reasons that made subjects do what they did. This is the only appropriation adequate with respect to the past: to reconstruct the reasons and motives for certain events in history, in order to understand what made them come about to counter fatal developments at the moment of their inception. Gadamer's account of effective history renders this impossible. Effective-historical consciousness takes on the role of the *über*-subject in history. It may be conceived as anonymous but it acts as an agent nevertheless. In this sense, Gadamer remains a foundationalist, albeit not in the epistemological sense of Husserl, but perhaps in a more dangerous "fundamentalism." Divorcing history from subjectivity is dangerous as it opens the door to irrationalism and fatalism just outlined. History and its logic would take on the role of a subject that acts "somehow," that is to say, in a way that we cannot comprehend; they would be the utter "alien subject." In this sense, Gadamer's account differs in no way from that of Heidegger (without Heidegger's mystical-eschatological elements), that is, of posing a fate of being (or history) that controls us like puppets. Such a scenario must be resisted at all costs. Contrary to Gadamer's own assertions, he parts with the tradition of Enlightenment the moment he takes the step toward effective history. Gadamer believed himself to be a part of the "completed Enlightenment" because he made a case for why prejudices cannot be overcome; we will always have them, just as all of our acts will always presuppose a horizon. This cannot be doubted. But Enlightenment is only complete when one realizes that prejudices need to be scrutinized by common sense at all times. Acknowledging *having* prejudices is one thing, *accepting* them as something that cannot change is another.

In conclusion, one has to insist that this effective-historical consciousness is decidedly a *consciousness*. As Husserl emphasized, the genesis of meaning is a genesis of rationally acting human *subjects*.[58] It is not an anonymous history of being but a history of human *agents* that always interact in the way of mutual discussion, disagreement, agreement, and new disagreement, with mutual checks and balances and reciprocal critique. This is also why history will never stop. History certainly does not always progress rationally, but it is at all times a history of human *consciousness*. In order to claim this, one does not have to endorse a Hegelian teleological view of humanity; and Husserl's teleology is regulative idea, not factual goal. Regardless of whether we are headed toward a higher humanity, it does not change the fact that this history is a history of human consciousness that is a history of human *inter*subjectivity in endless conversation questioning mutually held prejudices. This does not bar factual history from going awry, but it would indeed be a "capitulation of reason" to attribute fatal developments to a tradition that "comes upon us" as a dark, anonymous force. It does not mean that we are at all times in control of our destiny, but to take this possibility away from us would amount to an utter fatalism that is unacceptable in view of the catastrophes of the twentieth and the beginning twenty-first century. We are morally called upon to reconstruct where, and especially why, human reason went astray in order to counter any new dangerous developments from the outset. Gadamer's emphasis on an anonymous effective history in truth runs counter to the moral dimension of his philosophical hermeneutics, according to which any moral reflection starts, and ends, with dialogue between equal partners in the lifeworld, governed by common sense, the Greek ideal of *phronesis* that Gadamer himself invokes. *Phronesis* as the common sense displayed in the natural attitude leads us back to the pre-philosophical lifeworld and its internal "logic," a sphere that was opened up in its universal dimensions in Husserl's phenomenology and further explored by Gadamer. This "ethos" of the lifeworld calls on us to continue the conversation of humankind in ever-expanding "fusions of horizons."

From Gadamer's Toward a Husserlian Hermeneutics

In the previous chapters we saw how certain elements of Gadamer's can well be integrated into a Husserlian account of the lifeworld as a historical world of tradition. That is to say, one does not have to follow Gadamer's conscious move away from a transcendental to a factual account of the lifeworld in order to utilize in a beneficial manner his elements for the Husserlian framework. In fact, as the tendency of this interpretation has made clear, it is even better to "re-transcendentalize" Gadamer's account in order to "fit it" into the Husserlian account. The move away from the transcendental to the factual was, following Heidegger, Gadamer's slippery slope into historical fatalism. It is a path that should not be followed *if* one is committed, as Husserl, to the ideal of the Enlightenment, and it should be resisted vigorously for that very reason.

However, these critical remarks on Gadamer have already revealed *ex negativo* some elements of how one would have to draft a Husserlian transcendental-phenomenological hermeneutics and what it would look like. In the following, last chapter, then, these elements shall be spelled out in the positive in order to weave the threads together into a Husserlian hermeneutic phenomenology as a philosophy of culture. This last chapter, then, cannot be more than a draft of what such a hermeneutics would mean and encompass. Part of it has already been said in the previous chapters, where actual descriptions of the lifeworld were given. Hence, what will be said about a Husserlian "hermeneutic phenomenology" in the concluding chapter is not to be read as opening up new horizons. Instead, this last chapter is intended to pull together what has been said in an encompassing and summarizing manner and to show what Husserl's philosophical vision entails concerning his view of the Enlightenment. As the reader recalls, this view has already been expounded at the end of part 1 (chapter 6). Hence, similar to chapter 6, this last chapter is a way of coming full circle and has, together with chapter 6, the function of summarizing what has been said and pointing to further horizons of research following the Husserlian philosophical project.

Husserl's "Hermeneutical Phenomenology" as a Philosophy of Culture

> Our historical existence [*Dasein*] moves within innumerable traditions.
> —Hua VI, 366

Introduction

Scanning the multitude of texts from the vast amount of Husserl's writings of the 1920s and '30s—the period of his work of interest here—one cannot help but be struck by the multitude of themes with which Husserl was wrestling in these last years of his life: certainly the well-known theme of the method of the transcendental reduction, but also issues concerning the lifeworld, time-consciousness, constitution of space, teleological and theological problems, intersubjectivity and communal life, history, and still others.[1] Choosing a representative amount of these texts in a fairly comprehensible selection is no easy task, as every editor of volumes of the *Husserliana* will certainly testify, and it is much less easy to find guiding clues among this vast amount of texts, themes, and topics. Husserl was keenly aware of this seeming "mess." Thus it is striking that in these late texts he was clearly intent on *merging* these different dimensions of problems and was attempting to view them together in different ways and from different angles. It is as if Husserl each day anew shook the kaleidoscope of his phenomenology and looked through the lens again and again, only to discover new connections, ramifications, and surprisingly unanticipated combinations which he then pursued, again getting sidetracked.

Yet, all of these topics of the mature Husserl have to be seen within a matrix of problems and ultimately need to be connected to get "the full picture"—a synopsis that not even Husserl himself was able to achieve. Indeed, Husserl's ultimate failure to produce a comprehensive "system of phenomenology" was in part due to his unceasing attempts to accomplish such a grand overview. But maybe we should be grateful for this, because such a system might have "enshrined" what was to remain a working philosophy with open horizons. Moreover, it was his personal tragedy that he was never satisfied with what he had achieved and always attempted to gain new insights from new perspectives. Phenomenology *itself* was like the infamous perceptual object that always shows new adumbrations and whose full comprehension lies in infinity.

One line of thought that emerges in these late manuscripts, and with an eye to a synoptic reading just hinted at, is something that one might term Husserl's "hermeneutical phenomenology." Now it is clear that after Heidegger and especially after Gadamer's philosophical hermeneutics one can no longer use this notion with innocence. It is a loaded term with which we today associate concepts such as "understanding," "fusion of horizons," and "history of effects" and which we take to present a very well worked-out theory that Gadamer presented first in 1960 and steadily revised until the last years of his life.[2] In view of this, I am not claiming that we can find anything in Husserl that would resemble such a consciously developed theory, but rather elements or pieces that one may put together in the way attempted here. Yet what one can call a hermeneutical phenomenology, or elements of it, is certainly not restricted to Gadamer.

Indeed, as the previous chapter has shown, it is rather the case that something like Gadamer's theory rests on Husserlian foundations. Hence it will not be entirely surprising that one can spell out such a "hermeneutic phenomenology" in Husserl, though, of course, in the framework of his phenomenology as a *transcendental* undertaking, which shares many elements with the *other* transcendental philosophy discussed here, namely the transcendental theory of culture of the Marburg school. Hence, the manner in which Husserl's hermeneutic phenomenology will be presented here will be as a philosophy of culture in the manner specified in the latter half of the chapters of this volume. If the focus here is on its "hermeneutic" element—as it has already been shown over the course of this book how Husserl himself broadens his method from description to interpretation—this means that this concluding chapter will spell out, not so much the *material elements* of such a philosophy of culture, but rather its *methodology*. As we shall see, this problem will bring us full circle again to the problems with which this volume started out, namely, the issues of the method of phenomenology and Husserl's phenomenology as a peculiar shape of *Enlightenment philosophy*.

A "hermeneutics" in Husserl's late thought appears in a different context than one might at first assume. That is, when identifying such a hermeneutics in Husserl, I am not comparing terminological overlaps of terms, which really mean different things. Indeed, when one thinks of the term "hermeneutics" in Husserl's writings, what immediately springs to mind is Husserl's terming phenomenology a "hermeneutics of conscious life" in his 1931 lecture on "Phenomenology and Anthropology."[3] Here he employs this notion rather rhetorically to offer his phenomenology as an alternative to Heidegger's hermeneutics of facticity and Scheler's anthropology. This is *not* primarily what I have in mind here when I present a hermeneutical phenomenology in a Husserlian vein. Of course, what can be termed his "hermeneutic project" has commonalities with Husserl's employment of the term "hermeneutics," but "hermeneutics of conscious life" is misleading, as it implies a focus on consciousness, not on the world where it lives and dwells. But as the reader, who has followed the train of thought of this book up to now, knows, a focus on consciousness, solipsistically construed and as removed from the world, is a complete misunderstanding of Husserl's project.

Instead, Husserl's reflections turn out to be much more "hermeneutical" in the sense in which we perceive hermeneutics today. They take their point of departure from the concepts of *tradition, prejudice,* and *understanding,* concepts familiar from Gadamer, but presented with no less sophistication in the context of Husserl's thought (and, as we know from the previous chapter, they are concepts that were influential to Gadamer as well, independently of their mediation through Heidegger). Yet Husserl does not just utilize the same terms as Gadamer casually; they are employed for well-reflected systematic reasons. The reason why Husserl can offer an *alternative project* to Gadamer, which is also superior to Gadamer, is that Husserl carries out at all times such hermeneutical reflections in intimate connection to the *transcendental* problem, that is, of relating every phenomenon back to constituting subjectivity.[4] Hermeneutical questions, in Husserl's scenario, are not questions pertaining to the lifeworld *alone* and the traditions within it. Rather, they are reflections—if one may use this word, so discredited by Gadamer—that are embedded in the correlational a priori between constituting subjectivity and constituted world. This correlation can only be accessed through the Husserlian method of reflection. As such, these considerations necessarily involve the performance of the transcendental reduction. Husserl's is a philosophical hermeneutics that is impossible without relating the lifeworld back to experiencing subjects, where "experience" is more than just innocent onlooking; to the contrary, the lifeworld is the product of constitution through subjectivity on all levels, whereby phenomenology's access to this constitution is through the looking glass of consciousness. If the access to the lifeworld as a site of subjective constitution requires the reduction, this sheds a whole new light on Husserl's idea of an unprejudiced and radical new beginning in philosophy, what the epoché, as the first step of the reduction, is supposed to achieve after all. What I present in the following, hence, one could even call the "hermeneutic way" into the reduction. It will once and for all dislodge the erroneous notion that the reduction is intended to catapult us, via some magic trick, out of the world as a historical world of many opinions, into a safe realm of "pure consciousness." The reduction is the way to the world as lifeworld and world of culture; phenomenology as a hermeneutic enterprise is the manner to comprehend it; the lifeworld as a sphere of culture, finally, points to its interpretation as a realm where the human being can feel at home and come into its own; this is the ultimate position of enlightenment that a philosophy committed to the parameters of modernity can attain. The world as a world of culture is no "cold and lonely planet," but partaking in the deeds of culture in the lifeworld is the condition of the possibility of becoming human.

In order to throw Husserl's project into relief, I shall first discuss what are the minimal requirements for what one can plausibly call a philosophical hermeneutics; these requirements are formulated so as to be minimally controversial for any "theory of understanding and interpretation." But they will motivate why one is justified in placing Husserl into this tradition, although one knows that Husserl did not see himself in the lineage of "classical" hermeneutics of, say, Schleiermacher, Ranke, or Dilthey. But the little that Husserl knew of, for example, Dilthey's hermeneutics, makes it amply clear that he had a high estimation of the latter's project despite Husserl's completely different intellectual background.

In the second part I will present elements of Husserl's hermeneutical phenomenology as they emerge in his late manuscripts. These elements are in the form of Husserl's famous research notes; that is to say, they present no worked-out theories, but they are to be treated like trails that Husserl lays in the region of the phenomenological terrain. These trails meander, follow no steady course, and sometimes go in circles; yet they tread around phenomena and describe and interpret them. In following Husserl and then drawing out the conclusions that Husserl himself did not formulate, the interpreter is taking certain liberties, but this interpreter, at least, still remains on the grounds of the terrain, respecting Husserl's "zoning laws." The manuscripts dealing with these issues Husserl himself deemed as belonging to the method of the phenomenological reduction, witnessed by the fact that, in the ordering of his

Nachlass in the spring of 1935,[5] he created an entire section containing texts on this topic (the "B group"), where the texts dealing with these topics are to be found. In attempting to do justice to Husserl's own philosophical self-understanding, these manuscripts from Husserl's late phase that are the main focus of this chapter are taken from this group of texts. But as I attempted to illustrate earlier with the kaleidoscope metaphor, the issues Husserl wrestles with in these manuscripts are not only relevant in the context of the reduction but pertain to the entire scope of Husserl's thought.

A concluding part will spell out the consequences this project of a "hermeneutic phenomenology" has for Husserl's overall project as a philosophy of culture committed to the ideal of the Enlightenment.

Minimal Requirements for a Philosophical Hermeneutics

First a few remarks on hermeneutics prior to its philosophical "exploitation." I will then move on to formulate what I take to be "minimal requirements" for a hermeneutics as a *philosophical* enterprise.

Hermeneutics[6] has its origin in the context of theology and jurisprudence, where it is a methodological tool to interpret *texts*. Whoever peruses these literary documents needs help, for these (as it is agreed they are) opaque, difficult biblical passages or legislative stipulations require a special interpretive effort, a "key" in order to unlock them. They do not just open up by themselves, that is, by a superficial reading. Their difficulty lies often (though not exclusively, as Gadamer claims) in the temporal gap, for example, in how to grasp the meaning of an account, say of a Jesus story, that is set in the society of ancient Israel or the Roman Empire at large, or in how to apply the abstract law, say of the American Constitution, to a concrete situation more than 200 years later. In both cases, it is about what this text means *for us*. It is about the application to us (our times, etc.); otherwise, it would be a historicizing reading, which contrasts well with the hermeneutic task: the historicist differs from the hermeneuticist in that the former can rightfully limit his efforts to understanding Jesus in *his* time; he is interested in the *historical Jesus* and not, as is the case in hermeneutics, in what the *historical Jesus means for us today*.

The assumption for this task is, as mentioned, that the text does not readily "speak its mind," as it were. The American Constitution is a good example of why such a special effort is needed; for the situations of people

then—the Founding Fathers who drafted this document and the people
to which it pertained—and today—legal experts and the people to which
the Constitution applies today—differ so much that certain scenarios involving new "phenomena"—the Internet, birth control, or other such examples—could not in the least have been imagined by those who drafted
the Constitution. Hence, if this "old" document is not to be deemed obsolete—this is in itself the topic of a special juridical discussion—then there
must be something "hidden" in it that renders it applicable to today, what
is usually referred to as its "core," "intention," "gist," or the like. But what
this could be is not immediately obvious.[7]

The method of *hermeneúein,* "interpreting" or *auslegen,* involves special means of how one goes about unlocking these closed texts, making them understandable by explicating their presumably multilayered
meaning or aspects. This process of "unlocking" entails certain canonical
methodological steps. To these belong, for example, explicating the *intention* of the authors, the *horizon* of their understanding, and the problem of *applying* this intention to our horizon of understanding. Traditional devices in text interpretation are, for instance, to move from light
to darkness, that is, to start out from that which one understands to that
which one does not. Or the principle of the "more difficult reading,"
that is, when confronted with two interpretations of the same passage
and one is simple, the other difficult, to stick to the more difficult one,
at least at first. Broadly stated, the goal of interpreting is to bring light
into dark passages, or to make understandable what is at first not understood. Understanding is not something that just comes as a gift from the
gods (although the origin of the term "hermeneutics" comes from the
Greek god Hermes who delivers divine messages to humans); rather, understanding must be *produced.* And the object of this understanding is a
literary document in the broadest sense, the manifestation of a human
statement from times past that makes a claim (explicitly or not) to "universality," that is, to not being bound to its day and age. Hence, not every
object of the past is an object for hermeneutics.

Dilthey and especially Heidegger, both of whom were very knowl-
edgeable regarding these theological and juridical traditions, are responsible for placing hermeneutics into the philosophical context. A *philosophical* hermeneutics has to do, not with *texts,* but with *life itself.* Life is
something that is in need of interpretation, *because* it is first and foremost not understood. Or rather, it is not *truly* understood when simply
lived through. That is to say, life's everyday understanding is based on an
explicit pre-understanding that is not transparent to us as we go about
our daily business. What philosophy needs to clarify, hence, are these
pre-understandings, preconceived opinions and biases that govern our

everyday understanding. They *seem* understood, but in truth aren't. In this sense, the problem philosophical hermeneutics faces is not all that different from the Socratic situation. Socrates asks his interlocutor to tell him what a universal concept, such as virtue, is and that person replies by mentioning virtuous *things,* thereby implying a pre-understanding of what virtue *itself* is and which makes it possible to identify virtuous *things* as "partaking" in the idea of virtue. But one need not assume a Platonic *tópos hyperouránios* to conceptualize the difference between the application of something and the knowledge about it. Where philosophical hermeneutics fundamentally differs from something like Platonic or modern Enlightenment (in its pre-Kantian sense), however, is to see these prejudices and presuppositions not as a bad thing, as something to be eliminated at all costs, but as necessary "conditions of possibility" of any understanding. In this sense, Gadamer has aptly, and in accordance with Dilthey and Heidegger, spoken of a "rehabilitation of prejudices" as something that does not need to be overcome—an impossible task—but as something that can be *understood,* yet not uplifted, because the general structure of a judgment (*Urteil*) resting on a prejudice (*Vorurteil*) holds universally.

Thus, the move from "traditional" (text-based) to philosophical hermeneutics consists in essence in universalizing hermeneutics' scope of application, from texts to life itself; this move is a consistent one, if one can agree that texts are a mere expression of this life as it is lived. Hermeneutics thus takes on an existential dimension, and hence it is no accident that it could come to such fruition in Heidegger's project of a "hermeneutics of facticity" of concrete human *Dasein.* Just like certain texts, this "everyday" quotidian form of existence is opaque and is thus in need of a *specific method designed to unlock* what is "always already" *locked.* This is what makes hermeneutics a *philosophical* hermeneutics, as it has a universal function as opposed to the limited function before. But it shares in common with its traditional form the assumption that its task is the explication of something that is in need of elucidation or interpretation. And finally, that which is in need of interpretation does not always *seem* to have this need; only questioning it, making it explicit, reveals obscurities. A poem might be "clear" after a first reading, but upon closer inspection, it reveals an abyss of darkness; the same goes for life itself. But what ultimately makes this task a philosophical one is the task of not just explaining this initial obscurity, but of *justifying* it. It is not a neutral task, hence, but one that asks for the justification of certain claims, once made explicit.[8]

These considerations allow us to formulate *three minimal require-*

ments for a philosophical hermeneutics. A philosophical hermeneutics
has the task

1. of bringing to attention the insurmountable fact *that* each understanding rests on a certain *implicit* pre-understanding, that is, of *indicating*
   or *identifying* this fact;
2. of making this fact—that all understanding rests on a pre-
   understanding—*explicit,* and thereby raising the issue of its *justification;*
   and finally,
3. of explaining the *origin* and *genesis* of this pre-understanding, that is,
   of reconstructing how this pre-understanding came about in the first
   place.

To spell this triad out: a specific task may be the interpretation of
the utterance X on the part of person A. Task 1 is to explicate that this
utterance rests on a pre-understanding, which *might not be* explicit to the
one who uttered it (i.e., it is not a *necessary* characteristic of X that A's pre-
understanding is implicit). Part of this task is to spell it out, in the (simplified) form of "A says X, but A says so because A has a certain horizon H
of understanding and X is an expression of H, and H may be described
as . . ." Thus, the horizon of understanding is what is mostly and at least
partially the dark ground upon which one walks. Task 2 is the justification
of this horizon, in the form: "Is it justified to claim X based on the horizon H?" The answer can be no—or yes. In other words, the justificatory
work regarding H and X as stemming from H need not reject either. It
could reject one or the other (when, e.g., X does not necessarily follow
from H) or both, but need not. But the further task within this task is to
justify H itself. As becomes clear, tasks 1 and 2 are comparable to Kant's
quid facti and *quid iuris* questions. Task 3, then, places this "static" consideration into a genetic context by delving into the (temporal, historic)
depths and unearths the origins of H. But this is an extension of the justificatory task, insofar as it is not merely descriptive, but also interpretive
and explanatory (or "reconstructive," to use a term from the previous
chapters). This task, as a philosophical one, should ideally (itself an infinite task) be neutral and ideology-free. Thus, "justification of H" does not
mean to explain that H is good (and hence to be endorsed) or bad (and
hence to be rejected), but simply an explication of the origins and internal structures that have shaped H as the background assumption that
makes X possible.

To give an example, which is a typical one in the framework of
political philosophy (as a critique of discriminatory -isms): A may be a

white, heterosexual male, X is a derogatory remark about someone else who does not share A's traits just mentioned. The task then is to explicate how it was possible for A to say X by laying out his horizon of understanding H that made this possible. The next task, then, is to explain (justify) how X became possible as an expression of H; for example, it may not be obvious that X is an expression of H. The last task, finally, is to explain the origins of H (in A's history, his psychology, etc.).

All of this is a reconstruction of the *conditions of the possibility of X*. It is, in this sense, a transcendental task. A hermeneutics that deserves the title "philosophical" thus can rightfully be titled "transcendental," even if it does not posit a transcendental subject (of the Kantian or Husserlian sort). Two things may be pointed out in this task: first, it is clear that it is a scientific task in that it has a clearly defined methodology, but that its results will not be fixed, apodictic, and clear and distinct as in, say, mathematics. Second, hermeneutics' task is an endless one. This explains, to use a canonical distinction already operative in Dilthey and the neo-Kantians, why such a hermeneutics is, albeit a science, a discipline located more on the side of the *human sciences* (the *Geisteswissenschaften*) than on the natural sciences. Due to its peculiar subject matter—human life and understanding in the broadest sense—an interpretation of its motives, drives, intentions, aims, goals, and so on will be an endless approximation, but thereby not futile or unscientific.

Let this suffice for a *positive* account of an ideal type of theory of hermeneutics on a high level of formality. This means, *negatively:* while I *do* take it as a necessary requirement for a philosophical hermeneutics to stipulate *what* the origin or the "motor" is that drives the production and development of prejudices, it is here that hermeneutical philosophers differ, namely in the explanation of the origin of H. For instance, *Dilthey,* who was the first to work out a hermeneutics as a method germane to the human sciences, proposed as such an origin certain *types* of worldviews that have evolved over the course of history, expressing different aspects of this thing called life.[9] As *Heidegger* moved from a hermeneutics of factical *Dasein* to a history of being, the decisive force behind humans' understanding of world was declared to be *Being*. It is Being that over the course of history reveals itself in different ways to which human beings can merely answer. Every utterance (*Wort*) is in fact a reply (an *Ant-Wort*) to the voice of being that precedes all human actions.[10] *Gadamer,* who took his point of departure from the Heidegger after the *Kehre,* claimed that history was not a history of Being, but rather a history of effects (*Wirkungsgeschichte*) in which our cultural heritage has been handed down to us.[11] Drawing from a genuinely Husserlian insight, *texts themselves* or in general works of art and culture have their own "manner

of givenness" through history, and what distinguishes the classical from
the ephemeral is that the classical will always speak to humans as long
as they exist, but in different ways depending on who reads what when
and where. A final answer might be Foucault's "archeological" method,
which claims, influenced by Marx and Nietzsche, that this motor driving
history is an anonymous process, characterized by unanticipatable ruptures, breaks, and inconsistencies.

I take these different types of philosophical hermeneutics as proposals to answer the *third* demand of the bare bones of what makes a
philosophical hermeneutics, that is, attempts to explain the *origin and
genesis* of our pre-understandings as the sum total of H, the horizon of
our understanding of life. As different proposals of addressing this demand they are not exclusive solutions to this demand but merely different
answers; and all of these answers can be read, in a certain light, as critiques of the Husserlian account, which they, however, do not take in its
strongest shape (as demonstrated in chapters 5 and 11). Indeed, their
manner of using Husserl as a backdrop to motivate their own projects
mostly presents Husserl's project as a travesty. But as we shall see, Husserl
will offer another answer to the third task that allows us to consider his
mature philosophy as a hermeneutical phenomenology as well. Discussing this Husserlian project will also shed light on how he conceived of
the method of the phenomenological reduction in the context of the
actual work that phenomenology does, that is, to explain the functioning
of the lifeworld. Hence, the project of a hermeneutical phenomenology
is intimately linked to Husserl's method of the reduction. In the following, I shall present this Husserlian project as, inherently, a problem
of method.

The Reduction as a Move
from *Selbstverständlichkeit* to
Unverständlichkeit to *Verständlichkeit* and
Epoché as "Epoché from All Traditions"

Husserl was aware of the hermeneutical movement of his day and was
in touch with their main proponents, such as Dilthey and Simmel, and
later Dilthey's pupil and son-in-law Misch,[12] and he knew of Heidegger's
hermeneutics of facticity that he was probing in his early years in Freiburg
in his dealings with Aristotle and Saint Paul. But also political events and
the social upheaval associated with them made a project of the "return
to originary life"—if this may be shorthand for the project of a philo-

sophical hermeneutics—attractive. One can surmise that the terms "facticity" and "return to life" were catchphrases in the 1920s in Europe's philosophical and cultural scene among peoples who were just recovering from the shock of the Great War. Husserl was no exception in seeing in this event the "greatest disaster of our culture and civilization," and there were even some who believed that this horrible event might have been—a terrible thought—a necessity of life itself. Life might be inherently destructive and not guided by reason or logos (divine or otherwise). This sentiment—theoretically conceived by Schopenhauer's universal pessimism—started what is now known as existentialism. That sentiment entailed, in the eyes of many, that no rational agency was able to avoid such atrocities; in fact, the project of the Enlightenment with its inherent rationalism might have even been—in part or fully—accountable for this disaster.[13]

The result was doubt in reason itself. Especially the youth were craving new sources of meaning amidst the rubble of the war. Salvation was not to be found in the university auditoriums, at least insofar as professors dealt with abstract theory and not the realities of life. The youth turned away from "rigorous science" and instead turned to those who promised to address life in its concretion in its brute and sometimes ugly reality. "Rigorous science" not only did not address this existential urge; it even stood in the way of facing it. It was for this reason that Husserl viewed the cultural scene in the postwar period with great skepticism. The painfully needed renewal of culture could only be achieved by returning to serious work, philosophical or otherwise. For this reason, Husserl rejected philosophy of life or existence; giving up the ideal of rigorous science meant conjuring up the specters of irrationalism, skepticism, and relativism. Nevertheless, philosophy had to address life and the lifeworld and attempt to make sense of it philosophically. In this sense, phenomenology's task was to make understandable the lifeworld as well, only to offer a different solution than the fashionable philosophies surrounding him. Husserl's answer was a decidedly *rationalist* one; a hermeneutics that devotes itself to explaining this life cannot succumb to simply pointing out life's irrational character. The dark ground is one into which the "torch of reason" had to shine its bright light. What it elucidates is of a rational character as well, only that this very fact might not be obvious. Only in this way could one ground philosophically a sense of the lifeworld as a world of culture guided by reason. One sees immediately how the project of Husserl's phenomenology is a hermeneutical one in the sense explicated in the previous section, and how it must be seen as a response to the existential crisis of culture. How does this method proceed?

Now, getting to the issues themselves, Husserl's hermeneutical phe-

nomenology involves the conceptual dichotomy of understanding and
pre-understanding as well. This dichotomy can easily be translated into
Husserl's terminology as follows: we live first and foremost in the natural
attitude. To be caught up in this attitude means, as we already know, to be
"naive" with respect to the world's being constituted by achievements of
transcendental subjectivity. Another way of making essentially the same
point, thereby giving it a hermeneutical "slant," is to say that our average,
everyday understanding of ourselves and the world rests on the foundation of a profound non-understanding. Everyday understanding is in fact
a taking-for-granted of something that I, upon reflection, do not really
understand. In this sense, Husserl employs three related terms to frame
this situation in which we live *in* the natural attitude, whereby the latter
two already indicate the shift away from it:

1. The primary form of understanding that we have is in fact a
   taking-for-granted (*Selbstverständlichkeit*).
2. Upon reflection, this taking-for-granted turns out to be a non-
   understanding (*Unverständlichkeit*).
3. However, this non-understanding can be transformed into a true understanding (*Verständlichkeit*) through philosophical explication.[14]

Let me call this triadic structure Husserl's description of the *hermeneutic situation*. The situation is that of the natural attitude itself, as one can
also characterize it as a universal situation of taking-things-for-granted.
Phrasing this very idea already makes the first step into a hermeneutical
consideration (task 1, above). But to make explicit that we understand
certain *things* as self-evident that upon reflection are not understood is
not yet philosophy, to Husserl. Being insecure about certain things and
questioning their being is only a partial skepticism with respect to the
natural attitude; this is the situation in the particular sciences. Philosophy
comes into being when this skepticism becomes universal:

> I practice phenomenological Epoché. In a reflexive turn, I have [in
> view] the Ego in its "subjectivity" and its first apodicticity. This includes
> for me, the philosopher, an overview over those non-understood items
> [*Unverständlichkeiten*] that I have stumbled upon in my dissatisfaction
> with the situation in the sciences [or] the state of philosophical knowl-
> edge of the world. These motivated me to practice Epoché in the first
> place. I was driven from these non-understood items [*Unverständlich-
> keiten*] . . . to the universal non-understanding of the world. . . . *Thus I
> stand now in a universal situation of skepticism . . . in the state of "I under-*
> stand nothing" or, anything that I ever understood rests on the founda-

tion of a non-understanding [*Unverständlichkeit*] that is in fact that of taking-everything-for-granted [*Selbstverständlichkeit*]. (Hua XXXIV, 481)

Thus, the philosopher must move from particular non-understood *items* to the totality of non-comprehension. This is where science differs from philosophy. This "universal non-comprehension with the content 'world'" (482) can be "'unlocked'" (229) through phenomenological reflection, and as such it is "self-interpretation [*Selbstauslegung*] of the transcendental Ego according to that which it is for itself and that which it posits in itself as 'non-Ego' ['*Nicht-Ich*']" (230–31). That is to say, reflection does not take me into a sphere of solipsistic interiority, but immediately reverts to the correlational a priori, which Husserl phrases here with the Fichtean distinction of *Ich* and *Nicht-Ich*. This self-interpretation, *Selbstauslegung,* is thus already an interpretation of myself-as-constituting-world, and it can lead to understanding successfully because it is something "posited" (constituted) in principle by subjectivity, albeit not my own. As such it is an explication of that which is "most known," but thereby taken for granted, and this is the "general meaning of 'world'" (231). The title for the totality of that which we take for granted, but which also always has a certain (yet unknown) meaning for us, is "world." In the reduction, however, the meaning of "world" itself takes on a new meaning: it is now no longer the simple background of our normal activities, but becomes understood in its universality as the product of transcendental subjectivity's constitutive accomplishments—something that was utterly unknown in the natural attitude and even in the sciences. No science—with the exception, perhaps of psychology, which thereby is on the verge of phenomenology[15]—stumbles upon this universal background of meaning, and even less discovers this "world" as phenomenon, that is, as something constituted.

The reduction is in this sense a deliberate creation of a state of non-understanding in which I as reflecting Ego, however, first get to know the world as well as my real self that was only seemingly understood (in the sense of being taken for granted) *in* the natural attitude. But this taking-for-granted is ultimately a self-deceit because I live unaware of my "real being" as constitutor of the world in the totality of world-constituting subjects (thus subjectivity is only possible within intersubjectivity). Yet, practicing the reduction is something that is prefigured in the essential potentialities of each individual human person. "Thus belongs [to human life] the possibility of practicing the transcendental reduction and thereby to 'free' itself from self-alienation" (233). This statement is itself a phenomenological one, that is, a result of eidetic variation on me as transcendental Ego.

The term "self-alienation," which sounds almost Marxian, is to be understood in the same sense in which, after the reduction, the meaning of "world" takes on a new meaning: in the reduction, I alienate myself from my "old self," thereby revealing the "true self," which is the radiating center for all my world-constituting acts. This process of "freeing myself from 'self-alienation'" is, hence, that which gives rise to the famous "paradox of subjectivity," which is well known from the *Crisis*.[16] I am both an object in the world and subject for the world, and as long as I have not understood my "double nature," I live in the state of self-alienation, in which I apperceive myself as only a worldly Ego. As will become clear, this freeing-oneself from it is, moreover, not getting *rid* of pre-understandings, but is an explication of their *genesis*.

Again, the term for this broadest sphere of that which we take for granted is the world itself. The world as the "universal situation" (246) is as such also the "universal prejudice, it is a genuine universality of prejudices" (303). Why is this the case, and what does it mean? This moves us into the genetic dimension of Husserl's phenomenology. Husserl frames the relation of understanding and pre-understanding alternately in the terms of *givenness* and *pre-givenness*.[17] Every givenness that we have before us and that we can treat with the phenomenological method of description presupposes a pre-givenness. What is pre-given in the universal sense is, again, the world. *"The world as such is pre-given, it is the universe of pre-givenness"* (302). Thus, every givenness presupposes a pre-givenness that is first and foremost not understood. The phenomenological term for this is *horizon*. Every act of explicit attention when I focus on a particular thing has pre-given a horizon of possible things that can affect me. Thus,

> *all givenness has its horizon of affectivity,* its horizon of actual affection, among which the affection that effects my turning-attention to something, and moreover its horizons of potential affection, which are equally not nothing and co-function subjectively as presupposition of actual affection. (303)[18]

All of these items belonging to the horizon can be subsumed under the title of "pre-givenness." This piece of analysis of the character of the world as pre-given, of which Husserl merely reminds us here, however, has a *temporal* dimension. Pre-givenness is not merely a co-givenness of other objects in my horizon of vision, but has a history of prior givenness that has been sedimented and become habitualized. It is a pre-givenness of other fellow human beings' accomplishments and their experiences and judgments that they have made in the past and that shape my current horizon of understanding. The world as I know it is not something that I alone have constituted; rather, it has a *genesis* of (passive) constitution. So much is known, but now Husserl introduces a new term for this phenomenon. The key term for the totality of these constituting activities in a historical-genetic perspective now is *tradition*. That which is pre-given is something that *has been given* in the tradition of human world constitution. "Tradition is that which is valid-a-priori [*Gelten-im-Voraus*] out of tradition in the broadest conceivable sense" (302). Thus, to get a full overview over the totality of pre-givenness, or of the full meaning of that which is included in this "universal presupposition" that is comprised in the term "world," one first needs to gain the realization that this universal prejudice is a genetically produced and continually developing history of intentional acts. Every givenness rests on the basis of an implicit pre-givenness, and this pre-givenness means that it is not only co-present in the background but also in a *temporal* fashion. Husserl is saying nothing new for those who know of his genetic phenomenology, but only using a novel term, *tradition,* when he points out that the totality of that which is comprised in the givenness of the world for an experiencing agent is, or rests on, a sedimented tradition of past givennesses. Conscious life *itself* and the world it lives in are, to coin a term, "traditioned" through and through.

> This life in its own traditionality, in the fullest sense of the word, carries within itself that which is passed on through tradition and it passes itself on through tradition. As such we call it conscious life. World for myself, for us, is a universal tradition and the foundation of all tradition. (444)

Hence, the world as a world of tradition, that is to say, of a genesis of meaning constitution on the part of others, currently, in the past and into the future, also means that the world as a lifeworld is a historical world of tradition with its sedimentations. To revert briefly to the discussion concerning Husserl's relation with the Marburg neo-Kantians, it is entirely appropriate to call the world thus construed *culture*. I shall return to this point in the conclusion.

Thus, as regards the actual method of this hermeneutical task, in order to grasp the full "body" of the world as we experience it as taken for granted in the natural attitude, one needs to transform this self-understanding into a non-understanding *for* the naively living person in the natural attitude (thereby releasing the Ego from its original self-alienation) and, in the second step, *interpret* this non-understanding as a horizon of tradition. But these traditions within the horizon of tradition are all a product of "conscious life." As such, the task of genetic phenomenology is an "unveiling of the *transcendental* horizons of presuppositions" (245, italics added). "Tradition" here is thus a *transcendental* term as a term for the totality of that which constitutes the world in a genetic register. In this sense, it does not have the negative meaning as being a field of bad presuppositions that the philosopher must leave behind in the process of his becoming enlightened. It is a formal concept for the descriptively ascertained insight that every givenness that the phenomenologist takes as starting point has a horizon of pre-givenness. This pre-givenness has a genetic dimension, that is, a history and temporality. The pre-givennesses of the tradition are at first taken for granted, yet when they are made explicit through reflective inquiry they can become transformed into non-understanding. But the philosopher cannot bring these prejudices to vanish. Rather, he transforms them into *understood* prejudices by tracing genetically the origin and genesis of their coming about.

When we know the tradition, is Husserl's point, we understand the prejudices as prejudices and as such *justify* them, not in the sense of defending them, but we can clarify the laws of genesis by which they came about. They are not a matter of fate or accident, but have their origin and genesis, which stand under laws of genesis. As Husserl writes, famously, in *Cartesian Meditations,* the sense of the world is a sense that can be "understood but never altered" (Hua I, 177). This statement can be taken to express Husserl's sense of justification of prejudices. It is an understanding that arises from transforming traditions as taken for granted into something that we can understand *when* one has subjected them to a genetic analysis. Yet, the fact that the philosopher cannot alter it does not mean that he must just take it and accept it. The clarification of the tradition is a justification in the sense of an *understanding from the deepest sources.*

> The being of the world, by being clarified transcendentally, becomes understood and, at the same time, justified out of ultimate, absolute sources of its being, and in this radical justification there lies at the same time the whole range [*die Tragweite*] of this being as known and knowable. (245)

This is why the epoché must encompass all that which is part of the world as this encompassing horizon of presuppositions. One can only fully claim to practice the full epoché when one has *first opened up* the whole horizon of what it means to live in a world. Living in the world as the universal presupposition is living in a tradition. Thus, Husserl speaks also of the full, encompassing epoché as an "Epoché from all Tradition" (441).

> What the Epoché is to accomplish is the most radical and most univer-
> sal inhibition of each and every preconceived opinion [*Vormeinung*]
> or of all traditions—all prejudices [*Vorurteile*]—in the broadest sense.
> The basic insight here is the realization that this world of experience as
> constantly existing for us is a universal prejudice, a genuine universality
> of prejudices. (303)

That is to say, to just inhibit my particular general thesis of the
natural attitude is not an epoché in the full sense, that is, without realizing the range of this thesis as reaching back into tradition. To practice
epoché can only mean to bracket the whole tradition as the encompassing horizon of pre-givenness upon which I as conscious Ego rest. Before
practicing the most encompassing epoché, thus, means to first of all
bring to full awareness and to fully unfold the fact that my current givenness rests on the hitherto unthematized pre-givenness that is in its fullest
form tradition.[19]

Thus only such an epoché from all tradition is the fullest realization and understanding of the universal presupposition of the world.
Only when one has grasped that the world is a world of tradition can
the epoché as a break with this universal field of presuppositions be fully
enacted. In *this* sense, with the caveat in mind that such a task is infinite, one can say, alluding to Merleau-Ponty's famous critique, that the
reduction *can in principle* be completed. Indeed, the epoché is not a suspension of these presuppositions in the sense of a full freedom from
them, or as an act "in one stroke," but a continuous self-alienation from
them, *in order to understand them,* an understanding from the "deepest
sources," which lie in subjectivity. Genetic phenomenological analysis is
in this sense a reconstruction of these presuppositions in telling a story
of how they came about. Givenness rests on pre-givenness, but this is not
an opaque dark region, but a sphere of *previous givennesses* that can be
accessed through reflection and reconstruction. As former givennesses
they can be reconstructed as subjective achievements that lie in the past.[20]
The "hermeneutical" task, hence, is to clarify these origins through interpretation, and this means, by retracing all givenness of consciousness out
of *achievements* of consciousness. Nothing, in other words, is merely *given,*
but every givenness is *constituted.* Everything worldly as we encounter it
springs from ourselves.

Now this will strike many readers as an unusual rephrasing of the
epoché. Was not the epoché meant as a *suspension* of all traditions, of
making a radical *break* with the natural attitude in order to reach an absolute and unprejudiced foundation for philosophy, to reach the stance of
the non-participating observer? Husserl's hermeneutical insights revise

the epoché significantly to those who might have had such a mistaken notion of it (a mistaken notion, that is, which is still widespread). As should
have become clear in the previous analyses, the epoché is not intended
to reach a standpoint *outside* all tradition. Rather, it is intended to "make
strange" the prejudices of the natural attitude, and one's own understanding in the natural attitude in a "self-alienation," but *not* in order to
put them aside, but in order to *explain how they came about.* The move from
making-non-understood to a renewed and for the first time true understanding appropriates for ourselves what was ours, but not known to be.
Though this method functions very differently from Hegel's, it is not inap-
propriate to call this move one from the state of *in itself* to that of *for itself*
to, finally, that of *in and for itself.* To reiterate what has been said in chapter
6, the goal is not an "absolute standpoint," but rather *absolute transparency*
concerning oneself as world-constituting and the world as a product of
such constitution. The state to be reached, then, is from an alienation to a
universal *appropriation of myself and the world and their most intimate connection*
that is established through the insight into the correlational a priori.

Moreover, a suspension of all tradition does not mean ridding oneself of it, but *freeing oneself* from tradition's grasp *precisely by understanding
it.*[21] It is a "freeing-oneself from self-alienation" in understanding that
one is part and parcel of the world-as-constituted; the world is not alien,
but ours through and through. Non-understanding *can be transformed into
understanding* through a genetic clarification of their origin and their
coming about. The point in this hermeneutical reading of the reduction is that freedom can only be attained through an understanding of
prejudices *as prejudices,* and that means, of their genesis, and as such
transforming them into *understood* prejudices. But it is important to note
that this process of understanding them does not mean transforming
them into *rationally justified theories. They remain prejudices.* They can be
understood because they are subjective through and through, and practicing the epoché does not mean to live in the state of full *epistéme,* but
to continue to live in the midst of *dóxa* that has become understood.
Understanding *dóxa* means relating it back to meaning-bestowing subjective acts that needn't be rational, but which reach further back into
the pre-rational realm (passivity). But passivity is still a dimension of consciousness. To connect this with the notion of "justification," if taken to
be understood in the sense of Kant's *quid iuris,* that is, a justification of a
priori cognition, it becomes clear that this question now takes on a new
sense: it is a justification of the fact that all intentional accomplishments
that make the world possible ultimately stem from constituting subjectivity.[22] The justification of a priori cognition is, thus, only a higher-level
and rather specific application of the question of the justification for the

constitution of the world—the most basic insight revealed by phenomenology. This insight will also, as we shall see, have consequences on Husserl's full understanding of rationality.

Thus, to summarize the key elements of Husserl's hermeneutical phenomenology: the basic starting point is that our everyday understanding of ourselves and the world is in fact a taking-for-granted. Once we question single items it turns out they are only seemingly understood. This is the motivation for the particular sciences. The philosopher, however, has to expand this questioning into a universal dimension. What he finds is that the whole world as a horizon of constitutedness in this sense is not understood. This non-understanding, however, can be transformed into a genuine understanding through realizing that all givennesses in this world rest on a pre-history of pre-givennesses that Husserl calls *tradition*. Thus, to clarify the origin and genesis of this tradition, one needs to practice an epoché from all traditions, which is an endless task. But practicing such an epoché means in principle nothing other than relating the tradition back to previous achievements that lie in subjectivity. Tradition is not an anonymous force, but something constituted by previous subjective acts. When giving a genetic account of how this tradition has evolved in the framework of transcendental phenomenology, one is giving a reconstructive analysis of how this tradition has come about. Thereby, tradition and the world it has shaped become *understood*.

In simpler terms, the epoché as epoché from all tradition means seeing the tradition in its broad sense as a product of subjective acts. To connect tradition with the transcendental-phenomenological method means the commitment to see all tradition as an achievement of subjectivity, *even if this does not seem so*. The interpretive task, hence, is to produce exactly this insight at every juncture. Practicing transcendental analysis with respect to the tradition means fundamentally realizing that all tradition, no matter how naive and flawed it might be, is in principle an accomplishment of subjects. One can make explicit, assess, judge, or even reject the presuppositions of the tradition, but it is not an anonymous force that comes over us, but the history and tradition of human subjects who live in a historical nexus of interaction. Becoming free through the radical act of epoché means understanding tradition, and this even permits a living-along with it, but one has now understood it. Only an understanding in this sense enables critique. An external critique, that is, one voiced from outside of a tradition, almost always gets things wrong. But it is always *a tradition* in the sense specified, which means that it is always in principle accessible to any subject that makes the effort.

Understanding that comes about in this historical reflection is then not an exclusively *rational* act, but that of relating every *dóxa* back to meaning-bestowing acts of subjectivity. Reason, the way Husserl understands and utilizes it here, is not *divorced* from other forms of mental life—as in the traditional oppositions, such as reason and emotion, head and heart—but stands merely at the top of a genetic layering that reaches all the way down into "passivity" and its history. "Rational," then, is every act that has been justified through reflection. "Rational" justification, in this sense, also has a broader, namely *ethical,* meaning of justifying our life and our lifeworld, in which human life can flourish as *understood* from the bottom up in its traditionality. This type of rationality makes mankind *moral.*[23]

In this sense, Husserl's hermeneutic phenomenology is not only a valid alternative vis-à-vis Heideggerian or Gadamerian versions thereof, but it is also superior to them. History is not a history of Being that speaks to us in the manner of revealing and concealing itself on its own whim, nor is it a history of anonymous effects in which the subject is but a flickering light in the closed circuits of historical events. Husserl's answer to the third demand of a philosophical hermeneutics—that of explaining the origins of presuppositions—is that the origins of all presuppositions that guide our everyday life lie in past subjective acts that can be made explicit by thematizing and scrutinizing the tradition as to its laws of genesis, its motivations, and its inner logic of playing itself out. History is a history of tradition, that is to say, a history of subjectivity through and through. To play on Gadamer's metaphor, tradition is a bright and shining torch that is handed down through history. One can interpret Heidegger and Gadamer in this sense as anti-Enlightenment philosophers because they do not see any leeway for changing any presuppositions because subjects have no control over them and are entirely given over to history's forces.

From this angle, Husserl presents us with an *enlightened* Enlightenment. Presuppositions cannot always be overcome, but they can be made understandable *when* we subject them to a genetic analysis after practicing the epoché. We can make sense of the sense of the world as being given to us through tradition, *because* we can give a genetic account of how tradition has come about as a history of human subjectivity's achievements. The world is as it is because subjects have shaped it. We may not always be able to overcome prejudices and alter them, but we can at least make sense of them because we can realize with apodictic evidence that they are results of *human production.* This does not mean they are rationally produced (mostly they are not), but we *can* understand them *because other exemplars of our species* have created them out of their own motives and motivations. They are not ways in which the world speaks to us, but they are ways in which subjects relate to the world as a lifeworld. All great or foolish accomplishments in the history of the world as we know it are *our* accomplishments and can *therefore* be understood. This is Husserl's lasting humanistic promise.

Conclusion: Hermeneutical Phenomenology as a Philosophy of Culture

After spelling out Husserl's method of a hermeneutical phenomenology and its concomitant view of true Enlightenment philosophy, I want to conclude by connecting these issues with that of interpreting the lifeworld as a world of culture. This concluding point will be to sketch how we can understand, following Husserl, the lifeworld as a world of culture and how, accordingly, transcendental phenomenology as a hermeneutic enterprise can fulfill the promised task of a *transcendental philosophy of culture*. In so doing, I am not saying anything substantially new, just attempting to sketch in broad strokes what has been argued in different ways over the course of this work.

To summarize briefly what has been achieved in this chapter, one can view—in the manner shown—Husserl's transcendental phenomenology as a form of hermeneutic philosophy. Its task is, as in all other hermeneutic enterprises, to produce an understanding through the work of interpretation. Insofar as Husserl's static phenomenology of description needs to be expanded, following its systematic necessity, it leads into, or culminates in, a genetic phenomenology, whose method is interpretive insofar as it requires a reconstruction of past, sedimented acts as having shaped (constituted) the world as we now encounter it. The world, however, as currently experienced, is naively lived through; its understanding rests on a pre-understanding that is made explicit the moment the reduction has been enacted. The ideal goal is to disengage oneself from the world as a world of tradition—sedimented and historical—completely, but this is an endless task. Thus, like all interpretation, phenomenology's task is never completed, but its direction and its goal are clear: not to reach a position outside of the world, but to bring about ideally a full comprehension of the world, as a world constituted—statically, genetically, subjectively, intersubjectively—from transcendental life. Thus, phenomenology's goal is to lead, not away from the world into the niche of a Cartesian subject, but straight back to the world and the subjects constituting it.

Husserl's phenomenology, in this sense, satisfies the minimal requirements of a philosophical hermeneutics in making explicit the structure of prejudices, clarifies them and explains them as coming about through its historical genesis. What it reconstructs, thus, is *life itself* as a rich and "thick" structure, which encompasses life and its locus, in Husserlian parlance, transcendental consciousness and the lifeworld. Its work thus takes place within the correlational a priori, and it is thus a concrete work on the project of transcendental idealism, insofar as this correlation only comes into view after the transcendental turn. Transcendental idealism, in the phenomenological understanding of the term, is thus not just a philosophical position, but the title for a concrete project, a work in progress. The elucidation of life, thus, is a transcendental-philosophical one, and life, too, is a transcendental notion. Its facticity is only to be understood as a *constituted facticity*. Every *philosophical* work at clarifying life must thus take place in a transcendental register. Hence, any "philosophy of life" or "existentialism" which starts out and ends with facticity or concrete existence will forever stop short of the dimension of a philosophical account, which must be transcendental and whose concrete work as descriptive-interpretive must be phenomenological in nature (in its hermeneutic expansion). Thus, not only is Husserl's phenomenology *also* a philosophy of life and existence, but it also thereby first places these phenomena in their proper context. Thus, only a philosophy in the Husserlian sense explicated is *true existentialism, true Lebensphilosophie.*

But let us now turn to the noematic correlate of life. It is nothing other than the lifeworld. Through the concrete work of phenomenology, the world becomes understood and elucidated as lifeworld, that is, as a historical world of tradition and the accomplishment of subjects as parts of intersubjective communities. I said before that it is appropriate to call the lifeworld in this sense also a world of culture, thereby making the connection to the philosophy of culture we encountered in part 2. Let us focus on this notion of culture a bit in conclusion. Methodologically, it has been demonstrated that the neo-Kantian method of objectification, as developed by Cohen and then pluralized in Cassirer's system, is to be viewed as a counterpart to Husserl's method. In fact, they merely emphasize the two different sides of the same coin. Now the project of Cassirer's is explicitly termed a "critique of culture" as an expansion of the "critique of reason." Insofar as Husserl, too, calls his project a "critique of reason" for more than superficial reasons, it is not far-fetched to call his phenomenology also a "critique of the lifeworld," as this is where constitution "ends," and if the lifeworld is essentially a world of culture, the label "critique of culture" is quite appropriate for Husserl's phenomenology as well. But what does this mean?

Husserl's phenomenological account of the lifeworld, it must be emphasized, is different from Cassirer's account of culture in that Cassirer posits the different symbolic forms as "directions" of spirit's objectification. Cassirer's approach has been criticized, as discussed in chapter 10, as constructivist and hence unphenomenological. One can, however, compare the symbolic forms (myth, science, etc.) to what Husserl calls special worlds, though Husserl would reject the accusation that these are constructions. They are the result of descriptive accounts of different spaces of meaning. Rejecting the alleged constructivist approach of Cassirer's (leaving aside whether this critique is fair), however, does not imply a rejection of the objectivist tendency of Cassirer. Leaving aside the potential problems with Cassirer, Husserl's account of spaces of meaning with their internal logic and their structure of referential implication is not *in principle* different from Cassirer's. Thus, methodologically speaking, Husserl's hermeneutic phenomenology can rightfully be called a philosophy of culture. Yet, so far this is not more than a formal analogy.

But what this really means can only become clear when spelling out the meta-philosophical upshot of this project, and doing so, in conclusion, will bring us again full circle to Husserl's phenomenology as a form of Enlightenment philosophy. To begin, one may ask why the Marburg neo-Kantians were so intent on forming the Kantian transcendental philosophy as a critique of reason into a critique of culture. One insight—following the trajectory of transcendental philosophy in German idealism—was that reason as that which is the human being's most central trait, its "core," was too narrowly construed as to grasp the human being in its totality. The focus on the human being's objectifications—what the human being *does* and where one can visibly see its work—is meant to shift the focus from the subject as a "cold rational" creature into one who dwells in the world in manifold creative and distinct manners, in art with its many sub-forms, in science, in his social networks and projects and political creations, such as the state, government, with their institutions, and so on. In a word, this is *culture,* and the critique of the human being is most properly and most fully unfolded if it grasps the human being involved in its creations, its projects, its deeds, in a world, the human being as an *animal culturale.* Hence, the philosophy of culture is most properly a philosophy of the human being—and vice versa.

But this means, for the individual human being: the individual is what it is only as *engaged in projects* (to use this term for the totality of cultural deeds). These projects are necessarily *communal* projects (with their tradition, etc.). The human individual thus only comes into his own when engaged in projects. These projects, which in some form whatsoever contribute to society and its progress, lift the human being out of his individual existence. Partaking and participating in these projects first *form* the individual into a human being. A person in any robust sense of

the term is only someone engaged in projects, and since these projects—
a religious community, a civil group, a team, a state—are larger than this
individual, they also take him out of his finite existence. Partaking in
culture, in short, lifts the human being out of his solipsistic state and also
out of his finitude by making him "infinite" in the sense of placing him
into a larger context and the nexus of trans-generational projects and
goals. Only this shapes him into an "individual," which is not just some
anonymous number, but a collaborator in cultural projects and a *person*
only on this basis. The question of culture, thus, is also the question of
humanity, what makes one human. The answer, from the vantage point
of a philosophy of culture, is that the human being only *becomes* a human
being by actively partaking and participating in the projects of culture.
This is what it means to be human—not dwelling in one's finite and concrete individual existence.

This summary of the two manners of conceiving of the human being
(as infinite or finite) was, as the reader might have noticed, the core of
the Davos debate between Cassirer and Heidegger in 1929. Where Heidegger claimed the latter, it was Cassirer, the philosopher of culture, who
claimed the former, and one knows the ridicule his appearance caused
especially among the youth. This debate and its various ramifications
shall not be discussed here, and in the end one might have to agree that
regarding the question as to which view of the human being is the right
one is a matter of commitment, not of philosophical arguments. But this
way of portraying things is, again, a very existential and ultimately relativistic viewpoint. Be that as it may, it is clear from Husserl's many rejections
and critiques of existentialism, that he, too, would have sided whole-
heartedly with the vision offered by Cassirer. But this vision is not merely
a naive wish, it is a Kantian regulative idea. The vision of the world as a
world of culture and the human being within it as a cultural dweller is
spoken—in Cassirer as well as in Husserl—under the heading of Ought,
not Is. It is the ideal of how the world and the human being in it ought
to be as a regulative idea lying in infinity.

The lifeworld as a world of culture thus presents a vision and a
proposal for the individual human being to participate in the projects of
the world as a world of human creation. But these projects of culture are
combined efforts carried out by human beings communally and in mutual critique. They are enacted, thus, in a *rational* manner in the broadest
sense of the term. As already emphasized several times in this book, Husserl's vision of mankind is not that everybody should become a philosopher; far from it. But placing the human being in a culture as specified
means establishing one central feature as the main "method" of life, a
method that is already known since Kant but "brought down to earth" by

Husserl: that of justification. Phenomenology was characterized above as a *justification of life,* and in this sense, practicing phenomenology as a method is but the scientific application of what it means, for Husserl, to be a human being, and hence what it means to be enlightened. The project of living one's life as a cultural being in a world as cultural life-world means to latch on to communal projects which can only exist as *at all times justifying themselves, and "justification" means: the justification of the projects themselves, justifying them with respect to other projects, and the justification, finally, of the individual human being as being a part of a (or several) project(s).* This is Husserl's view of Enlightenment: the ability to justify oneself in the midst of the lifeworld as a bathos of culture. Justification is thus not an exclusively *rational* or *logical* act (though it can be and at some times needs to be), but one of *fitting in* in the broadest conceivable sense.

Culture, then, is the safe haven and our home, and nothing could be further from living an enlightened life than dwelling and feeling at home in the niches of subcultures, which deliberately depart from "the mainstream." Subcultures, which consciously depart from the "grand discourse" of Culture, are the enemy of culture. Living a life in culture as the encompassing element of the human being is living life to the fullest. This is not some lofty and aesthetic ideal, but the product of hard work and constant justification vis-à-vis others and ultimately with respect to oneself. Husserl's vision of the human being is the ability to justify oneself at all times and from the deepest sources, which at all times must lie in subjectivity. This is what it is to live a critical life in the fullest sense, self-critical and critical of others and the world which we create and shape. Constitution is everywhere. There is nothing in principle alien in the world. After the phenomenological critique, the world has been understood from deepest sources as being at all times a product of human creation. The deepest and most encompassing comprehension of the world, which amounts to justifying it and ourselves in it, thus stems from Husserl's core insight: the correlation of subjectivity and lifeworld (the *One Structure*). This is not just a theoretical insight, but a practical and concrete project, as Husserl has worked it out in his late thought (including his ethics). To realize it is to pursue the path of Enlightenment. Its path is an endless one, but is also one that will never become obsolete or outdated as long as human beings exist. Modernity, as the project of Enlightenment, remains an unfinished project. As has been shown over the course of this book, Husserl is one of its most ardent and passionate defenders. Husserl's phenomenology is thereby equally to be understood as an unfinished project. It has yet to come to fruition.

Notes

Chapter 1

1. In most introductions to Husserl's philosophy the natural attitude is treated as a mere transitional phase to describe the phenomenological reduction (see Bernet, Kern, and Marbach 1989, 58ff.). I know of no work on Husserl that explicitly devotes a chapter or section to it. Waldenfels in his study dwells on the proper right (*Eigenrecht*) of the natural attitude, but he, too, fails to give a thorough description of it (see Waldenfels 1971, 67ff.).

2. "*Die Aufgabe einer 'Ontologie der Lebenswelt.'*" Not only is the task of this ontology only feasible by going back into the natural attitude, but also the founding of all scientific and philosophical efforts on the ground of the relativity of the lifeworld can be seen as a recognition of the natural attitude as an "*Ur-Dóxa*" that can never be uplifted or bracketed.

3. Fink, however, sees as the central operative concepts the notions of "phenomenon," "epoché," "constitution," "achievement" (*Leistung*), and "transcendental logic" (phenomenological language) (see Fink 1976, 203), himself presupposing the natural attitude as the basis for the issues he raises. Hence it can be said that to Fink himself the natural attitude remains as an operative concept overshadowed by these aforementioned notions. Moreover, one might suspect that Fink's analysis of the phenomenological predication in §10 of the Sixth *Cartesian Meditation* (Hua-Dok II/1) implicitly bears a definition of the language of the natural attitude. Likewise does his notion of a phenomenological transcendental idealism as a dialectical relation between natural and phenomenologizing attitudes (see ibid., §12, 170ff.). However, this "definition" could only *ex negativo* be derived from the positive definition of the attitude of the phenomenologizing Ego. In other words, the natural attitude, to Fink, only becomes crucial in the enworlding of the transcendental "truths" into the natural attitude in the "transcendental pedagogical-implications" of phenomenology. For a comparison between Husserl's and Fink's views of transcendental phenomenology, see Luft (2002).

4. "Die beiden Titel: 'transzendentale Einstellung' und 'natürliche Einstellung' sind grundsätzlich transzendentale Begriffe" (Hua-Dok II/2, 104). See also Fink (1966, 113).

5. See esp. the Fifth Logical Investigation (Hua XIX/1): "Über intentionale Erlebnisse und ihre 'Inhalte'" ("On intentional lived-experiences and their 'contents'").

6. I use the term "life" here in order to imply all kinds of human action, not only conscious, that is, mental acts, but also all human activity, down to physical life on the level of mere instincts which Husserl tries to grasp under the title "*Triebintentionalität*" (intentionality of drives [see Hua XV, no. 34, 593ff. and app. XLIII, 597ff.]). Since I employ this concept of intentionality as a mere basic framework for the phenomenon of attitude, it is not necessary to go into this issue of intentionality more deeply.

7. Husserl himself is not blind to these pragmatical interests, as is often insinuated. To him, these pragmatical usages are a matter of the relative being as opposed to its limit of absolute, optimal appearance, which interests the philosopher. For Husserl, the relative being comes at the very end of the account of the constitution, whereas to Heidegger, it is the *próteron pròs hemâs* (see Hua XI, 23–24). "Das thematische Interesse, das in Wahrnehmungen sich auslebt, ist in unserem wissenschaftlichen Leben von praktischen Interessen geleitet, und das beruhigt sich, wenn gewisse für das jeweilige Interesse optimale Erscheinungen gewonnen sind, in denen das Ding so viel von seinem letzten Selbst zeigt, als dieses praktische Interesse fordert. Oder vielmehr es zeichnet sich als praktisches Interesse ein relatives Selbst vor: Das, was praktisch genügt, gilt als das Selbst. So ist das Haus selbst und in seinem wahren Sein, und zwar hinsichtlich seiner puren körperlichen Dinglichkeit, sehr bald optimal gegeben, also vollkommen erfahren von dem, der es als Käufer oder Verkäufer betrachtet. Für den Physiker und Chemiker erschiene solche Erfahrungsweise völlig oberflächlich und vom wahren Sein noch himmelfern." For Husserl's relation to and reading of Heidegger, compare chapter 5 of the present volume.

8. The intermediate dimension between purely passive givenness and active interest is called *attention*. Compared with other phenomena described in great detail (such as perception), Husserl devotes fairly little space to this phenomenon. See Hua XXXVIII (which was not published at the time this text was originally composed), where Husserl describes this phenomenon at some length.

9. "Interest" here means not only the thematic interest in the pursued object, but also, implicitly, the co-thesis of the existence of that which is intended; interest as a general structure of human life always implies the thesis of the being of the world. See also Hua IX, app. XI, 410ff., esp. 412–14; Hua XV, app. XXV, 414–15.

10. This term is not so much used by Husserl in the way I am employing it above, but rather in Fink's stressing of the concrete situation in which I can perform the epoché (see Hua-Dok II/2, 23ff., and Husserl's critical notations in footnotes 66 [23], 69, 70 [both on 24]). In note 70, Husserl writes, as a passing remark: "Natürlich waches Leben ist Akte vollziehen—jeder Akt hat *seine* Situation, aktives Leben ist ein *einheitliches Leben, ein von Situation in Situation Übergehen* und in ihr Ziele Haben, also von Ziel zu Ziel und im verwirklichenden Tun (Handeln im weitesten Sinn) von Erzielung, Verwirklichung zu ihren Zielen Übergehen."

11. Such would be the task of a phenomenological psychology, which need not have performed the reduction and thus need not stand in the transcendental sphere. It would be an eidetic account of the attitudes *within* the natural attitude. One of these tasks would be to see if there is a link or necessary connection

between a certain attitude and a certain fundamental mood (*Grundstimmung*) in Heidegger's sense. Defining the natural attitude itself, however, is only possible in and through the epoché.

12. See Hua VI, app. XVII, 459ff., esp. 460. "Jede jener 'Welten' [of special interests] hat ihre durch den Berufszweck bestimmte besondere Universalität, jede den unendlichen Horizont einer gewissen 'Allheit.'" On the same page Husserl coins for this phenomenon the often-used term "*Sonderwelt*," which I here translate as "special world." The notion of the openness of the horizon here also implies that it is an open horizon for my possibilities within an attitude; this is an openness of "*Vermöglichkeiten*"; see ibid., 164.

13. In doing so, I am aware of the fact that this is not the only meaning Husserl attributes to the notion of world. World as lifeworld is also the anthropological world with its sedimentations of meaning, tradition, and culture; hence this world is also a historical world (see Hua XXIX, no. 28, 321ff.; and no. 34, "Zur Kritik an den *Ideen*," 424ff., esp. 425–26). Despite these further differentiations and definitions of the notion of the lifeworld, this notion, too, falls under the category of Fink's "operative concepts."

14. In this sense the Kantian notion of schema as schematism of the pure notions of the "*Verstand*" (*Schematismus der reinen Verstandesbegriffe*) is embedded in this more universal schematism which pertains not only to objects of perception but to the totality of world appearing for the human being in this world. Whereas the Kantian model is merely epistemological, it is more deeply founded in a schematism that I shall call ontological.

15. Likewise, it can be said that the Ego is never only (pure) Ego, but cannot but live itself out in an attitude—but is not, again, only made up of attitudes.

16. See Hua XV, app. XI (214ff.) as one paradigm text of the many texts of Husserl's late period where he deals with this issue. For a thorough interpretation of this concept and how from it arises the concept of the one world as the full sense of the lifeworld, or rather, on the contrary, how the full notion of homeworlds with their correlative alienworlds constitute the full sense of the lifeworld, see Held (1991). See also Steinbock's thorough study (1995) on Husserl's concept of the homeworld in the framework of a "generative phenomenology."

17. Concerning the closedness and relative expansion of this homeworld, Husserl employs the image of an onion that has several layers concentrically surrounding the core; see Hua XV, text no. 27, 429ff. This metaphor is tricky, however, for one should not understand the universality of the world as the "big onion." This image only serves to illustrate the layeredness of the homeworld.

18. On this note, it might be helpful to know that "naive" as well as "natural" both stem from the same Latin root, as mentioned above, that is, *nasci*.

19. See Hua III/1, 26.

20. See, for a locus classicus, Plato's *Meno*, where the skill of mathematics functions as the paradigm case of that kind of knowledge which does not have to be learned, but is "innate" to the human being (82b–85e).

21. Husserl is convinced that this process of science as the mathematization of nature is intrinsic to Western thought. See Husserl's famous reconstruction of this process in §9 of the *Crisis*. Whether or not this thesis is true in the

light of the history of science is doubtful at least. But the point above is that the scientific attitude stems from the home attitude and thus stands on the basis of the latter. Husserl saw this process as a specifically European phenomenon which, however, has left its rightful path and has to be brought back to it. He envisions this as the rightful reminiscence of the Greek idea of the Europeization (*Europäisierung*) of mankind—a concept that has been highly criticized as being Eurocentric. For a defense of this idea as a (forgotten) positive category of unity, see Held (1989, 13–39). But for the systematic context above—that is, the question of how the natural attitude can be overcome—it is irrelevant whether or not Husserl was Eurocentric.

22. This fact of the being of the world Husserl also calls an absolute fact in the sense that this original certainty and belief can never be crossed out by doubt or annullment. Analogously as the scientific attitude is naive towards its own participation in the General Thesis and thus its origin in the natural attitude, Fink speaks of a philosophical naïveté to which the philosopher falls prey if he has not himself, although he might not stand on the ground of the General Thesis, analyzed himself (see Hua-Dok II/2, 5): "Wir stehen jetzt nach der Überwindung der *Weltnaivität* in einer neuen, in einer *transzendentalen Naivitität*." Husserl also calls this higher naïveté a "second General Thesis" (Hua XXXV, 406).

23. This is not to say that understanding of other cultures is in principle impossible; the above analysis takes place, as it were, on the transcendental level of reconstructing how it is possible in the first place that an encounter of the other or the alien may occur. The fact of globalization today might have already obscured this question. What is said above is, hence, not meant as a comment on today's world.

24. This is obviously Fink's understanding of the abnormal, as something that strikes us as something from outside our horizon and thus leads us to the reduction, whereas to Husserl the abnormal is something already constituted within the normality of our homeworld. In the outline to a planned systematic work Fink writes, as a note: "Die Anomalität als Motivation der Skepsis an der 'Weltexistenz'" (Hua-Dok II/2, 5). In his notation, Husserl replaces the term "Anomalität" with "Modalisierbarkeit aller Einzelerfahrung" (ibid., footnote 6)—obviously an action (a variation) *within* the world as opposed to an absurd or tragic event *intruding* into our world; see ibid., 30–31. In a later text from Husserl, from the year 1931 (Husserl read the above-quoted text in 1930), he does make the connection between alienity and abnormality (Hua XV, no. 10, 139): "Problem der Erweiterung der Welt durch Besetzung des leeren Welthorizonts mit einer anderen historischen Totalität, einer *fremden, total* fremdartiger, in diesem Sinn *abnormer* Menschen einer *abnormen* Umwelt" (italics added). To Husserl, it is obviously a problem of our expanding the horizon of our own world. See Steinbock (1995), who makes the distinction between "anomalous" and "abnormal," the first being a discordance within our homeworld, the latter being the normality of the alienworld, intruding into our own normal homeworld and thus striking us as abnormal: "When we characterize something as discordant . . . , discordance has merely a descriptive or normatively insignificant quality. It is not yet normatively significant as 'abnormal,' but rather 'anomalous'" (132). It is possible that

Husserl did not see the difference between abnormal and anomalous as clearly as expressed in this passage by Steinbock. Whatever difference there may be, for Husserl it was clear that the abnormal/anomalous was to be located at the very heart of the self; it is the condition of the possibility of any encounter with the alien. The sphere of "primordiality," which Husserl analyzes in the Fifth *Cartesian Meditation* and which is often used as a proof for interpreting Husserl as a "solipsist" or as privileging the self over the other, is a mere abstraction.

Chapter 2

1. Whereas the first generations of Husserl scholars (e.g., Fink, Boehm, Landgrebe, Kern) dealt extensively with the problem of the reduction, lately, especially in the French phenomenological scene, the reduction has again been a dominant theme; compare the works by Henry (1973) and Marion (1998). For a good overview of these newer tendencies, compare Bernet (1994b).

2. "Der Zukunft bin ich sicher" ("I am certain of the future"), letter to his friend G. Albrecht, December 29, 1930 (Hua-Dok III/9, 75–76).

3. The metaphor of a religious conversion is the image Husserl uses in the *Crisis* (see Hua VI, 140).

4. See Hua VIII, 19.

5. On a supposed "metaphysical neutrality" already in Husserl's early works, see Zahavi (2002, 93–108).

6. I shall refer to this article (Kern 1962) subsequently.

7. See *Crisis* (Hua VI, app. XVII, 459ff.), where Husserl speaks of "*Sonderwahrheiten*" (special, particular truths).

8. See Hua XI, 23–24.

9. This aspect in Husserl's account of the lifeworld was taken up in Gadamer's hermeneutics. See his discussion of Husserl in *Truth and Method*, part 2, §1.3. A, "The Concept of Life in Husserl and Count Yorck" (1989, 242ff.).

10. See Hua VIII, 98ff.

11. Because the conception of life is considered here from the perspective of the natural attitude, the topics of passivity and self-affectivity are not germane to this discussion. For a reconstruction of this pre-affective life, see Zahavi (1998) as well as Kühn (1998).

12. See Hua XV, 196–218, text no. 14 and app. XI; see also the critical interpretation by Held (1991, 305–7).

13. See Hua VI, 161–62, §46, and ibid., 169 n.

14. See Husserl's first account of the natural attitude in *Ideas I* (Hua III/1, §27ff.), as well as his later, more elaborate analyses in the manuscript material published in Hua XV, as well as in *Crisis* (Hua VI, §§34–37). See also his especially penetrating accounts of attitudes in his research manuscripts from the fall of 1926 (Hua XXXIV, 3–109).

15. See *Crisis* (Hua VI, 158–59, §44).

16. Whereas Husserl employs *dóxa* and *epistéme* to characterize the fundamental nature of this distinction—and hence the radically new nature of phe-

nomenology—he speaks of *"Neustiftungen"* (new/novel institutings) over against the original primal institutings in early Greek thought; see his late text on "Teleology in the History of Philosophy," in Hua XXIX, 362–420, text no. 32.

17. He also commends the British empiricists in their development of a scientific psychology. However, as for the development of transcendental philosophy, the decisive figures of modern philosophy are the ones mentioned above. See Cairns (1976, 104).

18. Apart from the "classical" schema first established by Kern, Fink mentioned at least one more way, that via the sciences. Be that as it may, Husserl did not have such a clear vision of the different ways, one of the reasons being that he developed them over the course of more than twenty years and they often intermingle. For example, the way via the lifeworld (the one presented in the *Crisis*) is also *in a sense* that via history, insofar as the lifeworld should be conceived rightfully as "historical lifeworld."

19. See Hua XXIX, 425–26. This passage will be discussed subsequently.

20. See Cairns (1976, 11–12, n. 18), where this example is mentioned.

21. See Held (1980).

22. See Hua VII, 159.

23. See Hua III/1, 52, §30; see also Hua VIII, 44–50, where Husserl formulates the "content" of the General Thesis as "the world exists" (*Die Welt ist*).

24. See the recent study by Brainard (2002, part 2, chaps. 3 and 4). This concept of freedom influenced Sartre's concept of "radical freedom" in *Being and Nothingness* (Sartre 1956, 315).

25. In his early years, Husserl was influenced by Schopenhauer's philosophy (see Schuhmann 1977, 9, 34, 51). Although there is no mention of Schopenhauer in Husserl's later years, it rings a striking bell when Husserl characterizes the natural attitude (the "world of representation," in Schopenhauer's words) as an attitude of "willing" which affirms being, and the epoché as a bracketing, suspending, and "letting go" of this basic life impulse.

26. This anticipates the problem of the relationship between the "mundane" and the transcendental Ego. This problem, which was also of particular interest to Husserl's last assistant, Eugen Fink, cannot be discussed here. See, however, Luft (2002; esp. chap. 4).

27. This tendency finds its most extreme execution in the lecture course from 1922/23, *Einleitung in die Philosophie* (Hua XXXV), where Husserl performs the "apodictic reduction" in order to gain an absolute foundation within the sphere of transcendental life. In this attempt of an ultimate foundationalism (*Letztbegründung*), he was mainly influenced by the neo-Kantians; a connection that shall be explored in part 2.

28. See the manuscript on the "meaning of the apodicticity of the I-am" from 1934 (Hua XXXIV, 467ff.), where Husserl emphasizes the importance of making the apodictic "I-am" the foundation of philosophical thought, although with the most significant addition that this "apodicticity" includes the world as a *cogitatum* (ibid., 469).

29. This "Platonistic" interpretation was widely held by some of Husserl's contemporaries after the publication of *Ideas I*. See, for example, Natorp's review

of *Ideas* from 1917–18 (Natorp 1973), or more strongly even Heidegger in his Marburg lecture course from 1925/26; compare Heidegger (1976, 31–125).

30. See also the London lectures from 1922, where he speaks of phenomenology as the *"mathesis universalissima"* (Hua XXXV, 305).

31. In this he is consistent with the first presentation of the reduction in the 1907 lectures on the *Idea of Phenomenology* (see Hua II, 4–5).

32. It should be mentioned, however, that in *Cartesian Meditations*, Husserl distinguishes adequate and apodictic evidence. Adequate evidence is not *eo ipso* apodictic (the evidence of transcendent objects is neither adequate nor apodictic, that of immanent objects adequate but not necessarily apodictic), although both yield "evidences." This is a reflex of the broadening of the concept of phenomenological evidence as Husserl broadens the "field" of subjectivity. See Hua I, §6–7.

33. For an account of Husserl's mature theory of living present, see Held (1966).

34. See Hua I, 70–71.

35. For instance, Husserl seems to map the field of experience according to the general distinction between positional and *quasi*-positional (imaginative) acts, as the two general species; compare Hua VIII, 112–20. A possible problem here are putative naturalistic assumptions that potentially factor into this sphere, which is, according to Husserl, nothing like the mundane sphere.

36. This effort can best be seen in the lecture course from 1925, *Phänomenologische Psychologie*, Hua IX.

37. On the topic of *"Gemeingeist"* see Hua XIV, 165–232.

38. One should not forget that "transcendental questions" also involve questions regarding truth claims and reason, concepts that a psychology as a science of consciousness does not (have to) deal with. See Hua XXXV, 301: "Es ist ein Widersinn, aus der Psychologie irgend etwas über das Wesen der Erkenntnis, über das Wesen des Ich, des Bewusstseins und seiner Wesensmöglichkeiten und -notwendigkeiten intentionaler Konstitution von Gegenständlichkeiten lernen zu wollen und somit von ihr etwas lernen zu wollen über die Vernunft, nicht als eine empirische Charaktereigenschaft, sondern als einen Titel für Wesensstrukturen der Erkenntnisgeltung, in der sich erkenntnismäßig Abzielung und Erzielung abspielen, in der eine teleologisch geordnete Sinngebung unter dem Telos 'wahres Sein' erfolgen und jede Gegenstandsregion ihre mögliche Selbstgegebenheit, ihre gültige Anerkennung als seiende und ihre logische Bestimmung erfahren kann."

39. This notion is introduced in the beginning of the 1920s. Already in the lecture course from 1923/24 (*Erste Philosophie*), the term seems well established and has its distinct meaning; see Hua VIII, 126–31.

40. For the discussion of patent and latent Ego, see Hua VIII, 90–92. For a more detailed account of the splitting of the Ego, see also Hua XXXIV, 41ff., text no. 2.

41. Carr (Husserl 1986, 176) translates this term as "infatuation" (without making a reference to the pun).

42. On the paradox of subjectivity, see Carr (1999). In this book, Carr

sets out to place this paradoxical character of subjectivity in a broader historical context starting with Kant and argues that the "transcendental tradition" offers a critique of subjectivity that is "much more subtle and devastating . . . than the one put forward by Heidegger" (ibid., 140). More on Husserl as part of the "transcendental tradition" in chapter 7 of the present volume.

43. See also Hua XXXIV, 125–26, text no. 7. On the alleged "parallelism" of psychology and phenomenology, see also chapter 3 of the present volume.

44. See Hua VII, 9–10.

45. For an account of responsibility in Husserl's philosophy, see Held (1989, 79–94) and Kuster (1996).

46. This is Husserl's path into phenomenology in the *Cartesian* (!) *Meditations* from 1931 (originally published as *Méditations Cartésiennes*, translated by E. Levinas and G. Peiffer). Compare esp. Hua I, §§3–5.

47. Natorp's work on psychology from 1912, which was closely read by Husserl, bears the title *Allgemeine Psychologie nach Kritischer Methode* (1912a). More on Natorp's influence on Husserl is to be found in chapter 8 of the present volume.

48. See Kern (1962). Unlike Kern, I differentiate the way via the lifeworld proper from that via regional ontologies. I consider it as part of the way via the positive sciences and as such I treat it as part of the second way.

49. See the text on "static and genetic method" in Hua XI, 336–45. See also Welton (2000), which deals largely with Husserl's development of a genetic phenomenology.

50. On the question of the "absolute being" of transcendental subjectivity, see Hua VIII, 497–506, and Landgrebe (1982, 38–57).

51. More on the transcendental nature of the lifeworld in chapter 4 of the present volume.

52. Only two of the five *Kaizo* articles were published in the Japanese journal *The Kaizo* (Japanese for "Renewal"); they have been published as a whole in Hua XXVII, 3–94. On Husserl's "political" philosophy, see also Schuhmann (1988).

53. A certain "missionary" impetus can also already be found in his article "Philosophy as Rigorous Science" (1911; see Husserl 2002). Already the *Logical Investigations* makes the claim for a radical reform of psychology, and from there the totality of sciences.

54. See the Galilei paragraph in the *Crisis* (§9, Hua VI, 2–60) for a detailed reconstruction of this process.

55. This thesis of science's forgetfulness of the lifeworld rings familiar with Heidegger's critique of modern philosophy as "leaping over" the problem of the world, although to Heidegger getting back to the world is only possible by doing away with the dualism between subjectivity and objectivity altogether (under the heading of a "destruction of metaphysics"), whereas to Husserl this forgetfulness is a crisis of a logical consequence of scientific progress in modernity.

56. See Hua VI, 508. See also Carr's interpretation of this quote in his translator's introduction (Husserl 1986, xxxf, as well as xxxi note 21). Although it has become "old hat" for Husserlians to correct this misreading, it shall be

mentioned for the sake of completeness: Husserl's often-quoted phrase in an appendix text of the *Crisis*, "the dream [of philosophy as rigorous science] is over [*ausgeträumt*]," does not express his own opinion, but in this he mockingly formulates the position of his critics. See Hua VI, 508, app. XXVIII.

57. This answer is but one reading of Husserl's concept of the lifeworld. See Claesges (1972) as well as Boehm (1979).

58. See Hua VI, 105.

59. While it is known that Husserl, in trying to reveal this natural lifeworld, is influenced by Avenarius's notion of the "*natürliche Weltbegriff*," it is historically interesting to mention that in a treatment of Avenarius's philosophy, the philosopher Leopold Ziegler, in his chapter "Ueber einige Begriffe der 'Philosophie der reinen Erfahrung'" ("On Some Concepts of 'Philosophy of Pure Experience'"), in *Logos* 2, no. 3 (1911–12): 316–49 (in Husserl's library), uses precisely the term "reduction" to characterize the movement necessary to uncover this "world": "The plan of an intentionally ahistorical comportment towards the world is not easily carried through. A brief reflection must teach the philosopher the impossibility to just simply think about the *world*. For what is the world? . . . Suddenly a task of its own difficulty arises before the thinker. That is, to lead the 'world' back [*zurückführen*] to such simplified basic notions, so that it in its totality becomes manageable [*handlich*] to thought, manageable [*handhablich*] for human spirit. On this first reduction, which necessarily has to be carried through in the development of any philosophy, depends not only its further conception [*Durchbildung*], its organization; rather, it remains also guiding [*bestimmend*] for the relationship and the contradiction between schools and directions, which history enumerates. The simplification, violent as well as unavoidable, of the 'all and everything' to original, complementing notions such as infinite and finite, moving and resting, becoming and being, one and many, temporal and eternal, being-for-itself and being-for-us, conscious and unconscious, body and soul, thinking and being, state of affairs and object—this simplification shows to the connoisseur [*Kenner*] a multitude of systematic accounts and historical philosophemes, which in all parts are governed by the reduction of beginnings. Perhaps no thinker other than Avenarius has so much tried to make the effort, as theoretically unsuspiciously as possible, to break reality down into a number of last basic notions" (316–17). See also the editor's introduction (Sowa) in Hua XXXIX, which traces this historical background in greater detail.

60. On Husserl's (and Fink's) concept of "enworlding" (*Verweltlichung*), see Bruzina (1989), as well as Luft (2002; esp. chap. 4).

61. It was Merleau-Ponty who clearly saw this "mundanizing" import of the phenomenological reduction. See *Phénoménologie de la perception* (1945, i), where he makes a reference to the *Sixth Cartesian Meditation*.

62. This is the title of the first part of the lecture course on *Erste Philosophie* (see Hua VII).

63. Compare some of the passages listed in the editor's introduction to Hua XXXIV, xx–xxiii.

64. See Hua XXIX, 353: "Is vocation [*Berufung*] an empty word? Has a philosopher ever . . . been a 'genuine' philosopher without the demonism of having

received such a vocation? Is philosophy to the genuine philosopher any random so-called life-occupation [*Lebensberuf*], is it for him not rather fate, which for him has decided over being and non-being?"

65. The systematic connection between Husserl's methodological and his moral reflections are spelled out in Luft (2010b). In this piece, I also show that Husserl's concept of rationality is different than traditional concepts. The main difference is that rationality is not seen in contradistinction to emotions or affects, but embraces the latter. More on Husserl's peculiar concept of rationality in chapters 5 and 7 in the present volume.

66. "Selbstgestaltung des Ich durch absolute Reflexion zum absolut echten Menschen" (manuscript A V 5/16b, probably from the 1930s, of the *Nachlass* in the Husserl-Archives, Leuven).

67. Only this kind of reflected freedom can account for one's "good conscience" as opposed to the "intuitively" conscientiously acting person. Thus, only the philosopher can truly have a "good conscience" and her life can come to a "rest" here. See Hua XXXIV, 518, the critical note to p. 40, line 27.

68. See Landgrebe (1981, 66–121).

69. Husserl's relation to Heidegger will be taken up in chapter 5 of the present volume.

70. See Landgrebe (1982, vii): the shift to the lifeworld is an approach, "von deren Tragweite sich Rechenschaft zu geben ihm [Husserl] nicht mehr vergönnt war."

71. This is the title of section A VII of the *Nachlass* in the Husserl-Archives in Leuven.

72. See Held (1996); in this comprehensive article, Held summarizes this debate lucidly and concludes that Husserl was ultimately not able to overcome "Cartesianism." One can even go further to say that neither did he *strive* to.

73. The topic of "implication" of the natural in the transcendental standpoint is very dominant in Husserl's late texts on the phenomenological reduction. See Hua XXXIV, 454ff., text no. 32 ("Die Implikation der Transzendentalen Subjektivität").

74. See Hua VI, 176.

75. Husserl owes this notion of reconstruction to Natorp, to whom the "reconstructive" method of psychology was the only way to analyze subjectivity without "objectifying" it (thereby losing its very nature). Compare Natorp's *Allgemeine Psychologie nach kritischer Methode* (1912a), which Husserl studied closely. For an account of Natorp's influence on Husserl, see Kern (1964, 321–73). The relationship between Husserl and Natorp is discussed in detail in chapter 8 in the present volume.

76. This has caused Husserl to be charged with "Eurocentrism." This discussion cannot be reiterated here. However, Husserl explicitly does not want to give a *factual*-historical account but rather one of "laws of genesis," that is, an ideal reconstruction. In a late text he even calls this reconstructive reading an "interpretation": "It is an interpretation, i.e., a sort of substruction of facts *for which all testimonies are lacking*" (Hua XXIX, 396, emphasis added).

77. One example of this is to be found in Düsing (1997); Husserl is one

systematic voice in a systematic transcendental theory of self-consciousness. See ibid., 113–16.

78. Compare Van Breda (1973, 281): "Seine Freiheit wiederzugewinnen heißt also, sich von der Welt frei machen oder wenigstens ihre autonome Quelle, das transzendentale Ego, wiederfinden. Diese Entdeckung ist bekanntlich nach Husserl nur durch die transzendentale Reduktion möglich."

Chapter 3

1. In France, the main representatives of new interpretations of the phenomenological reduction are Henry (1973), Courtine (1990), and Marion (1998); one should also mention Richir (1981/83), Bernet (1989), and Kühn (1998).

2. Wiehl (2000) and Düsing (1997) are examples of approaches that have included Husserl's philosophy from the phenomenological reduction onward in the tradition of contemporary theories of subjectivity.

3. Zahavi (1999) has shown how one can, in an extremely original way, relate Husserl's subjectivity-theoretical approach to current problems in the problematic of self-consciousness (e.g., the Heidelberg school).

4. In addition to the progressive publication of *Husserliana,* several very meritorious studies evaluating the material of the *Nachlass* have contributed to this more complete picture. One should mention here, in addition to the still classic study by Held (1966), the work of Schuhmann; Schuhmann (1988) is exemplary and particularly insightful on the late work. Further to be mentioned would be Hart (1992) and Lee (1993).

5. This line of argumentation is pursued, for example, by Marion (1998).

6. The horizon of a homeworld is always, in its previous style, infinitely expandable.

7. See Merleau-Ponty (1945, viii). Merleau-Ponty's reflections, which the context of this discussion makes clear, are motivated by his reading of the Finkian Sixth *Cartesian Meditation*—which Merleau-Ponty held to be an authentic text of Husserl's when he read it at the newly founded Husserl-Archives in Leuven in 1939 (a notion that Van Breda, the founder of the Husserl-Archives in Leuven, immediately dispelled upon reading *Phénoménologie de la perception*).

8. Most manuscripts quoted here have now been published in Hua XXXIV.

9. On this, see the ever-relevant Schuhmann (1973).

10. Several convolutes of manuscripts bear the title "Paradoxes," for example, the voluminous convolutes B I 14 and B II 7 (a significant selection of which has now been published in Hua XXXIV).

11. In these late reflections it is not clear how Husserl would see the relation of this "intentional psychology" to experimental psychology, such as the Würzburg or Wundt schools. This fact is not insignificant, given that Husserl's own background was in part in experimental psychology. On this point see Münch (1997), who reconstructs this context historically. In the process, he arrives at the thesis that transcendental phenomenology is ultimately completely independent from experimental psychology and fully "autonomous" from it, even claim-

ing that a "one-sided relation of dependence" exists, such that phenomenology could provide psychology with "norms" (111ff.) on the one hand and yet, on the other, could learn "nothing" more from psychology. This reading is problematic. Even if transcendental phenomenology is certainly a departure from idealist philosophy—in the context of Husserl's supposed conflict with neo-Kantianism—it would certainly be absurd to claim that a phenomenological doctrine of consciousness could learn nothing from experimental approaches; to the contrary, Husserlian phenomenology—perhaps even against Husserl's own pronouncements—would be very well served to take up impulses from experimental psychology, if only to receive more "data" than pure introspection might yield. But, to be sure, all results must subsequently be interpreted transcendentally, so as not to remain in a naturalistic stance.

12. Husserl's critique of Heidegger is ultimately directed against the absurdity of such an undertaking as a scientific one: "How does the ultimate justification take place for the being of the human being itself as the human being of its environment, as the human being who experiences fellow human beings as unified, thinks etc. this and that, by means of constructing an anthropology? Or does one want to say, in accordance with the latest changes in philosophical fashion: it is not at all a matter of science, science is a particular mode of comportment of particularly interested human beings in the concrete context of their lives, which is observed in abstract incompleteness if one observes it only as theoretical . . . ?" (B I 32/59b, from early in 1931). See also chapter 5 in the present volume, on the relation between both phenomenologists.

13. This metaphor originates from Schuhmann (see 1973, 195). As interpreted above, it is an intriguing image, but ultimately misleading.

14. One can formulate this argument even more sharply: that Husserl simply needs this "deficient discipline" in order to be able to set forth his understanding of phenomenology over against it. If there had not been the discipline of psychology as he depicted it, Husserl also would have had great difficulties in elucidating the sense of what he meant by transcendental phenomenology. The paradox would thus to a certain extent be a construction born out of need.

15. Revealingly, many texts in which Husserl deals with the relation of the mundane and the transcendental Ego are entitled "The Meaning of the Epoché"; see above all the texts in the convolute B II 9.

16. Thus the phenomenologist, like every other human, can have a profession (*Beruf*) or even a "lifelong vocation [*Berufung*]." This can consist of, for example, being a teacher or an educator.

17. Husserl uses this phrase—in an allusion to Heidegger's concept of the "hermeneutics of facticity"—in his public lecture "Phenomenology and Anthropology" from 1931, Hua XXVII, 177: "A true analysis of consciousness is, so to speak, a hermeneutics of the life of consciousness . . . ."

18. In this respect, the reduction certainly has an "epistemico-ethical" sense.

19. Compare the following quotation: "The hidden, absolute reason [which is] patent within the human being becomes human reason hidden in him. In the

human being, the drives of reason in human reason become patent, but in the phenomenologizing Ego absolute reason as such becomes patent, and as becoming patent, in phenomenological activity it understands its implicit and perpetual *telos* as absolute drive" (A V 20/2a 1935).

20. This metaphor of the creatures of "flatland" who are unaware of a third dimension appears, for instance, in Hua VI, 120–23. Husserl here mistakenly attributes it to Helmholtz, who indeed employs it, but thereby takes it over from the mathematician and mystic Fechner, alias "Dr. Mises." For an elucidation of this background and its employment in Helmholtz, see Gabriel (1980).

21. In 1922 Husserl introduced his new reflections regarding his "large systematic work." The relevant texts on this matter (if not already published in Hua VII and VIII) have now been published in the Hua edition of the 1922/23 lecture course *Introduction to Philosophy* (together with the London lectures), edited by Berndt Goossens, Hua XXXV. The most important of the manuscripts composed in 1926 on this theme can be found in B II 9, which are now published in Hua XXXIV.

22. See Husserl's letter to Rickert from February 11, 1921, in which he congratulates Rickert on the publication of the first part of his "system": "You have worked out your system, executed to your satisfaction and out of the ultimate springs of insight an orderly deduction of the main currents of philosophical problems, and achieved the outline for an idealist worldview. What it means to strive for such a goal for a whole lifetime [!], to need to strive for this, I know from my own experience" (Hua-Dok III/5, 185).

23. A volume (a collection of essays from experts) on the relation between Husserl and classical German philosophy is in preparation (edited by Faustino Fabbianelli and the author). However, for a sketch of Husserl's "system" see chapter 6 in the present volume.

24. One can doubt if enworlding has its systematic locus here (or only here). The intensive discussions of enworlding in Husserl for the most part take place where (following Husserl's titles) the "meaning of the epoché" or "the meaning of the reduction" are discussed. On the one hand, these speak even more strongly for the notion that enworlding is substantially associated with the reduction (and should be presented here); on the other hand, the topic of enworlding also intends something like a phenomenological self-critique, or as Husserl expresses it, a "phenomenology of phenomenology" (B II 6) which follows the first, "naive" phenomenology. It would have its systematic place, then, at the end of the systematic exposition. Another possibility of situating enworlding systematically could be through a methodological decision to present the self-critique right at the outset of the consideration. This was Husserl's approach in the 1922/23 lecture course *Introduction to Philosophy* (Hua XXXV), which starts out with an apodictic critique of phenomenological knowledge (apodictic reduction). This path in this lecture is perhaps Husserl at his "most Cartesian." Or finally, it could come after the first *preliminary* overview of the transcendental sphere: this was the modus operandi in the *Cartesian Meditations,* in which Husserl stresses to the end of this rough sketch (the *Meditations* feature an astonishingly short 160 pages!)

that he has "not lost sight of" the self-critique but that it should follow at this juncture. Indeed, this was the motive for the Sixth (!) Meditation to follow the preceding five.

25. Taken strictly, this "becomes" is ambiguous, in that it cannot be the case that the activity is "first" transcendental and after this "becomes" worldly; rather, insofar as the phenomenologizing activity operates as an activity, it is already (even if initially unrecognized) a human activity in the constituted world.

Chapter 4

1. This thesis was stated in earlier research (e.g., by Biemel), but it was soon discarded. As Welton speculates, Husserl used the term "lifeworld" for the first time in his 1919 lecture, *Natur und Geist.* See Welton (2000, 339, as well as the endnote, 460, no. 14). The passage in the lecture Welton refers to here is now published in Hua-Mat IV, 17–18 n., interestingly in a struck-out (and perhaps not presented) passage. Although Husserl had already treated the *theme* of the lifeworld much earlier—Welton refers, as Husserl repeatedly did himself, to the 1910/11 lecture *Grundprobleme der Phänomenologie* (*Basic Problems of Phenomenology*), published in Hua XIII, where he first touched on the issue of intersubjectivity—it is not unlikely that the *term* "lifeworld" is in fact first used in 1919.

2. On this "systematics" of Husserl's genetic phenomenology, see the presentation in Welton (2003, 255–88), and his broader but substantially fairly identical exposition in (2000, chaps. 13–15). Welton explains in both presentations of his thesis that Husserl's "system" is less something systematic, as it is known in the efforts of systematization, say, of German idealism, but that Husserl's "system" must rather be understood as a *systematic method* ("The Systematicity of Husserl's Transcendental Philosophy," 282; one must see "Husserl as developing not a system of philosophy but a philosophical method"). I will return to this thesis later. Welton's general interpretation states that "Husserl's most enduring discovery was how a transcendental characterization of subjectivity and a transcendental characterization of world mediate each other" (2003, 223). On this point, see Bermes (2004; in particular chaps. 3 and 4). We will return to the work of Welton as well as Bermes.

3. At the time when this chapter was written, the manuscripts on the lifeworld were not yet published. They are now available—in selection—in Hua XXXIX. Although this Hua volume is an exemplary edition by Rochus Sowa, including a superior editor's introduction, situating these texts both historically and in Husserl's corpus, nothing that is said in this chapter on the problematic nature and difficult connection of themes in these manuscripts changes, to my mind. To the contrary, the difficulties concerned with a phenomenology of the lifeworld become only greater, as new details emerge in Husserl's descriptions. The situation with respect to these texts has changed, however, insofar as they are now publicly available and can be discussed by the scholarly community (rather than having to rely on reports "by hearsay").

4. See Landgrebe (1963), as well as (1982, 75ff.; esp. 100ff.).

5. See the famous appendix XXXII in Hua VIII, 497 ff., in particular 506; see also Landgrebe's texts that comment on these passages in detail and which have since become classics of Husserlian research (Landgrebe 1982, 38–57 and 102–16).

6. See here Carr (1974; esp. chap. 5, 110ff.) in which this attempt is made. Carr speaks, accordingly, of a "historical reduction" which wants to clarify the origins of validity of the world as historical. See also his more recent studies in (1987), in particular text no. 3, 71ff., as well as text no. 10, 213ff., and no. 11, 226ff. Further, see also Lembeck (1988). On the concept of facticity, see especially ibid., 231–34. I am pleased to see that a recent study by Staiti (2010) takes up my cues to develop a thorough systematic exposition of "spirituality [*Geistigkeit*], life and historical world" in Husserl's transcendental phenomenology. This study can be seen, in many respects, as an elaboration of the systematic sketch presented in this chapter.

7. From this perspective, Husserl's characterization of phenomenology as "hermeneutic of the life of consciousness [*Hermeneutik des Bewusstseinslebens*]" (see Hua XXVII, 177) comes clearly into relief in its full critical sharpness. While for Heidegger phenomenology as a "hermeneutics of facticity" should interpret the quotidian average life of humans (human life in its "*durchschnittlicher Alltäglichkeit*"), a "hermeneutical" method for Husserl ought to be applied to the life of consciousness, which however has as its correlate the lifeworld constituted in its achievements from this consciousness. A Husserlian "hermeneutic" also ultimately concerns the lifeworld, but as the correlate to world-constituting transcendental consciousness. In the just-quoted lecture *Phänomenologie und Anthropologie*, which was intended as a reply to Max Scheler and especially Heidegger, Husserl goes on: "After all of what has been said we also understand that the reversal from the naive research into the world to the self-exploration of the transcendental Egological region of consciousness means nothing less than a turning away from the world and a transition to a theoretical specialty far removed from the world [*weltfremd*] and which is therefore disinterested. On the contrary: it is the turn that enables for us a truly radical research into the world, indeed, as it becomes clear, above and beyond that a radical scientific inquiry into the absolute being, being in the ultimate sense" (ibid., 178). On Husserl's project of a "hermeneutic phenomenology" in relation to Heidegger's project as well as that of the neo-Kantians, see chapters 5 and 9 in this volume.

8. The clearest and most comprehensive account of the development of Husserl's genetic phenomenology, in my opinion, is to be found, once again, in Welton (2000; esp. part 1). What is important in Welton's interpretation is that he shows how Husserl's turn to genetic phenomenology is consistent with and in principle already pre-delineated in the *Logical Investigations*. He thereby goes against the "standard interpretation," which looks at Husserl's late philosophy as a mere "afterthought" or as contradictory to his earlier phenomenology. In the *Cambridge Companion to Husserl* (Smith and Woodruff Smith 1995), for example, not a single contribution is dedicated to Husserl's late philosophy (with the exception of the contribution "Transcendental Idealism" by Herman Philipse [1995]), which at least casts a glance at the late work).

9. According to Husserl's self-interpretation, genetic phenomenology begins already in the Göttingen period, that is, prior to 1916; see his letter to Paul Natorp from June 29, 1918 (Hua-Dok III/5, 137): "and I may note that I already overcame the level of static Platonism more than a decade ago and have posed as the main theme of phenomenology the idea of transcendental genesis." This information should be understood primarily as a "formal statement" to his correspondent, who published his reconstructive psychology in *Allgemeine Psychologie nach kritischer Methode* in 1912, one year before the publication of *Ideas I.* Husserl read this book in detail in the late summer of 1918 and treated it in his seminar of 1922/23 (see the appendix to chapter 8 in the present volume). From his detailed marginal notes it is clear that he sees a "genetic" psychology already at work in Natorp's presentation; the latter, however, operates with a skewed methodology, according to Husserl. What Husserl described as genesis or genetic method appears in Natorp under the concept of "reconstruction"; see Natorp (1912a, 83). Natorp thus poses for his psychology the task of a "genetic reconstruction" but does this, as Husserl criticizes, without first performing the transcendental reduction; psychology is thus the movement on a scale towards the "minus" as opposed to the "plus" direction of the transcendental method (of the construction of reality, developed by Hermann Cohen). Natorp's psychology is thus in Husserl's estimation a naive, pre-transcendental science of consciousness, or more precisely, as Welton writes, "from Husserl's perspective after the transcendental turn, Natorp's analysis could be viewed only as an unwelcome mixture of psychological and transcendental analysis" (2003, 270). However, the influence of Natorp on Husserl's genetic phenomenology should not be underestimated, an influence from which Husserl attempted to distance himself through the at least dubitable dating of his genetic turn. The relation of Husserl and Natorp in this respect is traced in chapters 8 and 9 of the present volume.

10. See Hua V, 155ff. The *Nachwort* was used by the first translator of *Ideas I,* Boyce Gibson, as a "new preface" to the translation of 1930.

11. See Hua XI, 339, as well as Hua I, 109, §37.

12. This genetically acquired habit with its meanings, beliefs, and character properties cannot be separated from the I itself, as Husserl says in a supplement to *Ideas II:* "To change one's conviction is to change 'oneself.' But throughout change and unchange the Ego remains identically the same precisely as pole" (Hua IV, 311; 324).

13. On this, see in particular Husserl's extensive lectures on "transcendental logic," held several times in the first half of the 1920s (published in Hua XI, XVII, and XXXI; see also the reconstruction of the lecture in Hua XXXI, 141–42). On the reconstruction of Husserl's turn to genetic phenomenology, I again refer to the detailed study by Welton (2000; esp. part 1, 13–256). It should also be remembered that Husserl began to pose questions concerning the philosophy of history in the time that he worked out his "genetic logic." These reflections were also presented in the first part of the famous lecture from 1923/24, *Erste Philosophie* (Hua VII/VIII). These connections are also reconstructed in Welton, in particular in connection with Husserl's considerations concerning a "philosophy of culture" in the *Kaizo* articles from the same period (2000, 306ff.).

Welton shows here very plausibly how these themes—transcendental logic, philosophy of culture, and philosophy of history—systematically hang together in Husserl's late work.

14. This particular usage of the term *"Meinung"* has nothing to do with *Meinung* as *meaning/significance.* Rather, to "mean" something means, in the present context, to intend something specific within a horizon, as one says in English, pointing to something specific: "I mean this one" (and not another), when pointing to a particular from a selection of items.

15. For a greater elaboration of this horizonal structure of intentionality, compare chapter 1 in the present volume.

16. This is also overlooked in many presentations that critically judge Husserl as another representative of the "myth of the given" (as coined by Wilfried Sellars). The pre-givenness of the world is the fundamental assumption for any givenness. What Husserl thus assumes is not that something is given, but that every *potential* givenness has a *pre-given* horizon—which indeed does not appear itself or is not given like an object. For a defense of Husserl against this known critique from Sellars, see Soffer (2003).

17. I say "also" because it seems to me that the temporal meaning or dimension is not the only one. The "pre" (*vor-*) in the German word "pre-givenness" (*Vorgegebenheit*) simply has the meaning of "available" or "on-hand"; for example, *"ich gebe etwas vor"* = *"ich stelle etwas zur Verfügung,"* which may both be rendered as "I provide something." In translation into other languages (e.g., English "pre-givenness," French *prédonation*), it is mainly the temporal sense that is emphasized. That the world is "pre-given," for Husserl, means that it is simply *there;* in closer consideration, this presence indeed has a *temporal* structure, but at first brush, it is not the dominant meaning.

18. More on Husserl's notion of transcendental idealism, especially in comparison with Kant, in chapter 7 of the present volume.

19. This text (Hua XXXIV, text no. 34, 467ff.) is connected with Husserl's determination of the "apodicticity of the I-am," which is *"nothing more than the apodicticity of the Ego cogito in the epoché* with respect to being of the world that is valid in consciousness" (ibid., 469). This point reiterates that such an ontology of the lifeworld is inseparably connected, for Husserl, with reflection on the transcendental, world-constituting consciousness, which however is ultimately only accessible in the "undeclinability" of one's individual self-evidence, the first-person access. See here also Landgrebe (1982, 41–44). On the connection among lifeworld, transcendental phenomenology, and intersubjectivity, see also Zahavi (2003a). Zahavi's thesis here (among others) is that "the transcendental analysis of the historical past, of the previous generations, and more generally the transcendental phenomenological treatment of meaning, which transcends the finiteness of the subject, *must always take its point of departure from the first-person perspective"* (246, italics added).

20. See Hua XXXIV, text no. 18, 264ff. In this important text, which starts out from the Heideggerian question of the "being of the entities [*Sein des Seienden*]," Husserl wants to show that this ontological question leads in consequence to the transcendental question and ultimately requires the transcendental reduc-

tion. As Welton says, in Heidegger the world is thus only thematic in an "ontic" sense, that is, as the pre-given world of our concern, and not, as in Husserl, *also* in an "epistemic" sense, that is, as the meaningful formation of an accomplishing subjectivity; see Welton (2000, 347–70; esp. 369). Heidegger's interpretation (*Auslegung*) of the world in the framework of a "hermeneutic of facticity" is thus for Husserl entirely in good order, only misguided and one-sided, if Heidegger indeed thought he could carry out this project without the transcendental question.

21. Husserl finds himself here in some ways "in good company," insofar as the problematic of a history of self-consciousness had already been thematized since the early period of German idealism, in Reinhold, Fichte, and above all in Schelling's *System des transzendentalen Idealismus,* and later of course in Hegel. On this see Claesges (1974), and also Luft (2010d). Husserl wanted to engage more intensely with German idealism in his own words at the latest by his Freiburger period (1916) (see the letter cited in note 9 to Natorp). A serious *Auseinander-setzung,* however, never took place, and the little knowledge Husserl had came secondhand; one might mention here the interest his assistant, Eugen Fink, took in German idealism. Regarding the content Husserl received from idealistic thought, to this belonged, most likely, the conception, or at least the idea, of a transcendental history of consciousness. On this, see his philosophical-historical excerpts on Fichte, Jacobi, and Schelling, where the theme is mentioned, in B IV 9/12. How far this conception of idealism, despite already the initial differences, is similar to Husserl's idea of a genetic phenomenology, must be left open here. A first and broader attempt to compare a thinker of German idealism with Husserl was recently made by Stähler (2003). On Husserl's reception of Fichte, see Welton (2003, 270–74). Schelling, as the third great idealist, was not read by Husserl.

22. It is known that this distinction is introduced by Husserl in the context of his analyses of constitution in *Ideas II* (Hua IV) and means there the naturalistic and the personalistic manners of consideration, respectively. Against this meaning, I use the concepts of "inner" and "outer" in reference to the transcendental and natural attitude in the sense of the late Husserl, thus in the sense of speaking of the "first-person" and "third-person perspective" as made famous through Thomas Nagel. For a comparison in this respect between Husserl and Nagel, see Luft (2003).

23. On the Husserlian theory of enworlding, see the author's monograph on this issue (Luft 2002; esp. chap. 4, in particular 264ff.), as well as more recently Dodd (2004).

24. See Hua XXXIV, text no. 8, 148ff. Husserl here treats the individual monad in the "mode of the natural attitude" or in the mode of the transcendental attitude, respectively. Ultimately, it is the task of the phenomenologist "to cognize the natural attitude as *a mode of the transcendental attitude*" (ibid. 154–55). For a closer interpretation of this passage, see the text above.

25. That Husserl himself had problems discerning and consequently holding to this distinction is clear from the following marginal note to a manuscript: "Genesis, above all, cannot [in constitutive interpretation] have a worldly sense

of a worldly causality, but a transcendental sense. Then, however, the question becomes, how this transcendental genesis 'mirrors itself' in human and animal genesis and in psychological and social (pedagogic) genesis" (Hua XV, 491, from a manuscript from 1932). The metaphor of "mirroring" of the worldly in the transcendental stems from Natorp's reconstructive psychology, where it has a good meaning insofar as, for him, transcendental philosophy and psychology are manners of consideration that are opposed to each other (the plus and minus directions on an axis). The discussion of "mirroring" in the framework of Husserl's phenomenology, then, seems to me rather out of place, insofar as the transcendental sphere ought to have an entirely different character than the mundane I.

26. See Hua IV, 143ff., as well as Hua IX, 108. This is also emphasized by Held in his sovereign presentation (2003). As Bermes (2004) also aptly says (205): "By means of the interpretation of the 'world-attitudes' of the embodied, interpersonally acting and historically temporalizing subject, [Husserl's] phenomenology reformulates the world problem or the concept of the world as a theme which can be described according to different claims."

27. See Landgrebe (1982, 45–47).

28. See Hua XXXIV, 148 (especially the entirety of text no. 8).

29. The German *Welt* (world) descends etymologically from the Middle High German *weralt*, which is a combination of *wer* (human being, compare Latin *vir*) and *alt* (age, time, lifetime). The addition of "intersubjectively" to the world is thus, strictly speaking, tautological according to the original meaning of "*Welt*."

30. It is well known that Husserl also speaks of groups of people as "personalities of a higher order" or as an "analogue of an individual person" (Hua XV, 154; see also the detailed analysis on this topic in Hua XIV).

31. Reading *bin* (am) instead of *sind* (are) in the original manuscript.

32. In this sense, see also Lembeck (1988); it must be shown, as Lembeck says, "that history is grounded constitutively in transcendental subjectivity, which in turn always occurs as a human in the world." This is supplemented in Bermes (2004, 196): "[Husserl's] research project is expanded in the course of his studies towards a transcendental empirical historiography. In this project transcendental subjectivity is demonstrated as a historically self-temporalizing subjectivity—and indeed incarnated in a personal culture and its rational history."

33. On this concept, see Hua XXXIV, 153ff., as well as chapter 5 in the present volume, wherein the attempt is made to understand Husserl's discussion of the "transcendental person" or "transcendental humanity" as a concept brought into play especially against Heidegger's critique.

34. See Hua-Dok II/1, 216 (from manuscripts in connection with Fink's Sixth *Cartesian Meditation* from 1934).

35. The connection between lifeworld and transcendental subjectivity is also shown very nicely in Bermes (2004, e.g., 219). Bermes' thesis throughout this work is that world in Husserl connects with the subjective life of the Ego as a "utopian 'I-life' in active fullness that is not bound to a standpoint" (ibid., 220). See also ibid., 221: "Transcendental subjectivity can indeed be qualified as utopian in another sense. Namely, it expresses itself in the functional attitude in the

'world' and in this process, 'world' can make itself into a theme of its own. The transcendental subject is the subject for which world as a theme of its own is an issue for itself in its inserting itself in the world [*dem es in seinem Einstellen in Welt um Welt als einem Thema ihrer selbst geht*]." This latter formulation, which recalls Heidegger's formulation with respect to Dasein, "*dem es in seinem Sein um dieses Sein selbst geht*" (for which its own being is an issue), makes clear that world and subjectivity are nothing but structural moments of a comprehensive structure, or, in Heidegger's terminology, "world" is also in Husserl nothing other than an "existential" of a (not just the specifically human) subject, but this can only be fully comprehensible through the transcendental turn.

36. This is the Husserlian title of the A VII group in Husserl's *Nachlass,* in which he gathered the large part of his texts on the analysis of the lifeworld.

37. See Husserl's discussion of the absolute as an "absolute *factum,*" already in Hua XV, 403 (from 1931): "*The absolute that we disclose is an absolute fact.*"

38. The manuscript, encompassing sixty-nine pages, appears to originate in whole from October 1932. It bears the following summary of the contents on the cover page 1a: "Problem der Weltanschauung. Möglichkeit einer Ontologie. Seiendes—in der Welt als Universum, bezogen auf die Universalität fungierender Subjektivität. Überhaupt über Sein. Kritik der naiven 'klassischen' Idee von Seiendem etc. Sein und adäquate Wahrnehmung. 'Evidenz der inneren, Nichtevidenz der äußeren Wahrnehmung'. Reine Erfahrung. Klassische Idee des Seinden und Wissenschaft." Parts of this manuscript are now already published in Hua XXXIX (on Husserl's late texts on the constitution of the lifeworld).

Chapter 5

1. The first major (i.e., book-length) work that deals with the Husserl–Heidegger relationship is Misch's (Dilthey's son-in-law, pupil, and initiator of Dilthey's *Gesamtausgabe*) *Lebensphilosophie und Phänomenologie* (1929–30). This book was studied intensively by Husserl; see van Kerckhoven (1999/2000). (This volume of the *Dilthey-Jahrbuch* contains Husserl's as well as Heidegger's marginal remarks on Misch's book.) However, as Gadamer has often reported, he and his fellow students were already in the early 1920s discussing the novelty of Heidegger's phenomenological approach vis-à-vis traditional or (to use Husserl's own phrase) "classical" phenomenology (meaning mostly Husserl). For newer scholarly work on the Husserl–Heidegger relationship, see Alweiss (2003), as well as the important works by Crowell; I shall quote from this research below. I shall also consider Tugendhat's and Gethmann's "classical" works on this topic.

2. This goes especially for the figures who were present as students or foreign scholars in Freiburg and Marburg in the 1920s and early 1930s, of whom I only want to mention the most important: Patocka, Ingarden, Fink, Müller, Landgrebe, Celms, Cairns, and Gadamer. Most of these went on to become pivotal figures in the phenomenological movement or, as in the case of Gadamer, have developed their own way of thought. None of these achievements, however, was conceivable without the influence of Husserl and Heidegger. On a larger scale, few philoso-

phers after the Second World War have been indifferent towards this discussion, which has been of outstanding importance to twentieth-century philosophy's self-understanding. Again, it is not only philosophers in the German-speaking world who have in one way or another taken a stand on this relationship. Focusing on Germany, I only mention (again) Gadamer, Adorno, Apel, Habermas, Tugendhat, Schmitz, Held, and Waldenfels. In France, one should mention Levinas, Ricoeur, and Marion; and in North America, Arendt, Jonas, Schutz, Gurwitsch, Spiegelberg, Wild, and Sokolowski, among others.

3. Quoted in Kisiel (1993, 452). This letter to Bultmann, written at the end of 1927, is Heidegger's response to Bultmann's query as to how Heidegger would write an encyclopedia article about himself. Bultmann "published it almost verbatim under his own name in the lexicon, *Die Religion in Geschichte und Gegenwart*" (ibid., 453) in 1928.

4. This term was coined by Crowell (2001, 115), following Kisiel's coinage (from *The Genesis*) of "metaphysical decade" as a term for the decade afterwards.

5. The radical reading of Heidegger's project is, of course, that he is doing something radically different from any previous philosophical attempts. Such a reading can be supported by Heidegger himself, who claims in the introduction to *Being and Time* that the whole of Western metaphysics is flawed and needs to be replaced. I only wish to say that I do not endorse such a reading and find it philosophically unproductive. I shall not argue for my reading here, but can only state it thetically.

6. In the following, I am drawing from texts published in 2002 in Hua XXXIV.

7. See *Being and Time* (Heidegger 1993, 442) and Heidegger's comment in his own copy of *Being and Time*, ibid. 98 (ad "*Natur*").

8. Gethmann claims that Heidegger's point is really a twofold critique: (a) Husserl's identifying of the *constituting* agent with the transcendental subject, and (b) his identifying the *constituted* with the totality of objects. See Gethmann (1993, 26–27). Yet, since Husserl sees transcendental consciousness and that which it constitutes as moments within *one* structure (Hua XXXIV, 469), Gethmann merely draws out a distinction that is already implied in Husserl's concept of transcendental consciousness.

9. Or perhaps even earlier, if one agrees with Heidegger's claim that the concept of the subject was taken over by Descartes from the Greek (Aristotelian) concept of *hypokeimenon*.

10. A "classical" interpreter of this sort is Dreyfus (1991, 6): "From Plato's theoretical dialectic, which turns the mind away from the everyday world of 'shadows,' to Descartes' preparation for philosophy by shutting himself up in a warm room where he is free from involvement and passion, to Hume's strange analytical discoveries in his study, which he forgets when he goes out to play billiards, philosophers have supposed that only by withdrawing from everyday practical concerns before describing things and people can they discover how things really are. The pragmatists questioned this view, and in this sense Heidegger can be viewed as radicalizing the insights already contained in the writings of such pragmatists as Nietzsche, Peirce, James, and Dewey."

11. Though it would be interesting to see how Husserl's phenomenology of intersubjectivity compares to Heidegger's framing of *Dasein* as *Mit-Dasein*, this problematic, as leading beyond the scope of this chapter, will have to remain bracketed in this context.

12. See Hua IV, which contains the unpublished draft of *Ideas II*. For Husserl's further developments of the concept of personhood in the context of the distinction between nature and spirit (naturalistic and personalistic attitude respectively), see Hua-Mat V.

13. On Husserl's transcendental idealism, see Bernet (2004).

14. Husserl's famous letter to Pfänder is published in Hua-Dok III/2, 180–84. A brief historical summary: Husserl was asked by the editorial board of the *Encyclopaedia Britannica* to write an entry on phenomenology. Husserl agreed, but solicited Heidegger's help. The collaboration occupied Husserl and Heidegger throughout 1927, but ultimately failed and was abandoned. Husserl went on to submit his own draft of the article. This collaboration can be seen as the last true *philosophical* discussion between the two philosophers. The personal break between them began in 1929 after Heidegger's inaugural lecture in Freiburg (on taking over Husserl's chair), "What Is Metaphysics?," which Husserl attended and which he clearly saw as deviating from his own method. In 1931 Husserl paid a visit to several local Kant societies in Germany where he delivered his lecture "Phenomenology and Anthropology" (published in Hua XXVII), in which he attacked (without mentioning names) specific modern philosophical approaches which he saw as merely "existential" or "anthropological." Heidegger later wrongly claims (in his *Spiegel* interview) that Husserl spoke in the Berlin Sports Palace and openly attacked both himself and Scheler. See also the definitive historical account of their relationship by Schuhmann (1978).

15. In one manuscript (Hua XXXIV, 264ff.), Husserl ponders the question of ontology in the tradition of Aristotle and from there launches a critique of Heidegger. Even from this approach the question of being leads to the question of consciousness that *has* being (the problem of intentionality) and finally to the transcendental reduction. Passages from this and other texts from 1931 that were most probably written as reactions to Husserl's study of *Being and Time* will be discussed later.

16. It might be that Husserl and Heidegger rejected the term "anthropology" for different reasons—Husserl presumably because it lacks the transcendental "index," Heidegger because it lacks any reference to fundamental ontology. I certainly do not want to propose anthropology as a "new" fundamental discipline, but merely to point to the perceived center of gravity in the Husserl–Heidegger discussion. So to those objecting to the term "anthropology," I would immediately concede that this is merely a word I am picking up from Husserl but assert that one would merely be disagreeing about terminology.

17. As early as 1919 in his first lectures in Freiburg, Heidegger criticizes the sciences for providing a "maximum of theorization" and a concomitant "greatest possible elimination [*Austilgung*] of the situation," meaning the concrete situation of *Dasein*. This situation has to be remedied by philosophy, that is, it cannot be treated in the Husserlian style of "rigorous science" that falsely emulates the

(theoretical) method of the sciences. See Heidegger (1987, 207). Heidegger is influenced in his critique of "theory" by Dilthey, as Makkreel points out in his instructive article (2004).

18. Tugendhat, for example in (1967, 263ff.), thinks that there is no apparent epoché or reduction in Heidegger *not* because Heidegger would reject it, but rather because he accepts it from the very start and only radicalizes Husserl's position. From the very start Heidegger feels no need to fend off the specter of an "objective world" that Husserl was (supposedly) struggling with. Another reading favored by Bernet (1994a), as well as Marion (1998), claims that there is in fact a "reduction" in *Being and Time,* although Heidegger does not employ this term. According to this reading, Heidegger's form of reduction can be seen in *Angst* as that emotional or attuned state of *Dasein* in which it is brought before the facts of its radical loneliness.

19. Landgrebe (1963, 34) concludes in his chapter "Husserls Phänomenologie und die Motive zu ihrer Umbildung" (originally published in 1939): "So besteht ein *notwendiger Zusammenhang zwischen der Universalität der phänomenologischen Methode und der Haltung des unbeteiligten Zuschauers,*" and then goes on to say (and I am quoting the second half of the sentence above): "[F]assen wir diese Zusammenhänge ins Auge, so wird die Behauptung verständlich, dass in der Ablehnung des 'unbeteiligten Zuschauers' durch Heidegger ein Angriff auf einen Kerngedanken Husserls beschlossen liegt, auf denjenigen, an dem der Anspruch seiner Methode auf Universalität hängt."

20. For a similar reading, see also Crowell (2002).

21. Husserl discusses the difference between naturalistic and personalistic attitudes in *Ideas I* and especially *Ideas II. Ideas II* in its passages on the constitution of the spiritual world gives an account of the constitution of world from the personalistic attitude, that is, from the first-person perspective.

22. For a discussion of these two fundamental attitudes and motivation as "spiritual causality," see the classic study by Rang (1973). Moreover, it is not by accident that I employ Nagel's terminology here, as I do believe that Husserl and Nagel have much in common in this regard. I have tried to elaborate on this connection (Luft 2003).

23. More on this notion of "givenness" and its relation to Husserl's version of transcendental idealism (vis-à-vis Kant's notion thereof) can be found in chapter 7 of the present volume.

24. In this sense, Heidegger criticizes Husserl's ideal of rigorous science, which derives its model of rigor from mathematics. In his lecture course of 1923, *Ontology: The Hermeneutics of Facticity,* he writes that Husserl wants to elevate phenomenological description "to the level of mathematical rigor. . . . Is it justified to hold up mathematics as a model for all scientific disciplines?" (1999, 56). To be fair, Husserl does not claim this; rather, his point is that *phenomenology* must be an eidetic science, and an eidetic science cannot be anything but rigorous. Yet not all rigor is mathematical. The critique—and this is indeed a valid point and presumably what Heidegger meant—must rather be: why does phenomenology have to be an eidetic discipline? Heidegger's criticism is that it is absurd to engage in an eidetic science with regard to factical *Dasein.* An analysis of *Da-*

sein should certainly be *rigorous*, but not in the sense of eidetic (which Husserl equivocates). Ironically, the criticism often leveled against Husserl—that is, that phenomenology is merely about "description"—applies in this respect more to Heidegger than to Husserl!

25. I thus agree with Crowell's assessment that the discipline of psychology that Husserl portrays here is a mere construction made to give a clear "pedagogical" definition of transcendental phenomenology, as psychology's counterpart. Crowell holds that "pure phenomenological psychology is an unholy hybrid of insights and motives culled from transcendental philosophy, on the one hand, and elements that accrue to it from a purely conjectural association with positive science, on the other" (2002, 130). Crowell's main argument regarding the unresolved feud between the two philosophers is based on the problematic or unclarified concept of the transcendental employed by Husserl and criticized by Heidegger. Husserl, Crowell holds, in turn makes the mistake of framing the transcendental in terms of psychological description, thus stopping short of his own insights because of his own assumptions regarding phenomenological analysis. Thus, Heidegger's critique amounts to questioning the assumed relatedness of the transcendental to psychology (see 2002, 135), whereas Husserl's own concept of intentionality already *thematically* goes beyond his own *methodological* presuppositions. I very much agree with this reading and believe that my reconstruction of the transcendental person as a concrete agent of intentional acts complements Crowell's reading. Yet, whereas Crowell merely mentions the theme of intentionality as the topic of psychological or phenomenological research, it has to be insisted that this understanding of intentionality in the mature Husserl is a concept that goes far beyond act-intentionality in the sense of the *Logical Investigations*. Husserl's concept of intentionality includes *all* human behavior such as feeling, willing, acting, and so on. All of this is part of "intentional analysis," an account, to Husserl, that describes the human being in its broad dimensions as "horizonal" intentionality and "connected to" or "carried out" ("enacted," to use a currently fashionable term) by an embodied agent. For a broader treatment of these themes, see also Crowell (2001) and my review article dealing with Crowell (Luft 2006).

26. To be fair, one should mention that Husserl does envision a "phenomenological psychology" that investigates intentional structures *without* performing the transcendental turn (see his 1925 lecture on *Phenomenological Psychology,* Hua IX)—but it is also fair to say that this is merely a construction in order to clarify the status of *transcendental* phenomenology. Such a discipline is indeed a hybrid, to say the least!

27. See, for example, Hua XXXV, 305, where Husserl speaks of "transzendentale Erfahrungswissenschaft" or "transzendental begründete Erfahrungswissenschaft" ("transcendental empirical science" or "transcendentally grounded empirical science").

28. Indeed, the term "monad" already appears in the *Logos* article "Philosophy as Rigorous Science" (Husserl 2002) as well as in the 1910/11 lecture "Basic Problems of Phenomenology," published in Hua XIII. Thanks to Dermot Moran for pointing this out.

29. Already in texts from the early 1920s, when Husserl develops the concept of the monad, he emphasized its "concretion"; see Hua XIV, app. II (from 1921), 42ff. Here he writes: "Das konkrete Ich ist ein durch die immanente Zeit sich hindurch erstreckendes Identisches, ein sich nach seinem 'geistigen' Bestimmungsgehalt, nach seinen Akten und Zuständen Änderndes, in sich immerfort tragend den absolut identischen Ichpol und andererseits sich auslebend in seinem Leben, dem konkreten Zusammenhang der Akte, die im Pol identisch zentriert sind" (43–44). In a marginal note to this passage he writes, obviously at a later stage: "Aber diese ganze Betrachtung gibt keine Konkretion, wie ich selbst schliesslich sehe. Das Ich ist doch immerzu 'konstituiert' (in völlig eigenartiger Weise konstituiert) als personales Ich, Ich seiner Habitualitäten, seiner Vermögen, seines Charakters" (44). In a text from 1930 Husserl then points out that the monad in its fullest concretion has to be conceived of as transcendental, as "das transzendentale absolute Sein in Form einer Menschenmonade oder transzendentales Subjektsein in der Wesensgestalt 'transzendentales Menschentum'" (Hua XXXIV, 154). As such it has the possibility of living in the "mode of the natural attitude" (ibid., 148). Hence, whereas Husserl has nothing to correct regarding the characterization of the human being in terms of the monad, what he does criticize about his earlier account is the methodological indifference with regard to its status as transcendental. In my reading, the term "transcendental person" merely places greater emphasis on this methodological consideration which Heidegger overlooked. For a reconstruction of Husserl's monadology and his relation to Leibniz, see Mertens (2001) and Shim (2002).

30. This is in accordance with the fact that Heidegger always held Husserl's *Logical Investigations,* that is, Husserl's descriptive phenomenology before the transcendental turn, in great esteem: it supposedly gave Heidegger "eyes" for the first time. "*Husserl hat mir die Augen eingesetzt,*" Heidegger would later write (see 1988, 86–87).

31. This issue is taken up by Fink in his critique of Husserl in the Sixth *Cartesian Meditation.* Here this critique is utilized for a different end (the reconciliation of the natural and transcendental attitudes), but essentially amounts to the same: Fink claims that the transcendental Ego, because it is not existing but a "nonentity," in his words a *me-on* (because it *constitutes* being), cannot be described by normal language, which is, as a mundane phenomenon, itself constituted. To say that the transcendental Ego cannot be grasped by "logifying" description (by using the language of the natural attitude, and there is no other) amounts to saying that it does not "exist" at all—which is what Heidegger essentially claims. For a critique of this Finkian line of argument, see Crowell (2002, 244–63).

32. Crowell (2001) has pointed out that Heidegger too insists that describing *Dasein* is itself an act of *reflection,* that is, a reflective turn that runs counter to the natural attitude.

33. Gander (2001, 217) made the interesting claim that Heidegger in *Being and Time* is performing an "anthropologization of phenomenology" because of the "hermeneutic correction" of Husserl's original account, yielding space for a "legitimate notion of 'anthropology.'" In other words, it is the *hermeneutical*

dimension of Heidegger's fundamental ontology that accounts for such an "anthropologization" of phenomenology.

34. It has been argued that Heidegger takes up the fundamental theme of intentionality in his characterization of *Dasein*'s being-in (*Sein-in*) or being-with (*Sein-bei*) instead of, as has always been Husserl's paradigm, in terms of the correlation of intention and fulfillment. This theme cannot be discussed here in detail, but, if true, points to another consistent development from Husserl to Heidegger (instead of a radical break between both). See von Herrmann (1988).

35. See Heidegger (1993, 27) and Heidegger (1999, 56–57).

36. While the absence of this philosophizing agent was already noted in passing by many readers of *Being and Time* when it was published, this issue is dealt with in detail in Bernet's insightful text (1989). Bernet reads Fink's Sixth *Cartesian Meditation* equally as a critique—inspired by Husserl, to be sure—of this dark spot in Heidegger's hermeneutics of *Dasein*.

37. In fact, Husserl does acknowledge human facticity and "existential" questions about life and death, especially in his late lectures on *Phenomenological Psychology* (Hua IX) and in the drafts on the *Crisis* (*Hua* XXIX). These issues need to be clarified transcendentally, but this does not mean that they are in themselves "fundamental."

38. In a marginal note to *Being and Time* Husserl writes, characteristically: "Heidegger transponiert oder transversiert die konstitutiv-phänomenologische Klärung aller Regionen des Seienden und Universalen, der totalen Region Welt ins Anthropologische, dem Ego entspricht *Dasein* etc. Dabei wird alles tiefsinnig und philosophisch verliert es seinen Wert" (Husserl 1994, 13).

39. Of course, the religious person who has broken with the natural attitude will go elsewhere.

40. See Hua-Dok II/1, 192.

41. See also the following interesting passage from the *Nachlass* (B II 4/82) from 1929: "diese Welt . . . ist nichts von ihm, dem absoluten Ich und Ichleben Getrenntes, nicht etwas neben ihm und zu ihm Beziehung Habendes. Es hat zu ihm Beziehung als in ihm Konstituiertes zum Konstituierenden, und diese Beziehung liegt ganz und gar innerhalb der absoluten, der transzendentalen Subjektivität." This corresponds to another passage from the C-manuscripts where Husserl states that the world is a "transcendental non-Ego" (*transzendentales Nicht-Ich*). See also Hua XXXIV, 230–31, where Husserl speaks of transcendental phenomenology as a "self-interpretation [*Selbstauslegung*] of the transcendental Ego according to that which it is for itself and that which it posits in itself as 'non-Ego' ['*Nicht-Ich*']." On this topic, see Zahavi (2003a).

42. Note that Husserl here employs the term *Dasein* almost as a matter of course, as well as his curious reversal of "abstract" and "concrete"!

43. Indeed, as Husserl says explicitly in a conversation with Cairns in 1931: "Constitutional analysis is not the same as descriptive analysis. . . . Such naiveté is present also in Heidegger so far as he takes *Dasein* (human existence) as basic instead of having its constitution, its genesis parallel to the world-genesis" (Cairns 1976, 27–28).

44. Recall that, to Heidegger, transcendental constitution was a possibility of the *factical* self!

Chapter 6

1. On the systematic order in which Husserl left his *Nachlass* to posterity, compare Luft (2004b). Although Husserl ordered his vast manuscripts under the external pressure of establishing an archive outside of Germany to save himself (and his wife) from the Nazis, this order, which is still in use in the Husserl Archives, was not done without systematic intent.

2. The *Husserliana* does not reflect a systematics, but is a rather pragmatic edition of his works. The history and character of the *Husserliana* with its subseries can be found in Vongehr (2007).

3. On Husserl's notion of phenomenology as "first philosophy," see Luft (2010d) and Luft (2011).

4. See, however, the newer work by Sandmeyer (2009).

5. Natorp composed this last work, which was deemed by its critics as a "departure from neo-Kantianism" (of the traditional Marburg form), in 1924, the year of his death. The text was not published until 1954, however. More on this work in chapters 8 and 9 in the present volume. Hence, it is impossible that Husserl knew of this work firsthand, though he was, of course, in touch with Natorp through their correspondence and there was also a deep connection between the universities of Freiburg and Marburg, both through students who shuttled back and forth as well as Husserl's pupil Heidegger, who befriended Natorp. It is possible that through Heidegger, Husserl was informed about Natorp's plans. For the above context it is irrelevant, however, whether or not Husserl knew of this specific work of Natorp's. What is important is that it was quite clear to Husserl that this systematic ambition that the neo-Kantians professed was their profound link to the ambitions in classical German philosophy.

6. I take this from Fink's unpublished text entitled "Elemente einer Husserl-Kritik" from the spring of 1940, where Fink writes: "Die nüchtern-pathetischen Forderungen der Husserlschen Phänomenologie: 'wirklich handanlegende Arbeit,' 'wirkliche Erledigung der Probleme in mühseligen Studien' usw.—dies alles braucht philosophisch noch keinen Pfifferling wert zu sein. Der Schweiß der Arbeit ist noch kein Argument. Husserls Arbeitspathos ist auch eine Seite des antispekulativen Stiles seines Denkens. . . . Der Antagonismus von Spekulation und Analyse kann erst dann fruchtbar sein, wenn der spekulative Begriff die Bedingung der Möglichkeit analytischen Verstehens eröffnet." Quoted from the copy kept at the Husserl-Archives in Leuven under the signature Y Fink 5/p. 2.

7. See Hua I, 178. The outlines of such a "critique of the critique" (apodictic critique) can be retraced in Hua XXXV, though Husserl was—as always—not pleased enough with this presentation (in his lectures) to publish it, as originally planned.

8. On the Husserl–Fink relation, compare the numerous works by Bruzina. I have also dealt with this relation in detail in Luft (2002), where I also discuss Bruzina's work. I cannot get into the details of this debate here, but just reiterate my conclusion here that I reject the "Finkian" reading of Husserl and Bruzina's Finkian intepretation, which no longer follows the program Husserlian phenomenology pursues. This is an interpretation in which I side with scholars such as Crowell, Zahavi, and some others who reject—not lightly, it should be noted—this "Gnostic" reading (Crowell) of transcendental phenomenology.

9. "Dialectics" is a term that comes up in Husserl's writings in essentially two unrelated senses. First, "dialectics" is used almost as a synonym for Plato's philosophy; see, however, the interesting passage in *Formal and Transcendental Logic* (Hua XVII, 6), where he adds that this Platonic device is nothing other than "logic or theory of science in my [!] sense." Second, dialectics is assigned the decidedly negative sense of mere "speculative, logically terminological play" (see ibid., 208) without adhering to the things themselves—certainly with German idealism or especially its negative developments in the second half of the nineteenth century serving as examples. As I shall demonstrate in this chapter, this knee-jerk reaction Husserl had against German idealism is belied by his own speculative reflections on the nature of phenomenology as a system.

10. The manuscripts pertaining to these themes still await publication. They are scheduled to be published under the title "Grenzprobleme der Phänomenologie."

11. See *Husserliana* VII, 394. Husserl's systematic sketches (reprinted in Hua XV, xxxvi–xl, and Hua-Dok II/2, 4–9) show that phenomenological metaphysics always comes as the latest step of the system. All true, that is, transcendental philosophy *must* start with the Ego.

12. The term "dialectics" has been used several times in scholarship on Husserl, but hardly ever do I find the term actually problematized. It is usually merely employed without further reflection. For a recent example, see Trappe (1996), who has a whole final chapter entitled "The Dialectics of Phenomenology," where he seems to employ this term to designate certain "dialectical," which is to say, contradictory, antithetical notions thematized in phenomenology such as world-Ego, teleology-freedom, facticity-absolute. The reader never learns, however, what exactly "dialectics" is supposed to mean.

13. Here is the entire passage in the original: "Nun ist aber der doppelte Sinn des Ausdrucks 'transzendental' nicht zufällig; er verweist vielmehr auf die Selbstbezüglichkeit des Bewusstseins oder des 'Ich,' das sich in der transzendentalen Reflexion in das thematisierende und das thematisierte spaltet und damit auf die Frage nach seiner Einheit führt. So wird man gleich fragen, ob denn nicht gerade diese Spaltung das Problem ist, das die Dialektik zu lösen versucht, so daß doch anscheinend die Dialektik untrennbar ist von jeder Art von 'transzendentaler Überlegung.' "

14. See Kroner (1934, 155); also quoted in Schuhmann (1973, viii). An offprint of this article is in Husserl's library under the Archives signature SA 346 and bears no reading marks of Husserl. The offprint is dedicated to Husserl: p. 153 reads "Mit ergebensthen Grüßen v[om] Verf[erfasser]."

15. See B I 5/142.

16. These relationships have been touched upon in greater detail in chapter 3 of the present volume. I am simply alluding to them here.

17. More on Husserl's proximity to the Kantian project in chapter 7 of the present volume.

18. See Husserl's review of the German translation of the "Speeches of Gothamo Buddho," in Hua XXVII, 125–26, and also Husserl's manuscript "Sokrates—Buddha" (Luft 2010a).

19. See Hua-Dok II/1, 192: "Ich bin der transzendentale 'Zuschauer'— das ist kein zureichender Ausdruck—; ich bin der Phänomenologisierende, der alles, was ich selbst bin, enthüllt und dadurch zum wahrhaften, zum erkenntnismäßig Seienden macht."

20. See Hua VI, 508ff. (app. XXVIII).

21. See Hua XXVII, 3–122.

22. See the first part of Husserl's lecture *First Philosophy* (Hua VII).

23. The connection between Husserl's theoretical and practical philosophy, as well as Fichte's influence on Husserl, have been spelled out in Luft (2010d) and Luft (2011). On Husserl's ethics and his philosophy of the *Liebesgemeinschaft,* see Melle (2002).

Chapter 7

1. The letter is dated April 3, 1925. The Kant–Husserl relationship has been a mainstay of both Kant and Husserl scholarship and has attracted a fair amount of attention lately, no doubt because of new publications in the *Husserliana* that shed new light on the character of Husserl's *transcendental* phenomenology. For some recent interesting comparative monographs, see Lohmar (1998) and Paimann (2002). The first and exhaustive study is by Kern (1964). Welton (2000), though more a detailed account of *genetic* phenomenology, touches upon Husserl's relation to Kant in chap. 6. Newer *Husserliana* volumes featuring texts that deal with "transcendental issues" are Hua XXXII, *Natur und Geist,* lectures from 1927 that show Husserl wrestling with issues from the Southwest German school of neo-Kantianism; Hua XXXIII, *The Bernau Lectures on Time-Consciousness,* the much-awaited texts from the "middle" phase of Husserl's analysis of time-consciousness; Hua XXXIV, *On the Phenomenological Reduction,* which compiles texts from the late 1920s and 1930s; Hua XXXV, *Introduction to Philosophy,* lectures from 1922–1923 in which Husserl carries out an attempt at phenomenological ultimate foundationalism (*Letztbegründung*); and finally Hua XXXVI, *Transcendental Idealism;* it is this latter volume that is especially interesting here, because it shows the genesis of Husserl's notion of transcendental idealism (going back to 1908!) and also because of a peculiar "proof" that Husserl provides there.

2. See Hua III/1, 133–34: "It becomes evident that Kant's spiritual gaze lay on this field [i.e., transcendental subjectivity], although he was not capable of claiming it and understanding it as a working field of a genuine, rigorous eidetic science. Thus, e.g., the transcendental deduction of the first edition of the

Critique of Pure Reason actually already stands on phenomenological grounds; but Kant misinterprets this ground as psychological and thereby loses it again."

3. See the "Epilogue" to *Ideas I* from 1930, where he writes, with reference to transcendental idealism introduced in *Ideas I* from 1913, that he has "nothing to revoke" (Hua V, 151). On the "realism" of phenomenological idealism, see Hua V, 152–53. The way Husserl portrays his idealism here is as a wedge between traditional realism and idealism, which stand opposed to each other in a sort of dialectical opposition. One might recall the dispute over the index to *Ideas I*, which was first compiled by Gerda Walther, a student of Husserl's in Göttingen, that is, from the early "realist" period of phenomenology, adverse to idealism (of any sort). In 1918 she provided this index, in which she created two subentries on "phenomenological idealism," one listing passages where Husserl supposedly speaks "contra" idealism, others where he is "pro" idealism. Husserl was not happy with this division and had his new assistant, Landgrebe, work on a new index in 1928, in which this distinction was omitted and replaced by the sole entry "phenomenological idealism." This index was then printed in the third edition of 1928. See Schuhmann (1973, 189–92) for a detailed account of this episode.

4. As Welton rightly says, in his analysis of Husserl's method of the transcendental reduction, "perhaps we can simply say that for him the analysis *is* the method" (2000, 289; italics added).

5. See Hua VII, 235 (from 1924), and earlier, Hua XXXVI, 66 (from 1908).

6. It should be pointed out that Kant himself speaks of a phenomenology in the framework of his *Metaphysical Grounding of Natural Science;* it is the last of the four principles of natural science (the first three being phoronomy, dynamics, and mechanics). This has almost nothing to do with the Husserlian sense of the word. For the sense in which Kant's first *Critique* can be construed as a "transcendental phenomenology" see Allison's interesting chapter, where he construes Kant in a Husserlian fashion (Allison 1975), drawing parallels between the two projects. It is not too far-fetched to say that his defense of Kant's transcendental idealism in his seminal study *Kant's Transcendental Idealism* (Allison 1983) is already a response to critics such as Husserl. In my reading of Husserl's phenomenological idealism, Husserl is not so much criticizing Kant as developing what he considers to be the correct insights. Allison acknowledges as much when he calls Husserl's criticisms those that are "raised against Kant *from within* a transcendental perspective" (Allison 1983, 331; italics added).

7. There are two historical accounts where Husserl tells this story in similar fashion: first in the lecture *Erste Philosophie* (Hua VII, here esp. 63–70, 191–99) and then later in the *Crisis* (Hua VI, 74–104).

8. One would be completely wrong to claim that Husserl has nothing to say about moral philosophy. Particularly in his lectures on ethics from the 1920s (Hua XXXVII) and the *Kaizo* articles from the same period (Hua XXVII), he develops an elaborate account of the moral person and the moral community. These reflections, however, are detached from the context in which he discusses phenomenology as transcendental idealism. For a more recent attempt to reconcile both projects, see Luft (2010b).

9. The only real practical considerations Husserl has in the framework of his transcendental phenomenology could be described as ethics of scientific conduct—the role of the scientist in her activities and henceforth in her role as "functionary of mankind." Hence, Funke's attempt to establish a "primacy of practical over theoretical reason" in Husserl merely manages to talk about an individual's self-reflection as a scientist or a philosopher and is, therefore, not very convincing as establishing a universal ethics in Husserl similar to Kant's (see Funke 1984; esp. 28). It is also not in Husserl's vein. See the conclusion below on Husserl's reflections on Kant's practical postulates.

10. I thus follow the line of interpretation of authors such as Allison, Ameriks, Prauss, Pippin, Gardner, and others, whose basic understanding of the Kantian project in the first *Critique* is that it presents one long and gradually unfolding argument for transcendental idealism; see Gardner's summary of this reading (1999, xii–xiii).

11. See Kant 1998, 111, B xix, where Kant elaborates on the "altered method of our way of thinking, namely that we can cognize of things *a priori* only what we ourselves have put into them."

12. Thus, the "third alternative," according to which things-in-themselves might, for all we know, be constituted *as well* as existing in space and time (which are by definition exclusively our forms of intuition), is impossible. This would be the position of transcendental realism, which Kant clearly rejects, because the point of transcendental idealism is that it considers the *epistemic conditions* under which things are experienceable for *us*. On the third, "Trendelenburg" alternative, see Gardner (1999, 107–11).

13. This standpoint has not died out but has been revived—or preserved, however one chooses to look at it—in modern science with the label "naturalism." This is Thomas Nagel's critique of modern science in striving for what he calls a "view from nowhere." It is the explicit attempt to rid oneself of a perspective in order to have "real," "objective" truth. Nagel's point is slightly different: while he does see it as an ideal to strive for "objectivity," like Husserl he sees it as an ideal limit. His critique turns on applying this ideal to subjectivity in reducing experience to brain synapses, and so on. It is this attempt that is not only wrongheaded but absurd to Nagel, as it reduces consciousness to objective "facts" that are "there" without viewpoint.

14. See Kant 1998, 360, B306: "If we call certain objects, as appearances, beings of sense (*phaenomena*), because we distinguish the way in which we intuit them from their constitution in itself, then it already follows from our concept that to these we as it were oppose, as objects thought merely through the understanding, either other objects conceived in accordance with the latter constitution, even though we do not intuit it in them, or else other possible things, which are not objects of our senses at all [!], and call these beings of understanding (*noumena*)."

15. See Kant 1998, 112, B xx, where Kant speaks about "things insofar as we are acquainted with them [*sofern wir sie kennen*] (*insofar as they are given to us*)" (italics added).

16. See, for example, Heidegger (1997, 153).

17. See Kant 1998, 168, B 59–60, where Kant distinguishes between intuition (*Anschauung*) and experience (*Erfahrung*), the latter of which has veridical value. It is also the final passage of the "Transcendental Aesthetic" before he moves on to the "Transcendental Logic," where experience in the "thick" sense (as providing material for a priori cognition) is elaborated.

18. See Langton (1998), who calls this "Kantian humility" and devotes a study to the notion. Her point, however, is that Kant's epistemological conception of a priori cognition is not Kant's main point. Her reconstruction of Kant's distinction contends, rather, that what Kant means by the distinction between appearances and things-in-themselves is that we cannot have any knowledge of "intrinsic properties" of things, but only in the manner in which they affect us (see Langton 1998, 205–6). What strikes me as curious, despite this compelling analysis, is that she rejects the notion of idealism for this standpoint. She seems to understand the term "idealism" in a rather Platonic-Berkeleyan sense. I think that it makes perfect sense to accept her analysis and still see Kant's philosophical standpoint as "*transcendental* idealism," which is compatible with empirical realism (see Kant 1998, 426, A370: the transcendental idealist is a "dualist").

19. I am focusing here on the *positive* aspect of the *Critique,* not the negative, delineating part of the "Dialectics," which arguably is equally important to Kant. See the conclusion of this chapter for the negative aspect of Kant's project.

20. See Hua VII, 254; Hua VI, 100–110 and 103–4; and, more pointedly, Hua XXXIV, 55, where he speaks of "the *Copernican* Turn, enacted in its radical form in the phenomenological reduction." See also Moran (2008) for a discussion of Husserl's notion of transcendental idealism.

21. Hua III/1, 60; see also Hua VIII, 36ff. See also the lucid reconstruction in Held (2003, 17–21).

22. See Hua XXXIV, 14n: "The world as universe is in the natural attitude in general no theme; therefore it is properly speaking no *attitude.* The world is pre-given; it is the region of all natural attitudes in the actual thematic sense."

23. See Carr (2003, 196), who sums up his analysis of this paradox as follows: "We must conclude . . . by accepting what Husserl calls the paradox of subjectivity: that we are both subjects for the world and objects in the world. The transcendental tradition introduces us to this radical opposition and provides us with new means for getting beyond it. It gives us two descriptions of the self which are equally necessary and essentially incompatible. According to my account, neither of these forms of self-consciousness takes precedence over the other. From the perspective of each, the other appears somehow bizarre, unreal. From that of the natural attitude, the transcendental subject seems artificial, contrived, a mere fiction. From that of the transcendental attitude, the world as a whole, and my empirical self within it, looms as 'phenomenon,' its reality placed in suspension." To be sure, the "intentionality" in Kant extends not only to intuition but to the pure concepts of the understanding as well, in that they have to be *schematized* in order to become applicable to objects of intuition. The true sense of "transcendental" in Kant, thus, is not so much that of condition of possibility in general, but that of the condition of the possibility of the categories' capacity for being applied to the intuition that we as contingent agents are ca-

pable of having. Thus, the story to be told for Martians would be completely different—and could only be told by Martians (but only if they are endowed with reason)! Also, we would not be able to understand their story.

24. Another way of phrasing this, from the "opposite" angle, would be to say that the thesis of transcendental idealism is already a prototype of the theory of intentionality. This is what Carr has in mind when he speaks of the "transcendental tradition," in which he includes, as its inceptor, Kant (Carr 2003, 181ff.).

25. We can leave aside here the distinction between real and possible consciousness, which becomes instrumental in the concrete "proof" for transcendental idealism that Husserl develops in some of the texts in that volume. For an analysis of this proof, and an alternative version of transcendental idealism that follows from this, see Bernet (2004).

26. Hua III/1, 351 is the locus classicus: "Hence it becomes clear that something like spatial objectivity is intuitable not only for us but also for God—as the ideal representative of absolute knowledge—only through appearances, in which [this objectivity] is given and must be given 'perspectivally' in numerous but ordered manners changing and thereby in changing 'orientations.'"

27. De Palma's attempt to refute the idea that Husserl's phenomenology is a transcendental idealism but instead must be construed as an "eidetic empiricism" (De Palma 2005, 200) is therefore completely misguided: eidetic empiricism would just be a different title for what Husserl is doing in his *eidetic* science of *transcendental subjectivity*. That means that De Palma's error lies in trying to sever the transcendental and the empirical in Husserl's method: this would be to miss the entire point of Husserl's transcendental *phenomeno*-logy.

28. It is clear in this light why to Husserl embodiment belongs necessarily to transcendental subjectivity, which would be completely nonsensical to Kant's notion of "transcendental." The issue of embodiment will be taken up again very briefly later in this chapter.

29. See Hua XI, 16ff. See also the analysis of Husserl's transcendental idealism by Woodruff Smith, who proposes that "transcendental idealism be renamed 'intentional perspectivism' and developed as a many-aspect monism coupled with a theory of intentionality via noemata. . . . If Husserl himself took the plunge into idealism, we need not join him. He has shown the way to the *Ding an sich*" (Woodruff Smith 1995, 384). I agree with Woodruff Smith's interpretation, which is much more sophisticated than my rather schematic account above. My only contention would be that Husserl can already be construed as professing an "intentional perspectivism," albeit without the consequences Woodruff Smith is trying to work out from this assessment, and I would add my hope that he will overcome his objection (more, it seems, a knee-jerk reaction) to the term "transcendental idealism." It seems to me that he is just replacing Husserl's "-ism" with another one. And to add one last suspicion, I feel that he still might not have grasped the radicality of Husserl's point and that he lapses back into a naive Kantian (not Kant's own!) position when he writes: "The position [of perspectivism] would be that while the *being* of natural objects does not depend on the being of consciousness, their *being known or intended does*" (384). Husserl's idealistic point is that one cannot distinguish between the two *without* lapsing into

a naive idealism that separates being from the notion of givenness—the standpoint of the natural attitude thus.

30. As Kant famously remarks in the B "Introduction" of *Critique of Pure Reason,* the two stems of cognition "perhaps spring from a common, yet to us unknown root" (Kant 1998, 152, B 29).

31. Crowell has called the realm of phenomenology, in analogy to Sellars's idea of the "space of reasons," the "space of meaning." See Crowell (2001, esp. the introduction, 3–19). I have adopted this term and have used it throughout this book.

32. One could object to this whole analysis that Husserl is oriented at a spatial concept of perception here, and indeed the history of the concept of "attitude" (*Einstellung*) comes from the experimental psychology of the nineteenth century, when it was mainly used with respect to perception; and, moreover, the examples above are mostly concerned with objects of external perception. However, the same holds with respect to other objects of experience in the broad sense. One can have different attitudes to the war in Afghanistan or the issue of doping in professional sport. This, I venture to say, is where Gadamer's hermeneutical philosophy took its cue with its notion of different horizons and the prospect of "fusing" them.

33. Mohanty (1996, 29), too, makes a connection between the noematic sense and the meaning of transcendental idealism. In his analysis, the shift from thing to noematic sense *is* precisely the sense of Husserl's transcendental idealism. The above analysis concurs with Mohanty's brief assertion, though it expands upon it significantly.

34. I leave aside here the question of *optimality,* in which a thing is given as optimal in a certain way of experiencing it. For instance, the plant lover will be completely happy when she has a certain aesthetic experience of a flower garden that "fully" pleases her, while the botanist will not stop but merely starts here with his experience. Compare Hua IX, 120–23, and Hua XI, 23–24. Of course, the optimum will only be relative as well; the plant lover can begin to refine her knowledge and feel dissatisfied with her current level of knowledge about plants, and so on. This would lead into a "genetic" account of the constitution of science from lifeworldly experience of the sort that Husserl provides in §9 of the *Crisis* or his famous text on the "Origin of Geometry" (Hua VI, 365–86).

35. On the genetic aspect of transcendental phenomenology, see chapter 4 in the present volume.

36. Concerning the question as to the role of embodiment for the subject's experience, as condition of possibility of experience of external objects, and the role of the lived-body in relation to the problem of transcendental idealism (and intersubjectivity!), see Hua XXXVI, 151ff.

37. For a reconstruction of Husserl's phenomenology of intersubjectivity and its development in social-political thought (Apel, Habermas), see the concise analysis by Zahavi (1996).

38. See Hua IX, 121.

39. On the dynamic a priori, which was conceived by the neo-Kantians (Hermann Cohen, Heinrich Rickert, and others) precisely in their interaction with

contemporary science, see Ameriks (2006) and Friedman (2010). This dynamization "can be understood as having developed a rigorous new kind of Kantian program that uncovers principles that are *a priori* in the significant framework within a particular era" (Ameriks 2006, 296). The problem with this approach is, to Ameriks, "that it has tended to lose touch with Kant's concerns with ordinary experience, which clearly interested him as much as any particular scientific developments, and which can remain constant throughout scientific change. Edmund Husserl's later work moved in this broadly Kantian direction" (296). What is interesting about Ameriks's observation is that Husserl, in my reading, intends to straddle both issues that Ameriks identifies precisely through a genetic perspective: objective-scientific claims arise *out of* lifeworldly experience. Science arrives at a "crisis" once it no longer sees this connection, just as lifeworldly concerns cannot ignore the scientific import and importance for today's world (e.g., through technology). So Husserl's attempt (at least) is intended to appreciate these two aspects of Kant's system as well. On this issue, see the conclusion of chapter 6 in the present volume.

40. See Hua XI, 125–26, where Husserl charges Kant with attending only to "the higher-order problem of the constitution of a spatio-worldly object" and not the lower problems of "primitive" object-constitution. This argument, according to which Kant—and the entire idealistic tradition—started "too high up," is an often-repeated critique of Husserl's.

41. See Hua XXXVI, 191–94, and Hua III/1, 301–4.

42. Mohanty (1996, 20) also makes this point.

43. See Kant 1998, 117, B xxx.

44. As Kern says, correctly though rather casually: "It seems that Husserl did not wish to go beyond the factical existence of the phenomenon of world constitution in transcendental (intersubjective) consciousness purely on the basis of theoretical reason; but instead he sought to ground metaphysics, like Kant, through the postulates of practical reason" (Kern 1964, 302). As Kern indicates, spelling out this idea would lead to a type of "phenomenological metaphysics." The relevant Husserlian texts on such a metaphysics remain unpublished, but an edition of them is imminent.

45. This text dates from 1923, less than two years prior to Husserl's letter to Cassirer: see note 1 above. Given all this, he asks, *"Is this bearable?"* Indeed, to an "idealistic" thinker such as Husserl, such a pessimistic view is itself a moral failure! Compare what Kant says about the virtue of optimism (*Frohsinn*) in his *Metaphysik der Sitten:* it is not a moral demand or an imperative, but rather a prescribed "attitude" accompanying the moral person (Hua VIII, 626).

46. It is pure speculation whether Husserl had Schopenhauer in mind here, of course, though it may be pointed out that Husserl knew Schopenhauer's work very early on. Husserl's earliest lectures from 1892 were on Schopenhauer's *World as Will and Representation* (Schopenhauer 1969). Schuhmann (1988, 33–35) has explored this connection—the little that one can make out about it, since Husserl's lecture manuscripts from this time are lost—as well as in relation to Husserl and Indian thought (2004a, 137ff). This issue has been further explored in my edition of Husserl (Luft 2010a, correcting an erroneous conjec-

ture of Schuhmann's). In this text on "Socrates and Buddha," Husserl himself makes the connection between Indian thought and Schopenhauer's metaphysics of resignation. While I cannot agree with Schuhmann that Husserl's concept of transcendental idealism is inspired by Schopenhauer (see Schuhmann 1988, 33), I find the connection with Buddhist thought intriguing. Concerning the Buddhist ideal of resignation and letting go, in the latter article Schuhmann reconstructs Husserl's later thought (from the 1920s and 1930s) on these matters and highlights the fact that Husserl himself made a connection between the method of the reduction and Buddhist thought. The result is the same as in his encounter with Kant in the context above: while one could presume that the reduction is equally a move from action to mere contemplation, its true task is to work out philosophy as rigorous science—to become *active* in this manner. Thus, while the *attitude* of the phenomenologist might be akin to Buddhism, the latter does not get to work actively. Schuhmann writes: "Buddhism did not [according to Husserl] establish itself *as* transcendental; this label had to be attached to it by Husserl and from the outside. Thus Buddhism was a philosophy *malgré lui*, it did not work out the idea which in fact, and in fact alone (but not in essence), was hidden in it [rigorous science]" (Schuhmann 2004a, 159). This interpretation can now be confirmed by Husserl's own words in Luft (2010a).

47. In this sense I cannot agree with Höffe (2004, 332), who places Husserl among others (Peirce, the early Wittgenstein, Heidegger, and Russell) who merely emphasize the positive intent of Kant's critique (legitimization) and follow Kant exclusively in this manner, while ignoring the negative part (limitation). They "fall prey to an optimism concerning reason that is alien to the *Critique* and remind one more of a fundamentalism of Descartes and German Idealism than of Kant" (Höffe 2004, 332). Given what I say above, it is clear that the limiting function of a critique of reason is present in Husserl as well, though of a different type from Kant's. Husserl's optimism concerning reason is more a spiteful reaction to the crisis of reason in the twentieth century than the expression of unalloyed confidence.

Chapter 8

1. See his correspondence with Husserl, published in Hua-Dok III/5. Husserl and Natorp as well as their families were on friendly terms. Their later correspondence seemed to center primarily around university business, especially hiring affairs, where both more than once asked for, and trusted, the other's good judgment. For example: one of the reasons for Heidegger's call to Marburg was Husserl's recommendation to Natorp and Natorp's high opinion of what later has been called the "*Natorp-Bericht*," Heidegger's excerpt on his (never published) work on Aristotle (Heidegger 1989a). Natorp and Husserl viewed each other as the most distinguished representatives of the neo-Kantian and phenomenological movements, respectively. At least up to 1923, Husserl read Natorp's writings time and again (compare the appendix at the end of this chapter) and remembers Natorp's "grand vision" of a philosophical psychology in a manu-

script from 1926 (see Hua XXXIV, 4). Also, Natorp was an engaged reader of Husserl's publications, wrote penetrating reviews (of *Logical Investigations* and *Ideas I*) and quoted them in his own writings. For an account of Natorp's discussion of Husserl's philosophy, see Sieg (1994, esp. 413–16).

2. Regarding the relationship between Husserl and Kant as well as neo-Kantianism, compare the extensive study dedicated to this topic by Kern (1964), to which I shall refer throughout this chapter.

3. Though Husserl felt, especially in his late Göttingen and Freiburg years, somewhat closer to the Southwest school of neo-Kantianism—especially to Rickert, whom Husserl succeeded in Freiburg in 1916 (on his relation to Rickert, compare Husserl's lecture *Natur und Geist* of 1927, Hua XXXII, as well as the highly instructive introduction by M. Weiler)—he was nevertheless over the entire Halle, Göttingen, and Freiburg periods in closest contact with Natorp. It should also be noted that it is striking that Husserl never mentions Hermann Cohen (1842–1918), the perceived head and founder of the Marburg school of neo-Kantianism and arguably one of the most renowned philosophers in Germany at the turn of the century. This is most likely due to a biographical fact: in his later philosophy, especially after the turn of the century after having completed his "system," Cohen had turned to an exploration of the Jewish roots of modern moral philosophy and was an ardent proponent of the project of a Jewish state and the question of preserving the Jewish identity. After his retirement from Marburg, Cohen moved to Berlin where he worked at the Center for the Study of Judaism, where Theodor Herzl also worked (compare Ollig 1979, 32–34). An irritable man, Cohen despised Jewish converts such as Husserl, who together with his wife was baptized—like many Jews in the (nonetheless quite secular) German *Reich*. Cohen's disdain for Husserl is revealed in a letter to Natorp of August 23, 1914, where he writes: "Der oesterreichische Konvertit ist auch so eine geschwollene Eitelkeitsfigur, ohne Aufrichtigkeit & Wahrhaftigkeit" ("The Austrian convert is also a blown-up figure of vanity, without a sense of honesty and truthfulness" [Holzhey 1986/2, 430]). Cohen makes this statement in the context of his fight against anti-Semitism *within* the Jewish community, which has to become, he believes, more "positive" (ibid.), instead of relinquishing and denying its Jewish origins, as the Husserls had done. According to the late Karl Schuhmann, with whom the author corresponded about this passage, there can be "no doubt" that it is Husserl whom Cohen is referring to here. See also Cohen's letter to Natorp of December 1908 (ibid., 369–70), where he warns Natorp of Husserl, and suggests "*einige Reserve und nicht vollkommene Vertrauensseligkeit*" ("some reservation and not complete gullibility").

4. See the account of this split within the phenomenological movement in Landgrebe (1978, 27–28); see also the note on Natorp (ibid., n. 22). In 1929 Heidegger, during the Davos debate with Cassirer, claims that Husserl had "in a certain sense fallen into the clutches of the neo-Kantians between 1900 and 1910" (Heidegger 1973, 247). It is interesting that Heidegger dates this influence to the *first* decade of the twentieth century, that is, before the publication of Husserl's *Ideas I* in 1913, which is usually seen as inaugurating Husserl's transcendental turn. See the protocol of the "*Davoser Disputation* zwischen Ernst Cas-

sirer und Martin Heidegger" (Heidegger 1991). Although one could think that Heidegger's phrasing "fallen into the clutches" is a bit strong, it is the intention of the present chapter to show that Husserl in fact not only came close to neo-Kantian (or simply Kantian) thought by 1910, but that by 1913 he explicitly embraced this philosophical tendency and came to more and more disregard, sometimes even belittle, his origins in the Brentano circle. Thus, although Heidegger meant this characterization as a critique of Husserl, it is actually spot-on.

5. Husserl's background was, of course, in mathematics, and he slowly worked his way into philosophy by way of Brentano's psychology. Natorp's background was partly in mathematics as well, but besides being formally trained as a philosopher, he also held a degree in classics. His scholarship with respect to Greek philosophy, especially Plato, is considered solid and careful, although not unproblematic in respect to its *philosophical* claims. See the second edition (1921) of Natorp's influential *Plato's Theory of Ideas* (2004).

6. How such a "philosophy of culture" and its method, a peculiar form of hermeneutics, would have to be construed in Husserl's vein will be sketched in the final chapter 12 of the present volume.

7. See also Husserl's letter to Natorp from June 1918, Hua-Dok III/5, 135–38, esp. 137, lines 9–39.

8. In Husserl's late manuscripts, he deals less and less with any other philosophers and, by the 1930s, with literally none of his contemporaries, except for (as with Heidegger and Scheler) in a polemical context. Another reason for Husserl not mentioning any neo-Kantians (e.g., in the *Crisis* of 1936) might be due to the fact that by the mid-1930s neo-Kantianism can be said to have nearly vanished from the European continent. In terms of influence, the movement had seen its final day as a philosophical school of any importance after 1918 (the end of World War I and the year of Cohen's death) and even more so by 1924 (the year of Natorp's death). For instance, Windelband and Rickert are mentioned in passing in a manuscript of the *Crisis* period, but here in the framework of a dated debate (compare Hua VI, 344). In the letter quoted in note 7 (above), from 1925, Husserl calls neo-Kantianism "*totgesagt*" (moribund), but indicates that Cassirer (and not Nicolai Hartmann, who had inherited Natorp's chair) is one of the only ones that has kept this heritage alive.

9. See the appendix to this chapter for an overview of the relevant publications of Natorp in Husserl's research.

10. For a comparison of the transcendental and the phenomenological methods (esp. Natorp and Husserl), see Holzhey (2010).

11. See BQ 326, Husserl's copy of *Einleitung in die Psychologie* (Natorp 1888), title page. Here Husserl writes: "Apriorische Psychologie Korrelat der apriorischen Erkenntnistheorie." The latter is what is discussed above as the method of "objectivation."

12. In also including pre-scientific cognizing as part of constructing activity (of the *fieri* of consciousness), Natorp already goes significantly beyond Cohen's "Marburg paradigm"; see Sieg (1994, 414): "Vielmehr gelte es [for Natorp], den subjektiven Charakter aller seelischen Phänomene hinreichend zu berücksichtigen. Dies bedeutet eine entscheidende Erweiterung des philoso-

phischen Konzepts der 'Marburger Schule' die sich bislang ausschließlich mit der objektiven Begründung bereits vorhandener wissenschaftlicher Erkenntnis beschäftigt hatte."

13. Compare also ibid.: "Dass nun diese Rekonstruktion eine wirkliche und nicht ganz leichte Aufgabe ist, wird gerade dann besonders klar, wenn man sich vergegenwärtigt, wie unmittelbar und unvermerkt die Objektivierung alles [!] Subjektiven sich zu vollziehen pflegt. Schon jede Benennung, jede Fixierung des Blicks, man *möchte* sagen jeder Fingerzeig, jede noch so entfernt auf ein Erkennen gerichtete Funktion schließt wenigstens den Ansatz, den Versuch einer Objektivierung ein."

14. See Natorp's first "sketch" of this genetic account (1912a, chap. 10, 229ff.). The operative term for the levels of *Erkenntnis* is, interestingly, *"Potenz"* (potency), the central notion Schelling uses in his ("reconstructive") history of self-consciousness in, for instance, the *System des transzendentalen Idealismus*. Compare also Husserl's reflections on *Potenz* in the manuscript pages between pages 244 and 245 of BQ 342.

15. This has led Cramer to argue that Natorp's theory renders self-consciousness essentially impossible (1974; esp. 556–69). However, the way the argument proceeds in the present chapter hopes to show that the reconstructive method for subjectivity does not *want* to claim any such accessibility. To *accuse* Natorp of this omission, as Cramer does, is thus to misunderstand his intentions. Rather, Natorp claims that self-consciousness "takes place" or "occurs" on a level deeper than that of explicit, objectifying knowledge. What Natorp wants to *preserve*, precisely through this methodological caveat, is something like pre-reflexive self-awareness, which is close to Husserl's paradigm of intuition as foundation for the phenomenological method. For an account of pre-reflexive self-awareness from a phenomenological point of view, and a critique of the "Heidelberg school" (of which Cramer was part), compare Zahavi (1999; esp. 31–37).

16. See Natorp (1912a, 191).

17. It seems that Nagel's (1986, 15) arguments against the "various forms of reductionism—behavioristic, causal, or functionalist," aim at the same intention that Natorp is pursuing in his philosophical psychology. This lead cannot be pursued here. For a comparison between Husserl and Nagel, see Ratcliffe (2002).

18. See Natorp (1912a, 200): "Der zweifache, gleichsam Plus- und Minussinn des Erkenntnisweges, vom Subjektiven zum Objektiven und zurück, entspricht der zweiseitigen Bedingtheit der Erkenntnis, durch die Erscheinung einerseits, den 'Gesichtspunkt' der Einheit des Mannigfaltigen andererseits. Die subjektivierende Erkenntnis deckt sich demnach mit der objektivierenden nach dem ganzen Umfang des zu Erforschenden, aber ist der Richtung nach ihr diametral entgegengesetzt."

19. Natorp (1912a, 24) names the three "moments" of subjectivity: (1) the *content* of consciousness, (2) the *Ego* which *has* the consciousness, and (3) the *relation* between both, that is, the *Bewußtheit,* "the fact of having (something) conscious," or literally "conscious-ity." Only this last, however, is the "irreducible" moment in consciousness, and this is the topic of psychology (see Natorp 1912a,

27ff., §3). This threefold distinction is most likely derived from Reinhold (in his *Attempt at a Novel Theory of the Faculty of Representing* from 1789, Reinhold 2010/ 1789). On Reinhold and his connection to Husserl's phenomenology, see Luft (2010d).

20. *"Einheitlicher Beziehungspunkt."* One can question already at this point whether this is a fair reading of Natorp. The pure Ego is something Natorp mentions, but it does not play a significant role in his account; whereas Husserl's argument shuns any concept of a "pure" Ego and focuses instead on what he calls the "empirical" Ego, that is, the Ego's actual life as (intentional) experience-of-(something).

21. See Hua II, 44. See also ibid., 5: "That which is transcendent (not really [*reell*] immanent) I may not use. For that reason [!] I must perform the *phenomenological reduction;* I must *exclude all that is posited as transcendent.*"

22. The pure Ego is not coextensive with the transcendental Ego. In his analysis of the constitution of the Ego as person in *Ideas II,* the "pure Ego" is the lowest level of subjectivity in its pure function as "Ego pole" and as "radiating center" (*Ausstrahlungszentrum*) of acts (Hua IV, 97). However, from the way the transcendental Ego is introduced in *Ideas I* (Hua III/1, §33, 66 ff.), it is clear that Husserl in this period uses "pure" and "transcendental" Ego nearly (and irritatingly) interchangeably. See also the insightful passage in Hua III/1, 124, where Husserl mentions the difficulties with the "pure Ego" and makes a reference to *Ideas II* (which was never published during Husserl's lifetime). It is precisely in this passage where, in the footnote, Husserl makes reference to the discussion with Natorp on the issue of the pure Ego. For a support of this reading of pure and transcendental Ego, see Welton (2000, 230).

23. A full-scale study has been devoted to this reconstruction by Lavigne (2002).

24. It is in this context that Husserl also uses the term "constitution."

25. The way Natorp describes this "natural consciousness" is incidentally quite similar to Husserl's account of the natural attitude (Natorp 1912a, 194): "Dem natürlichen Bewußtsein gilt es . . . als selbstverständlich, daß die Gegenstände zuerst da und gegeben, das Wahrgenommen werden oder Erscheinen sekundär sei." ("It is a matter of course for natural consciousness that firstly objects are there and given, whereas the being-perceived and the appearing are secondary.")

26. I am leaving aside here the question of "normal" and "phenomenological" reflection. When I mention earlier in this passage that "simple reflection" suffices to access intentional life, it certainly does not mean that it suffices in order to thematize subjectivity in its universal dimension after the transcendental reduction. For the latter, a radical reflection and a break with the natural attitude are necessary. For a discussion of this distinction compare Hua I, §15, 71ff.

27. See Natorp (1912a, vi). The published work of 1912 is volume 1 of a projected two-volume series and as such merely a *"Grundlegung der Grundlegung"* ("grounding of a grounding"). The planned but never completed second volume was to contain the actual execution of psychology under the title "General Phenomenology," although Natorp concedes that he is not sure if he can also lay

out the "systematic of the unities of lived experience" (*Systematik der Erlebnisein-heiten*) (ibid., vii) in this second part. It is, in other words, the most crucial part of his psychology whose success he leaves open at this point—and eventually abandons! In general, the *Allgemeine Psychologie* was considered a work of remark-able density, originality, and acumen. It was discussed, apart from members of the Marburg school (for instance, by Cassirer in his *Philosophy of Symbolic Forms*), by representatives of phenomenology and experiential psychology. Reinach and Binswanger (a phenomenologist and psychologist, respectively) applauded its philosophical quality, though they also pointed out the problematic elements of Natorp's sketch. Compare Sieg (1994, 416–17).

28. It is not in itself a critique to point out that re-construction is itself a form of construction, as Heidegger seems to suggest in his critical discussion of Natorp's psychology in his lecture from the *Kriegsnotsemester* 1919 (see Heidegger 1987, 107–9). Natorp would immediately concede that reconstruction is con-structive, albeit negatively. What is more problematic is what this position further implies, i.e., that there is no real difference *on the methodological level* for Natorp's insistence on the difference between subjectivity and objectivity. But this is not Heidegger's point, which is moot for Natorp.

29. This phrase already indicates a shift of perspective away from psychology being a mere "parallel" discipline of epistemology. It also, at least programmati-cally, follows Cohen's system, who wanted to complete the "constructive" work in the areas of theory, practice, and aesthetics with a psychology as the "unity of cultural consciousness" (*Einheit des Kulturbewusstseins*). Cohen, however, died (in 1918) before he could compose this last part of his "system of philosophy."

30. This modification was not so much a giving up of the reconstructive method as it was Natorp abandoning the notion of an inversion of constructive and reconstructive methods. This led him to a radicalization of the reconstruc-tive method. The change in Natorp's method can already be seen in his review of Bauch's Kant book of 1918 (Natorp 1918), and is further carried out in his lectures on "Allgemeine Logik" of 1920 (see Natorp 1980) and in his posthu-mous works *Vorlesungen über praktische Philosophie* (1925) and *Philosophische System-atik* (edited from the *Nachlass* by Hans Natorp [Natorp's son] in 1958 [Natorp 2000]); see also the fine introduction by Gadamer (ibid., xi–xvii), who was, after all, a student of Natorp's). Natorp's late development clearly distanced him from neo-Kantianism in the "classic" sense; for an account of this development com-pare Stolzenberg (1995), as well as Wolzogen (1985). Finally, compare also Fer-rari (2010).

31. Gadamer has also called him "the most rigorous methodological fa-natic of the Marburg school" in his introduction to Natorp's *Philosophische Sys-tematik* (Natorp 2000, xi).

32. "Der Gegensatz Objekt-Subjekt, der hier überall spielt, findet erst seine verständliche Aufklärung durch die phänomenologische Reduktion bzw. in der Kontrastierung der natürlichen Einstellung, aus der natürlichen Reflexion, die Vorgegebenheiten, Seiendes, Objekte im Voraus hat, und der transzendentalen Einstellung, die auf das *Ego cogito* zurückgeht, also in die absoluten Reflexion übergeht, die die Urtatsachen setzt und Urerkenntnis, also absolute Erkenntnis

von möglicher Erkenntnis, die nichts vorgegeben hat, sondern sich selbst habendes Erkennen ist."

33. See, for example, Hua VII, 382.

34. For Husserl's account of motivation as "fundamental law of the spiritual world," see Hua IV, 211ff. (§§ 54–61).

35. See Hua XXXIV, 4.

36. I have tried to show this in greater detail (Luft 2004a).

37. As Welton has suggested to me, this may be an interesting application of Kant's principle that the unity of the subject is to be found in the unity of the object; see Kant 1998, 248, B 136 ff.

38. See the Natorp quotation on page 11 of Holzhey (1991) as well as his discussion on pages 11 and 12.

39. See Kant 1998, 245ff., B 129ff. Natorp himself points out that this distinction is the decisive difference between his own and Husserl's position in his penetrating review of Husserl's *Ideas I*. This review first appeared in 1913, but was reprinted in 1917–18 (Natorp 1973, here 41). See also Sieg's comment on this difference (Sieg 1994, 414–15).

40. See Natorp (1912a, 199): " 'unendlich ferner Punkt' "—" 'infinitely distant point.' "

41. In his review of Bauch's Kant book, Natorp defines philosophy as follows: "Ist doch Philosophie überhaupt nichts anderes als das Bewußtsein der zentral begründeten *Einheit,* der *unzerstückten, nie zu zerstückenden Ganzheit* des Kulturlebens"— "Indeed, philosophy is nothing but the consciousness of the centrally founded *unity,* of *the unsevered, never to be severed unity* of cultural life" (Natorp 1918, 426; emphasis added).

42. In Husserl's discussion of the transcendental and phenomenological methods, he himself presents the two as correlative or at least compatible, although the phenomenological method goes deeper. In this account, the transcendental method as regressing to "logical origins . . . , leading back to logical beginnings and principles" (Hua VII, 382), in turn calls for a deeper inquiry into the origins *of* these origins—that is, the *transcendental* reduction. Thus, he goes on: "*These* origins of cognition, the *logical ones,* call for a further regress to origins, namely a transcendental phenomenological inquiry into the constitution of that which is referred to as objective in these principles: the *origins of objectivity in transcendental subjectivity*" (ibid.). Compare also the discussion of this passage in the following section of the present chapter.

43. Natorp compares his and Husserl's methods especially in his review of *Ideas I;* see Natorp (1973, 37–38 and 54ff.).

44. See Natorp (1912a, 229ff.).

45. As both Kern (1964, 348) and Welton (2000, 198ff.) argue, what Husserl had in mind with this retrospective self-interpretation were most likely his analyses of inner time-consciousness, which Husserl first presented in his lecture course of 1904/05 (published in Hua X). This discussion is not crucial for the above train of thought, and hence need not be broached here.

46. Compare Husserl's reflections in his text on "static and genetic phe-

nomenological method" especially with regard to the question of *Leitfäden* (guiding clues), Hua XI, 336–45.

47. See the subsequent passage where Husserl reflects on the relation between (his own) progressive and regressive methods.

48. These concepts are familiar from Husserl's late reflections on the problems of passive genesis; see Hua XI and XV.

49. I am indebted to R. Sowa of the Husserl-Archives in Leuven for bringing this passage to my attention; it is now published in Hua XXXIX, 2.

50. See a list of these and more passages in Kern (1964, 370–72).

51. To be sure, there are still many other areas of philosophy where Husserl drew heavily from the neo-Kantians—and not exclusively from the Marburg school, though I have focused on the latter here. One would also have to mention Husserl's reflections on the philosophy and theory of science; reflections that he carried out mostly in conversation with the Southwest school of neo-Kantianism, especially Windelband and Rickert (compare Hua XXXII). Finally, Husserl was also heavily influenced by volume 2 of Cassirer's *Philosophy of Symbolic Forms,* which deals with mythical thought.

52. This was—*nota bene*—*after* Husserl penned his "Bernau manuscripts" on time. The latter were written on the occasion of two visits to Bernau in the Black Forest, in the late summer of 1917 and the spring of 1918 (see the editors' elucidations, Hua XXXIII, xx).

Chapter 9

1. It is noteworthy that around 1925, at a time when Martin Heidegger still conceived of himself (more or less) as a phenomenologist in the traditional (Husserlian) sense, he notes: "Contemporary phenomenology has, with certain caveats, a good deal in common with Hegel, not with the *Phenomenology* [*of Spirit*] but with that which Hegel meant with logic. The latter is to be identified with certain reservations with contemporary phenomenological research" (Heidegger 1976, 32). This is not merely a historical remark about Heidegger; he merely, and rightfully, points to a common problem in Hegel, Husserl, and the neo-Kantians.

2. See the interesting systematic introduction in Crowell (2001) where he shows how many of the ideas that, for example, John McDowell discusses (1996) have been discussed between the neo-Kantians and phenomenology in the period I am dealing with in the present chapter.

3. Heidegger's critique of the intuitive method comes most clearly to the fore in his emphasis on *Dasein* as being-in-the-world, which can at best "re-lucently" thematize its intentionally constituted interiority. *Dasein*'s true intentionality consists of "being-with" objects (as ready-to-hand or present-to-hand) or other *Dasein* "in the world." Heidegger's critique of Husserl—though this particular critique is not emphasized—and Husserl's rebuttals are dealt with in greater detail in chapter 5 in the present volume. This criticism is further advanced, for example, in Sartre's account of the *transcendence* of the Ego.

4. For an account and a discussion of their relationship, see Iso Kern (1964, 321–73), as well as their lengthy correspondence, published in Hua-Dok III/5, 39–165. This is by far the most extensive correspondence Husserl had with any contemporary philosopher. As is well known, Husserl and Natorp also masterminded Heidegger's call to the University of Marburg in 1923. For a further comparison between Natorp's and Husserl's conception of psychology, see Zeidler (2001, 144–46).

5. See Hua XIX/2, 24, see n. 1 for the text of the first edition (which was subsequently modified in the second edition of 1913).

6. This concept of a pure Ego that is lacking in the first edition of *Logical Investigations* can also be termed "transcendental" Ego from Husserl's later standpoint. Although, to be sure, both are not the same, what Husserl is about to discover is the Ego which experiences world and thus cannot be part of the world, and is therefore "pure." This conception of the pure Ego as standing opposed to the world it experiences is, in simple terms, the way Husserl understands the "transcendentality" of transcendental consciousness. See Husserl's letter to Mahnke of 1925 (Hua-Dok III/3, 450–51): "Then the phenomenological reduction, carried out on the basis of the general thesis [of the natural attitude], is merely the method . . . to study human interior life in its *purity*" (emphasis added).

7. See also his addition to this §8 of the Fifth Logical Investigation in the second edition, Hua XIX/2, 376. Here Husserl states that through Natorp he has learned to be less "shy of metaphysics" with regard to a metaphysics of a pure Ego. Here he also mentions that he left this section in its entirety for the sake of documenting a certain, dated, discussion, since it also does not diminish the importance of the train of thought Husserl pursues in the Fifth Investigation. See also §57 of *Ideas I* (Hua III/1, 123–24), where he discusses the pure Ego as the "residuum" of the phenomenological reductions and again refers to his modified stance vis-à-vis the first edition of *Logical Investigations* (Hua III/1, 124 n. 1).

8. See Husserl's account of the pure Ego in Hua IV, §§22–29.

9. Although this cannot be discussed further here, it is worth pointing out that the title of Natorp's work is already programmatically aimed at the title of Franz Brentano's *Psychology from an Empirical* [!] *Point of View* and is, to be sure, completely opposed to an empirical framing of subjectivity. Brentano's work was first published in 1874. It plays virtually no role in Natorp's *Einleitung in die Psychologie nach kritischer Methode* from 1888 and is mentioned only twice in passing in the new edition of the work from 1912, which bears the new title *Allgemeine Psychologie nach kritischer Methode,* and here only in the context of Natorp's discussion of Husserl's doctrine of intentionality (see Natorp 1912a, 274 and 286). As is already discussed, Husserl saw himself in his early years as a member of Brentano's school of thought but emancipated himself from this school at the latest after the publication of the *Logical Investigations*. Except for the theme of intentionality, that is, Husserl's phenomenological psychology is much closer to Natorp's than to Brentano's. In a seminar from the winter semester of 1922/23, dealing with Natorp's *Allgemeine Psychologie,* Husserl refers to Natorp's *Einleitung in die Psychologie* as "one of the most important books [in psychology] of the

nineteenth century" (Hendrik Josephus Pos's unpaginated notes in the Husserl Archives in Leuven under the signature N I 26, here Husserl's seminar of November 24, 1922).

10. As a reminder (and as also has been emphasized in the previous chapter), to include simple acts of "mere" perception into the realm of objectification is already Natorp's step beyond Cohen. To Cohen, only "logifying" acts count as objectifying, that is, as ascertaining laws about reality.

11. On the *factum* as a form of "producing" (*fieri*) consciousness, see also Natorp (2000, 12).

12. In his discussion of the constructive character of subjective description, Makkreel is rightly making a connection to Kant's conception of the reflective power of judgment, which needs to *construct a priori* a teleology of (and for) empirical intuition. Thus, already at this level, Natorp as well as Cassirer (although the latter might have been more aware of it) go beyond the conception of subjectivity conceived as pure reason. See Makkreel (2010, 260).

13. Cohen dismisses this subjective side wholesale. As he says in his famous *Kants Theorie der Erfahrung* (1987, 103): "It is hence a sign of critical maturity to assume undissolvable elements of consciousness." Kant's theory of experience, in this reading, has simply nothing to do with experience but with concepts. This "Hegelian" reading of Kant has also a striking resemblance with McDowell's position in *Mind and World*.

14. I shall quote the passage for the sake of its striking language: "When reading nearly all books on psychology, one cannot lose the impression that one is walking through morgues: One sees corpse next to corpse and a hundred hands busy with stripping the dead of even the faintest appearance of livelihood, even the faintest memory of any life, a memory that was at least preserved before taking apart the corpse, when all joints were together according to their original combination." Husserl comments on this passage with "Notabene."

15. See Hua XXXV, 111, 473–78.

16. Although this terminological distinction between formal and material a priori can be found in Husserl—see Hua XVIII, 220—it was especially Max Scheler who emphasized the "material a priori" as phenomenology's main discovery vis-à-vis the purely formal a priori in Kant. See his magnum opus, *Formalism in Ethics,* and also his text "Phenomenology and Epistemology" from 1916 (Scheler 1973 and 1957). It is noteworthy that in this latter text from his *Nachlass,* Scheler formulates the distinction between formal and material a priori precisely in the context of a critique of Cassirer's philosophy of symbolic forms (this passage shall be discussed subsequently); see Scheler (1957, 383–84): "Phenomenology's apriorism is indeed able to take up the correct intuitions that were present in Plato's and Kant's apriorism. Yet an abyss divides phenomenology from these other doctrines. . . . Next to the so-called formal a priori of the intuitive facts of pure logic, every factual region reveals to the intuitive regard in each case a whole system of material principles a priori, based on essential intuition, principles that tremendously expand Kant's apriorism. And in each case is the a priori in the *logical* sense a *result* of the a priori of the intuited facts that constitute the objects of judgments and principles."

17. I am using the terms "introspection" and "reflection" very loosely here. All that I mean to say is that access to subjective structures requires a turning-away from the world and a turn-to *experience* of world. Since Husserl later distinguishes between "natural" and "radical" reflection, he concedes a rudimentary form of this type of reflection already in the natural attitude, whereas only "radical" reflection performs a break with the natural attitude. We can, however, neglect this complicated issue in Husserl's theory of the phenomenological reduction in this discussion. For a discussion of this distinction, see Hua VIII, 92–97, and chapter 1 in the present volume.

18. Natorp weighs them somewhat differently, however: he calls them consciousness, the "fact-of-having-something-consciousness" (*die Bewußtheit*), and the content of the latter. See Natorp (1912a, 33–37, §6), although this threefold distinction is already to be found in *Einleitung in die Psychology* (Natorp 1888). This characterization is not identical to Husserl's theory of intentionality. Husserl criticized Natorp's view in the *Logical Investigations* of 1900–1901, which was in turn criticized by Natorp in *Allgemeine Psychologie* from 1912. On the margin of *Allgemeine Psychologie*, in the passage where Natorp critically discusses Husserl, Husserl writes: "In the *LI*, I had posited Ego = stream of consciousness. With 'experienced' in the *LI* I meant 'to be part of the being of the stream.' I denied a pure Ego. But what I said there was of course wrong" (BQ 342, 34). Thus Husserl's later stance on intentionality as breaking down into pure Ego, the intentional act, and the content of this act can be seen as a modification of his earlier view with an incorporation of Natorp's notion of a pure Ego.

19. As an aside, it should be pointed out that Husserl's later reflections on time-consciousness in the 1930s and the thematization of the "lived present" (*lebendige Gegenwart*) can be understood as a reflex of this attempt to gain access to the absolute, concrete, and hence "flowing" ("living") life of subjectivity by practicing a reduction to the "here and now constituting subjectivity" (the lived present) precisely in its "standing-streaming" character. It is for this reason that Husserl considers the "reduction to the lived present" the "most radical reduction" possible (see Hua XXXIV, 185–88). See also the still-decisive monograph on this topic by Held (1966, 67–78).

20. That is, Natorp does not operate with the Husserlian distinction between "natural" and "radical" reflection, the latter of which breaks with the general thesis of the natural attitude.

21. Husserl also characterizes the reduction as accessing the dimension of intentional manifold from the uniform "object pole" (from the experienced object to the multiple intentional acts which "constitute" it). See *Ideas I* (Hua III/1, 231): "If we take this 'object' and all of its objective 'predicates'—noematic modifications of the object's predicates, predicates which are straightforwardly posited as real in normal perception—so the object as well as the predicates are certainly unities vis-à-vis manifolds of constituting conscious lived-experiences (concrete noeses)."

22. Natorp uses this phrase (Natorp 1913, 202).

23. The *Allgemeine Psychologie* was conceived as book 1 of altogether (presumably) two books. Natorp announces in the preface that he will "shortly" make

the second volume available, but this second part never appeared. One can speculate that it was due to internal problems in his method that he felt compelled to change his stance on a "general" psychology. In turn, Natorp focused on what he was later to call "general logic" and abandoned the project of a critical psychology altogether. This transformation is reconstructed in detail by Stolzenberg (1995, 189–249). Holzhey, in his comparison between Husserl's and Natorp's draft of a psychology, also comments critically: "Natorp's foundation of a philosophical psychology gives us only meager contributions to a theory of subjectivity, contributions that are oriented at traditional psychological dispositions. Husserl's phenomenological analyses give us incomparably richer material and have, accordingly, been received much more intensively in the positive sciences" (1991, 18; see also Holzhey 2010). In a letter to Husserl from July 2, 1918, Natorp characterizes his attempts as follows: "actually it is not psychology, but a doctrine of categories for psychology" (Hua-Dok III/4, 139).

24. For a critique of Natorp's method, following Heidegger's criticism of reflection, see also Zahavi (2003b, esp. 155–60).

25. The development of Husserl's genetic phenomenology begins in this period, when Husserl, in 1917–18, penned his famous "Bernau manuscripts" on time-consciousness (now published in Hua XXXIII). See the elucidations regarding the connection between the analysis of time-consciousness and genetic analysis in the editors' introduction, ibid., xlvi–xlix.

26. Husserl makes this statement in the context of the alleged characterization of his phenomenology as "Platonism," a critical point Natorp had made in his review of the *Logical Investigations*. However, in his discussion of Husserl's "new standpoint" in *Allgemeine Psychologie* (Natorp 1912a, §14, 287–90), Natorp insists that—although Husserl came "a good deal closer" (289) to a "genetic Platonism"—his account of subjectivity is still "static." Natorp cites here Husserl's *Logos* article, "Philosophy as Rigorous Science" from 1911, which (to be fair to Husserl) was merely intended as a programmatic chapter against "historicism" and *Lebensphilosophie*. On the margin of this passage in *Allgemeine Psychologie*, Husserl thus complains: "There is no mention of the difference that I make in the Logos [article] concerning phenomenology and psychology!" (BQ 342, 290). With regard to Natorp's conception of philosophy as "genetic," Husserl most likely extracted this from Natorp's *Deutscher Weltberuf* of 1918 (see Hua-Dok III/5, 172 n., 178), which he also read at the time (at the end of the First World War). In this book, written for a broader audience, Natorp lays out a teleological view of world history.

27. Edmund Husserl, "Nachwort zu meinen 'Ideen zu einer reinen Phänomenologie und phänomenologischen Philosophie' (1930)," in Hua V (138–62, here 142).

28. See Kern (1964, 348). The above statement is incorrect, but not because Husserl did not broach genetic themes in this period, as he did, for example, in his *Thing and Space* lecture course from 1907; see Hua XVI. What makes it problematic is that Husserl claims that he has "posited the theme of genetic analysis for phenomenology," which implies an explicit statement about "genetic analysis." While it is true that genetic analysis was at work in this period as well as,

more explicitly, in 1917–18, Husserl does not come to characterize his attempts as "genetic phenomenology" until the 1920s. In other words, his reflections on method came after his actual methodological work.

29. Aristotle in Physics 219b2 defines time as *arithmòs kinéseos katà tò próteron kaì tò hysteron,* that is, as the (counted) number of movement regarding the earlier and the later, much like pearls on a string, whereas for Husserl the "now" is only an ideal limit. In this analysis, Husserl is indebted to William James's and Henri Bergson's analyses of internal time as consisting of an "impression" of now with "fringes" rather than discrete boundaries. See Held (2003).

30. This is, to be sure, a very condensed summary of Husserl's phenomenology of inner time-consciousness. His 1904/05 lecture course and other texts pertaining to this topic are to be found in Hua X.

31. The same goes, although not in a temporal fashion, for the conscious life of another person: I can never bring another's own subjective experience to direct intuition. This is precisely the problem setting up Husserl's reflections on intersubjectivity; see especially the Fifth *Cartesian Meditation,* see Hua I, 87–88. See also Hua XXXIV, 287, where Husserl uses the term "reconstruction" precisely in the context of describing the experience of another Ego.

32. To draw on what has been explained in chapter 4, though Husserl insists on the eidetic character of genetic analysis, what he calls "laws of genesis," these laws are not of the "hard" character of eidetics in static analysis. They are, rather, "fuzzy laws," "lawfulnesses" in a weaker form, precisely because the givennesses they refer to cannot be brought to direct givenness, but must be reconstructed as explained above.

33. See Hua XI, 345.

34. See the passages Kern has collected in Kern (1964, 370–73). See also Hua XXXIV, 287.

35. For an in-depth presentation of Husserl's turn to genetic phenomenology and a full outline of this genetic method, see Welton (2000), as well as Steinbock (1995) and chapter 4 in the present volume.

36. Compare the quotation in chapter 8 in the present volume (229). See also the following passage from Hua XI (an appendix to the lectures): "In a certain way, we can therefore distinguish 'explanatory' phenomenology as a phenomenology of regulated genesis, and 'descriptive' phenomenology as phenomenology of possible, essential shapes . . . in pure consciousness and their teleological ordering in the realm of possible reason. . . . In my lectures [on transcendental logic, Hua XI], I did not say 'descriptive,' but rather 'static' phenomenology" (Hua XI, 340).

37. Judging from the stylistic character of Husserl's marginal remarks, Husserl read *Einleitung in die Psychologie* (Natorp 1888) in the first decade of the twentieth century. He also was confronted with Natorp's ideas through discussion groups conducted by Johannes Daubert in 1905 and later. See Schuhmann (2004b, 299–301).

38. For this distinction, see the classic monograph by Rang (1973).

39. Welton also mentions the influence of Natorp (Welton 2000, 443 n. 38), but does not get into this influence in any detail. See, however, his account

in (2003) where he gives the Natorp influence a broader treatment; see ibid., 266–70. Here (270) he concludes that "from Husserl's perspective after the transcendental turn, Natorp's analysis could be viewed only as an unwelcome mixture of psychological and transcendental analysis," while conceding that there is an influence on Husserl from the part of Natorp. From what has been said above, it should be clear that this influence was crucial to Husserl's transcendental recasting of phenomenology.

40. See the aforementioned letter to Natorp from 1918 (Hua-Dok III/5, 137), as well as Husserl's letter to Cassirer of 1925 (Hua-Dok III/5, 4–5). One should also bear in mind that the bulk of Husserl's manuscripts on metaphysics and teleology are still unpublished (section E III of his *Nachlass*).

41. Following Husserl's terminology especially in *Ideas I*, the *noetic* "side" of transcendental subjectivity is the *act of* (thinking, remembering, etc.), whereas the noematic aspect is the object *insofar as it is experienced*. Thus, the immanently given, not the transcendent object, must be viewed as *intentum*. See *Ideas I* (Hua III/1, 200–224, the chapter on "Noesis and Noema"). This interpretation is indebted to Holzhey's lucid article already referred to (2010), where he compares especially Natorp's and Husserl's methods as paradigms of both philosophical schools. He interprets the task of Natorp's psychology as—in Husserl's terms—"constitutive-noematic" (15), which leaves out the constitutive-noetic aspect, the aspect that is supplied by Husserl. Although Holzhey does not spell out this consequence, I do not hesitate to admit that it is this basic insight which has aided the author in developing the interpretation presented here.

42. See Heidegger's little-known text on the history of the philosophical chair (*Lehrstuhl*) in Marburg, written on the occasion of the 400th anniversary of the University of Marburg in 1927 (1991, here 309–10), an account that gets the relation between Natorp and Cassirer just right: "In the last years, *Cassirer* strives to sketch a general 'philosophy of culture' on the basis of the neo-Kantian paradigms. His 'Philosophy of Symbolic Forms' strives to subsume the activities [*Verhaltungen*] and formations of spirit under a systematic interpretation following the idea of 'expression' as guiding clue. In his way, Cassirer converges with the attempts of *Natorp*, attempts that take their bearings more on the general categorial grounding of the system and not in the concrete interpretation of single 'symbols' of spirit."

43. Indeed, such a judgment is also unfair with respect to Natorp and Cohen as well. Cohen first conceived of the transcendental method and limited it, at least in his commentaries to Kant's first *Critique*, to the positive sciences. Yet to reduce Cohen to his work on theoretical philosophy deliberately ignores his extensive works on ethics, aesthetics, and, especially, religion. See the accounts of the scope of Cohen's philosophy by Stolzenberg (1995) and Holzhey (1986/1).

44. See Gadamer's (after all, a pupil of Natorp's) introductory text to Natorp's late work, *Philosophische Systematik* (Natorp 2000, xii–xiii): "[In his draft of a *General Psychology*] Natorp was moving along paths that converge with Dilthey's psychology of the spiritual sciences as well as with Husserl's phenomenology. Yet his question with respect to this psychology did not have the purpose of a new grounding of the spiritual sciences, nor that of a methodological reorientation

of philosophical research. Instead, it had to do with the systematic notion of the unity of philosophy as such that appears to him in the correlation of objectivation and subjectivation. That is, it is about the full dominance of the concept of method, of process, the dominance of the *fieri* even over the *factum* of science. In this sense, Natorp appeared to be the most rigorous methodological fanatic and 'logicist' of the Marburg school."

45. See Natorp (1912b, 194): "This is precisely what we mean by philosophy as 'method': every fixed 'being' must become soluble into a 'path,' a *movement* of thought."

46. In Cassirer's obituary of Natorp (1925, 288).

47. See Holzhey (1986/1, 56 and passim). See also Ollig (1979, 30–33).

48. See Kant 1998, 574, B 641: "Yet if pure reason for itself can be practical and really is practical, as the consciousness of the moral law demonstrates, it remains nevertheless always one and the same reason that, be it in theoretical or practical intent, judges according to principles a priori." See also *Critique of Judgment* (Kant 1990, 2). Here Kant differentiates the application of reason in its "purely theoretical" *Gebrauche* (use, employment) vis-à-vis its practical use and the power of judgment, thereby bridging the gap between both applications of reason and as such constituting another "moment" of reason; see ibid., 11, 14–15.

49. For Cassirer's view of modern idealism in a nutshell, see the introduction to volume 1 of *The Problem of Knowledge* (Cassirer 1994a, 1–18).

50. See especially Paul Natorp (1925); here he mainly deals with art, philosophy of economy (*Wirtschaftsphilosophie*), and pedagogy. His philosophy of religion is sketched in his *Philosophische Systematik*. Natorp died in 1924 and was unable to complete his philosophical system.

51. This whole chapter deals with Natorp and Cassirer's critique of Natorp's method (see Cassirer 1954/III, esp. 58–67).

52. Though Cassirer somewhat obfuscates the origin of his theory in Kantian philosophy in his first introduction to the *Philosophy of Symbolic Forms* as he introduces it by way of symbolic notation in mathematics that he has learned from the mechanical scientist Hertz (see Cassirer 1954/I, 5–6), it is hard to miss the overall direction of his intention when he explicitly states that in his philosophy of the symbolic, "the critique of reason becomes thus the critique of culture" (Cassirer 1954/I, 11).

53. In his discussion of newer concepts of transcendental philosophy, Oberer claims that "since the publication of the 'Philosophy of Symbolic Forms' Cassirer has always been judged (against his own self-understanding) as a phenomenologist. That is, in his 'Philosophy of Symbolic Forms' one has pointed with special emphasis to the (alleged) *non*-neo-Kantian character of this work" (1969, 586). Contrary to this assessment, one can show that Cassirer claimed for himself at least phenomenological *influence*. See the footnote in vol. 2 on mythical thought (Cassirer 1954/II, 16) and the quotation in the letter to Husserl in the conclusion to this chapter. In the footnote in vol. 2, Cassirer does not refer to himself as a phenomenologist. Rather, he commends Husserl's phenomenol-

ogy for "bringing into sharp view for the first time again the differences of spiritual 'structural forms'" and for having "shown a new way that is distinguished from psychological questions and methods" (ibid.). Furthermore, as the present chapter intends to show, his philosophy of symbolic forms is also decidedly of neo-Kantian character. To be sure, Cassirer's philosophy—as a philosophy of culture—has expanded its scope by opening itself up to other forms of "structural forms" of *Geist*. Due to the phenomenological character of his approach, one can say that Cassirer treads on middle ground between both schools, as Husserl himself has moved towards a neo-Kantian conception of symbolic formation as well. In other words, both move into the direction of the other and their methods converge.

54. Although Cassirer uses this term to describe Natorp's project, it becomes clear from the context that he also includes his own philosophy of culture in this framework, though, to be sure, without Natorp's problematic restrictions. The term "phenomenology" in general is certainly not exclusive to Husserl's treatment of consciousness. For instance, Thomas Nagel uses it as a title for a scientific discipline with the first-person perspective; see his *The View from Nowhere* (1986) and *Mortal Questions* (1979).

55. See Cassirer (1979).

56. For a discussion of Cassirer's "hermeneutics of objective spirit" and a comparison between Cassirer's theory of perception and Husserl's theory of eidetic intuition, see Bernet (2010). This discussion lies beyond the scope of this chapter.

57. This volume is a collection of Cassirer's unpublished drafts for the fourth volume of the *Philosophie der symbolischen Formen*.

58. One may be attempted to apply here Gadamer's famous metaphor of the subject as a "flickering light" (in the closed circuits of history), though this is entirely misleading. The subject is not vacuous or evanescent, but only a subject in established cultural institutions.

59. In this context, Cassirer likes to refer to Kant's image of the "light dove" that feels the bothersome resistance of the air but can in fact only fly in this very element (Cassirer 1995, 218, 265).

60. It is in this light that Max Scheler—in the already-quoted discussion of the relation between phenomenology and neo-Kantianism—came to define phenomenology precisely as a "desymbolization of the world." See note 16 above.

61. In this sense, of clarifying the logic of scientific discovery, Cassirer remains remarkably close to his teacher Cohen, who already anticipated a "dynamic a priori" in this very logic. Thus, the dynamics pertains not to the active subject, but to the concepts themselves that are in flux in the process of scientific work. That this work is concretely carried out by living human beings would be trivially true at best for Cohen and presumably Cassirer.

62. See the discussion of the relation between transcendental and mundane in chapters 3 and 4 in the present volume.

63. The realm of passivity Husserl also calls "the unconscious," which is "nothing less of a phenomenological nothing but itself a limit mode [*Grenzmo-*

dus] of consciousness"; see Hua XVII, 318–19. Because the realm of passivity is where self-consciousness has not asserted itself actively, Husserl can also call the natural attitude—as that way of being which knows nothing of its involvement with constituting the world—passive; see Hua XXXIV, 49 n., as well as 64.

64. The topic of passive genesis is dealt with most broadly in Husserl's lecture course on transcendental logic from the early 1920s. This lecture is published in Hua XI and XXXI, and in part in Husserl (1948).

65. I can merely hint at the problem of attitudes in this context. For a detailed analysis of these issues, see the first chapter of Luft (2002), as well as chapter 1 in the present volume.

66. This issue of whether the symbolic forms are to be understood as a systematics (hence a construction) or a certain description with "systematizing" tendencies is discussed especially in Cassirer's drafts for a fourth volume of the *Philosophy of Symbolic Forms;* see Cassirer (1995/1996).

67. These topics are dominant especially in the *Crisis,* though they are to be found nearly everywhere in his research manuscripts as of the late 1920s. See Hua VI, 504–7.

68. However, the extent to which these analyses reached can now be retraced in the monumental edition of Husserl's manuscripts on the constitution of the world; compare Hua XXXIX.

69. For a critique of Cassirer's omission of a moral philosophy in his system, see Birgit Recki's (at times rather polemical) chapter (1997). The brunt of her critique is that Cassirer's paradigm of human beings' practical activity precisely obliterates any genuine difference between activity as such and specifically moral activity.

70. This comes from a letter to Husserl from April 10, 1925. Cassirer quotes here Husserl's letter of April 3 of the same year (Hua-Dok III/5, 5).

71. As an example I would merely like to mention Cassirer's account of myth in which Cassirer openly admits his indebtedness to Husserl (Cassirer 1954/II, 16 n.) and towards which Husserl, in turn, was very sympathetic, as well as generally towards a phenomenology of primitive consciousness, as witnessed in Husserl's enthusiasm for the works of the French ethnologist Lucien Lévy-Brühl.

72. Whereas *Geist* (spirit) is ubiquitous in Cassirer's oeuvre, Husserl only rarely deals with it, for example, where he talks of phenomenological psychology thematizing "universal intersubjective spirituality" (Hua XXXIV, 102), or what he also calls *Gemeingeist* (communal spirit) in his reflections on intersubjectivity; see Hua XIV, 165–204. In his reflections pertaining to the theory of science, he often discusses the distinction of nature and spirit as different regions that have to be analyzed by different methods. In his 1927 lecture course *Nature und Spirit* (Hua XXXII), Husserl discusses this distinction and deals here critically with Rickert's distinction between "nomothetic" and "idiographic" methods. In other words, "spirit" serves as a general term for consciousness in an intersubjective dimension. Thus, the topic of *Geist* as communal spirit is thematic in Husserl's reflections on intersubjectivity, though he does not appreciate the term itself, presumably due to its proximity to Hegel.

Chapter 10

1. For an account of Cassirer's time in the United States, see Gawronski (1949) and T. Cassirer (1981, esp. 278ff.).

2. Another reason for his lacking popularity in the United States might be because Cassirer died after only four years residence (or rather visit, as was initially planned) in the United States, that is, before he could actually establish a circle of American students and followers.

3. See Cassirer (1979) and (1995/1996). I shall be quoting from the latter texts, which first appeared in 1995 as critical edition, ed. by Krois as volume 1 of the German edition of the unpublished papers of Ernst Cassirer. Only a few other scholars have worked on Cassirer in Anglophone scholarship, though the tide seems to be changing currently; see the newer work by Sidelsky (2009) and my review of this work (Luft 2010c).

4. In the German-speaking world, the main proponents of Cassirer research are Orth, Schwemmer, Recki, Rudolph, Kaegi, and Möckel, to name the most prolific ones. For an overview of the newer Cassirer research, see Braun et al. (1988) as well as Frede and Schmücker (1997). For Cassirer's reception in France, see Seidengart (1990). In Italy, it is especially the works of Ferrari which have presented the most influential Cassirer interpretations. More generally speaking, the interest in neo-Kantianism has been especially strong in Italy for some years. See Besoli et al. (2002).

5. Although this work is dedicated to her teacher, A. N. Whitehead, and has surprisingly few explicit references to Cassirer, the latter is nevertheless the dominant figure behind her work. Her own contribution can be seen in the detailed work on aesthetics in what she calls the general movement of *symbolic transformation* (see Langer 1942, viii). Langer has also translated Cassirer's *Language and Myth* into English.

6. See the appendix for a brief discussion of Goodman's reading of Cassirer.

7. See Habermas in Frede and Schmücker (1997). This positive assessment is not a mere eulogy of Cassirer; rather, in reading Habermas's text it becomes immediately clear that, in the way he frames Cassirer's approach and in his critique, Habermas is pursuing his own agenda. His critique of Cassirer consists of insisting that there can be no "place" or language of the philosophy of symbolic forms because language itself is a symbolic form. However, he already sees in Cassirer's own analysis of language a turn to a pragmatic analysis of language at work which, had Cassirer drawn the conclusions, would have led him to overcome his "epistemological narrowing" (*"erkenntnistheoretische Verengung,"* 100); see Frede and Schmücker (1997, 98–100). This reading, however, aligns Cassirer too closely with the Marburg school, as we shall see (though this is a good counterweight to most interpretations that make the opposite mistake).

8. For a rather "postmodern" reading of Cassirer, see Paetzold (1993).

9. See Soboleva (2001, 281; as well as 290 and n. 60, on the same page).

10. Gadamer makes few allusions to Cassirer's *Philosophy of Symbolic Forms.* He, like most contemporaries of Cassirer, understood Cassirer to be mainly a historian of philosophy, most notably through his four-volume study of *The Problem*

of Knowledge. However, it is quite certain that Gadamer knew of Cassirer's systematic ideas of the *Philosophy of Symbolic Forms*. It would be worth a whole study of its own to show this, but paradigms of Gadamer's philosophical hermeneutics, such as "understanding" and "history of effects" (*Wirkungsgeschichte*), have parallels or even equivalents in Cassirer's theory: the symbolic forms are not "ontological" categories but functional forms by which we live in and comprehend the world. The fact that Gadamer focuses on the mode of understanding in the human sciences and Cassirer on the plurality of understandings in all forms of interaction in the world might account for the fact that Gadamer has not explicitly reverted to Cassirer. Cassirer also conceived of the *Philosophy of Symbolic Forms* as a "hermeneutics." The passage where he mentions this will be discussed subsequently.

11. For an overview of the influences on Cassirer as well as Cassirer's influence on his contemporaries, see Krois (1988).

12. The earlier Cassirer was perceived by his fellow scholars in the neo-Kantian movement throughout Germany as a new "rising star"; see Sieg (1994, 328–45; esp. 333–34). For an account of the neo-Kantian movement in general, see the definitive study by Köhnke (1986/1991).

13. It is especially Orth who has made an effort to point out the phenomenological elements in Cassirer's philosophy. See especially (Orth 1996, 162–75). For another comparison between phenomenology (Husserl's, to be precise) and the philosophy of symbolic forms, see Möckel (2001, 233–58) and Bösch (2001, 148–61).

14. This goes at least for his interpretation of modern philosophy as of the Renaissance, which is the topic of his four-volume *The Problem of Knowledge*. Yet in the introduction to the problem of symbolic forms in the first volume of his magnum opus he even goes back to the pre-Socratic paradigm of *noein* and *einai* (Parmenides) to frame the problem of philosophy as that of knowledge. This is not to be seen as a narrowing of his view of philosophy stemming from the neo-Kantian background (which conceives of philosophy as scientific epistemology) but rather a systematic framing of his own problem of the symbolic forms, which expands the problem of critique of knowledge (the problem of critical philosophy) to that of a critique of culture. See the systematic introduction to the first volume, *Philosophie der symbolischen Formen I, Die Sprache* (1954/I, 3–52).

15. In the following, I am drawing on main lines from Cassirer's *Substanzbegriff und Funktionsbegriff*, especially chaps. 1–2 and the concluding chapters, 6–8 (Cassirer 1994b). It is interesting to note that already in this work Friedman sees Cassirer departing from the strict "party line" of Marburg neo-Kantianism in his insistence on the procedural character of schematizing sensibility with the aid of categories; see Friedman (2000, chap. 3, 32).

16. Husserl's concept of the lifeworld is equally a conceptualization—to be sure, of pre-scientific experience—and as such an abstraction. Although Cassirer insists that we can never "escape" symbolic formation, he does draw a distinction between "natural" and symbolic experience. This refers back to a discussion of whether one can speak of the symbolic forms as "worlds" in Goodman's sense; here I agree with Kaegi's assessment (see Kaegi 1995) that the symbolic forms cannot be understood this way due to the "natural" symbolism of pre-conceptual

experience. Thus, although the comparison with Goodman is misleading for a number of other reasons (see the appendix for this chapter), I still want to insist on Cassirer's making a point of the human mind's inability to leave or step outside the symbolic forms. This is made especially clear in Cassirer's metaphysical considerations of the philosophy of symbolic forms (in the planned but never completed fourth volume; see the longer quote of Cassirer [1995, 37]). In other words, although there might be symbolisms on essentially two levels, even the "natural symbolism" *is* a symbolism. That is, even on this level we cannot step outside the basic thesis of idealism, which states a coincidence—or, in Husserl's words—a correlation between thinking and being.

17. This shift or replacement of the substantialist by the functionalist account takes place in Descartes' philosophy. See Cassirer's treatment of Descartes in volume 1 of *The Problem of Knowledge* (1994a, 504). The first edition of this work was published in 1906, four years before *Substance and Function*. In the latter work, Cassirer, as it were, only draws the systematic conclusions he had already reached through his historic studies.

18. In Cassirer's view, modern philosophy is characterized as *"Erkenntniskritik,"* literally "epistemo-critique." This entails that the Copernican turn to consciousness is not something that occurred only in Kant's philosophy. Rather, it is a process that began essentially with Descartes and came to a certain high point in Kant, and was further developed in post-Kantian philosophies (essentially German idealism).

19. It should also be mentioned that Kant characterized the categories as "functions of the understanding"; see Kant 1998, 206, B 94; see also Kant 1998, 206–10, §9, B 95ff., and Kant 1998, 456, B 428.

20. This Goethe quotation (from *Maximen und Reflexionen*, no. 575) will be employed subsequently by Cassirer time and again. See also Cassirer (1995, 199).

21. As is well known, with Cassirer's call to the University of Hamburg, he came in contact with Aby Warburg and his famous library from which he was to benefit to a degree that, as he himself admitted, was incomparable to any other aid or influence on his work. See the introduction to the second volume of the *Philosophy of Symbolic Forms* (1954/II, xiii).

22. Already in the first presentation of the theory of the plurality of symbolic formation, this enumeration is merely laid out and in no way motivated in its systematic necessity. See Cassirer (1946, 8). After stating his claim concerning the "self-dissolution of the spirit" (ibid.), he goes on without further ado: "From this point of view, myth, art, language and science appear [!] as symbols . . . in the sense of forces each of which produces and posits a world of its own" (ibid.).

23. See (Cassirer 1954/III, chap. 5, 222–37). This concept is often regarded as a novel theme within the theory of symbolic forms (see Krois 1988, 23–24), whereas it seems to me Cassirer has merely, as it were at the end of constructing his philosophy of symbolic forms (in the third volume of 1929 in its first appearance), found a "pregnant" term for what has been already thematic all along, only that the concept of symbolic pregnancy pays more attention to the individual object (as a concrete symbol) rather than the symbolic form within which it appears or to which it is bound.

24. See Merleau-Ponty (1945, 337).

25. Another indication of the proximity between Cassirer and Husserl becomes manifest when one compares this example with Husserl's example of the house, which can be viewed in different attitudes; see chapter 1 of the present volume.

26. See Kant 1998, 691, B 860.

27. Indeed, in his treatment of Hegel in the third volume of *The Problem of Knowledge*, Cassirer criticizes Hegel's concept of systematics. Hegel's system is essentially unable to deduce the principle from which one concept arises from another. Therefore, this system has ultimately no explanatory power "outside" of itself. See Cassirer (1994a, 370–71). See also Bayer's comments on the character of Cassirer's "systematic overview" (Bayer 2001, 172–73).

28. It is a long-standing discussion in Cassirer research whether he truly departed from the classic form of neo-Kantianism or whether, in his deepest intentions, he remained loyal to them. Whereas Krois (1988) claims that Cassirer indeed was under way to an original conception of his own (see also Marx 1988), other studies have shown that Cassirer, in his main intentions with his philosophy of symbolic forms, remained true to the Marburg school; see Orth (1996) and Seidengart (1994, esp. 447ff.). One especially interesting question is whether Cassirer remained close to Natorp's late philosophy in which he allegedly also departed from the Marburg doctrine; see Heidegger, "Zur Geschichte des philosophischen Lehrstuhls seit 1866," in (Heidegger 1991, 304–11), who, in this fairly unknown text from 1927, points out Natorp's late development as overcoming the specific Marburg doctrine of neo-Kantianism (see 310). As should be clear from the assessment in this chapter, my reading is balanced, in that I strongly believe that Cassirer remained close to his Marburg roots in his transcendental outlook and his goal of drafting a philosophy of culture; but this does not contradict the reading that Cassirer nevertheless introduced new elements *into the general systematic frame* of the Marburg school.

29. See the note in the second volume of the *Philosophy of Symbolic Forms* on Husserl (Cassirer 1954/II, 16), where he sees Husserl (of *Ideas I*) in direct accordance with Cassirer's own project.

30. This is not to say that Cassirer does not imagine a certain "dialectic," namely between language and spirit (see Cassirer's text on "'Geist' und 'Leben,'" Cassirer 1995, 3–32). However, this dialectic takes place within each symbolic form and is not a way of explaining the relation of different forms to each other as in Hegel, where the dialectical method is designed to show the evolvement of one "form" of spirit out of another. On Cassirer's relation to Hegel see Verene (1969; esp. 37ff.).

31. Art and technology are discussed in *An Essay on Man* (chap. 9) and *The Myth of the State* (chap. 18). Cassirer also mentions history among symbolic forms and devotes a chapter to it in his *Essay in Man*. However, it is not clear whether history is in itself a symbolic form or rather the (temporal) form in which the symbolic forms themselves "evolve." This ambiguity cannot be discussed here. For a discussion of history in Cassirer's philosophy, see Krois (1987; esp. chap. 5, 172ff.). As I have had a chance to browse through Cassirer's unpublished *Nach-*

lass kept in the Beinecke Rare Book Library at Yale University (after finishing this chapter), it is fair to conclude that there are no major unpublished texts shedding new light on this issue.

32. Compare this conception of an openness of symbolic formation to Rickert's concept of an "open system." This system conception assumes a system which is, however, not "static" but rather dynamic and open to new additions but nevertheless retains its basic "system form." This accords also with Cohen's idea of a "dynamic a priori," that is, the progress of concept formation in the progress of science.

33. Bernet (2010; esp. 54–55), however, does claim that the *Philosophy of Symbolic Forms* "seems, in the end, to be drawn up from the viewpoint of absolute knowledge. It describes a system of symbolic forms from a vantage point that is a 'view from nowhere.'" The upshot is that this philosophy cannot reflect upon its own status without falling into a relativism. This would be true *only if* philosophy thereby becomes a symbolic form among others, as Bernet seems to believe (ibid.), but as I have shown above, in my reading, the status of philosophy is neither that it is a symbolic form nor a view from nowhere, but a sort of "zigzag" between both—a dialectics, if one likes. Bernet thus seems to read Cassirer as committing to more than he actually does.

34. In the fourth volume of the *Philosophy of Symbolic Forms* Cassirer expounds his theory of the "basis phenomena" which are conceived of certain "primal phenomena" by which every symbolic form must be ordered. See Cassirer (1995, 123–95). For a thorough commentary on this concept, see Bayer (2001, 129–52).

35. Although he mentions law (*Recht*) as a symbolic form, there is no separate treatment of it, nor, more specifically, of morality. See Recki's critique of Cassirer's "failing" to write an ethics and the refutation of this critique (Recki 1997, also discussed in chapter 9 in the present volume). As should have become amply clear in this chapter, this reading completely misinterprets Cassirer's whole intention, which is to link his critique of culture to an ethical consideration of culture. Being a member of a culture the way Cassirer understands it *is* to be ethical.

36. See Cassirer (1944, 1).

37. See "Davoser Disputation zwischen Ernst Cassirer und Martin Heidegger" (Heidegger 1973, 289): "Ich glaube [says Heidegger], daß das, was ich mit Dasein bezeichne, sich nicht übersetzen läßt mit einem Begriff Cassirers."

38. Pages 1–22 will be the main focus of my attention.

39. See, for example, Graeser (1994). See also Kaegi (1995), whose chapter is essentially a critique of this reading. Again, it is not Goodman who is responsible for this, but it is this interpretation which misreads both.

40. See Goodman 1978, 7–17.

41. Quotations from ibid., 21. With regard to actually "building" new worlds, Goodman remarks: "A broad mind is no substitute for hard work" (ibid.).

42. See, however, Cassirer's text on "'Spirit' and 'Life'" in the fourth volume of the *Philosophy of Symbolic Forms* (Cassirer 1996, 3–33), where he attempts to characterize the subjective "force" of spirit—in this following the late Natorp—

as "life." Yet, also following Natorp's paradigm of "reconstructive" analysis, this characterization can never be direct in accessing subjectivity but only reconstructive in going back from spirit's manifestations in objective forms.

43. My current work in progress is devoted to spelling out this transcendental philosophy of culture following the Marburg school, including Cassirer. A manuscript is in preparation under the title "The Space of Culture."

Chapter 11

1. This quotation is taken from Gadamer's text of 1986, "Zwischen Phänomenologie und Dialektik: Versuch einer Selbstkritik" ("Between Phenomenology and Dialectics: An Attempt at a Self-Critique" [1988a]).

2. It is not necessary to engage with the proponents of the standard interpretation because the standard interpretation simply ignores the Husserlian influence. Since Husserl is passed over in silence, the reasons why it is all right to overlook him are rarely argued for; Husserl is for the most part treated by omission, so it is hard to engage with someone who simply ignores the claim I am trying to make (rather than refute it). It is usually taken as evident that the main tenets that essentially make up Husserl's phenomenology—for example, subjectivism, transcendentalism, and foundationalism—are simply not shared by Gadamer. This is true in a superficial way; but it is not true (a) that these -isms are all there is to Husserl (as this book should have made clear by now) and (b) that these are necessarily "bad things" if understood correctly, and (c) it does not justify ignoring other aspects in Gadamer's hermeneutics that *are* genuinely Husserlian—for instance, the concept of horizon—which do not necessarily belong to other problematic issues, for example, foundationalism. The standard interpretation is thus guilty of an illegitimate reductionism with regard to its image of Husserl; not to mention that one can also argue that it is a travesty of Husserl's main intentions to tag them with these -isms. For instance, is Husserl a foundationalist? Yes, but not in the sense of a vulgar foundationalism (Cartesianism). The ultimate foundation of meaning in the mature Husserl is the lifeworld (to be sure, as the correlate of transcendental constituting intersubjectivity); hence, a Husserlian "foundationalism" (if the term is at all adequate) would certainly be very different from the one inspired by Descartes.

3. Despite the fact that I see no need to directly confront the proponents of the standard interpretation (see the above note), there are a number of volumes on Gadamer that all appeared around 2000, that is, his 100th birthday, from which I have drawn and will quote from in this chapter. These volumes are *Gadamer's Century: Chapters in Honor of Hans-Georg Gadamer* (Malpas et al. 2002); *The Philosophy of Hans-Georg Gadamer* (Hahn 1997) (with especially valuable comments on the chapters by Gadamer himself); *Gadamer's Repercussions: Reconsidering Philosophical Hermeneutics* (Krajewski 2004); *The Cambridge Companion to Gadamer* (Dostal 2002); and *Gadamer Verstehen/Understanding Gadamer* (Wischke and Hofer 2003). These voluminous collections of chapters give a good overview and representation of the current status of international Gadamer scholarship.

4. This anti-foundationalist tendency in modern philosophy can be traced back to Kierkegaard and Nietzsche in the nineteenth century and has been shared in twentieth-century thought by many phenomenologists, existentialists, and in a different variant by the Frankfurt school. Since I am drawing in broad strokes here, it is not necessary to go into detail in these critiques of the Enlightenment.

5. As much as one can criticize Gadamer for falling back into foundationalism, I should like to note that I believe this is *not* something with which one could charge Heidegger. While Gadamer falls back into foundationalism because he shies away from the radical consequences of Heidegger's late philosophy, Heidegger indeed no longer is committed to any such figures of thought that he criticizes as being part of Western metaphysics. However, this self-declared departure from Western metaphysics also means that Heidegger willingly and consciously departs from any type of reasonable discourse from where one could *argue* with him. Heidegger is no longer foundationalist because he is beyond *arguing*.

6. See Gadamer (1995, 64) where he speaks of "the limit of all opacity that constantly retrieves. As a philosopher, Schelling described this limit with the cognate 'the unforethinkable' ['*das Unvordenkliche*']."

7. Gadamer's coinage *Wirkungsgeschichte*—presumably derived in analogy from similar terms such as *Problemgeschichte, Rezeptionsgeschichte*, or *Begriffsgeschichte*—is translated here throughout as "effective history," following the standard translation. As Gadamer himself points out, effective history is also meant as a counterpoint to the neo-Kantian paradigm of writing the history of philosophy as *Problemgeschichte*, that is, as a history of problems that philosophers tackled throughout history in an ongoing discussion, engendering a progress in furthering the issue. Examples of such *problemgeschichtliche* accounts can be found in Windelband's, Kuno Fischer's, and Cassirer's histories of philosophy. Where Husserl engages in the history of philosophy, for example, Hua VII (part 1 of the lecture *Erste Philosophie*), his method may also be considered *problemgeschichtlich*, though Husserl's term for it is "*kritische Ideengeschichte*" ("critical history of ideas"). What characterizes this approach—and this is, presumably, what Heidegger and Gadamer found most objectionable—is its decidedly *teleological* bent, that is, guided by the presupposition that one could reconstruct the history of philosophy retrospectively *post factum*, that is, backward from an existing status quo. Although most neo-Kantians shared their dislike of Hegel, there is indeed a lingering Hegelianism in this type of reconstruction. It would be a worthy enterprise to reconstruct Gadamer's effective history as critical rejection or productive reception of *Problemgeschichte*. This issue lies beyond the scope of this chapter, but see Grondin (2010) for an attempt at placing Gadamer in the Marburg school of neo-Kantianism, from which he emerged.

8. "Foundationalism" is, again, the standard translation for the term *Letztbegründung* as a term for a philosophical quest to find a *fundamentum incocussum* of knowledge in the knowing subject, a quest that was historically inaugurated by Descartes and further developed by Reinhold, Fichte, and Schelling and reached a peak around 1880–1920 as a program proposed most vigorously by the neo-Kantians and also Husserl (for a comparison between these attempts, see Luft 2010a). It has just recently been established by Berndt Goossens, the editor of Hua XXXV (containing Husserl's London lectures of 1922 and his lecture

course of 1922/23 entitled *Introduction to Philosophy*), that this term was actually coined by Husserl as early as 1922 in the adjective form *"letztbegründend"* (see Hua XXXV, 27–28). To be sure, while Husserl may have *coined* the term, he was referring to an already firmly established tradition in modern transcendental philosophy to which he wished to express his commitment. As Gethmann writes in his entry "Letztbegründung" (1980), this term has not been used as a label for this type of attempt until "the last decades" (251), that is, presumably as of the 1960s. When talking about *Letztbegründung* in these contexts, it is usually identified as the overarching project of transcendental philosophy around 1900 and essentially as a dated project. Compare, however, the influential book that appeared in Germany in 1957, Wolfgang Cramer's *Grundlegung einer Theorie des Geistes* (1975). Cramer, sometimes also referred to as "neo-neo-Kantian," sees his project as again attempting a new theory of *Letztbegründung* in this work. Before him, after the "high time" of neo-Kantianism had faded at the latest by 1933 in Germany, the lineage of this tradition was upheld by Richard Hönigswald, incidentally Gadamer's first teacher in Breslau before Gadamer's move to Marburg. Hönigswald later received a call to the University of Munich, where he was removed from his position in 1933 due to a devastating "expert opinion" of Heidegger, then the president of the University of Freiburg. On Hönigswald's and Cramer's projects of *Letztbegründung*, compare Wiehl (2000, 293–319).

9. Heidegger makes this statement in the famous debate with Cassirer in Davos in 1929. As we now know (from chapters 8 and 9 in the present volume), Husserl's "falling into the clutches" of the neo-Kantians was more than just temporary and was only exacerbated in his mature period as of 1922 onward.

10. In terms of the development of German philosophy in the first two decades of the twentieth century, this article was quite an event and in fact a "coup" for the neo-Kantians. Husserl had emerged as a major figure on the scene with the publication of the *Logical Investigations* and had become a professor in Göttingen in 1906. However, his early phenomenology had a clear anti-idealist and anti-transcendental bent. Natorp early on tried to downplay the difference between phenomenology and "criticism" (as the neo-Kantians also called their tendency) and famously said about volume 1 of the *Investigations*, the *Prolegomena*, that the neo-Kantians had "little to learn" from it. As we now know, Husserl "discovered" the phenomenology reduction in 1905 and from then on worked out his phenomenology as transcendental philosophy. It was no small issue that Husserl in 1911 formally and publicly declared his alliance with his erstwhile enemies, an event that raised many eyebrows among his early followers, the phenomenological societies in Munich and Göttingen.

11. This article is reprinted in Hua XXV, 3–64.

12. This is an allusion to an article by Husserl's former assistant Landgrebe that was very influential in the early days of Husserl reception after the Second World War, and was entitled "Husserl's Departure from Cartesianism" (first published in 1958). Its claim is, in a nutshell, that the late Husserl, under the influence of Heidegger, departed from Cartesianism (read as foundationalism) and was onto something new that was akin to Heidegger's project of fundamental ontology. This reading—which has been proven wrong many times over—was

highly influential in the reception of Husserl and still shapes the image of Husserl's phenomenology and its development to this day.

13. Besides Gadamer, one would have to mention Oskar Becker, Fink, and Landgrebe (all assistants to Husserl at one point) and many contemporary Heidegger and Gadamer scholars.

14. This is how Gadamer explicitly sees Husserl; compare the preface to *Truth and Method:* "the conscientiousness of phenomenological description that Husserl has placed upon us as a duty" (1990, 5).

15. Compare Gadamer's well-known and oft-quoted presentation, "The Phenomenological Movement" (1986b). As Gadamer points out here (and elsewhere), the image of the Husserlian "open horizons" that were merely filled in by Heidegger was first utilized by Becker, Husserl's pupil and Heidegger's colleague in Freiburg; a claim that is repeated in Tugendhat's influential book on the problem of truth in Husserl and Heidegger. Becker himself saw his own work in the same manner as a part of the phenomenological movement. His book *Mathematische Existenz,* published in the same yearbook volume as *Being and Time* in 1927, intended to apply the phenomenological method to the sphere of mathematics.

16. Indeed, Gadamer interprets Heidegger's sketch of a "hermeneutics of facticity," the "fundamental ontology of Dasein" as presented in *Being and Time,* as an aberration of Heidegger's early intentions. The infamous *"Kehre,"* or turning, that Heidegger took some years after *Being and Time* is in truth, to Gadamer, a *"Ruckkehr,"* a return, to these early intentions. Gadamer's critique states that *Being and Time* has come all too close to transcendental philosophy ("philosophy of reflection") in the style of Husserl's transcendental phenomenology and the transcendentalism of the neo-Kantians. Heidegger's early impulse Gadamer sees best captured in Heidegger's statement *"es weltet"* ("it worlds") as the original event of Being (the world) that reveals *itself* to us, rather than being something that we, as representing subjects, can control (as an intentional object or horizon of objects); compare Heidegger's last early Freiburg lecture of 1923, *Ontology: The Hermeneutics of Facticity* (1999). This is the first lecture of Heidegger's that Gadamer attended (in the summer semester of 1923 in Freiburg, where he heard Heidegger for one semester after finishing his dissertation with Natorp; Gadamer moved back to Marburg in the fall of that year following Heidegger, who had been called to Marburg) and to which he refers often throughout his works (where he first felt Heidegger's language hitting him "like a lightning bolt"). Heidegger's later philosophy of *"Ereignis"* (translated as "event" or—rather inaptly—as "enownment") to Gadamer merely reiterates this early insight and places it in the larger context of a *historicity* of this *Ereignis.* Gadamer repeats this assessment of Heidegger's thought on several occasions; compare (1989, 259–69), as well as the chapters on Heidegger (Gadamer 1986b, 175–332, esp. the important critical article "Die Sprache der Metaphysik" ["The Language of Metaphysics"], ibid., 229–37).

17. See note 18.

18. While there are few, and mostly implicit, traces of Husserl in *Truth and Method,* Gadamer's writings that explicitly deal with Husserl stem from *after* the publication of *Truth and Method.* Compare, for example, the three chapters explicitly devoted to Husserl and the phenomenological movement in general in

volume 3 of his *Collected Works* from 1963, 1972, and 1974. While Gadamer knew Husserl from the latter's published writings and his lectures (Gadamer also attended Husserl's lecture in the summer semester of 1923 in Freiburg alongside those of Heidegger), one can detect a new phase of studying Husserl beginning around 1968. This new phase, in which he also turned to newer volumes in the *Husserliana* making available hitherto unpublished material, was presumably motivated by external factors, in this case Gadamer's lectures and professorships in the United States and Canada after his retirement from the University of Heidelberg in 1968. The title of his course at Catholic University in 1969 was "The Phenomenological Movement," and, as preparation for the course, he freshened up on his knowledge of Husserl, making a serious effort to read newer material. On April 4, 1969, Gadamer writes to Heidegger: "My renewed Husserl studies make the tragic side of his thought increasingly clear, this continual self-complication from which he can never quite free himself, without falling back on the simplest, oldest motifs of his thought" (quoted in Grondin 2003, 468); compare also Grondin's account of Gadamer's travels as an emeritus in the chapter of his biography entitled "Second Youth" (312–29). It is one of the strengths of Gadamer's expositions of Husserl that he emphasizes the continuity of his thought from his first book, *Philosophy of Arithmetic,* to the *Crisis.* Thus, although one cannot call Gadamer a Husserl scholar, he did have a keen sense of Husserl's philosophical intentions and instincts. For an assessment of what Gadamer acknowledged of Husserl's philosophical corpus (not just the published works that he knew already before the war), one can certainly mention *Husserliana* volumes I (*Cartesian Meditations*), III, IV, and V (*Ideas I–III*); *Formal and Transcendental Logic* (Hua XVII); *Experience and Judgment* (Husserl 1948); the *Crisis* (Hua VI); as well as, as is clear from the later texts, the volumes on the critical history of ideas and the theory of the phenomenological reduction (Hua VII and VIII, the lecture course of 1923/24), time-consciousness (Hua X), and the three voluminous tomes that collect manuscript material on the problem of intersubjectivity (Hua XIII–XV). Thus, although the corpus of Gadamer's texts devoted explicitly to Husserl is rather slim (compared to the writings on Heidegger), one can certainly say that Gadamer was well aware of the intricacies of Husserl's phenomenology.

19. Though it would be an unfair ad hominem argument, it is worth mentioning that it is not unlikely that Gadamer's views, and in general those of his generation in Europe, were shaped by the events in Europe in his lifetime: the global economic crisis in the early 1930s, the failure of the Weimar republic, most importantly the National Socialist revolution and World War II, and last but not least, the student revolts in the late 1960s.

20. See, for example, Jung (2002), which, apart from being an excellent exposition of the scope of hermeneutics, makes no mention of Husserl.

21. The linkage between Husserl's concept of horizon and Gadamer's doctrine of understanding is also emphasized by Sokolowski (1997, esp. 228–29) and Ramberg (1997, 462).

22. Concerning the continuity of Husserl's thought, see the footnote in the *Crisis* in which Husserl emphasizes the continuity of his work since the breakthrough discovery of intentionality and the correlational a priori in the course of

working on the *Logical Investigations* in the last decade of the nineteenth century; see Hua VI, 169–70.

23. See Hua III/1, 202–9.

24. See Heidegger's similar analysis of ready-to-handness and the curious omission of the concept of "nature" in *Being and Time* (1993, chap. 3, 63–130). "Pure" nature is something that is never given to us as such, "stripped" of any meaning, but always as something that has a certain significance for us; for example, the forest as a place for leisurely contemplation *or* as a supply of wood for heating, and so on; that is, even in the most innocuous circumstances, the structure of "in order to" (*um-zu*) obtains, even in the attitude of what Kant has called (in the *Critique of Judgment*) "disinterested pleasure" (*interesseloses Wohlgefallen*).

25. See the passage from Husserl's *Analyses of Passive Synthesis,* Hua XI (24), which gives an elaborate analysis of "external perception" and concludes in the following sentences: "The house itself and in its true being, and specifically with respect to its pure bodily thingly nature, is quickly given optimally, i.e., experienced as complete for that person who regards it as a buyer or a seller. For the physicist and the chemist, such ways of experience would seem completely superficial and miles away from its true being." Husserl's criterion for what guides a certain attitude is, as mentioned, the *interest,* which again underscores his orientation ultimately at *knowledge.*

26. Some scholars claim that it is from here that Heidegger derives the concept of "clearing" that motivates his reading of the Greek concept of truth, *alétheia,* as unconcealment. Especially the works by Landgrebe and Held have tried to harmonize Husserl and Heidegger in this way by comparing them on the basis of the concept of horizon. See Landgrebe (1963, 9–39) and Held (1992). One should point out, however, that Heidegger's idea of clearing has different roots and is informed by the Greek experience of nature (*physis*) as something that appears on its own and shows itself to man. Husserl's concept of horizon derives directly from his analysis of intentionality and is a structure of *subjectivity.*

27. However, in his presentation of Husserl's late philosophy (in "The Phenomenological Movement"), Gadamer is remarkably clear about declaring Husserl's transcendental turn as necessary for his theory of the lifeworld. That is, while he recognized the *immanent* necessity for Husserl to attach the science of the lifeworld to the transcendental theory of constitution, Gadamer himself, in his own positive hermeneutic approach, consciously did not follow along Husserl's path. This displays, on the one hand, his superb understanding and intimate knowledge of Husserl's philosophy as a whole. On the other, it marks the clear and well-reflected point of departure for Gadamer toward a more Heideggerian concept of world.

28. I am referring here mainly to Husserl's project of a "transcendental logic" in his shift from static to genetic phenomenology in the 1920s. See Hua XI as well as the detailed account in Welton (2000).

29. See the epigraph of this chapter.

30. This quotation is taken from the key text on "static and genetic phenomenological method," in which Husserl discusses the shift from "static" to "genetic" methods.

31. Whereas Husserl emphasizes the "teleological" process of perception as a phasing-out of older, inadequate perceptions, hence as a process of "verification" (although at this level Husserl is not dealing with propositional judgment or logical truth), Gadamer in turn emphasizes the "negative," "falsifying" aspect of experience in the sense that new experiences primarily devalue old ones (see 1989, 352–58). In this sense, both merely emphasize different sides of the same coin. Also, by recognizing the "negative" aspect, Gadamer implicitly criticizes Husserl's underlying presupposition of a *teleological* process of experience, a process that supposedly moves from pre-predicative experience all the way up to logical, rational judgment.

32. One should mention that Heidegger harshly criticized this account that he considered a construction; see chapter 5 in the present volume. This is worth mentioning because such a reading clearly ignores Husserl's genetic phenomenology.

33. See the *Crisis* (Hua VI, 12–17, 269–76). Similar formulations can be found in nearly all of Husserl's latest writings that are to be found in Hua VI and XXIX.

34. Husserl deals with the topic of history very late in his life, in his late reflections in the context of his last work, the *Crisis of European Sciences* (Hua VI), but his reflections do not go beyond mere musings about the manner in which one could expand phenomenology into a philosophy of history.

35. Gadamer uses the terms "*Tradition*" and "*Überlieferung*" synonymously; both can readily be rendered "tradition" in English.

36. In some late texts, Husserl, too, acknowledges that the lifeworld is a context of tradition; accordingly, the epoché that we must practice in order to access transcendental consciousness is an "epoché from all traditions." Compare Hua XXXIV, 431–40, and the following chapter.

37. There can be no doubt that in this respect Gadamer is inspired by Heidegger's account of the "fore-structure of understanding" (see *Being and Time*, Heidegger 1993, §2, 5–8) as well as Heidegger's terminology in these passages. However, this fore-structure to which Gadamer calls attention here is nothing but an explication of Husserl's analysis of horizonal intentionality—this goes for Heidegger's account as well! In other words, both Heidegger and Gadamer merely draw from an unacknowledged Husserlian insight here.

38. McDowell (1996) has reverted to this Aristotelian theme in a similar way as Gadamer. The experiences that we make and that we inherit through tradition actually form us, they form our second nature; compare (1996, xi–xxiv). One presupposition that Gadamer makes here (in the framework that Brandom calls "gadamerian platitudes") is that tradition is at all times given, as it were "automatically," and is not something that requires any actual work of an active *acquisition*. Yet, things are not that easy; as Goethe famously says, "What you have inherited from your forefathers, acquire it in order to own it" ("*Was Du gelernt von Deinen Vätern, erwirb es, um es zu besitzen*"). In other words, the sheer givenness of a tradition does not necessarily account for "owning" it, that is, understanding it. To do so requires an explicit "fusion of horizons" that throws into relief both my own horizon and that of the tradition that is mine only poten-

tially. While it is true that Gadamer seems to take this "givenness" of tradition for granted, it can be remedied by the fact that he thinks that a fusion of horizons does not just take place "horizontally" between partners in a dialogue but also "vertically" between my present and the tradition I find myself in. For a discussion of these "gadamerian platitudes," see Brandom (2002, 92–94, 105–6).

39. Especially part 1 of the second division of *Truth and Method* (Gadamer 1990, 177–269).

40. Gadamer in response to Detmer's chapter (1997, 275–86). It is interesting to note that Gadamer's response to Detmer's chapter, in which Detmer presents Gadamer as an anti-Enlightenist, is unusually harsh. Gadamer starts out his reply as follows: "It is extremely astonishing to me that my project of a philosophical hermeneutics as well as some other such projects are being discussed under the title 'critique of Enlightenment' and not with reference to the idealist concept of the 'completed Enlightenment' which was coined by Fichte" (287).

41. The passage continues: "Therefore the prejudices [*Vorurteile*] of the individual, far more than his judgments [*Urteile*], form the historical reality of his being."

42. See Hua X, esp. 23ff. (§§7–18).

43. See *Truth and Method*, xvi (on the unpaginated frontispiece).

44. See ibid., 304.

45. As already discussed in chapter 3, it was especially Husserl's last assistant, Eugen Fink, who confronted Husserl with this question in the Sixth *Cartesian Meditation* and other texts during the collaboration with Husserl (1929–38). This critical inquiry was motivated, among other things, by Heidegger's seeming rejection of the phenomenological reduction and the concept of the natural attitude that is implied in it. See chapter 2 of Luft (2002), where I discuss this particular dispute between Husserl and Fink.

46. In this respect one can rightfully apply Habermas's verdict, that the experience Gadamer articulates is primarily that of a philologist (Gadamer's original formation in classics at the University of Marburg). In this context, Habermas also famously speaks of Gadamer's philosophy as an "urbanization of the Heideggerian province." See Habermas (1987, 393).

47. This challenge is evinced, for example, in Rilke's well-known poem "Archaischer Torso Apolls," which ends with the phrase (in this poem, spoken by the artwork to the spectator): *"Du mußt Dein Leben ändern"* ("You must change your life"). Gadamer on several occasions makes reference to this poem. See the chapters on Rilke that are assembled in (Gadamer 1993, 271–319).

48. See Gadamer (1986b, 159, 171).

49. See Gadamer (1989, 48–61).

50. McDowell (2002) makes the same point that a fusion can change the position of the viewer, rather than bringing about a whole new "horizon" altogether: "When we come to understand the other subject, that can involve a change in how we view the world. When the horizons fuse, the horizon within which we view the world is no longer in the same position" (2002, 180).

51. This is true even if I immerse myself in it, through traveling, for example, to a country with a culture radically different from my own.

52. Division 3 of *Truth and Method* is entitled "Hermeneutics' Ontological Turn Guided by Language" (Gadamer 1989, 387–494). Division 2 ends with the subsection ß, "The Logic of Question and Answer" (375–86).

53. See Blumenberg's comments on Heidegger's "history of Being": "It [the *Seinsgeschichte*] allows for the thought that subjects remain unchanged because the history of being . . . severs the whole realm of causal agency from subjects and attributes it to an objective sphere. This objective sphere is no longer the history formed by humans but historicity as the unauthorized [*eigenmächtig*] power of Being. It is supposedly Being that changes in order that the subjects do not have to change. Indeed, they could not change in any case and for which giving good reasons would be all but vain, reasons that had already been experienced and endured throughout history. The empirical futility of changing subjects gives rise to the evidence of the only remaining possibility of change, i.e., of letting the totality of objects change radically by means of a mysterious fatality coming from out of their background, and by so doing, to change the behavior of the subjects. If that were the case, understanding this type of thought, like Heidegger's, would merely be a symptom of something that would not be effected, but only indicated, by this understanding" (Blumenberg 1996, 35–36, from a text entitled "What If Heidegger Were Understood?" referring to a text by Heidegger's friend Egon Vietta, in which the latter claims that *if* Heidegger's philosophy were understood, the age of technology would be "finished").

54. See Apel (1973).

55. Here Gadamer also mentions Nietzsche as a philosopher who emphasized the notion of horizon as man's essential situatedness and perspectivalness.

56. It should be noted that *Einrücken* is a military term, denoting an army's moving into a city or region.

57. See Gadamer 1989, 293.

58. Indeed, Husserl's "genetic logic" intends to show, precisely, how rationality has developed by necessity (i.e., according to "laws of genesis") from the most "primitive" experiences on the pre-predicative level of perception. This is the path Husserl attempts to reconstruct in his *Experience and Judgment*, which has the subtitle "On the Genealogy of Logic." Even the "passive" level is subjective through and through.

Chapter 12

1. These topics are to be found in the following volumes of the *Husserliana* that appeared over the last decade: Hua XXXIV, *Zur Phänomenologischen Reduktion: Texte aus dem Nachlass (1926–1935);* Hua XXXV, *Einleitung in die Philosophie (1922/23);* Hua XXXVI, *Transzendentaler Idealismus;* Hua-Mat VII, *Späte Texte über Zeitkonstitution (1929–1934) (die C-Manuskripte);* and Hua XXXIX, texts on the lifeworld. *Husserliana* volumes that are about to appear within the next years will feature texts on the constitution of space and manuscripts on teleology and theology (limit problems of phenomenology).

2. Gadamer's *Truth and Method* (*Wahrheit und Methode: Grundzüge einer Phil-*

osophischen Hermeneutic) appeared in 1960 and was reedited six times, the last time in 1990, each time with significant revisions. Between 1960 and 2002, Gadamer's death, he published a substantial amount of additional material to further flesh out what he had grounded in 1960. Given his prolific literary output after his sixtieth birthday, it is not far-fetched to compare him in this sense to Kant, who, as is well known, published the *Critique of Pure Reason* at age sixty.

3. See Hua XXVII, 177. The reason offered above for Husserl's employing this term to distinguish his phenomenology from that of Heidegger and Scheler is certainly the most dominant one in this context, that is, in this public lecture. However, there is also another reason; namely, that Husserl's revision of his phenomenological method leads him from static to genetic analysis that entails a broadening of the method from description to interpretation; see chapter 8 in the present volume.

4. For a sketch of Husserl's transcendental-hermeneutic phenomenology, see also Reeder (2010), who frames the problem as Husserl's phenomenology being both hermeneutic and focused on *intuition,* and transcendental as focused on a *critique* of this intuition. Although Reeder's account is focused on these aspects more specifically, I am in full agreement with the overall intention and conclusion of his presentation.

5. For a historical account of these events, which would prove definitive for Husserl reception, see Luft (2004b).

6. I rely here on Gadamer's dictionary entry "Hermeneutik" in the *Historisches Wörterbuch der Philosophie* (Gadamer 1974).

7. Thus, the question as to what it is that this specific document has to say to us requires the decision, which has to be made beforehand, that this document has something to say to us; I call the former the what-question, the latter the that-question. It is interesting to see what problems some people encounter when they assume that the first step has been answered without further questioning and then want to spell out what this content is supposed to be. A good deal of discussion and disagreement on the what-question rests, in fact, on the prejudice that the that-question has been answered in the affirmative. I assert that a large portion of this disagreement could be avoided completely if more attention were to be paid to the that-question. Perhaps some canonical texts simply have nothing to say on a certain issue. This point seems to be completely lost on some who try to wrench water from a stone in answering questions of the type "what does (e.g.) the Bible have to say on X?" or "what does Nietzsche have to say to women?" and so on.

8. It should be clear that this characterization is one of "ideal types," not concrete forms of hermeneutics in Western intellectual history (in Boekh, Schleiermacher, etc.).

9. See Dilthey (1985).

10. This view is most succinctly articulated in Heidegger's manuscript *Beiträge zur Philosophie (Vom Ereignis)* (1989b), which was not published until Heidegger's 100th birthday.

11. See *Truth and Method,* esp. part 2, section 2, d ("The Principle of Effective History").

12. It was Georg Misch—Dilthey's son-in-law and editor of Dilthey's *Collected Works*—who offered the first comparison between Husserl, Dilthey, and Heidegger in his *Phänomenologie und Lebensphilosophie* of 1929–30 (Misch 1929–30), which both Husserl and Heidegger closely studied.

13. This seems to have been Husserl's view himself, as he reconstructs the "inner motives" for the modern crisis in his *Crisis of European Sciences*. Such a view was echoed by several other philosophers at the time, for example, in José Ortega y Gasset's *History as a System* (1936).

14. Husserl presents these three notions especially in Hua XXXIV, text no. 36, §1, 481–83.

15. On the relation of psychology to phenomenology, see chapters 2 and 3 in the present volume.

16. See Hua VI, paragraphs 53–54, as well as Carr's superb study (1999) on the topic.

17. This pair of terms is familiar from chapter 4 of the present volume; but in the present context, it is used in a slightly different, that is, "hermeneutical," context.

18. Compare also Husserl's Göttingen lectures on perception and attention (Hua XXXVIII), where he treats of the phenomenon of attention in great detail. However, it should be noted that at this earlier stage of thought (the lectures were delivered before *Ideas I*), Husserl had not yet worked out the concept of horizon, which is indispensable for the above analysis. What Husserl says above, thus, in the most rudimentary form can also be seen as his recasting the phenomenon of attention in the framework of genetic phenomenology.

19. Husserl distinguishes further between patent and latent tradition, corresponding to the distinction between active and passive (or patent and latent) genesis. Compare Hua XXXIV, 443, and also the following passage: "To practice Epoché with respect to the validity of an object means not only bracketing my validity but the whole horizon of my unknown and unknown others and hence all worldly subjects . . . To 'bracket' myself thus means to bracket all subjects" (ibid., 439).

20. How this insight can be utilized to critique Gadamer's hermeneutics of effective consciousness is spelled out in the previous chapter.

21. Lohmar (2004) makes a similar point. The epoché as an act of one's personal freedom does not stand in contradiction to living among prejudices. The epoché does not *nullify* them but intends to *understand* them. The point I am making here—going beyond Lohmar's exposition—is that this understanding can only come about through a *genetic* analysis, that is, of an analysis that *reconstructs* how these prejudices came about.

22. See also chapter 7 of the present volume for a comparison between the Kantian and Husserlian question of *quid iuris*.

23. I have attempted to connect these methodological considerations with Husserl's ethical reflections (Luft 2010b).

Bibliography

All translations, unless otherwise noted, are by the author.

Husserliana (published by Martinus Nijhoff, Kluwer Academic Publishers, and Springer)

Edmund Husserl Gesammelte Werke (quoted as Hua)

Hua I: *Cartesianische Meditationen und Pariser Vorträge*, ed. Stephan Strasser, 1950.
Hua II: *Die Idee der Phänomenologie: Fünf Vorlesungen*, ed. Walter Biemel, 1973.
Hua III/1 and 2: *Ideen zu einer reinen Phänomenologie und phänomenlogischen Philosophie*, I. Buch: *Allgemeine Einführung in die reine Phänomenologie*. In two volumes. 1. Halbband: Text der 1.–3. Auflage; 2. Halbband: *Ergänzende Texte (1912–1929)*, ed. Karl Schuhmann, 1976.
Hua IV: *Ideen zu einer reinen Phänomenologie und phänomenologischen Philosophie*. Zweites Buch: *Phänomenologische Untersuchungen zur Konstitution*, ed. Marly Biemel, 1991.
Hua V: *Ideen zu einer reinen Phänomenologie und phänomenologischen Philosophie*. Drittes Buch: *Die Phänomenologie und die Fundamente der Wissenschaften*, ed. Marly Biemel, 1971.
Hua VI: *Die Krisis der europäischen Wissenschaften und die transzendentale Phänomenologie: Eine Einleitung in die phänomenologische Philosophie*, ed. Walter Biemel, 1976.
Hua VII: *Erste Philosophie (1923/24)*. Erster Teil: *Kritische Ideengeschichte*, ed. Rudolf Boehm, 1954.
Hua VIII: *Erste Philosophie (1923/24)*. Zweiter Teil: *Theorie der phänomenologischen Reduktion*, ed. Rudolf Boehm, 1956.
Hua IX: *Phänomenologische Psychologie: Vorlesungen Sommersemester 1925*, ed. Walter Biemel, 1968.
Hua X: *Zur Phänomenologie des inneren Zeitbewusstseins (1893–1917)*, ed. Rudolf Boehm, 1969.
Hua XI: *Analysen zur passiven Synthesis: Aus Vorlesungs- und Forschungsmanuskripten (1918–1926)*, ed. Margot Fleischer, 1966.
Hua XII: *Philosophie der Arithmetik: Mit ergänzenden Texten (1890–1901)*, ed. Lothar Eley, 1970.

Hua XIII: *Zur Phänomenologie der Intersubjektivität: Texte aus dem Nachlass.* Erster Teil: 1905–1920, ed. Iso Kern, 1973.

Hua XIV: *Zur Phänomenologie der Intersubjektivität: Texte aus dem Nachlass.* Zweiter Teil: 1921–1928, ed. Iso Kern, 1973.

Hua XV: *Zur Phänomenologie der Intersubjektivitiät: Texte aus dem Nachlass.* Dritter Teil: 1929–1935, ed. Iso Kern, 1973.

Hua XVI: *Ding und Raum: Vorlesungen 1907,* ed. Ulrich Claesges, 1973.

Hua XVII: *Formale und transzendentale Logik: Versuch einer Kritik der logischen Vernunft: Mit ergänzenden Texten,* ed. Paul Janssen, 1974.

Hua XVIII: *Logische Untersuchungen: Erster Band: Prolegomena zur reinen Logik,* ed. Elmar Holenstein, 1984.

Hua XIX, 1 and 2: *Logische Untersuchungen.* Zweiter Band: *Untersuchungen zur Phänomenologie und Theorie der Erkenntnis,* ed. Ursula Panzer, 1984.

Hua XX, 1: *Logische Untersuchungen: Ergänzungsband: Erster Teil: Entwürfe zur Umarbeitung der VI. Untersuchung und zur Vorrede für die Neuauflage der Logischen Untersuchungen (Sommer 1913),* ed. Ullrich Melle, 2002.

Hua. XX, 2: *Logische Untersuchungen: Ergänzungsband: Zweiter Teil: Texte für die Neufassung der VI. Untersuchung: Zur Phänomenologie des Ausdrucks und der Erkenntnis (1893/94–1921),* ed. Ullrich Melle, 2005.

Hua XXI: *Studien zur Arithmetik und Geometrie: Texte aus dem Nachlass (1886–1901),* ed. Ingeborg Strohmeyer, 1983.

Hua XXII: *Aufsätze und Rezensionen (1890–1910),* ed. Bernhard Rang, 1979.

Hua XXIII: *Phantasie, Bildbewusstsein, Erinnerung: Zur Phänomenologie der anschaulichen Vergegenwärtigungen: Texte aus dem Nachlass (1898–1925),* ed. Eduard Marbach, 1980.

Hua XXIV: *Einleitung in die Logik und Erkenntnistheorie: Vorlesungen 1906/07,* ed. Ullrich Melle, 1984.

Hua XXV: *Aufsätze und Vorträge (1911–1921),* ed. Thomas Nenon and Hans Reiner Sepp, 1987.

Hua XXVI: *Vorlesungen über Bedeutungslehre 1908,* ed. Ursula Panzer, 1987.

Hua XXVII: *Aufsätze und Vorträge (1922–1937),* ed. Thomas Nenon and Hans Reiner Sepp, 1989.

Hua XXVIII: *Vorlesungen über Ethik und Wertlehre 1908–1914,* ed. Ullrich Melle, 1988.

Hua XXIX: *Die Krisis der europäischen Wissenschaften und die transzendentale Phänomenologie: Ergänzungsband, Texte aus dem Nachlass (1934–1937),* ed. Reinhold N. Smid, 1993.

Hua XXX: *Logik und allgemeine Wissenschaftstheorie. Vorlesungen Wintersemester 1917/18. Mit ergänzenden Texten aus der ersten Fassung von 1910/11,* ed. Ursula Panzer, 1996.

Hua XXXI: *Aktive Synthesen: Aus der Vorlesung "Transzendentale Logik" 1920/21: Ergänzungsband zu "Analysen zur passiven Synthesis,"* ed. Roland Breeur, 2000.

Hua XXXII: *Natur und Geist: Vorlesungen Sommersemester 1927,* ed. Michael Weiler, 2001.

Hua XXXIII: *Die Bernauer Manuskripte über das Zeitbewusstsein (1917/18)*, ed. Rudolf Bernet and Dieter Lohmar, 2001.

Hua XXXIV: *Zur phänomenologischen Reduktion: Texte aus dem Nachlass (1926–1935)*, ed. Sebastian Luft, 2002.

Hua XXXV: *Einleitung in die Philosophie: Vorlesungen 1922/23*, ed. Berndt Goossens, 2002.

Hua XXXVI: *Transzendentaler Idealismus: Texte aus dem Nachlass (1908–1921)*, ed. Robin D. Rollinger and Rochus Sowa, 2003.

Hua XXXVII: *Einleitung in die Ethik: Vorlesungen Sommersemester 1920/1924*, ed. Henning Peucker, 2004.

Hua XXXVIII: *Wahrnehmung und Aufmerksamkeit: Texte aus dem Nachlass (1893–1912)*, ed. Thomas Vongehr and Regula Giuliani, 2004.

Hua XXXIX: *Die Lebenswelt: Auslegungen der vorgegebenen Welt und ihrer Konstitution: Texte aus dem Nachlass (1916–1937)*, ed. Rochus Sowa, 2008.

Hua XL: *Untersuchungen zur Urteilstheorie: Texte aus dem Nachlass (1893–1918)*, ed. Robin D. Rollinger, 2009.

Husserliana—Materialien (quoted as Hua-Mat)

Hua-Mat I: *Logik: Vorlesung 1896*, ed. Elisabeth Schuhmann, 2001.

Hua-Mat II: *Logik: Vorlesung 1902/03*, ed. Elisabeth Schuhmann, 2001.

Hua-Mat III: *Allgemeine Erkenntnistheorie. Vorlesung 1902/03*, ed. Elisabeth Schuhmann, 2001.

Hua-Mat IV: *Natur und Geist: Vorlesungen Sommersemester 1919*, ed. Michael Weiler, 2002.

Hua-Mat V: *Urteilstheorie: Vorlesung 1905*, ed. Elisabeth Schuhmann, 2002.

Hua-Mat VI: *Alte und neue Logik: Vorlesung 1908/09*, ed. Elisabeth Schuhmann, 2003.

Hua-Mat VII: *Einführung in die Phänomenologie der Erkenntnis: Vorlesung 1909*, ed. Elisabeth Schuhmann, 2005.

Hua-Mat VIII: *Späte Texte über Zeitkonstitution (1929–1934): Die C-Manuskripte*, ed. Dieter Lohmar, 2006.

Husserliana—Dokumente (quoted as Hua-Dok)

Hua-Dok I. Karl Schuhmann. 1977. *Husserl-Chronik: Denk- und Lebensweg Edmund Husserls.*

Hua-Dok II. Eugen Fink. 1988. *VI. Cartesianische Meditation.* Part 1: *Die Idee einer transzendentalen Methodenlehre.* Ed. Hans Ebeling, Jann Holl, and Guy van Kerckhoven. Part 2: *Ergänzungsband.* Ed. Guy van Kerckhoven.

Hua-Dok III. Edmund Husserl. 1994. *Briefwechsel.* Ed. Karl Schuhmann in conjunction with Elisabeth Schuhmann.

III.1. *Die Brentanoschule.*

III.2. *Die Münchener Phänomenologen.*

III.3. *Die Göttinger Schule.*

III.4. *Die Freiburger Schüler.*

III.5. *Die Neukantianer.*

III.6. *Philosophenbriefe.*

III.7. *Wissenschaftlerkorrespondenz.*

III.8. *Institutionelle Schreiben.*

III.9. *Familienbriefe.*

III.10. *Einführung und Register.*

Hua-Dok IV. *Edmund Husserl Bibliography.* Compiled by Steven Spileers. 1999.

Other Works by Husserl

Husserl, Edmund. 1940. "Grundlegende Untersuchungen zum phänomenologischen Ursprung der Räumlichkeit der Natur ('Umsturz der Kopernikanischen Lehre')." In *Philosophical Essays in Memory of Edmund Husserl.* Ed. Marvin Farber. Cambridge, Mass.: Harvard University Press, 307–25.

———. 1948. *Erfahrung und Urteil: Untersuchungen zur Genealogie der Logik.* Ed. Ludwig Landgrebe. Hamburg: Meiner.

———. 1970a. *Logical Investigations.* Trans. J. N. Findlay. New York: Humanities.

———. 1970b. *Logical Investigations.* Trans. J. N. Findlay. London: Routledge and Kegan Paul.

———. 1973a. *Experience and Judgment: Investigation in the Genealogy of Logic.* Trans. James S. Churchill and Karl Ameriks. London: Routledge and Kegan Paul.

———. 1973b. *The Idea of Phenomenology.* Trans. William Alston. The Hague: Martinus Nijhoff.

———. 1974. "Kant and the Idea of Transcendental Philosophy." Trans. Ted E. Klein and William E. Pohl. *Southwestern Journal of Philosophy* 5 (Fall): 9–56.

———. 1977. *Phenomenological Psychology: Lectures, Summer Semester 1925.* Trans. John Scanlon. The Hague: Nijhoff.

———. 1980. *Ideas Pertaining to a Pure Phenomenology and to a Phenomenological Philosophy: Third Book: Phenomenology and the Foundations of the Sciences.* Trans. Ted E. Klein and William E. Pohl. The Hague: Nijhoff.

———. 1981. "The World of the Living Present." In *Husserl: Shorter Works,* ed. Peter McCormick and Frederick A. Elliston. South Bend, Ind.: University of Notre Dame Press, 161–97.

———. 1983. *Ideas Pertaining to a Pure Phenomenology and to a Phenomenological Philosophy: First Book: General Introduction to a Pure Phenomenology.* Trans. Fred Kersten. The Hague: Nijhoff.

———. 1985. *Texte zur Phänomenologie des inneren Zeitbewusstseins (1893–1917).* Ed. Rudolf Bernet. Hamburg: Meiner.

———. 1986. *The Crisis of European Sciences and Transcendental Phenomenology: An Introduction to Phenomenological Philosophy.* Trans. David Carr. Evanston, Ill.: Northwestern University Press.

———. 1989. *Ideas Pertaining to a Pure Phenomenology and to a Phenomenological Philosophy: Second Book: Studies in the Phenomenology of Constitution.* Trans. Richard Rojcewicz and André Schuwer. Dordrecht: Kluwer Academic.

————. 1991. *On the Phenomenology of the Consciousness of Internal Time (1893–1917)*. Trans. John B. Brough. Dordrecht: Kluwer Academic.

————. 1994. "Husserls Randbemerkungen zu Heideggers *Sein und Zeit* und *Kant und das Problem der Metaphysik*." Ed. Roland Breeur. *Husserl Studies* 11: 3–63.

————. 1997. *Thing and Space: Lectures of 1907*. Trans. Richard Rojcewicz. Dordrecht: Kluwer Academic.

————. 1999. *Cartesian Meditations: An Introduction to Phenomenology*. Trans. Dorian Cairns. Dordrecht: Kluwer Academic.

————. 2001a. *Logical Investigations*. Ed. Dermot Moran. Trans. J. N. Findlay, with a preface by Michael Dummett. London: Routledge.

————. 2001b. *Analyses Concerning Passive and Active Synthesis: Lectures on Transcendental Logic*. Trans. Anthony J. Steinbock. Dordrecht: Kluwer Academic.

————. 2002. "Philosophy as Rigorous Science" (1911). Trans. Marcus Brainard. In *The New Yearbook for Phenomenology and Phenomenological Philosophy*, ed. Burt C. Hopkins and Steven G. Crowell. Seattle: Noesis.

————. 2005. *Phantasy, Image Consciousness, and Memory (1898–1925)*. Trans. John B. Brough. Heidelberg: Springer.

Husserl's *Nachlass* (Literary Estate)

Husserl ordered his unpublished manuscripts (German: *Nachlass*) in 1935 into the sections listed below. This is the manner in which Husserl's literary estate is preserved and quoted to this day. The pages of these convolutes have been numbered after Husserl's death. Hence, the way in which Husserl's *Nachlass* is normally cited (and it is the manner in which it has been done in this book) is by citing the group and the subgroup (e.g., A V), the latter of which is made up of many convolutes, which are cited in Roman numerals, and the pages are then cited in Arabic, a designating recto, b verso. So, for instance, A VII 12/23b is page 23 verso of convolute 12 of group A VII. Books in which Husserl made annotations are shelved as "BQ" and a Roman numeral in alphabetical order. For instance, Husserl's copy of Natorp's *Allgemeine Psychologie nach kritischer Methode* is shelved under BQ 342. "BQ 342, 12" hence refers to Husserl's annotation on page 12 in Natorp's book.

> A: Mundane Phänomenologie (Mundane Phenomenology)
> A I: Logik und Formale Ontologie (Logic and Formal Ontology)
> A II: Formale Ethik, Rechtsphilosophie (Formal Ethics, Philosophy of Right)
> A III: Ontologie (Eidetik und ihre Methodologie) (Ontology [Eidetics and Its Methodology])
> A IV: Wissenschaftslehre (Theory of Science)
> A V: Intentionale Anthropologie (Person und Umwelt) (Intentional Anthropology [Person and Surroundings])
> A VI: Psychologie (Lehre von der Intentionalität) (Psychology [Doctrine of Intentionality])

A VII: Theorie der Weltapperzeption (Theory of World-Apperception)

B. Die Reduktion (The Reduction)

B I: Wege zur Reduktion (Ways to the Reduction)

B II: Die Reduktion selbst und ihre Methologie (The Reduction Itself and Its Methodology)

B III: Vorläufige transzendentale Intentionalanalytik (Preliminary Transcendental Analytic of Intentionality)

B IV: Historische und Systematische Selbstcharakteristik der Phänomenologie (Historical and Systematic Self-Characterization of Phenomenology)

C: Zeitkonstitution als Formale Konstitution (Temporal Constitution as Formal Constitution)

D : Primodiale Konstitution ("Urkonstitution") (Primordial Constitution ["Primal Constitution"])

E: Intersubjektive Konstitution (Intersubjective Constitution)

E I: Konstitutive Elementarlehre der unmittelbaren Fremderfahrung (Constitutional Elementary Doctrine of Immediate Experience of Others)

E II: Konstitution der Mittelbaren Fremderfahrung (die volle Sozialität) (Constitution of Mediate Experience of Others [Full Sociality])

E III: Transzendentale Anthropologie (Transzendentale Teleologie, Theologie, Metaphysik) (Transcendnental Anthropology [Transcendental Teleology, Theology, Metaphysics])

F: Vorlesungen und Vorträge (Lecture Courses and Lectures)

K: Manuscripts not part of the original order of 1935

L: Bernauer Manuskripte (Bernau Manuscripts)

M: Abschriften von Husserls Assistenten (Typescripts by Husserl's Assistants)

N: Nachschriften (Student Notes)

Other Literature

Allison, Henry E. 1975. "The *Critique of Pure Reason* as Transcendental Phenomenology." In *Dialogues in Phenomenology*, ed. Don Ihde and Richard M. Zaner. The Hague: Nijhoff, 136–55.

———. 1983. *Kant's Transcendental Idealism*. New Haven, Conn.: Yale University Press.

Alweiss, Lilian. 2003. *The World Unclaimed: A Challenge to Heidegger's Critique of Husserl*. Athens: Ohio University Press.

Ameriks, Karl. 2006. *Kant and the Historical Turn: Philosophy as Critical Interpretation*. Oxford: Oxford University Press.

Apel, Karl-Otto. 1973. *Transformation der Philosophie*. Vol. 1, *Sprachanalytik, Semiotik, Hermeneutik*. Frankfurt am Main: Suhrkamp.

Bauch, Bruno. 1918. "'Immanuel Kant' und die Fortbildung des Systems des Kritischen Idealismus." *Kant-Studien* 22: 426–59.

Bayer, Thora I. 2001. *Cassirer's Metaphysics of Symbolic Forms*. New Haven, Conn.: Yale University Press.

Bermes, Christian. 2004. *"Welt" als Thema der Philosophie: Vom metaphysischen zum natürlichen Weltbegriff*. Hamburg: Meiner.

Bernet, Rudolf. 1989. "Différence ontologique et conscience transcendentale: La réponse de la *Sixième méditation cartésienne* de Fink." In *Husserl*, ed. Eliane Escoubas and Marc Richir. Grenoble: J. Millon, 89–116.

———. 1994a. "Phenomenological Reduction and the Double Life of the Subject." Trans. François Renauld. In *Reading Heidegger from the Start: Essays in His Earliest Thought*, ed. Theodore Kisiel and John van Buren. Albany: State University of New York Press, 245–67.

———. 1994b. "La réduction phénoménologique et la double vie du sujet." In *La vie du Sujet: Recherches sur l'interpretation de Husserl dans la phénoménologie*. Paris: Presses Universitaires de France, 5–36.

———. 2004. "L'Idéalisme Husserlien: Les objets possibles ou réels et la conscience transcendantale." In *Conscience et existence: Perspectives phénoménologiques*. Paris: Presses Universitaires de France, 143–68.

———. 2010. "The Hermeneutics of Perception in Cassirer, Heidegger, and Husserl." In *Neo-Kantianism in Contemporary Philosophy*, ed. Rudolf A. Makkreel and Sebastian Luft. Bloomington: Indiana University Press, 41–58.

Bernet, Rudolf, Iso Kern, and Eduard Marbach. 1989. *Edmund Husserl: Darstellung seines Denkens*. Hamburg: Meiner.

Besoli, Stefano, Massimo Ferrari, and Luca Guidetti, eds. 2002. *Neokantianismo e fenomenologia: Logica, psigologia, cultura e teoria della conoscenza*. Macerata: Quodlibet.

Blumenberg, Hans. 1996. *Ein mögliches Selbstverständnis*. Stuttgart: Reclam.

Boehm, Rudolf. 1979. "Husserls drei Thesen über die Lebenswelt." In *Lebenswelt und Wissenschaft in der Philosophie Edmund Husserls*, ed. Elisabeth Ströker. Frankfurt am Main: Klostermann, 23–31.

Bösch, Michael. 2001. "Symbolische Prägnanz und passive Synthesis: Genetische Phänomenologie der Wahrnehmung bei Cassirer und Husserl." *Philosophisches Jahrbuch* 109: 148–61.

Brainard, Marcus. 2002. *Belief and Its Neutralization: Husserl's System of Phenomenology in Ideas I*. Albany: State University of New York Press.

Brandom, Robert. 2002. *Tales of the Mighty Dead: Historical Chapters in the Metaphysics of Intentionality*. Cambridge, Eng.: Cambridge University Press.

Braun, Hans J., Helmut Holzhey, and Ernst Wolfgang Orth, eds. 1988. *Über Ernst Cassirers Philosophie der symbolischen Formen*. Frankfurt am Main: Suhrkamp.

Breda, Hermann Leo Van. 1973. "Husserl und das Problem der Freiheit." In *Husserl*, ed. Hans Noack. Darmstadt: Wissenschaftliche Buchgesellschaft, 277–81.

Bruzina, Ronald. 1989. "The Enworlding (*Verweltlichung*) of Transcendental Phenomenological Reflection: A Study of Eugen Fink's '6th Cartesian Meditation.'" *Husserl Studies* 3: 3–29.

Cairns, Dorion. 1976. *Conversations with Husserl and Fink*. Phaenomenologica 66. The Hague: Nijhoff.

Carr, David. 1974. *Phenomenology and the Problem of History*. Evanston, Ill.: Northwestern University Press.

———. 1987. *Interpreting Husserl: Critical and Comparative Studies*. Phaenomenologica 106. Dordrecht: Nijhoff.

———. 1999. *The Paradox of Subjectivity: The Self in the Transcendental Tradition*. New York: Oxford University Press.

———. 2003. "Transcendental and Empirical Subjectivity: The Self in the Transcendental Tradition." In *The New Husserl: A Critical Reader*, ed. Donn Welton. Bloomington: Indiana University Press, 181–98.

Cassirer, Ernst. 1925. "Paul Natorp." *Kant-Studien* 30: 273–98.

———. 1944. *An Essay on Man: An Introduction to a Philosophy of Human Culture*. New Haven, Conn.: Yale University Press.

———. 1946. *Language and Myth*. Trans. Susanne K. Langer. New York: Dover.

———. 1954. *Philosophie der symbolischen Formen*, I: *Die Sprache;* II: *Das mythische Denken;* III: *Phänomenologie der Erkenntnis*. 2nd ed. Oxford: B. Cassirer.

———. 1955. *The Philosophy of Symbolic Forms*, I: *Language;* II: *Mythical Thought;* III: *Phenomenology of Knowledge*. Trans. Ralph Manheim. New Haven, Conn.: Yale University Press.

———. 1979. "Critical Idealism as a Philosophy of Culture." In *Symbol, Myth and Culture: Essays and Lectures of Ernst Cassirer 1935–1945*, ed. Donald P. Verene. New Haven, Conn.: Yale University Press, 64–94.

———. 1983. *Wesen und Wirkung des Symbolbegriffs*. Darmstadt: Wissenschaftliche Buchgesellschaft.

———. 1994a. *Das Erkenntnisproblem in der Philosophie und Wissenschaft der neueren Zeit I*. Darmstadt: Wissenschaftliche Buchgesellschaft.

———. 1994b. *Substanzbegriff und Funktionsbegriff: Untersuchungen über die Grundfragen der Erkenntniskritik*. Darmstadt: Wissenschaftliche Buchgesellschaft.

———. 1995. *Zur Metaphysik der symbolischen Formen*. Ed. John M. Krois et al. Hamburg: Meiner.

———. 1996. *The Philosophy of Symbolic Forms, Vol. Four: The Metaphysics of Symbolic Forms, Including the Text of Cassirer's Manuscript on Basis Phenomena*. Ed. John M. Krois and Donald P. Verene. New Haven: Yale University Press.

Cassirer, Toni. 1981. *Mein Leben mit Ernst Cassirer*. Hildesheim: Gerstenberg.

Claesges, Ulrich. 1972. "Zweideutigkeiten in Husserls Lebenswelt-Begriff." In *Perspektiven transzendental-phänomenologischer Forschung: Für Ludwig Landgrebe zum 70. Geburtstag*, ed. Ulrich Claesges and Klaus Held. Phaenomenologica 49. The Hague: Nijhoff, 85–101.

———. 1974. *Geschichte des Selbstbewußtseins: Der Ursprung des spekulativen Problems in Fichtes Wissenschaftslehre 1794–95*. The Hague: Nijhoff.

Cohen, Hermann. 1987. *Kants Theorie der Erfahrung*. Hildesheim: Olms.

Courtine, Jean-François. 1990. *Heidegger et la phénoménologie*. Paris: Presses Universitaires de France.

Cramer, Konrad. 1974. "Erlebnis: Thesen zu Hegels Theorie des Selbstbewusstseins mit Rücksicht auf die Aporien eines Grundbegriffs nachhegelscher Philosophie." In *Hegel–Studien* 11. Bonn: Bouvier, 537–603.

Cramer, Wolfgang. 1975. *Grundlegung einer Theorie des Geistes*. 3rd ed. Frankfurt am Main: Klostermann.

Crowell, Steven Galt. 2001. *Husserl, Heidegger, and the Space of Meaning: Paths Towards Transcendental Phenomenology*. Evanston, Ill.: Northwestern University Press.

———. 2002. "Does the Husserl/Heidegger Feud Rest on a Mistake? A Chapter on Psychological and Transcendental Phenomenology." *Husserl Studies* 18: 123–40.

De Palma, Vittorio. 2005. "Ist Husserls Phänomenologie ein transzendentaler Idealismus?" *Husserl Studies* 21: 183–206.

Detmer, David. 1997. "Gadamer's Critique of the Enlightenment." In *The Philosophy of Hans-Georg Gadamer*, ed. Lewis E. Hahn. Chicago: Open Court, 275–86.

Dilthey, Wilhelm. 1985. *Introduction to the Human Sciences*. Vol. 1 of *Selected Works*, ed. Rudolf A. Makkreel and Frithjof Rodi. Princeton, N.J.: Princeton University Press.

Dodd, James. 2004. *Crisis and Reflection: A Chapter on Husserl's Crisis of the European Sciences*. Phaenomenologica 174. Dordrecht: Kluwer.

Dostal, Robert J., ed. 2002. *The Cambridge Companion to Gadamer*. Cambridge, Eng.: Cambridge University Press.

Dreyfus, Hubert. 1991. *Being-in-the-World: A Commentary on Heidegger's Being and Time, Division I*. Cambridge, Mass.: MIT Press.

Düsing, Klaus. 1997. *Selbstbewußtseinsmodelle: Moderne Kritiken und systematische Entwürfe zur konkreten Subjektivität*. Munich: Fink.

Ferrari, Massimo. 2010. "Is Cassirer a Neo-Kantian Methodologically Speaking?" In *Neo-Kantianism in Contemporary Philosophy*, ed. Rudolf A. Makkreel and Sebastian Luft. Bloomington: Indiana University Press, 293–314.

Fink, Eugen. 1966. *Studien zur Phänomenologie 1930–1939*. The Hague: Nijhoff.

———. 1976. *Nähe und Distanz: Phänomenologische Vorträge und Aufsätze*. Ed. Franz-Anton Schwarz. Freiburg: Alber.

Frede, Dorothea, and Reinold Schmücker, eds. 1997. *Ernst Cassirers Werk und Wirkung*. Darmstadt: Wissenschaftliche Buchgesellschaft.

Friedman, Michael. 2000. *A Parting of the Ways: Carnap, Cassirer, and Heidegger*. LaSalle, Ill.: Open Court.

———. 2010. "Ernst Cassirer and Thomas Kuhn: The Neo-Kantian Tradition in the History and Philosophy of Science." In *Neo-Kantianism in Contemporary Philosophy*, ed. Rudolf A. Makkreel and Sebastian Luft. Bloomington: Indiana University Press, 177–91.

Funke, Gerhard. 1984. "Practical Reason in Kant and Husserl." In *Kant and Phenomenology*, ed. Thomas M. Seebohm and Joseph J. Kockelmans. Washington: Center for Advanced Research in Phenomenology and University Press of America, 1–29.

Gabriel, Gottfried. 1980. "Metamathematik I." In *Historisches Wörterbuch der Philosophie* V. Darmstadt: Wissenschaftliche Buchgesellschaft, 1175–76.

Gadamer, Hans-Georg. 1974. "Hermeneutik." In *Historisches Wörterbuch der Philosophie* III. Darmstadt: Wissenschaftliche Buchgesellschaft, 1061–73.

———. 1976. *Philosophical Hermeneutics*. Ed. and trans. David E. Linge. Berkeley: University of California Press.

———. 1986a. "Zwischen Phänomenologie und Dialektik: Versuch einer Selbstkritik." Vol. 2 of *Gesammelte Werke*. Tübingen: Mohr/Siebeck, 2–23.

———. 1986b. "Die phänomenologische Bewegung." Vol. 3 of *Gesammelte Werke*. Tübingen: Mohr/Siebeck, 105–46.

———. 1989. *Truth and Method*, 2nd rev. ed. Trans. Joel Weinsheimer and Donald G. Marshall. New York: Crossroad.

———. 1990. *Wahrheit und Methode: Grundzüge einer Philosophischen Hermeneutik*. Tübingen: Mohr/Siebeck.

———. 1993. *Ästhetik und Poetik II: Hermeneutik im Vollzug*. Vol. 9 of *Gesammelte Werke*. Tübingen: Mohr/Siebeck.

———. 1995. *Hermeneutik im Rückblick*. Vol. 10 of *Gesammelte Werke*. Tübingen: Mohr/Siebeck.

Gander, Hans-Helmuth. 2001. *Selbstverständnis und Lebenswelt: Grundzüge einer phänomenologischen Hermeneutik im Ausgang von Husserl und Heidegger*. Frankfurt am Main: Klostermann.

Gardner, Sebastian. 1999. *Kant and the Critique of Pure Reason*. London: Routledge.

Gawronski, Dimitri. 1949. "Ernst Cassirer: His Life and His Work." In *The Philosophy of Ernst Cassirer*, ed. Paul A. Schilpp. Evanston, Ill.: Open Court, 31–37.

Gethmann, Carl Friedrich. 1980. "Letztbegründung." In *Historisches Wörterbuch der Philosophie* V. Darmstadt: Wissenschaftliche Buchgesellschaft, 251–54.

———. 1993. *Dasein: Erkennen und Handeln: Heidegger im phänomenologischen Kontext*. Berlin: De Gruyter.

Goodman, Nelson. 1978. *Ways of World-Making*. Indianapolis, Ind.: Hackett.

Graeser, Andreas. 1994. *Ernst Cassirer*. Munich: C. H. Beck.

Grondin, Jean. 2003. *Gadamer: A Biography*. Trans. Joel Weinsheimer. New Haven, Conn.: Yale University Press.

———. 2010. "The Neo-Kantian Heritage in Gadamer." In *Neo-Kantianism in Contemporary Philosophy*, ed. Rudolf A. Makkreel and Sebastian Luft. Bloomington: Indiana University Press, 92–110.

Habermas, Jürgen. 1987. *Philosophisch-politische Profile*. Frankfurt am Main: Suhrkamp.

———. 1997. "Die befreiende Kraft der symbolischen Formgebung: Ernst Cassirers humanistisches Erbe und die Bibliothek Warburg." In *Ernst Cassirers Werk und Wirkung*, ed. Dorothea Frede and Reinold Schmücker. Darmstadt: Wissenschaftliche Buchgesellschaft, 79–104.

Hahn, Lewis E., ed. 1997. *The Philosophy of Hans-Georg Gadamer*. Vol. 24 of Library of Living Philosophers. LaSalle, Ill.: Open Court.

Hart, James. 1992. *The Person and the Common Life: Studies in a Husserlian Social Ethics*. Phaenomenologica 126. Dordrecht: Kluwer.

Heidegger, Martin. 1973. *Kant und das Problem der Metaphysik*. Frankfurt am Main: Klostermann.

———. 1976. *Logik: Die Frage nach der Wahrheit*. Ed. Walter Biemel. Frankfurt am Main: Klostermann.

———. 1987. *Über das Wesen der Universität und des akademischen Studiums*. In *Zur Bestimmung der Philosophie*. Ed. Bernd Heimbüchel. Frankfurt am Main: Klostermann.

————. 1988. *Zur Sache des Denkens*. Tübingen: Mohr/Siebeck.

————. 1989a. "Phänomenologische Interpretationen zu Aristoteles (Anzeige der hermeneutischen Situation)." *Dilthey-Jahrbuch* 6: 235–69.

————. 1989b. *Beiträge zur Philosophie (Vom Ereignis)*. Ed. Friedrich-Wilhelm von Hermann. Frankfurt am Main: Klostermann.

————. 1991. *Kant und das Problem der Metaphysik*. Frankfurt am Main: Klostermann.

————. 1993. *Sein und Zeit*. 17th ed. Tübingen: Niemeyer.

————. 1996. *Being and Time*. Trans. Joan Stambaugh. Albany: State University of New York Press.

————. 1997. *Kant and the Problem of Metaphysics*. Trans. Richard Taft. Bloomington: Indiana University Press.

————. 1999. *Ontology: The Hermeneutics of Facticity*. Trans. John van Buren. Bloomington: Indiana University Press.

Held, Klaus. 1966. *Lebendige Gegenwart: Die Frage nach der Seinsweise des transzendentalen Ich bei Edmund Husserl, entwickelt am Leitfaden der Zeitproblematik*. Phaenomenologica 23. The Hague: Nijhoff.

————. 1980. "Husserls Rückgang auf das *phainómenon* und die geschichtliche Stellung der Phänomenologie." In *Phänomenologische Forschung* 10: 89–145.

————. 1989. "Husserls These von der Europäisierung der Menschheit." In *Phänomenologie im Widerstreit: Zum 50. Geburtstag Edmund Husserls*, ed. Christoph Jamme and Otto Pöggeler. Frankfurt am Main: Suhrkamp, 13–39.

————. 1991. "Heimwelt, Fremdwelt, die eine Welt." In *Phänomenologische Forschungen* 24/25: 305–37.

————. 1992. "Die Endlichkeit der Welt: Phänomenologie im Übergang von Husserl zu Heidegger." In *Philosophie der Endlichkeit*, ed. Beate Niemeyer and Dirk Schütze. Würzburg: Königshausen & Neumann, 130–47.

————. 1996. "Abschied vom Cartesianismus: Die Phänomenologie Edmund Husserls." *Neue Zürcher Zeitung* 76.

————. 2003. "Husserl's Phenomenology of the Lifeworld." In *The New Husserl: A Critical Reader*, ed. Donn Welton. Bloomington: Indiana University Press, 32–64.

Henry, Michel. 1973. *The Essence of Manifestation*. Trans. Girard Etzkorn. The Hague: Nijhoff.

Herrmann, Friedrich-Wilhelm von. 1988. *Der Begriff der Phänomenologie bei Heidegger und Husserl*. 2nd ed. Frankfurt am Main: Klostermann.

Höffe, Otfried. 2004. *Kants Kritik der reinen Vernunft: Die Grundlegung der modernen Philosophie*. Munich: C. H. Beck.

Holzhey, Helmut. 1986. *Cohen und Natorp*. 2 vols. Basel: Schwabe.

————. 1991. "'Zu den Sachen selbst!' Über das Verhältnis von Phänomenologie und Neukantianismus." In *Sinn und Erfahrung: Phänomenologische Methoden in den Humanwissenschaften*, ed. Max Herzog and Carl Friedrich Graumann. Heidelberg: Springer, 3–21.

————. 2010. "Neo-Kantianism and Phenomenology: The Problem of Intuition." In *Neo-Kantianism in Contemporary Philosophy*, ed. Rudolf A. Makkreel and Sebastian Luft. Bloomington: Indiana University Press, 25–40.

Jung, Mathias. 2002. *Hermeneutik zur Einführung*. Hamburg: Junius.

Kaegi, Dominic. 1995. "Jenseits der symbolischen Formen: Zum Verhältnis von Anschauung und künstlicher Symbolik bei Ernst Cassirer." *Dialektik* 1: 73–84.

Kant, Immanuel. 1968. *Critique of Pure Reason*. Trans. Norman Kemp Smith. London: Macmillan.

———. 1987. *Critique of Judgment*. Trans. Werner S. Pluhar. Indianapolis, Ind.: Hackett.

———. 1990. *Kritik der Urteilskraft*. Ed. Karl Vorländer. Hamburg: Meiner.

———. 1998. *Kritik der reinen Vernunft*. Ed. Jens Timmermann. Hamburg: Meiner. (The *Critique of Pure Reason* is cited according to the original first and second edition as "A" and "B," respectively.)

Kerckhoven, Guy van, ed. 1999/2000. "Edmund Husserls Randnotizen zu Georg Mischs *Lebensphilosophie und Phänomenologie*." *Dilthey-Jahrbuch* 12: 145–86.

Kern, Iso. 1962. "Die Drei Wege zur transzendental-phänomenologischen Reduktion." In *Tijdschrift voor Filosofie* 24: 303–49.

———. 1964. *Husserl und Kant: Untersuchung über Husserls Verhältnis zu Kant und zum Neukantianismus*. Phaenomenologica 16. The Hague: Nijhoff.

Kisiel, Theodore. 1993. *The Genesis of Heidegger's "Being and Time."* Berkeley: University of California Press.

Köhnke, Klaus Christian. 1986. *Entstehung und Aufstieg des Neukantianismus: Die deutsche Universitätsphilosophie zwischen Idealismus und Positivismus*. Frankfurt am Main: Suhrkamp.

———. 1991. *The Rise of Neo-Kantianism*. Trans. R. J. Hollingdale. Cambridge, Eng.: Cambridge University Press.

Krajewski, Bruce, ed. 2004. *Gadamer's Repercussions: Reconsidering Philosophical Hermeneutics*. Berkeley: University of California Press.

Krois, John Michael. 1987. *Cassirer: Symbolic Forms and History*. New Haven, Conn.: Yale University Press.

———. 1988. "Problematik, Eigenart und Aktualität der Cassirerschen Philosophie der Symbolischen Formen." In *Über Ernst Cassirers Philosophie der symbolischen Formen*, ed. Hans-Jürg Braun, Helmut Holzhey, and Ernst Wolfgang Orth. Frankfurt am Main: Suhrkamp, 15–44.

Kroner, Richard. 1934. "Bemerkungen zur Dialektik der Zeit." In *Veröffentlichungen des internationalen Hegelbundes* III. Tübingen, 153–61.

Kühn, Rolf. 1998. *Husserls Begriff der Passivität: Zur Kritik der passiven Synthesis in der Genetischen Phänomenologie*. Freiburg: Alber.

Kuster, Friederike. 1996. *Wege der Verantwortung: Husserls Phänomenologie als Gang durch die Faktizität*. Phaenomenologica 138. Dordrecht: Kluwer.

Landgrebe, Ludwig. 1963. *Der Weg der Phänomenologie: Das Problem einer ursprünglichen Erfahrung*. Gütersloh: Mohn.

———. 1980. "Phänomenologische Analyse und Dialektik." In *Phänomenologische Forschungen* 10, ed. Ernst Wolfgang Orth. Freiburg: Alber, 21–88.

———. 1981. "Departure from Cartesianism." In *The Phenomenology of Edmund Husserl*, ed. Donn Welton. Ithaca, N.Y.: Cornell University Press, 66–121.

———. 1982. *Faktizität und Individuation*. Hamburg: Meiner.

Langer, Susanne K. 1942. *Philosophy In a New Key: A Study in the Symbolism of Reason, Rite, and Art*. Cambridge, Mass.: Harvard University Press.

Langton, Rae. 1998. *Kantian Humility: Our Ignorance of Things in Themselves*. Oxford: Clarendon.

Lavigne, Jean-François. 2002. *Husserl et la naissance de la phénoménologie*. Paris: Presses Universitaires de France.

Lee, Nam-In. 1993. *Edmund Husserls Phänomenologie der Instinkte*. Phaenomenologica 128. Dordrecht: Kluwer.

Lembeck, Karl-Heinz. 1988. *Gegenstand Geschichte: Geschichtswissenschaftstheorie in Husserls Phänomenologie*. Phaenomenologica 111. Dordrecht: Kluwer.

Lohmar, Dieter. 1998. *Erfahrung und kategoriales Denken: Hume, Kant und Husserl über vorprädikative Erfahrung und prädikative Erkenntnis*. Phaenomenologica 147. Dordrecht: Kluwer.

————. 2004. "Ich enthalte mich aller Tradition." In *Tradition und Traditionsbruch zwischen Skepsis und Dogmatik: Interkulturelle philosophische Perspektiven*, ed. Claudia Bickmann, Hermann-Josef Scheidgen, Tobias Voßhenrich and Markus Wirtz. Amsterdam, 193–208.

Luft, Sebastian. 2002. *"Phänomenologie der Phänomenologie": Systematik und Methodologie der Phänomenologie in der Auseinandersetzung zwischen Husserl und Fink*. Phaenomenologica 166. Dordrecht: Kluwer.

————. 2003. "'Idealismo Realista': Una Respuesta Heterodóxa a la Pregunta del Idealismo Trascendental." *Escritos de Filosofía* 43: 75–98.

————. 2004a. "A Phenomenology of Subjective and Objective Spirit: Husserl and Cassirer." *New Yearbook for Phenomenology* 4: 209–49.

————. 2004b. "Die Archivierung des Husserlschen Nachlasses 1933–1935." *Husserl Studies* 20: 1–23.

————. 2006. "The Condition of Possibility of Transcendental Philosophy," review essay of *Husserl, Heidegger and the Space of Meaning*, by Steven G. Crowell. *Husserl Studies* 22: 53–75.

————. 2010a. "Edmund Husserl: Socrates—Buddha: An Unpublished Manuscript from the Archives." Ed. and introduced by Sebastian Luft. *Husserl Studies* 26: 1–17.

————. 2010b. "Das Subjekt als moralische Person: Zu Husserls späten Reflexionen bezüglich des Personenbegriffs." In *Geist—Person—Gemeinschaft: Freiburger Beiträge zur Aktualität Husserls*, ed. Philippe Merz, Andrea Staiti, and Frank Steffen. Würzburg: Ergon, 221–40.

————. 2010c. Review of *Ernst Cassirer: The Last Philosopher of Culture*, by Edward Sidelsky. *Journal of the History of Philosophy* 48, no. 1: 116–17.

————. 2010d. "Phenomenology as First Philosophy: A Prehistory." In *Edmund Husserl 150 Years: Philosophy, Phenomenology, Sciences*, ed. Carlo Ierna, Hanne Jacobs, and Filip Mattens. Phaenomenologica 200. Heidelberg: Springer, 2010, 41–67.

————. 2011. "Phänomenologie als Erste Philosophie und das Problem der Wissenschaft von der Lebenswelt." In *Archiv für Begriffsgeschichte* 53/2011, forthcoming.

Makkreel, Rudolf A. 2004. "Heidegger, Dilthey und der Vollzugssinn der Geschichte." In *Heidegger-Jahrbuch* I. Freiburg: Alber, 307–21.

———. 2010. "Wilhelm Dilthey and the Neo-Kantians: On the Conceptual Distinctions Between *Geisteswissenschaften* and *Kulturwissenschaften*." In *Neo-Kantianism in Contemporary Philosophy*, ed. Rudolf A. Makkreel and Sebastian Luft. Bloomington: Indiana University Press: 253–271.

Makkreel, Rudolf A., and Sebastian Luft, eds. 2010. *Neo-Kantianism in Contemporary Philosophy*. Bloomington: Indiana University Press.

Malpas, Jeff, Ulrich Arnswald, and Jens Kertscher, eds. 2002. *Gadamer's Century: Essays in Honor of Hans-Georg Gadamer.* Cambridge, Mass.: MIT Press.

Marion, Jean-Luc. 1998. *Reduction and Givenness: Investigations of Husserl, Heidegger, and Phenomenology.* Trans. Thomas A. Carlson. Evanston, Ill.: Northwestern University Press.

Marx, Wolfgang. 1988. "Cassirers Philosophie—ein Abschied von kantianisierender Letztbegründung." In *Über Ernst Cassirers Philosophie der symbolischen Formen,* ed. Hans-Jürg Braun, Helmut Holzhey, and Ernst Wolfgang Orth. Frankfurt am Main: Suhrkamp, 75–88.

McDowell, John. 1996. *Mind and World.* Cambridge, Mass.: Harvard University Press.

———. 2002. "Gadamer and Davidson on Understanding and Relativism." In *Gadamer's Century: Essays in Honor of Hans-Georg Gadamer,* ed. John Malpas, Ulrich Arnswald, and Jens Kertscher. Cambridge, Mass.: MIT Press, 173–94.

Melle, Ullrich. 2002. "Edmund Husserl: From Reason to Love." In *Phenomenological Approaches to Moral Philosophy: A Handbook,* ed. John J. Drummond and Lester Embree. Dordrecht: Kluwer, 229–48.

Merleau-Ponty, Maurice. 1945. *Phénoménologie de la perception.* Paris: Éditions Gallimard.

Mertens, Karl. 2001. "Husserls Phänomenologie der Monade: Bemerkungen zu Husserls Auseinandersetzung mit Leibniz." *Husserl Studies* 17: 1–20.

Misch, Georg. 1929–30. *Lebensphilosophie und Phänomenologie.* Leipzig: Teubner.

Möckel, Christian. 2001. "Die anschauliche Natur des ideierend abstrahierten Allgemeinen: Eine Kontroverse zwischen Edmund Husserl und Ernst Cassirer." *Phänomenologische Forschungen:* 233–58.

Mohanty, J. N. 1996. "Kant and Husserl." *Husserl Studies* 13: 19–30.

Moran, Dermot. 2008. "Husserl's Transcendental Philosophy and the Critique of Naturalism." *Continental Philosophy Review* 41: 401–25.

Münch, Dieter. 1997. "Edmund Husserl und die Würzburger Schule." *Brentano Studien* 7: 89–122.

Nagel, Thomas. 1979. *Mortal Questions.* Cambridge, Eng.: Cambridge University Press.

———. 1986. *The View from Nowhere.* New York: Oxford University Press.

Natorp, Paul. 1888. *Einleitung in die Psychologie nach kritischer Methode.* Freiburg: Mohr.

———. 1912a. *Allgemeine Psychologie nach kritischer Methode.* Tübingen: Mohr.

———. 1912b. "Kant und die Marburger Schule." *Kant-Studien* 17: 193–221.

———.1913. "Philosophie und Psychologie." *Logos* 2, no. 4: 176–202.

———. 1918. "Bruno Bauchs 'Immanuel Kant' und die Fortbildung des Systems des Kritischen Idealismus." In *Kant-Studien* 22 (1918): 426–59.

———. 1925. *Vorlesungen über praktische Philosophie*. Erlangen: Philosophische Akademie.

———. 1973. "Zur Frage der logischen Methode: Mit Beziehung auf Edmund Husserls *Prolegomena zur reinen Logik*." In *Husserl*, ed. Hermann Noack. Darmstadt: Wissenschaftliche Buchgesellschaft, 1–15.

———. 1980. "Allgemeine Logik." In *Erkenntnistheorie und Logik im Neukantianismus*, ed. Werner Flach and Helmut Holzhey. Hildesheim: Olms, 226–69.

———. 2000. *Philosophische Systematik*. Hamburg: Meiner.

———. 2004. *Plato's Theory of Ideas: An Introduction to Idealism*. Ed. Vasilis Politis, trans. Vasilis Politis and John Connolly. Sankt Augustin: Academia.

Noack, Hans, ed. 1973. *Husserl*. Darmstadt: Wissenschaftliche Buchgesellschaft.

Oberer, Hariolf. 1969. "Transzendentalsphäre und konkrete Subjektivität: Ein zentrales Thema der Neueren Transzendentalphilosophie." In *Zeitschrift für philosophische Forschung* 23: 578–611.

Ollig, Hans-Ludwig. 1979. *Der Neukantianismus*. Stuttgart: Metzler.

Ortega y Gasset, José. 1961. "History as a System." In *History as a System and Other Essays Toward a Philosophy of History*, trans. Helene Weyl. New York: Norton, 165–233.

Orth, Ernst Wolfgang. 1996. "Phänomenologie in Ernst Cassirers Philosophie der symbolischen Formen." In Ernst Wolfgang Orth, *Von der Erkenntnistheorie zur Kulturphilosophie: Studien zu Ernst Cassirers Philosophie der symbolischen Formen*. Würzburg: Königshausen & Neumann, 162–75.

Paetzold, Heinz. 1993. *Ernst Cassirer zur Einführung*. Hamburg: Meiner.

Paimann, Rebecca. 2002. *Formale Strukturen der Subjektivität: Egologische Grundlagen des Systems der Transzendentalphilosophie bei Kant und Husserl*. Hamburg: Meiner.

Philipse, Herman. 1995. "Transcendental Idealism." In *Cambridge Companion to Husserl*, ed. Barry Smith and David Woodruff Smith. Cambridge, Eng.: Cambridge University Press, 239–322.

Ramberg, Bjørn. 1997. "The Source of the Subjective." In *The Philosophy of Hans-Georg Gadamer*, ed. Lewis E. Hahn. Chicago: Open Court, 459–71.

Rang, Bernhard. 1973. *Kausalität und Motivation: Untersuchungen zum Verhältnis von Perspektivität und Objektivität in der Phänomenologie Edmund Husserls*. Phaenomenologica 53. The Hague: Nijhoff.

Ratcliffe, Matthew. 2002. "Husserl and Nagel on Subjectivity and the Limits of Physical Objectivity." *Continental Philosophy Review* 35: 353–77.

Recki, Birgit. 1997. "Kultur ohne Moral? Warum Ernst Cassirer Trotz der Einsicht in den Primat der Praktischen Vernunft Keine Ethik schreiben konnte." In *Ernst Cassirers Werk und Wirkung: Kultur und Philosophie*, ed. Dorothea Frede and Reinold Schmücker. Darmstadt: Wissenschaftliche Buchgesellschaft, 57–78.

Reeder, Harry P. 2010. "Husserl's Hermeneutic Phenomenology" (unpublished typescript).

Reinhold, Karl Leonhard. 2010/1789. *Versuch einer neuen Theorie des Vorstellungsvermögens*. Ed. Ernst-Otto Onnasch. Hamburg: Meiner.

Richir, Marc. 1981/83. *Recherches phénoménologiques: Fondation pour la phénoménologie transcendentale (I–III), du schématisme phénoménologique transcendental (IV–V)*. 2 vols. Brussels: Ousia.

Rorty, Richard. 1979. *Philosophy and the Mirror of Nature*. Princeton, N.J.: Princeton University Press.

Sandmeyer, Bob. 2009. *Husserl's Constitutive Phenomenology: Its Problem and Promise*. London: Routledge.

Sartre, Jean-Paul. 1956. *Being and Nothingness*. Trans. Hazel E. Barnes. New York: Philosophical Library.

Scheler, Max. 1957. "Phänomenologie und Erkenntnistheorie (1913/14)." In *Gesammelte Werke X*, ed. Manfred S. Frings. Bern: Franke, 377–430.

———. 1973. *Formalism in Ethics and Non-Formal Ethics of Values: A New Attempt Toward the Foundation of an Ethical Personalism*. Trans. Manfred S. Frings and Roger L. Funk. Evanston, Ill.: Northwestern University Press.

Schopenhauer, Arthur. 1969. *The World as Will and Representation*. Trans. Eric F. J. Payne. New York: Dover.

Schuhmann, Karl. 1973. *Die Dialektik der Phänomenologie*. 2 vols. The Hague: Nijhoff.

———. 1978. "Zu Heideggers Spiegel-Gespräch über Husserl." In *Zeitschrift für philosophische Forschung* 32: 591–612.

———. 1988. *Husserls Staatsphilosophie*. Freiburg: Alber.

———. 2004a. "Husserl and Indian Thought." In *Karl Schuhmann: Selected Papers on Phenomenology*, ed. Cees Leijenhorst and Piet Steenbakkers. Dordrecht: Kluwer, 137–62.

———. 2004b. "Daubert-Chronik." In *Selected Papers on Phenomenology*, ed. Cees Leijenhorst and Piet Steenbakkers. Dordrecht: Kluwer, 299–301.

Seidengart, Jean. 1994. "Die philosophische Bedeutung des Unendlichkeitsbegriffs in Ernst Cassirers Neukantianismus." In *Neukantianismus: Perspektiven und Probleme,* ed. Ernst Wolfgang Orth and Helmut Holzhey. Würzburg: Königshausen & Neumann, 442–56.

———, ed. 1990. *Ernst Cassirer: De Marbourg à New York: L'itinéraire philosophique*. Paris: Cerf.

Shim, Michael. 2002. "Towards a Phenomenological Monadology: On Husserl and Mahnke." In *Subjektivität—Verantwortung—Wahrheit: Neue Aspekte der Phänomenologie Edmund Husserls,* ed. David Carr and Christian Lotz. Frankfurt am Main: Lang, 243–59.

Sidelsky, Edward. 2009. *Ernst Cassirer: The Last Philosopher of Culture*. Princeton, N.J.: Princeton University Press.

Sieg, Ulrich. 1994. *Aufstieg und Niedergang des Marburger Neukantianismus: Die Geschichte einer philosophischen Schulgemeinschaft*. Würzburg: Königshausen & Neumann.

Smith, Barry, and David Woodruff Smith, eds. 1995. *Cambridge Companion to Husserl*. Cambridge, Eng.: Cambridge University Press.

Soboleva, Maja. 2001. "Zur philosophischen Hermeneutik Ernst Cassirers." *Phänomenologische Forschungen*, new series 1: 281–94.

Soffer, Gail. 2003. "Revisiting the Myth: Husserl and Sellars on the Given." *Review of Metaphysics* 57: 301–37.

Sokolowski, Robert. 1997. "Gadamer's Theory of Hermeneutics." In *The Philosophy of Hans-Georg Gadamer,* ed. Lewis E. Hahn. Chicago: Open Court, 223–36.

Stähler, Tanja. 2003. *Die Unruhe des Anfangs: Hegel und Husserl über den Weg in die Phanomenologie.* Phaenomenologica 170. Dordrecht: Kluwer.

Staiti, Andrea S. 2010. *Geistigkeit, Leben und geschichtliche Welt in der Transzendentalphänomenologie Husserls.* Würzburg: Ergon.

Steinbock, Anthony J. 1995. *Home and Beyond: Generative Phenomenology After Husserl.* Evanston, Ill.: Northwestern University Press.

Stolzenberg, Jürgen. 1995. *Ursprung und System: Probleme der Begründung systematischer Philosophie im Werk Hermann Cohens, Paul Natorps und beim frühen Martin Heidegger.* Göttingen: Vandenhoeck & Ruprecht.

Trappe, Tobias. 1996. *Transzendentale Erfahrung: Vorstudien zu einer transzendentalen Methodenlehre.* Basel: Schwabe.

Tugendhat, Ernst. 1967. *Der Wahrheitsbegriff bei Husserl und Heidegger.* Berlin: De Gruyter.

Verene, Donald P. 1969. "Kant, Hegel, and Cassirer: The Origins of the Philosophy of Symbolic Forms." *Journal of the History of Ideas* 30: 33–46.

Vongehr, Thomas. 2007. *History of the Husserl Archives.* Heidelberg: Springer.

Waldenfels, Bernhard. 1971. *Das Zwischenreich des Dialogs: Sozialphilosophische Untersuchungen in Anschluss an Edmund Husserl.* The Hague: Nijhoff.

Welton, Donn. 2000. *The Other Husserl: The Horizons of Transcendental Philosophy.* Bloomington: Indiana University Press.

———. 2003. "The Systematicity of Husserl's Transcendental Philosophy: From Static to Genetic Method." In *The New Husserl: A Critical Reader,* ed. Donn Welton. Bloomington: Indiana University Press, 255–88.

Wiehl, Reiner. 2000. *Subjektivität und System.* Frankfurt am Main: Suhrkamp.

Wischke, Mirko, and Michael Hofer, eds. 2003. *Gadamer Verstehen/Understanding Gadamer.* Darmstadt: Wissenschaftliche Buchgesellschaft.

Wolzogen, Christoph von. 1985. *Die autonome Relation: Zum Problem der Beziehung im Spätwerk Paul Natorps.* Würzburg: Königshausen & Neumann.

Woodruff Smith, David. 1995. "Mind and Body." In *Cambridge Companion to Husserl,* ed. Barry Smith and David Woodruff Smith. Cambridge, Eng.: Cambridge University Press, 323–93.

Zahavi, Dan. 1996. *Husserl und die transzendentale Intersubjektivität: Eine Antwort auf die sprachpragmatische Kritik.* Phaenomenologica 135. Dordrecht: Kluwer.

———. 1998. "The Fracture in Self-Awareness." In *Self-Awareness, Temporality, and Alterity,* ed. Dan Zahavi. Dordrecht: Kluwer, 21–40.

———. 1999. *Self-Awareness and Alterity: A Phenomenological Investigation.* Evanston, Ill.: Northwestern University Press.

———. 2002. "Metaphysical Neutrality in *Logical Investigations*." In *One Hundred Years of Phenomenology: Husserl's "Logical Investigations" Revisited,* ed. Dan Zahavi and Frederik Stjernfelt. Phaenomenologica 164. Dordrecht: Kluwer, 93–108.

———. 2003a. "Husserl's Intersubjective Transformation of Transcendental Philosophy." In *The New Husserl: A Critical Reader,* ed. Donn Welton. Bloomington: Indiana University Press, 223–51.

———. 2003b. "How to Investigate Subjectivity: Natorp and Heidegger on Reflection." *Continental Philosophy Review* 36: 155–76.

Zeidler, Kurt W. 2001. "Das Problem der Psychologie im System Cohens (mit Blick auf P. Natorp)." In *Hermann Cohen und die Erkenntnistheorie,* ed. Wolfgang Marx and Ernst Wolfgang Orth. Würzburg: Königshausen & Neumann, 135–46.

Ziegler, Leopold. 1911/12. "Ueber einige Begriffe der 'Philosophie der reinen Erfahrung.'" *Logos* 2, no. 3: 316–49.

Index

About the Author

Sebastian Luft is an associate professor of philosophy at Marquette University.